A Usable Past

Essays in European Cultural History

WILLIAM J. BOUWSMA

University of California Press

Berkeley   Los Angeles   Oxford

University of California Press
Berkeley and Los Angeles, California

University of California Press, Ltd.
Oxford, England

© 1990 by
The Regents of the University of California

Library of Congress Cataloging-in-Publication Data

Bouwsma, William James, 1923–
    A usable past : essays in European cultural history / William J.
Bouwsma.
        p.   cm.
    ISBN 0-520-06438-0 (alk. paper). ISBN 0-520-06990-0 (pbk.: alk.
paper)
    1. Europe—Civilization.   2. History—Philosophy.   I. Title.
D7.B72   1990
901—dc20   89–29621
                                                        CIP

Printed in the United States of America
1   2   3   4   5   6   7   8   9

To Jean and Henry May
also for the best reasons

Contents

Acknowledgments

The first person to suggest that some of these essays might be worth republication in more accessible form was the late baseball commissioner, A. Bartlett Giamatti, then in another line of work. My Berkeley colleagues Gene Brucker and Barbara Shapiro gave me further encouragement in this direction; the latter also brought the idea to the attention of James Clark, director of the University of California Press. To him I owe special gratitude for his confidence in a project about whose feasibility, however pleased I was by the thought of bringing these pieces together in a book, I had considerable misgivings. Werner Gundersheimer, director of the Folger Library, meanwhile gave me the best possible counsel about the presentation of the collection. My secretary, Vanessa Friedman, and my research assistant, Kathryn Edwards, helped to prepare the collection for the printer. My wife endured, over more than four decades, the abstractedness and other strains occasioned in their author by the initial composition of these pieces; she also gave sensitive and reliable stylistic help with the essays. I should like to express here my deep appreciate to all these persons.

Introduction

The title of this collection is derived from Friedrich Nietzsche's essay "On the Uses and Disadvantages of History for Life."[1] The central argument of this passionate work, judiciously qualified, reflects my own deepest convictions about the value of historical scholarship. Nietzsche opened his essay with a quotation from Goethe: "I hate everything that merely instructs me without augmenting or directly invigorating my activity." This meant to him that a vital historiography must serve the "life and action" of society. There is, Nietzsche argued, a "natural relationship of an age, a culture, a nation with its history—evoked by hunger, regulated by the extent of its need," but "always and only for the ends of life and thus also under the domination and supreme direction of these ends."[2] History, in this view, much like water and electricity, is a public utility.[3]

This means in the first place that history is not the private preserve of professional historians, just as divinity, law, and medicine do not "belong" to clergymen, lawyers, and physicians. Like other professional groups, historians are properly the servants of a public that needs historical perspective to understand itself and its values, and perhaps also to acknowledge its limitations and its guilt. Historians have an obligation, I believe, to meet public needs of this kind.

This view of the relation between historiography and society largely explains the sort of history to which I have devoted most of my career,[4] although the way in which I have described my work has changed somewhat over the years. As a graduate student and during the earlier years of my professional career, I thought of myself as an *intellectual* historian. Gradually, however, the idealism underlying this notion gave way to a growing historicism, and I began to recognize that the conception of "intellect" was itself a historical artifact stemming primarily from the hellenic strain in Western culture: a mental construct, indeed, that, far from serving its needs, had been often exploited to justify dominance over society. I began instead, therefore, to call myself a *cultural* historian, understanding "culture," somewhat as anthropologists do, less as a set of beliefs and values than as the collective strategies by which societies organize and make sense of their experience.[5] Culture in this sense is a mechanism for the management of existential anxiety; it serves deeper needs than the "ideas" to which I had first been attracted.[6]

Because it challenges the privileged status of "high" culture, this understanding of culture has sometimes been taken to justify the tendency of some recent historians to ignore the culture of elites in favor of popular culture. This seems to me, however, a non sequitur; the conception is equally applicable to every level of culture.[7] Even the "distinction" supposedly conferred on dominant social groups by their "higher" culture *functions* in somewhat the same way as other cultural constructions. It relieves the anxiety of elites by giving them much the same orientation and sense of identity that popular culture supplies to those lower on the social scale.[8] I make this point because my own continued attention to elite culture may appear somewhat old-fashioned at a time when so much of what seems most fresh and exciting in historical writing deals with popular culture. Part of the reason for my persistence along so well-trodden a path is that elite culture has the advantage, while it serves many of the same functions, of being, for obvious reasons, far more fully documented than the culture of "ordinary" people. Elites not only kept and preserved records of themselves, but they were also in a position to articulate more fully, and often more sensitively, the general concerns of their times.

A cultural history based on this larger understanding of the function of culture seems to me singularly "usable." Just as every individual human being has been shaped (if not exclusively) by the experiences constituting his personal history, so a society can be described as the complex sum of its collective experience, that is, of its history; and the cultural formations with which it responds to this experience are the measure of its impact. On the other hand, it has seemed to me that some areas of culture are more instructive for self-understanding than others. The most informative for me has been religion, including theology but also, and even more profoundly, spirituality, *because* it transcends intellectuality. Religious symbolism and practice seem to me to concentrate and integrate singularly well what a society is finally "about." So, of course, do various secular substitutes for religion, though, I suspect, less comprehensively. This consideration, too, explains the emphasis of many of these essays.

I need hardly point out that this approach to the writing of history does not claim to be "scientific"; indeed it is probably incompatible with the impulse to convert history into a science. For it also seems to me that the frequent, though I think always in the long run unsuccessful, efforts of some historians to enhance the prestige of what they do by claiming for it the status of a science threatens its social function; this too was part of Nietzsche's message. Indeed such efforts may also endanger respect for historical explanation; the tendency most recently of some among the *Annalistes,* for example, to minimize in the name of scientific objectivity the significance of identifiable human actors and discrete events in history[9] is all too likely, however paradoxically, to open the way for nonhistorical modes of explanation. Since the beginning of recorded time, after all, human beings have looked to history to provide explanations for events; and if historians decline this task, others will be found all too willing to undertake it. As Hans Blumenberg has observed,

> The consolation we derive from giving precedence to conditions over events is based only on the hypothesis that conditions are the result of the actions of an indeterminate large number of people instead of just a few whom we can name. But it is just as natural to suppose that history then becomes a process in nature, a sequence of waves, a glacial drift, a tectonic fault movement, a flood, or an alluvial deposit. Here . . . science works against elementary needs and therewith in a way that favors susceptibility to remythicization.[10]

The reduction of history to a science also endangers its social function in another way. Scientists are, for the most part, notoriously indifferent to the communicability of their results except to professional peers. But history, in its origins a rhetorical art, edifies a wider public only insofar as it combines, as the old formula puts it, instruction with delight. Most historians, beginning with Herodotus and Thucydides, have always known this.[11] It should also be emphasized that history performs its function not abstractly and, so to speak, intransitively, but on behalf of particular societies, to whose needs and capacities it must be adapted. This too recalls us to its rhetorical origins; a socially effective historiography must be shaped by that central virtue of the rhetorical tradition, *decorum,* that is, attention to the needs and capacities of its audience.

The essays in this volume, however, concern European history and were written by an American in the first instance for an American audience. This raises the question how the European past can be "used" by Americans. The answer touches, of course, on the complex and changing relation of American to European culture and the ambivalence of a nation of immigrants, mostly until recently of European descent, toward a world they have, at least physically, left behind. The extended colonial experience of earlier Americans had tended to identify them with European culture, primarily English, even when they thought of themselves as starting afresh in a "new" world. But a successful rebellion against English rule stimulated a sense of difference from, and sometimes superiority to, Europe; and eventually new waves of immigrants, coming from every part of Europe and often bringing with them far less cultural baggage than those who came earlier, diffused and further complicated the connection with Europe.

Against this background American historians of Europe, it seems to me, have, roughly speaking, "used" the European past in two rather different ways. One, motivated partly by a search for roots on the part of second- and third-generation Americans, partly by the discovery of what presented itself as a richer and more exotic culture than the United States had developed, has been the intensive study of one or another European national history. This tends to be accompanied by as close a personal identification as possible with the chosen nation as a kind of adopted *patria*. American historians who have taken this route tend to identify themselves with the historiographical community of the society on which they work. Its leading historians become their mentors; its questions become their questions; they follow its methods; and its approval represents, for them, the highest possible accolade. This attitude toward Europe has resulted in a distinguished body of American scholarship. It has enlarged the American understanding both of the possibilities of the human condition, always one of the most valuable uses of historical study, and of the deeply rooted complexities of the world Americans inhabit.

Though I have great respect for this way of doing European history, it is not my way. I have deliberately chosen not to concentrate on the history of any particular European nation, somewhat in the self-consciously American spirit of the young Henry James as stated in a letter to his friend Thomas Perry in 1867. "To be an American," James declared, "is an excellent preparation for culture. . . . It seems to me that we are ahead of the European races in the fact that more than either of them [*sic*], we can deal freely with forms of civilization not our own, can pick and choose and assimilate and in short (aesthetically etc.) claim our property wherever we find it."[12] In the same slightly greedy way, though with the excuse that Americans now need to examine and correlate many areas of European culture, I have deliberately moved from place to place and have exploited local episodes, as far as possible, to illuminate not local situations but issues of European and finally also of American resonance.[13]

This approach, though not always appreciated by historians in Europe, can at the very least complement and compensate for the narrowness of a historiography confined to particular nation-states. I am pleased to associate myself on this matter with Robert R. Palmer, who approached "the democratic revolution" of the later eighteenth century as a European rather than simply a French phenomenon. The relevant scholarship, Palmer observed, had been conducted "in national isolation, compartmentalized by barriers of language or the particular histories of governments and states." The result, he concluded, was that, "whereas all acknowledge a wider reality, few know much about it."[14] My own original area of interest, the Renaissance, has suffered similarly. Although Jacob Burckhardt had been concerned with the significance of the Renaissance in Italy for the whole of Europe, as a result of the recent growth of national and local specialization the period of the Renaissance has been more and more frequently treated in merely national and local terms, and efforts to generalize about it tend increasingly to be viewed with distrust.[15] It is less and less likely to be interpreted as a major episode in Western culture, the common property of all the heirs and beneficiaries of that culture.

In addition to their concern with larger perspectives of this kind, the sorts of problems with which these essays deal also call for unusual chronological range. Here above all, perhaps, cultural history differs from social history, at least as recently practiced, with its preference for relatively static structural description and, in contrast, its tendency to discern radical discontinuity between the modern age and all that has gone before. From this standpoint, it has recently been maintained, almost everything prior to the end of the eighteenth century has irretrievably disappeared. All but the relatively recent past, to cite the title of an influential book, is a "world we have lost."[16]

I am in no position to speculate about the durability of this judgment for social history. But gross discontinuities of the kind it implies seem to me generally implausible in cultural history, in which change is usually very slow. The ability of cultural formations to adapt to even the most drastic mutations in other realms constantly surprises us, though this may be chiefly a reflection of our naivete about such matters. The result

is that a historian of European culture, even of its contemporary manifestations, cannot afford to ignore the fact that its roots extend back at
least as far as biblical and classical antiquity.

This is true in spite of the tendency of some modern intellectuals to
believe, like many social historians, that, as Alan Megill has put it, we
are now "under the reign of discontinuity":[17] that, in short, to be "modern" means, among other things, to recognize the irrelevance of the past.
This sense of a break with the past, particularly on the part of alienated
intellectuals, is not, however, to be confused with discontinuity itself;
indeed, as a repetition of similar attitudes, for example among Renaissance humanists, it reflects, in a radical form, one possible attitude to
the past perhaps unique to Western culture.[18]

In addition, whereas a historiography of discontinuity can largely
dispense with narrative history, the continuities between past and present
can only be demonstrated by narrative. Narrative is also implied by the
idea of history as a public utility: the need for it can only be satisfied
by stories about the past. Indeed even the possibility of general interest
in those relatively static moments in the past on which historians have
recently tended to focus has largely depended on the place of such moments within a familiar narrative. This is the case with most of the essays
in the present collection.[19] Their significance depends on a sense of the
deep continuities between past and present.

I have always believed that to think historically means to locate every
historical datum, whether person, artifact, event, or process, in the largest
possible context of significance. I do not regard this aim as discredited
because it was also Ranke's,[20] though I may differ from Ranke on the
capacity of even the greatest historians to achieve this goal. I owe at
once this slightly old-fashioned Rankeian aspiration, my need to qualify
it, and even some part of my interest in the larger patterns of European
history to the fact that I was introduced to the systematic study of history
by Harvard's famous (to some, perhaps, now infamous)[21] History 1,
first as a naive and insecure freshman from the Middle West, and then
for three years as a graduate student teaching discussion sections in the
course. Some of the criticism directed at the course, however deficient
in historical perspective, is justified. But History 1 had at least one solid
virtue. It constantly required reflection about the larger significance of
its content; students learned from it to think about the broader importance of everything they were required to learn and to build up larger
and larger generalizations about *European* history as well as about its
various national components. The implicit motto of the course, as I
experienced it, was "Always connect." The conviction that this is the

ultimate responsibility of a historian has never left me; and it underlies, however imperfectly I may have carried it out, all my scholarship.

On the other hand, History 1 was also blatantly whiggish. It was tacitly and uncritically elitist in a way that suited the old Harvard;[22] it emphasized politics, neglecting if not ignoring social and cultural history; and it still assumed as inevitable and desirable, even in 1940, the extension of Western values, Western democracy, and Western science over the non-Western world. I suspect that this optimistic and partly prophetic vision of world history is still more widely shared by historians than many of them would care to admit; criticisms of History 1 for its elitism, sexism, and ethnocentricity seem to me to require, at least in principle, only relatively minor adjustments of the old whig vision. Indeed I am inclined to see the elimination of these sins as a logical extension of that vision which leaves its essential features intact.

My own departure from whiggism is more radical. It is based on a rejection of what was, nevertheless, one of the most genial elements in the scheme: its confidence, also Rankeian, in the ultimate harmony of the major strands in Western culture.[23] History 1, in spite or because of its conventional bias toward the attitudes of the Enlightenment, left me with the impression that the biblical and the classical strands in Western culture—the former rather selectively understood—had collaborated naturally and relatively easily in the creation of modern civilization. The generation of my teachers, many of them European refugees,[24] was especially concerned to reaffirm this double foundation of the civilized values of the West as it confronted the barbaric dictatorships of right and left.

I learned a great deal from these teachers: from Paul Kristeller to identify Renaissance humanism with a program of educational reform and to be skeptical, though without his belief in their compatibility, of the conventional antithesis between humanism and Scholasticism; from Douglas Bush and Werner Jaeger that lovers of the classics and even of Greek philosophy were often serious Christians; from Hans Baron, somewhat later, that Renaissance humanism was by no means simply the academic movement that it was conventionally represented to be but was often engaged with the most vital issues of Renaissance life and thought. It is doubtless also significant, though this did not occur to me at the time, that my doctoral dissertation dealt, in Guillaume Postel, with an egregious harmonizer of sixteenth-century France.[25]

But for the most part, and from an even earlier time in my intellectual development, I was concerned less with the harmonies than with the tensions and contradictions in Western culture. This was primarily because, as a child of second-generation Dutch Calvinist immigrants who were trying to assimilate the high culture of early-twentieth-century America, these tensions posed problems for me; I was troubled, for example, about the compatibility of an "inalienable right" to "life, liberty, and the pursuit of happiness" with Christianity. But long before I decided to become a historian, it occurred to me that much of the confusion I discerned in myself might be reduced if I knew where the various pieces of intellectual baggage I carried about had come from. I could then sort them out according to their origins, and this would presumably help me to decide to which I was genuinely committed and which I could comfortably discard. History from this standpoint, I thought, might serve, like psychoanalysis at another level, to liberate the conscious mind from the inconvenient legacies of the collective past, first of all for myself but in the classroom for others.

My habit of thinking about the European cultural past in terms of its polarities found expression as early as my undergraduate honors thesis at Harvard. It was entitled "The Conflict between Humanism and Orthodoxy in Milton." Later I would understand the tensions in Western culture rather differently, but my interest in identifying such problems has persisted. My doctoral dissertation may have been a temporary deviation from this concern, but even as a deviation it was only partial. The frantic effort of Postel to unify all thought as the foundation for the unification of the human race, as I see now, was indirect testimony to its actual polarities; and I took his syncretism as an intellectual achievement in the same spirit as the syncretism of *Finnegans Wake,* which I was trying to decipher at about the same time.

I did not read Nietzsche until much later, but on this matter, too, he articulated and deepened my sense of the rich confusions latent in Western culture. "Historical knowledge," Nietzsche wrote, "streams in unceasingly from inexhaustible wells, the strange and incoherent forces its way forward, memory opens all its gates and yet is not open wide enough, nature struggles to receive, arrange and honor these strange guests, but they themselves are in conflict with one another and it seems necessary to constrain and control them if one is not oneself to perish in their conflict."[26] As I entered the world of scholarship on my own, I increasingly saw that my task as a historian would be to try to sort out the major elements in the heterogeneous bundle of impulses that constitute Western culture and lay bare its contrarieties. The relief of the anxiety engendered by cultural conflict also figured more and more centrally in my project. A historian, as it seemed to me, might, by exposing contradictions arising out of the eclecticism of Western culture, contribute to conscious and informed choice. The first group of essays in this volume is particularly concerned to do this.

In Jack Hexter's redolent language, then, I became a "splitter," though chiefly in the sense that I was bisecting a larger lump into two not inconsiderable parts corresponding to the biblical and classical strains in Western culture.[27] There was, of course, nothing original about this. I was only following, in a less combative spirit, Tertullian, who had opposed Jerusalem to Athens; Matthew Arnold, who with contrary intent had opposed hellenism to Hebraism; and a host of lesser figures. Somewhat more my own, perhaps, was the awareness that, in the end, I was dealing not with concrete historical movements, whatever terminology I might choose, but with ideal types that, in their abstract purity, could not be identified fully even with the Jewish and Christian Scriptures on the one hand or with the classical corpus on the other. Both Greek philosophy and the Bible turned out to be, in this sense, impure, mixtures of impulses emerging out of concrete cultural environments that were, in both cases, far more heterogeneous and complex than is often supposed. Ideal types helped me, nevertheless, to think about other historical antitheses: notably rhetoric and philosophy, both originating in the classical world of thought, as the sources of contrary educational ideals; the confrontation between the humanities and the sciences; and, a bit more concretely, the two bundles of contrasting attitudes I eventually associated with Augustinianism and Stoicism.[28] I am not sure that such ideal types make in any general sense for a usable past, but they have made the past more usable for me.

The orientation of Western culture to two poles between which it might be seen to fluctuate also opened up for me a general way of understanding cultural change, about which anthropologists, usually more concerned with structures than with processes, were not very helpful. I found the help I needed, however, in the cyclical conceptions of two of the most profound students of historical change in the Western tradition: Augustine of Hippo and Niccolò Machiavelli.

Augustine, in his basic distinction between the *civitas terrena* (or, in some versions, the *civitas diaboli*) and the *civitas dei,* also distinguished two kinds of change, the contrast between which has exercised metahistorians ever since. For the heavenly city, since it is guided by God to its appointed end beyond time, change is linear and progressive; as Augustine wrote, "If the soul goes from misery to happiness, nevermore to return, then there is some new state of affairs in time." The wicked, on the other hand, "will walk in a circle . . . because the way of false doctrine goes round in circles."[29] So the earthly lives of individuals, who are born, sin, suffer, and die, can be seen endlessly to repeat the same hopeless round. The secular careers of organized groups of human beings are also cyclical, and in much the same way; states, and more conspicuously great empires, rise, the more grand the greater their ascent, and then plunge to their ruin; the wheel comes full circle. All of this is the stuff with which secular historians deal.[30]

Machiavelli, drawing on Polybius, described more fully the cycle through which governments move in a passage that is also suggestive for cultural history. Government, in this scheme, is necessary to deal with disorder and insecurity; and the first kings, chosen by their peoples as best suited for the task, did this effectively. But as the original disorder that had evoked kingship was forgotten and monarchy became hereditary, kingship deteriorated into tyranny and order collapsed. The people of a state that had fallen into this condition then chose to be ruled by aristocrats; but, the reason for the establishment of this form of government likewise forgotten, aristocracy degenerated into oligarchy, and again disorder ensued. Finally the people turned to democracy; but this too eventually declined, through licence, into anarchy. Nothing was left, then—nothing could ever be done—but to begin the whole cycle over again. "This," Machiavelli concluded, "is the circle in which all states revolve."[31]

He deplored this, and much of his thought was directed to devising a political constitution that would reduce, as far as possible, the instability of the cycle and the disorders it was likely to bring. The inspiration of this reflection is thus finally the anxiety implicit in the unknowability of the future; the unknown is frightening not in itself—it is only an abstraction—but because behind it lurk nameless, infinite, and infinitely destructive possibilities. Machiavelli's balanced constitution was ultimately a device to hold anxiety at bay by containing every potentially dangerous political force. But Machiavelli's view of human nature compelled him to recognize that, though the playing out of the cycle could be delayed, the cycle could never be ended.

The anxiety that propels the Machiavellian political cycle from stage to stage supplied me with an unexpected insight into the dynamics of cultural history. If Western culture is characterized not by its harmonies but by its fundamental, historically engendered antinomies, the history of Western culture may be conceived as a series of efforts, none successful for long, to constrain and control its internal conflicts. In this context, a culture can be understood as the psychological equivalent of a constitution;[32] cultural systems, by ordering human behavior through customs and rules, reduce anxiety by regulating human activity and making it predictable.

My interest in the relation between anxiety and culture was first stimulated by Huizinga's *Waning of the Middle Ages*,[33] and it occupies a prominent place in these essays.[34] But only in the course of working on my Calvin book did I realize that an overarticulated culture such as Huizinga described can be a cause of as well as a response to anxiety. There are, as I came to see, not one but two kinds of cultural anxiety: to use Calvin's terrifying metaphors, the anxiety of the abyss, the result of an underarticulated culture (or, to put it more positively, of an excess of freedom), and the anxiety of the labyrinth, the result of excessive and suffocating cultural constraints. Thus, as Machiavelli so clearly saw, an excess of disorder brings on a reaction toward control; but the inconveniences that result tend inevitably to precipitate a countermovement. So, by a somewhat circuitous route, I have wound up once again not so much with an original insight as with the familiar observation that the pendulum of cultural history swings from freedom to regulation and back again. The wicked, the weak, the unfortunate, that is to say humanity in history, truly seem to walk in circles.

The youthful confusion which impelled me to study history was a particular instance of what Leon Festinger has called "cognitive dissonance."[35] Until I began to consider it more generally, I assumed this to be an acutely uncomfortable condition. But in actuality, as I now believe, the minds of most of us are a tangle of confusions of which, far from being terrified, human beings are for the most part unaware. Indeed, even when we become conscious of our confusions, we usually manage, once past the idealistic expectations of youth, to live with them in relative comfort. Nietzsche noticed this too. "Habituation to such a disorderly, stormy and conflict-ridden [mental] household," he observed, "gradually becomes a second nature." Only sometimes can the "indigestible stones" of a man's knowledge, like the protests of an overloaded stomach, "be heard rumbling about inside him."[36]

Particular circumstances, therefore, must be invoked to explain those historical moments when this chronic condition turns into acute discomfort. Such a moment constitutes a cultural *crisis,* a word from the Greek literally signifying a crossroads where two ways converge and separate again, so that a a traveler is compelled to make a decision. This literal meaning suggests the particular value of a "crisis" for the historian; it enables him to observe in action conflicting forces hitherto at work invisibly, below the surface of human affairs.[37]

That the Renaissance was such a crisis, indeed that it was, as I continue to believe, the crisis par excellence of European cultural history, explains the enduring importance of the Renaissance to which the title of my second group of essays refers. I have chosen to do most of my work in this conventional borderland between the medieval and modern chapters of European history because of its critical significance. I do not think that it has been displaced from this position by any later episode. Here, through the philological researches of Renaissance humanists, themselves driven by a crisis of values and a sense of social and political crisis, the contradictions in the mixture of values and attitudes that constitute Western culture came closer to consciousness than ever before, indeed than in most times since. Study of the Renaissance, therefore, allows us to watch several generations of European thinkers, generally unsystematic but often eloquent, usually interesting, and sometimes profound, wrestling with problems that are with us yet; hence the durability of the Renaissance.

My reliance on ideal types in these essays comes about as close to a "methodology" as I have managed to develop. I must confess, in fact, that the notion of method in historical scholarship has always made me uncomfortable. This may explain why the essays on history and historians in the third section of this collection have little to say about the methods of historians and are chiefly concerned with the ideas and attitudes underlying their work.

I am also reluctant to characterize as a "method" my own close reading of texts. I do assume that no historian can, passively or otherwise, "mirror" the past, and that a historian who works with texts must actively tease out from them whatever meanings they can be made to yield. As Francis Bacon remarked of the secrets of nature, so too there are secrets in texts that "reveal themselves more readily under the vexations of art than when they go their own way."[38] I have also been less concerned with the objective content of a text than with the reconstruction from it of the *forma mentis* of its author, with those aspects of himself and his world that he unwittingly reveals, with his tacit assumptions and values. What is required to reveal such matters is a sensitive and empathic reading not only of the lines of a text but, so to speak, between them; what is left unsaid is often more important that what is explicit. I have also found figurative language particularly helpful; it frequently conveys what is too profoundly believed to be consciously expressed. In addition, the *tone* of what is said, however problematic, can sometimes reveal more than its content; tone can even contradict content. My purpose, in every case, has been to discover the function of ideas in the case of any thinker, and above all whether they help to control or to liberate his experience.

This way of reading can hardly be described as a technique, nor can it be reduced to rules. Yet I believe that it has often made it possible for me to probe, to put the terminology of Erik Erikson to a use rather different from his, the most "sensitive zones" of human concern.[39] I mean by this the fundamental assumptions, usually implicit rather than explicit, that inform a whole body of thought. For me two sorts of conceptions of this kind have been most revealing. The first is a thinker's conception of the human personality, the second his notion of what it means to "know" something: his basic anthropological and epistemological orientation.

The last section of this book consists of essays in what I have called "applied history," in which my identification of the anthropological and epistemological foundations of Western culture often figures. These pieces were mostly responses to requests for historical perspective on some matter of general interest. They are not the kind of writing a historian would do in the course of what he might think of as his own work but rather examples of how to make the resources of historical scholarship available for a particular public use. I could not have written them had I not been first of all a historian. They also reflect my conviction that a historian performing generally as a man of letters, as historians usually did before they were overcome by the compulsion to specialize, may still contribute to the discussion of large issues of concern to others. They may also be examples of what "learning from history" might mean after the demise of philosophy of history, including its whig version. In the end, however, the past becomes publicly usable only insofar as a historian can communicate it, and this means that he must be not merely a scholar but above all, even in his scholarly communication, a teacher, able to communicate what he knows to others, with a teacher's sense of responsibility to teach what is harsh and unpalatable as well as what pleases. This explains my coda. It is ironical that I was called on to write this piece, which has not hitherto been published, as a duty incumbent on my presidency of the American Historical Association, a dignity to which my performance as a teacher had been only marginally relevant. It seems much to the point now as I look once again at these essays.

NOTES

1. Included in *Untimely Meditations,* tr. R. J. Hollingdale (Cambridge, 1983), pp. 59–123; I am aware that Nietzsche expressed himself quite differently in other places.

2. Ibid., pp. 59, 77.

3. I have made this point most explicitly in the last selection in the volume, "The History Teacher as Mediator," which also recognizes the dangers in the conception.

4. What follows are my own reflections about the impulses underlying my work. For other perspectives, both by colleagues whom I particularly esteem, see Martin Jay, "Hierarchy and the Humanities: The Radical Implications of a Conservative Idea," *Telos* 62 (1984–1985), 131–144, and above all Randolph Starn, "William Bouwsma and the Paradoxes of History," *Culture, Society, and Religion in Early Modern Europe: Essays by the Students and Colleagues of William J. Bouwsma,* a special issue of *Historical Reflections* 15 (Spring 1988), 1–11.

5. In making this move I was influenced above all by Mary Douglas, especially *Purity and Danger: An Analysis of Concepts of Pollution and Taboo* (London, 1966); Clifford Geertz, *The Interpretation of Cultures* (New York, 1973); and Marshall Sahlins, *Culture and Practical Reason* (Chicago, 1976). I have elaborated on the distinction between intellectual and cultural history in "From History of Ideas to History of Meaning," ch. 15 below.

6. In an earlier form, this conception underlies my essay of 1980, "Anxiety and the Formation of Early Modern Culture," ch. 6 below; it was carried further in *John Calvin: A Sixteenth-Century Portrait* (New York, 1988).

7. The notion of distinct cultures corresponding to class is less and less accepted by historians; cf. Roger Chartier, *The Cultural Uses of Print in Early Modern France,* tr. Lydia G. Cochrane (Princeton, 1987), pp. 3–5. The basic inseparability of elite and popular culture in the sense in which I use the term underlies, for example, Natalie Z. Davis, "The Study of Popular Religion," in *The Pursuit of Holiness in Late Medieval and Renaissance Religion,* ed. Charles Trinkaus (Leiden, 1974), pp. 307–336. It also poses the problem to which Lawrence L. Levine gives so suggestive an answer in *Highbrow Lowbrow: The Emergence of Cultural Hierarchy in America* (Cambridge, Mass., 1988).

8. This reflection was stimulated by Pierre Bourdieu, *Distinction: A Social Critique of the Judgement of Taste,* tr. Richard Nice (Cambridge, Mass., 1984).

9. For example, Emmanuel Le Roy Ladurie, in "L'histoire immobile," *Annales: Economies, sociétés, civilisations* 29 (1974), 673–682, tr. John Day, "Motionless History," *Social Science History* 1 (1977), 115–136. The irrelevance of a history that ignores events has recently been pointed out with particular poignancy by Arno Mayer in connection with the Holocaust in *Why Did the Heavens Not Darken? The "Final Solution" in History* (New York, 1989).

10. Hans Blumenberg, *Work on Myth,* tr. Robert M. Wallace (Cambridge, Mass., 1985), p. 102. Cf. my discussion of "the myth of apocalyptic modernization" in "The Renaissance and the Drama of Western History," ch. 16 below.

11. Cf. George H. Nadel, "Philosophy of History before Historicism," *History and Theory* 3 (1964), 291–315.

12. Quoted from a letter of 1867 by Leon Edel, *Henry James: A Life* (New York, 1985), p. 87.

13. In what follows I have drawn on "Early Modern Europe," my contribution to *The Past before Us: Contemporary Historical Writing in the United States,* ed. Michael Kammen (Ithaca, 1980), pp. 78–94. I have not included it in the present collection because it is chiefly of only bibliographical interest.

14. *The Age of the Democratic Revolution,* 2 vols. (Princeton, 1959–1964), I:8.

15. Broader perspectives on the Reformation have also been narrowed by its identification with German history and a view of its manifestations elsewhere

as a tribute to the originality and influence of Germany. My effort to understand it in European terms (see ch. 9 below) met with strong resistance at the Fourth International Congress for Lutheran Research in 1971.

16. Cf. Peter Laslett, *The World We Have Lost* (London, 1965).

17. Alan Megill, "Foucault, Structuralism, and the Ends of History," *Journal of Modern History* 51 (1979), 451. The point is also central to Megill's *Prophets of Extremity: Nietzsche, Heidegger, Foucault, Derrida* (Berkeley, 1985).

18. This seems to me also implicit in the observation of Carl E. Schorske, *Fin-de-Siècle Vienna: Politics and Culture* (New York, 1980), xvii–xviii: "an understanding of the death of history must also engage the attention of the psychoanalyst. At the most obvious level, the latter would see the sharp break from a tie with the past as involving generational rebellion against the fathers and a search for new self-definitions." Much of this sense of discontinuity, however, also seems to me to reflect—and is used to justify—ignorance of the past. In this connection, see my review essay on Dominick LaCapra and Steven L. Kaplan, eds., *Modern European Intellectual History: Reappraisals and New Perspectives* (Ithaca, 1982), in *History and Theory* 23 (1984), 234–236.

19. Though much of my *Venice and the Defense of Republican Liberty: Renaissance Values in the Age of the Counter-Reformation* (Berkeley, 1968) is narrative history.

20. Cf. the preface to Ranke's *Histories of the Latin and Germanic Nations from 1494 to 1514,* in *The Varieties of History from Voltaire to the Present,* ed. Fritz Stern (New York, 1956), pp. 55–58.

21. See the critical treatment of the course by Gilbert Allardyce, "The Rise and Fall of the Western Civilization Course," *American Historical Review* 87 (1982), 695–725.

22. I hasten to add, however, that I do not object to elitist history per se but only when its appropriateness is unquestioned and therefore not a matter of deliberate choice.

23. Cf. Hayden White, *Metahistory: The Historical Imagination in Nineteenth-Century Europe* (Baltimore, 1973), pp. 167–168.

24. By "my teachers" I do not mean only those from whom I received formal instruction at Harvard.

25. This was revised and published as *Concordia Mundi: The Career and Thought of Guillaume Postel, 1510–1581,* Harvard Historical Monographs, 33 (Cambridge, Mass., 1957).

26. "Uses and Disadvantages of History," p. 78.

27. J. H. Hexter, "The Burden of Proof," *London Times Literary Supplement,* Oct. 24, 1975.

28. See "The Two Faces of Humanism: Stoicism and Augustinianism in Renaissance Thought," ch. 1 below.

29. *De civitate Dei,* XII, 13; I quote in the translation of Henry Bettenson (London, 1967).

30. Cf., most recently, though without reference to Augustine, Paul Kennedy, *The Rise and Fall of the Great Powers: Economic Change and Military Conflict from 1500 to 2000* (New York, 1987).

31. *Discorsi,* II, 2; I quote in the translation of Allan Gilbert (Durham, N. C., 1965).

32. Freud also, it may be recalled, had viewed the mind, in Peter Gay's recent formulation, "as a set of organizations in conflict with one another; what one segment of the mind wants, another is likely to reject, often anxiously" (*Freud: A Life for Our Time* [New York, 1988], p. 109).

33. J. Huizinga, *The Waning of the Middle Ages: A Study of the Forms of Life, Thought, and Art in France and the Netherlands in the Fourteenth and Fifteenth Centuries* (London, 1924).

34. The first to touch on this subject were ch. 12, "Three Types of Historiography in Post-Renaissance Italy," and ch. 19, "Christian Adulthood"; it became prominent, however, only with ch. 6, "Anxiety and the Formation of Early Modern Culture."

35. Leon Festinger, *A Theory of Cognitive Dissonance* (New York, 1957).

36. "Uses and Disadvantages of History," p. 78.

37. Cf. Randolph Starn, "Historians and 'Crisis,'" *Past and Present* 52 (1971): 3–22.

38. *The New Organon*, ed. Fulton H. Anderson (Indianapolis, 1960), p. 95. I do not mean, of course, quite what Bacon meant by "art," i.e., scientific procedure.

39. Erik H. Erikson, *Childhood and Society,* 2d ed. (New York, 1963), esp. pp. 48–108. Erikson uses the phrase to designate those zones of the body most sensitive to psychological and cultural stimuli.

POLARITIES OF
WESTERN CULTURE

1 The Two Faces of Humanism

Stoicism and Augustinianism in Renaissance Thought

Like a number of other essays in this volume, this piece was distilled from an otherwise unsuccessful—because excessively ambitious—effort to write a general book about the place of the Renaissance and Reformation in the context of the whole of Western culture. I regard this essay, however, as my most successful description of what seem to me that culture's perennial dichotomies. The essay also reflects my reliance on ideal types, although this strategy was not always recognized by reviewers. The essay was published in a Festschrift for Paul Oskar Kristeller, on the occasion of his seventieth birthday, entitled Itinerarium Italicum: The Profile of the Italian Renaissance in the Mirror of Its European Transformations, *ed. Heiko A. Oberman with Thomas A. Brady, Jr. (Leiden: E. J. Brill, 1975), pp. 3–60. It is reprinted here by permission of the publisher.*

• • •

Recent emphasis, stemming primarily from the work of P. O. Kristeller, on the central importance of rhetoric for Renaissance humanism, has enabled us to understand the underlying unity of a singularly complex movement; and it has proved singularly fruitful for Renaissance scholarship. At the same time, since this approach depends on the identification of a kind of lowest common denominator for humanism, it may also have the unintended effect of reducing our perception of its rich variety and thus of limiting our grasp of its historical significance. I should like, accordingly, to begin with Kristeller's fundamental insight, but then to suggest that rhetoric, for reasons closely connected with the circumstances under which the rhetorical tradition was appropriated in the age of the Renaissance, was also the vehicle of a set of basic intellectual conflicts crucial to the development of European culture in the

19

early modern period. For there were divisions within Renaissance humanism which, since they were perennial, seem hardly incidental to the movement and which can perhaps be explained more persuasively than by the familiar suggestion that, as "mere rhetoricians," humanists felt comfortable in invoking any set of ideas that seemed immediately useful for their purposes, a notion that is in any case psychologically not altogether persuasive. The humanists were not inclined, I think, to invoke simply *any* set of ideas but tended rather to be divided by a fairly constant set of issues.

From this point of view humanism was a single movement in much the sense that a battlefield is a definable piece of ground. The humanists, to be sure, were often engaged in a conscious struggle with the schoolmen, but this was an external conflict in which the opposing sides were more or less clearly separated. But the struggle within humanism which I shall discuss here, though related to that external struggle, was subtler, more confused, and more difficult, though possibly of greater significance for the future of European culture. Often scarcely recognized by the humanists themselves, more frequently latent than overt for even the most acutely self-conscious among them, and never fully resolved, this internal struggle also helps to explain the adaptability of Renaissance humanism to changing needs, and hence its singular durability.

The two ideological poles between which Renaissance humanism oscillated may be roughly labeled "Stoicism" and "Augustinianism." Both terms present great difficulties, and neither, as an impulse in Renaissance intellectual culture, is yet susceptible to authoritative treatment. I will employ them here in a rather general sense, to designate antithetical visions of human existence, though both are rooted in concrete movements of thought that invite more precise analysis. But any effort to deal with the ideological significance of Renaissance humanism must now grapple with their confrontation.

I. STOICISM AND AUGUSTINIANISM:
THE ANCIENT HERITAGE

It seems curious that historians have been so slow, until quite recently, to recognize the importance of the opposition between these impulses in humanist thought.[1] One reason for this, perhaps, has been the persistent notion that Renaissance culture was centrally preoccupied with the recovery of an authentic classicism; and the classical world of thought has been ultimately brought into focus through the issues raised by ancient philosophy. Thus it has been assumed that the two greatest philosophers of classical antiquity, Plato and Aristotle, must represent, however distantly, the essential options available to the thinkers of the Renaissance. This approach to the Renaissance problem may still be encountered in the familiar notion of a medieval and Aristotelian scholasticism confronted by a Platonic humanism.

Whether because or in spite of its neatness, almost everything in this formula is misleading, if not wrong. In the first place it is wrong in fact. Medieval philosophy, even in the thirteenth century, was by no means entirely Aristotelian, and on the other hand the culture of Renaissance humanism probably owed at least as much to Aristotle as to Plato. But it is equally wrong in principle, for it seeks to comprehend the eclectic and non-systematic culture of the Renaissance in overtly systematic terms. It seems to be based on the quaint but durable notion that every man must, in his deepest instincts, be either a Platonist or an Aristotelian. In fact the conflict between Plato and Aristotle is, for the understanding of the Renaissance, a false scent, especially if we are primarily concerned with the tensions within humanism. Neither Plato nor Aristotle was closely connected with the rhetorical tradition, for whose ancient sources we must look instead to the Sophists and the less overtly philosophical pronouncements of the Latin orators. Furthermore, though Renaissance thinkers (including some humanists) sometimes disputed the relative merits of Plato and Aristotle, this rather academic debate was not a major or a regular concern of humanism; hence it can hardly be expected to illuminate its central concerns. More seriously, when compared with the humanists of the Renaissance Plato and Aristotle seem more to resemble than to differ from one another, not only because both were systematic philosophers but also because, however serious their disagreements, they came out of the same cultural world. By the later fifteenth century this was commonly observed by the humanists themselves, and Raphael, in an early representation of the division of labor, celebrated their complementarity by placing Plato and Aristotle side by side in the Stanza della Segnatura. Finally, the attempt to understand the polarities of Renaissance culture in terms of Plato and Aristotle seems to be based on the common but mistaken identification of antique thought with classical hellenism. It ignores the rich variety of the ancient heritage, and above all the significant fact that the earliest and probably the most influential ancient sources on which Renaissance humanism was nourished were not hellenic but hellenistic.

Thus although it is useful, both for the longer historical perspectives the exercise affords and for the deeper resonances it releases, to associate the impulses at work in Renaissance humanism with the various resources of the Western cultural tradition, we must locate these resources first of all in the hellenistic rather than the hellenic world of thought. Stoicism and Augustinianism both meet this requirement, but they are also closer to Renaissance humanism in other respects. Both were bound up with the ancient rhetorical tradition, Stoicism through the ethical teachings of the Latin orators and essayists particularly beloved by the humanists, Augustinianism through the rhetorical powers of Augustine himself and, more profoundly, the subtle rhetorical quality of his mature theology.[2] Furthermore the tension between Stoicism and Augustinianism was a perennial element in the career of Renaissance humanism and indeed persisted well beyond what is conventionally taken as the end of the Renaissance; the ambiguous confrontation between the two impulses is still as central for Antoine Adam's distinguished Zaharoff lecture on the thought of seventeenth-century France as it is in Charles Trinkaus's rich studies of fourteenth- and fifteenth-century Italian humanism.[3] Finally, Stoicism and Augustinianism represented, far better than Plato and Aristotle, genuine alternatives for the Renaissance humanist to ponder.

Nevertheless it must be admitted that neither Stoicism nor Augustinianism is easy to define with precision, and here may be another reason for our slowness to grasp their importance. In the case of Stoicism the difficulty arises from the singular complexity of the problem of isolating a pure body of thought from the tangled bundle of hellenistic ideas that were the common property of Stoics, Epicureans, Cynics, Neoplatonists, later Peripatetics, Gnostics, hellenized Jews, Christians, and other groups in later antiquity.[4] Stoicism was itself eclectic in its sources and syncretist in its aims. It combined an Aristotelian (and perhaps pre-Socratic) materialism with Socratic ethical theory, the hint of an Asiatic passion for righteousness with, in its later stages, the severe moralism of Rome. Its sense of the unity and harmony of nature and its emphasis on the structural and dynamic affinities of macrocosm and microcosm readily fused with Babylonian astrology. Stoicism embraced the allegorical principle by which every philosophical and religious position in the hellenistic world could be perceived as a legitimate insight into the nature of things, and it popularized the notion that the various schools of ancient philosophy constituted, all together, a single Great Tradition of consistent, developing, and overlapping wisdom. Seneca himself, with Cicero the major source of Europe's early knowledge of Stoic teaching, frequently borrowed from non-Stoic sources. In addition Stoicism had a history. In its later, Roman form its physical, metaphysical, and epistemological foundations receded into the background, though these dimensions of its influence continued to work more subtly; and the absolutism of its ethical demand was modified. It is thus hardly remarkable that Renaissance humanists were often far from clear about the precise lineaments of Stoicism, nor is it surprising that modern scholars who are not technical historians of philosophy more often refer to than try to define Stoic philosophy. Stoicism, for the humanist, was sometimes a fairly particular set of beliefs, but it was also the particular form in which the pervasive and common assumptions of hellenistic paganism presented themselves most attractively and forcefully to the Renaissance.

The definition of Augustinianism is at least equally difficult, partly because Augustine himself was a product of the same philosophically confused culture that produced Stoicism (with the difference that several additional centuries had made the spiritual atmosphere even more turgid), partly for other reasons. His *Confessions,* not to mention the remarkable eclecticism of the pagan culture reflected in his other works, provide in themselves a sufficient explanation for his vision of ancient philosophy as "the city of confusion."[5] In addition Augustine was a singularly complex and unsystematic thinker who presents many different faces to his readers. He has been compared to a turbulent stream into whose rushing waters an abundance of silt has been washed, with the result that, although its waters are opaque, it deposits much rich nourishment along its banks for the support of a wide variety of life. A recent work, proceeding systematically, has identified some eleven distinct and in some respects incompatible types of "Augustinianism."[6] Like a river, the mind of Augustine was in constant movement. His voluminous writings were evolved out of his rich and varied experience, the changing circumstances of his external life, and above all his inner development. His thought can therefore be apprehended fully only as a set of tendencies rather than a system; its coherence is biographical rather than structural. His successive works constantly combined and recombined old and new elements in his thought, in a constant struggle to discover where he stood and where he was moving. He saw this himself. "I am the sort of man," he wrote in a letter, "who writes because he has made progress, and who makes progress—by writing."[7] And he knew that he had, in some important respects, changed his mind; hence, late in his life, he felt compelled to correct, in his *Retractions,* the errors committed in his earlier works.

Nevertheless the direction of Augustine's movement is reasonably clear, and this may suggest that a useful and legitimate definition of Augustinianism, as a particular impulse in European thought, may be sought in the tendencies of his maturity or even, more profoundly, in the vision he presents of a mind engaged in a certain kind of movement. That movement can be generally described as a slow, steady, though incomplete advance from a hellenistic understanding of Christianity, which sought to reconcile the Gospel with the commonplaces of later antique culture, toward an increasingly biblical understanding of Christianity. For it is now generally recognized that Augustine's conversion did not lead to an immediate break with his hellenistic heritage; for some time (like many, perhaps the majority, of the Christians of his age), he understood his new faith as a better statement of what he had previously believed. Christianity, from this standpoint, brought the Great Tradition of ancient philosophy to its culmination. Only gradually, particularly under the influence of the Pauline Epistles, did he become aware of the tensions within this mixture and seek to overcome them. Thus Augustinianism, like Stoicism, may be seen to have had, for the Renaissance, both a more precise and a more general significance. It can be taken to represent, at the same time, a set of propositions antithetical to those brought into focus by Stoicism, and the process by which some thinkers were freeing themselves from the old assumptions of hellenistic culture and moving toward a more specifically Christian vision of man and the human condition.

The notion of the compatibility and even the affinity between Stoicism and Christianity goes back to the yearning of early Christian converts for some bridge between the old word of thought and the new. Stoic elements in the expression (if not the thought) of the Apostle Paul tended to obscure their radical differences, and the apocryphal correspondence between Paul and Seneca confused the issue further.[8] The affinities, indeed, might seem immediately impressive, as they did in the Renaissance. The Stoics were commendably pious; they spoke much about the gods and even about God, praising His wisdom, His power, and His love for mankind. Their emphasis on divine providence and its ultimate benevolence seemed a particular point of contact with Christianity, and the idea of a single providential order led in turn to an ostensibly Christian ethic of absolute obedience and acceptance of the divine will. The Stoics displayed a singular moral seriousness; and their emphasis on virtue, through their famous contrast between the things that are within and those that are not within human control, recognized its inwardness; they acknowledged the problem of sin and stressed man's moral responsibility. They preached the brotherhood of man as well as the universal fatherhood of God, and they had much to say about the immortality of the soul.

But at a deeper level Stoicism and Augustinian Christianity were in radical opposition. The issue between them, in its most direct terms, was the difference between the biblical understanding of creation, which makes both man and the physical universe separate from and utterly dependent on God, and the hellenistic principle of immanence, which makes the universe eternal, by one means or another deifies the natural order, and by seeing a spark of divinity in man tends to make him something more than a creature of God.[9]

This fundamental difference has massive implications, and from it we may derive the major issues on which Stoicism and Augustinianism would be in potential opposition within Renaissance humanism. The anthropological differences between the two positions were of particular importance. The Stoic view of man attributed to him a divine spark or seed, identified with reason, which gave man access to the divine order of the universe, from which the existence, the nature, and the will of God could be known. Stoicism therefore pointed to natural theology; and since reason was seen as a universal human attribute, which meant that all men have some natural understanding of God, Stoic anthropology virtually required a religious syncretism. As the distinctive quality of man, reason also gave him his specifically human identity; a man was most fully human, best realized the ends of his existence, and became perfect through the absolute sovereignty of reason over the other dimensions of the human personality. Virtue consisted, accordingly, in following the dictates of reason, to which the rebellious body and its passions were to be reduced by the will. But the will was not perceived as an independent faculty; it was the faithful and mechanical servant of reason, and therefore Stoicism rested on the assumption that to know the good is to do the good. Through rational illumination and rational control man was capable of reaching perfection. The body presented problems, but these could be solved through a disciplined *apatheia,* a cultivated indifference to physical needs and impulses, to the affections, and to external conditions. But since only man's reason was divine, immortality was reserved for the soul. Conversely Stoicism had a typically hellenistic contempt for the body.

Augustinianism contradicted this view at every point. Seeing man in every part of his being as a creature of God, it could not regard his reason (however wonderful) as divine and thus naturally capable of knowing the will of God. Such knowledge was available to man only in the Scriptures, particular revelations from God himself, which spoke not to mankind as a general category but to the individual. And because neither reason nor any other human faculty was intrinsically superior to the rest, Augustinianism tended to replace the monarchy of reason in the human personality with a kind of corporate democracy. The primary organ in Augustinian anthropology is not so much that which is highest as that which is central; it is literally the heart (*cor*), whose quality determines the quality of the whole. And that this quality is not a function of rational enlightenment is seen as a matter of common experience. The will is not, after all, an obedient servant of the reason; it has energies and impulses of its own, and man is a far more mysterious animal than the philosophers are inclined to admit. Human wickedness thus presents a much more serious problem than the Stoics dream of, and the notion that man in his fallen condition can rely on his own powers to achieve virtue is utterly implausible. Nor, in any event, is there virtue in withdrawal from engagement with the nonrational and external dimensions of existence. The physical body and the emotional constitution of man were created by God along with man's intellectual powers, and their needs too have dignity and are at least equally worthy of satisfaction. For the same reason immortality cannot be limited to the soul; man must be saved, since God made him so, as a whole.

The contrasts are equally significant in respect to the position of man in society. Although the self-centeredness in the Stoic ideal of individual existence was often uneasily and joylessly combined with a Roman concern for civic duty, the Stoics generally left the impression that social existence was a distraction from the good life, which could be satisfactorily pursued only by withdrawal from the world of men. Despite his recognition of the basic equality of man, the Stoic was also persuaded that the good life based on the contemplation of eternal verities was possible only for a few select souls; he was therefore contemptuous of the vulgar crowd. By contrast the mature Augustine, though still yearning for a contemplative life, insisted unequivocally on the obligations of the individual to society, obligations at once of duty, prudence, and love; and at the same time the conception of the blessed life opened up by his less intellectual vision of man was not for the few but accessible to all.

Stoicism, again, had little use for history. Its conception of a rational and unchanging law of nature underlying all things led to a peculiarly rigid notion of cyclical recurrence that denied all significance to discrete events, which in any case belonged to the uncontrollable outer world irrelevant to the good life, just as it precluded the idea of a direction and goal for history. Its cultural values were not the products of particular experience in the world of time and matter but eternal, perennially valid, and so perennially recoverable. Thus its only remedy for present discontents was a nostalgic return to a better past. But Augustine vigorously rejected the eternal round of the ancients. He brooded over the mystery of time as a creature and vehicle of God's will and proclaimed that history was guided to its appointed end by God Himself and therefore, expressing His wisdom, must be fraught with a mysterious significance.

But underlying all these particular contrasts was a fundamental difference over the order of the universe. For the Stoics a single cosmic order, rational and divine, pervaded all things, at once static and, through a divine impulse to achieve perfection planted in everything, dynamic, its principles operative alike in physical nature, in human society, and in the human personality. The existence of this order determined all human and social development; and the end of man, either individually or collectively, could not be freely chosen but consisted in subjective acceptance and conformity to destiny. The perfection of that order meant that whatever is is right, however uncomfortable or tragic for mankind; at the heart of Stoicism is that familiar cosmic optimism which signifies, for the actual experience of men, the deepest pessimism. Against all this, Augustinianism, though by no means denying in principle the ultimate order of the universe, rejected its intelligibility and thus its coherence and its practical significance for man. The result was to free both man and society from their old bondage to cosmic principles, and to open up a secular vision of human existence and a wide range of pragmatic accommodations to the exigencies of life impossible in the Stoic religious universe. In this sense Augustinianism provided a charter for human freedom and a release for the diverse possibilities of human creativity.[10]

II. STOICISM AND AUGUSTINIANISM: THE MEDIEVAL HERITAGE

I do not mean to imply that either Stoicism or Augustinianism presented itself to the Renaissance humanist with even the limited coherence of this short sketch, which is introduced here only to suggest the antithetical impulses in the two movements for the clarification of what follows. Earlier (and indeed much of later) humanism was afflicted with the same kind of ideological confusion that prevailed in the hellenistic world, and Stoic and Augustinian impulses were persistently intermingled and fragmentary. Their operation on the Renaissance mind also depended on the manner in which they were transmitted, their reception on the needs of a changing historical situation.

Obviously neither tradition was a complete novelty in the Renaissance. This is clearest in the case of Augustine, although it is essential to recognize that the diversities and ambiguities in his thought require us to treat medieval Augustinianism with some precision. The earlier Middle Ages seems to have been attracted chiefly to the more hellenistic aspects of Augustinianism and generally resisted (though without altogether rejecting) the full implications of his theology of justification. It was largely oblivious to his secularism or to the problem of his personal development. And with the revival of Aristotle in the thirteenth century, the influence of Augustine (and indeed of the Fathers in general) suffered some decline. A strong loyalty to Augustine persisted among the Franciscans and above all among the Augustinian Hermits, whose claims to ancient origin were regarded with some reserve and who therefore needed to demonstrate their close affinities with their alleged founder.[11] But Thomas, put off by Augustine's Platonism and troubled by the possibility that Augustine had changed his mind, recommended that his earlier writings be approached with caution; and Albertus Magnus rejected his authority in philosophy, though respecting it in theology.[12] This more selective treatment of Augustine may well have prepared the way, by its recognition, however negatively, of his development, for the more personal Augustinianism of the Renaissance. At the same time the relative eclipse of Augustinianism made it possible for Renaissance Augustinianism to present itself as something of a novelty.

The decline of Augustinianism is vividly illustrated by the *Divine Comedy,* from which, in spite of deeper traces of Augustinian influence in Dante's thought, Augustine as a personality is strikingly absent. He does not appear among the representatives of sacred wisdom in Paradise, introduced by Saint Thomas in what may be interpreted as Dante's basic philosophical and theological bibliography,[13] nor does he appear in the next group of cantos which deal with the theological virtues. He is not assigned to answer any of Dante's questions, or to explain to him any of the mysteries of Christian doctrine and human destiny. Indeed he can scarcely be said to *appear* at all; Saint Bernard merely mentions him in the course of explaining the order in which the souls of the blessed are grouped around Christ. And even at this point, although he is introduced in the estimable company of Saint Francis and Saint Benedict, both of whom do play didactic roles in other cantos, he seems of only historical interest, as marking off a phase in the evolution of the church.[14] For Dante Augustine has almost literally disappeared. It is hardly surprising that Dante was unimpressed by the *Confessions.*[15]

Medieval Stoicism has received far less attention than medieval Augustinianism, possibly for the same reasons that account for the neglect of Stoicism in the Renaissance. But in spite of the absence of systematic study of this subject, it is not difficult to demonstrate the importance of a Stoic element in medieval thought, sometimes at the deepest level.[16] Cicero and Seneca (along with Boethius who, as a transmitter, may have been at least as important for Stoicism as for Neoplatonism and for Aristotle) were favorite philosophical authorities during the entire Middle Ages; and, in contrast to Augustine's, their influence was not decreasing in the thirteenth century. Roger Bacon defended Seneca's "elegance of statement about the virtues which are commonly required for honesty of life and the community of human society";[17] the *Romance of the Rose* is full of Stoic precepts;[18] Thomas made heavy use of Cicero;[19] and Dante cited Cicero many times, often linking his authority with Aristotle's.[20] But this parallelism chiefly suggests the ambiguous place of Stoic influences in European thought, and their presence is often most powerful when it is not explicit. We may discern it in medieval preoccupation with the systematic and unitary order of the cosmos, which probably owes more, at least directly, to Stoicism and other hellenistic influences than to the great hellenic philosophers, and in the intellectual vision of man so often conveyed by the Ciceronian commonplace that the erect stature of the human body had been decreed by nature so that men "might be able to behold the sky and so gain a knowledge of the gods."[21] We may see it again in medieval interest in the religious truths available to all mankind through reason alone, so important for missionary strategy;[22] or, at another level, in the distinction between the things belonging to man and those in the domain of fortune,[23] or in medieval debates over the character of true nobility, which so regularly invoked Stoic belief in the natural equality of man.[24]

The Stoic element in Renaissance humanism may thus represent more actual continuity with the Middle Ages than does Renaissance knowledge of Augustine. At any rate it is not clear, before the assimilation by later Renaissance humanists of Marcus Aurelius and the chief Stoic (or Stoicizing) Greek writers, Epictetus and Plutarch, that Renaissance thinkers knew significantly more about the Stoics than their medieval predecessors had known. But the men of the Renaissance had far more of Augustine. During the Middle Ages Augustine had been known, even to many of those who venerated him most deeply, chiefly through the *Decretum* of Yves of Chartres with its 425 extracts from Augustine, through Peter Lombard's *Book of Sentences,* so overwhelmingly based on Augustine, or through Robert Kilwardby's *tabulae* and *capitulationes.* Even Bonaventura knew Augustine at least partly from sources of this kind; he cited one of Augustine's early works eleven times, but ten of his citations were to the same text, presumably garnered from one or another of the compendia available to him.[25] But the fourteenth century saw a concerted effort, particularly among his followers in the Augustinian order, to recover the whole corpus of Augustine's works and, in a manner that would be characteristic of Renaissance scholarship, to develop a systematic acquaintance with his whole thought, not from the standard medieval proof-texts but from the direct study of his entire writings. For the first time a careful attempt was made to identify the exact location, by title, chapter, and verse, of quotations from Augustine, and to verify their accuracy. The great figure in this enterprise was Gregory of Rimini (d. 1358), who has been called the first modern Augustinian. Gregory not only knew the writings and followed the doctrines of Augustine more closely than any previous scholar; he also restored long-neglected works to circulation, in a movement that would result in the critical rejection of the substantial body of apocrypha from the Augustinian corpus and eventually culminate in the great critical editions of Augustine in the sixteenth and seventeenth centuries.[26] Already in the later fifteenth century a single series of sermons by the Augustinian friar Johann Staupitz contained 163 citations from 24 separate works of Augustine.[27]

But neither Stoicism nor Augustinianism was, in the Renaissance, primarily a function of the availability and transmission of literary sources. They were rather responses to the deep and changing needs of Renaissance society and culture. These needs had been created by the growing complexity of European life in the later Middle Ages and above all by the development of towns and the new vision of human existence towns increasingly evoked. For towns produced a set of conditions that made parts of Europe more and more like the hellenistic world in which both the Stoics and Augustine had been reared: the constant menace of famine and pestilence, urban disorders and endemic warfare in the countryside, incessant conflict among individuals, families, and social groups, a growing social mobility that left a substantial proportion of the urban population rootless and insecure, above all the terrible anxieties of a life in which the familiar conventions of a close and traditional human community had given way to a relentless struggle for survival in a totally unpredictable and threatening world.

It was this situation to which scholastic culture seemed irrelevant, and which conversely Stoicism and Augustinianism sought, in their different ways, to interpret and remedy; and the needs of this grim predicament primarily explain why men sought and read Stoic and Augustinian writings. Paradoxically Stoicism, though pagan in a Christian culture, proved the more traditional and conservative of the two prescriptions; Augustinianism, though it appealed to the most authoritative of the Latin Fathers, was at least potentially the more novel. But the conservatism of the Stoic adaptation to a new situation—certainly an element in its attraction—was disguised by the graceful and unsystematic form of the sources in which it was chiefly available: dialogues, personal letters, pensées, essays filled with memorable sayings and concrete examples.[28] Stoicism could therefore present itself as an alternative to scholastic habits of thought.

III. THE STOIC ELEMENT IN HUMANIST THOUGHT

Stoicism addressed itself to the problems of modern Europe, as to those of later antiquity, by reaffirming the divine, harmonious, and intelligible order of nature and drawing appropriate conclusions, practical as well as theoretical. The Stoicism of the Renaissance, perhaps especially when it was least aware of its Stoic inspiration, was based, like ancient Stoicism, on natural philosophy and cosmology, a point of some importance in view of the common supposition that Renaissance thinkers only drew isolated, practical ethical precepts from Stoic sources. Valla's Epicurean (in this case made, perhaps deliberately, to sound like a Stoic) declared nature virtually identical with God.[29] Vives from time to time elaborated on the meaning of this proposition. The universe, he wrote, was governed "by the divine intelligence which commands and forbids according to reason."[30] Calvin, for all his concern to maintain the distinction between God and nature, drew on the same conception. "This skillful ordering of the universe," he argued, "is for us a sort of mirror in which we can contemplate God, who is otherwise invisible."[31] For Charron nature was "the equity and universal reason which lights in us, which contains and incubates in itself the seeds of all virtue, probity, justice."[32]

And man is also a part of this rational order of nature. Montaigne found this humbling: "We are neither superior nor inferior to the rest. All that is under heaven, says the sage, is subject to one law and one fate. . . . Man must be forced and lined up within the barriers of this organization."[33] Others saw in it some justification for glorifying man. "This is the order of nature," wrote Vives, "that wisdom be the rule of the whole, that all creatures obey man, that in man the body abides by the orders of the soul, and that the soul itself comply with the will of God."[34] Another way to coordinate man with the universe was the notion of man as microcosm in Pomponazzi and even Calvin.[35] Calvin was willing, too, to acknowledge the influence of the rational order of the heavens on the human body.[36]

Implicit in these passages, and sometimes more than implicit, is the assumption that this divinely ordered universe is accessible to the human understanding, that man's perception of the rational order of the universe tells him a good deal about the nature and will of God, and that man's reason is thus the link between himself and God. This conception of nature leads us accordingly to the notion of man as essentially an intellectual being. As Aeneas Sylvius declared, the mind is "the most precious of all human endowments";[37] and Petrarch's definition of man as a rational animal is enthusiastically developed, in the *Secretum,* by Augustinus: "When you find a man so governed by Reason that all his conduct is regulated by her, all his appetites subject to her alone, a man who has so mastered every motion of his spirit by Reason's curb that he knows it is she alone who distinguishes him from the savagery of the brute, and that it is only by submission to her guidance that he deserves the name of man at all. . . . when you have found such a man, then you may say that he has some true and fruitful idea of what the definition of man is."[38] As this passage suggests, this view of man requires the sovereignty of reason within the personality. For Pomponazzi human freedom depended on the subservience of will to intellect,[39] and for Calvin this had been the situation of Adam in Paradise, the consequence of his creation in God's image: "In the mind [of Adam] perfect intelligence flourished and reigned, uprightness attended as its companion, and all the senses were prepared and molded for due obedience to reason; and in the body there was a suitable correspondence with this internal order." Before the Fall, apparently, Adam had been a model of Stoic perfection.[40] "The understanding," he wrote more generally, "is, as it were, the leader and governor of the soul" and the instructor of the will.[41]

On the other hand this elevation of reason was often likely to be accompanied by a denigration of other dimensions of the personality, especially the passions and the body with which they were regularly associated, which threatened to challenge the sovereignty of reason. From this standpoint the body and the rational soul could be seen as radically opposed. Petrarch claimed to have learned from his own body only "that man is a vile, wretched animal unless he redeems the ignobility of the body with the nobility of the soul." He saw his soul as imprisoned in and weighed down by the body, the one "an immortal gift, the other corruptible and destined to pass away."[42] With Vives, attack on the body achieved an almost pathological intensity.[43] But happily the rational soul, however threatened by the body and the affections, was in the end clearly superior to them. As Lipsius remarked, "For although the soul is infected and somewhat corrupted by the filth of the body and the contagion of sense, it nevertheless retains some vestiges of its origin and is not without certain bright sparks of the pure fiery nature from whence it came forth."[44]

Reason, in any case, because of its access to the divine order of the universe, is a legitimate source of religious insight, a point exploited at some length by Calvin, who quoted Cicero that "there is no nation so barbarous, no race so savage that they have not a deep-seated conviction that there is a God." In sound Stoic fashion Calvin found the order of the heavens, but also the wonders of the human body, a natural witness to the greatness of God. "The natural order was," he declared, "that the frame of the universe should be the school in which we were to learn piety, and from it pass over to eternal life and perfect felicity."[45] Because the religious insights from nature are the common possession of mankind, it must also be true that all peoples may be expected to reveal some knowledge of God; and this belief contributed heavily to the study of the classics. Petrarch, thinking of himself as following Augustine, was deeply impressed by Cicero's Stoic arguments for the providential order of the world, phrased, as he thought, "almost in a Catholic manner."[46] Aeneas Sylvius maintained that Socrates had taught the Christian way of salvation and recommended "the poets and other authors of antiquity" because they were "saturated with the same faith" as the Fathers of the church.[47] Erasmus saw various values in classical education, among others the fact that Plato "draws the reader to true knowledge by similes."[48] His follower Zwingli placed a number of the ancients among the elect.[49] Through all of this we may discern traces of the hellenistic idea of a great tradition of developing and coherent wisdom, with its corollary that, properly understood, all schools of philosophy are in agreement and that philosophy itself is consistent with and complementary to Christian truth. Thus Bruni had argued for the essential agreement of all the philosophers,[50] a conception of which Pico's *Theses* was a kind of *reductio ad absurdum*.

But rational knowledge was also a resource in a more practical sense. From an understanding of the general rationality of nature, man could discover the rational laws of his own nature and, by following them, variously perfect himself. Augustinus advised Franciscus "to order your life by your nature,"[51] and this principle was basic to much humanist thought about education. Alberti's Uncle Lionardo recommended that a child be formed by encouraging the best elements in his nature, on the general principle that "excellence is nothing but nature itself, complete and well-formed."[52] Erasmus made the point broadly: "All living things strive to develop according to their proper nature. What is the proper nature of man? Surely it is to live the life of reason, for reason is the peculiar prerogative of man."[53] Calvin, who in his youth had identified the injunction to follow nature as Stoic doctrine,[54] did not hesitate in his maturity, like Boccaccio and Valla, to exploit the principle as an argument against celibacy.[55] Charron repeated the general point: "the doctrine of all the sages imports that to live well is to live according to nature."[56]

But clearly the formation men most required in a brutal and disorderly world was training in morality, and it was in this area that Stoic doctrine seemed most relevant to contemporary needs, most immediately prescriptive. The rational order of nature was to be the foundation for the orderly behavior of men; this was its practical function. Stoic moralists were attractive, then, because of their emphasis on the supreme value of virtue, sometimes, as Augustinus tells Franciscus, because it is the only basis for human happiness, sometimes, as Petrarch wrote elsewhere, because virtue, "as the philosophers say," is "its own reward, its own guide, its own end and aim."[57] Pomponazzi, who had clearer reasons, agreed that virtue could have no higher reward than itself and praised it as the most precious quality in life;[58] and Calvin recognized the peculiar emphasis of the Stoics on virtue.[59] Guarino applied the conception directly to education, seeing "learning and training in virtue" as the peculiar pursuit of man and therefore central to *humanitas*.[60]

This concern with virtue reflects also the persistence of the intellectual conception of man so closely bound up with the rational order of the Stoic universe. This is apparent in two ways. In the first place Stoic virtue is acquired through the intellect; it is a product of philosophy, absorbed from books. Thus Erasmus believed that even small children could absorb it through beginning their education by reading ancient fables. He particularly recommended the story of Circe, with its lesson "that men who will not yield to the guidance of reason, but follow the enticements of the senses, are no more than brute beasts." "Could a Stoic philosopher," he asked rhetorically, "preach a graver truth?"[61] But in the second place, as this passage also suggests, the practice of this Stoic virtue depended on the sovereignty of reason and its powers of control over the disorderly impulses arising out of other aspects of the personality. Alberti's Uncle Lionardo made the point clearly. "Good ways of living," he declared, "eventually overcome and correct every appetite that runs counter to reason and every imperfection of the mind."[62] Vives identified this ethics of rational control with the teaching of Christ:

> Our mind is a victim of its own darkness; our passions, stirred by sin, have covered the eyes of reason with a thick layer of dust. We need a clear insight, serene and undisturbed. . . . All the precepts of moral philosophy can be found in the teachings of Christ. In his doctrine, and in his words, man will find the remedy to all moral diseases, the ways and means to tame our passions under the guidance and the power of reason. Once this order has been secured man will learn proper behavior in his relations with himself, with God, and with his neighbor; he will act rightfully not only in the privacy of his home but also in his social and political life.[63]

And in this emphasis on rational control we may perhaps discern an important clue to the attraction of Stoic ethical doctrine for the age of the Renaissance. It presented itself as an antidote for a terrible fear of the consequences of the loss of self-control. Montaigne suggested this in his ruminations over the perils of drunkenness, which may cause man to spill out the secrets on which his survival and dignity depend. "The worst state of man," Montaigne concluded, "is when he loses the knowledge and control of himself."[64] And the ability of men to control their lower impulses with the help of philosophy gave some hope for a better and more orderly world. So it seemed to Aeneas Sylvius: "Respect towards women, affection for children and for home; pity for the distressed, justice towards all, self-control in anger, restraint in indulgence, forbearance in success, contentment, courage, duty—these are some of the virtues to which philosophy will lead you."[65]

The Stoic model for the order of society, like its model for the order of the individual personality, was also derived from the order of the cosmos. An authentic and durable social order that would properly reflect the stability of the cosmos had thus to meet two basic requirements. It had to be a single order, and it had to be governed by reason. This meant in practice that the human world must be organized as a universal empire, and that it must be ruled by the wise, by men who are themselves fully rational and in touch with the rational principles of the cosmos.

Thus the Stoic type of humanist tended, from Petrarch in some moods to Lipsius in the waning Renaissance, to admire imperial Rome. The conquest of the Roman Empire, Petrarch once remarked, had been "actuated by perfect justice and good will as regards men," however defective it may have been in regard to God.[66] Castiglione's Ottaviano Fregoso found an earlier example of the universal model to admire; he praised Aristotle for "directing Alexander to that most glorious aim—which was the desire to make the world into one single universal country, and have all men living as one people in friendship and in mutual concord under one government and one law that might shine equally on all like the light of the sun."[67] Erasmus decried any attachment to a particular community; he had succeeded himself, he said, in feeling at home everywhere.[68] Lipsius similarly attacked love of country as an expression of the lower demands of the body and of custom rather than nature, which commands us to regard the whole world as our true fatherland.[69]

But the sovereignty of reason in the cosmos also required that the world be governed by the wise. All political disorder, Erasmus argued, was the result of stupidity; hence, he declared, "You cannot be a prince if you are not a philosopher."[70] Vives saw the ruler as simply a sage with public authority.[71] There was some discrepancy between this ideal and political actuality, but it could be remedied; since it was rarely possible to elevate sages into kings, it was necessary to convert kings, by education, into sages. This was the aim of Erasmus's *Institutio principis Christiani,* and Rabelais presented Grangousier as a model philosopher-king. Properly educated, the ruler might be made to excel all other men in wisdom and therefore in virtue, and his central duty was then to instruct his subjects in virtue.[72] But always, in this conception of kingship, the Stoicizing humanist kept in mind the ultimate source of wisdom and virtue. The philosophy of the prince, for Erasmus, was the kind that "frees the mind from the false opinions and the ignoble passions of the masses, and following the eternal pattern laid up in heaven points the way to good government."[73] It is not (too much has been made of the point) just a practical moral wisdom, despite its disclaimer of metaphysics, but an application to human affairs of the general principles of order in the cosmos. "As the sun to the sky," Erasmus wrote, in what was no mere figure but the reflection of a whole world of thought, "so is the prince to the people; the sun is the eye of the world, the prince the eye of the multitude. As the mind is to the body, so is the prince to the state; the mind knows, the body obeys."[74]

The idealism in this conception of government generally makes it appear singularly unsuited to the actualities of political life, but in at least one respect it helped to meet genuine practical needs. By its conception of a rational law of nature, it assisted in the rationalization of law and social relations. The problem is suggested by Salutati's confrontation between law and medicine, in which the latter offers a kind of diagnosis of the human scene: here, without the stability of some eternal principle, all things would belong "to the realm of the accidental." Law, "based upon eternal and universal justice," placed government upon a more secure foundation than the whims of the ruler or the accidents of custom.[75] It seems likely that the Stoic conception of a natural law governing all human intercourse and authenticating all particular laws gave some impetus, perhaps most powerful when the cosmic vibrations in the conception were least felt, to the systematic codification of the chaos of existing legislation, to the general rule of law, and to more equal justice. Yet we may sense something equivocal, however opportune, even here. This is apparent in the impersonal rationality in the Stoic idea of social virtue based on law, which corresponded to the increasing legalism and impersonality of the new urban scene. It tended to base social order not on the unreliable vagaries of personal ties, personal loyalties, and personal affection, but on abstract and general social relationships: in a word, on duty rather than on love. The social thought of Stoic humanism thus reflected and probably helped to promote the rationalization of society on which large-scale organization in the modern world depended. But it also made the human world a colder place.

On the other hand the Stoic conception of social improvement was diametrically opposed to the actual direction in which European society was moving. Its ideal, like Seneca's, was nostalgic. As the retrospective prefix in the familiar Renaissance vocabulary of amelioration attests—*renascentium, reformatio, restoratio, restitutio, renovatio,* etc.—it could only look backward for a better world. Petrarch chose deliberately to live in spirit in the ancient past; one of the participants in an Erasmian colloquy deplored the disappearance of "that old time equality, abolished by modern tyranny,"[76] which he also associated with the Apostles; Castiglione thought men in antiquity "of greater worth than now."[77] Even the improvement Renaissance writers occasionally celebrated was regularly conceived as the recovery of past excellence, and hope for the future usually was made to depend on some notion of revival. Petrarch found strength in the greatness of Rome. "What inspiration," he exclaimed, "is not to be derived from the memory of the past and from the grandeur of a name once revered through the world!"[78] Lorenzo de Medici's motto in a tournament of 1468 was *le tems revient.*[79] Machiavelli's chief ground for hope, when he deplored the decadence of contemporary Italy, was that "this land seems born to raise up dead things, as she has in poetry, in painting, and in sculpture."[80] Giles of Viterbo applied the conception to ecclesiastical renewal: "We are not innovators. We are simply trying, in accordance with the will of God, to bring back to life those ancient laws whose observance has lapsed."[81]

All of this suggests the lack of a sense of the positive significance of change in Stoic humanism. Since excellence was associated with the divine origins of all things, change could only mean deterioration; and improvement necessarily implied the recovery of what was essentially timeless. The static character of this ideal was reflected in its vision of the good society which, once it had achieved perfection, could not be permitted to change. So Erasmus hoped that the conflicting interests of human society might "achieve an eternal truce" in which proper authority and degrees of status would be respected by all.[82] One of the essential duties of the Erasmian ruler is to resist all innovation.[83] The central virtue in the Stoic ideal of society is thus peace, which is not simply the absence of war but ultimately dependent on the correspondence of social organization to the unchanging principles of universal order. This is a dimension of the humanist peace movement that it is well to remember in assessing the significance of the pacifism of Petrarch, the emphasis on peace in the circle of Erasmus, or Lipsius's peculiar admiration for the *pax romana*. Peace, too, for the Stoic humanist, required the strong rule of a single "head." And again Stoicism can be seen to supply, at least in theory, a remedy for one of the most glaring defects of Renaissance Europe.

One service performed by Stoic humanism was, then, to supply a foundation for personal and social order in the very nature of things. But this was only one, and perhaps not the major, dimension of its significance. For there was a crucial ambiguity in its moral thought, and indeed in its understanding of virtue, which pointed not to the improvement of the conditions of life but rather to acceptance of the necessary and irremovable discomforts of existence. If the rationality of the universe could be regarded as a resource for a better order, it could also be taken to imply that in some sense the structure of the universe is already perfect and so beyond improvement. From this standpoint Stoicism became a strategy by which, through a combination of enlightenment and disciplined accommodation, the individual could come to terms with the humanly pessimistic implications of a cosmic optimism. It was a strategy of protection for the isolated self in a thoroughly unsatisfactory world. Virtue, in this light, was the ultimate resource by which the ego could minimize its vulnerability to adversity. And this represented a very different kind of adaptation to the changing patterns of European life.

This application of Stoicism was based on the crucial Stoic distinction between those external elements of existence, generally identified with fortune, that are not absolutely within the control of the individual, and the inner world that belongs entirely to himself, the realms, respectively, of necessity and freedom. The inner world alone is the area in which the highest dimension of the personality, man's reason, can exercise total sovereignty, and therefore in which alone man can realize his highest potentialities and attain the ends of his existence; thus it is also the only realm in which he can hope to achieve total happiness. For this is where man discovers the laws governing the universe. As Salutati declared, "They inhere in our minds as of nature. Thus we know them with such certainty that they cannot escape us and that it is not necessary to seek them among external facts. For, as you see, they inhabit our most intimate selves."[84] Lipsius outlined the ideal: "I am guarded and fenced against all external things and settled within myself, indifferent to all cares but one, which is that I may bring in subjection this broken and distressed mind of mine to right reason and God and subdue all human and earthly things to my mind."[85]

The ideal had various implications, notable among them the definition of virtue as that self-sufficiency which, by freeing the individual from all dependence on things external to himself, makes him invulnerable to fortune and so supplies him with inner freedom, the only freedom to which man can aspire. This is the burden of Augustinus's injunction to Franciscus in the *Secretum:* "Learn to live in want and in abundance, to command and to obey, without desiring, with those ideas of yours, to shake off the yoke of fortune that presses even on kings. You will only be free from this yoke when, caring not a straw for human passions, you bend your neck wholly to the rule of virtue. Then you will be free, wanting nothing, then you will be independent; in a word, then you will be a king, truly powerful and perfectly happy."[86] Virtue in this sense was the power to raise the mind above all the external accidents of existence in order to dwell securely in the realm of the eternal. It enabled man to identify himself subjectively with the divine order of the universe, and accordingly a special kind of numinous awe surrounded it, of a sort that could hardly adhere to the more practical virtues of social existence. So this species of virtue meant at once identification with higher and separation from lower things, especially from all those dimensions of existence that distracted or troubled the mind and threatened the self-sufficiency of the discrete individual. Franciscus confessed to Augustinus that his dependence on others was, in his life, "the bitterest cup of all";[87] and Petrarch, who periodically longed for a Stoic repose, reproached Cicero for betraying his own best convictions by giving up the "peaceful ease" of his old age to return to public service.[88] The Stoic impulse in Renaissance humanism favoring such contemplative withdrawal would find regular expression among later writers, from Salutati to Montaigne.[89]

In view of the importance of the city as a stimulus to Renaissance moral reflection, it is also of some interest that it was, for Petrarch, a peculiar threat to his inner freedom; and he gave vivid articulation to the historical implications of these Stoic sentiments. "I think of liberty even while in bonds," he wrote, "of the country while in cities, of repose amidst labors, and finally . . . of ease while I am busy." A pattern of concrete associations emerges here. The modern world, with its greed, bustle, and conflict, means bondage to demanding work in the city; but against this is the vision of freedom, simplicity, and solitary repose in an idealized rural world. We may find here, therefore, some hint of the social realities underlying this discussion.[90]

A more positive dimension of this emphasis in Stoic humanism was its contribution to that inwardness which, with its genuine affinity to one aspect of Augustinianism, deepened consciences and provided one source for the moral sensitivity of the Catholic as well as the Protestant Reformation. Inwardness pointed to the role of conscience in the moral life, the inner voice which is concerned rather with motives than with outward acts and results. The young Calvin recognized this element in Stoicism. "Nothing is great for the Stoics," he wrote, "which is not also good and inwardly sound"; and he attacked "*monsters of men, dripping with inner vices,* yet putting forth the outward appearance and mask of uprightness." In his maturity he noted that men can discover some ideas of God within themselves and denounced the indolence of those who refused this inward search.[91] Montaigne's habitual self-examination also owed much to Stoicism. "For many years now," he declared, "my thoughts have had no other aim but myself, I have studied and examined myself only, and if I study any other things, it is to apply them immediately to, or rather within myself." Only by looking within, rather than at his deeds, could he discover his "essence," for here resided his "virtue."[92] The Stoic pursuit of truth within would also leave a fundamental mark on the thought of Descartes.

And from this source also came the remedy for the disagreeable agitation of mind resulting from the trials of modern life. The Stoic humanist recognized that perturbation of mind was a response to external stimuli; but he also saw that, since it was in the mind, it was potentially subject to rational control. Augustinus criticized Franciscus for his distractability and called on him to concentrate his attention, with the clear implication that this was within his power.[93] Philosophy, then, could quiet the wars of the self and induce a genuine and reliable tranquility of mind, as Pico argued.[94] Vives identified this belief with the Gospel: "The immediate and direct goal of Christianity is to calm down the storm of human passions, thus to provide the soul with a joyful serenity which makes us similar to God and to the angels."[95] It was in this sense that, for Pirckheimer, philosophy "[in Cicero's words] heals souls, dispels needless care, and banishes all fear."[96] Calvin recognized the attractions of this Stoic teaching. "Peace, quiet, leisure especially serve pleasure and usefulness," he wrote, and identified Stoic tranquility with what "the theologians almost always call 'peace.'"[97] Lipsius emphasized the intellectuality of the conception, the opposition it posited between reason and the affections. "Constancy," he declared, "is a proper and immovable strength of mind which is neither elevated nor depressed by external or casual accidents."[98]

At times the Stoic remedy for the evils of modern life found concrete application. Augustinus saw in it a better antidote for the problems of Franciscus than flight to the country; Stoic discipline would make it possible for him to live happily even in the city. "A soul serene and tranquil in itself," he observed, "fears not the coming of any shadow from without and is deaf to all the thunder of the world"; and he cited Seneca and Cicero to make the point that if "the tumult of your mind should once learn to calm itself down, believe me this din and bustle around you, though it will strike upon your senses, will not touch your soul."[99] Lipsius turned to Stoic doctrine specifically as consolation for the disruption of his personal life by the wars in the Low Countries, which had forced him to flee from place to place.[100] Stoicism was thus a doctrine of consolation not only for adversity in general; it was called forth by the particular troubles of the contemporary world, the chronic annoyances and indignities of urban life, and the acute dangers of war.

But it was also a regular and conscious feature of the Stoic prescription for human trouble that it was available only to the few; in practice Stoic humanism consistently rejected the implications of that vision of human brotherhood which had been one of the most genial features of ancient Stoicism. The aristocratic impulses in Renaissance society therefore found support in the powerful analogy between the order of the universe, the order of the human personality, and the social order, which suggested that society too must consist of both a higher rational principle and a lower, duller and less reliable component to which the higher force, personified by an elite, was in the nature of things superior. The blessedness to which the Stoic aspired was available only to a select few capable of the rational enlightenment and self-discipline of the wise; the masses were condemned to the external and turbulent life of the body, the passions, the senses. And one of the marks of the Stoic humanist was his constant, rather nervous concern to differentiate himself from the vulgar crowd and to reassure himself, somewhat in the manner at times discerned in the Protestant elect, of his spiritual superiority.

From this standpoint one's opponents, whoever they might be, could represent the mob. Petrarch seems variously to have identified the crowd with the enemies of the poetic way to truth (presumably the schoolmen), with vulnerability to the blandishments of the more disreputable rhetoricians, and with popular piety, as well as (more conventionally) with "the rank scum that pursues the mechanic arts."[101] Aeneas Sylvius, as Pius II, associated it with disrespect for the pope, in a passage that also invokes the Stoic longing for repose. "Some," he wrote of his enemies in Siena, "as is the way of the populace, even hurled abuse at him, and the ruling party actually hated him. The way of the world is certainly absurd with nothing about it fixed or stable." "Eloquence, like wisdom, like nobleness of life," he had written earlier, "is a gift of the minority."[102] Pico feared that access to philosophy by the commonality would contaminate it.[103] Erasmus made separation from the crowd one of his "General Rules of True Christianity": "This rule is that the mind of him who pants after Christ should disagree first with the deeds of the crowd, then with their opinions"; the mark of the philosopher is his contempt for "those things which the common herd goggles at" and his ability "to think quite differently from the opinions of the majority." That this was not altogether metaphorical is suggested by his indignation at Luther for "making public even to cobblers what is usually treated among the learned as mysterious and secret."[104] Calvin, too, was impressed by the dangers of the crowd. "These are the unchanging epithets of the mob: *factious, discordant, unruly,* and not groundlessly applied!" he commented in connection with Seneca; and he proceeded to illustrate the point copiously from Roman history.[105] For Montaigne dissociation from the crowd was an essential condition of intellectual freedom.[106] The general ideal of the intellectual life in this tradition was well expressed by Charles de Bouelles: "The wise man who knows the secrets of nature is himself secret and spiritual. He lives alone, far from the common herd. Placed high above other men, he is unique, free, absolute, tranquil, pacific, immobile, simple, collected, one. He is perfect, consummated, happy."[107]

IV. THE AUGUSTINIAN STRAIN
IN THE RENAISSANCE

Stoicism, then, had both attractions and weaknesses as the basis for accommodation to the conditions of Renaissance life, and these were not unrelated to one another. It identified the major problems of modern existence, often vividly and concretely, as the schoolmen did not. It reaffirmed in a new form a traditional vision of universal order which seemed an attractive prescription for the practical evils of a singularly disorderly society. It affirmed personal responsibility, its inwardness corresponded to the growing inwardness of later medieval piety, and it promised consolation for the tribulations of existence. But the structure of assumptions that enabled Stoic humanism to perform these services was not altogether adequate to the changing needs of a new society. Its conception of a universal order was singularly contradicted by the concrete world of familiar experience, and its idealism, however plausible in theory, ran the risk of seeming as irrelevant to life as the great systems of the schoolmen. Its intellectual vision of man was hardly adequate to a world in which men constantly encountered each other not as disembodied minds but as integral personalities whose bodies could not be ignored, whose passions were vividly and often positively as well as dangerously in evidence, and whose actions were profoundly unpredictable. The Stoic idea of freedom was too elevated to have much general application, and also severely limited by the large area of determinism in Stoic thought. And Stoicism appeared often to ignore or to reason away rather than to engage with and solve the practical problems of life; its disapproval of cities, of political particularity and individual eccentricity, of change, demonstrated the high-mindedness of its adherents, but it did not cause these awkward realities to go away. And it was scarcely helpful, especially since even the Stoic had no remedy for the misery of the overwhelming majority of mankind, to deny that suffering was real because it belonged to the lower world of appearances, or to direct the attention of wretched men from mutable to eternal things, or to insist that the world ought to be one and to be ruled by the wise. Like ancient Stoicism, therefore, the Stoic humanism of the Renaissance was ultimately hopeless. It is thus hardly surprising that, like the Stoicism of the hellenistic world, it was contested, within humanism itself, by another and very different vision of man, his potentialities, and his place in the universe. The great patron of this vision was Saint Augustine.

Here too Petrarch's *Secretum,* which I have frequently exploited to illustrate the Stoic elements in humanist thought, is singularly instructive. For, despite the ambiguities of this work, which foreshadow the perennial tension between the Stoic and Augustinian impulses in the Renaissance, it makes one clear point. It calls back to life the great Latin father who had virtually disappeared from Dante's intellectual universe, and it recalls him, however dimly realized, as a person. The personal appearance of Augustine in Petrarch's world of thought, only a generation after the completion of the *Divine Comedy,* may thus be taken as a kind of watershed between medieval and Renaissance culture. But it also suggests the crucial polarities within humanism itself.

For although Petrarch often makes Augustine into an ancient sage, a spokesman for the commonplaces of hellenistic moral thought who repeatedly quotes Cicero, Seneca, and other Latin writers, the Scriptures hardly at all, and although the Franciscus of the dialogues often seems more truly Augustinian than Augustine himself, the work gives eloquent testimony to the need of an anguished man of the fourteenth century not only for abstract wisdom but for a direct encounter with another human being in the past whose spiritual experience, as an individual, might be a source of nourishment for himself. Petrarch's Augustinus, however equivocal, is in the end not Truth itself, for a direct encounter with truth, Petrarch suggests, is more than man can bear.[108] He is a man, however venerable, who performs the role of one man with another. He listens and reacts to the confession of Franciscus, argues with him, not always successfully, and compels him to look more deeply and honestly into himself.

This humanization of Augustine, however incomplete, was a notable achievement. Because Augustine was a Christian, a saint, and still the most venerated source of religious wisdom in the West outside of Scripture itself, he provided the ultimate test for a typically Renaissance impulse, which Petrarch applied more successfully to such pagan worthies as Cicero or Seneca, and even to Aristotle. That he could manage it at all with Augustine testifies to the intensity of a new vision of existence even in its earliest stages. A fresh breeze had begun to blow in the old European atmosphere.

The uses of Augustine in the Renaissance did not always reflect this new awareness of his personality. He continued, with some regularity, to be cited in the old way as a guarantor of the highest truths. The later fifteenth-century Roman humanist Benedetto Morandi, for example, thought it "not only wicked but foolhardy" to oppose him;[109] and Melanchthon generally thought (though he did not always adhere to this opinion) that agreement with Augustine was virtually identical with Christian orthodoxy.[110] But it became increasingly common to praise him for his eloquence,[111] a human competence in which Renaissance rhetoricians might aspire to emulate him, or to call attention to dimensions of his personality or his earthly life, a tendency not confined to humanists. Gerson described his own mother as a "Saint Monica,"[112] and Vives observed that "if Augustine lived now, he would be considered a pedant or a petty orator."[113] And it became possible to take issue with Augustine, at least by implication; Poggio testifies to this in his attack on the presumption of Valla in implying that "the blessed Augustine also (such is the pride of this man, or rather of this brute) would have fallen into error about fate, the Trinity, and divine providence."[114] So thoroughgoing an Augustinian as Staupitz thought that Augustine "had no idea of the depths of the mystery of the Incarnation."[115]

But the humanization of Augustinianism has a larger significance for our purposes. It directs us to a crucial difference between Stoic and Augustinian humanism and helps to explain the very different order in which it is necessary, in the following pages, to analyze the latter. With Stoicism we must begin with the cosmos, and this in turn implies a certain view of man. But with Augustinianism we must begin with man, and from here we reach a certain view of the cosmos.[116] In Augustinian humanism the nature and experience of man himself limit what can be known about the larger universes to which man belongs and how he can accommodate to them.

Thus Augustinian humanism saw man, not as a system of objectively distinguishable, discrete faculties reflecting ontological distinctions in the cosmos, but as a mysterious and organic unity. This conception, despite every tendency in his thought to the contrary, is repeatedly apparent in Petrarch, in the *Secretum* and elsewhere, and it explains Melanchthon's indifference to the value of distinguishing the various faculties of the human personality.[117] One result was a marked retreat from the traditional sense of opposition between soul and body. Bruni found support for the notion of their interdependence in Aristotle,[118] and Valla, as Maffeo Vegio, vigorously rejected the possibility of distinguishing the pleasures of the soul from those of the body;[119] Pomponazzi's notorious refutation of the soul's immortality must be understood against this background. A corollary of this position is that the soul cannot be seen as a higher faculty in man, a spark of divinity which is intrinsically immune from sin and can only be corrupted from below. Petrarch confessed that, in the end, his troubles came rather from his soul than his body;[120] and Calvin was only applying this insight in his insistence that the Fall of Adam had its origins in deeper regions of the personality. "They childishly err," he wrote against a hellenistic understanding of Christianity, "who regard original sin as consisting only in lust and in the disorderly motion of the appetites, whereas it seizes upon the very seat of reason and upon the whole heart."[121] It follows, therefore, that the distinctive quality of man cannot be his reason. Valla identified it with his immortality,[122] Calvin with his capacity to know and worship God.[123] It also follows that the abstract knowledge grasped by reason is not sufficient to make men virtuous and therefore blessed, a point made with considerable emphasis by Petrarch in praising oratory above philosophy; thus Aristotle suffered as a moralist in comparison with Cicero, whom Petrarch now exploited in his less Stoic mood.[124] Since to know the good could no longer be identified with doing the good, it might also now be necessary to make a choice between knowledge and virtue, and the Augustinian humanist regularly came out on the side of virtue.

Despite their underlying belief in the integral unity of the personality, the Augustinian humanists accepted and argued in terms of the old vocabulary of the faculties; but the faculties they chose to emphasize implied a very different conception of the organization of man from that of the Stoics. They spoke above all of the will. Petrarch recognized clearly that Augustine's own conversion had been a function of his will rather than his intellect,[125] and Calvin was similarly Augustinian in recognizing the crucial importance of the will in the economy of salvation.[126] But the essential point in this conception of the will was its separation from and its elevation above reason. "It is safer," Petrarch declared, "to strive for a good and pious will than for a capable and clear intellect. . . . It is better to will the good than to know the truth."[127] Melanchthon was developing the implications of this view in saying that "knowledge serves the will. . . . For the will in man corresponds to the place of a despot in a republic. Just as the senate is subject to the despot, so is knowledge to the will, with the consequence that although knowledge gives warning, yet the will casts knowledge out and is borne along by its own affection."[128] One consequence was a new degree of freedom for the will, always severely restricted by the Stoic conception of the will as the automatic servant of reason. Salutati recognized this with particular clarity. Nothing, he wrote, could "even reach the intellect without the consent or command of the will," and once knowledge had penetrated the intellect, the will could freely follow or disregard it.[129] Valla saw in the freedom of the will the only conception of the matter consistent with the evident reality of sin, which would be impossible, and man would be deprived of responsibility and moral dignity, if reason in fact ruled will.[130]

The will, in this view, is seen to take its direction not from reason but from the affections, which are in turn not merely the disorderly impulses of the treacherous body but expressions of the energy and quality of the heart, that mysterious organ which is the center of the personality, the source of its unity and its ultimate worth. The affections, therefore, are intrinsically neither good nor evil but the essential resources of the personality; and since they make possible man's beatitude and glory as well as his depravity, they are, in Augustinian humanism, treated with particular respect. Thus even when Augustinus recommended Franciscus to meditate on the eternal verities, he called on him to invest his thought with affect, as a necessary sign that he has not meditated in vain.[131] Valla was especially emphatic about the positive quality of the passions, a primary consideration both in his perception of the particular importance of oratorical as opposed to philosophical communication and in the understanding of Christianity. "Can a man move his listeners to anger or mercy if he has not himself first felt these passions?" he asked. "It cannot be," he continued; "So he will not be able to kindle the love of divine things in the minds of others who is himself cold to that love."[132] For Valla religious experience was not intellectual but affective; the love of God is to be understood as man's ultimate pleasure. Calvin was working out the same line of thought in arguing, against the schools, that "the assent which we give to the divine word . . . is more of the heart than the brain, and more of the affections than the understanding. . . . faith is absolutely inseparable from a devout affection."[133] Prayer, he observed in the Geneva Confession, "is nothing but hypocrisy and fantasy unless it proceed from the interior affections of the heart";[134] and because of its power to rouse the heart he vigorously supported congregational singing.[135] Melanchthon remarked on the irrepressible power of the affections: "When an affection has begun to rage and seethe, it cannot be kept from breaking forth."[136] Against the scholastic view of the affections as a "weakness of nature," he argued that, on the contrary, "the heart and its affections must be the highest and most powerful part of man." Thus he saw that the consequence of control over the affections (if such control were truly possible) would be not rationality but insincerity, the presentation not of a higher and rational self to the world but of an inauthentic self.[137] We may find in this psychological discussion, therefore, a shrewd contribution to Renaissance concern, another reflection of social disruption, with the problems of friendship and hypocrisy.

This sense of the power and positive value of the passions was frequently the basis of an explicit attack on the Stoic ideal of *apatheia,* a point on which Stoicism seemed peculiarly unconvincing. Salutati doubted that "any mortal ever attained to such perfection besides Christ."[138] Brandolini denied that Stoic virtue could be truly divine because of its rejection of feeling, "for whoever lack affects necessarily lack virtues."[139] Erasmus denounced Stoic apathy in the *Praise of Folly*,[140] as did the young Calvin, citing Augustine; the older Calvin also attacked "the foolish description given by the ancient Stoics of 'the great-souled man'" and also denounced "new Stoics who count it depraved not only to groan and weep but also to be sad and care-ridden." We, he declared, citing Christ's tears, "have nothing to do with this iron-hearted philosophy."[141]

This same vision of man relieved the body of its old responsibility for evil and dignified its needs. Calvin particularly emphasized the error of associating sin primarily with the body; this mistake tended to make men "easily forgive themselves the most shocking vices as no sins at all." He traced the growth of this error historically, from the philosophers of antiquity, "till at length man was commonly thought to be corrupted only in his sensual part, and to have a perfectly unblemished reason and a will also largely unimpaired."[142] Such a view required a fresh understanding of the Pauline meaning of "flesh." It had to be construed, not narrowly as the physical body, but more broadly as those tendencies that alienated every part of man from God.[143] Melanchthon thought that "flesh" must especially signify reason, the site of unbelief.[144]

At the same time the impulses of the body could be viewed more tolerantly. Augustinus waived, for Franciscus, the strict Stoic doctrine regarding man's physical needs in favor of the golden mean,[145] and Calvin argued that "God certainly did not intend that man should be slenderly and sparingly sustained; but rather . . . he promises a liberal abundance, which should leave nothing wanting to a sweet and pleasant life."[146] He insisted on the legitimacy of pleasure, at least in moderation; severity on this score would lead to "the very dangerous error of fettering consciences more tightly than does the word of the Lord." Calvin was thinking of the monks, but the point applied equally to Stoic moralism.[147] It applied especially to sex, so often the special worry of traditional moralists because of its association with the body. Civic humanism had long applauded the family as the source of new citizens, and Valla had suggested a positive view of sex because it gave pleasure. But the sense, among the Augustinian humanists, of the integrity of the personality also provided a deeper foundation for the value of the sexual bond. As Bucer declared, "There is no true marriage without a true assent of hearts between those who make the agreement," and marriage is accordingly "a contract not only of body and of goods but also of the soul."[148] Calvin praised marriage, attributing disapproval of it to "immoderate affection for virginity."[149] A higher estimate of the body and of sex led also to some perception of the dignity of women.[150]

This better view of the body had even wider ramifications. It was related to Renaissance debate over the value of the active life, for the alleged inferiority of activity to contemplation assumed the inferiority to the mind of the body, which does the active business of the world. It also had deep theological significance, for it redirected attention from the immortality of the soul to the resurrection of the body; the more Augustinian humanist was likely to emphasize the central importance of the resurrection. Thus, although Petrarch often spoke of the soul, he had also learned "the hope of resurrection, and that this very body after death will be reassumed, indeed agile, shining, and inviolable, with much glory in the resurrection."[151] Calvin saw with particular clarity (and here his relation to Pomponazzi is evident) that "the life of the soul without hope of resurrection will be a mere dream."[152] And this Augustinian anthropology also posed the question of human freedom and man's need for grace in a new way. If it freed the will from obedience to reason, it perceived that this only meant the bondage of the will to the affections of the heart. And this meant that man can only be saved by grace, not by knowledge; for knowledge can at best reach only the mind, but grace alone can change the heart.[153]

It thus precluded the natural theology towards which Stoic humanism tended; its theology regularly opposed the folly of the cross to the rational wisdom of the philosophers.[154] Augustinus thus urged on Franciscus the irrelevance to his own deepest needs of that knowledge of nature on whose religious significance the Stoic set so much store.[155] In reply to his own more Stoic vision of the order of the universe, Calvin insisted on the actual inability of men, as the vain and contradictory speculations of the philosophers clearly demonstrated, to discover religious truths from nature.[156] Valla had argued that philosophy was the mother of heresy.[157] The Augustinian humanist was clear that, however valuable they might be for other purposes, the classics, based on reason alone, were valueless for Christianity. There was, Petrarch suggested, a qualitative difference between knowledge and faith, which he saw as something like the difference between seeing and listening: the difference, that is to say, between learning by means of one's own natural powers and learning directly, and so with peculiar certainty, from God.[158] Thus an Augustinian anthropology was fundamental to the new emphasis among humanists on the Bible, on the "school of the Gospel," which Budé contrasted with the Stoa as well as the Academy and the "subtle debates of the Peripatetics."[159]

Ultimate truth, then, is mysterious, beyond rational comprehension, and therefore first planted in the heart by grace, not discovered by the mind. "It is not man's part to investigate the celestial mystery through his own powers," Petrarch declared after emphasizing the gulf between God the creator and man his creature;[160] and Petrarch's sense of the incalculability of the world was carried by Salutati to a more general skepticism. "Every truth which is grasped by reason," Salutati wrote, "can be made doubtful by a contrary reason"; consequently man's rational knowledge cannot be absolute but, at best, is "a kind of reasonable uncertainty."[161] Valla humanized knowledge by representing truth as a matter not of objective certainty but of believing and feeling "concerning things as they themselves are."[162] And this notion of truth was hardly appropriate to the kind of conviction required by the Gospel. Accordingly philosophy, when it approached religious questions, was, for Melanchthon, a "chaos of carnal dreams"; the sacred mysteries, he insisted, should be adored, not investigated.[163] Calvin, since "human reason neither approaches, nor strives, nor takes straight aim" toward religious truth, suggested that a skeptical agnosticism was the best posture for men without revelation: "Here man's discernment is so overwhelmed and so fails that the first step of advancement in the school of the Lord is to renounce it."[164] This skepticism is obviously fundamental to the humanist case for the superiority of rhetoric to philosophy; like Scripture, rhetoric recognized the weakness of reason and spoke to the heart.

The Augustinian humanist recognized a very different tendency in Stoicism and occasionally displayed some insight into the affinities of Stoicism with medieval intellectuality. Valla sometimes used "Stoicism" to represent philosophy in general, by which he meant both ancient and medieval philosophy;[165] and Brandolini pointed to the rational (and for him specious) methodology which the Stoics shared with "almost all the philosophers and theologians of our time."[166] Calvin noted the "Stoic paradoxes and scholastic subtleties" in Seneca.[167] Here, then, is another area in which the tensions between Stoic and Augustinian humanism were threatening to break out into the open.

But all this was evidently the reflection of a more general insistence, within Augustinian humanism, on man's absolute dependence on his creator, which contrasted sharply with the Stoic tendency to emphasize man's sufficiency. This sense of human dependence is especially apparent in the Augustinian attitude to virtue, the supreme good of the Stoic.

Valla thought the Stoic ideal of the sage a contradiction in terms, if only because the triumph of virtue implied constant struggle; Stoic serenity was therefore unattainable.[168] Brandolini doubted that virtue could overcome suffering.[169] The examples of ancient virtue adduced as models by the Stoic humanist thus required some analysis. It might be remarked in general, as Petrarch and Erasmus did, that "true" virtue could not be attributed to any pagan, since his actions were obviously not done in the love of Christ.[170] Valla went beyond such generality to suggest that pagan virtue was vitiated by its concern for glory,[171] a point the young Calvin also emphasized. "Remove ambition," he wrote, "and you will have no haughty spirits, neither Platos, nor Catos, nor Scaevolas, nor Scipios, nor Fabriciuses." He saw the Roman Empire as "a great robbery," a notion also bearing on the Stoic ideal of a universal state.[172] Melanchthon viewed the virtues that enabled Alexander to conquer an empire simply as evidence that he loved glory more than pleasure.[173] These humanists did not deny the practical value of the alleged virtues of the pagans, but they insisted on distinguishing between the restraint of human nature and its purification, which only grace could accomplish. From this standpoint the Stoic ideal was shallow and therefore, in the end, unreliable. Christianity, as Melanchthon remarked, was not primarily concerned with virtue, and the pursuit of instruction on this topic in the Scriptures "is more philosophical than Christian."[174]

In fact a deeper knowledge of the self revealed that, like his knowledge of God, man's virtue and happiness also come entirely from God. To realize this was the goal of self-knowledge. Such knowledge, Calvin declared, "will strip us of all confidence in our own ability, deprive us of all occasion for boasting, and lead us to submission";[175] and Petrarch's own spiritual biography may be understood as a prolonged search for this kind of knowledge. It taught man, for example, the precise opposite of Stoic wisdom. Against the Stoic notion that blessedness can be founded only on the things that are man's own, Petrarch argued directly that in fact the only things that are a man's own are his sins; thus "in what is in one's own power" there is chiefly "matter of shame and fear."[176] There is an obvious connection between this interest in self-knowledge and the Pauline teaching on the moral law as the tutor of mankind, a conception again quite at odds with the Stoic notion of the function of law. If Petrarch's self-knowledge brought him to despair, he could take hope if only "the Almighty Pity put forth his strong right hand and guide my vessel rightly ere it be too late, and bring me to shore." God was the only source of his virtues (these are clearly not his own), of his blessedness, of his very existence: "In what state could I better die than in loving, praising, and remembering him, without whose constant love I should be nothing, or damned, which is less than nothing? And if his love for me should cease, my damnation would have no end."[177] Peace itself, the essence of Stoic beatitude, could only be the consequence, not of "some human virtue," Brandolini contended, but of grace.[178]

But there are, for the general development of European culture, even broader implications in the sense, within Augustinian humanism, of man's intellectual limitations. It pointed to the general secularization of modern life, for it implied the futility of searching for the principles of human order in the divine order of the cosmos, which lay beyond human comprehension. Man was accordingly now seen to inhabit not a single universal order governed throughout by uniform principles but a multiplicity of orders: for example, an earthly as well as a heavenly city, which might be seen to operate in quite different ways. On earth, unless God had chosen to reveal his will about its arrangements unequivocally in Scripture, man was left to the uncertain and shifting insights of a humbler kind of reason, to work out whatever arrangements best suited his needs. Hence a sort of earthy practicality was inherent in this way of looking at the human condition.

Indeed it is likely that the sharp Augustinian distinction between creation and Creator, since it denied the eternity of the universe, also promoted that secularization of the cosmos implicit in the Copernican revolution. If human order no longer depended on the intelligible order of the cosmos, the motive for discerning any such order was seriously weakened; conversely much of the resistance to Copernicanism stemmed from a concern, so strong in Stoic humanism, to protect a universal order that supplied mankind with general guidance for its earthly arrangements. Galileo relied heavily on Augustine to support his argument that the proper concern of religion is how one goes to heaven, not how heaven goes.[179]

If Machiavelli is the most famous example of the secularizing tendency in the Renaissance, he also had predecessors among earlier humanists of an Augustinian tendency. But the secularism implicit in Augustinian humanism achieved its clearest articulation in figures connected with the Reformation, not because Protestantism originated the secular impulse, but because, since Stoic arguments had been a major resource to support the old order, they now required a more direct attack. Calvin distinguished with particular clarity between the heavenly and earthly realms and the kinds of knowledge appropriate to each:

> There is one understanding of earthly things; another of heavenly ones. I call those things earthly which do not pertain to God and his kingdom, to true justice, or to the blessedness of the future life, and are in some sense confined within the limits of it. Heavenly things are the pure knowledge of God, the nature of true righteousness, and the mysteries of the heavenly kingdom. The first class includes government, domestic economy, all the mechanical skills and the liberal arts. In the second are the knowledge of God and of his will, and the rule by which we conform our lives to it.

He was emphatic about the separation between the two, whose correspondence had been so long cited in support of the ecclesiastical hierarchy. There was no basis, he declared, "to philosophize subtly over a comparison of the heavenly and earthly hierarchies," thus challenging not only the Neoplatonism of Dionysius but also the fundamental principles of Stoic world order.[180] By the same token he had no use for idealistic prescriptions for earthly order; he dismissed utopia as "a foolish fantasy the Jews had."[181] For Melanchthon "the civil and external dispensation of things has nothing to do with the Spirit's righteousness, no more than do plowing a field, building, or cobbling shoes."[182] This was not to deny the utility of humbler things but rather to assert that they worked best when it was recognized that they belong to a sphere of their own.

The pragmatic secularism to which Augustinian humanism pointed opposed the political idealism of Stoic humanism in all its dimensions: its belief in the universal principles needed to validate all government, its universalism, its insistence on the rule of the wise, its indifference to changing circumstance, its pacifism. Bruni gave concrete expression to the secularist mood in his own acceptance, without setting them in a larger framework of objective justification, of the common political values of Florence. "I confess that I am moved by what men think good," he wrote in his *Florentine Histories*: "to extend one's borders, to increase one's power, to extol the splendor and glory of the city, to look after its utility and security."[183] Here is the Machiavellian principle that the affairs of this world should be based on the dynamic interplay of earthly interests whose sordid realities are honestly faced; in short, the eternal reason of the Stoics must, for the practical good of men on earth, give way to reason of state.

This signified that laws and institutions must be accommodated to the variety of the human condition, and thus the desirability of many states with various kinds of government. This, rather than a universal empire, was, for Calvin, what God had intended. "If you fix your eye not on one city alone," he wrote, "but look round and glance at the world as a whole, or at least cast your sight upon regions farther off, divine providence has wisely arranged that various countries should be ruled by various kinds of government. For as elements cohere only in unequal proportion, so countries are best held together according to their own particular inequality." By the same token civil laws are not primarily the reflection of eternal law but should vary according to practical circumstance. "Every nation," Calvin declared, "is left free to make such laws as it foresees to be profitable for itself."[184] Melanchthon carried this relativism to extremes, finding in it the most likely guarantor of earthly order:

> Indeed, the political art covers external action in life, concerning possessions, contracts, and such like, and these are not the same among all nations. Laws are of one kind among the Persians, of another in Athens, or in Rome. Accordingly a Christian dresses differently in one part of the world than in another, reckons days differently in one place than he does in another. Whatever the policy of the place, that he uses; as Ezra judges cases according to Persian law when in Persia, so in Jerusalem he judges according to Jewish law. These things do not belong to the Gospel, any more than do clothes or the spacing of days. This distinction between the Gospel and political affairs is conducive to maintaining tranquility and increasing reverence for the magistrates.[185]

Augustinian humanism was thus closely related, as Stoic humanism was not, to the political realities of contemporary Europe.

In the same way Augustinian humanism attacked the spiritual elitism of the Stoic tradition, both in its loftier forms and in its application to government; and it was thus more sympathetic to those populist movements that found religious expression in the dignity of lay piety, political expression in the challenge of republicanism to despotism. For it was obvious that if rational insight into cosmic order could not supply the principles of either religious or political life, neither the church nor civil society could be governed by sages. This conviction had deep roots in Italian humanism. Charles Trinkaus has presented at least one group of humanists as lay theologians who were concerned to assert the religious competence of ordinary men by their emphasis on Christianity as a religion of grace accessible to all.[186] Valla contrasted the exclusiveness of Stoicism with the popularity of Epicureanism,[187] and he rested his case for eloquence against philosophy largely on the fact that it employed the language of ordinary men rather than the specialized vocabulary of an elite who "teach us by an exquisite sort of reasoning both to inquire and answer, which illiterates and rustics do better than philosophers."[188] There is a hint of this attitude even in Castiglione, who was willing to leave the evaluation of his *Courtier* to public opinion "because more often than not the many, even without perfect knowledge, know by natural instinct the certain savor of good and bad, and, without being able to give any reason for it, enjoy and love one thing and detest another."[189] Augustinian humanism denied any privileged position to a philosophically enlightened class. Calvin attacked the monks on the basis of the equality of all callings before God and broke with traditional humanist elitism by praising the manual as well as the liberal arts.[190] For the church this tendency would culminate in the priesthood of all believers. Melanchthon minimized the specialized competence of the clergy,[191] and Calvin insisted on the popular election of ministers "so as not to diminish any part of the common right and liberty of the church."[192] For civil society this impulse meant the rejection of theocracy, and a fully secular government. "Just as Socrates, at the beginning of the *Republic,* sent poets out of the state," Melanchthon asserted, "so we would not eject the theologians from the state but we would remove them from the governing group of the commonwealth,"[193] a principle also applied in the Italian republics. Calvin's preference for a republic over other forms of government is well known. "This is the most desirable kind of liberty," he wrote, "that we should not be compelled to obey every person who may be tyrannically put over our heads, but which allows of election, so that no one should rule except he be approved of us."[194] This position did not preclude social hierarchy, but it meant that differences in status among men could only be seen as an accident of history; they are not rooted in the order of the universe, and accordingly social structures can be modified as needs change.

So the willingness to accommodate human institutions to the varieties of circumstance also implied a willingness to acknowledge the significance of change in human affairs. "Now we know," Calvin declared, "that external order admits, and even requires, various changes according to the varying conditions of the times."[195] The historicism of the Renaissance, to which recent scholarship has given much attention, was distinctly not a function of the Stoic tendencies in humanism, which could only view mutability with alarm, but rather of the Augustinian tradition, in which God's purposes were understood to work themselves out in time. Thus for Salutati God "foresaw all that was and will be in time entirely without time and from eternity, and not only did he infallibly foresee and wish that they occur in their time, but also that through contingency they should be produced and be."[196] Contingency was no longer a threat to order but the fulfillment of a divine plan, and discrete events thus acquired meaning. This repudiation of Stoic stasis opened the way to the feeling for anachronism that we encounter not only in Valla's analysis of the Donation of Constantine and Guicciardini's attack on Machiavelli's rather Stoic application of the repetition of analogous situations but also in a more general relativism that left its mark on Calvin's understanding of church history and on his exegetical methods. He saw the rise of episcopacy, for example, as a practical response to the problem of dissension in the early church, an "arrangement introduced by human agreement to meet the needs of the times"; and he noted that there are "many passages of Scripture whose meaning depends on their [historical] context."[197] For Calvin fallen man seems to confront God in history rather than in nature.

At the same time these tendencies in Augustinian humanism also suggest the repudiation of the Stoic vision of peace as the ideal toward which man naturally aspires. This too was an expression of the greater realism in the Augustinian tradition; it had no conflict in principle with the acceptance by Renaissance society of warfare as a normal activity of mankind.[198] Within the Renaissance republic conflict had been institutionalized by constitutional provisions for checks and balances among competing social interests;[199] the Stoic ideal, on the contrary, would have sought to eliminate conflict by submitting all interests to the adjudication of reason, settling for nothing less than final solutions to human problems. And the restlessness of human society was paralleled, in the vision of Augustinian humanism, by the inescapable restlessness of individual existence. The Augustinian conception of man as passion and will implied that he could only realize himself fully in activity, which inevitably meant that life must be fraught with conflict, an external struggle with other men, but also an inner struggle with destructive impulses in the self that can never be fully overcome. For Valla virtue was only ideally a goal; practically it was an arduous way.[200] And the Calvinist saint, unlike the Stoic sage, could by no means expect a life of repose; on the contrary he must prepare himself "for a hard, toilsome, and unquiet life, crammed with numerous and various calamities. . . . in this life we are to seek and hope for nothing but struggle."[201] The ideal of earthly peace, from Calvin's standpoint, was a diabolical stratagem in which the struggle with sin was left in abeyance and God's will went undone. Here too it was apparent that Stoicism tended to confuse earthly with heavenly things.

Yet, far less equivocally than Stoic humanism, the vision of Augustinian humanism was social; and, based on the affective life of the whole man, its conception of social existence was animated not by abstract duty but by love. Augustinus reproved the anti-social sentiments of Franciscus by pointing out that life in society is not only the common lot of mankind but even the most blessed life on earth: "Those whom one counts most happy, and for whom numbers of others live their lives, bear witness by the constancy of their vigils and their toils that they themselves are living for others."[202] Salutati found in charity, understood in an Augustinian sense as a gift of divine grace, a way to reconcile— that there should have been a problem here testifies to the strength of the contrary Stoic impulse—his religious values with his love of Florence and his other attachments to the world. Love alone, he wrote, "fosters the family, expands the city, guards the kingdom, and preserves by its power this very creation of the entire world."[203] Thus Stoic withdrawal was countered by Augustinian engagement, which offered not the austere satisfactions of Stoic contemplation but the warmer and more practical consolations of a love applied to the needs of suffering mankind. Zwingli was writing in this tradition in describing the moral ends of education. "From early boyhood," he declared, "the young man ought to exercise himself only in righteousness, fidelity, and constancy: for with virtues such as these he may serve the Christian community, the common good, the state, and individuals. Only the weak are concerned to find a quiet life: the most like to God are those who study to be of profit to all even to their own hurt."[204] Calvin, who was explicit that man is by nature a social animal, saw in the limitations of individual knowledge a device by which God sought to insure human community. "God," he wrote, "has never so blessed his servants that they each possessed full and perfect knowledge of every part of their subject. It is clear that his purpose in so limiting our knowledge was first that we should be kept humble, and also that we should continue to have dealings with our fellows." Because of the needs of social existence he early rejected Stoic contempt for reputation; conscience was by itself an insufficient guide for human conduct, he argued, because, strictly a private and individual faculty, it was likely, operating in a social void, to cut man off from his neighbor. For Calvin the struggles of the Christian life were above all required by loving service to the human community.[205] Augustinian humanism sought to meet the crisis of community in the age of the Renaissance not by protecting the individual from destructive involvement with the social world but by full engagement, if possible out of love, in meeting its deepest and most desperate needs.

V. STOIC AND AUGUSTINIAN HUMANISM:
FROM AMBIGUITY TO DIALECTIC

At least two general conclusions emerge from this contrast between Stoic and Augustinian humanism. The first comes out of the fact that we can illustrate either with examples drawn indiscriminately from anywhere in the entire period of our concern, and this suggests that the tension between them found no general resolution in the age of the Renaissance and Reformation. But it is equally striking that we have often cited the same figures on both sides. Neither pure Stoics nor pure Augustinians are easy to find among the humanists, though individual figures may tend more to one position than the other. Erasmus, for example, seems more Stoic than Augustinian; Valla appears more Augustinian than Stoic. A closer study of individuals may reveal more personal development, from one position to another, than it has been possible to show here. Petrarch, Erasmus, and Calvin may especially invite such treatment. But the general ambivalence of humanists makes clear the central importance for the movement of the tension between the two positions. It was literally in the hearts of the humanists themselves. At the same time this ambiguity also reveals that Stoicism and Augustinianism do not represent distinguishable factions within a larger movement but ideal polarities that help us to understand its significance as a whole.

Yet I suggest that we can discern in this confrontation, if not a clear resolution, at least some instructive patterns of development. The humanism of the earlier Renaissance uneasily blended Stoic and Augustinian impulses which it neither distinguished clearly nor, in many cases, was capable of identifying with their sources. Its Augustinianism consisted of a bundle of personal insights that had, indeed, legitimate affinities with Augustine himself, as Petrarch vaguely sensed; but its Stoicism was singularly confused. Whatever Stoicism may have meant to Valla, his Cato Sacco, who probably is intended to represent the contemporary understanding of Stoicism, offers little more than a set of clichés about the misery of man and the malevolence of nature, hardly a legitimate Stoic idea; it is chiefly his emphasis on virtue that stamps him as a "Stoic." Conversely there is more genuine Stoicism in Maffeo Vegio, Valla's Epicurean, who defends the rational order of nature.[206] This seems to suggest that earlier Renaissance humanism, until the middle decades of the quattrocento, was profoundly confused about the variety in hellenistic thought, and confused as well about the gulf between antique paganism and the biblical world of ideas represented by the mature Augustine. Its historical sense was not yet adequate to sort out basic polarities.

But there were also resources within the Petrarchan tradition for overcoming this confusion. They are suggested by Petrarch's recall of Augustine in the *Secretum* as a vital personality whose personal experience and peculiar mode of thought can be apprehended in all their particularity by the philological imagination. Petrarch himself gave a large impetus to the novel tendency of Renaissance humanism to associate schools of thought with individual personalities, to dissolve the identity of ancient philosophy as a whole with a perennial wisdom and thus up to a point with Christianity itself, to sort out one school from another, and so to see every set of ideas, individually identified, as a product of the human mind at work under the limitations of historical circumstance. On this basis Petrarch was compelled to recognize (quoting Augustine) that no ancient philosopher, not Aristotle or even Plato, could be fully trusted for the truth; and he laid down an important principle for clarifying the understanding of the ancient philosophers, whom he characteristically insisted on regarding as men. "Far be it from me," he wrote, "to espouse the genius of a single man in its totality because of one or two well-formulated phrases. Philosophers must not be judged from isolated words but from their uninterrupted coherence and consistency. . . . He who wants to be safe in praising the entire man must see, examine, and estimate the entire man."[207]

We can begin to discern something of the implications of this principle in Salutati. "To harmonize Aristotle with Cicero and Seneca, that is the Peripatetics with the Stoics, is," he observed, "a great deal more difficult than you think."[208] But the point had a larger resonance; it tended to dissolve not only the bonds that hellenistic syncretism had forged among the various schools of philosophy but also those between philosophic and Christian wisdom. It may also be observed that this impulse to sort out one strand of thought from another came not from the Stoic strain in the European inheritance, which was itself permeated by an opposite motive, but from an Augustinian recognition of the conflict between the pagan (and clearly human) and the Christian worlds of thought. In the early Renaissance this impulse was most fully developed by Valla, who recognized the eclectic confusion in Stoicism itself and thus significantly reduced its authority.[209] Valla defended eclecticism, but he did so playfully, in full awareness of its philosophical deficiencies, and on behalf of the rhetorician rather than the philosopher. His treatment of Stoicism and Epicureanism was designed primarily to demonstrate the peculiar identity of Christianity, not its affinities with the rational systems of antiquity. And his own philological acumen provided the instrument for a further development of the historical sensitivity that made it increasingly difficult for the Renaissance humanist to persist in the confusions of the earlier stages of the humanist movement.

We encounter evidence of greater sophistication about ancient philosophy and its bearing on Christianity in various places after Valla, some of them unexpected. Later humanists increasingly perceived the differences rather than the agreements among the various schools of antiquity.[210] Savonarola, who as a Dominican could hardly have been expected to look kindly on Plato, protested against the effort to make either Plato or—more surprisngly—Aristotle into a Christian. "It is to be wished that Plato should be Plato, Aristotle Aristotle, and not that they should be Christian. . . . Let philosophers be philosophers and Christians Christians."[211] Erasmus, at other moments something of a Platonist, similarly protested the notion that Plato (or any other pagan writer) could have written under the inspiration of the Holy Spirit. He also denied the authenticity of the letters between Seneca and Paul, on which some part of the affinity between Stoicism and the Gospel was thought to depend; and he insisted, though venerating him still, that Seneca be read as a pagan who, if this were not clearly recognized, might otherwise mislead the Christian reader.[212] Here Erasmus displayed a concern for the individuality of the historical personality that was also reflected in the first volume of his edition of Augustine, in which he began with the *Confessions* and *Retractions,* on the ground, so alien from medieval thought, that it is necessary, in order to comprehend a writer, to have some preliminary knowledge of his biography and the general scope of his work.[213]

But the perception of differences did not automatically lead to the elimination of pagan elements from what was taken as the Christian tradition. Sometimes, as with Pico, it resulted in a more self-conscious and enthusiastic acceptance of the syncretist principle, which was given new life in the Neoplatonism of the later Italian Renaissance. And while Neoplatonism continued to reflect impulses central to the Stoicism of the earlier Renaissance, Stoicism itself remained attractive, with the possible difference that it could now be appropriated more consciously and deliberately. Traversari was attracted to the Stoic notion of virtue because he believed that it reinforced monastic life,[214] and Pico supported the Gospel with precepts from Seneca.[215] Pomponazzi underwent a late conversion from Aristotelianism to Stoicism, Stoic elements in the thought of Machiavelli were prominent enough to stimulate refutation by Guicciardini (himself not untouched by Stoicism), Erasmus and above all Vives were heavily influenced by the Stoics, and Clichetove's ideal for the priesthood resurrects something of the Stoic conception of the sage.[216] Meanwhile in Italy, Augustinianism, or at least the kind of Augustinianism that had attracted the earlier Renaissance, seems to have undergone some decline. Augustine was of major importance for Ficino, as he was for Giles of Viterbo, but chiefly because he seemed helpful to reconcile Platonism with Christianity. He was also more generally important to support the notion of a perennially valid "ancient theology," one of the less "Augustinian" uses to which he could have been put.[217] The reasons for this shift must be sought in the growing insecurity and disorder of later fifteenth-century Italy, which at once increased the attractions of Stoic consolation and Stoic emphasis on order and control, and at the same time decreased opportunities for the individual activity and social engagement called for by the mature Augustine.

But not all of Europe felt similarly damaged, and the Protestant Reformation stimulated some humanists to resume the debate between Augustinianism and Stoicism. The link between this tendency in Protestantism and Renaissance humanism may be discerned in the high degree of philological and historical sophistication in the thought of the Reformers. Melanchthon was peculiarly sensitive to the infiltration of Christian doctrine by Greek philosophy, and he traced the process from the Fathers (with the partial exception of Augustine) to the contemporary schoolmen. Though, like most subsequent historians of medieval philosophy, he discerned in it first a Platonic and then an Aristotelian phase, the essential elements of his indictment apply equally to the central assumptions of Stoicism: to its emphasis on the power of reason and accordingly on the self-sufficiency of man, especially man's ability to procure his own salvation.[218] On the other hand he humanized Augustine, whom he could perhaps admire precisely because Augustine had been aware of his own fallibility, recognized his mistakes, and changed his mind. Melanchthon recognized the relation between Augustine's opinions and the concrete historical circumstances that had produced them. Augustine was for Melanchthon, as Petrarch had tried to see him, not the personification of reason, but a person.[219]

The same point can be made even more strongly about Calvin. Augustine had helped him, even as a youth, to recognize the vanity in ancient disputes about the supreme good.[220] And his instincts for distinguishing between the philosophical residues in the thought of Augustine and the biblical dimensions of his thought were unusually sound. He paid small attention to Augustine's earlier, more philosophical compositions, though he otherwise drew massively on the works of Augustine; he disliked his allegorizing and his more speculative flights; and he thought him "excessively addicted to the philosophy of Plato," so that (for example) he had misunderstood the Johannine Logos.[221] But if Augustine did not interest him as a philosopher, Calvin was profoundly impressed by him as a theologian—and as a person. His respect for Augustine as a historical personality compelled him to insist on absolute fidelity—again we hear the authentic Renaissance note—to the intentions, and so to the full context, of any pronouncement of Augustine. "If I pervert his words into any other sense than Saint Augustine intended in writing them," he declared against his opponents, "may they not only attack me as usual but also spit in my face."[222] His sensitivity to what was authentically Augustinian made him particularly effective in sorting out genuine from pseudo-Augustinian writings, an exercise in which he made some improvement over Erasmus. He exploited his knowledge of Augustine's changes of mind against his Catholic enemies who still, apparently, thought an Augustinian pronouncement from any period in the saint's life equally representative of his views.[223] But above all Augustine was for Calvin a model of the open, developing spiritual life, of the mind in movement which we have seen as perhaps the central feature in Augustine's significance for the Renaissance. In the 1543 edition of the *Institutes* he included the quintessentially Augustinian motto: "Ie me confesse estre du reng de ceux qui escrivent en profitant, et profitent en escrivant."[224]

Although this study is not generally concerned with the problem of the connections between Renaissance humanism and the Reformation, it may thus be of some help in explaining why some humanists, but not others, turned to Protestantism. Humanists of more Stoic tendencies, like Erasmus, seem to have been less likely to become Protestants than those of the more Augustinian kind. But the more Augustinian humanist might end up in either the Protestant or Catholic camp.

For Augustine was also an important figure, though in a more complex way, in the Catholic Reformation. The reaffirmation of the authority of tradition at Trent guaranteed to the Fathers collectively an essential place, linking the apostolic to the medieval church, in the historical continuity of the faith; and Augustine shared in a general patristic flowering. He received extensive treatment in Bellarmine's *De scriptoribus ecclesiasticis*;[225] and his works went through numerous printings in Catholic countries, culminating with the authoritative Benedictine edition of Saint Maur (1679–1700).[226] But Augustine had many uses. The thought of the mature Augustine was of fundamental importance for the circle of Bérulle, who, in the tradition of Augustinian humanism, opposed it to Stoic tendencies in Catholic thought.[227] The significance of this species of Augustinianism for the Catholic world is evident in the deep influence of Augustine at Louvain, where it found expression in the works of Baius and Jansen, and in the controversy *De auxiliis*. Since Thomist theology was so deeply rooted in Augustine, the growing influence of Thomism also operated to keep Augustine alive as a theologian of grace. But the condemnations of Baius and of Jansenism and the inconclusiveness of the dispute *De auxiliis* indicate the reserve of ecclesiastical authority toward this kind of Augustinianism; and meanwhile the Platonic Augustine of the Florentine Platonists, who could be invoked to support the old mixture of philosophy with Christianity, was still very much alive. Some of the opponents of Jansenism also exploited the authority of Augustine to support a heavily moralistic and rather arid scholasticism from which Augustine himself seems strikingly absent.[228]

At the same time Stoicism was becoming stronger than ever in later sixteenth-century Europe, once more presenting itself as both a source of personal consolation and a force for order in a period when religious wars were creating general anarchy, when the challenge to ecclesiastical authority threatened to produce a deeper kind of disorder, when the ruling classes were made profoundly insecure by what they discerned as the danger of mass uprising from below, and when all the world seemed in the grip of unrestrained passion. Under these conditions both the moral disciplines and the larger theories of control advanced by the Stoics once more appeared singularly attractive, and Stoicism reinforced the more general impulse of the Catholic Reformation to discipline every dimension of life.[229] This period saw, with Lipsius, the first fully systematic presentation of Stoicism; Lipsius was perhaps the first modern European to recognize clearly, though earlier Stoic expression often gave inadvertent testimony to it, that the heart of Stoicism is not its ethics but its philosophy of nature.[230]

Lipsius, and to a lesser extent Charron and Du Vair, therefore mark the beginning of a new phase in the influence of Stoicism. Since it was now an increasingly articulated system, it was more successful than the eclectic bits and pieces gleaned from Seneca and Cicero not only in establishing the cosmic foundations of order but also in promoting the peace of the contemplative life. Lipsius recognized a number of Christian objections to Stoicism in his *De constantia*, but it is significant that the ideal of *apatheia* was not among them; indeed, his own ideal of constancy explicitly includes freedom from hope and fear.[231] And the recovery of a more consistent Stoic anthropology, in which reason was seen as the essential faculty of man and thus capable of imposing order on the passions and finally on society, was supplemented in this movement by a renewal of the effort of Stoic humanism to join philosophical with Christian wisdom. Neostoic writers even assimilated Augustine, whom they often quoted.[232]

On the other hand Stoic doctrine was also popular, among Protestants as well as Catholics, in a more secular form. It is worth remembering that even those Augustinian humanists who had rejected the mixture of philosophy with religion recognized the value of rational insight for the humbler business of this world; and it was therefore entirely consistent with a fundamentally Augustinian position to draw on isolated Stoic maxims for their relevance to practical situations. Calvin himself continued to exploit Seneca for his sermons and elsewhere.[233] In this form Stoicism nourished the secularization of morality and the discovery of principles of social order independent of religion. This species of Stoicism was responsible for the attempt by such figures as Charron and Grotius, in a time when religious passion was a source of general disturbance, to base ethics on the laws of nature. Eventually this would lead to the notion that the principles of human behavior might be based solely on the knowledge of human nature.[234]

In this secularized form Stoicism could be reconciled with Augustinianism. The two could be seen to complement each other, as law is complemented by grace, or the earthly by the heavenly city. But such a reconciliation, which depended on the deracination of Stoicism, was obviously a reconciliation on Augustinian terms. And Stoicism had a peculiar facility for growing new roots; thus the tension between the two old antagonists was never fully resolved.

NOTES

1. For example, the *Grande Antologia Filosofica,* though it includes a section on Renaissance Epicureanism, gives no special treatment to either Stoicism or Augustinianism; and Eugenio Garin's distinguished *L'umanesimo italiano: filosofia e vita civile nel rinascimento* (Bari, 1952) has much on Platonism but little directly on Stoicism or Augustinianism. On the other hand, both receive substantial recognition in Charles Trinkaus, *In Our Image and Likeness: Humanity and Divinity in Italian Humanist Thought* (Chicago, 1970), to which I am heavily indebted. The chief difference between his treatment of the subject and my own is one of emphasis; Trinkaus seems to me primarily concerned with the humanist effort to harmonize Stoic and Augustinian impulses (cf. I, xx–xxi).

2. For the ambiguous connections between Stoicism and rhetoric there is much in George Kennedy, *The Art of Rhetoric in the Roman World, 300 B.C.– A.D. 300* (Princeton, 1972); see also Jerrold E. Seigel, *Rhetoric and Philosophy in Renaissance Humanism: Ciceronian Elements in Early Quattrocento Thought and Their Historical Setting* (Princeton, 1968), esp. ch. 1, and Nancy S. Struever,

The Language of History in the Renaissance: Rhetoric and Historical Consciousness in Florentine Humanism (Princeton, 1970), esp. ch. 1. For the rhetorical element in Augustine, I have had fundamental guidance from Peter Brown, *Augustine of Hippo: A Biography* (Berkeley, 1967); see also Marcia Colish, *The Mirror of Language: A Study in the Medieval Theory of Knowledge* (New Haven, 1968). Henri Irénée Marrou, *Saint Augustin et la fin de la culture antique,* 4th ed. (Paris, 1958), also remains basic. For the importance of Cicero and Stoicism in Augustine, see also Maurice Testard, *Saint Augustin et Cicéron: Cicéron dans la formation et dans l'œuvre de Saint Augustin* (Paris, 1958).

3. Adam, *Sur le problème religieux dans la première moitié du XVIIe siècle* (Oxford, 1959); Trinkaus, *op. cit.*

4. On this problem cf. Raymond Klibansky, *The Continuity of the Platonic Tradition in the Middle Ages* (London, 1939), 36. For one recent effort to sort out this mixture, see Andreas Graeser, *Plotinus and the Stoics: A Preliminary Study* (Leiden, 1972), a title whose modesty suggests the difficulty of the problem. Moses Hadas, *Hellenistic Culture: Fusion and Diffusion* (New York, 1959), is generally useful on the subject, in spite of its tendency to exaggerate Semitic elements in the hellenistic bundle.

5. *De civitate dei,* XVIII, 51; cf. XVIII, 41.

6. Eugene Teselle, *Augustine the Theologian* (London, 1970), 347–348.

7. Ep. 143, quoted by Brown, 353. For the general point, in addition to Brown and Teselle, I am much indebted to F. Edward Cranz, "The Development of Augustine's Ideas on Society before the Donatist Controversy," *Harvard Theological Review,* 47 (1954), 255–316, and R. A. Markus, *Saeculum: History and Society in the Theology of St. Augustine* (Cambridge, 1970).

8. For this apocryphal correspondence, *Epistolae Senecae ad Paulum et Pauli ad Senecam 'quae vocantur,'* ed. C. W. Barlow (Rome, 1938).

9. For an excellent introduction to the fundamental importance of this issue, see *Creation: The Impact of an Idea,* ed. Daniel O'Connor and Francis Oakley (New York, 1969).

10. The classic work of Charles Norris Cochrane, *Christianity and Classical Culture* (Oxford, 1940), is particularly useful on this fundamental difference.

11. Damasus Trapp, "Augustinian Theology of the 14th Century: Notes on Editions, Marginalia, Opinions, and Book Lore," *Augustiniana,* VI (1956), 189.

12. M. D. Chenu, *Toward Understanding St. Thomas,* tr. Albert M. Landry and Dominic Hughes (Chicago, 1964), 43, 54, 142 (I cite the English edition rather than the French original, *Introduction à l'étude de Saint Thomas d'Aquin* [Paris, 1950], because of its richer documentation); Henri-Irénée Marrou, *Saint Augustin et l'augustinisme* (Paris, 1955), 161–162.

13. Canto X.

14. Canto XXXII.

15. He cites the *Confessions* from time to time in the *Convivio* but appears to regard it as no more than a conventional work of moral guidance.

16. This has been noted by Nicola Abbagnano, "Italian Renaissance Humanism," *Cahiers d'histoire mondiale,* XI (1963), 269; cf. Charles B. Schmitt, *Cicero Scepticus: A Study of the Influence of the Academica in the Renaissance* (The Hague, 1972), 33–34, on the importance (and neglect by modern scholars) of Cicero for the Middle Ages. Hans Baron, "Cicero and the Roman Civic Spirit

in the Middle Ages and the Early Renaissance," *John Rylands Library Bulletin,* XXII (1938), 72–97, has useful remarks on the medieval, as contrasted with the Renaissance, image of Cicero.

17. Quoted by John Mundy, *Europe in the High Middle Ages, 1150–1309* (London, 1973), 478, noting the prominence of Seneca in Bacon's *Opus maius.*

18. Cf. the passages on fortune in the translation of Charles Dahlberg (Princeton, 1971), 87, 102–104, 121–122.

19. For his use of the Senecan notion of seeds of virtue and knowledge, see also the passages listed by Maryanne C. Horowitz, "Pierre Charron's View of the Source of Wisdom," *Journal of the History of Philosophy,* IX (1971), 454 n. 44. Professor Horowitz is working on a general study of the career of Stoicism from antiquity to the later Renaissance.

20. Esp. in the *Convivio;* cf. Inferno, IV, 141, where Cicero appears in the company of "Seneca morale."

21. *De natura deorum,* ed. H. Rackham (Cambridge, Mass., and London, 1957), 257–259. For medieval use of the image, cf. R. W. Southern, *Medieval Humanism and Other Studies* (New York, 1970), 37–41.

22. Cf., for example, Marsilius of Padua, *Defensor pacis,* I, v, 10.

23. See, for example, *Romance of the Rose,* 110, and the Knight's and Monk's tales in Chaucer's *Canterbury Tales.*

24. Cf. *Romance of the Rose,* 308–312, and the passages collected in Mundy, 265–269. Johan Huizinga, *Waning of the Middle Ages,* tr. F. Hopman (New York, 1959), 64–67, directs attention to the importance of this motif in medieval literature.

25. Chenu, 47–48, 52 nn. 3 and 4, 152.

26. Trapp, 150–151, 181, describing Gregory as the "first Augustinian of Augustine" to distinguish him from the more equivocal Augustine of the Middle Ages.

27. David Curtis Steinmetz, *Misericordia Dei: The Theology of Johannes von Staupitz in Its Late Medieval Setting,* Studies in Medieval and Reformation Thought, IV (Leiden, 1968), 155.

28. The point is made by Trinkaus, I, 307.

29. *De vero falsoque bono,* ed. Maristella de Panizza Lorch (Bari, 1970), 18. See the discussion of this discourse in Trinkaus, I, 110–113.

30. Quoted in Carlos G. Noreña, *Juan Luis Vives* (The Hague, 1970), 216.

31. *Institutes,* I, v, 1. For a balanced view of Calvin's Stoicism, which is sometimes exaggerated, see Charles Partee, "Calvin and Determinism," *Christian Scholar's Review* V (1975–76), 123–128. I will make no distinction in these pages between men of humanist backgrounds such as Zwingli, Melanchthon, and Calvin, who became Protestants, and other humanists. However conventional, such a distinction seems to me to rest on assumptions that cannot be justified in the light of recent scholarship. This is an obvious inference from Kristeller's fundamental contributions to our understanding of humanism, and the fact that we have been so slow to draw it is perhaps chiefly attributable to the overspecialization that artificially separates students of the Renaissance from those of the Reformation.

32. Quoted by Horowitz, 453, from *De la sagesse;* Charron cites Seneca.

33. "Apologie de Raimond Sebond," *Essaies,* ed. Maurice Rat (Paris, 1958), II, 140–141. I follow here the translation of E. J. Trechman (Oxford, 1935).

34. Quoted by Noreña, 201–202.

35. See the passage from *De fato* in Trinkaus, II, 547; for Calvin, *Institutes*, I, v, 3.

36. *Calvin's Commentary on Seneca's De clementia*, ed. Ford Lewis Battles and André Malan Hugo (Leiden, 1969), 103 n. 39, citing *Contre de l'astrologie judiciaire* (1549).

37. *De liberorum educatione*, tr. William Harrison Woodward, in *Vittorino da Feltre and Other Humanist Educators* (New York, 1970), 140.

38. *Secretum*, 460. My references to this work are to the edition in Francesco Petrarca, *Opere*, ed. Giovanni Ponte (Milan, 1968), but I have generally followed the translation by William H. Draper (London, 1911). For the confrontation between Stoicism and Augustinianism in Petrarch, see Klaus Heitmann, *Fortuna und Virtus: eine Studie zu Petrarcas Lebensweisheit* (Cologne, 1958); and for his Augustinianism, Pietro Paolo Gerosa, *L'umanesimo agostiniano del Petrarca* (Turin, 1927).

39. See Trinkaus, II, 544, for a passage from *De fato* in which Pomponazzi expresses his disagreement with the more Augustinian notion of the will as mistress of the intellect.

40. *Commentary on Genesis*, 1:26. I quote in the translation of John King (Edinburgh, 1847).

41. *Institutes*, I, xv, 7.

42. *Epistolae familiares*, XI, 1 and XXI, 15, in *Le famigliari*, ed. Vittorio Rossi (Florence, 1937), II, 23, IV, 94; I use the translations in David Thompson, *Petrarch: An Anthology* (New York, 1971). Cf. Augustinus on soul and body in *Secretum*, 468, 498.

43. Cf. the remarkable passage in Noreña, 202. For Vive's hatred of sex, see also 209–211.

44. *De constantia libri duo* (Antwerp, 1605), 7.

45. *Institutes*, I, iii, 1; I, xiv, 21; I, v, 2; II, vi, 1. Egil Grislis, "Calvin's Use of Cicero in the Institutes I:1—A Case Study in Theological Method," *Archiv für Reformationsgeschichte*, LXII (1971), 5–37, shows how closely Calvin follows *De natura deorum*.

46. *Invectiva contra eum qui Maledixit Italiae*, in Thompson, 230–231; *Secretum*, 470; *De sui ipsius et multorum ignorantia*, tr. Hans Nachod, in *The Renaissance Philosophy of Man*, ed. Ernst Cassirer et al. (Chicago, 1948), 83–85.

47. *Op. cit.*, 141–142.

48. Quoted by Charles Partee, "The Revitalization of the Concept of 'Christian Philosophy' in Renaissance Humanism," *Christian Scholar's Review*, 3 (1974), 364.

49. *An Exposition of the Faith*, tr. G. W. Bromiley, *Zwingli and Bullinger*, Library of Christian Classics, XXIV (London, 1953), 275–276.

50. Seigel discusses this, 104–106.

51. *Secretum*, 494.

52. *I libri della famiglia*, ed. Cecil Grayson, in *Opere volgari*, I (Bari, 1960), 63; I use the translation of Renée Neu Watkins, *The Family in Renaissance Florence* (Columbia, S.C., 1969), 75–76.

53. *De pueris instituendis*, in *Desiderius Erasmus concerning the Aim and Method of Education*, ed. William H. Woodward (New York, 1964), 192–193.

54. *Comm. Seneca*, 280–281.

55. *Institutes,* IV, xiii, 3, 21.

56. Quoted by Horowitz, 452–453.

57. *Secretum,* 442; *Ep. fam.,* XXI, 15, in IV, 95.

58. See his argument in *De immortalitate animae,* tr. William Henry Hay, II, *Renaissance Philosophy of Man,* 359–377; discussed by Trinkaus, I, 539–541.

59. *Comm. Seneca,* 112–113.

60. *De ordine docendi et studendi,* in Woodward, *Vittorino da Feltre,* 177.

61. *De pueris instituendis,* Woodward, 212.

62. *Della famiglia,* 64.

63. Quoted by Noreña, 207.

64. "De l'yvrongnerie," *Essaies,* II, 10.

65. *De liberorum educatione,* Woodward, 157.

66. *De vita solitaria,* II, ix, tr. Jacob Zeitlin, *The Life of Solitude* (Urbana, 1924), 250–251.

67. *The Book of the Courtier,* tr. Charles S. Singleton (New York, 1959), 332.

68. Letter to Servatius Roger, 8 July 1514, *Opus Epistolarum Erasmi,* ed. P. S. and H. M. Allen (Oxford, 1906–1958), I, 567–569.

69. *De constantia,* 15–19.

70. The adage *Aut fatuum aut regem nasci oportere,* in Margaret Mann Phillips, *The Adages of Erasmus* (Cambridge, 1964), 219; *Institutio principis Christiani,* tr. Lester K. Born (New York, 1968), 150.

71. Noreña, 213.

72. *Gargantua,* I, ch. xlv; cf. Erasmus on the philosopher-king in the adage cited above, Phillips, 217, and Castiglione, *Courtier,* 307.

73. From the dedication of the *Institutio principis Christiani,* tr. Born, 134.

74. From the adage cited above, Phillips, 219.

75. See the discussion of Salutati's *De nobilitate legum et medicinae* in Garin, 36–38.

76. "Inns," *The Colloquies of Erasmus,* tr. Craig R. Thompson (Chicago, 1965), 150.

77. *Courtier,* 82.

78. *Epistolae variae,* XLVIII, tr. Thompson.

79. Harry Levin, *The Myth of the Golden Age in the Renaissance* (Bloomington, 1969), 38.

80. From the concluding reflections in the *Arte della guerra,* in Machiavelli, *The Chief Works and Others,* tr. Allan Gilbert (Durham, 1965), II, 726.

81. Quoted by John W. O'Malley, *Giles of Viterbo on Church and Reform* (Leiden, 1968), 141.

82. From the adage *Festina lente,* in Phillips, 183–184.

83. *Institutio principis Christiani,* 211.

84. Quoted by Garin, 37.

85. *De constantia,* 46.

86. *Secretum,* 494.

87. *Secretum,* 514.

88. *Ep. fam.,* XXIV, 3. I use the translation of M. E. Cosenza, *Petrarch's Letters to Classical Authors* (Chicago, 1910), 1–4.

89. For Salutati, cf. Seigel, 70–76; for Montaigne, see for example "De la solitude," *Essaies,* I, esp. 276. For a typical debate on the subject, cf. Alberti, *Della famiglia,* 179–185.

90. *Ep. fam.*, XVII, 10, in III, 263; cf. his dismal vision of urban life, with special reference to Avignon, in *Secretum*, 516–518.

91. *Comm. Seneca*, 348–349, 52–53; *Institutes*, I, v, 3.

92. "De l'exercitation," *Essaies*, II, 50; "Des cannibales," I, 241.

93. *Secretum*, 472.

94. *Oration on the Dignity of Man*, tr. Elizabeth Livermore Forbes, in *Renaissance Philosophy of Man*, 231.

95. Noreña, 207.

96. Quoted by Hans Rupprich, "Willibald Pirckheimer: Beiträge zu einer Wesenserfassung," *Schweizer Beiträge zur Allgemeinen Geschichte*, XV (1957), 85.

97. *Comm. Seneca*, 84–85, 40–41.

98. *De constantia*, 6.

99. *Secretum*, 522, 516.

100. *De constantia*, 2.

101. *Ep. fam.*, XIII, 6, in III, 72; *Secretum*, 442–444, 476–478, 512.

102. *Memoirs of a Renaissance Pope: The Commentaries of Pius II*, tr. Florence A. Gragg (New York, 1959), 58; *De liberorum educatione*, 148.

103. Cf. *Oration*, 250. For the esoteric notion of communication based on this view, see Edgar Wind, *Pagan Mysteries in the Renaissance* (New Haven, 1958), 24–30.

104. *Enchiridion militis Christiani*, tr. Ford Lewis Battles, in *Advocates of Reform*, ed. Matthew Spinka, Library of Christian Classics, XIV (London, 1953), 349 and cf. 350, 357; adage *Aut fatuum aut regem nasci oportere*, Phillips, 217; letter to Jodocus Jonas, 10 May 1521, Allen, IV, 487–488.

105. *Comm. Seneca*, 24–25.

106. "De la coustume et de ne changer aisément une loy receüe," *Essaies*, I, 125.

107. *Metaphysicum introductorium*, E1^r, quoted by Augustin Renaudet, *Préréforme et l'humanisme à Paris pendant les premières guerres d'Italie*, rev. ed. (Paris, 1953), 420 n. 2.

108. *Secretum*, 434.

109. Quoted by Trinkaus, I, 287.

110. Peter Fraenkel, *Testimonia Patrum: The Function of the Patristic Argument in the Theology of Philip Melanchthon* (Geneva, 1961), 94–96.

111. Cf. Trinkaus, II, 562, 568, 631.

112. James L. Connolly, *John Gerson, Reformer and Mystic* (Louvain, 1928), 22.

113. In his commentary on *De civitate Dei*, quoted by Noreña, 135.

114. Quoted by Salvatore I. Camporeale, *Lorenzo Valla, umanesimo e teologia* (Florence, 1972), 34.

115. From the sermon "Eternal Predestination and its Execution in Time," in Heiko A. Oberman, *Forerunners of the Reformation* (New York, 1966), 179.

116. Trinkaus, I, 104, notes a similar contrast between the cosmological and rational emphasis of scholastic and the anthropological emphasis of humanist thought, a point with some bearing on the historical significance of Stoicism.

117. Cf. *Loci communes theologici*, tr. Lowell J. Satre, in *Melanchthon and Bucer*, ed. Wilhelm Pauck, Library of Christian Classics, XIX (London, 1969), 23–24.

118. Cf. Hans Baron, "Franciscan Poverty and Civic Wealth in Humanistic

Thought," *Speculum*, XIII (1938), 21, quoting Bruni's commentary on the *Economics* of Aristotle.

119. *De vero bono*, 76.
120. *Secretum*, 516.
121. *Comm. Genesis* 3:6.
122. Trinkaus, I, 153, 155.
123. *Institutes*, I, iii, 3.
124. *De ignorantia*, 104 and more generally.
125. *Secretum*, 448–450.
126. As in *Institutes*, II, v, 15.
127. *De ignorantia*, 70.
128. *Loci communes*, 23–24.
129. Quoted by Trinkaus, I, 64.
130. Cf. Giorgio Radetti, "La religione di Lorenzo Valla," *Medioevo e rinascimento: studi in onore di Bruno Nardi* (Florence, 1955), II, 617–618.
131. *Secretum*, 462.
132. *De vero bono*, 91; cf. Trinkaus, I, 115–116, 127, 138.
133. *Institutes*, III, ii, 8; cf. 33, 36.
134. Article 13, in *Calvin: Theological Treatises*, ed. J. K. S. Reid, Library of Christian Classics, XXII (London, 1954), 29.
135. *Comm. Genesis* 4:21.
136. *Loci communes*, 30; cf. Calvin, *Institutes*, II, vii, 10.
137. *Loci communes*, 29, 28.
138. Quoted by Struever, 59; cf. Seigel, 72–73.
139. Quoted by Trinkaus, I, 317–318.
140. *Opera*, ed. J. Leclerc (Leiden, 1703–1705), IV, 430.
141. *Comm. Seneca*, 360–361; *Institutes*, III, viii, 9.
142. *The Necessity of Reforming the Church*, in *Calvin: Theological Treatises*, 198; *Institutes*, II, ii, 4.
143. For Calvin see, among other places, *Comm. Genesis* 6:3 and *Comm. Romans* 8:10; for Melanchthon, *Loci communes*, 31, 37–38.
144. *Loci communes*, 144.
145. *Secretum*, 490; cf. Baron, "Franciscan Poverty," 7.
146. *Comm. Genesis* 1:30.
147. *Institutes*, III, x, 1.
148. *De regno Christi*, in *Melanchthon and Bucer*, 322.
149. *Institutes*, IV, xii, 27.
150. For Calvin, cf. *Comm. Genesis*, 1:31; for Melanchthon, see Fraenkel, 293.
151. Quoted by Trinkaus, I, 190–191.
152. *Comm. Matthew* 22:23, in *A Harmony of the Gospels Matthew, Mark and Luke*, tr. A. W. Morrison (Grand Rapids, 1972), III, 29.
153. Cf. Melanchthon's formulation, *Loci communes*, 27.
154. Cf. Trinkaus, I, 55, on Salutati.
155. *Secretum*, 476.
156. *Institutes*, I, v, 4; cf. 12.
157. See passages from the *Elegantiae*, in Camporeale, 7.
158. Cf. passage from *De otio* in Trinkaus, I, 39; cf. Calvin, *Institutes*, III, ii, 14.

159. From *De transitu Hellenismi ad Christianismum,* quoted by Josef Bohatec, *Budé und Calvin: Studien zur Gedankenwelt des französischen Frühhumanismus* (Graz, 1950), 70.

160. Quoted by Trinkaus, I, 36.

161. Quoted by Seigel, 74.

162. Quoted by Trinkaus, I, 162.

163. *Loci communes,* 99, 21.

164. *Institutes,* II, ii, 18; III, ii, 34.

165. Seigel, 152.

166. Quoted by Trinkaus, I, 299.

167. *Comm. Seneca,* 336–337.

168. *De vero bono,* 108.

169. Trinkaus, I, 169.

170. For Petrarch see the passage from *De otio,* quoted by Trinkaus in "The Religious Thought of the Italian Humanists and the Reformers: Anticipation or Autonomy?" *The Pursuit of Holiness in Late Medieval and Renaissance Religion: Papers from the University of Michigan Conference,* ed. Charles Trinkaus and Heiko A. Oberman, Studies in Medieval and Reformation Thought, X (Leiden, 1974), 352; for Erasmus, *Erasmus and the Seamless Coat of Jesus,* tr. Raymond Himelick Lafayette, Ind., 1971), 58.

171. *De vero bono,* 2.

172. *Comm. Seneca,* 94–95, 32–35.

173. *Loci communes,* 27–28.

174. *Ibid.,* 22.

175. *Institutes,* II, i, 2.

176. Trinkaus, I, 45–46, quoting *De otio.*

177. *Secretum,* 466–468; *Ep. fam.* XXII, 10, in IV, 127.

178. Quoted by Trinkaus, I, 318.

179. In his letter to the Grand Duchess Christina, in Galileo Galilei, *Opere,* ed. Antonio Favaro (Florence, 1890–1909), V, 307–348.

180. *Institutes,* II, ii, 13; IV, vi, 10.

181. *Contre les Anabaptistes,* quoted by Michael Walzer, *The Revolution of the Saints: A Study in the Origins of Radical Politics* (Cambridge, Mass., 1965), 47.

182. *Loci communes,* 129.

183. Quoted by Donald J. Wilcox, *The Development of Florentine Humanist Historiography in the Fifteenth Century* (Cambridge, Mass., 1969), 88–89.

184. *Institutes,* IV, xx, 8; IV, xx, 15. For Calvin's rejection of universal empire, see also IV, vi, 8.

185. From his commentary on Aristotle's *Politics,* quoted by Quirinus Breen, *Christianity and Humanism: Studies in the History of Ideas* (Grand Rapids, 1968), 84.

186. The point is made in connection with Petrarch, I, 147; cf. Seigel, 75, on Salutati.

187. *De vero bono,* 110.

188. Quoted by Trinkaus, I, 152.

189. *Courtier,* 7.

190. *Institutes,* IV, xiii, 11; II, ii, 14.

191. *Loci communes,* 146.

192. *Institutes,* IV, iii, 15.

193. Quoted in Breen, 83–84.

194. *Comm. Deuteronomy* 1:16, quoted by David Little, *Religion, Order, and Law: A Study in Pre-Revolutionary England* (New York, 1969), 73.

195. *Institutes,* IV, vii, 15.

196. Quoted by Trinkaus, I, 196.

197. *Institutes,* IV, iv, 2; IV, xvi, 23. Cf. *Comm. Genesis* 2:3.

198. Cf. J. R. Hale, "War and Public Opinion in Renaissance Italy," *Italian Renaissance Studies: A Tribute to the Late Cecilia M. Ady,* ed. E. F. Jacob (London, 1960), 94–122.

199. For Calvin's Renaissance attitude to checks and balances, cf. *Institutes,* IV, iv, 12; IV, xi, 6.

200. Cf. Trinkaus, I, 161.

201. *Institutes,* III, viii, 1; IV, ix, 1.

202. *Secretum,* 514.

203. Quoted by Trinkaus, I, 74–75.

204. *Of the Education of Youth,* in *Zwingli and Bullinger,* 113.

205. *Institutes,* II, ii, 13; *Comm. Romans,* Epistle; *Comm. Seneca,* 250–251.

206. This is well brought out by Trinkaus, I, 107–109, 365 n. 21.

207. *De ignorantia,* 101, 87.

208. Quoted by Seigel, 105.

209. *De vero bono,* 14–15.

210. Paul Oskar Kristeller, *The Philosophy of Marsilio Ficino* (New York, 1943), 23.

211. Quoted by D. P. Walker, *The Ancient Theology: Studies in Platonism from the Fifteenth to the Eighteenth Century* (Ithaca, 1972), 46.

212. André Hugo discusses these matters in his introduction to Calvin's *Comm. Seneca,* 57–59.

213. Quoted by Luchesius Smits, *Saint Augustin dans l'œuvre de Jean Calvin* (Louvain, 1957), I, 42.

214. See Charles L. Stinger, "Humanism and Reform in the Early Quattrocento: The Patristic Scholarship of Ambrogio Traversari (1386–1439)," Stanford Doctoral Dissertation (1971), 116.

215. Noted by Jean Dagens, *Bérulle et les origines de la restauration catholique (1575–1611)* (Paris, 1952), 54.

216. Jean-Pierre Massaut, *Josse Clichtove, l'humanisme et la réforme du clergé* (Liège and Paris, 1968), II, esp. 125–134.

217. Kristeller, *Ficino,* 15, and "Augustine and the Early Renaissance," *Studies in Renaissance Thought and Letters* (Rome, 1956), 355–372; O'Malley, 58–61; Trinkaus, II, 465; Walker, *passim.*

218. *Loci communes,* 19–20, 22–23.

219. *Ibid.,* 22; Fraenkel, 19, 302.

220. *Comm. Seneca,* 24–25.

221. Smits, I, 146, 265–270; *Comm. John* 1:3.

222. *Institutes,* IV, xix, 12.

223. Smits, I, 191–194, 145, 252.

224. Quoted by Smits, I, 63; cf. the passage quoted, p. 23 above.

225. Augustine is given almost twice as much space as any other writer.

226. See Henri-Jean Martin, *Livre pouvoirs et société à Paris au XVIIe siècle (1598–1701)* (Geneva, 1969), I, 113–116, 494; II, 601, 609.

227. Dagens, 55 and *passim*. For Augustine in seventeenth-century France see, more generally, Nigel Abercrombie, *Saint Augustine and French Classical Thought* (Oxford, 1938).

228. The literature on seventeenth-century Augustinianism is massive, but see especially J. Orcibal, *Jean Duvergier de Hauranne, abbé de Saint-Cyran, et son temps* (Paris, 1947), and Henri de Lubac, *Augustinisme et théologie moderne* (Paris, 1965).

229. Cf. John Bossy, "The Counter-Reformation and the People of Catholic Europe," *Past and Present*, 47 (May, 1970), 51–70.

230. Jason Lewis Saunders, *Justus Lipsius: The Philosophy of Renaissance Stoicism* (New York, 1955), 67. In general, see also Julien Eymard d'Angers, "Le Stoïcisme en France dans la première moitié du XVIIe siècle," *Études Franciscaines*, II (1951), 287–299, 389–410.

231. *De constantia*, 9.

232. Noted by Abercrombie, 6; Lipsius described Augustine as "nostrorum scriptorum apex" (*Manductio ad Stoicam philosophiam*, I, iv).

233. The point is made by Hugo, introduction to Calvin's *Comm. Seneca*, 36–40.

234. On this point, in addition to Léontine Zanta, *La Renaissance du Stoïcisme au XVIe siècle* (Paris, 1914), see Anthony Levi, *French Moralists: The Theory of the Passions, 1585 to 1649* (Oxford, 1964).

2 Changing Assumptions in Later Renaissance Culture

This paper was originally presented to the Central Renaissance Conference at the University of Missouri in the spring of 1974. In it I tried to discriminate stages in the development of Renaissance high culture and to explain them as responses to shifting social, political, and psychological needs. The implication of the paper that some among the cherished artifacts of that culture were less expressive of its central insights than others has met with some resistance. The paper was published in Viator: Medieval and Renaissance Studies *7 (1976), 421–440, and is reprinted here with the permission of the Regents of the University of California.*

● ● ●

The familiar notion of a "later" Renaissance immediately presents itself as an innocent effort at chronological arrangement, as a convenience for determining relationships in time. But of course it is much more. It calls upon us to distinguish the differing characteristics of successive moments, to trace a process of development from inception to maturity and possibly on to decline; and it introduces the complicated problem of the relations between Italy and the Northern Renaissance.[1] It is thus closely connected with one of the most fruitful tendencies in all aspects of modern Renaissance scholarship: the effort to distinguish stages in a larger movement which, without such analysis, is filled with an ambiguity that makes useful discussion almost impossible. This tendency is perhaps nowhere more apparent than in the study of Renaissance humanism, a subject which, though by no means their only significant expression, brings into unusually clear relief the assumptions underlying what was most novel and creative in Renaissance culture. By the same token concentration on humanism is a convenient way to deal with the inner development of Renaissance culture.

The most persuasive attempts to work out the stages in the evolution of Renaissance humanism have concentrated on particular places, as, for example, the work of Baron on Florence, of Branca on Venice, or of Spitz on Germany.[2] Such efforts have proved remarkably useful, but by their very nature they can be no more than suggestive about the development of humanism as a general phenomenon of Renaissance Italy or even of Renaissance Europe, responsive to more than local influences. In addition, what has so far been said on this subject is not very helpful for the problem of the later Renaissance. Students of humanism have been concerned chiefly with its earlier, formative stages, as though, once the movement were well established, its full story had been told. Here, as elsewhere in Renaissance scholarship, we can perhaps sense a reluctance to deal with the notions of maturation and then of decay, decline, and end. Back of this may lurk the old idea of the Renaissance as the beginning of the modern age—which, by definition, must still be with us.

I should like to approach the problem of the later Renaissance, then, by calling attention first to changing attitudes towards rhetoric, now generally recognized as the core of Renaissance humanism.[3] The Renaissance humanist was first of all a rhetorician, concerned to perfect in himself and others the art of speaking and writing well. From this standpoint his interest in the classics was secondary and at any rate hardly a novelty; we are now fully aware of the deep classicism of medieval culture. What was significant in the Renaissance humanist was not his classical interests but the novelty of his preferences within the classical heritage. For him the most important classical writers were the Latin orators, the supreme teachers, by both precept and example, of the rhetorical art. It is now clear, therefore, that humanism must be understood initially as a movement in the history of education which proposed to substitute, for the philosophers beloved by the dialecticians, a new group of classical authors, the orators, and then their allies, the ancient poets, historians, and moralists, as the center of a new curriculum, the *studia humanitatis*.

For some scholars this conception of humanism makes it appear less serious. The reason is, perhaps, that in our own culture rhetoric is popularly regarded as an ambiguous art, and we try to protect ourselves from those who abuse it by attaching to it the adjective "mere," though the need for such protection suggests a fear hardly consistent with the adjective itself. The phrase "mere rhetoric" implies that a rhetorician is at best only a frivolous and minor artist who does no more than decorate serious content with ultimately superfluous adornments; at worst he is a seducer. Back of the phrase "mere rhetoric" also lies, perhaps, a quasi-metaphysical assumption that form is distinguishable from substance, a conception that betrays the persistent influence of one important strand of ancient thought on the Western mind. But it seems to me the very essence of Renaissance humanism, insofar as it differed from the humanism of the Middle Ages, that it rejected this distinction.[4] It took rhetoric seriously because it recognized that the forms of thought are part of thought itself, that verbal meaning is a complex entity, like the human organism, which also cannot survive dissection. This, I think, is the significance of Lorenzo Valla's translation of *logos* not as *ratio* but as *oratio,* a conception which not only suggests the dynamism and the substantive importance of rhetoric but is also significantly closer to the biblical than to the philosophical world of thought.[5] It is in this light that we must understand Valla's praise for the eloquence of Saint Paul.[6] Rhetoric, rhetoric alone, seemed able to address man, every man, at the vital center of his being.

And there is a further profound implication of this position, which Valla, the deepest mind among the earlier humanists, did much to elucidate. Since the forms of thought can at any rate be perceived as historically determined, the indivisibility of form and content suggests that all intellectual activity is relative to its times. So Renaissance rhetoric opened the way to a denial of absolutes in favor of a novel cultural relativism.[7] Man, for the rhetorician, not man as a species but man in a particular time and place, becomes the measure of all things, a conception that suggests a further element in the lineage of rhetoric, and also brings out the irony in the familiar humanist designation of the schoolmen as "sophists."[8]

Thus there was nothing frivolous in the cult of rhetoric in the Renaissance, or at least in the early Renaissance in Italy. Nor was there anything trivial about its practical uses. As the art of effective communication, rhetoric was not only the instrument of divine revelation but also the essential bond of human community, and therefore of supreme value for an increasingly complex society struggling to develop more effective patterns of communal life. Enthusiasm for rhetoric was most intense among townsmen responsible for welding the inchoate mass of individuals thrown together within the urban walls into a genuine community. Rhetoric thus provided a natural foundation for the new urban culture of the Renaissance, and it operated at every level of human interaction, both private and public. Businessmen had to communicate persuasively with their customers, suppliers, and associates; lawyers had to argue conflicts of interest in the courts; citizens conversed and corresponded with their friends on personal matters or sought the agreement of their peers on questions of public policy; rulers had to maintain the support of their subjects; governments corresponded with each other, sent out embassies, courted foreign opinion.

Rhetoric therefore, because it gave form to every subject of human concern and made it communicable, was not on the periphery but at the very center of human existence. Accordingly a rhetorician could only be a generalist, and a rhetorical education became, in the Renaissance, the first truly general education in European history. A Florentine statute at the end of the fourteenth century, even before Poggio's discovery of Quintilian, justified the appointment of a public teacher of rhetoric on the ground that "the art of rhetoric is not only the instrument of persuasion for all the sciences but also the greatest ornament of public life," and that it "embraces the precepts for advocating or opposing anything we wish."[9] Rhetoric brought into focus all knowledge and all experience.

This elevation of rhetoric also had other major ideological implications; thus if, as Kristeller has shown, it had no explicit philosophical substance, it had considerable significance, as he also recognized, for philosophy in a larger sense.[10] Above all the new rhetorical culture rested on a novel conception of man. Rejecting the abstract man of classical anthropology with its separate, hierarchically distinguished faculties, rhetoric accepted and appealed to man as it encountered him in the individual moments of his existence. Man was no longer merely a rational animal but an infinitely complex being, a dynamic and unpredictable bundle of psychic energies, simultaneously sensual, passionate, intellectual, and spiritual; like the rhetoric he used, a mysterious unity. If his nature could be defined at all, he was a social and verbal animal who needed to share with others the whole range of his experience. As Leon Battista Alberti's Uncle Lionardo remarked, "Nature, the best of builders, not only made man to live exposed in the midst of others, but also seems to have imposed on him a certain necessity to communicate and reveal to his fellows by speech and other means all his passions and feelings."[11]

But this position not only subverted the old hierarchy of the human personality; it also eroded the gradations of status in society corresponding to it. The broader function of speech meant that communication should not primarily serve the intellectual needs of the few but the general needs of many. The first requirement of speech was that it be commonly understood. Petrarch, himself no lover of crowds, pointed to this perception early in the history of the movement. "The strongest argument for genius and learning is clarity," he declared. "What a man understands clearly he can clearly express, and thus he can pour over into the mind of a hearer what he has in the innermost chamber of his mind."[12] Castiglione's Count Lodovico was only repeating an old humanist cliché when he urged the Courtier to employ "words which are still used by the common people."[13] Language was the common property of men.

The tendency in rhetoric to break down the old barriers and divisions previously seen as inherent in the nature of man, society, and the cosmos itself, points to a further aspect of its deeper significance. Rhetoric was uniquely suited to reflect a world whose order was tending to escape objective comprehension. Its malleability, its adaptability to the nuances of experience, allowed it to mold itself flexibly around the infinitely varied and constantly shifting particularities of life,[14] and at the same time it encouraged the conviction that reality could not be grasped by the fixed and general categories of rational and systematic thought. Rhetoric was agnostic in regard to general propositions; from its standpoint man could not hope to penetrate to the ultimate order of things but only make particular sense of his immediate experience. But the result was that rhetorical expression could be supremely creative, as language could not be if it aimed only to reflect an absolute and static reality. Language itself was a human creation, a point on which Valla rebuked the schoolmen, who, as though forgetting Genesis 2:19, seemed to believe that God Himself had invented words.[15]

The apparently neutral rhetorical doctrine of decorum concealed another set of striking implications.[16] Decorum meant simply that effective communication required the adaptation of a speaker's discourse to his subject and above all to his audience: to its special characteristics, its immediate circumstances of time and place, its mood, and the purpose of the speaker. It too suggests that language seeks man out as he is from moment to moment and addresses him not as the representative of a species, in the timeless language of absolute truth, but as an individual. When Petrarch declared, "I am an individual and would like to be wholly and completely an individual,"[17] he was thus expressing one of the deepest impulses underlying Renaissance rhetoric. At the same time, decorum pointed to an attitude of complete flexibility in confronting the infinite variety of life.

Step by step, then, the humanists of earlier Renaissance Italy developed this new vision of man who, with all the resources of his personality, engages fully with the total range of experience. We can trace their progress most vividly in their growing recognition of the role of the passions and the will in the human personality, which advanced into prominence as the intellect receded. Petrarch was still ambivalent and allowed Augustine, improbably disguised as a Stoic sage, to rebuke him for his attachment to love and glory, which Petrarch nevertheless insisted on regarding as "the finest passions" of his nature.[18] But by the next generation Salutati was prepared to acknowledge that, however desirable, the suppression of feeling was impossible. "Indeed," he wrote, "I know not if any mortal ever attained to such perfection besides Christ."[19] And by 1434 Alberti's Uncle Gianozzo was locating the essence of man precisely in his emotions. The first gift of nature to each of us, he declared, is "that moving spirit within us by which we feel desire and anger."[20] Valla brought this motif to its climax in his *De vero bono,* which argued that even man's moral and spiritual life cannot be advanced by deliberate intellectual activity but only by surrender to the supreme pleasure of divine love.[21]

Closely associated with the passions was the will, which translates the impulses of the passions into action. For in this new vision of man the will was no longer merely the servant of reason; it had replaced reason, in Nancy Struever's phrase, as the "executive power" of the personality.[22] The quality of man's existence thus depended now not on the adequacy of his reason but on the strength and freedom of his will. For Salutati the will was a faculty "whose force . . . is so great and its hegemony over the other powers of the soul so large that even though the instruments of the senses receive the images of sensible things, the effect of such reception scarcely proceeds further without the commands of the will."[23] The will represented the active power of the soul.

Thus its primacy pointed, finally, to a revised conception of the existence best suited to man in this life. Since man was no longer an intellectual being, he could no longer hope to fulfill himself through contemplation but only through active engagement with the demands of life, especially in society. Even the ambivalent Petrarch, though frequently lamenting the interruption of his repose, sometimes admitted that a life free from choice and struggle is unsuited to human nature,[24] and his successors were steadily clearer on this issue. Alberti's dying father emphasized the point in his parting message to his sons. "Adversities are the material of which character is built," he declared. "Whose unshakeable spirit, constant mind, energetic intelligence, indefatigable industry and art can show its full merit in favorable and quiet situations?" Uncle Lionardo said this less solemnly: "Young men should not be allowed to remain inactive. Let girls sit and grow lazy."[25]

I do not mean to offer the line of thought I have traced here as a balanced description of earlier Renaissance humanism; Petrarch's equivocations are also significant,[26] and they were never fully overcome by his successors. I have simply tried to offer a brief sketch of the radical novelties implicit in the movement, in the hope that they may help us to assess the quality of the later Renaissance. For, beginning about the middle of the fifteenth century, humanism began subtly to change. The impulses we have just reviewed were still at work and capable of further development, as we are reminded by such figures as Machiavelli, Pomponazzi, and Guicciardini. Yet even in writers in whom we can still discern the earlier attitudes, the novelties of the earlier Renaissance were often being modified.

Once again we may conveniently begin with the problem of rhetoric, towards which attitudes were changing. We still can find, to be sure, enthusiastic celebrations of the power of words. Vives, for example, could describe language as more important for society than justice itself. "Words," he declared, "win the approval of others and control their passions and emotions. . . . I see nothing more relevant to society than the ability to speak properly and eloquently. Emotions can be set ablaze by the spark of words; reason is aroused and directed by language. There is no occasion in public or private life, at home or outside, where words can be left out. Words can be the cause of great evils and the beginning of incomparable blessings. It is very important, therefore, always to use a decent language adapted to the circumstances of time, place, and people . . . which will prove that eloquence is a most important part of prudence."[27]

Yet even among the champions of eloquence one is aware of a growing sense of its limits. This is evident in a tendency, once again, to see eloquence as the mere embellishment of truth. Rhetoric no longer seemed to give access to the solid realities of life, which once more appeared to have some absolute and independent existence; and the relationship between eloquence and knowledge, form and content, once thought an indissoluble marriage, began to look like a passing affair.

This is particularly evident in the attitude of later humanists to the Gospel, which for Valla had been, in the fullest sense, rhetorical communication.[28] Now such a view hardly seemed serious; as ultimate truth, the Gospel could not be dependent on the contingencies of eloquence, and rhetoric could only be of incidental help for its communication. Thus the French scholar Gaguin commended eloquence in preaching to the young Erasmus only on the ground that "the memory of those who have an old-womanish, hesitating and stuttering style will truly last only a few days," and that "only those who have combined eloquence and knowledge are respected and renowned among men of letters," a position that reduces rhetoric to a memory aid or an element in personal reputation. Erasmus agreed. "Religious matters," he responded, "can be made to shine more brightly with the aid of the classics, provided that only purity of style is sought." For Erasmus eloquence could not itself convey the Gospel into the heart; it merely put the reader into a hospitable mood.[29] And Vives denied the universal competence of rhetoric. "Everyone can see clearly," he wrote against Quintilian, "that to speak of the heavens, the elements, and the angels is not the orator's concern."[30]

A natural accompaniment of this separation of the form from the content of verbal expression was a growing emphasis on the value of literary refinement for its own sake, or at most for the esthetic satisfaction it could provide. Thus Castiglione's discussion of language in the *Courtier* suggests more concern with the propriety of language than with its deeper powers of communication. He devotes much attention to this subject, indeed, but the effect is largely to trivialize what had earlier been of profound human importance. There is no concern with virtue or duty in Count Lodovico's vision of the Courtier's literary education. He reviews the old curriculum; the Courtier is to acquaint himself with both the Greek and Latin classics "because of the abundance and variety of things that are so divinely written therein," and he is to pay particular attention to the poets, orators and historians. But the count's explanation lacks the old high seriousness: "besides the personal satisfaction he [the Courtier] will take in this, in this way he will never want for pleasant entertainment with the ladies, who are usually fond of such things." The humanities will, to be sure, also "make him fluent, and . . . bold and self-confident in speaking with everyone." But this contribution to the personal effectiveness of the Courtier seems something of an afterthought; after all, as the count remarks, arms are the chief profession of the Courtier, and all his other accomplishments are only "ornaments thereto." The Courtier is a specialist. Another of Castiglione's interlocutors drives the point deeper. For Federico Fregoso the Courtier "should be one who is never at a loss for things to say that are good and well-suited to those with whom he is speaking, he should know how to sweeten and refresh the minds of his hearers, and move them discreetly to gaiety and laughter with amusing witticisms and pleasantries, so that, without ever producing tedium or satiety, he may continually give pleasure."[31]

One can observe of this ideal that at least it does not discriminate against women. Indeed it seems particularly suited to women; the old curriculum of the rhetoricians here provides a culture for aristocratic ladies, but for men chiefly when they are in the company of ladies. By sixteenth-century standards nothing better illustrates the low estate to which the *studia humanitatis* had fallen. And decorum, which in the earlier Renaissance meant primarily the appropriateness of language to its audience or the intentions of the speaker, tended now to mean appropriateness to the speaker's status in life, and eventually what was appropriate to the upper classes. It was no longer the vehicle of a flexible attitude to existence but simply a virtue of the drawing room. Ficino, to be sure, defined decorum more grandly, but only to elevate it altogether above ordinary human life. "Decorum," he declared, "is God Himself, from whom and through whom all decorous things come to being."[32]

But Ficino's conception was exceptional and perhaps only inadvertently applicable to rhetoric. In general rhetoric tended now to be seen as little more than embellishment and thus relatively frivolous; and so it became in some circles a kind of play, a source of pleasure and a form of self-display, but therefore for serious men an object of suspicion, as a distraction from the naked apprehension of truth. This concern seems to have some bearing on the Ciceronian controversy in the generation of Erasmus, who himself attacked a Ciceronian floridity in favor of the plain style. His preference, at least in principle, for "the sententious density of matter" over "the cadency and chiming of words" suggests a long step back from rhetoric to philosophy. "Farfetched conceits may please others," he wrote, but "to me the chief concern seems to be that we draw our speech from the matter itself and apply ourselves less to showing off our invention than to present the thing."[33] Form and content have apparently become separable.

This divorce between eloquence and wisdom was, of course, nowhere more pronounced than among the Florentine Platonists. Ficino, concerned with truth, was troubled by the rhetorical enterprise.[34] Pico distinguished sharply between truth and eloquence, which he thought likely only to obscure, distort, and taint truth.[35] From their perspective the authentic task of language is simply to describe objective reality, and the fact that the majority of men lack the capacity to understand philosophical discourse suggested not the limitations but the distinction of philosophy. "What if," Pico wrote in defense of philosophers, "we are commonly held to be dull, rude, uncultured? To us this is a glory and no cause for contempt. We have not written for the many. . . . We are not unlike the ancients who by their riddles and by the masks of their fables made the uninitiate shun the mysteries; and we have been wont by fright to drive them from our feasts, which they could not but pollute with their far more repulsive verbal inventions."[36]

One result of this sentiment was a return to abstraction; another, more widespread but perhaps equally remote from daily life, was a new type of communication, both verbally and in the plastic arts, through a variety of cryptic devices: riddles, allegory, hints.[37] This notion of communication was as applicable to reading as to writing; and it meant, among other things, a recovery of medieval ways of studying the classics, the discovery in ancient texts not simply of a noble but human communication from the past but of hidden insights into a perennial and ultimate truth. Landino made the point in his commentary on Horace's *Art of Poetry:* "When [poetry] most appears to be narrating something most humble and ignoble or to be singing a little fable to delight idle ears, at that very time it is writing in a secret way the most excellent things of all, which are drawn forth from the fountain of the gods."[38] Erasmus, for all his evangelical impulses, preferred the allegorical to the literal meaning of the Scriptures.[39]

But the familiar classics, already too widely known, were insufficiently esoteric to satisfy the longing for an exclusive wisdom by which aristocrats of the spirit could raise themselves above the corrupt and vulgar masses. The result was a turn to less accessible writings in Greek, Hebrew, and eventually other Semitic languages, to the Orphic hymns, the Hermetic corpus, the cabala. As Pico observed, the canonical scriptures could only meet the needs of "tailors, cooks, butchers, shepherds, servants, maids," persons whose "dim and owlish eyes could not bear the light."[40] For superior souls some further revelation was required. Nor were such conceptions confined to a fringe of intellectual extremists. The eminently respectable General of the Augustinian Friars, Giles of Viterbo, one of the most influential figures at the Curia, shared Pico's conviction that the Gospel of Christ required cabalistic explication.[41] We may also note in these interests the disappearance of the incipient cultural relativism of the earlier Renaissance.

In this new atmosphere classicism itself became increasingly academic. No longer an inspiration for the active life, it developed into a new and often less serious form of the contemplative life; a humanist was now less likely to be an orator than a philologist or a man of letters. The leading humanists of the later fifteenth century were men like Poliziano, who discovered the esthetic virtues of the Latin silver age; Merula, who edited texts and standardized spelling; and Ermolao Barbaro, who restored the Greek text of Aristotle. We continue to call these men humanists, but it is sometimes hard to see them as more than superficially like Petrarch, Salutati, Bruni, or Valla. They loved the classics, they knew them better than their predecessors, and they wrote better Latin. But earlier humanism, with its high seriousness about the tasks of rhetoric, had rebelled against the detachment of literature from life, the style from the substance of communication. Barbaro, Pico, and sometimes even Poliziano and Erasmus look increasingly like professional intellectuals.

But, as this account of the fate of rhetoric in the later Renaissance has at various points already suggested, these changing attitudes to language and communication were accompanied by, and gave expression to, a deeper set of cultural changes. If rhetoric in the earlier sense of the art of touching men in their hearts and so stimulating them to action was now declining, the reason was that man himself was increasingly perceived, once again, as essentially an intellectual being. Since intellect is a faculty man shares with other men, man was also beginning to lose some of his passionate individuality. And since the object of intellect is the general and rational order of reality itself, the decline of rhetoric signified too the recovery, albeit under somewhat new forms, of the old sense of the cosmos as a unity organized according to fixed patterns, accessible to the mind, which dictate the norms of man's individual and social existence. The attitudes of the earlier Renaissance, it is well to repeat, by no means disappeared. But a major shift in the intellectual climate seems to me unmistakable.

At the center of the change was a decline of the secular principle underlying the culture of the earlier Renaissance: the sense, to cite the typically Renaissance sentiment of a seventeenth-century Englishman, that man lives in divided and distinguished worlds, each of which operates in accordance with principles of its own.[42] The movement of thought was now towards synthesis rather than analysis; men preferred the One to the many, simplicity to complexity.[43] Thus if, in describing the assumptions of earlier Renaissance culture, we must begin with its anthropology, in dealing with those of the later Renaissance we must start with its cosmic vision.[44] We are back in a world of thought in which the imagery of divine activity and human existence is once again cosmological. Colet recalls Dante in his description of "the uniting and all-powerful rays of Christ . . . streaming as it were from the Sun of Truth, which gather and draw together towards themselves and towards unity, those who are in a state of multiplicity."[45] The aged Erasmus hinted at something very like the naturalism repudiated by earlier humanists in his explanation of man's yearning for rest:

Why is it that even in inanimate things you may see that each
and every one is drawn to its own peculiar abode? As soon as a
rock dropped from a height hits the earth, it comes to rest. How
eagerly a flame is attracted to its own place! What is this which
sometimes rocks the earth so hard it dislodges mountains and
stones except the north wind struggling to break through to the
place where it was born? Thus it is that a bladder full of air,
when forcibly pressed down into water, springs back up. Now
the human spirit is a flammable thing which, though hindered
by this absurd little body of clay, still does not rest until it
mounts up to the seat of its beginning. By nature, indeed, all
men hunt for repose; they seek something in which the spirit
can rest.[46]

This impulse to imbed man once again in the objective order of the
cosmos, from which earlier humanism had freed him, explains the popularity now of the notion of man as microcosm, a conception whose
prominence in the later Renaissance hardly requires illustration. It is
also closely related to the revival of various forms of occultism, both
esoteric and popular, which sought, in Pico's words, to "wed earth to
heaven."[47] It nourished too the ideal of harmony (though this could be
expressed in human as well as absolute terms) and above all the revival
of the conception of hierarchy, which was, for Ficino, almost synonymous with order itself.[48] Valla's doubts about the authenticity of the
writings attributed to Dionysius the Areopagite[49] were now forgotten;
a new group of readers craved to believe in it. For Ficino, Dionysius
rivaled Saint Paul as "the wisest of the Christian theologians"; Giles of
Viterbo called him "the unique light of Greek theology"; Colet devoted
a major part of his life to the study of his works; and Lefèvre d'Étaples
edited his *Celestial Hierarchies* and described his writings as "most sacred"
and "so eminent in dignity and excellence that no word of praise is
adequate to describe them."[50] Even Erasmus, though less enthusiastic,
did not hesitate to apply the Dionysian hierarchical vision to both the
ecclesiastical and political order.[51] Thus we are once again back in a
single holy order of reality whose principles are mandatory in every
aspect of existence. It is true, of course, that something of the earlier
Renaissance persists in the uses of hierarchy by the Neoplatonists. Ficino's hierarchy is not simply a static structure but a system for the
transmission of vital influences; and Pico sought to protect human freedom by allowing man the liberty to ascend or descend "the universal
chain of Being" and so freely to shape himself.[52] But what is most
significant here, it seems to me, is not the impulses retained from the

earlier Renaissance but the overwhelming presence of the hierarchy itself. For Pico man ought clearly to rise rather than to descend on the ladder of being; its existence prescribes the uses of human freedom.

But it is above all in the application of these conceptions to the understanding of man that we can best see the difference from the earlier Renaissance. Once again the human personality was conceived not as a dynamic unity but, reflecting the structure of the cosmos, as a set of distinct and graded faculties, properly ruled by reason, the soul, or the spirit; the terminology varied from thinker to thinker, depending somewhat on whether he wrote under Aristotelian, Stoic, or Platonic influence. Vives attached the idea directly to the larger order of things. "This is the order of Nature," he declared, "that Wisdom be the rule of the whole, that all creatures obey man; that in man, the body abides by the orders of the soul, and that the soul itself comply with the will of God. Whoever violates this order, sins."[53] Men played changes on the general conception. In the *Courtier,* Ottaviano Fregoso noted that "even as our mind and body are two things, so likewise the soul is divided into two parts, one of which has reason in it, and the other has appetite."[54] For Erasmus "the body or flesh is our lowest part. . . . The spirit represents in us the likeness of the divine nature. . . . Lastly, God founded the soul as the third and middle faculty between the other two, to hold the natural senses and impulses."[55]

But the sovereignty of the highest part of man meant that the essence of man was once again seen to reside in his intellect, or, as sometimes in Ficino, something above the intellect, but always a high and separate faculty. Thus for Castiglione's Bembo (we may compare him with Petrarch or Valla on the point) knowledge is prior to love, for, "according to the definition of ancient sages, love is nothing but a certain desire to enjoy beauty; and, as our desire is only for things that are known, knowledge must precede desire, which by nature turns to the good but in itself is blind and does not know the good."[56] This intellectual vision of man was also accompanied by a remarkable optimism; it agreed with the classical traditions by which it was nourished that to know the good is to do the good. Thus Erasmus remarked that it is fitting "for all to recognize the motions of the mind, then to know none of them to be so violent but that they can either be restrained by reason or redirected to virtue." This, he continued, "is the sole way to happiness: first, know yourself; second, do not submit anything to the passions, but all things to the judgment of reason."[57] In his colloquy *The Wooer and the Maiden,* the maiden Maria tells her lover, a bit pompously, "What emotions decide is temporary; rational choices generally please forever"; and her young man rather surprisingly agrees in what might be taken also, however, as a bit of Erasmian irony: "Indeed you philosophize very well, so I'm resolved to take your advice."[58] Obviously the will remains an important element in this conception; every exhortation to choose the way of reason implies both its existence and its power. But the will is no longer at the center of the human personality; it has been reduced to servitude: if virtuous, to reason; if vicious, to the passions. Much of the educational thought of the later Renaissance rests on this conception.

Inevitably now the passions, identified with either the body or the lowest part of the soul, once again presented themselves rather as a problem than as a resource for good as well as evil. Even Erasmus, although a bit ambivalent, did not give them much praise. Indeed he applauded his own poems for their *lack* of passion: "There is not a single storm in them," he wrote, "no mountain torrent overflowing its banks, no exaggeration whatever." He preferred the poetry that seemed most like prose and disliked the choruses in Greek drama because of their violent emotionality.[59] Vives similarly distrusted the passions, though technically admitting their ethical neutrality. "The more pure and lofty a judgment is," he declared, "the less passion it tolerates; such a judgment examines with much care the possible good aspects of each object and does not accept any excitement, except on rare occasions and with serene moderation." "Whenever a passion crops up with all its natural power," he wrote again, "the wise man represses it with the control of reason and forces it to withdraw in the face of a prudent judgment."[60]

Nor is there much question, for the later Renaissance, of the vileness of the body, which was once again, as with Ficino, an "earthly prison" and the "dark dwelling" of the soul. Ficino excluded the body from his definition of man. "Man," he asserted, "is the soul itself. . . . Everything that a man is said to do, his soul does itself; the body merely suffers it to be done; wherefore man is soul alone, and the body of man must be its instrument."[61] Erasmus could make the point lightly, as when his lovers agree that the soul is a willing prisoner of the body, "like a little bird in a cage."[62] But at times he was in deadly earnest. "If there is any evil in the mind," he wrote in his *Education of a Christian Prince*, "it springs from infection and contact with the body, which is subject to the passions. Any good that the body possesses is drawn from the mind as from a fountain. How unbelievable it would be and *how contrary to nature*, if ills should spread from the mind down into the body, and the health of the body be corrupted by the vicious habits of the mind."[63] Again we are reminded of the dependence of human existence on the larger order of nature. Vives was more violent: "Our souls carry the heavy burden of bodies with great misery and pain; because of bodies, souls are confined to the narrow limits of this earth, where all filth and smut seem to converge."[64] In this insistence on the separation and even antagonism between the higher and lower parts of man, between the rational soul or the spirit and the body and its passions, we can discern a significant counterpart to the distinction between the substance and form of verbal discourse, or between its rational content and its rhetorical embellishment, the soul and body of thought.

This attitude to the body had its positive corollary in a peculiar emphasis on the immortality of the soul, a doctrine sometimes denounced by the Fathers because it appeared to contradict Christian belief in the resurrection of the body. The typical representatives of the later Renaissance occasionally defended the resurrection, and Ficino spoke of the natural desire of the soul to be reunited with the body, a desire that had in the nature of things eventually to be satisfied.[65] But the true interests of the later humanists lay in another direction; and even when they discussed the subject, they emphasized not so much the glorification of the resurrection body as its transformation into something less bodily and more spiritual. They were preoccupied with the immortality of the soul. Ficino devoted most of his *Platonic Theology* to proving it; and there are echoes of the idea, on a more earthly level, in Gargantua's letter exhorting Pantagruel to virtue: "If, beside my bodily image, my soul did not likewise shine in you, you would not be accounted worthy of guarding the precious immortality of my name. In that case, the least part of me (my body) would endure. Scant satisfaction *that,* when the best part (my soul which should keep my name blessed among men) had degenerated and been bastardized."[66] The proclamation of the immortality of the soul as an official dogma of the Church at the Fifth Lateran Council in 1513 can perhaps be attributed to this interest of the later Renaissance.[67]

This new tendency in the idea of man also helps to explain the revival of the contemplative ideal and the recovery of interest in philosophy. Pico was typical. "I have always been so desirous, so enamored of [philosophy]," he wrote, "that I have relinquished all interest in affairs private and public, and given myself over entirely to leisure for contemplation."[68] Giles of Viterbo oddly thought of Jesus as a man who avoided cities, market places, and the company of men; "the happy man," he wrote a friend, "is he who, conscious of how short life is, lives for himself, apart from the tumult of human affairs."[69] Even Castiglione's Ottaviano, confronted with the stock problem whether the active or contemplative life is to be preferred by a prince, could only offer the unlikely suggestion that "princes ought to lead both kinds of life, but more especially the contemplative," which ought to be "the goal of the active as peace is of war and as repose is of toil."[70] The persistent longing of Erasmus for peace devoted to study is not only a personal taste but the ideal of a generation, and the peace movement among the intellectuals of his time was no more simply a response to the political situation than was Dante's *De monarchia*.[71]

In this atmosphere Scholasticism no longer appeared so distasteful. We have learned to take more seriously Erasmus's protestations that he attacked not the Schools but their abuses;[72] and if he could not bring himself to praise the schoolmen, he sufficiently venerated the idea of philosophy to reunite it with theology in his *philosophia Christi*. Pico saw his mission in life as the renewal of philosophy after decades of attack;[73] and Ficino, Lefèvre, and Vives were all eager to bring philosophy once again into the service of faith.[74] Aristotle, Plato, the Stoics, now no longer merely names to conjure with, all found ardent admirers and increasingly serious students. And even Thomas Aquinas began to develop a prestige he had never before enjoyed outside the Dominican Order.[75] Erasmus himself admitted that Thomas had "a certain unction in his writings."[76] Thus two cultural worlds, largely kept apart in the earlier Renaissance, were now converging. Raphael's great *Stanza della Segnatura*, with its effort to combine all culture, human and divine, under the parallel auspices of theology and philosophy, was a product of this movement.

Again, I must emphasize, there was here no absolute change, no total repudiation of the ideals of the earlier Renaissance. Yet it seems clear that a profound shift was under way, which calls for some explanation. Part of the explanation is probably to be found in a kind of dynamic within humanism itself. When men first sought to enlarge their powers of verbal expression by imitating the classics, they discovered not only the principles of classical expression but also new and undreamt-of potentialities within themselves. But as classical philology was more and more fully explored and objectively mastered, it could be submitted to general rules; and classicism became no longer liberating but confining. The feeling for propriety in the use of language was also nourished by the printing press, another major development of this period, which standardized every aspect of verbal expression and, as printed books poured off the presses by the millions, imposed its norms on a growing literate public.[77] Yet, even if we do not look beyond humanism itself, I think we can see a deeper impulse at work, pushing the movement in the same direction. For implicit in the culture of the rhetoricians, with its rejection of an objective cosmic order by which man could take his bearings, was not only liberation but also the danger of total anarchy and disorientation. From the beginning the more sensitive among the humanists had been aware of this problem and had tried to solve it by calling for the union of eloquence with wisdom. But there was no necessary reason, in the absence of an objective order accessible to philosophy, or of spiritual guidance supplied by faith, for such an alliance; and in fact the earlier humanists were themselves not only exuberant about the newly discovered freedom and creativity of the individual but also increasingly anxious about the uses men were likely to make of these gifts. Petrarch allowed Augustine to reproach Franciscus for glorying in his eloquence; Salutati was troubled by the fact that many orators were not good men; Poggio was increasingly depressed that rhetoric seemed rather a tool for the abuse than for the strengthening of human community.[78] Thus, in spite of its attacks on philosophy, even early humanism recognized the need for something more than the power of rhetoric. From this standpoint the later Renaissance seems to have been seeking to supply a defect in the culture of the earlier Renaissance. At the same time we must ask whether this defect was not in fact a necessary element in its identity.

Yet I think that we must finally look beyond humanism itself to developments in the larger social and political world. We may point immediately to the deterioration of conditions in Italy. Centuries of internal conflict within the towns of Italy had produced, by the middle decades of the fifteenth century, a climate of intolerable insecurity; and this was aggravated by the long period of large-scale warfare and destruction initiated by the French invasion of 1494, which effectively destroyed the freedom of the Italian states. Order, not freedom, was the most urgent need of this new age; society became more rigidly stratified and governments more authoritarian; all change appeared increasingly terrifying. And in the same period too the papacy, at last fully recovered from the conciliar ordeal, was reasserting the authority of the medieval vision of reality.[79] The general proposition that all things are part of a single holy order of reality at once objective, intelligible, hierarchically organized, and ruled from above was, under these conditions, not entirely anachronistic. It provided relief from the immediate and pressing dangers of the times. Its conception of government also bolstered the authority of princes, with whom the papacy was now prepared to come to terms by concordats. In Italy, with the exception of Venice, princes were everywhere in the ascendancy; and, whatever their particular differences with the pope, princes found the new hierarchical vision of order congenial. Under these conditions rhetoric lost much of its public utility; social solidarity and social order were no longer created from below, by persuasion, but imposed from above, by force; and intellectuals, their own social roles reduced, were increasingly contemptuous of the masses, who corresponded socially to the doubtful passions of the body politic. By the same token the art of speaking well became a badge of social distinction, the peculiar property of a social and political aristocracy gathered in princely courts. And the image of man, which at least since Plato had been closely correlated with the image of society, once again reflected the perception of the general order of things.

This account of the changing assumptions of later Renaissance culture is obviously not a sufficient or balanced description of the later Renaissance. Just as, along with its novelties, the culture of the earlier Renaissance preserved some residues of medieval culture, itself not entirely homogeneous, much from the earlier Renaissance survived in the later fifteenth and sixteenth centuries, often in uneasy tension with the tendencies I have described.[80] And it is at this point in the argument that we must take cognizance of the relationship between the Italian Renaissance and cultural developments in other areas. The fact that Germans, Frenchmen, Spaniards, and Englishmen were nourished by Italian movements of thought largely in the period of this retreat from earlier novelties is worth some reflection. Thus it may be that the regressive tendencies in later Renaissance culture made Italian modes of thought more congenial than they would otherwise have been to Europeans elsewhere, who might have been put off by the less veiled novelties of earlier humanism. The modification of earlier Renaissance culture, as it was transposed from the urban republics of its birth into the milieu of the princely courts, doubtless also assisted its adaptation to the aristocratic circles of the northern monarchies, though these changes had a more ambiguous meaning for the free cities of the Empire, now under growing pressure from territorial princes.

But, as I have from time to time emphasized, the more vital impulses of the earlier Renaissance had not altogether disappeared from the culture of the later Renaissance even in Italy, however much they had been compromised; and these too were known beyond the Alps, where they nourished, if they did not precisely cause, the novelties in what, for all the ambiguities in the term, is conventionally described as the "Northern Renaissance." Northern Europeans, however equivocal their feelings about Italy, regularly admired her Renaissance achievement as a break with the medieval past; and the deepest assumptions of earlier humanist culture found theological expression in the Protestant Reformation.[81]

Thus if the earlier Renaissance was an Italian affair, and the attitudes of the later Renaissance found expression, as the examples cited here reveal, in both Italy and the North, the later Renaissance seems to have had a very different significance outside of Italy, where it presents itself rather as the beginning of a new phase in cultural history than as the decline of a movement already well established. In the North, therefore, and perhaps most conspicuously in England, we can discern with increasing clarity much the same sense of the potentialities of human freedom, the same restless and creative exploration of the possibilities of individual existence as in earlier Renaissance Italy. And this too requires explanation.

The major cause for the continuation of the vital impulses of the Renaissance in Northern Europe after the first decades of the sixteenth century is to be found, I think, in its political pluralism. This, together with geographical and spiritual distance from Rome, the symbol and champion of universalism, posed an insuperable obstacle to the full recovery of any conception of a single, holy, and cosmic order. On this point the distinction between Catholicism and Protestantism is largely irrelevant. France and Spain, the piety of Philip II notwithstanding, resisted papal influence as successfully as England or the Elector of Saxony; all together represented the secular principle of divided and distinguished realms that made any conception of a unified hierarchy embedded in an objective structure of reality ultimately implausible. And political particularity provided a foundation for the development of national cultures which, because of their secularity, also gave room for the same kind of personal individuality that had characterized the earlier Renaissance in Italy. Nowhere is this development more apparent than in the emergence of the great vernacular literatures, in which Northern Europeans discovered for themselves the creative and liberating power of language, much as the rhetoricians of Italy had begun to do two centuries before.

NOTES

1. Interest in these matters is reflected in *The Late Italian Renaissance*, ed. Eric Cochrane (London 1970).

2. Hans Baron, *The Crisis of the Early Italian Renaissance: Civic Humanism and Republican Liberty in an Age of Classicism and Tyranny*, rev. ed. (Princeton, 1966); Vittore Branca, "Ermolao Barbaro e l'umanesimo veneziano," in *Umanesimo europeo e umanesimo veneziano* (Venice, 1963), 193; Lewis W. Spitz, *The Religious Renaissance of the German Humanists* (Cambridge, Mass., 1963), 5–7.

3. We owe this perception above all to Paul Oskar Kristeller, especially in

The Classics and Renaissance Thought (Cambridge, Mass., 1955), repr. in *Renaissance Thought: The Classic, Scholastic, and Humanist Strains* (New York, 1961). The ideological implications of rhetoric emerge more fully in Hanna H. Gray, "Renaissance Humanism: The Pursuit of Eloquence," *Journal of the History of Ideas* 24 (1963), 497–514; Nancy S. Struever, *The Language of History in the Renaissance: Rhetoric and Historical Consciousness* (Princeton, 1970); and, more ambiguously, Jerrold E. Seigel, *Rhetoric and Philosophy in Renaissance Humanism: Ciceronian Elements in Early Quattrocento Thought and Their Historical Setting* (Princeton, 1968). The work of Baron (n. 2 above) has been of particular importance for exploring the political and social implications of rhetorical humanism.

4. Much on this point may be gleaned from Richard McKeon, "Rhetoric in the Middle Ages," *Speculum* 17 (1942), 1–32; but now see also James J. Murphy, *Rhetoric in the Middle Ages: A History of Rhetorical Theory from Saint Augustine to the Renaissance* (Berkeley, 1974). Also cf. Seigel, 173–213.

5. Cf. Donald R. Kelley, *Foundations of Modern Historical Scholarship: Language, Law, and History in the French Renaissance* (New York, 1970), 28. On other occasions Valla translated *logos* as *sermo*; see Salvatore I. Camporeale, *Lorenzo Valla, Umanesimo e teologia* (Florence, 1972), 297. Erasmus followed Valla on this point, whose deep significance is discussed in J. C. Margolin, *Recherches érasmiennes* (Geneva, 1969), 35, and James K. McConica, "Erasmus and the Grammar of Consent," *Scrinium erasmianum* 2 (1969), 90.

6. Cf. Camporeale, 345.

7. Kelley, 19–50, is particularly illuminating on this aspect of Valla's historicism.

8. A significant exception is the appeal in Leon Battista Alberti's *I libri della famiglia,* ed. Cecil Grayson, in *Opere volgari* 1 (Bari, 1960), 132, to Protagoras on man as the measure of all things; here at any rate there appears to be some faint recognition of the sophistic origins of the rhetorical tradition.

9. Quoted by Struever (n. 4 above), 105.

10. Cf. Kristeller, *Renaissance Thought* (n. 3 above), esp. 10, 22–23.

11. Alberti, *Della famiglia* 45; in quoting this work I use the translation of Renée Neu Watkins, *The Family in Renaissance Florence* (Columbia, S. C., 1969).

12. Francesco Petrarch, *De sui ipsius et multorum ignorantia,* tr. Hans Nachod, in *The Renaissance Philosophy of Man,* ed. Ernst Cassirer, Paul Oskar Kristeller, and John Herman Randall, Jr. (Chicago, 1948), 96.

13. Baldassare Castiglione, *The Book of the Courtier,* tr. Charles S. Singleton (New York, 1959), 54; cf. 57.

14. Cf. Alberti, *Della famiglia* 84 (n. 11 above), explicitly relying on Cicero: "Nothing in the world is so flexible and malleable as the spoken word. It yields and inclines in any direction you choose to move it."

15. Camporeale (n. 5 above), 150–151.

16. Struever is illuminating on this point (n. 3 above), 67–68 and passim.

17. Quoted by Michael Seidlmayer, *Currents of Medieval Thought,* tr. D. Barker (Oxford, 1960), 157. Cf. Petrarch's application of this impulse to his conception of God's solicitude: "He watches over me personally and is solicitous for my welfare. . . . He cares for each individual as if he were forgetful of mankind *en masse*" (*Epistolae familiares* 12.10, tr. Morris Bishop, *Letters from Petrarch*

[Bloomington, 1966], 191). For similar sentiments in Valla see the passages quoted by Charles Trinkaus, *In Our Image and Likeness: Humanity and Divinity in Italian Humanist Thought* (Chicago, 1970), 1.141 and 143.

18. *De secreto conflictu curarum mearum libri III,* ed. E. Carrara, in Francesco Petrarch, *Prose* (Milan, 1955), 132.

19. Quoted by Struever (n. 3 above), 59.

20. Alberti, *Della famiglia,* 168 (n. 11 above).

21. Lorenzo Valla, *De vero falsoque bono,* ed. Maristella de Panizza Lorch (Bari, 1970), 114.

22. Struever (n. 3 above), 60.

23. Quoted by Trinkaus (n. 17 above), 1.67.

24. Hans Baron, "Cicero and the Roman Civic Spirit in the Middle Ages and Early Renaissance," *John Rylands Library Bulletin* 22 (1938), 18.

25. Alberti, *Della famiglia* 25, 72 (n. 11 above).

26. Cf. Klaus Heitmann, *Fortuna und Virtus: Eine Studie zu Petrarcas Lebensweisheit* (Cologne, 1958).

27. Quoted by Carlos G. Noreña, *Juan Luis Vives* (The Hague, 1970), 182.

28. Cf. Hanna H. Gray, "Valla's Encomium of St. Thomas and the Humanist Conception of Christian Antiquity," in *Essays in History and Literature Presented to Stanley Pargellis,* ed. Heinz Bluhm (Chicago, 1965), 37–51.

29. This exchange is quoted by Eugene F. Rice, Jr., "Erasmus and the Religious Tradition," in *Renaissance Essays from the Journal of the History of Ideas,* ed. Paul Oskar Kristeller and Philip P. Wiener (New York, 1968), 180. Cf. his letter to Amerbach, 31 August 1518, in *Opus epistolarum Erasmi,* ed. P. S. and H. M. Allen (Oxford, 1906–58), 3.385, where he describes eloquence as the handmaiden of wisdom.

30. Quoted by Noreña (n. 27 above), 278. This is also, of course, Pico's point in his famous letter to Ermolao Barbaro, tr. by Quirinus Breen, in "Giovanni Pico della Mirandola on the Conflict of Philosophy and Rhetoric," *Journal of the History of Ideas* 13 (1952), 384–412.

31. Castiglione (n. 13 above), 70–71, 32, 140. Cf. Struever (n. 3 above), 190, on the transition from "civic-mindedness" to "urbanity."

32. Quoted by Paul Oskar Kristeller, *The Philosophy of Marsilio Ficino* (New York, 1943), 69. For a similar shift in the meaning of decorum for painting and literature, cf. Peter Burke, *Culture and Society in Renaissance Italy, 1420–1540* (London, 1972), 280.

33. Quoted by J. Huizinga, *Erasmus and the Age of the Reformation,* tr. F. Hopkin (New York, 1953), 105. For this dimension of the Ciceronian controversy, see also George Williamson, *The Senecan Amble: A Study in Prose Form from Bacon to Collier* (Chicago, 1951), 11–31. In the light of this revised attitude to rhetoric, Erasmus's mistaken view of Valla as essentially a grammarian assumes special significance; cf. Camporeale (n. 5 above), 5–6.

34. Cf. the documentation in Seigel (n. 3 above), 258.

35. Letter to Barbaro in Breen (n. 30 above), 395–396.

36. *Ibid.,* 397.

37. Cf. Edgar Wind, *Pagan Mysteries in the Renaissance* (New Haven, 1958), 13–38.

38. Quoted by Burke (n. 32 above), 158.

39. Cf. Erasmus, *Enchridion militis Christiani*, tr. Ford Lewis Battles, in *Advocates of Reform*, ed. Matthew Spinka, Library of Christian Classics, 14 (London, 1953), 303, 305, 334, 335. But Erasmus may have withdrawn somewhat from this position in his later years; see, for example, his late work *De sarcienda ecclesia concordia*, in *Opera omnia*, ed. Jean Leclerc (Leiden, 1703–1706), 5.470–471.

40. Quoted by Wind (n. 37 above), 39.

41. John W. O'Malley, *Giles of Viterbo on Church and Reform* (Leiden, 1968), 40.

42. Thomas Browne, *Religio medici* (London, 1906), 39.

43. Cf. Ficino's preoccupation with unity, displayed by Kristeller (n. 32 above), esp. the quotations on 68, 88, 92, 105–106.

44. Trinkaus (n. 17 above), 1.104, notes a similar contrast between the cosmological foundations of scholastic and the anthropological foundations of humanist thought. I am suggesting here that a comparable distinction can be made between later and earlier humanism.

45. John Colet, *Enarratio in primam epistolam S. Pauli ad Corinthios*, tr. J. H. Lupton (London, 1874), 57–58.

46. Erasmus, *Opera* (n. 39 above), 5.484–485; I quote in the translation of Raymond Himelick, *Erasmus and the Seamless Coat of Jesus* (Lafayette, Ind., 1971), 57.

47. Giovanni Pico della Mirandola, *Oration on the Dignity of Man*, tr. Elizabeth Livermore Forbes, in *Renaissance Philosophy of Man* (n. 12 above), 249.

48. Cf. Kristeller (n. 32 above), 84.

49. See Mario Fois, *Il pensiero cristiano di Lorenzo Valla nel quadro storico culturale del suo ambiente* (Rome, 1969), 492.

50. For Ficino (and Colet), see Leland Miles, *John Colet and the Platonic Tradition* (London, 1961), 20–21; for Giles, see O'Malley (n. 41 above), 58; and for Lefèvre, Eugene F. Rice, Jr., "The Humanist Idea of Christian Antiquity: Lefèvre d'Étaples and His Circle," *Studies in the Renaissance* 9 (1962), 128.

51. Cf. Erasmus, *Institutio principis Christiani*, tr. Lester K. Born (New York, 1968), 158, though he hinted at reservations about Dionysius in his letter to Jodocus Jonas, 21 May 1521, Allen (n. 29 above), 4.491–492.

52. As noted by Ernst Cassirer, "Giovanni Pico della Mirandola," *Journal of the History of Ideas* 3 (1942), 123–145, 319–347; for the elements in Ficino and Pico characteristic of the earlier Renaissance, cf. Paul Oskar Kristeller, "Ficino and Pomponazzi on the Place of Man in the Universe," *Journal of the History of Ideas* 5 (1944), 286, and "The European Significance of Florentine Platonism," *Medieval and Renaissance Studies* 4 (1968), 214.

53. Quoted by Noreña (n. 27 above), 201.

54. Castiglione (n. 13 above), 313.

55. Erasmus, *Enchiridion* (n. 39 above), 319.

56. Castiglione, 336.

57. Erasmus, *Enchiridion*, 314–315.

58. *The Colloquies of Erasmus*, tr. Craig R. Thompson (Chicago, 1965), 98.

59. Huizinga (n. 33 above), 105.

60. Quoted by Noreña (n. 27 above), 269.

61. Quoted by Miles (n. 50 above), 72–73; cf. Kristeller (n. 32 above), 328.

62. Erasmus (n. 58 above), 96.

63. Erasmus (n. 51 above), 176; italics added.

64. Quoted by Noreña (n. 27 above), 127; for the hatred of sex accompanying this attitude, see 209–211.

65. Kristeller (n. 32 above), 195–196.

66. François Rabelais, *Gargantua et Pantagruel,* 2.8, tr. Jacques Le Clercq (New York, 1944), 191.

67. Kristeller, "European Significance" (n. 52 above), 215–216.

68. Pico della Mirandola (n. 47 above), 238.

69. Quoted by O'Malley (n. 41 above), 144–147.

70. Castiglione (n. 13 above), 309–310.

71. On this interest more generally in the later Middle Ages and Renaissance, see Heiko A. Oberman, "The Shape of Late Medieval Thought: The Birthpangs of the Modern Era," in *The Pursuit of Holiness,* ed. Charles Trinkaus and Heiko A. Oberman (Leiden, 1974), 15–19; and, in the same volume, more specifically on the circle of Erasmus, James K. McConica, "Erasmus and the 'Julius': A Humanist Reflects on the Church," 444–467.

72. Letter to Louis Ber, 30 March 1529, Allen (n. 29 above), 8.120. On this point cf. Henri de Lubac, *Exégèse médiévale: Les quatre sens de l'Écriture* (Paris, 1959–1964), 4.432.

73. Pico della Mirandola (n. 47 above), 237–238.

74. Cf. Kristeller (n. 32 above), 322–323; *The Prefatory Epistles of Jacques Lefèvre d'Étaples and Related Texts,* ed. Eugene F. Rice, Jr. (New York, 1972), xix; Noreña (n. 27 above), 231–232.

75. Cf. Paul Oskar Kristeller, *Le Thomisme et la pensée italienne de la renaissance* (Montreal, 1967). Cf. John W. O'Malley, "Some Renaissance Panegyrics of Aquinas," *Renaissance Quarterly* 27 (1974), 174–192.

76. Letter to Jodocus Jonas, 13 June 1521, Allen (n. 29 above), 4.520.

77. Cf. Elizabeth L. Eisenstein, "Some Conjectures about the Impact of Printing on Western Society and Thought: A Preliminary Report," *Journal of Modern History* 40 (1968), 1–56.

78. Petrarch (n. 18 above), 72–74; Struever (n. 3 above), 55, 155–167.

79. Leopold David Ettlinger, *The Sistine Chapel before Michelangelo: Religious Imagery and Papal Primacy* (Oxford, 1965), is suggestive on this point.

80. I have analyzed this tension, as a perennial element in Renaissance thought, in "The Two Faces of Humanism: Stoicism and Augustinianism in Humanist Thought," in *Itinerarium Italicum: The Profile of the Italian Renaissance and its European Transformations,* ed. Heiko A. Oberman and Thomas A. Brady, Jr. (Leiden, 1975), 3–60; ch. 1 above.

81. This point is developed in my paper "Renaissance and Reformation: An Essay in their Affinities and Connections," in *Luther and the Dawn of the Modern Era: Papers for the Fourth International Congress for Luther Research,* ed. H. A. Oberman (Leiden, 1974), 127–149; ch. 9 below.

3   The Venetian Interdict and the Problem of Order

This essay explored the broader cultural significance of the confrontation between the papacy and the Venetian Republic during the interdict of 1606– 1607. Viewing the transition from the medieval to the modern world as involving, among other things, a shift from a metaphysical to a practical conception of order, it brought into sharper focus one of the themes of my book Venice and the Defense of Republican Liberty, *published by the University of California Press in 1968. During the years when I was working on that book, I was corresponding about scholarly matters with Lech Szczucki of the Polish Academy of Sciences; and he solicited from me an article for a volume of essays,* Histoire–Philosophie–Religion, *published by the academy's Institute of Philosophy and Sociology as volume 12 of the Archiwum Historii Filozofii i Myśli Społecznej (Warsaw, 1966), pp. 127–140. It is reprinted here by permission of the publisher.*

•   •   •

Central to the great upheavals marking the transition between the medieval and the modern world were profound disagreements about the nature of order, whether in the social and political realm, in the church, in the cosmos, or in the exalted spheres of metaphysics. High medieval culture, broadly speaking, had tended toward a unified and hierarchical conception of order which assigned to all men, experiences, places, things, and ideas their appropriate positions in a vast, graded system of values. Conversely the attack on medieval civilization at its deepest level, operating simultaneously in both the material and ideal realms, was directed at this system and the general principles it incorporated. Their common participation in this attack is perhaps the primary link among the essential tendencies of the Renaissance, the Protestant Reformation,

97

and the scientific revolution. By the same token the Counter-Reformation was, at its center, an effort to reassert and reinvigorate a conception of political and cultural as well as ecclesiastical order that had been under long attack from many directions. This crucial impulse in Rome establishes the coherence of the various efforts on the part of ecclesiastical authority to obstruct the growing political particularism of the modern age, to control literary and artistic expression, to fight heresy, to centralize the loose administration of the church, and to restrain the new science. Each of these apparently disparate phenomena had expressed in a different area of human concern some parallel repudiation of the traditional vision of order.

Complex relationships of this sort among great historical movements, unless they are altogether obvious, can generally be established clearly only by elaborate demonstration and evidence drawn from numerous sources. But occasionally a concrete historical crisis forces a whole range of underlying issues to the surface and brings suddenly into clear focus the inner meaning of major historical developments. The Venetian interdict of 1606–1607 was a crisis of this useful kind. Ostensibly intended to force the defiant Venetian Republic to cease the punishment of criminal clergy in civil courts and to withdraw laws restricting clerical wealth and the building of churches, the interdict quickly became the occasion for fundamental discussion not only about the nature of Christendom and the church but also about the underlying principles of all order.[1]

Even at the Curia preliminary interviews between Pope Paul V and the Venetian ambassador, Agostino Nani, quickly touched on fundamentals. Nani boldly defended Venetian policy by a direct appeal to "reason of state," and the pope denounced the Republic on precisely the same ground. For both sides the propriety of an autonomous and secular politics was clearly at stake.[2] But the most penetrating discussion of basic issues was carried on by means of a massive exchange of writings which were, for both sides, directed to a European audience. The presses of Rome, Bologna, and other Italian cities poured out a flood of pamphlets and books, often of considerable length, against the stubborn Republic; and the best minds in the Catholic world (as well as some of the dullest) were pressed into this cause. Among the champions of the pope were Baronius, Bellarmine, Possevino, and even Campanella. Often tedious, repetitious, quite without intellectual distinction, and frequently merely hortatory or vituperative, the various compositions of the papal writers nevertheless provide an impressive collective statement of the deepest attitudes and convictions of the Counter-Reformation. Venice also found effective champions. Some, like the Servite monk Fra Paolo Sarpi, the

Franciscan Marc'Antonio Capello, and the lay patrician Antonio Quirino, were native Venetians. Others, like the Neapolitan Giovanni Marsilio, a former Jesuit, were outsiders resident in the city and enlisted in its defense. In Paris the Venetian ambassador, Pietro Priuli, managed to persuade the Gallican jurists Louis Servin and Jacques Leschassier to write in behalf of Venice. Like the writings composed in the Roman interest, those defending Venice also dealt with the most fundamental issues.

The confrontation between the two sides was not entirely direct. Much of their difference originated in attitudes and assumptions too deep and intimate for conscious recognition. Proceeding from different premises, the papal and Venetian writers often give the impression of writing in different languages that perversely insist on using the same vocabulary. The result was that each side triumphantly scored points against the other, chalked up favorable marks on its private boards, and felt a righteous indignation when the opposition refused to admit defeat. Charges of dishonesty accumulated, bad feeling mounted, and each side was increasingly inclined angrily to dismiss the arguments of the other. For Rome Venice was moved only by impious greed later compounded by rebellion. For Venice the lofty pretensions of Rome masked a lust for power.

The basic obstacle to their communication was a major difference in intellectual constitution. Roman discourse was rational and systematic in a style inherited from the high Middle Ages, while Venice represented the concrete and flexible political mentality of Renaissance republicanism. Thus Bellarmine and his colleagues attacked the Venetians as bad logicians,[3] inundated the discussion with masses of authorities,[4] and accumulated classifications and subtle distinctions. Bellarmine, for example, did not care to discuss *liberty* without distinguishing half a dozen senses of the term.[5] The mental world of these men was fixed and certain, and they conceived of intellectual discourse as the task of revealing its firm, clear outlines.

But the works of Sarpi and his associates (though they frequently found it necessary to reply in kind) often display quite a different spirit. Sarpi ridiculed Bellarmine's distinctions as pedantic,[6] and his own compositions are permeated with a sense of the relativity of human practice "to what the variety of the times may bring."[7] As he remarked to his government at an early point in the struggle, he was convinced that "examples move more than reasons."[8] He constantly preferred concrete data to speculative conclusions;[9] he remarked in his first *consulto* that "it is not suitable to proceed in these cases by conjectures, deductions, or syllogisms, but by explicit laws."[10] By the same token the Venetian theologians were critical of their opponents' habit of pressing Scripture into a rigid dogmatic framework. "One ought not take refuge in allegory but stick to the proper and literal sense," Marsilio loftily informed Bellarmine;[11] and Sarpi constantly insisted that a proper interpretation of Scripture always required a sense of context. "Sacred Scripture should be read as a whole, not in passages," he advised the most distinguished of the Roman theologians.[12] Such minds were also little impressed by the familiar medieval arguments from analogy, to which the papal theologians still constantly referred. "Propositions that are to be estabished as dogmas should not be based on similitudes of similitudes," Sarpi observed stiffly in connection with the association of Peter and the rock;[13] and Capello was not at all persuaded that the relationship between body and soul had any real bearing on the relations between Venice and the pope.[14] Roman theologians appealed to historical precedent, and Venetians cited canons or exploited syllogisms where they were useful. But neither side was entirely comfortable with the weapons of the other.

But although issues could not always be joined directly, the basic character of the conflict is clear; and the clash was nowhere more fundamental than in the utterly different meanings the two sides assigned to the idea of order; on its deepest level the Venetian interdict was nothing less than a struggle over the nature of order. For the Roman theologians *order* implied a great system comprehending the entire natural and supernatural universe, organizing all its elements into a single all-inclusive scheme, imposing harmony and meaning on the whole and each of its parts. For the Venetians *order* had a limited and practical significance. Order was simply the necessary condition of social existence, and any attempt to fill it with a more sublime content could only subvert the true order relevant to the human situation.

Lelio Medici, Inquisitor General in Florence, offered an unusually comprehensive exposition of the papalist vision of order. "Now it is very clear and a conclusion approved by all the theologians," he declared in a typical piece of exegesis, "that all the works of God have order in themselves." Thus in the story of the Creation the fact that "God saw all the things that he had made and they were very good" (Gen. 1:31) meant that they were *ordered*. It could not be otherwise, Medici declared, "because if they were not ordered, there would necessarily be confusion among them, which would mean imperfection in all things and especially in God." It was equally clear to this writer that order had a specific character. Its essential principle was hierarchy, the distinction between higher things and lower, above all the due subordination of inferior to superior. "Order," Medici continued, "carries with it this condition, that lower things, being less perfect and noble, should be subordinated to higher, to the more perfect and noble, a point on which there is no difficulty."[15] Possevino was both more specific and more complex: "In the world there are the elements and the higher spheres; but because the whole remains in order, they are conserved together. In man there are a soul and body of diverse natures, and God found a way to join them together. Nor, because the heart, the brain, the liver administer motion, heat, and life to the body, do they suffice to keep man alive, because the intellectual soul is necessary, without which, as without its proper form, the whole would remain a cadaver. . . . In heaven there are, equally, various hierarchies, nor does one prejudice another because, each power being subordinated to higher powers, they preserve that admirable union from which all stability and joy derive."[16]

This general conception of order was central to the papalist view of all social organization. "The order which shines through in all the works of God," leaders of his own monastic group wrote against Sarpi, "is also found in every human congregation. For because order cannot exist without chief and head, since the principle of order consists in this, it happens that in every multitude gathered together, insofar as order exists, there is a chief and head on which the ordered multitude depends. This appears in families, in armies, and in all other regulated assemblies." Inherent in nature, the same principle of order also applies inevitably to the church: "In the same way the most beauteous order appears in this Holy Congregation of the faithful, which is the Christian Church, as in the family, or an army, or even, as Saint Paul suggests, a human body." Thus it was clearly necessary "that there should be one head and chief, and in consequence levels of authority and subjection. Because in every ordered assembly it is necessary that some should rule and others should be subject; some should command and others obey; some should give laws and others observe them, and with their observance direct and conduct themselves to the destined end."[17]

Ventura Venturi, Olivetan abbot of Siena, made the system as a political conception particularly neat, at the same time suggesting how participation in the hierarchy meant the dignity and fulfillment of even its humblest members. "Nor are temporal princes and senators disunited from this hierarchy," he wrote, "but a part and principal member of it. For just as the celestial hierarchy consists of angels and archangels, thrones, principates, powers, dominions, so in the human hierarchy there correspond the thrones of the empires, of kingdoms, of princes; of governments, of republics, and of all the other powers which, therefore, with just and harmonious proportion, are successively ordered by, disposed by, and finally depend on the supreme hierarch, the pope."[18] But the principle of subordination above all required the obedience of the whole temporal order to spiritual direction and the discipline of all things to man's ultimate end. This meant that politics could never be self-contained and that secular government could never be a law unto itself. Giovanni Antonio Bovio made this point with particular clarity:[19]

> Politics and religion cannot rule in distinct countries separated by mountains, rivers, or other boundaries; because every community of men, like every man in himself, being made by God and subject to him, must have within itself religion, with which it renders to God due tribute of worship and adoration. Since, therefore, politics and religion must exist together in the same republic, it is necessary that they should not co-exist as equals, lest differences and discords be interminable; and hence one has to be subordinated to the other, since where there is no order there is confusion, and where all powers are not subordinated to one supreme power there cannnot be good government. . . .
> Now we see which of the two must be subordinated and subject to the other. Politics undertakes to procure the felicity of this earthly life, religion that of celestial life. Politics ordains the whole body of the republic under an earthly prince, religion orders both the entire republic and its head under the supreme Head and Lord God. Politics rules and governs earthly things, religion directs them to the eternal. Politics is occupied for the most part with what pertains to the body and to corporal things, religion with that which concerns the salvation of souls. Who does not see clearly, therefore, that just as man is subject to God and the body to the soul, and just as this life is ordained as the way to the heavenly fatherland and these earthly things as a stairway to celestial, so politics is subject and subordinate to religion, and the prince and temporal government to the head of religion and of the church?

Bovio thus presents us systematically with the case of the Counter-Reformation against Machiavelli and against Renaissance politics in general. His argument was of course by no means novel; novelty was precisely what Rome wished to avoid. But the emphatic articulation of the position here should make it quite apparent that general considerations of the most far-reaching significance were at stake in the papal indictment of Venice. The offense of the Republic did not consist simply of particular acts of disobedience to papal authority but set off a series of wide reverberations. The real guilt of Venice lay in her rebellion against the principle of order implicit in the very nature of reality. Bellarmine equated Venetian defiance of the pope with the original sin of Eve.[20]

The Venetian theologians made little effort to refute the papal conception of order directly. Indeed their indifference to this abstract challenge on its own sublime level is one of the clearest indications of the distance between the two antagonists. For Venice order posed a practical, not a speculative, problem; true order was precisely what her own admirable constitution had so effectively created, and the Venetian constitution required no sanction beyond its own perfection and success. Thus the real Venetian reply to the Roman conception of order was not a direct refutation but insistence on the familiar Renaissance conception of the liberty of states. The order of Venice depended not on her participation, as a subordinate member, in a monolithic and hierarchical system but on her detachment and independence from all systems. It was because Venice was free, because no alien power had the right to interfere with her genial political processes, that her government had become a model of stability for the rest of Europe.

The Venetian political ideal was not altogether secular; the theologians of the Republic derived its separate existence (and the existence of all other states) from God. But the relation of any particular state to the deity (like that of the Protestant believer) was direct; it was not mediated through a hierarchy of authorities. And God himself, as Sarpi insisted, required that the independence of states should be staunchly maintained: "Because the civil being of every republic or kingdom comes from God and is directed to his glory, therefore it is not permissible, without sin and offense to God, that its proper liberty, which is the civil being of every principate, should be taken away and usurped. Nor ought there to be any doubt that negligence in its defense is a grave offense against God, and most grave when it is voluntarily allowed to be usurped."[21] It could hardly have been reassuring to Rome that Sarpi put the matter in such general terms. He not only clearly denied that Venice belonged to a system directed by the pope to supernatural and supranational ends; he also argued that such a system was directly contrary to the will of God.

But God's purposes in willing the existence of a political world of discrete states were not inscrutable and arbitrary; particular states were required because of their superior efficiency in maintaining the kind of order that the Venetians considered relevant to the human condition. This point emerges clearly in the theories of sovereignty that the Venetian writers developed from their ideal of political liberty. Sovereignty, as the authority to govern effectively and without external interference, presented itself as the only guarantee of true order in human affairs. For Sarpi sovereignty meant first of all the comprehensive authority of rulers to take any action required by the common interest. "Nature," he wrote, "when it gives an end, also provides all those powers necessary to attain it." Would God, he inquired rhetorically, do less?[22] He had already supplied his answer: "God, on whom the prince who is responsible for the public tranquility immediately depends, has also given him power to impede and to remedy all the things that disturb it."[23] Therefore, he declared, "In a well-ordered republic this kind of sovereignty requires that the prince can dispose of any thing and person according to the necessity and utility of the public good."[24] But the adequacy of sovereignty also implied its indivisibility and, once again, its independence. "I cannot refrain from saying," Sarpi advised his government at an early point in the struggle with Rome, "that no injury penetrates more deeply into a principate than when its majesty, that is to say sovereignty, is limited and subjected to the laws of another. A prince who possesses a small part of the world is equal in this respect to one who possesses much, nor was Romulus less a prince than Trajan, nor is your Serenity now greater than your forebears when their empire had not extended beyond the lagoons. He who takes away a part of his state from a prince makes him a lesser prince but leaves him a prince. He who imposes laws and obligations on him deprives him of the essence of a prince, even if he possessed the whole of Asia."[25]

Sarpi's reference here to laws points to the fact that for the Venetians, as for Bodin, full legislative authority, the key to maintaining social order, was the heart of sovereignty. The right to do "anything needful" meant above all the right to make and enforce laws. By claiming comprehensive authority to interfere with the laws of Venice the pope had thus touched on the most sensitive nerve of the body politic. Princes, the Senate had reminded the French ambassador, "are necessarily deprived of sovereignty when they are subjected to the censures of popes, who can compel them with excommunications to adjust the laws in their way."[26] The Venetian government had seen this issue clearly. At an early point it had insisted to the pope on its right to make laws, a right which "God gave to the first men who established the Republic and through them transmitted to the present and continuously exercised with moderation, never exceeding legitimate limits."[27] Each of the particular Roman complaints against Venice was an attack on some aspect of the legislative authority of the secular state, and therefore on its ability to maintain true order.

The more limited and practical Venetian conception of order also found expression in a conception of law far different from that of the Curia. For the Roman theologians law too was embedded in the general structure of reality; law was first of all an eternal principle of universal application. Particular laws, notably including the legislation of particular societies, were thus legitimate only when they reflected and conformed to the general principle of law, which also had its hierarchies. Certain authorities, certain kinds of law, were inevitably closer to the general source of law than others, reflected its substance more accurately, and therefore should take precedence over other authorities and other kinds of law. This meant that princes were never free to legislate arbitrarily, or simply on the basis of local need and conditions. Responsible only for an inferior level of the Christian Republic, itself a vast commonwealth in which local interests had always to be subordinated to universal, princes not only were required to adapt their enactments to divine and natural law; their laws were also subject to review by ecclesiastical authority. By the same token canon law in every state had always to take precedence over civil law.[28] According to these criteria local custom was the poorest possible form of legal authority.[29]

The Venetians did not deny the existence or even the priority of divine and natural law. Sarpi, indeed, was prepared on occasion to defend the "natural" rights of princes, and he acknowledged that certain acts, for example murder, were intrinsically contrary to the law of nature.[30] But most human actions and situations could not, in his view, be treated in this categorical way. The majority of acts, he argued, are by nature neither just nor unjust but merely raise issues of convenience; and such matters were, he believed, precisely the concern of the civil law, which must therefore respond not to ultimate principles but to immediate conditions.[31] But although it need not be referred to larger patterns of universal order, Sarpi did not mean that civil law was merely arbitrary; its true criterion, however, should be the interest of the immediate community it is designed to serve.

But, as the Venetians were well aware, communities differ and times change. Thus in connection with the regulation of clerical wealth Sarpi pointed out that "every prince can in such matters establish in his own state whatever the conditions of the times and places require, and also change things once constituted if changing conditions demand it."[32] Capello made the point even more generally: "Laws are to behavior like medicine to illnesses. Therefore, just as a different illness requires a different medicine, so different times, different customs, different conditions, require various, diverse, and sometimes contrary laws."[33] On this basis the Venetians attached a high value to local custom.

The Venetian definition of order had particular consequences for the status of the clergy in the community. Rome had taken the position that the absolute priority of spiritual to temporal required for the clergy a special position, privileged and apart, within every secular state; the clergy were not properly citizens of any earthly community but only of the City of God. Possevino thought it monstrous "that the head should be subject to the feet, the greater to the less, those who are consecrated to the divine cult to profane men."[34] Bellarmine argued that priests cannot be judged by laymen because in relation to the laity a priest is divine, and also that it is much worse for a layman to disobey a prelate than for a prelate to injure a layman.[35] The Servite theologians agreed with him that although the clergy may normally live in conformity with the civil law, they do so only voluntarily rather than through any legal obligation.[36] The hierarchical distinctions among men were thus as absolute as those in the heavens.

But for Venice just as sovereignty could not be shared, the needs of order required that the law be applied equally to all persons within the geographical limits of the state. Quirino was emphatic: "The Republic, as free and independent prince, has, by the nature of its principate, authority over all its subjects indifferently."[37] For Sarpi the very survival of the state depended on the maintenance of this principle. "A natural body could not endure within itself one part not destined to belong to the whole," he wrote; "even less can a civil body endure that has in its midst a man who recognized others than the prince [as his superior] in human and temporal things."[38] The authority of the Venetian state (or any other) to punish criminals of every description was, for the Venetians, an inevitable consequence of the purpose for which the state had been instituted. That the clergy should be exempted from an obligation not only common to all men but also finally a religious duty appeared to them particularly unseemly.[39]

Behind the Venetian position on this matter was the conviction that a priest, whatever else he might be in addition, was in the first place a civil being, that he shared the common needs of men as citizens, and that he ought therefore to have some share in the common obligations of citizenship. Quirino was also clear on this point: "It suffices to say that a city is composed of citizens, and that citizens are those who enjoy the benefit of civil life through being preserved in peace among themselves, through being defended from foreigners, through experiencing the good care of their resources and possessions, and finally through enjoying those blessings and felicities to which the collectivity of the citizens has been directed. This is not possible to obtain without community in the laws and good public ordinances, and with common judges."[40] Sarpi agreed, drawing the appropriate practical conclusion: "Ecclesiastics are citizens and parts of the republic; but the republic is governed with the laws of the prince. Therefore they are subject to him so that, resisting, they sin before God no less than laymen."[41] Fom the Venetian standpoint this conception of ecclesiastics as citizens certainly implied no reduction in dignity. On the contrary, it opened up to the clergy an area of virtuous activity from which they would otherwise have been excluded; as Capello noted, it recognized their capacity for "civil felicity."[42] But the "liberty" from the normal obligations of political life demanded for the clergy in Rome would have denied them the benefits of the only species of order relevant to the human condition. What Rome called *liberty* was for Sarpi only *license*.[43]

The Venetian concern with civil order and the jurisdiction of the state over its clerical subjects as over other men seems finally to have serious ecclesiological overtones. The Venetian argument tended, practically if not out of logical necessity, to break down all distinctions between priest and layman; and this tendency too found explicit expression in the Venetian case against Rome. The theologians of the Republic indignantly rejected the inclination at the Curia to identify the church with its clerical officers. Sarpi described this as usurpation.[44] Quirino insisted that the clergy were merely that segment of the church chosen to serve the rest.[45] Another Venetian writer argued that since every Catholic Christian is equally a member of the church, he is equally entitled to call himself an *ecclesiastic*.[46] Any true definition of the church, these men insisted, had to take into account its huge lay majority; the church, Sarpi maintained more than once, "is the congregation of the faithful diffused throughout the whole world."[47]

Venetian reluctance to acknowledge special status for the clergy even in the church seems to derive ultimately from an obscure but deeply rooted tendency among the urban republics of the Renaissance to regard the church as an essentially spiritual body. Venetian theologians were inclined to think of the work of salvation as wholly spiritual and invisible, and they minimized the contribution to it of any institutional agent. As Sarpi insisted against Bellarmine, salvation depends more on "the interior motions of the soul" than on any means at the disposal of the pope.[48] Hence ecclesiastical censure might be ignored with impunity;

Sarpi assured his countrymen that only their private deficiencies could truly exclude them from the church. "The theologians give as a certain and infallible rule," he wrote, "that when a man is certain in his own conscience that he has not sinned mortally in the matter for which he is excommunicated, he may be sure in his conscience that he has suffered no hurt to his soul and is neither excommunicated with God nor deprived of the benefits of the church."[49] God, in this view, could be glorified properly only by the invisible works of the spirit performed by the individual believer. For Sarpi the Gospel was on this point unequivocal: "We see from the divine Scriptures that the glory of God consists in the propagation of the Gospel and the good life of Christians and in sum, as Saint Paul says, in the mortification of the outer man and the life of the inner, and in the exercise of works of love. . . . And finally, as even the ordinary man knows, travail and suffering are the marks and proofs of the friends of God; and no one, the Gospel says, follows Christ without taking his own cross on his shoulders." Under these circumstances the clergy were not properly rulers, administrators, and disciplinarians; their duty consisted solely in appealing to individual believers, in "preaching the Gospel, holy admonitions and instructions about Christian customs, the ministry of the most holy sacraments, the care of the poor, the correction of crimes which exclude from the kingdom of God" through pious and charitable example. These sentiments were the more remarkable because they are contained in an official document in which Sarpi was concerned not to argue theology but only to appeal to the common religious assumptions of the Venetian patriciate.[50]

Thus in the Venetian conception of things the irrelevance to Venice and to political existence in general of any comprehensive schemes of metaphysical or cosmic order found a religious parallel in deep convictions about the position of the individual soul. Every believer, like every state, was seen to be related to God directly and individually, not through a system of visible hierarchical relationships in which the individual derived his position from membership in a general class. The Venetian challenge to the pope that reached its climax with the interdict of 1606 was thus analogous, at once spiritually and politically, to the Protestant challenge of the previous century. But it is peculiarly apparent in this case that the relationship between the religious and political dimensions of the confrontation went deep. The religious issue and the political issue must finally be seen as parallel expressions of a profound disagreement about the ultimate structure of order in every aspect of the universe. That both sides recognized the gravity of their differences accounts for the extraordinary bitterness of their confrontation.

NOTES

1. The best general introduction to the bibliography of the Venetian interdict is Carlo de Magistris, *Carlo Emanuele I e la contesa fra la Repubblica Veneta e Paolo V (1605–1607)* (Venezia, 1906), introduction, pp. xxv–lii.

2. Enrico Cornet, *Paolo V e la Repubblica Veneta. Giornale dal 22. ottobre 1605–9. giugno 1607* (Vienna, 1859), pp. 1–2; and *Paolo V e la Repubblica Veneta*, "Archivio Veneto," ser. 1, V (1873), 41–44.

3. Thus, in his *Risposta alla difesa delle otto propositioni di Giovan Marsilio Napolitano* (Rome, 1606), p. 142, Bellarmine dismissed his opponent as one whom Aristotle would have excluded from his school for inability to learn logic.

4. Cf., for example, *Difesa delle censure pubblicate da N. S. Paolo Papa V nella causa de'Signori Venetiani fatta da alcuni theologi della religione de'Servi in risposta alle considerationi di F. Paolo da Venetia* (Perugia, 1607), passim.

5. *Risposta ad un libretto intitolato Trattato, e risolutione sopra la validità delle Scommuniche, di Gio. Gersone Theologo, e Cancellier Parisino* (Rome, 1606). I cite from the text in *Raccolta degli scritti usciti fuori in istampa e scritti a mano, nella causa del P. Paolo V co'signori venetiani* (Coira, 1607), p. 310. This collection will be cited hereafter as *Raccolta*.

6. See his *Apologia per le opposizioni fatte dall'illustrissimo e reverendissimo signor cardinale Bellarminio alli tratti e risoluzioni di Giovanni Gersone sopra la validità delle scommuniche*, in *Istoria dell'interdetto e altri scritti editi ed inediti*, ed. Giovanni Gambarin (Bari, 1940), III, 50, where he speaks ironically of Bellarmine's "apparatus of six liberties." This collection will be cited hereafter as *Scritti*.

7. This typical phrase appears in *Considerazioni sopra le censure della santità di papa Paulo V contra la serenissima Republica di Venezia*, in *Scritti*, II, 221, in connection with varieties of secular jurisdiction over the clergy.

8. *Scrittura sopra la forza e validità della scommunica giusta ed ingiusta*, in *Scritti*, II, 39.

9. Cf. his ridicule of Bellarmine's "airy" speculations in the *Apologia*, in *Scritti*, III, 178–179.

10. *Consiglio in difesa di due ordinazioni della serenissima Republica*, in *Scritti*, II, 6.

11. *Difesa a favore della risposta dell'otto propositioni contro la quale ha scritto l'illustrissimo et reverendissimo sig. cardinal Bellarmino* (Venice, 1606), in *Raccolta*, p. 203.

12. *Apologia*, in *Scritti*, III, 87. In a number of passages in this work Sarpi insists on interpreting Scripture only in context; cf. pp. 100, 106–107, 132, 133.

13. Ibid., pp. 129–130. See also p. 132, where he objects to carrying to excessive lengths the figure of Christians as sheep.

14. *Delle controversie tra il sommo pontefice Paulo Quinto, et la serenissima Republica di Venetia parere* (Venice, 1606), p. 94.

15. *Discorso, sopra i fondamenti e le ragioni delli ss. Veneziani, per le quali pensano di essere scusati della disubbidienza, che fanno alle censure e interdetto della santità di nostro signor Papa Paolo* (Bologna, 1606), in *Raccolta*, p. 191.

16. Written under the pseudonym Teodoro Eugenio di Famagosta, *Risposta all'aviso mandato fuori dal sig. Antonio Quirino senatore veneto, circa le ragioni che*

hanno mosso la Santità di Paolo V pontefice a publicare l'interdetto sopra tutto il dominio venetiano (Bologna, 1607), p. 39.

17. *Difesa de'Servi*, p. 42.

18. *Della maiestà pontificia* (Siena, 1607), p. 31.

19. *Lettera al R. P. M. Paolo Rocca nella quale si discorre . . . sopra a due lettere del Doge e Senato di Vinetia* (Milan, 1606), pp. B2v–B3.

20. Under the pseudonym Matteo Torti, *Avviso alli sudditi del Dominio Veneto* (Rome, 1607), in *Raccolta*, p. 123.

21. *Considerazioni sulle censure*, in *Scritti*, II, 251.

22. Ibid., p. 212.

23. *Scrittura sopra l'esenzione delle persone ecclesiastiche dal foro secolare*, in *Scritti*, II, 131.

24. *Difesa di due ordinazioni*, in *Scritti*, II, 12.

25. *Forza e validità della scommunica*, in *Scritti*, II, 40.

26. Sarpi, *Istoria dell'Interdetto*, in *Scritti*, I, 115.

27. Ibid., p. 24.

28. Cf. Lelio Baglione, *Apologia contro le considerazioni di F. Paolo* (Perugia, 1606), pp. 48–49; *Difesa de'Servi*, pp. 37, 120; Medici, *Discorso*, p. 200.

29. Cf. *Difesa de'Servi*, p. 186; Bovio, *Risposta*, p. 73; Baglioni, *Apologia*, pp. 52, 55; Bellarmine, *Risposta ai sette*, p. 63.

30. *Forza e validità della scommunica*, in *Scritti*, II, 38–39; *Scrittura sulla alienazione di beni laici alli ecclesiastici sotto pretesto di prelazione o altro*, in *Scritti*, II, 105.

31. *Consiglio sul giudicar le colpe di persone ecclesiastiche*, in *Scritti*, II, 52–53.

32. *Sulla alienazione di beni laici*, in *Scritti*, II, 105.

33. *Delle controversie*, p. 125.

34. Under the pseudonym Giovanni Filoteo di Asti, *Nuova risposta alla lettera di un theologo incognito* (Florence, 1606), p. 18.

35. *Risposta a un libretto intitolato Risposta di un Dottore di Theologia* (Rome, 1606), in *Raccolta*, pp. 152 ff.; *Risposta alle oppositioni di Fra Paulo Servita* (Rome, 1606), pp. 100–102.

36. *Difesa de'Servi*, pp. 20–22.

37. *Aviso delle ragioni della serenissima Republica di Venetia, intorno alle difficoltà che le sono promosse della Santità di Papa Paolo* (Venice, 1606), in *Raccolta*, p. 26.

38. *Considerazioni sopra le censure*, in *Scritti*, II, 222. For his full argument, see *Sopra l'esenzione delle persone ecclesiastiche*, in *Scritti*, II, 130–138.

39. Sarpi evidently saw the performance of civic duties as good works in a religious sense; cf. *Forza e validità della scommunica*, in *Scritti*, II, 21.

40. *Aviso*, p. 26.

41. *Sul giudicar le colpe di persone ecclesiastiche*, in *Scritti*, II, 50.

42. *Delle controversie*, pp. 44–45.

43. *Istoria dell'interdetto*, in *Scritti*, I, 4, where he makes the terms synonymous.

44. *Scrittura in materia della libertà ecclesiastica*, in *Scritti*, II, 139.

45. *Aviso*, p. 28.

46. Fulgenzio Tomaselli, *Le mentite Filoteane, overo Invettiva di Giovanni Filoteo d'Asti contra la Republica Serenissima di Venetia, confutata*, in *Raccolta*, p. 397.

47. *In materia della libertà ecclesiastica,* in *Scritti,* II, 139; cf. his *Apologia,* in *Scritti,* III, 69–70, and Capello, *Delle controversie,* p. 120.

48. *Apologia,* in *Scritti,* III, 171.

49. *Forza e validità della scommunica,* in *Scritti,* II, 21.

50. *Considerazioni sulle censure,* in *Scritti,* II, 214–215.

4 The Secularization of Society in the Seventeenth Century

This essay was my response to an invitation from the Organization Committee for the Thirteenth International Congress of Historical Sciences held in Moscow in the summer of 1970. The invitation gave me an opportunity to think about the meaning of secularization within a society that remained still, for the most part, profoundly Christian. The paper also required some extension of my range as a historian, both topically and chronologically.

The paper was published with others prepared for the congress; I have added, however, notes omitted from its original printed version.

• • •

The subject of this report may, on first inspection, have an excessively familiar look. Secularization, like the rise of the middle class with which it is often associated,[1] has served for generations to describe a process perceived as crucial to the emergence of the modern world. It has not, however, occupied a very prominent or general place in studies dealing with the seventeenth century; hence this paper may be an opportunity to take a fresh look at a number of problems, among them the place assigned to the seventeenth century in recent historical thought. On this point I will observe in general that the seventeenth century has not managed to assume any very specific or commonly accepted identity as a European phenomenon, and the habit of asking questions or even of making pronouncements about it usually depends more on the apparently irresistible fascinations of the decimal system than on any strong sense of the coherence of these hundred years. The earlier part of the century is usually perceived (depending on the purposes of the historian) as an appendix to the age of the Renaissance or as the concluding phase of a longer period of religious conflict, the latter part (though perhaps with greater difficulty) as the prelude to the Enlightenment or, with a special eye to the civilization of France, as a unique moment by itself.[2] The century as a whole has largely defied broad generalization, and in a historiographical sense it remains an underdeveloped borderland between two overdeveloped areas.[3]

The conception of secularization itself also presents problems. Like other abstractions employed in historical discourse, it has tended, with little perception of what might be at stake, to grow in implication and, in the process, to become increasingly elusive.[4] Thus it is now regularly employed to signify a process of dissociation (as though there were no essential difference) from control by the clergy as a social group, from control by the church as an institution or moral force, or from religious influence altogether; and it is likely to be used interchangeably with *laicization, worldliness,* and *irreligion.* Some of our difficulties with the term may come from a tendency to lump all these matters together and to attribute to the whole, somewhat heterogeneous, bundle a species of teleological authority; it thus functions not merely as a description of particular developments, which can be fairly precise, but also as explanation, which is often less so. In this way *secularization* and *the secular spirit* that gives birth to it have been made to seem inexorable and irreversible forces shaping modern culture and society. The absence of any obvious antonym for secularization may be suggestive in this connection.

When our professional vocabulary is debased, the wisest course might well be to change it. But past experience along this line is not encouraging, and in any case I think that, pruned of its excrescences, the conception of secularization may still prove useful for our general understanding both of European development and of the place of the seventeenth century within larger patterns of change. I should like, therefore, to try to restore its value by offering an example, from the seventeenth century itself, of what I take to be a secular society and therefore of proper use of this language: the Republic of Venice.[5]

Venice has the special advantage for this purpose that for some months during 1606 and 1607 she was under an interdict imposed by the pope. Since the purpose of an interdict is to compel secular authority to bow to the will of the church, this event precipitated what might be described as a crisis of secular values, and the Venetian interdict set off a broad discussion that reveals what was involved in the process of secularization as it was perceived in the seventeenth century itself. Venice may conveniently serve, therefore, both as a touchstone for identifying other manifestations of secularization and as a starting point for tracing its career in the seventeenth century.

Rome had many grievances against Venice. She was immediately provoked by the Venetian habit of submitting criminal clergy to the judgment of secular courts and by Venetian laws limiting bequests by laymen to the church and regulating the construction of church buildings. Thus secularization has as its first and most limited meaning the imposition of lay control over matters previously regarded as belonging to the church. But these complaints were primarily pretexts for dealing with more general offenses of which, in the view of Rome, they were only symptoms. The Curia was profoundly antagonized by the persistent refusal of Venice to participate in crusades against the infidel, by her insistence on maintaining diplomatic and commercial relations with the non-Catholic and even the non-Christian world, by her exclusion of clergy and clerically oriented families from the councils of her government, by the moral and philosophic license of the Venetian printing industry, by the refusal of Venetian authorities to impose a rigid theological orthodoxy at Padua.

And here we may begin to discern a larger meaning in the process of secularization: Venice evidently represented for the papacy an insistence in principle on the autonomy of various realms of human concern, and particularly of politics, economic life, and culture. This, for contemporaries, was the crux of the matter: whether it was permissible to conduct the various affairs of this world in accordance with principles derived only from the human ends they served, or, on the contrary, whether they must be controlled by and made to serve larger spiritual ends. If the latter were true, Venice would be expected to obey the pope; but in fact the Venetian leaders insisted that they had no superior in temporal things. Thus secularization threatened the traditional vision of society both as a structural unity under a single head and as a functional unity in which all activity must be subordinated to ultimate goals.

But even more than this was at stake. Beyond the repudiation of traditional relationships, priorities, and goals in society was the repudiation of a vision of the universe and its structure, and thus of a traditional mode of organizing the human understanding. Secularization rested on a deep conviction that eternal truths are inaccessible to the human intellect, and that only the limited insights afforded by experience in this world are relevant to the earthly career of the human race. Thus the secularization of society also pointed to the radical subversion of any comprehensive vision of cosmic and metaphysical order, of the perception of all reality as a single system governed by common principles, in which human society finds its duly appointed place and its ultimate meaning. For Rome the secular claims of Venice made of her, from this standpoint, a rebel against the divinely constituted order of reality in general. The secularization of society was part of a larger process, and it cannot be fully assessed without some attention to Galileo's demand for an autonomous science and the vigorous controversies of the seventeenth century about the possibility and the validity of metaphysics.

The champions of Rome in the bitter war of words that accompanied the interdict understood very clearly that all these lofty issues were at stake, but the spokesmen for Venice seem to have understood it as well. When the pope first made known his grievances to the Venetian ambassador in Rome, the latter did not hesitate to defend the actions of his Republic by appealing explicitly to reason of state; and his government insisted repeatedly that since the matters over which the pope professed outrage were merely political, they did not properly concern him at all. In Venice it was obvious that reason of state had no basis in Eternal Reason, and therefore that it was unnecessary for the laws of any state to conform to a universal principle of law. The Venetians did not deign, therefore, to reply to papal invocations of a universal order. It seemed clear enough that the only order that mattered was the immediate and very secular order of the Venetian state. Thoroughly at home in the practical world of affairs, the Venetians found abstract and systematic argument utterly unpersuasive, and calculated indeed to destroy such order as human beings can attain in this world.

But although the Venetian position reveals the intimate connection between secularization in society and hostility to certain kinds of thought, it also makes quite evident that the question of secularization is by no means the same as the religious question, the question of the existence and intensity of piety. The problem was not with the degree of piety but rather with its kind. For although Rome, committed to religious formulations inextricably bound to universal principles of order and unwilling to recognize the validity of an alternative type of religion, felt some compulsion to represent the position of Venice as impious, in fact the interdict coincided with a renewal of Christian devotion among the patricians of Venice; and her leaders insisted, with a fervor that cannot be dismissed as cynical, on their attachment to the Christian faith. Their commitment, however, was to a version of Christianity that rested on a profound conviction of the inadequacy of the human mind to grasp final truth and thus to discern the orderly unity of the universe, a problem which was regarded as in any case irrelevant to the spiritual condition of human beings; Venetian piety was a matter of faith and will rather than of intellectual appropriation. This type of Christianity not only acknowledged that man lives, to quote a great seventeenth-century writer, "in divided and distinguished worlds,"[6] but implied that there could be no alternative. And thus, by accepting the incongruity between earthly and heavenly things and at the same time prepared to render unto Caesar the things that are Caesar's, this type of piety was consistent with a high degree of secularization. It obviously did not exclude the need to express Christian virtue in the world, but it perceived this not so much systematically, based on the application of general principles, as practically and almost incidentally, through the particular acts of sanctified individuals. It should also be observed that this type of piety had flourished with special vigor since the fourteenth century and was to be found among both Catholics and Protestants in the sixteenth and seventeenth centuries.

It is especially important to recognize the distinction between secularization and the decline of piety in approaching the seventeenth century, a peculiarly devout age, if those who see in it the advancement of secularization and those who emphasize its piety are not to appear utterly at cross-purposes.[7] Indeed the importance of the distinction is increasing with the tendency of recent scholarship to emphasize the religious sincerity and even the religious inspiration of many of those seventeenth-century figures who have long been considered major champions of a new, secularized view of man and the universe: of Sarpi and Galileo, of Descartes, Locke, Bayle, and Newton, perhaps even of Bacon and Hobbes.[8] Although such revisionism may owe a good deal to some obscure zeitgeist of our own, it is at any rate more plausible to interpret these figures in terms of the general preoccupations of their age than as eccentric "forerunners" of the future. And this perception can lead, in turn, to a clearer understanding of secularization itself.

The case of Venice should also remind us of one further point: that secularization did not begin with the seventeenth century; in fact it was well advanced when the century opened. The position represented by Venice was rooted in the values and attitudes of the Renaissance in Italy; Rome identified it with Machiavellianism. And the major steps in the practical secularization of Europe had for the most part been taken earlier: the replacement of clergy by laymen in governmental agencies, the transfer of jurisdictional authority of various kinds from ecclesiastical to secular courts,[9] the seizure of ecclesiastical lands in Protestant areas. Hospital administration in France[10] and philanthropy in England[11] largely passed from clerical to lay administration during the sixteenth century in a development based on the conviction that these matters had more to do with public order in this world than, as an opportunity for good works, with the salvation of souls in the next. Education too had for some time tended to be withdrawn from clerical direction for comparable reasons.[12] And, in a parallel development, the sixteenth century began a movement away from Roman law, with its universalistic overtones, toward reliance on particular bodies of local law.[13]

Thus much that seems most secular in the life of the seventeenth century must be seen as a continuation or consolidation of an impulse already long at work. This is notably true of the peace of Westphalia and the eclipse of the Empire, full acceptance of balance of power as the most likely guarantor of political survival, and the full laicization of the European diplomatic corps.[14] It is also true of mercantilism, peculiarly secular in its rejection of universal good in favor of particular benefits;[15] the antecedents of seventeenth-century mercantilism can be discerned at least as early as the fifteenth century in France, and navigation acts were already an important instrument of royal policy in early sixteenth-century England. The real problem for the historian of the seventeenth century is whether this impetus from the past was sustained.

On this question, in spite of the fact that the Venetian interdict ended in a defeat for the papacy, which never again dared to challenge the secular world in so overt a way, the evidence is ambiguous, and even on a practical level rather different from what might be expected from a secularizing movement of such obvious vigor. What had previously seemed a general movement no longer appears so comprehensive, and it becomes necessary to make both chronological and geographical distinctions.[16] Venice herself was compelled to readmit the Society of Jesus, which she had expelled as a source of danger to her secular values, and in 1684 she was persuaded to join the great crusade organized by Pope Innocent XI to expel the infidel from Europe, although this enterprise promised little benefit to herself.[17] If the policies of Richelieu rigorously distinguished the interests of the faith from those of the French state,[18] those of Louis XIV, in the closing years of his reign, are less clear; his revocation of the Edict of Nantes challenged the secularity of politics accepted, at least practically, by Henry IV; and his later wars took on some of the enthusiasm and savagery that had characterized the religious conflicts of the previous century.[19] The synods of Dort, not only in 1619 but again in 1686, were much concerned with the religious obligations of rulers, especially in the Netherlands;[20] and even in England the religious profession of the ruler was increasingly a focus of concern. There was no general retreat from the secular constructions of an earlier time, but one has an impression of the deceleration and occasional faltering of the secularizing process as a practical matter, perhaps especially after the middle of the century.

Secularization is as much a matter of the values attached to human activity as of the concrete forms of activity itself, and it is easier to trace what was occurring in the thought of the seventeenth century than in its institutions, which, being more inert, better preserved the character they had taken on in the previous period. And what must be recognized in the thought of the seventeenth century is a persistent tension between the pragmatic attitudes represented by secular Venice, based on an extremely modest estimate of the generalizing intellect, and the systematic impulse represented by Rome. Both types of intellectual orientation may be found at any time during the century, and few groups or individuals did not in some measure participate in both and feel the common tensions of the age; neither secularism nor its opposite can often be encountered in a pure form. One can discern, nevertheless, a gradual shift in the balance between these antithetical positions during the course of the century; and it seems likely that by 1700 a smaller proportion of Europeans organized their perceptions of life, society, and the world like Venetians at the time of the interdict than had been the case a century earlier. The seventeenth century saw a decline in the secularizing mentality that is related, in a manner probably more profound than that of either cause or effect, to the weakening of secularization in society.

It is true that in important ways secular attitudes intensified during the earlier seventeenth century, allied with and encouraged by the ascendancy of a skeptical and fideistic piety that rejected the possibility of authentic systems of abstract thought. It remained both common and respectable to insist on the gulf between faith and reason, and in this period the sense of the ultimate helplessness and irrationality of the human race reached a kind of climax.[21] Much of the intellectual leadership of Western Europe now shared a deep antipathy to system building and attacked metaphysics with a holy zeal.[22] Galileo's insistence that theology is queen of the sciences only through the special dignity of its subject and not through any right to govern what occurs in the other sciences, and that religion teaches "how one goes to heaven, not how heaven goes,"[23] reflects an attitude that he shared with Bacon, Gassendi, Mersenne, and Pascal.[24] But the principle applied equally to matters other than natural philosophy; it pointed to the autonomy of all aspects of human experience insofar as they are objects of human thought. The secularization of science, with its substitution of efficient for final causes and of a mechanical for an organic and animistic model of physical reality, was symptomatic of a more general development.

It is notably evident during the earlier seventeenth century in attitudes to man and society. A sense of the spiritual incommensurability of heaven and earth could produce a sharper conviction, of course, as among some Jansenists, of the need to impose spiritual direction on the secular world, and the effect of earlier seventeenth-century pessimism was not unambiguously secular.[25] But it was more likely to result in a belief that the corrupt world should be ignored because it is both unintelligible and irredeemable, a view in which other Jansenists[26] were joined by some of the new partisans of both Epicureanism[27] and Stoicism,[28] or, among minds more engaged with the life around them, a conviction that although the *civitas terrena* had nothing in common with the *civitas dei*, it nevertheless operates according to identifiable principles of its own. Thus, as with the influential Charron, just because behavior could not manifest eternal wisdom, ethics might be treated as a secular science;[29] and for the same reason some French libertines developed a hedonistic conception of art.[30] The principle also had implications for the writing of history; with Paolo Sarpi, precisely because the true church is an utterly spiritual body existing beyond the world of time, the career of the institutional church could be described in completely secular terms.[31]

The same sense of the separateness and thus the independence of the secular is also in evidence in much of the political thought of this period, and the persistent attacks on the "Machiavellianism" of the age are a tribute to its continuing vitality in theory as well as practice. While Francis Bacon praised Machiavelli for describing "what men do, and not what they ought to do,"[32] an influential Frenchman (possibly Père Joseph himself) began a general treatise on European politics by remarking that "the best advice one can give in matters of state is based on special knowledge of the state itself."[33] Such attitudes were dominant in the circle of Richelieu, whose successes seemed to certify to the validity of the secular principles identified by Machiavelli and his followers.[34] But the secular principles underlying human society were also being elaborated in other quarters: by those who idealized non-Christian polities, that of the Turks or the Chinese, for example,[35] and possibly even through the naturalistic contract theory promoted (though for quite other than secular motives) by Jesuit theorists.[36]

Even the divine-right theory of this period, which was employed to bolster the position not only of kings but of all governments, as its application to the Venetian and Dutch republics reveals, seems to me to have been equivocal in respect to secularization. On the one hand it supplied a religious base to governments and spiritual sanctions to rulers.

But it served also as a justification for the compartmentalization of life in the kind of language that had now become most persuasive, and thus it protected the autonomy of politics. In addition, by accepting the actual fragmentation of the political world, divine-right theory confirmed one of the aspects of secularization that was most abhorrent to its foes. Divine right thus suggests the general ambiguity of the seventeenth century.

And indeed, even as the secularizing currents flowing out of the past were rushing more and more frantically, they were being compressed into an increasingly narrow channel. A reaction, whose sources may also be traced back through the sixteenth century to the age of the Renaissance, was gathering force. It found general expression in the recovery everywhere of the systematizing mentality, which rested on a positive estimate of man's intellect very different from the view that underlay the secularizing movement, and which insisted on relating all aspects of human experience to a central core of universal and therefore abstract truth. Thus it renewed not only a sense of the priority of eternal values, but above all a confidence in their general applicability to the secular world; and in this way it pointed to the destruction of the autonomy which, in the seventeenth century, was at the heart of the secularizing process.

This tendency is apparent everywhere: in the massive renewal of scholastic theology in Counter-Reformation Catholicism, but also (and perhaps even earlier) in the Protestant world, in a movement that justifies our speaking of a *Protestant* Counter-Reformation.[37] The recovery of metaphysics made philosophy almost as interchangeable with theology among Protestants as among Catholics; Aristotle became as important in the universities of Germany and England as in those of Spain or France; and some Protestants went as far as the authorities in Rome in reviving the spiritualized cosmology of the Ptolemaic universe, which could not be challenged without attacking Christianity itself.[38] Seventeenth-century Calvinism was meanwhile experiencing a parallel transformation. Though less hospitable to Aristotle than Lutheranism, it found in the logic of Ramus grounds of its own for a more optimistic view of the human intellect, its theology became increasingly speculative and systematic, it discovered that the medieval schoolmen were more respectable than it had supposed, and it began to take a growing interest in identifying general laws of nature.[39]

The most influential expression of this resurgence of the systematizing mentality was, of course, the method of Descartes. It is doubtless important for some purposes to distinguish between retrospective and innovative system building. But here their differences are less important than what they have in common: the conviction that an intellectual construction can be something more than the product of a particular culture, and that it is possible for human beings to attain certain knowledge. Both pre- and post-Cartesian rationalism represented the impulse toward the systematic integration of all experience. Both therefore tended in principle to reject the autonomy of the secular. The significance of Descarte's own dualism may still be debatable, but his followers found the Cartesian method useful rather for establishing relationships than for preserving distinctions; in the hands of a Malebranche, Cartesianism seemed as suitable as Aristotelianism to reconstitute a philosophy of universal order on Christian principles.[40]

In a climate characterized by an increasing penchant for system building, the autonomy of the secular came under increasing attack. This is obvious enough in the theory and practice of Counter-Reformers in Rome; we have already noticed the offensive against Venice. Bellarmine had laid down, as a general principle, that "all order consists in this, that some should command and others should be subjugated";[41] and there was no doubt among the authorities of the Counter-Reformation what this meant in practice and to what purposes the obedience of mankind should be directed. For Bellarmine the temporal and spiritual powers were still "united so that they compose one body," a body in which "spirit rules and moderates, and sometimes restrains, sometimes stimulates as it judges expedient for its own ends."[42] The enunciation of correct principles was also accompanied by a general offensive against a secularized politics, to which the label "false reason of state" was regularly applied, following Botero.[43]

The significance of the seventeenth century may be seen in the fact that such conceptions were probably more popular and more widely diffused as it ended than when it began.[44] Instead of assuming the autonomy of politics like Machiavelli, the men of the later seventeenth century, for example that weather vane of opinion Pufendorf, or the influential Seckendorf, were preoccupied with (to cite one of Pufendorf's own titles) "the relation of the Christian religion to civil life."[45] In France earlier concern to recover for use the specific and practical *mos gallicus* gave way to the efforts of jurists like Jean Domat, who sought to derive the laws of the state from the eternal principles supremely represented by Christian morality.[46] And while Massillon and others celebrated the revocation of the Edict of Nantes as a decisive blow against "false reason of state,"[47] a generation of reformers began to attack mercantilism as a violation of the universal concern for mankind taught by the Christian faith.[48] Meanwhile the quality, and perhaps also the quantity, of historical composition, that most secular activity of the previous century, declined, under pressure for the subordination of historiography to religion or to a political science or an ethics based on universal principles. Even the most notable histories of the seventeenth century, for example Clarendon's *History of the Rebellion,* gave to providential explanation an importance that Sarpi would have found remarkable.[49] And the moral doctrines central to seventeenth-century classicism were acceptable largely on the ground that their universal validity gave them a unique capacity for the expression and support of Christian morality.[50] As in other matters, the fact that truths could be derived from sources other than the Scriptures or the authoritative teaching of the church did not imply that a secularizing process was at work. It pointed not to a larger area of autonomy for the secular world but to the systematic coherence of all aspects of experience.

These considerations may also suggest that the contribution of natural law theorists to the political speculation of the seventeenth century was, like divine-right theory, equivocal from the standpoint of secularization. Like the proponents of divine right, the advocates of natural law recognized the sovereignty of particular states,[51] and they combined the idea of natural law with an individualistic contract theory that seemed to deny any ultimate source of political authority. But theories of natural law also expressed a very different impulse. If they were intended to serve a practical purpose, it was above all to restrain an excessively secular politics rather than as a positive contribution to the process of secularization. Thus Grotius can hardly be considered a "secularizer" because he argued from reason rather than from revelation. Scholars familiar with Scholastic thought find it difficult to detect much difference between Grotius and Thomas Aquinas on this point;[52] and although it might be argued that Thomas, too, was in some sense a secularizer, it seems more useful here to compare Grotius with Machiavelli. In this perspective it should be apparent that Grotius represented precisely the tendency in political discussion that Machiavelli most abhorred: Grotius was finally concerned not with how men act but rather with how they should act. He aimed to substitute a prescriptive and deductive politics based on universal principles for a descriptive and inductive politics based on experience, a politics of abstract intelligence and generalized morality for a politics of will and power. The effect was to fit politics once again into a general system of values consistent with, if not actually derived from, the revealed will of God. The tendency of some scholars to minimize the importance of God for Grotius himself may express more about their anticipation of what lay ahead than about their understanding of what was central for Grotius, and the importance of God as the ultimate source of law and morality may have been greater among later natural law theorists such as Pufendorf.[53]

At the same time I do not wish to leave the impression that the seventeenth century saw a complete retreat from the insistence on the separateness of realms basic to secularization. The satires of Molière in France,[54] the comedies of manners in later seventeenth-century England, and the hedonistic ethics of a few worldly aristocrats in both countries[55] suggest that the old impulses were still alive. And several major thinkers—Hobbes, Locke, and Bayle—reveal that the conviction of human inadequacy to grasp ultimate truths could still nourish a vigorous and ultimately influential vision of man and society. It is no accident, I think, that these men came out of a tradition that had been peculiarly emphatic about the distance between this world and the world beyond.

Neither Hobbes nor Locke, at any rate, was altogether immune from the systematic contagion of the age. Both sought to establish as much coherence as the human mind could manage, and the similarities between Hobbes and Descartes are obvious; of the two, Hobbes may indeed have been the more purely deductive.[56] But both Hobbes and Locke, in the end, seem to have staunchly resisted that philosophical conjunction of realms characteristic, for example, of the natural law theorists on the Continent and of the century in general; neither equated man's access to the workings of nature with God's;[57] and Bayle's sense of the limits of human understanding went much farther. This position led to a vision of political order that is reminiscent once again of the position of Venice at the beginning of the century: politics became again a practical affair, not an earthly projection of cosmic order but a construction by men on the basis only of as much as they could understand of themselves and their position in a purely natural universe. And it was devised not for the expression of eternal principles theoretically convenient for humankind, but to serve immediate and thoroughly practical human needs.[58]

Hobbes, Locke, and Bayle also had this in common: that to varying degrees all three were immediately regarded as dangerous.[59] They were dangerous because they undermined the systematic rationality of the universe that other men of the century were desperately seeking to reconstruct. To understand this more general concern, which the occasional truly secular thinker of the seventeenth century apparently threatened, we must doubtless go back to the material conditions of the age: to the prolonged depression of the century, to its social dislocation, its wars and revolutions. But by the end of the century the grimmest part of the general crisis was over, and men could increasingly relax. This is perhaps why Hobbes and above all Bayle and Locke, the transmitters of an attitude toward human existence more common in the previous age than in their own century, would seem more and more like the voices of the future.

NOTES

1. As in Carl J. Friedrich, *The Age of the Baroque, 1610–1660* (New York, 1952), p. 35: "It was undoubtedly a part of this bourgeois spirit of the newer political thought, secularized and urban in its orientation, that it tended to eliminate the church from any role in the political sphere." See also Alfred von Martin, *Soziologie der Renaissance* (Stuttgart, 1932), p. 28, for a standard juxtaposition of "säkularisiert" and "bürgerlich."

2. Cf. H. R. Trevor-Roper, "The General Crisis of the Seventeenth Century," in *Crisis in Europe, 1560–1660*, ed. Trevor Aston (London, 1965), pp. 59–95. Trevor-Roper is emphatic on the difference between the first and second halves of the century, pp. 62–63. G. N. Clark made somewhat the same point in the introduction to the second edition of *The Seventeenth Century* (Oxford, 1947), in which he spoke of the middle of the century as "one of the great watersheds of modern history," although this perception did not result in any major change from the first edition (1929), in which Clark had been content to designate the century as a period of "transition": a word that should now be treated with some suspicion.

3. For the curiously inconclusive quality of works even on major aspects of the century, see also Leonard N. Marsak, "The Idea of Reason in Seventeenth-Century France," *Cahiers d'histoire mondiale* 11 (1969), 407, on "the uncertainty still attached" to "the great age in France."

4. Thus in English the verb "to secularize" was first used in 1611 in the narrow sense of conversion from ecclesiastical possession or use; its meaning was enlarged, and became more ambiguous, in the eighteenth century, when it began also to signify both dissociation or separation from religion or spiritual *concerns* and a turn toward *worldliness* (*Oxford English Dictionary*, s.v. "secularize").

5. For a fuller account of what follows, see my *Venice and the Defense of Republican Liberty* (Berkeley, 1968), esp. pp. 339–482.

6. Thomas Browne, *Religio Medici* (London, 1906), p. 39. Browne's emphasis on division and distinction is both paradoxical and poignant, since it appears as part of a thoroughly traditional celebration of man as microcosm. Cf. S. L. Bethell, *The Cultural Revolution of the Seventeenth Century* (London, 1951), which attempts to relate T. S. Eliot's celebrated notion of a "dissociation of sensibility" to seventeenth-century Anglican theological discussion.

7. A few examples of this emphasis must suffice. Some writers have insisted on the piety of the century as a whole, without distinction of time or place. Thus, in E. Préclin and E. Jarry, *Les luttes politiques et doctrinales aux XVIIe et XVIIIe siècles,* Histoire de l'église, 19 (Paris, 1955), 1:286, the period saw the "sanctification du travail manual" and of "la vie profane." Rosalie Colie, *Light and Enlightenment: A Study of the Cambridge Platonists and the Dutch Arminians*

(Cambridge, 1957), p. 1, calls theology "the blood of the seventeenth-century body politic"; cf. Michael Walzer, *The Revolution of the Saints: A Study in the Origins of Radical Politics* (Cambridge, Mass., 1965), esp. p. 259. Other historians have emphasized the power of religion during particular decades or in particular parts of Europe. Thus Carl Bridenbaugh, *Vexed and Troubled Englishmen* (New York, 1968), p. 276: "one cannot gainsay the fact that many of the people of the generations that lived between 1590 and 1640 had undergone a spiritual quickening that made most of them less materialistic and more devout than their predecessors of the previous century." Among French historians Etienne Thuau, *Raison d'état et pensée politique à l'époque de Richelieu* (Paris, 1967), p. 13, appears to agree that the seventeenth is the "grand siècle chrétien de notre histoire," and P. Barrière, *La vie intellectuelle en France du XVIe siècle à l'époque contemporaine* (Paris, 1961), pp. 176–177, stresses the religious preoccupations of French literature throughout the seventeenth century. In his brilliant Zaharoff lecture *Sur le problème religieux dans la première moitié du XVIIe siècle,* Antoine Adam organizes French thought in terms of contrasting religious orientations; and even Paul Hazard's *Crise de la conscience européenne,* 3 vols. (Paris, 1935), 2:415, notes a resurgence of religious sentiment at the end of the century in France.

8. For Sarpi, see my *Venice and the Defense of Republican Liberty,* esp. pp. 528–555. For Galileo, see Giorgio de Sanatillana, *The Crime of Galileo* (Chicago, 1955), pp. 103, 130; Ludovico Geymonat, *Galileo Galilei* (Milan, 1957); and Giorgio Spini, "The Rationale of Galileo's Religiousness," in *Galileo Reappraised,* ed. Carlo L. Golino (Berkeley, 1968), pp. 44–66. For Descartes, see the considerable literature cited by Leonard Krieger, *The Politics of Discretion* (Chicago, 1965), p. 266, and the passages cited by Krieger, p. 217. For Locke, see John W. Yolton, *John Locke and the Way of Ideas* (Oxford, 1956), pp. 116–117; the introduction by Philip Abrams to *Two Tracts on Government* (Cambridge, 1967); and above all John Dunn, *The Political Thought of John Locke* (Cambridge, 1969). For Bayle, see the magisterial work of Elisabeth Labrousse, *Pierre Bayle,* 2 vols. (The Hague, 1963–1964), which reflects the views of a revisionist school that also includes Paul Dibon, Walter Rex, and Richard Popkin. For Newton, see Frank Manuel, *A Portrait of Isaac Newton* (Cambridge, Mass., 1968). For Bacon, see Christopher Hill, *Intellectual Origins of the English Revolution* (Oxford, 1965), pp. 85–130. For Hobbes, see Willis B. Glover, "God and Thomas Hobbes," *Church History* 29 (1960), 275–297; and F. C. Hood, *The Divine Politics of Thomas Hobbes* (Oxford, 1964).

9. On the secularization of the Parlement of Paris, see, for example, J. H. Shennan, *The Parliament of Paris* (London, 1968), pp. 33–35, 81–82. The process had been essentially completed well before 1600.

10. Ibid., p. 91.

11. Wilbur K. Jordan, *Philanthropy in England, 1480–1660* (New York, 1959), pp. 114–117.

12. For France, see Shennan, *The Parlement of Paris,* pp. 91–93; for England, Jordan, *Philanthropy in England,* p. 147; and cf. Leopold Willaert, *Après le Concile de Trente: La restauration catholique, 1563–1658,* Histoire de l'église, 18 (Paris, 1960), 1:201.

13. Julian Franklin, *Jean Bodin and the Sixteenth-Century Revolution in the*

Methodology of Law and History (New York, 1963); J. G. A. Pocock, *The Ancient Constitution and the Feudal Law: English Historical Thought in the Seventeenth Century* (Cambridge, 1957), pp. 1–29.

14. Garrett Mattingly, *Renaissance Diplomacy* (New York, 1955), esp. p. 216; John B. Wolf, *Emergence of the Great Powers, 1685–1715* (New York, 1951), p. 7.

15. Lionel N. Rothkrug, *Opposition to Louis XIV: The Political and Social Origins of the French Enlightenment* (Princeton, 1965), is especially good on this aspect of mercantilism, esp. pp. 7–35.

16. For the general view of the seventeenth century as "retreat" or "reaction," see Hazard, *Crise de la conscience*, vol. 1, and above all the classic work of Henri Hauser, *La modernité du XVIe siècle,* new ed. (Paris, 1963).

17. On the persistence and intensification of the crusading ideal in the later seventeenth century, see Frederick L. Nussbaum, *The Triumph of Science and Reason, 1660–1685* (New York, 1953), pp. 239–241, although, as its title suggests, this work sees the seventeenth century quite differently from my own interpretation.

18. On the secularism of Richelieu and his circle, see Thuau, *Raison d'état et pensée politique,* pp. 26–27.

19. On the general point, cf. Wolf, *Emergence of the Great Powers,* pp. 101–102. See also Philippe Sagnac and A. de Saint-Leger, *Louis XIV, 1661–1715,* new ed. (Paris, 1949), p. 1. William F. Church, "The Decline of the French Jurists as Political Theorists, 1660–1789," *French Historical Studies* 5 (1967), 1–40, sees in this development the general explanation for the declining role of lawyers in the formation of French political thought.

20. E. H. Kossman, "The Development of Dutch Political Theory in the Seventeenth Century," in *Britain and the Netherlands,* ed. J. S. Bromley and E. H. Kossman (New York, 1960), pp. 91–110, emphasizes the theoretical intolerance of the Netherlands, although he sees a progression toward a more secular conception of the state under the influence of rationalism.

21. Arthur O. Lovejoy, *Reflections on Human Nature* (Baltimore, 1961), p. 15.

22. These tendencies found expression in the Augustinianism emphasized by Jean Orcibal, *Jean Duvergier de Hauranne, abbé de Saint-Cyran, et son temps* (Paris, 1947), and by Antoine Adam, *L'âge classique, 1624–1660* (Paris, 1968), esp. pp. 61ff. It helps to explain the popularity of Charron (see Richard H. Popkin, *The History of Scepticism from Erasmus to Descartes* [Assen, The Netherlands, 1950], p. 57) and of Gassendi (see Tullio Gregory, *Scetticismo ed empirismo, studio su Gassendi* [Bari, 1960]) in this period as well as of Montaigne. In general see also René Pintard, *Le libertinage érudit dans la première moitié du XVIIe siècle* (Paris, 1943). The decline of Scholasticism in seventeenth-century Cambridge seems related to the same tendencies; see William T. Costello, *The Scholastic Curriculum at Early-Seventeenth-Century Cambridge* (Cambridge, Mass., 1958).

23. This famous passage is from his letter to the Grand Duchess Christina, *Opere* (Milan and Rome, 1936), I:888.

24. In addition to the works cited in n. 22 above, see also Paolo Rossi,

Francesco Bacone: dalla magia alla scienza (Bari, 1957), and Robert Lenoble, *Mersenne ou la naissance du mécanisme* (Paris, 1943).

25. Orcibal, *Saint-Cyran,* pp. 499–500, on Saint-Cyran's attack on Richelieu; Thuau, *Raison d'état,* pp. 103–152, discusses the religious opposition to "la 'Raison d'Enfer.'"

26. Cf. Lucien Goldmann, *Le dieu caché* (Paris, 1959).

27. Cf. Adam, *L'âge classique,* pp. 73–74.

28. Leontine Zanta, *Renaissance du stoicisme au XVI᷎ siècle* (Paris, 1914), pp. 75–98, associates Stoicism with the secularization of morality. Anthony Levi, *French Moralists: The Theory of the Passions, 1585–1649* (Oxford, 1965), pp. 2, 11, sees an alliance between Stoicism and skepticism.

29. Popkin, *History of Scepticism,* p. 60, and especially Eugene F. Rice, Jr., *The Renaissance Idea of Wisdom* (Cambridge, Mass., 1958), p. 203.

30. Adam, *L'âge classique,* pp. 98–99.

31. Bouwsma, *Venice and Republican Liberty,* ch. 10.

32. Quoted by Mary A. Scott in the introduction to her edition of Bacon's *Essays* (New York, 1908).

33. This pamphlet is discussed at length by Friedrich Meinecke, *Die Idee der Staatsräson in der neueren Geschichte* (Munich and Berlin, 1925), ch. 6.

34. See Thuau, *Raison d'état,* esp. pp. 166–409.

35. See, in general, Geoffroy Atkinson, *Les nouveaux horizons de la Renaissance française* (Paris, 1935), and cf. Boccalini's idealization of the Turks, as discussed by Meinecke, *Staatsräson,* ch. 3.

36. The point was made long ago by J. N. Figgis, *Political Thought from Gerson to Grotius, 1414–1625* (Cambridge, 1907), pp. 88–89.

37. This suggestive phrase is used by Henri Hauser, *La prépondérance espagnole, 1559–1660,* 3d ed. (Paris, 1948), p. 215, and by R. Hooykaas, *Humanisme, science et réforme: Pierre de la Ramée, 1515–1572* (Leiden, 1958), p. 18.

38. This movement is well discussed, especially for Lutheranism, by John Dillenberger, *Protestant Thought and Natural Science: A Historical Study* (New York, 1960), esp. pp. 50–74.

39. This is a major thesis of Perry Miller, *The New England Mind: The Seventeenth Century* (New York, 1939), esp. pp. 100–108.

40. Hazard, *Crise de la conscience,* vol. 1; Adam, *L'âge classique,* p. 565, for the attraction of Cartesianism for some Jansenists.

41. *De potestate pontificis temporali,* bk. I, ch. 2.

42. *De clericis,* chs. 18, 29.

43. On the general importance of this distinction in the earlier seventeenth century, see Meinecke, *Staatsräson,* ch. 5.

44. Cf. Thuau, *Raison d'état,* p. 333, on the decline of Machiavellianism, and the suggestive remarks of A. J. Krailsheimer, *Studies in Self-Interest from Descartes to La Bruyère* (Oxford, 1962), p. 7, on the shift in attitudes after the Fronde.

45. Krieger, *Politics of Discretion,* p. 66; Wolf, *Emergence of the Great Powers,* pp. 306–307.

46. Church, "French Jurists," pp. 13ff.

47. Quoted by Thuau, *Raison d'état,* p. 369.

48. Rothkrug, *Opposition to Louis XIV,* p. 9.

49. See B. H. G. Wormald, *Clarendon: Politics, Historiography, and Religion, 1640–1660* (Cambridge, 1964), pp. 179ff. Bossuet is an even more obvious example in a later generation; cf. Adalbert Klempt, *Die Säkularisierung der universalhistorischen Auffassung zum Wandel des Geschichtsdenkens im 16. und 17. Jahrhundert* (Göttingen, 1960), p. 11, and Karl Löwith, *Meaning in History* (Chicago, 1949), pp. 137–144.

50. Barrière, *Vie intellectuelle en France,* pp. 208–209.

51. Otto von Gierke, *Natural Law and the Theory of Society, 1500–1800,* tr. Ernest Barker (Cambridge, 1934), p. 40, emphasizes this point.

52. Cf. Frederick Copleston, *A History of Philosophy: Ockham to Suarez* (London, 1953), p. 149.

53. Cf. Krieger, *Politics of Discretion,* pp. 663, 78–79, 222.

54. Cf. Krailsheimer, *Studies in Self-Interest,* p. 215.

55. Hazard, *Crise de la conscience,* vol. 2, with particular attention to Saint-Evremond, Halifax, Temple, and Shaftesbury.

56. Cf. M. M. Goldsmith, *Hobbes's Science of Politics* (New York, 1967), introduction, p. xv; Hood, *Divine Politics of Hobbes,* p. 19, makes him out a kind of schoolman because of the deductive tendencies of his rationalism.

57. For Hobbes, cf. Hood, *Divine Politics of Hobbes,* pp. 2–3; F. S. McNeilly, *The Anatomy of Leviathan* (London, 1968), p. 31, which notes the failure of Hobbes even to acknowledge the question, so important to Descartes, whether there are objects corresponding to the images registered by the senses; and Samuel I. Mintz, *The Hunting of Leviathan: Seventeenth-Century Reactions to the Materialism and Moral Philosophy of Thomas Hobbes* (New York, 1926), pp. 26–27, contrasting Hobbes with Hooker. For Locke, cf. Yolton, *Locke and the Way of Ideas,* esp. pp. 1–25, and Richard Ashcraft, "Faith and Knowledge in Locke's Philosophy," in *John Locke: Problems and Perspectives,* ed. John W. Yolton (Cambridge, 1969), pp. 194–223.

58. Cf. Goldsmith, *Hobbes's Science of Politics,* p. 125.

59. For the attack on Hobbes, see Mintz, *Hunting of Leviathan,* esp. pp. 39–62, 134ff.; Thuau, *Raison d'état,* pp. 96–97, compares the "scandal provoked by *Leviathan*" with the detestation of Machiavelli; on Locke as dangerous, see Yolton, *Locke and the Way of Ideas,* pp. 1–25; for Bayle, see Labrousse, *Bayle,* 1:259–265.

5 Lawyers and Early Modern Culture

Like the previous paper, this essay deals with the transition to modern culture, but this time as it found expression in the experience and attitudes of a strategically important profession. I also argue here that it is a mistake to confuse the secular practicality of lawyers with hostility to Christianity; it should be rather understood as a function of an Augustinian distinction between the earthly city and the City of God. In an earlier form this essay was presented at the annual luncheon meeting of the Modern European Section of the American Historical Association in New York in 1971. It was published in the American Historical Review *78 (1973), 303–327, and is reprinted here by permission of the editor.*

•   •   •

Although European historians have increasingly recognized the impact of large-scale change or significant events on human culture, they have paid little attention to the importance of the less dramatic aspects of social experience for shaping the attitudes of men. The result has been, for most of us, a schism between social and intellectual history that has impoverished both. As Frederic C. Lane has reminded us, the routine tasks of daily life are likely to impress those engaged in them with a profound sense of what the world and especially men are like and to produce patterns of expectation and systems of value—dimensions of culture in its larger meaning.[1] Eventually these impressions are likely to find explicit formulation in philosophy, science, theology, and literature and the other arts—in culture in a narrower sense. But since the work by which men support their needs tends, particularly in the modern world, to be highly differentiated, it is difficult to treat the relation of work to culture in general terms. To get at this relationship, the historian must examine the experience of particular occupational groups that have held a position of strategic importance both in movements central to their social universe and in the articulation of its vision of the human condition. The rise and development of groups of this kind, especially where they have not previously been prominent, gives the historian an opportunity, unique in its concreteness, to study the sources and the nature of social change. In addition, such groups may be especially useful for identifying the sources in social experience of fundamental shifts in attitudes and values. Scientists and technologists invite this kind of study in our own time. So, for early modern Europe, do lawyers.

In view of the attention recently directed to social history, it is remarkable that so little study of occupational groups has been done. One reason, I take it, is the tendency of many social historians to rely for most purposes on the categories of social class, which, though only imperfectly related to occupational differences, can usually be made to absorb them. From this standpoint occupations are interesting chiefly because they help in the assignment of individuals to their appropriate classes, and small attention is given to the often rather different functions of men who are seen as members of the same class, or to the possibility of contrasting perceptions of life arising out of the quite different ways men spend their working days. Lawyers can doubtless be generally identified with the middle class or some rank above it, though precision on this matter has often proved difficult: in societies sensitive to social gradation, men of the law regularly presented problems, a fact that might well alert us to their special significance. But the mind of a lawyer was also shaped by a professional experience that made him rather different from most merchants or landed gentlemen.[2]

A second obstacle to the fruitful study of occupations has been our tendency to leave them to specialists concerned primarily with disciplines abstracted from their human and social meaning. Thus we have histories of theology but few of theologians, with the result that theology presents itself chiefly as an evolving set of disembodied ideas rather than as a response to human needs perceived through some kind of experience with life. We have histories of science but few of scientists considered as a group, and histories of law—indeed great classics on this formidable subject—but very little on lawyers as a profession characterized by a certain social role and a particular perspective on life and the world. What we have is useful and often admirable; we need not go all the way with Christopher Hill's somewhat imperial assertion that "it is time to take legal history out of the hands of the lawyers, as religious history has been taken away from the theologians, and to relate both to social development."[3] Yet the general point is valid enough, even though—as revealed by recent works of Gilmore and Martines for Italy, of Franklin, Kelley, and Huppert for France, and, among others, of Thorne, Pocock, and Little for England—a broader interest in lawyers and their activity is now stirring.[4] This article is concerned to call attention to some of the larger possibilities in the subject and thus to the need for further work that, with proper respect for differences among societies and legal traditions, will permit a higher level of generalization.

The history of lawyers is peculiarly adapted to display connections among various dimensions of human activity, but it also bears on fundamental controversies about the nature of the law itself. In the long history of speculation on the law, lawyers of the Renaissance were the first theorists since the Sophists to argue that legal systems should not be required to reflect the will of God in any direct way or to mediate between eternal reason and the practical needs of men;[5] the law functions best, some Renaissance lawyers maintained, as a response to the concrete needs of particular societies and in fact can be shown to have evolved in this way.[6] Ever since the Renaissance, men have divided over this issue or, like Sir Edward Coke, uneasily straddled it; and the same disagreement, or at any rate the profound psychological differences it may be taken to represent, underlies much contemporary dispute about the law, perhaps including recent debate over strict construction.[7] A more comprehensive study of the historical relations between law and social experience might also contribute something to this perennial issue; our subject may thus have some practical importance.

The legal profession of early modern Europe was a somewhat diverse body, and I shall define it rather loosely to include all those who supplied legal or quasi-legal services. At its highest and most broadly influential level of eminence it included judges and magistrates, sometimes with little or no formal education, who applied the law to the various needs of government. In addition it included juridical scholars with varying degrees of practical experience, practicing lawyers—among them canonists as well as civilians and common or customary lawyers—and also, in this period, notaries. Sometimes organized with lawyers in a single guild as in Renaissance Florence, notaries supplied various legal services to a far larger body of clients than their less numerous and more prestigious colleagues. Because the task of providing written legal instruments merged into the work of public secretary and scribe, notaries were important in relating law to literature and scholarship. They were therefore of special importance in mediating between the broader and the narrower meanings of culture.[8]

It is, at any rate, evident that men somehow connected with the law occupy a remarkable and disproportionate place among those prominent in European culture expression.[9] The connection was sometimes a matter of degree, and in particular cases it was clearly ambiguous. Many young men destined for fame in other connections studied law but failed or refused to complete the course or in the end made no professional use of their legal training. Among these were Petrarch, Luther, both Calvin and his victim Servetus, the satirist Samuel Butler (so widely read in his own time), Voltaire, Diderot, and David Hume, who eventually became librarian of the Faculty of Advocates in Edinburgh. Although students of Calvin have never doubted the influence of the law on his formation, others mentioned above reacted violently against the law, though this, too, may testify to its importance. Such names also leave us with an impression of the extent to which ambitious fathers regarded a career in the law as an avenue of worldly success for gifted sons who might have had other views for themselves.[10] In still other cases the influence of the law was rather a matter of family background, with its subtle impressions, and of milieu, than of direct professional engagement. Machiavelli, for example, was the son of a lawyer who—we may surmise —might, had he been more prosperous, have sent the boy to study law, then an expensive affair. At any rate young Niccolò found a type of employment in the Florentine government usually reserved for lawyers or notaries, and he was deeply concerned throughout his life with the social function of law. The dramatist Beaumont was son of a justice of common pleas. Pascal and Racine were both sons of lawyers and magistrates and spent much of their lives close to the legal circles of Paris.[11]

But in many cases the relation to law was close and direct. Guicciardini had a flourishing legal practice in Florence for many years. La Boétie and Montaigne, before he retired to devote himself to letters, were judges in the Parlement of Bordeaux. John Donne attended Lincoln's Inn and served as a law clerk before taking orders. Corneille was an *avocat* and magistrate, like his father before him, and Molière studied and may even have practiced law before turning to the stage. La Fontaine was a magistrate. Leibnitz finished law school to become a professor of law at the age of twenty-three. Giambattista Vico, though he never achieved the professorship to which he aspired, saw himself primarily as a student of civil law. The career of Montesquieu followed the pattern of Montaigne. Henry Fielding was a lawyer and magistrate in London.[12] And other great figures combined government service as lawyers with historical composition or religious and philosophical reflection: Thomas More, Paolo Sarpi, and Francis Bacon. Such an enumeration is, to be sure, impressionistic; but it could be carried much farther, and it has a certain cumulative impact, which is strengthened when we look at movements rather than men.

Thus the culture of Renaissance humanism, especially in its earlier stages, was largely a creation of lawyers and notaries.[13] Salutati was a notary, Bruni went from the study of law into the Florentine chancery, and Poggio and Flavio Biondo were notaries, as was Lorenzo Valla, the most original mind among the humanists of Italy. The son of a lawyer at the Curia, Valla felt enough confidence in his own understanding of the law to challenge the methods of its contemporary practitioners.[14] And the relations between humanism and the law were even closer in the French Renaissance. The great scholars and historians of sixteenth-century France were jurists, from Budé to Pasquier, Bodin, and Jacques de Thou. Most of the *libertins* of the earlier seventeenth century were lawyers. Lawyers played a large part in public support for the scientific movement of the seventeenth century in both France and England— the membership lists of the Royal Society, for example, are filled with their names—and the so-called Scottish Renaissance of the eighteenth century was dominated by lawyers.[15]

This is to say nothing of those great figures who devoted themselves primarily to juridical thought: Coke, Selden, Grotius, Pufendorf, Beccaria, and Bentham. The point is important, for it should be recognized that jurisprudence was not, in these centuries, only an esoteric and highly specialized discipline. Some knowledge of the law was essential equipment for the landed gentry of Britain in an age of lively litigation over titles to real property and of the gentry's general responsibility, as justices of the peace, for the preservation of local order. In addition some acquaintance with the philosophical principles of the law was a part of the culture of every educated man. Laymen like Hobbes had an extensive knowledge of the law and felt competent to write on the subject; and the young Gibbon in Lausanne, who considered attending courses in law, was probably not unusual in the time he devoted to reading great legal treatises, refusing to be put off, as he noted in his autobiography, "by the pedantry of Grotius or the prolixity of Pufendorf."[16]

The prominence of lawyers in the formation of modern culture, with its characteristic attention to the workings of this world, is in some respects not altogether surprising. Lawyers were members of an articulate as well as a learned profession in which success required some discipline of mind and was likely to bring the wealth and leisure to support general reflection. Lawyers often had, too, the social status and influence needed to make their views heard. But I would suggest that something more was involved: that men of the law were uniquely fitted by their social role and the nature of their experience with the world to interpret it plausibly to contemporaries. Engaged to a special degree in the task of meeting the essential needs of a changing society, they were in a better position than other groups in Europe to give expression to society's changing perceptions. It is therefore necessary to look briefly at what these men were called upon to do and at what their function represented at the level of values.

That lawyers contributed substantially to the slow transition from medieval forms of political and social organization has long been recognized in a general way, and some description of this contribution in detail is now possible. As in so much else, precedents were supplied by the medieval church, which, from the time of the investiture struggles, was increasingly administered by lawyers concerned to define its rights.[17] In the later Middle Ages most bishops, including those of Rome, were lawyers rather than theologians;[18] and the litigiousness of early modern Europe was prefigured by the litigiousness of the medieval church,[19] where a sense of the inappropriateness of domination by lawyers nourished generations of reformers.[20] Two points may be made about the rise of lawyers in the church. In the first place their emergence into positions of power corresponded to the increasing importance of institutional controls accompanying the centralization of the ecclesiastical apparatus and the evolution of the church into a mechanism for government. Here as elsewhere law became significant in direct proportion to the growth of social and institutional complexity. At the same time the prominence of lawyers reflected the growing acceptance of the inevitability of conflict even in the Body of Christ. For canon lawyers—and it should be noted that they were not necessarily ecclesiastics—were divided, both ideologically and practically, into antagonistic schools that represented conflicting principles and interests, and litigation in the church regularly involved canonists on both sides of a dispute. The establishment of lawyers in the church consecrated professional representation in adversary proceedings and accustomed men to rely on the expert services of the legal profession.

From the twelfth century, as towns grew in size and their societies, too, became more complex, the legal profession became increasingly important in the secular world, with the competence and respectability of lawyers nourished by the revival of Roman law. In the governments of the Italian towns, lawyers and notaries assumed responsibilities out of all proportion to their numbers, precisely because they possessed skills essential to the development of a more complicated social order. They drafted legislation in an age remarkably confident in the regulatory and reformatory value of laws, they participated in all public commissions, they staffed agencies of state, they went on embassies and prepared treaties, and they formulated and administered policy for republics and despotisms alike. Their interpretations of Roman law legitimized the sovereignty and independence of states.[21] And lawyers achieved equal prominence elsewhere in Europe, if somewhat more gradually, as societies beyond the Alps also grew more complex. The feudal conception of the king as dispenser of justice made his employment of lawyers appear natural even when their activities were resented. In France the administrative competence of lawyers was extended by the familiar institutional ambiguities of the Old Regime, in which, just as administrative agencies regularly performed some judicial tasks and thus needed lawyers, so the sovereign courts steadily expanded their administrative responsibilities in the name of the king. In the sixteenth century, for example, the Parlement of Paris took over hospital and university administration and also supervised the administration of the city. As *maîtres des requêtes*, lawyers were indispensable to the councils of the king and managed a wide range of his affairs. Meanwhile lawyers supported royal authority by historical and constitutional argument and attacked the feudal establishment by both their studies and their service in the courts.[22] In Spain, in the Netherlands, and in the Empire lawyers dominated royal councils and administration. Lawyers also ran colonial empires, both in bureaucracies at home and in the new societies developing overseas. A similar situation prevailed in England. Common lawyers molded the Star Chamber, promoted the Tudor revolution in government, and supplied personnel for every kind of administrative post. From Bosworth Field to the accession of Elizabeth, every chancellor of the exchequer was a lawyer. So was every one of the twenty-two speakers of the House of Commons.[23]

The activity of lawyers in the construction of a new political order is well known. We know less, unfortunately, about the part played by lawyers in the shaping of social and economic life and about their representation of private clients. But it is clear that, on the Continent, lawyers had early developed the legal basis for the corporate structure of the society that persisted through the Old Regime out of the resources of Roman law.[24] As judges, lawyers enforced the harsh demands of the criminal law; they stood for law and order and above all for the protection of property. Lawyers and notaries served the material security and perpetuation of families by drawing up marriage agreements and wills. They also ensured the performance of business agreements by contracts, deeds, and bills of sale; here they both met a practical need and provided the psychological prerequisite for economic activity. And eventually the common lawyers of England, some of them heavy investors in the great trading companies, were instrumental in freeing economic life from royal control.[25]

It is evident, at any rate, that lawyers were essential in developing the institutions and the conventions of early modern Europe. This was their peculiar task, and we can usefully linger for a moment on what this meant. Lawyers were needed to deal with the most urgent problems of their societies, not only incidentally and occasionally, like the majority of men, but in the most concentrated form imaginable, at every moment of their working lives. As private practitioners, they saw and represented clients who were in trouble, feared trouble, sought the clarification of some ambiguous situation, or aimed to twist the social system in some novel and advantageous way. As servants of government, lawyers were concerned to enforce and extend the rights of central authority or to shape institutions that could do so more effectively, usually in an abrasive struggle with a hostile adversary; the personal costs of failure could be high. As judges, they were compelled to scrutinize and weigh evidence, often of a disheartening and usually of an equivocal nature. Their role, in short, was to man the frontiers between the safe and familiar on the one hand, the dangerous and new on the other; between the tolerable and the intolerable; between the conventional world and the chaos beyond it. They constituted a kind of civil militia whose difficulties were compounded by the fact that the precise location of the frontiers to which they were assigned was rarely clear, and these frontiers were constantly changing. We may well ask what kind of men these were.

It is hardly remarkable that a special and rather unattractive temperament has been conventionally attributed to the lawyer.[26] He was, like Guicciardini, a skeptic and a cynic; like Bacon, cold and crafty; or, like Bacon's great rival Coke, mean and harsh, a bully and a coward, a man of whom even his widow, after thirty-six years of marriage, remarked at his death, "We shall never see his like again—praises be to God." From the lawyer's exposed position on the frontiers of behavior he saw the world, like Montaigne, at its most irrational, most selfish, venal, and hypocritical. The lawyer knew the small practical worth of ideals and fine principles, and he knew also the humiliations and indignities that were the price of success in the world of men, a price that, like Bacon or Coke, even the best of lawyers was nevertheless prepared to pay.[27] The degradation that ended Bacon's public career nicely illustrated his own melancholy reflection on the hazards of success: "The rising into place is laborious, and by pains men come to greater pains; and it is sometimes base, and by indignities men come to dignities. The standing is slippery, and the regress is either a downfall or at least an eclipse, which is a melancholy thing."[28] In short, the lawyer knew the world. His mind and character were shaped to a unique degree by contact with its changing pressures and brutal realities, its dangers and uncertainties; and it is for this reason that he was peculiarly fitted to play so large a role in forming the culture of worldliness and vigilant individualism to which the more optimistic and trusting culture of the preceding period gradually gave way.

At any rate the lawyer commanded vast, if sometimes equivocal, respect. In Florence the guild of lawyers and notaries ranked first on all ceremonial occasions, and its chief officer was honorary head of the whole guild system. As individuals, doctors of law in Renaissance Italy ranked with knights.[29] Traiano Boccalini, a kind of Art Buchwald of the later Renaissance, argued that lawyers better deserved the title of Excellency than the nobles who complained of the lawyers' presumption.[30] In France the lawyer's profession was considered—except by some nobles— as honorable as bearing arms: La Bruyère described both functions as equally sublime and useful. The great Anglican theologian Richard Hooker, a devotee of law in a grander sense, declared that "soundly to judge of law is the weightiest thing which any man can take upon him."[31] Even the hatred and scorn for lawyers so frequently encountered in every age in which they have been numerous are a tribute to their importance, if only through their capacity to threaten others; lawyers represented the omnipresent danger inherent in the increasingly complex and increasingly mysterious machinery of social organization, before which the individual felt more and more helpless. They clearly endangered the self-esteem of old nobles like Saint-Simon.[32] The deliberate exclusion of lawyers from More's Utopia only suggests their central place in the real world for one who understood it well.[33] And an oblique tribute of a similar kind may be discerned in Luther's frequent expressions of hostility to lawyers. One of the young men who sat at his table reported an incident of particular interest in this connection: "The doctor took his child in his hands and said, 'If you should become a lawyer, I'd hang you on the gallows. You must be a preacher and must baptize, preach, administer the sacrament, visit the sick and comfort the sorrowful.' "[34] The episode suggests the celebrated guilt of the youth who had abandoned law school, sold his lawbooks, and entered a monastery against the wishes of his own father. For Luther the law continued to represent the world and its spiritual dangers, which he had forsaken to pursue his salvation; lawyers remained, in his mind, at the center of this world's concerns. But this view was more than a private eccentricity. Luther's attitude also pointed to the degree to which the figure of the lawyer persisted in haunting the European religious consciousness. Indeed, this may have had as much to do with his unpopularity as the inconveniences he represented. The lawyer was an obvious scapegoat for the general guilt of a world in transition, made anxious not only by the immediate insecurities of life in society but also by the abandonment of old ways and values.

The significance of lawyers in European life depended on more than the importance of their practical role or the respect in which they were held. It rested on the deeper needs they satisfied. And here, to make the point more concrete, I will give particular attention to the period between the middle of the sixteenth and the middle of the seventeenth centuries. If the transition from the medieval to the modern world was generally characterized by a crisis of both social order and belief, this phase of the transition was peculiarly troubled by their convergence in religious wars, by international conflict of particular intensity, by inflation and depression, and by mounting social tension and dislocation.[35]

One consequence of the peculiar difficulties of this period was a singular exaltation of law as an antidote to disorder. The value attached to law now went far beyond the traditional and more measured confidence, as in the generation of Erasmus and Machiavelli, in the capacity of legislation to regulate and improve human conduct. In the frustrated Italian states of this period law presented itself as the only means to discipline the violent passions of mankind that had so obviously destroyed the freedom of Italy, and as the only instrument to control the wanton masses. To this tendency both the mood and the intellectual resources of the Counter-Reformation contributed. In France law, beginning with Bodin, was now first clearly perceived as the essence of sovereignty, Gallican jurists dominated political discussion, reformers saw law as the solution to every moral and religious problem, and the high magistracy at last completed its slow evolution into a new nobility of the robe. In England men were finally compelled by rapid social and institutional change and the accompanying growth in legal business to take a fresh look at the common law, to adapt a legal system based on the needs of an older agrarian society to new social and political uses, and to reduce that legal system to some kind of order.[36] This was the greatest age of the common lawyers, whose numbers multiplied. Admissions to the Inns of Court generally doubled; Gray's Inn saw as much as a fivefold increase.[37] The printing press helped in all this, supplying uniform editions of laws that made legal systems everywhere more reliable, systematic, and effective.[38] During the same period the polity most admired in the whole of Europe was Venice, primarily because she gave the impression of an order based on sound and equitably administered laws.[39] In addition this period is of unusual interest for the comparative study of lawyers because lawyers were often peculiarly conscious of themselves as an international community of professional men that transcended political and confessional boundaries and was held together by common goals and ideals, common problems, and a common intellectual culture. An international correspondence among the lawyers of this age included the exchange of views on religious, literary, historical, and scientific topics as well as on the events of the day and discussion of legal questions of mutual concern.[40]

Much in the special importance attached to law in this period was a response to the unusual intensity of disorder in a Europe whose growing social complexity meant a new degree of vulnerability to dislocation and thus a growing need for regulation. The primary source of disorder was patently the conflict of human interests; and, as in the church, the rise of the legal profession in secular society signified a concern for the peaceful resolution of conflict. Lawyers started to work when conflict loomed. A legal system may therefore be described as a means for institutionalizing conflict, but there was a crucial difference, at first subtle and disguised but increasingly radical and explicit, between medieval and modern assumptions about this process. Litigation in secular courts had been forbidden by the early church; Augustine, who knew the courts well, had pointed to lawsuits to illustrate the persistent sinfulness of earthly society.[41] The notion of a relative natural law appropriate to man's fallen state had resolved the practical problems of life in a society that, although professedly Christian, remained imperfect.[42] But the acceptance of conflict was, in this view, also relative; it could never be tolerated as normal and inevitable. Justice was itself finally an absolute; and this meant that a legal decision was ideally concerned not so much to resolve conflict as to transcend and abolish it by resort to ultimate principles. In this light coercion by legal authority was an effort to bend the refractory wills of men into conformity with a final vision of justice. But increasingly the lawyers of early modern Europe, whatever the formulas to which they sometimes still appealed, disregarded such conceptions. Their task was practical and limited; they aimed not to transcend conflict but to manage it. In their world the essential tensions were not between sin and ultimate justice but between antithetical human interests that generally seemed morally ambiguous on both sides. Their activity was directed to the effective resolution of conflict, not to the realization of a lofty vision; their rise signified and accelerated the breakdown of a traditional view in which social values were defined in accordance with final ends. As early as the thirteenth century it was a commonplace that a good jurist made a bad Christian.[43]

Lawyers were thus central to the cultural transformation that marks the end of the Middle Ages, and they took a leading part in the articulation of a novel set of empirical, pragmatic, and secular attitudes in which the orderly administration of this world's affairs was seen to depend on practical principles of its own. This new vision, which reached reasonable clarity only in the sixteenth century and still encountered deep resistance, was based on a perception of the world as an infinitely complex population of forces in conflict that, though ceaseless and terrifying, was nevertheless not altogether maleficent. A lawyer knew from experience that, in this world, constructive results sometimes came from the clash of forces and that to avoid conflict might, in social terms, invite worse consequences than to accept it. Like Paolo Sarpi, legal adviser to the Venetian Republic, he might therefore deplore an excessive pacifism, either in James I or at home.[44] As Sarpi wrote to a French lawyer, in one of the international exchanges now characteristic of the legal profession, the times needed a Democritus or a Heraclitus, a remark equally applicable to metaphysics and to politics in its sense of the world as a dynamic flux of particular entities in incessant interaction.[45] The positive value of confrontation between opposing forces is suggested at another level by Bacon's observation that "truth emerges more readily from error than from confusion."[46] Sarpi, who was also in touch with Bacon's circle, would have agreed with this early hint of the liberal principle that truth may be better conceived as a pursuit than as a discovery and that it may be preferable to take a doubtful position than none at all.[47] Also suggested was the active life in which men are willing to engage with an adversary, however dubious the battle; and we are reminded again of the original connections between the law and the social vision of Renaissance humanism.

A lawyer's experience with the real world of unpredictable and hostile forces was likely to make him suspicious of those great systems of thought which, by presuming to take general account of all possibilities in advance, inhibited adaptation to changing circumstance and interfered with meeting the daily need for practical order. He needed first of all to sort out and scrutinize the discrete data in a case; his mind was characterized by what a distinguished modern jurist has ruefully defined as the capacity to "think about a thing inextricably attached to something else without thinking of the thing which it is attached to."[48] Thus the lawyers of our critical period were notable for their repudiation of systems and their preference for such limited sense as could be constructed from particular phenomena. Guicciardini's famous rejection of abstract speculation and generalization[49] found a parallel in Sarpi's contrast between dialectic and law, in the emphasis of such French jurists as Pithou and Pasquier on the particularities of time, place, and circumstance, and in Bacon's contempt for Scholasticism and his opposition to the systematization of the law itself, except in chronological terms that would respect its particularity.[50] This helps to explain why the law, which the notary Salutati had championed against the deductive and humanly irrelevant science of the fourteenth century,[51] converged in the seventeenth with the new empirical science. Important lawyers in both France and England were fascinated, perhaps as much as physicians, by the achievements of scientists.[52] The same flexible and practical attitudes allied law with the—from another point of view lawless—doctrine of reason of state, which suggested the changing uses of the law, without regard to more ultimate considerations, in accordance with the changing needs of states.[53]

Similar attitudes informed the political vision of lawyers and shaped their loyalties; their rejection of the unworkable and irrelevantly general in favor of the immediately practical for their particular societies made them patriots. The lawyers of Venice resisted the interference of Rome, an interference that followed from a quite different conception of law, on the ground that the good order of Venice sufficiently demonstrated the excellence of her laws; these lawyers argued that the virtue of law was not absolute but relative to the needs of a particular society. Similarly French jurists from the time of Budé rejected the familiar claims of Roman superiority and insisted on the perfection of French law because it was so well adapted to French needs, and this legal nationalism was the point of departure for a more general cultural nationalism. In the same fashion the common lawyers of England praised English ways and the admirable consequences for England of the independence of English law from that of the Continent.[54]

This position led to general praise of custom as the only satisfactory basis for law. So Pasquier made the case: "Since customs were formed gradually in each province according to the diversity of our characters, it seems appropriate in case of obscurity or doubt to have recourse to people close to us, who by their proximity would seem to conform to our manners and character and so to our customs."[55] The meaning of this proposition, for which there are analogues in the legal discourse of other places, was that custom best represented the proper particularity of the law, its necessary correspondence to the concrete and differing needs of peoples. The same point could be made about vernacular languages, and it is hardly surprising to find lawyers among their champions. Latin was customarily employed in a legal tradition that, whatever its practical tendencies, still professed to appeal to universal principles. The language of eternal Rome could always be counted on to give a subliminal ring of ultimate authority to a legal pronouncement: it implied finality where none could be claimed. Hence it is of particular significance that Pasquier advocated the use of French in the law as in other serious subjects, and Coke, though on occasion still inclined to take shelter in Latin, for the most part abandoned the tradition of earlier commentators on the law of his country to write in English.[56] Through changes in language, too, law was taking on a more practical and particular quality, and more was at stake than the greater ease of communication.

These various tendencies may be summarized in one word that will relate them to a development fundamental to every dimension of early modern European life: secularism—in the sense of a growing acceptance of the autonomy of the various aspects of human concern. Lawyers represented the growing assumption that life in the world is only tolerable when it is conceived as a secular affair and that the world's activities must be conducted according to manageable principles of their own rather than in subordination to some larger definition of the ultimate purpose of existence. By applying this assumption to solve the constantly changing problems of their societies, lawyers were, in a manner far more effective than that of any abstract philosopher, the supreme secularizers of their world. By imposing their own secularism on the machinery of social life they helped to accustom their contemporaries to think in secular terms, thus contributing in a fundamental way to the secularization of every other dimension of human concern: to the secularization of politics and economic life, of science, philosophy, and literature and the other arts.

At the same time it is important to recognize that secularism in this sense is not synonymous with unbelief. Some lawyers, like occasional members of other groups, may have been unbelievers; but more characteristic of the profession was, I think, a preference, shared by both Catholic and Protestant lawyers, for a kind of piety that stressed the spiritual and inward quality of the faith, contrasted it sharply with the world and its ways, and by emphasizing the incongruity liberated secular life from direct religious control. The lawyers and notaries of Renaissance Italy, the Gallican (and later Jansenist) magistrates of Paris, and the lawyers of early Stuart England, both Puritan and Anglican, all tended to an Augustinian spirituality.[57] Some of them doubtless felt a personal affinity to Augustine—himself the product of a legal culture—whose influence was so powerful in this period generally.[58] But this only suggests a deeper community arising, once again, out of a peculiar experience with life. A serious-minded lawyer was forced to recognize that the earthly city for whose affairs he was responsible could at best achieve only a contingent order quite different from that of the heavenly city, and in addition he was constantly reminded of the unregenerate state of humanity and the need for divine assistance. He knew, in short, the difference between law and grace.

For if the lawyer, as secularizer, was in some sense an agent of change, he also represented the need for order and gave expression to the conservative impulses of his age. In a period singularly troubled by the collapse of traditional ways of life and yearning for stability, he promised a measure of security, both for individuals and for society as a whole. His services gave a sense of security to his client; even as he threatened the security of his client's adversary he compelled him to have recourse to the law. The lawyer also supplied security for the future; his role was to foresee and provide against as many as possible of the dangers that might lie ahead, and thus it reflected both distrust of the future and, at the same time, some confidence in the ability of men to plan ahead and to control the unfolding of their earthly lives. Dependence on lawyers has, therefore, some value in revealing attitudes fundamental to changing cultural patterns exhibited in such comprehensive matters as trust, time, and human freedom; resort to lawyers implied the reverse of fatalism.

But legal systems functioned above all as a source of order for society in general. While they did so in an obvious sense through the punishment of wickedness and vice, I would suggest—though it would be difficult to demonstrate concretely—that they also performed a larger service for the vast majority who were disposed to obey the law. Legal systems contributed subtly, in this way, to ending the peculiar restlessness of European society that had come to a climax in the earlier seventeenth century. By defining what was socially intolerable and by reshaping the official forms of social intercourse, laws and the men who worked with them must have gradually renewed that sense of limit in the social universe, so profoundly threatened by the crumbling of established conventions, without which life had become not only practically hazardous but in a deeper sense unsatisfactory. The "crisis in Europe" of Trevor Aston's title was also a crisis of mind and spirit, of which we may take as typical symptoms Don Quixote's disorientation, Mersenne's anxieties about the fifty thousand atheists in Paris, *The Anatomy of Melancholy*, the moral anarchy of the Jacobean stage, and the prosecution of witches, in which lawyers also had their part to play. Lawyers helped to relieve the terrors in this world by supplying a social foundation on which some sense of the order and meaning of life could be reconstructed. Through the orientation of the masses of the law-abiding, they enabled their contemporaries once again to feel at home in a familiar world.[59]

Indeed, even the contribution of the lawyer to change was largely a consequence of his conservatism, of his acceptance of the established order of society and his determination to achieve his purposes within it. Whether in the maintenance of public order or in resolving conflicts of interest, he was above all concerned to make the social system work.[60] Yet this was likely to make him a conservative with a difference. For, since cases frequently failed to conform exactly to type and in fact often presented novel and ambiguous features, a lawyer's concern with workability was likely to operate against a complete rigidity of mind. If they respected the structures within which they worked, lawyers also required those structures to be flexible, responsible, and continuously useful. Like Montaigne, Montesquieu, Selden, Fielding, or Beccaria, lawyers sometimes presented themselves as reformers.

The attitudes of lawyers also underwent a gradual change as circumstances and demands on the law shifted; the later seventeenth century was to see some modification of the pragmatic and relativistic tendencies that had characterized the profession during the previous hundred years, but here, too, the law is revealed as a sensitive and leading participant in the larger movement of European culture. Thus the legal speculation of France in the classic age displayed a growing tendency to appeal once again to the timeless sanctions of reason and religion;[61] the idea of a general and prescriptive natural law came to dominate the law schools of Germany and the Netherlands; and even in England efforts were made to systematize the common law on philosophical principles, though Matthew Hale's great *History of the Common Law of England* (1713) also suggests the limits of English participation in this European movement.[62] But such changes suggest, too, how the legal mind was constantly prepared to mediate between the general and the particular, the ideal and the concrete, order and energy, ideas and life itself. The life of the law is potentially fraught with tension between these poles; and this also helps to explain the regular prominence of lawyers in the creation of modern culture.

Among the polarities with which lawyers had to live, one proved singularly fruitful for the transition from medieval to modern conceptions of the world and is also of particular interest from the standpoint of the historian: the tension between continuity and novelty, between the need of traditionalistic societies to feel at one with the past and the practical requirements of adaptation to change. Such tension, which may account for the prominence, from an early point, of men connected with the law in the composition of history, may be discerned as early as the thirteenth century, in the chronicle of the Paduan notary Rolandino, and in the fourteenth century in the work of the early humanist Albertino Mussato, another Paduan notary, and in the interests of the Venetian doge Andrea Dandolo, who collected legal and political documents and wrote a history of his republic.[63] In their writings we may already find hints of the secular emphasis, the cool political analysis, and the consciousness of change in human affairs that distinguish the great Florentine histories of Bruni, Poggio, Machiavelli, and Guicciardini, again men all more or less associated with the law. When we add the names of Sarpi, Bacon, and Clarendon to this list of lawyer-historians and note the role of the Scottish bar in establishing the great tradition of historical study in eighteenth-century Scotland,[64] it should be clear that we are in the presence of some special affinity. Law formed men with broad interests in human affairs who were skilled in the examination of evidence, experienced in the difficult task of sorting out what might be germane to a problem from the irrelevant detail surrounding it, and trained to reconstruct events, as well as close to the constantly changing social and political scene.

But the most important consequences for historiography resulted from the application of historical interests to the law itself, a process that began with the notary Lorenzo Valla, whose close philological researches revealed that the Roman law was a product of time and circumstance, a historical artifact rather than a body of universally valid legal wisdom. And this vision, transmitted to a generation of French jurists by the teaching of Jacques Cujas, stimulated a national school of medieval studies with a novel interest in the development of law and institutions rather than in the wars and royal actions of traditional historical writing. Though this school produced no individual masterpieces, it extended the range of historical scholarship and displayed both a new methodological rigor and above all that secular feeling for the particulars of human experience otherwise characteristic of the legal mind.[65]

At the same time the lawyer-historians of the later Renaissance in France were no mere *érudits*. They intended the vision of the past constructed by their scholarly work to be useful; and in the peculiar nature of their historicism they were at one with Sarpi's researches in church history and the English common lawyers' study of the medieval constitution. Lawyer-historians resembled each other in their common contribution to reconciling the conservative instincts of an age desperately concerned with order to the adjustments demanded by the times, through myths supported by the most sophisticated research Europe had yet witnessed. In this way lawyer-historians made a new order palatable and historical study attractive. Thus Venice defended her ecclesiastical and political independence against the pressures of the Counter-Reformation by arguing that her admirable society rested on law and custom going back to the origins of the Republic; by contrast, lawyer-historians maintained, the juridical and administrative centralization demanded by Rome was of recent origin. Sarpi's *History of the Council of Trent* (1619) was a sustained demonstration of this essentially juridical point.[66] The lawyers of France employed similar arguments in defense of French customary law against imperial Roman law and of the Gallican liberties against ecclesiastical Rome. In both the underlying issue was the right of self-determination, a matter made subjectively important with the emergence of national feeling and of immediate practical significance, since public order seemed to depend on the exclusion of any kind of foreign interference. Thus the researches of French lawyers demonstrated the value of custom for the particular needs of France and the thesis that the canons of the ancient church had guaranteed the autonomy she now required. The study of history, especially legal history, revealed the subversion in the Middle Ages of a system admirably suited to contemporary needs.[67]

Much the same argument defended the English common law against the challenge of the royal prerogative. For Sir Edward Coke, too, the problems of contemporary society were to be solved by the recovery of an ancient heritage. "No subject of this realm," he wrote,

> but being truly instructed by the good and plain evidence of his
> ancient and undoubted patrimony and birth-right (though he
> hath for some time by ignorance, false persuasion, or vague fear
> been deceived or dispossessed) but will consult with learned and
> faithful councillors for the recovery of the same. The ancient
> and excellent laws of England are the birth-right and the most
> ancient and best inheritance that the subjects of this realm have,
> for by them he enjoyeth not only his inheritance and goods in
> peace and quietness, but his life and his most dear country in
> safety. (I fear that many want true knowledge of this ancient
> birth-right.)[68]

The defects in the scholarship supporting this vision were not difficult to identify; Hobbes was critical of Coke on this score,[69] and by the later seventeenth century men were casting about for a better foundation for the social order than this mythical past. But Coke was psychologically on sounder ground than Hobbes in his sense of the kind of argument required by the times; like Sarpi, like the lawyers of France, Coke helped contemporaries to accept change by representing it as continuity. Serious consideration of some other basis for law and order, and therefore for human liberty and human rights, depended on a new political and cultural climate.

Nevertheless the myth of a recovered past proved a perennial resource of European culture, and it should be of particular interest to those who think of themselves as historians of modern Europe. The lawyers did not create the myth themselves; they merely applied to their own discipline a notion common to reformers of every kind for centuries. It is, of course, the myth of renewal that is at the heart of both the Renaissance and the Reformation. But because of the central importance of the law in the development of modern European society, the application of the idea in this domain gave to the conception of an initial perfection, decay, and recovery the broadest possible social resonance. It could now serve as the organizing principle for understanding the whole process of secular history. In dealing with lawyers, therefore, we are also looking at the origins of the idea of modern history itself.

NOTES

This article owes much to the critical reading of my colleagues Gerard E. Caspary, Thomas G. Barnes, and John T. Noonan, Jr.; the latter two are themselves lawyers as well as historians.

1. Frederic C. Lane, *Venice and History* (Baltimore, 1966), 427–28.

2. See George Rudé, *Hanoverian London, 1714–1808* (Berkeley, 1971), 37. Rudé finds the occupational surveys of England by Gregory King (1696) and Patrick Colquhoun (1805) less instructive than Defoe's classification of Englishmen according to wealth (1709); but as a result lawyers, as a distinct group, largely disappear from Rudé's picture of London society.

3. Christopher Hill, *Puritanism and Revolution: The English Revolution of the Seventeenth Century* (New York, 1964), 28. See also the stimulating remarks of Barbara J. Shapiro, "Law and Science in Seventeenth-Century England," *Stanford Law Review,* 21 (1969): 728.

4. Myron P. Gilmore, *Humanists and Jurists: Six Studies in the Renaissance* (Cambridge, Mass., 1963); Lauro Martines, *Lawyers and Statecraft in Renaissance Florence* (Princeton, 1968); Julian Franklin, *Jean Bodin and the Sixteenth-Century Revolution in the Methodology of Law and History* (New York, 1963); Donald R. Kelley, *Foundations of Modern Historical Scholarship: Language, Law, and History in the French Renaissance* (New York, 1970); George Huppert, *The Idea of Perfect History: Historical Erudition and Historical Philosophy in Renaissance France* (Urbana, 1970); Samuel Thorne, "Tudor Social Transformation and Legal Change,"

New York University Law Review, 26 (1951): 10–23, and his *Sir Edward Coke, 1552–1952* (London, 1952); J. G. A. Pocock, *The Ancient Constitution and the Feudal Law: English Historical Thought in the Seventeenth Century* (Cambridge, 1957); David Little, *Religion, Order, and Law: A Study in Pre-Revolutionary England* (New York, 1969). These examples are limited to the area of my own concern, but it is encouraging to note that an interest in lawyers is also developing elsewhere, notably among American historians.

5. See the admirable survey of early Western legal theory in Julius Stone, *Human Law and Human Justice* (Stanford, 1965), 9–31.

6. See Kelley, *Foundations of Modern Historical Scholarship*, 289, *passim*.

7. See Little's general treatment of Coke in *Religion, Order, and Law*, 167–217; see also Shapiro, "Law and Science," 727.

8. Some indication of the importance of notaries in Italy may be gleaned from *Il notariato nella civiltà italiana: biografie notarili dall' VIII al XX secolo* (Milan, 1961). For the importance of notaries in the Italian communes, see Daniel Waley, *The Italian City-Republics* (London, 1969), 29. J. K. Hyde, *Padua in the Age of Dante: A Social History of an Italian State* (Manchester, 1966), 154–75, has much on notaries in Padua. For notaries in Florence, see Martines, *Lawyers and Statecraft, passim*; on their functions, see page 37. I have not seen Giorgio Costamagna, *Il notaio a Genova tra prestigio e potere* (Rome, 1970). It may be noted that in England scriveners also provided some legal services.

9. The only systematic study on this point that I have seen is the appendix in Huppert, *Idea of Perfect History*, 185–93. Huppert finds that, of the writers listed in the *Bibliothèque françoise* of La Croix du Maine who "made significant contributions to French culture between 1540 and 1584" and about whom information was available, 80 per cent were connected with the law.

10. At the same time it may be observed that the uses of the law for social mobility have been somewhat exaggerated. Great legal careers tended to run in families in Italy and France, and in Britain the law was largely a monopoly of the gentry. On this point, for Florence (probably typical of Italy), see Martines, *Lawyers and Statecraft*, 68. In France, of course, membership in the high magistracy was largely hereditary; see J. H. Shennan, *The Parlement of Paris* (Ithaca, 1968), 110–12, and see also Marcel Rousselet, *Histoire de la magistrature française* (Paris, 1957), 1: 259–322. The family of Montaigne was typical; see Donald M. Frame, *Montaigne: A Biography* (New York, 1965), 7–8. For indications that a similar situation prevailed in Portugal, and probably Spain, see Stuart B. Schwartz, "Magistracy and Society in Colonial Brazil," *Hispanic American Historical Review*, 50 (1970): 721. For England, see E. W. Ives, "The Common Lawyers in Pre-Reformation England," *Transactions of the Royal Historical Society*, ser. 5, vol. 18 (1968): 160, and Lawrence Stone, "The Educational Revolution in England, 1560–1640," *Past and Present*, no. 28 (1964): 58; for Scotland, see John Clive, "The Social Background of the Scottish Renaissance," in N. T. Phillipson and Rosalind Mitchison, eds., *Scotland and the Age of Improvement* (Edinburgh, 1970), 228.

11. Roberto Ridolfi, *Vita di Niccolò Machiavelli* (rev. ed.; Florence, 1969), 1: 25–35. On the costs of a legal education, see Martines, *Lawyers and Statecraft*, 70. Although I have reservations about Lucien Goldmann's general thesis in other respects, his interpretation of Pascal and Racine in the context of this group, in *Le dieu caché* (Paris, 1955), seems to me appropriate.

12. Martines reviews Guicciardini's legal career in *Lawyers and Statecraft*, 110–12; on Montaigne's legal career, see Frame, *Montaigne*, 46–62. For Vico, see Dario Faucci, "Vico and Grotius: Jurisconsults of Mankind," in Giorgio Tagliacozzo and Hayden V. White, eds., *Giambattista Vico: An International Symposium* (Baltimore, 1969), 61. William Empson, "Tom Jones," *Kenyon Review*, 20 (1958): 217–49, discusses Fielding's fiction in the light of his experience with the law; this article was called to my attention by Paul Alpers.

13. This is especially well brought out by Jerrold E. Seigel, *Rhetoric and Philosophy in Renaissance Humanism* (Princeton, 1968). See also Denys Hay, *The Italian Renaissance in Its Historical Background* (Cambridge, 1961), 69–72.

14. Salutati's notarial career has received special attention in Peter Herde, "Politik und Rhetorik in Florenz am Vorabend der Renaissance," *Archiv für Kulturgeschichte*, 47 (1965): 155, and in Ronald G. Witt, "Coluccio Salutati, Chancellor and Citizen of Lucca," *Traditio*, 25 (1969): 191–216. For Valla, see Kelley, *Foundations of Modern Historical Scholarship*, 19–50.

15. Kelley, *Foundations of Modern Historical Scholarship, passim*; Hans Baron, "Secularization of Wisdom and Political Humanism in the Renaissance," *Journal of the History of Ideas*, 21 (1960): 131–50; René Pintard, *Le libertinage érudit dans la première moitié du XVIIᵉ siècle* (Paris, 1943); Shapiro, "Law and Science," 738; Clive, "Social Background of the Scottish Renaissance," 228–31.

16. Samuel I. Mintz, "Hobbes's Knowledge of the Law," *Journal of the History of Ideas*, 31 (1970): 614–15; Edward Gibbon, *The Autobiography of Edward Gibbon*, ed. Dero A. Saunders (New York, 1961), 102.

17. See R. W. Southern, *The Making of the Middle Ages* (New Haven, 1953), 145–46, 151.

18. On this situation, see Giuseppe Alberigo, *I vescovi italiani al Concilio di Trento (1545–1547)* (Florence, 1959), 55.

19. See Robert Brentano, *Two Churches: England and Italy in the Thirteenth Century* (Princeton, 1968), 132–73.

20. For a typical expression of this feeling, see the review of the college of cardinals by the Venetian ambassador to Rome, Paolo Tiepolo, in 1576, in Eugenio Albèri, ed., *Relazioni degli ambasciatori veneti al senato*, ser. 2, vol. 4 (Florence, 1939–63), pp. 222–23: "Since there are many lawyers among them, because this profession is more highly valued at the Roman Curia than any other, very few theologians are found there, indeed perhaps none, although theology ought to be the principal profession of priests."

21. Martines, *Lawyers and Statecraft, passim*.

22. Franklin L. Ford, *Robe and Sword: The Regrouping of the French Aristocracy* (Cambridge, Mass., 1953), 35; Shennan, *Parlement of Paris*, 86–93; Shennan, *Government and Society in France, 1461–1661* (London, 1969), 40; William Farr Church, *Constitutional Though in Sixteenth-Century France: A Study in the Evolution of Ideas* (Cambridge, Mass., 1941); Kelley, *Foundations of Modern Historical Scholarship, passim*.

23. Schwartz, "Magistracy and Society in Colonial Brazil," 716. For lawyer-bureaucrats in Spain, see also Richard L. Kagan, "Universities in Castile, 1500–1700," *Past and Present*, no. 49 (1970): 55–61. Ives, "Common Lawyers in Pre-Reformation England," 153–71.

24. Martines, *Lawyers and Statecraft*, 12; Gaines Post, *Studies in Medieval Legal Thought: Public Law and the State, 1100–1322* (Princeton, 1964), ch. 1.

25. This much seems clear, whatever the merits of the view of Coke as a precursor of liberalism. On the controversy over this issue, see the bibliographical essay in Little, *Religion, Order, and Law,* 238–46, and Little's own discussion, *ibid.,* 167–217.

26. Martin Mayer, *The Lawyers* (New York, 1966), 3, quotes Lord Melbourne: "All the attorneys I have ever seen have the same manner: hard, cold, incredulous, distrustful, sarcastic, sneering. They are said to be conversant with the worst part of human nature, and with the most discreditable transactions. They have so many falsehoods told them, that they place confidence in no one." See also Mayer's discussion of the change of personality even among law students, *ibid.,* 76–77.

27. Martines, *Lawyers and Statecraft,* 112; Thorne, *Coke,* 4; Christopher Hill, *Intellectual Origins of the English Revolution* (Oxford, 1965), 225–26; Catherine Drinker Bowen, *Francis Bacon: The Temper of a Man* (Boston, 1963), 14–15, 31–32, 50.

28. Francis Bacon, "Of Great Place," in his *Essays,* ed. Mary Augusta Scott (New York, 1908), 45–46. See also Bacon's poem on the misery of life given in John Aubrey, *Brief Lives,* ed. Oliver Lawson Dick (London, 1950), 10–11.

29. Martines, *Lawyers and Statecraft,* 14, 29–30.

30. Traiano Boccalini, *Ragguagli di Parnaso e scritti minori,* ed. Luigi Firpo (Bari, 1948), 1: 177–80.

31. La Bruyère is quoted by Ford, in *Robe and Sword,* 70–71, n. 44, though Ford observes that La Bruyère occasionally expressed other sentiments; for Hooker's comment see his *Of the Laws of Ecclesiastical Polity,* in his *Works,* ed. John Keble (Oxford, 1845), 1: 278.

32. See Ford, *Robe and Sword,* 72–73.

33. More, *Utopia,* ed. Edward Surtz (New Haven, 1964), 114: "Moreover, they absolutely banish from their country all lawyers, who cleverly manipulate cases and cunningly argue legal points."

34. *D. Martin Luthers Werke. Kritische Gesamtausgabe: Tischreden* (Weimar, 1912–21), vol. 2, p. 96, no. 1422.

35. Hence the title of the essays collected from *Past and Present:* Trevor Aston, ed., *Crisis in Europe, 1560–1660* (London, 1965).

36. For the Italian states, see the remarks of Carlo Curcio, *Dal Rinascimento alla Controriforma: contributo alla storia del pensiero italiano da Guicciardini a Botero* (Rome, 1934), 61; see also Rudolph von Albertini, *Das florentinische Staatsbewusstsein im Übergang von der Republik zum Prinzipat* (Bern, 1955); for France, see the remarks of Antoine Adam, *Du mysticisme à la révolte: les Jansénistes du XVIIe siècle* (Paris, 1968), 37; and Ford, *Robe and Sword,* 63; for England, see Hill, *Intellectual Origins,* 227–28; and Thorne, "Tudor Social Transformation."

37. Stone, "Educational Revolution in England," 51–79. Thomas G. Barnes generously supplied me with his tabulation for Gray's Inn.

38. Elizabeth L. Eisenstein, "Some Conjectures about the Impact of Printing on Western Society and Thought: A Preliminary Report," *Journal of Modern History,* 40 (1968): 14–15; Wilfrid Prest, "Legal Education of the Gentry at the Inns of Court, 1560–1640," *Past and Present,* no. 38 (1967): 24.

39. This has been noted for England by John R. Hale, *England and the Italian Renaissance: The Growth of Interest in Its History and Art* (Oxford, 1964), 30; and for Florence by Albertini, *Florentinische Staatsbewusstsein,* 20–31, among

others. For fuller documentation, see my "Venice and the Political Education of Europe," in J. R. Hale, ed., *Studies in Renaissance Venice* (London, 1973), 445–466. Among those who admired the Venetian legal system was Jean Bodin, otherwise often critical of Venice.

40. See, for example, the correspondence of Paolo Sarpi with a group of French lawyers in his *Lettere ai Protestanti*, ed. Manlio Duilio Busnelli (Bari, 1931), and his *Lettere ai Gallicani*, ed. Boris Ulianich (Wiesbaden, 1961). The confessional distinctions reflected in these titles are irrelevant to the content of the letters and obscure the point that this was largely an exchange among lawyers. For Sarpi's contact with English legal circles, see Vittorio Gabrielli, "Bacone, la riforma e Roma nella versione hobbesiana d'un carteggio di Fulgenzio Micanzio," *English Miscellany*, 8 (1957): 195–250.

41. Augustine *De civitate dei* 19. 5.

42. See the classic discussion of Ernst Troeltsch, *The Social Teachings of the Christian Churches*, tr. Olive Wyon (London, 1931), 1: 150–55.

43. Victor Martin, *Les origines du Gallicanisme* (Paris, 1939), 1: 137–38.

44. William J. Bouwsma, *Venice and the Defense of Republican Liberty: Renaissance Values in the Age of the Counter-Reformation* (Berkeley, 1968), 526–28.

45. Paolo Sarpi to Jacques Leschassier, Sept. 14, 1610, in *Lettere ai Gallicani*, 93. The same pre-Socratic philosophers were also favorites of Bacon; see his *Novum Organum*.

46. Bacon, *Novum Organum*, in his *Works*, ed. James Spedding (New York, 1869), 8: 210.

47. See Sarpi's attitude to controversy in connection with Gallicanism, as in his letter to Jerôme Groslot de l'Isle, Mar. 13, 1612, in *Lettere ai Protestanti*, 1: 220–21.

48. Thomas Reed Powell, quoted in Mayer, *The Lawyers*, 86.

49. Directly applied to law in his *Ricordi*, ser. C, no. 111, in *Maxims and Reflections of a Renaissance Statesman*, tr. Mario Domandi (New York, 1965), 69: "Common men find the variety of opinions that exists among lawyers quite reprehensible, without realizing that it proceeds not from any defects in the men but from the nature of the subject. General rules cannot possibly comprehend all particular cases. Often, specific cases cannot be decided on the basis of law, but must rather be dealt with by the opinions of men, which are not always in harmony. We see the same thing happen with doctors, philosophers, commercial arbitrators, and in the discourses of those who govern the state, among whom there is no less variety of judgment than among lawyers."

50. For Sarpi, see, for example, the first of his official *consulti* on the validity of the Venetian laws against which the papal interdict of 1606 was directed, in Paolo Sarpi, *Istoria dell'Interdetto e altri scritti editi ed inediti*, ed. Giovanni Gambarin (Bari, 1940), 2: 6: "It is not appropriate to proceed in these cases by way of conjectures, deductions, or syllogisms, but through explicit laws." For the French jurists, see Kelley, *Foundations of Modern Historical Scholarship*, 258, 279–80. For Bacon, see Shapiro, "Law and Science," 743 n.61.

51. Salutati, *De nobilitate legum et medicine* (1399), discussed by B. L. Ullman in *The Humanism of Coluccio Salutati* (Padua, 1963), 31–32.

52. Rousselet, *Histoire de la magistrature française*, 2: 247–50; Shapiro, "Law and Science."

53. See Martines, *Lawyers and Statecraft*, 408–36.

54. See my *Venice and Republican Liberty*, 449–52; for France, see Kelley, *Foundations of Modern Historical Scholarship*, 59–60, 288–90, *passim*; for England, see Ives, "Common Lawyers in Pre-Reformation England," for a review of this classic position.

55. Pasquier, quoted in Kelley, *Foundations of Modern Historical Scholarship*, 289. For similar attitudes elsewhere, see my *Venice and Republican Liberty*, 451–52, and Hill, *Intellectual Origins*, 250–51.

56. Kelley, *Foundations of Modern Historical Scholarship*, 269, 272–73; Hill, *Intellectual Origins*, 258–59.

57. For Italy, see the richly suggestive work of Charles Trinkaus, *In His Likeness and Image: Humanity and Divinity in the Thought of the Italian Renaissance* (Chicago, 1970); for Gallicanism, see William J. Bouwsma, "Gallicanism and the Nature of Christendom," ch. 13 below. The Jansenism of the French magistracy has long been recognized, but see Goldman, *Dieu caché*, and Ford, *Robe and Sword*, 87–88; for England, see Little, *Religion, Order, and Law*.

58. Peter Brown, *Augustine of Hippo: A Biography* (Berkeley, 1967), 23, remarks of North Africa: "A legal culture, hard-headed and relentless, had proliferated in its new clerical environment. Viewed by an Italian bishop who knew him well and heartily disliked his theology, Augustine was merely the latest example of an all-too-familiar figure, the *Poenus orator,* 'the African man of law.' " For the Augustinian revival of the seventeenth century, see Henri Marrou, *Saint Augustin et l'augustinisme* (Paris, 1955), 172–76.

59. See the discussion of the positive function of crime in Lewis Coser, *The Functions of Social Conflict* (Glencoe, 1967), 124–27.

60. See Martines, *Lawyers and Statecraft*, 168–69, and Hill, *Intellectual Origins*, 255.

61. William F. Church, "The Decline of the French Jurists as Political Theorists, 1660–1789," *French Historical Studies*, 5 (1967): 1–40. The gradual triumph of this tendency should also not obscure the fact that it had been developing slowly over many decades in both Italy and France; see Gilmore, *Humanists and Jurists*, 26–37, and Kelley, *Foundations of Modern Historical Scholarship*, 102–03, 137.

62. See the classic work of Otto von Gierke, *Natural Law and the Theory of Society, 1500 to 1800*, introd. and tr. Ernest Barker (Cambridge, 1934), and Leonard Krieger, *The Politics of Discretion: Pufendorf and the Acceptance of Natural Law* (Chicago, 1965). For the Netherlands, see also E. H. Kossmann, "The Development of Dutch Political Theory in the Seventeenth Century," in J. S. Bromley and E. H. Kossmann, eds., *Britain and the Netherlands* (New York, 1960), 91–110. Hale's *History of the Common Law of England* has just appeared in a new edition with a useful introduction by Charles M. Gray (Chicago, 1971). For the general point, see Shapiro, "Law and Science," 729–48.

63. For Rolandino, see Girolamo Arnaldi, *Studi sui cronisti della Marca Trevigiana nell'età di Ezzelino da Romano* (Rome, 1963), 79–208; for Mussato, see Manlio Dazzi, "Il Mussato storico," *Archivio Veneto*, ser. 5, vol. 6 (1929): 357–471; for Dandolo, see Enrico Simonsfeld, "Andrea Dandolo e le sue opere storiche," *Archivio Veneto*, ser. 1, vol. 14, pt. 1 (1877): 49–149.

64. Clive, "Social Background of the Scottish Renaissance," 231.

65. See Kelley, *Foundations of Modern Historical Scholarship*, and Huppert, *Idea of Perfect History*, passim.

66. See my *Venice and Republican Liberty*, 568–623.

67. Kelley, *Foundations of Modern Historical Scholarship*, *passim*, and Bouwsma, "Gallicanism and the Nature of Christendom," 308–24 in this volume.

68. Coke, quoted by Hill, *Intellectual Origins*, 257–58. On the general point, see also Little, *Religion, Order, and Law*, 31, 201, and Pocock, *Ancient Constitution*. Pocock's book is particularly suggestive in its recognition of affinities between French and English thought.

69. For example, in *A Dialogue between a Philosopher and a Student of the Common Laws of England*, ed. Joseph Cropsey (Chicago, 1971), 96; see also Little, *Religion, Order, and Law*, 179.

II

THE DURABLE RENAISSANCE

6 Anxiety and the Formation of Early Modern Culture

This paper was prepared for my Faculty Research Lecture at Berkeley in 1975. The lectureship is a formidable assignment, not only because it is a considerable honor but also because the lecture must address an audience composed of one's professional peers as well as students and faculty from the whole range of disciplines in the university. The subject of the paper had long been on my mind, but I had not before attempted to think about it systematically. Some of those who heard the lecture believed that I was offering a description of the contemporary world disguised as an account of the past.

Eventually I published the paper, somewhat revised, in After the Reformation: Essays in Honor of J. H. Hexter, *ed. Barbara C. Malament (Philadelphia: University of Pennsylvania Press, 1980), pp. 215–246. It is reprinted here by permission of the University of Pennsylvania Press.*

•   •   •

All men may be anxious; but it is commonly observed that some are more anxious than others, both individually and in groups. It is widely believed, for example, that our own age is a time of peculiar anxiety.[1] But though this impression may derive less from the considered views of professional historians than from the general distress of the later twentieth century, it is obviously a historical judgment; it implies that various moments in the past can be contrasted in terms of the degree of anxiety they exhibit.

But systematic elaboration of such contrast is difficult. "Anxiety" is itself a problematic term; and without some clear conception of its sources in the human personality, its dynamics, and its relation to other subjective states, we may well misread our evidence and above all misunderstand the relation between anxiety and objective experience. The study of historical anxiety therefore requires some special theoretical resources. But the empirical side of such investigation also presents unusual difficulties. Some degree of anxiety seems latent in the human condition, and various expressions of it can doubtless be discovered in every time and place. At the same time it seems unlikely that, outside of the laboratory, anxiety can ever be submitted to precise measurement. Accordingly, the judgment that one age or social group was more or less anxious than another can hardly be supported by the kind of hard comparative data that may be adduced for more objective phenomena. In dealing with matters of this sort we are therefore likely to find ourselves in the awkward position of basing essentially quantitative conclusions on patently qualitative evidence.[2] And we may find no evidence at all precisely where we most need it.

Nevertheless these problems have not deterred able historians from speaking about past anxiety. At least one distinguished scholar has used the term to characterize the later hellenistic world.[3] And it is notably present, at various levels of generality, in recent scholarship dealing with the transition from those centuries that were clearly "medieval" to those almost as clearly not. Historians of this important segment of the European past seem, in fact, to be discovering symptoms of a peculiar anxiety in many places. Origo and Bec have noted the heightened anxiety of Italian merchants; Lewis, that of merchants in France; Dollinger, that of German merchants; Herlihy has found it deeply embedded in the Renaissance family, transmitted from anxious mothers to their children.[4] Historians with larger purposes are meanwhile coming steadily closer to a general characterization of this as an age of special anxiety. The tendency is apparent in the excellent monographs of Douglass and Steinmetz on later medieval piety, and in the more general studies of Seidlmayer, Meiss, Becker, Delaruelle, Trinkaus, Oberman, Delumeau, Ozment, Dickens, and Walzer.[5] Garin speaks of the Italian Renaissance as "the beginning of an age of [subjective] torment," whatever it may have represented positively.[6] And Lynn White, Jr., broadly presenting the three or four centuries after 1300 as a time of "abnormal anxiety," has offered us a general interpretation of the period in these terms.[7] We seem to be reaching a point at which the general implications of this scholarship, based on both northern and southern Europe, on movements conventionally associated both with the later Middle Ages and with the Renaissance, and on every social group for which evidence is available, must be confronted more deliberately.

A rather different kind of pressure, less clearly the product of professional investigation, is impelling us in the same direction. There has been a remarkable tendency among recent translators into English, concerned to convey meaning from one time, as well as one language, to another, to read "anxiety" into a wide range of words or phrases in documents of this period. The transformation of the Latin *anxietas* into "anxiety" may occasion little surprise, though perhaps it should; in medieval usage *anxietas* signified a vague weariness or distress of heart, and came close to monastic *acedia* or even *tristitia*.[8] But the meaning of *anxietas* seems to have broadened by the sixteenth century, as we can learn from Calvin, that indefatigable translator of his own Latin into the vernacular. In his French *Institution*, Calvin variously rendered the *anxietas* of the Latin *Institutio* into *angoisse, destresse, frayeur,* and *solicitude,* and his Latin *solicitudo* (evidently a close synonym) could become either *solicitude* or *perplexité*.[9] By the time "anxiety" and "anxious" entered English in the sixteenth and seventeenth centuries (and that they did so at this time is of obvious interest here), they evidently already conveyed these various possibilities; and we can certainly forgive recent translators, themselves doubtless in some *perplexité,* at least a part of their freedom, even though it may occasionally raise an eyebrow. From Latin Petrarch's *cura* and the *distractio* of Thomas à Kempis can both emerge as "anxiety."[10] And a host of vernacular expressions come out similarly. The identification of the German *Angst* and *Anfechtung* with "anxiety" is sufficiently familiar, although, to be sure, Reformation scholars have been unusually conscious of the nuances of these more technically theological terms. But from the French, Commynes's *ce travail et misere* now appears as "their anxieties and their worries";[11] and a recent translation of Alberti's *I libri della famiglia* converts *maninconia, affanno, cura, sollecitudine, sospetto, perturbazione,* and *agonia di mente* indiscriminately into "anxiety," *buona diligenza* into "anxious attention," and *stare in paura* into "to be anxious."[12] From Spanish both *ansia* and *cuidado* emerge as "anxiety."[13] I do not propose to quarrel here with these renderings; I want only to suggest how, even by so apparently innocent a route, we are being led into strange new historiographical territory.

A further impulse behind our sense of the period after about 1300 as an age of unusual anxiety stems from the more benign impression conveyed by the culture of the twelfth and thirteenth centuries. In that earlier period, those men whose attitudes are accessible to us appear to have felt reasonably comfortable about human existence.[14] The prospects for mankind, both in this world and the next, seemed generally happy; the medieval schools could demonstrate, with increasing confidence, the intelligibility and friendliness of the universe; intellectuals were pleased to see themselves, though dwarves, as standing on the shoulders of giants; and men could hope that, in various walks of life, "the quality of our life should be improved."[15] The defects of the contemporary scene were not passed over (indeed selective attention to them was a sign of confidence), as we know from such popular works as the *Roman de la Rose;* but the essential quality of that work was its bold and exuberant naturalism, and even Dante could still believe in the power of intelligence and love to remedy the ills of existence. Generalized laments about the human condition abounded, like Innocent III's little treatise *De miseria* (though he had hoped to complement this with a more positive statement about life); but there seemed little specifically wrong with the times, much that was right, and much to look forward to.

Some caution is in order here. We know little directly about how, for example, merchants of the twelfth and thirteenth centuries felt about their lives; and it is hard to believe that existence in towns (a subject that will figure prominently in what follows) did not, from the beginning, generate profound inner as well as outer discomfort. It is even more difficult to assess the psychological condition of the vast rural majority. But even granting this, I think it would be a mistake simply to dismiss the optimism of high medieval culture as the invention of an isolated class of intellectuals. Medieval high culture was not altogether detached from its social context, as its hospitality to the more concrete world of Aristotelian thought would seem to demonstrate; and the combination of intellectual and pastoral concern in the great mendicant orders provided a two-way bridge between intellectual constructions and the needs of daily life. The result was that, though human problems might still be acute, men who addressed themselves to such general questions could still contemplate the future with relative confidence.

This positive attitude to the future in the High Middle Ages is of special significance because it is the key to a clearer understanding of the nature of anxiety. It reminds us that anxiety is a function of man's attitude to time. As the *Oxford English Dictionary* tells us, anxiety is "uneasiness or trouble of mind about some uncertain event." Man is anxious, therefore, because his existence extends into the *future,* and the future is inherently *uncertain*. This suggests that, since all human life unfolds in time, anxiety is in some degree inescapable, perhaps especially in the Western tradition, with its peculiar sense of the significance of time. Chaucer's Knight understood the general element in human existence that gives rise to anxiety:

> It's good to keep one's poise and be protected
> Since all day long we meet the unexpected.[16]

The unusual anxiety of the period after 1300 is thus implicit in its novel concern with the passage of time, which found general expression in the familiar new historical consciousness of the Renaissance and was manifested more particularly in efforts to mark the flow of time with chronometers and to control its use by profitably filling the hours. The increasing reliance on clocks in later medieval and Renaissance Europe has been often remarked,[17] and their value celebrated. A fourteenth-century Milanese chronicler praised a new striking clock because it "marks off the hours from the hours, as is supremely necessary for all classes of men."[18] Calvin emphasized the utility of the sun, and Pascal that of his watch, for marking time.[19] And Petrarch hinted at the anxiety underlying the concern with time; time, as he wrote the emperor Charles IV, is "so precious, nay, so inestimable a possession, that it is the one thing which the learned agree can justify avarice."[20] Vergerio proposed that a clock be installed in every library, "that it may catch the eye of the reader, to warn him by the swift lapse of time of the need for diligence."[21] Rabelais's ideal teacher Ponocrates so arranged the schedule of his young pupil "that not a moment of the day was wasted."[22] But anxiety over the use of time was not confined to scholars. The anxious wife of the merchant Francesco Datini chided her husband for his misuse of time: "In view of all you have to do, when you waste an hour, it seems to me a thousand. . . . For I deem nought so precious to you, both for body and soul, as time, and methinks you value it too little."[23] This peculiarly modern concern would eventually find homely expression in *Poor Richard's Almanack,* but more was at stake here than "profit." For the proper regulation and use of time eliminated some of the uncertainty of life; it warded off, objectively, the blows of fortune, that comprehensive symbol of the uncertainty of life.

The fundamental relationship between the unreliability of fortune and human anxiety seemed, at any rate, obvious to contemporaries. So Alberti's Uncle Adovardo asked, quite rhetorically, "If a man is afflicted with so many anxieties, and always fears the instability of fortune . . . how can we consider him happy or call him anything but unfortunate?"[24] If the management of time suggested an objective means of escape from this predicament, Petrarch's *De remediis* (so popular also outside of Italy) promoted, at vast length, subjective remedies, chiefly along Stoic lines.[25] Machiavelli was following a similar direction of thought in proposing that although men "know not the end and move towards it along roads which cross one another and as yet are unexplored . . . they should not despair, no matter what fortune brings."[26] We have here further testimony to the general connection between anxiety and the uncertainty inherent in time itself as an inescapable dimension of life. Fortune expressed the radical untrustworthiness of the future.

But back of the future, beyond the limits of time as a dimension of each individual existence, lurks the uncertainty surrounding death. This is why, in some ultimate sense, all anxiety is anxiety about death,[27] and why the anxiety of this period, often when it was immediately focused on the use of time, tended to accumulate especially around death and judgment, the nameless horror beyond every particular danger. "It is sad," Thomas à Kempis wrote, "that you do not employ your time better, when you may win eternal life hereafter. The time will come when you will long for one day or one hour in which to amend; and who knows whether it will be granted?"[28] The peculiar obsession of Europeans with these matters from the fourteenth century onward has been of considerable interest to historians;[29] we seem to be dealing here with something more than a set of perennial platitudes. Death, both as a physiological process and as the entrance into a realm of final uncertainty, was surrounded, even more than fortune, though for the same reason, by a singular dread. For all his piety, Petrarch could not conquer his fear of death, which he described in obsessive and strenuous detail. "*Ubi sunt?*" he asked, and could only reply, "All has dissolved into worms and into serpents, and finally into nothing." He hated sleep because it reminded him of death, and his bed because it suggested the grave.[30] For Commynes death showed "what a petty thing man is, how short and miserable his life is, and how empty the differences between the great and the small, as soon as they are dead. For everyone is horrified by a corpse and vituperates it."

But the horror of death was compounded by a deeper anxiety over the uncertainty of judgment. "The soul," Commynes had concluded his little meditation on death, "must immediately go to receive God's judgment. Sentence is given at that very moment in accordance with the works and merits of the corpse."[31] Calvin spelled out the connection between this apprehension and the general anxiety of the age: "Where does death come from but from God's anger against sin? Hence arises that state of servitude through the whole of life, that is the constant anxiety in which unhappy souls are imprisoned."[32] Even laymen despaired over the mysteries of predestination and had to be advised to leave such matters to theologians.[33] The pains of Purgatory were sufficiently feared; Thomas More himself described them in grisly detail,[34] and the rich provided in their wills for masses to speed their souls to heaven: three thousand for a German merchant, ten thousand for Henry

VII of England (who was prepared to pay above the going rate to insure their being said properly), thirty thousand for the emperor Charles V.[35] In the Medici Chapel in Florence, the massive figures of Michelangelo brooding over their solemn work, priests dropped with fatigue saying masses for their departed rulers.[36] But the fear of hell was infinitely worse. A popular catechism pictured the damned feeding on their own flesh and explained, "The pain caused by one spark of hell-fire is greater than that caused by a thousand years of a woman's labor in childbirth."[37] Nor were such fears alien to more refined minds. Petrarch described his thoughts of hell: "Terror grips my heart / Seeing the others I tremble for myself / Others urge me on, my last hour may be now."[38]

The peculiar guilt of this period is sometimes attributed to the confessional, but this seems at best a half-truth; the confessional was as much an expression as a cause of anxiety. Men submitted to its scrutiny because they were in desperate fear of appearing before God with a single sin left unrecognized and unabsolved. Even confessors sometimes shrank from so dreadful a responsibility, itself a source of unbearable anxiety.[39] And men often stayed away from confession because it gave no relief. Some looked instead to conscience, though this could be no more reassuring; for conscience, as Leonardo Bruni wrote, is a judge who "knows all" and "was present at every crime," and who "forces tears from you and compels you to weep among sacred things."[40] Luther, who had vowed to become a monk through "the terror and agony of sudden death,"[41] was eloquent on the inadequacy of conscience to relieve anxiety. To the guilty, he wrote, "all creatures appear changed. Even when they speak with people whom they know and in turn hear them, the very sound of their speech seems different, their looks appear changed, and everything becomes black and horrible wherever they turn their eyes. Such a fierce and savage beast is an evil conscience. And so, unless God comforts them, they must end their own life because of their despair, their distress, and their inability to bear their grief."[42]

The importance of these fundamental dimensions of the anxiety of this period is suggested by the attention given to the problem, both explicitly and implicitly, in the religious thought of the sixteenth century, among Catholics almost as much as among Protestants. The uncertainty we have identified as central to anxiety figured prominently in the Protestant indictment of later medieval piety, and conversely Protestants stressed the certainties implicit in their own understanding of the Gospel. For Luther the "fear, terror, and horror" of death were the peculiar work of the devil; and faith alone could produce that "comfortable certainty" he could not attain by himself.[43] For Calvin the terrible "anxiety and trepidation of mind" produced by honest self-examination, and the ignorance of providence that is "the ultimate of all miseries," could only give way before the "incredible freedom from worry about the future" that comes from faith. Scripture frees us from seeking "some uncertain deity by devious paths" and brings us to an "assurance that is not assailed by some anxiety." "Surely it is terrifying to walk in the darkness of death," he wrote; "and believers, whatever their strength may be, cannot but be frightened by it. But since the thought prevails that they have God beside them, caring for their safety, fear at once yields to assurance."[44] Saint Teresa described her own movement from a deep depression of uncertainty about God's favor to the recognition that "I might safely take comfort and be certain that I was in grace."[45] The personal intensity of both Protestant and Catholic piety in the age of the Reformation can only be understood against the background of the peculiar anxiety that it sought to assuage.

It is essential, to get at the ultimate meaning of anxiety, to notice first its attachment to the problems of time, death, and judgment. But anxiety also has other dimensions; as a diffuse condition of the personality, it can suffuse any area of experience. Indeed, it tends to seek out more particular and immediate expression, for, by providing itself with a local habitation and a name, it is therapeutically transformed into fear. Fear is distinguishable from anxiety by the specificity of its object; and because the object of fear is concrete and may be dealt with by some appropriate action, fear can be reduced or overcome. The effect of anxiety, on the other hand, is likely to be paralysis and depression. Yet the relationship between anxiety and fear remains close, for behind the fear of a particular danger always lurks, again, uncertainty about its eventual outcome. The close connection between these two states accounts for the fact that we encounter in this period not only anxiety about ultimate matters but also a peculiar capacity to be troubled, like Martha, about many things. The worries of this prototypical housewife can tell us, indeed, a good deal about the nature of historical anxiety. Mary and Martha (a point frequently made in a related connection) are two sides of the same existential coin. Mary represents the direct approach to human anxiety; she goes to its source. But Martha prefers to diffuse her anxiety among a variety of household tasks, with which she can immediately cope. We are here, perhaps, close to the psychological roots of the preoccupation of Renaissance moral and political discourse with the *vita activa*.

Europeans of the fourteenth century, and for some time thereafter, were thus both profoundly anxious and at the same time frightened by almost every aspect of experience. It is hardly necessary to review here the evidence of their pervasive fear; historians are now discerning it in every sector of life. They have found it among rulers and merchants, and in every social relationship. It poisoned friendships and family ties, and even the sexual bond. The marriage bed itself now seemed less genial, as indeed we might expect; men who had learned a general distrust of life could hardly have been capable of a careless spontaneity in the most intimate realms of experience.[46] Anxiety also attended the pursuit of learning, which too often seemed only an occasion of further despair; the more-one knew, the less sense the world made.[47]

Each of these particular concerns can doubtless be attributed to objective causes. Politics *was* a dangerous game, the pursuit of wealth did involve great risks, friends played false, treachery within families did occur, lovers could inflict deep wounds, the wisdom in books might indeed mislead and confuse. But it is not immediately obvious that much of this was not also true in the preceding centuries (or indeed in most centuries), and what is most striking about these expressions of distress is their inclusiveness. They arise in connection with every significant human activity. Indeed they may surround, with equal intensity and a mysterious poignancy, quite insignificant matters. Alberti could debate alternative solutions to the larger and more concrete problems of life, but he suggests that the same degree of anxiety could also surround its more trivial responsibilities, and with paralyzing effect. His uncles were radically upset by the "confusions, worries, and anxieties" of giving a dinner party, in which "upheaval and annoyance overwhelm you until you are tired before you have even begun your preparations"; and the difficulties of moving to a new house evoked in them "anxieties that afflict your mind and distract and disrupt spirit and thought."[48] Alberti seems to be reminding us that the problem of anxiety, the somber thread that runs all through his book, was, after all, more general and diffuse than any particular dangers could account for.

Historians have tended to attribute the peculiar anxiety of this period to the specific character, and above all the disasters, of European life after the beginning of the fourteenth century: to epidemics (and, of course, the Black Death!) more terrible than anyone could remember, to the uncertainties of a depressed economy, to the transition from a corporate to an individualistic society, to political disorder, to the contraction of Christendom in the East, to the disarray of the institutional church, to the pressures of the confessional, or to the novelties of rapid change. And evidence is not lacking that each of these experiences disturbed and depressed some men, from time to time and in varying degrees. But it is hardly demonstrable, however distressing these matters seem to modern historians, who can envisage them cumulatively and imagine their concentrated impact on themselves, that they had a similar effect on those who experienced them in the past. The men of our period engaged with them not simultaneously but separately and at intervals, and were rarely in a position to draw general conclusions about their meaning.[49] Nor is it clear that, had they been able to do so, they would have reacted much differently from men in earlier centuries to their own difficulties, which were not objectively insignificant. The diffuseness of the anxiety of our period suggests that the relationship of anxiety to particular disasters was incidental rather than essential. Explanation in these terms appears to neglect the distinction, and the relationship, between anxiety and fear.

Nevertheless it remains true that the malaise of our period was peculiarly its own. It must be seen as a historical phenomenon, and so it was considered at the time, when it became an essential component of a new historical consciousness. "*Now* the world is cowardly, decayed, and weak, / All goes badly," wrote Eustache Deschamps;[50] and it is this *now* that commands our attention: not simply life in general but the times, and above all what they might hold in store, were out of joint. Petrarch stressed the "present woes" that promised, if this were possible, worse to come: "*O tempora, o mores!*" he exclaimed.[51] "*Now* the study of holy eloquence and its professors suffer the laughter and derision of all," declared a French reformer in about 1400.[52] Machiavelli denounced "the negligence of princes, who *have lost* all appetite for true glory, and of republics which *no longer* possess institutions that deserve praise."[53] Erasmus explained the spate of predictions of the world's end as a judgment on the particular conditions of the present age: "They say it's because men are behaving *now* just as they did before the Flood overwhelmed them."[54] Montaigne represented his own time as dull and leaden, all virtue spent.[55]

Implicit here, obviously, is comparison with a previous period when human affairs had presumably gone better, and with this comparison we begin to sense a contemporary explanation for the anxieties of the time that is somewhat different from the explanations favored by modern historians. There are hints of it in the town chronicles of fourteenth-century Italy, with their idealization of a simpler past,[56] as well as in Commynes, who believed that "our life-span is diminished, and we do not live as long as men did in former times; neither are our bodies as strong, and similarly our faith and loyalty to one another has been weakened."[57] The past now represented a lost ideal of peace, order, freedom, and above all brotherhood, in which men could exist without anxiety. The clue to the peculiar difficulties of the present thus seemed to lie in the deterioration of all social relationships; men had become anxious, contemporaries constantly repeated, because they had come to fear each other. "You are young," a Florentine merchant wrote one of his agents, "but when you have lived as long as I have and have traded with many folk, you will know that man is a dangerous thing, and that danger lies in dealing with him."[58] Everywhere one meets the charge that *now* men looked out only for themselves. "Men live among themselves in such a manner," wrote Luther, "that no consideration is given to the state or household. . . . Who does not see that God is compelled, as it were, to punish, yes, even to destroy Germany?"[59]

And the explanation for this novel egotism lies just below the surface of many expressions of contemporary anxiety: its cause was seen in the replacement of an agrarian by an urban society and in the attitudes and activities particularly associated with townsmen. A long tradition of antiurban sentiment lay behind this, nourished by both the Greek and the Latin classics, given substance by the medieval perception of towns as a disruptive intrusion into the old agrarian order, and finding expression in the Franciscan ideal of poverty. But by the fourteenth century there are signs that European observers were tending to regard towns as the cause of a general historical crisis and the source of their peculiar anxiety. Petrarch, adapting Juvenal, associated many of his worst moments with cities: with filthy, noisy, and bustling Avignon and even with Venice, where, he reported, "wherever I go in full day a crowd of dogs drawn from the populace assails me noisily . . . they are innumerable, turbulent, and noisy, and they are plagued with endless worry because they cannot bite me."[60] Here, apparently, his anxiety was matched by that of those who surrounded him.

But towns provoked anxiety above all because they were greedy; townsmen preyed on others to benefit themselves, and this was what made them unreliable and dangerous, a threat to the general security of human existence. Even a merchant could lament that "where money is at stake or some personal interest, one finds no relative or friend who prefers you to himself and has not forgotten his conscience."[61] The rural victims of urban greed made particular complaint, as in the *Reformatio Sigismundi:* "Nowadays a man going to a city to buy or sell will come away saying 'They have cheated me.' Everything in the city is sold at too high a price."[62] "Nowadays," declared a Lutheran, "trading and bartering have brought our land to such a pass that a man, if he would save himself from ruin, is compelled to cheat, defraud, and lie to his neighbors, for he himself is deceived at every turn."[63]

"Nowadays." Again we are in the presence of a contrast, deeply felt, between a distressed present and a supposedly happier past, but also between man's present and his true home: *nostalgia* in its primary meaning. Ideally man should, and perhaps once did, reside in a garden: the more sophisticated garden in which Boccaccio's splendid youths found refuge from the horrors of plague-stricken Florence (itself a terrifying reality but even more potent as a symbol of the general malaise of urban life), or the primal garden where, as Luther remarked, Adam and Eve had lived "in the happiest security, without any fear of death and without anxiety."[64] Piety and brotherhood seemed to come more readily in the country, and radical intellectuals during the early years of the Reformation occasionally went to the land; Karlstadt bought a farm, wore peasant gray, tilled the soil with his own hands (at least for a while), and called on university students to follow his example.[65] Moralists like Bucer thought agriculture more virtuous than other pursuits,[66] a sentiment that would receive systematic application by the Physiocrats. Johann Agricola attributed the fall of Rome to its abandonment of its old ways in which "rulers and statesmen used to be summoned directly from the plow and the field" and "plain, honest, hardworking farmers aspired to honor and uprightness, not to riches."[67] Petrarch found only in the country the peace of mind favorable to the descent of his muse.[68] The genial host in Erasmus's "Godly Feast" marvelled at "people who take pleasure in smoky cities" when "the whole countryside is fresh and smiling."[69] Galileo is reported to have considered the city "the prison of the speculative mind" and his own thought liberated "only by the freedom of the countryside."[70]

We are evidently in the presence of an early formulation of the fruitful modern myth of *Gemeinschaft* and *Gesellschaft*. And there is much in this fragmentary contemporary diagnosis, however it differs from our own more particular explanations, to instruct us about the general causes of the anxiety in this period. Its foundation was, of course, partly a myth even then, as Hutten recognized in reminding the nostalgic Pirckheimer that in the countryside too "each day is filled with anxiety over what the morrow might bring."[71] Nevertheless it is true that much in urban life induced anxiety among those brought up in the country, as much of the urban population had been; since the death rate in towns tended to exceed the birth rate, even the maintenance of stable population in towns, and much more their growth, depended on substantial immigration from the country. For erstwhile peasants the proliferation of complex laws and bureaucracies meant the substitution of an external, coercive, and mystifying set of social controls for the old internalized sentiments of a simpler community. And the unusual mobility of the urban population meant also that, in cities, much of life was passed among strangers, potential predators, themselves made anxious by the novelty and insecurity of urban existence.

The needs of survival in this new environment and the increasing differentiation of economic and social roles compelled men to adopt specialized stances in relation to each other. A relaxed and candid self-exposure now became dangerous; human intimacy was inhibited by the need for vigilance in masking the true self. The villain of the Elizabethan and Jacobean stage was likely to be a dissembler, but so in some degree was the average *honnête homme*.[72] The conception of "friendship" was itself corrupted by self-interest; as a Florentine merchant remarked, "It is good to have friends of all kinds, but not useless men."[73] The making of friends now depended on the artful presentation of a carefully edited "image," and advice on this delicate operation became necessary. "If there is someone in your *gonfalone* who can help you and push you ahead," Giovanni Morelli advised his sons, "first try to become intimate with him, if possible, by means of marriage. If that is not practicable, then have dealings with him and his [relatives]; try to serve him, offer him aid, if you can do so without too much loss to yourself, when you see that he is in need; give him presents, honor him by inviting him often to dinner." Morelli cited the example of his own father, who had been skillful in these tactics: "And by such wise and provident means, he had so arranged matters that, in his time of great need, he had friends, and not only relatives, who gave him help and support."[74] Alberti's Uncle Adovardo advised that "to make friends it is necessary to study the gestures, words, customs, and conversations of others."[75] No wonder, then, that, as Commynes complained, "ours is indeed a miserable life, when we take such trouble and pains to shorten it by saying so many things which are almost the opposite of what we really think."[76] At the end of his life the disillusioned Poggio Bracciolini confessed that he now spoke "only with the dead, who do not lie."[77]

But urban life was also closer to the more ultimate sources of human anxiety. In cities time was experienced differently from in the country; change became a function not merely of the eternal rhythms of nature but of the unpredictable human will, and with the future always dependent on the actions of other men it became increasingly uncertain. Even death might seem more grim; it was now all too likely to occur among strangers or false friends, and without the prayers of a stable community.[78]

Are we, then, to substitute a more general social explanation of the special anxiety of this transitional age for the particular catastrophes on which historians have recently concentrated? Is the anxiety that seems to have hung over and darkened the lives of so many in this period, like smog, a direct consequence of the practical conditions of urban life? There is much to recommend this explanation; it directs us to the most general European developments to account for a general phenomenon, and it is suggested by contemporary testimony itself.

Yet this seems to me, however essential, not yet a sufficient explanation. For the problem here appears to lie less in the objective changes in the quality of European life that were, in any case, not altogether novel in the fourteenth century, than in the ability of Europeans to cope with them. Although the anxiety and depression of our period eventually declined, so that we can now see it as in this respect an unusual age in contrast not only to the medieval past but also (if a bit less clearly) to succeeding centuries, this can hardly be explained as a consequence either of the decline of cities or of a reduction in the rate of change. I think, therefore, that we must move to a deeper level of explanation: to the problem of man's ability to impose a meaning on his experience that can give to life a measure of reliability and thus reduce, even if it cannot altogether abolish, life's ultimate and terrifying uncertainties. The fundamental problem to which we must thus address ourselves appears to be the problem of culture and of its capacity to manage and reduce the anxiety of existence.[79]

Medieval culture was conspicuously successful in the performance of this essential task. Applying a common set of distinctions (like other cultures of the type described by anthropologists as primitive)[80] to all areas of human concern, notably such polarities as inside and outside, high and low, male and female, it was able at once to distinguish, to classify, and to relate all phenomena, and so to create an intelligible and coherent cosmos, apparently rooted in the eternal principles of nature itself, out of the undifferentiated chaos of raw experience. The phenomenal world could thus be reduced to a kind of orderly map; men could feel at home in it because they could distinguish one area from another by clear conceptual boundaries which were reflected in the structures of life as well as thought.

Thus medieval cosmology gave intelligibility to the universe as a whole by supplying it with an external boundary, and within it distinguished among its constituent parts. Bounding and distinguishing were fundamental to scholastic method, with its definitions (that is, conceptual boundaries), categories, and species. The sacred was clearly differentiated from the profane, *sacerdotium* from *imperium*. The various faculties of the human personality were similarly distinguished: soul and body; intellect, will, and passion. Human acts could be classified as virtuous or vicious, and the several virtues and vices were also unambiguously defined, and exploited to categorize and explain human behavior. Social identity depended on the boundaries between communities and classes, within which the individual was contained and at home. God was himself bounded by his intelligence, which guaranteed not only the immutability and intelligibility of the whole structure but also its ontological status. Boundaries were thus invested with numinous awe and surrounded by religious sanctions.

As a fully articulated system of boundaries, medieval culture was admirably suited to the management of anxiety. It provided well-defined areas of safety and focused the latent anxiety in the human condition at their margins. Anxiety was thus transmuted into a fear of transgressing the boundaries defining the cultural universe, and in various ways men could usually stay away from them.[81] They were safe in their communities or estates, or as long as the boundary between the sacred and profane was respected, or insofar as the soul was not contaminated by the body or reason by the passions, or in the performance of virtuous and the avoidance of vicious acts. They could even face death with greater confidence, not only because their latent anxiety could be released by the obligations of boundary maintenance, but also because the *viator* through and beyond this life could take his bearings from the boundaries that continually surrounded him, discover the true way, and above all know his direction. Dante may have strayed briefly from his path, but he was enabled to find it again.[82]

But certain peculiarities of the medieval system of boundaries made it appropriate only under special conditions. Above all it was based on the notion of absolute qualitative distinctions rooted in ultimate reality and therefore perennially applicable to human affairs. The system depended on the clarity of these distinctions, and it could not tolerate ambiguity. Thus it could remain plausible only as long as it was practicable for men to avoid transgressing its boundaries, for, although our response to experience is conditioned by culture, we also require a culture appropriate to experience and the needs of survival.

And it is at this point that the significance of urban life becomes apparent; the accumulating social changes of the later Middle Ages eventually exceeded the flexibility of the inherited culture and forced men increasingly to violate the old boundaries. Lateral social mobility broke down the boundaries between communities; town walls still retained deep symbolic meaning in the thirteenth century but—I suspect for more than demographic or military reasons—seemed increasingly arbitrary and useless thereafter and gradually ceased to be built. Vertical mobility eroded the boundaries between classes; and we now begin to encounter disputes over precedence in ceremonial processions among socially ambiguous groups such as lawyers and university scholars.[83] The distinction between the sacred and profane was dissolving with the growing responsibility and dignity of lay activity and the secular state. The psychological boundaries by which the old culture had sought to understand the nature of man and predict his behavior were useless when he was no longer inhibited by the pressures of traditional community; and, experienced concretely in a more complex setting, human acts proved too ambiguous for neat ethical classification. Even the boundaries of the physical universe, so intimately linked to those in society and the human personality, were collapsing. No objective system of boundaries could now supply either security or effective guidance. When man still clung to the old culture, he seemed to have become, in spite of himself, a trespasser against the order of the universe, a violator of its sacred limits, the reluctant inhabitant of precisely those dangerous borderlands—literally no man's land—he had been conditioned to avoid. But his predicament was even worse if this experience had taught him to doubt the very existence of boundaries. He then seemed thrown, disoriented, back into the void from which it was the task of culture to rescue him. And this, I suggest, is the immediate explanation for the extraordinary anxiety of this period. It was an inevitable response to the growing inability of an inherited culture to invest experience with meaning.

There are hints that contemporaries themselves obscurely perceived their problems in these terms. Boundaries establish order by keeping each thing in its place, and the critics of cities were offended because, in them, confusion reigned. This is the deeper significance of the association of cities with dirt; with smoke, which obscures every visual boundary; perhaps even with noise, which intrudes on the inner life. Petrarch was nauseated by Avignon, "the narrow and obscure sink of the earth, where all the filth of the world is collected," with its "streets full of disease and infection, dirty pigs and snarling dogs, the noise of cart-wheels grinding against walls, four-horse chariots dashing down at every crossroad, the motley crew of people, swarms of vile beggars side by side with the flaunting luxury of wealth . . . the medley of characters—such diverse roles in life—the endless clamor of their confused voices, as the passers-by jostle one another in the streets."[84] The juxtaposition here of contamination and confusion is instructive. Filth, as Mary Douglas has pointed out, is culturally defined; dirt is matter out of place, and what may be unexceptionable when confined to the barnyard is noxious elsewhere.[85] Cities, as an anomaly in a traditional agrarian order, increasingly threatened to dissolve the patterns of a culture that had made the world comprehensible and comfortable, and accordingly they represented pollution and a reversion to chaos.

Petrarch's revulsion against cities has an ironic side, though it can be readily understood as expressing his apprehension of the consequences of his own onslaught against the old culture. For his attack on scholastic modes of thought radically challenged the principles underlying that culture. He repeatedly described scholastic efforts to identify the fundamental elements of reality in an orderly and systematic way, and so to define their boundaries, as "infantile babble"; "in total oblivion of the real basis of things," he maintained, the schoolmen "grow old, simply conversant with words."[86] What this charge amounted to, a charge in which Renaissance humanists were joined by a new breed of scholastics, and later by the Protestant Reformers, was that a culture once able to give an ontological foundation to the phenomena of human experience could no longer do so. It had lost touch with reality and become irrelevant; its definitions and boundaries could no longer supply meaning to life. The result was a crisis of confidence in the significance of human knowledge. For Salutati, "to speak properly, what to us is knowledge is really only a kind of reasonable uncertainty."[87] Pierre d'Ailly concluded "that the philosophy or doctrine of Aristotle deserves the name of opinion rather than science."[88] For Melanchthon the schoolmen "continually think up new and prodigious fancies and monstrous expressions by which, since they have no basis in reality, nothing can be understood."[89] Indeed the inherited culture had become positively mischievous since, though it still claimed ontological status, it no longer possessed any. Thus, though the old culture was now seen to be clearly no more than a human invention, its practical demands, because they could no longer be satisfied, filled men with dread. As Calvin wrote of the schoolmen, "They torture souls with many misgivings, and immerse them in a sea of trouble and anxiety."[90]

The collapse of the old boundaries can be seen in many areas of cultural expression: for example, in the more fluid definition of nobility that we encounter in both humanists and Reformers, or in Nicholas of Cusa's conception of the infinite in which all polarities are reconciled and obliterated, or in the paradoxes of Luther, or in the new astronomy of the sixteenth and seventeenth centuries. An occasional thinker felt, in the presence of this disintegration, the exhilaration of freedom; this was its effect on Bruno:

> There are no ends, boundaries, limits or walls which can defraud or deprive us of the infinite multitude of things. Therefore the earth and the ocean thereof are fecund; therefore the sun's blaze is everlasting, so that eternally fuel is provided for the voracious fires, and moisture replaces the attenuated seas. For from infinity is born an ever fresh abundance of matter.[91]

But infinity is not, for the majority of mankind, a comfortable habitat, as man's inability to live without culture would seem to attest; and Bruno's tragic fate testifies that his reaction to the new cultural situation was not only eccentric but profoundly threatening to his contemporaries. A more typical response to the implausibility and collapse of cultural boundaries was a frantic, if ultimately unsuccessful, effort to shore them up, of which the increasingly elaborate articulation of the old culture Huizinga noted in the fourteenth and fifteenth centuries, the regressive tendencies of later Renaissance Italy, and the more detailed application of the penitential system are examples.[92] Gerson proposed to cure the malaise of spiritual life by strengthening the boundary between theology and philosophy: "It is evident that although it surpasses philosophy, the teaching of faith has its predetermined boundaries in the sacred writings which have been revealed to us. One ought not dare define and teach anything beyond these boundaries."[93] Rulers were increasingly preoccupied with defining the boundaries of their states, which appeared the more plausible in the degree to which they could be attributed to "nature," that is, given a quasi-ontological status.

But none of these efforts was finally of much use, as Pascal in his radical honesty would testify at the conclusion of a long process of cultural disintegration. We may interpret his sensitivity to the frightening "eternal silence of these infinite spaces" as a metaphor for the larger cultural universe of which his new vision of the physical universe had become a part. Both had finally lost those old familiar boundaries by which men could orient themselves and find meaning, and human existence could be made tolerable now only if men could be distracted from reflecting "on what they are, whence they come, whither they go." "Ever drifting in uncertainty, driven from end to end," man, for Pascal, "feels his nothingness, his forlornness, his insufficiency, his dependency, his weakness," and "there will immediately arise from the depth of his heart weariness, gloom, sadness, fretfulness, vexation, despair." This was the terrible predicament that had come out of the cultural disintegration of the previous centuries:

> When I see the blindness and wretchedness of man, when I regard the whole silent universe, and man without light, left to himself, and, as it were, lost in this corner of the universe, without knowing who has put him there, what he has come to do, what will become of him at death, and incapable of all knowledge, I become terrified, like a man who should be carried in his sleep to a dreadful desert island, and should awake without knowing where he is, and without means of escape. And thereupon I wonder how people in a condition so wretched do not fall into despair.[94]

Nevertheless Voltaire's incredulity as he confronted Pascal's vision of the human condition testifies that earthly palliatives for such general despair could be found.[95] From time to time, to be sure, Europeans have sought to recover the confidence of their medieval predecessors by insisting once again on the ontological basis of human culture. This, I take it, is the significance of both the Protestant and the Catholic Counter-Reformations,[96] of the more absolutist tendencies of the Enlightenment, and of some recent authoritarian ideologies; our perennial nostalgia for the Middle Ages is perhaps a more innocent expression of the same impulse, which will doubtless continue to seek expression. But such attempts to resurrect the spirit of the old culture, however tempting, have so far proved incapable of meeting for long the need for cultural security. Relief would come rather from the gradual emergence of a new kind of culture, based on quite different principles, that was struggling to be born even as the old one disintegrated. The new culture of post-medieval Europe has often been described, with varying degrees of success; and I want in conclusion chiefly to suggest how it managed to reduce, though it could not eliminate, the terrible anxiety implicit in the disintegration of the medieval certainties.

The new culture of modern Europe was constructed on a quite different pattern of assumptions. It began with the recognition that culture is not an absolute but the creation of men, and therefore a variable and conventional product of changing conditions and shifting human needs. This change in the understanding of culture began in later medieval nominalism and Renaissance humanism, which collaborated, however unwittingly, in setting the West on a new path. For both movements language ceased to link the mind with ultimate reality and so to identify the objective boundaries defining existence.

Human culture was thus seen to consist simply in those matters that men (or a particular group of men) could agree on; its boundaries, having only a human character, could therefore no longer claim absolute respect.[97] Renaissance rhetoric was accordingly valued for its plasticity, its ability to flow into and through every area of experience, to disregard and cross inherited boundaries as though they had no real existence, and to create new but always malleable structures of its own. In both nominalism and humanism the word, now humanized, created its own human cosmos out of crude experience.

An important consequence of this humanization was a more modest approach to the kind of cosmos man could discern in chaos, that is, to the scope of culture. Since his culture was simply the product of his own creative impulses, it no longer seemed possible for man to make every dimension of reality permanently intelligible or to comprehend the whole under the same broad categories. The isolated proverb, the *pensée,* the familiar essay, became favorite vehicles for the transmission of human wisdom. The autonomous painting of modern art is a nice symbol of the new ways of culture formation; a painting is a distinctly bounded little universe, the product of deliberate choices among infinite possibilities, a little area of order separated by its own boundaries from the chaos without. Thus, in place of one overarching cosmos we now encounter a range of uncoordinated and often minuscule structures representing a limited order whose plausibility is only aesthetic or practical. A political construction, for example, could now no longer be justified by its conformity to the order of the heavens, a principle that had achieved few practical benefits, but only by its results. It should therefore also be apparent that this new culture is significant not only for its own novel characteristics but also for its new understanding of culture as such. It made possible the conception of *cultures,* each relative to its own time and place, as distinguished from *Culture.*

In addition, quantity now tended to be substituted for quality as the essential principle of orientation; more-or-less, which recognized no impassable boundaries between nothing and infinity, for the either-or suggested by the Aristotelian law of contradiction. The practical foundation for this development was supplied by the growing importance of numerical calculation to artisans and merchants; the numerical arts were the climax of a boy's education in mercantile communities, and their general value for the interpretation of experience was recognized. As the banker Giovanni Rucellai remarked of arithmetic, "It equips and spurs the mind to examine subtle matters."[98] Mathematical models broadly invaded fourteenth-century philosophy.[99]

That the practical resort to number implied a cultural revolution was by no means immediately clear, and its significance was for some time obscured by the sublimation of quantitative approaches to experience into a philosophical mathematics that sought to renew the ontological foundations of the crumbling traditional structure. In this view number became God's language in the book of nature. Salutati insisted on the indispensability of mathematics to theology; as another humanist proclaimed, "Mathematics raises us, prostrate on the earth, to the sky."[100]

But the growing reliance on measurement and number also provided a means of orientation when qualitative boundaries were disintegrating and all things had become, in a new sense, relative. The mathematician could begin at any point in the welter of the phenomenal world, by measurement in units of his own devising define its relation to other phenomena, and so, like the artist in words or in paint, describe an order in the universe (if not *the* order *of* the universe), in accordance with his chosen purposes. The practical meaning of the change is apparent in the new science of probability, for the calculation of probabilities might now present itself as man's best guide through an indeterminate universe. Montaigne, as part of his rejection of the inherited dogmatism that had so disrupted his world, proposed to base life instead on probability;[101] Pascal's notion of the wager applied the principle even to salvation.[102] For probability could provide some basis for choice when the old qualitative boundaries had disappeared and give some relief from the terror induced by "the eternal silence of these infinite spaces."

Pascal seems to have grasped the new situation in a general way, and there are hints of such general understanding elsewhere: for example, in Guicciardini's observation that fortune, that ubiquitous symbol of chaos in human affairs, is angry with those who seek to limit (that is, to impose boundaries on) her dominion.[103] The renewed emphasis on faith, among Catholics as well as Protestants, also reflects some insight into the new situation; a righteousness defined by works is a righteousness largely dependent on culture, and in this context justification by faith alone may be interpreted as a radical solution to the problem of the unreliability of culture. But of all the thinkers in the period of transition from medieval to modern culture, Nicholas of Cusa seems to have discerned most clearly what was happening and to have made the most positive attempt to establish human culture on a new basis. Nourished by both nominalism and humanism, he praised mathematics extravagantly, seeing in it a resource for the reorientation of thought to a universe no longer intelligible in traditional terms. For Cusanus the pursuit of ontological reality that had characterized Western philosophy in the course of its long previous history had come to nothing. In cosmology, to which he gave particular attention, this meant that the notion of either a fixed center or an external boundary of the universe was illusory. But the point had larger implications; it suggested the indeterminacy of the entire phenomenal world, and the construction of man's conceptual universe became simply a project of the autonomous and creative human mind, and especially of its capacity for measurement. In this light all "reality" was essentially a function of the mathematical relationships between entities with which man, for reasons of his own, happened to concern himself.[104]

And this conception, applied by Cusanus most immediately to space, and eventually applied also to cartography by locating points on a grid of latitudinal and longitudinal parallels, was meanwhile becoming a general principle of cultural articulation. It was also applied, in much the same way, to time, so fundamentally related to anxiety. Time could no longer be a function of the natural and qualitative rhythms of day and night, the seasons, and the years; it was now shaped in accordance with human needs. The hours were numbered according to a conventional scale imposed on an intrinsically formless temporal flow, and their conventional significance was enforced by the ringing of bells. Their content was also practically defined: hours were designated for opening and closing one's place of business, for meetings with other men, for this task and that.[105] And once time, like money, could be measured, it became a precious human asset to be calculatedly exploited, as Alberti's Uncle Giannozzo solemnly advised his nephews, stressing also the novelty of the conception: "Keep these thoughts in your memory. . . . These are not sayings of the philosophers but, like the oracles of Apollo, perfect and holy wisdom such as you will not find in all our books."[106] This, in other words, was nontraditional wisdom.

Time quantified was, like money, related to power; and the same tendency to quantification now intruded itself into political thought in the guise of a concern with balance. Equilibrium became a primary category for analyzing the relations both of states and of the social forces within them; the maintenance of political stability was seen to depend on quasi-mathematical calculation and adaptation rather than on the preservation of a pattern of qualitative relationships. Machiavelli aimed to contain the dangerous energies of the various elements in Florentine society not by rigid boundaries but by systematic provision for their dynamic interaction, through which they might contain each other by the opposition of force to force. And the relativity in this new understanding of the political universe paralleled that in the new cosmology.

It was a commonplace of political discussion that, because the structure of forces varies from people to people, every constitution, every set of laws, must suit the peculiarities of the situation to which it is applied.

Meanwhile, as the social cosmos too threatened to collapse into chaos; as qualitative distinctions in social status were gradually eroded by power, whose increase could be at least roughly measured; and as individuals, no longer defined and protected by traditional social categories, were left increasingly vulnerable to one another, a new set of boundaries was required to protect men from each other. The principle at work here would find expression in the ominous proposition that good fences make good neighbors, a symptom of the new culture that may usefully be contrasted with the open field system of medieval agriculture. And much of the worldly wisdom of the early modern age was directed to building fences. Its complementary emphasis on self-control and vigilance both kept the individual within the boundaries of his self-definition and guarded them against infringement by others;[107] this is the cultural significance of the famous bourgeois anal personality. It also helps to explain the deep revulsion, in this period, against begging. For the Alberti, "I beg" was a phrase peculiarly "hateful to a free man's mind"; whether represented by a wandering friar or a wretched layman, mendicancy posed a radical threat to individual autonomy and challenged the very basis of the new pattern of human relations.[108]

We also encounter hints of the new quantifying mentality in the definition of relationships among individuals. Where the absolute categories of status could no longer establish the relation of each individual to his fellows, men now defined themselves against each other by subtle processes of measurement. Life was a strenuous competition with others to become wiser, richer, more esteemed: a race in which one strove to surpass other men by as many paces as possible. "Honor" itself, the term by which Alberti's Uncle Lionardo evaluated success in life, ceased to be an absolute, to be contrasted with dishonor. He personified it as "a public accountant, just, practical, and prudent in measuring, weighing, considering, evaluating, and assessing everything we do, achieve, think, and desire."[109]

This attitude projected onto the social world that "bookkeeping mentality" often noted in the new mercantile culture, which served not only the needs of business but the deeper psychic needs of men inhabiting a newly problematic universe. Various human contrivances were developed to impose some pattern, when none was otherwise available, on the existence of the individual and his family: books for keeping mercantile accounts, systems for the filing of letters, records of the birth dates of children, plans for the orderly arrangement of household goods.[110] The value of such devices in meeting the immediate needs of life is obvious, but they also had a more profound significance. For the Alberti the keeping of family records had a moral quality; it reflected "the conscientiousness of a father." As Uncle Giannozzo informed his wife, "We should have order and system in all that we do."[111] This does not seem an altogether utilitarian principle.

By such devices postmedieval culture achieved substantial success in reducing anxiety. Its creation of new boundaries focused anxiety on their maintenance and converted it into relatively manageable fears: fear of being late or wasting time, which, translated into the modern work ethic, has been especially effective in holding at bay our more general uneasiness about the meaning of existence; fear that great social and political forces might, uncontained, break out and destroy the precarious balance that makes social existence tolerable; fear lest some relaxation of personal vigilance and control might jeopardize the boundaries that protect man from man; fear of losing out in the competitive business of life. The new culture taught men where to locate particular areas of danger and kept them busy shoring up the various barriers against chaos. And the general dissipation of anxiety by these means also reduced anxiety about death and judgment, the most serious symptom of the failure of the old culture.

The new culture could also reduce anxiety because its relativistic and quantitative principles gave it a measure of control over time. Flexible boundaries could accommodate to contingency and enabled men to construct legal instruments (notable among them wills, contracts, and various types of insurance) to control and shape the future. Practical reason could now impress Alberti as "more powerful than fortune"; planning now seemed "more important than any chance event." "Think well ahead and consider what you are going to need," his Uncle Giannozzo advised, evidently persuaded of the good results of such foresight.[112]

Various characteristics of the culture of early modern Europe attest to the decline of anxiety. One was a growing acceptance of cities, which found Italian expression in Leonardo Bruni's praise of Florence[113] and Botero's *Greatness of Cities*. And if antiurbanism can hardly be said to have died out (for the city has become a perennial symbol of the alarming complexities of modern life), Cowper's "God made the country, and man made the town" is at least no more representative of the eighteenth century than Dr. Johnson's relish of London life. The city was no longer necessarily a focus of anxiety, and Voltaire challenged Pascal's vision of the world as a "dreadful desert island" by pointing to the felicities of urban existence.[114]

But an even more fundamental symptom of the change in mood was the gradual decline of nostalgia for the past. The humanists of Italy began to locate the highest achievements of human civilization at the end rather than the beginning of its development;[115] Castiglione and Machiavelli both expressed reservations about the tendency of mankind to contrast the present unfavorably with the past;[116] writers of the later Renaissance—Pulci, Boiardo, Cervantes—ridiculed that chivalric heroism with which earlier generations had imaginatively identified themselves.[117] The Reformers, perhaps obscurely recognizing not only that Adam fell but that Jesus was betrayed in a garden, may have hinted at the same new conception of time. For Luther man could not be re-formed—that is, restored to an earlier condition—but only forgiven;[118] and Calvin from time to time inveighed against the value of precedent as a barrier against change.[119] Hobbes's famous depiction of natural existence as "solitary, poor, nasty, brutish, and short" was, in context, a radical rejection of the nostalgic mentality of earlier generations, and implicitly a celebration of the new urban culture.[120] Man's true home was no longer in the past but increasingly in the future, whatever it might hold in store. And the growing belief in progress from the later sixteenth century onward attests that thoughts of the future were less and less accompanied by anxiety.

The redefinition of culture on the basis of the new principles was not completed in the early modern period, and the progressive substitution of fluid and relative for absolute and qualitative cultural categories has continued to disorient mankind and to release anxiety. We can see the continuation of the process in the emotional reaction to Darwin's attack on the fixity of species in the nineteenth century, and in the profound anxieties released more recently by the challenge to absolute distinctions of sex, an area in which (perhaps because it is peculiarly fraught with uncertainty) the principles of premodern culture have been unusually durable. And the new culture, precisely because of its own relativism, has never been more than relatively successful in the management of anxiety.

There were, certainly, problems that the structures of modern culture could not solve and might rather intensify. Its strategies, indeed, have sometimes themselves induced a peculiar anxiety, as Saint Teresa re-marked about her own concern with the effective use of time. "If we find ourselves unable to get profit out of a single hour," she noted, "we are impeded from doing so for four. I have a great deal of experience of this. . . . "[121] Even more troubling consequences have come from the need of the individual to adapt to unpredictable circumstances and the changing expectations of others. The needs of survival in a problematic world have tended to alienate the public from any true self or, worse, to require the annihilation of the true for the sake of a social self. Thus, the relation between the boundaries of self-definition and any stable center of the personality have tended to become themselves problematic, and this has been the source of a peculiarly burdensome kind of anxiety in the modern world. Even the artist, his task no longer to discover and illuminate immutable truths but to create some relative cosmos from the chaos that surrounds him, may feel more terror than exuberance as he considers the contingency and fragility of his work. In spite of the impressive accomplishments of postmedieval culture, a higher level of anxiety was now to be a permanent feature of the West.

NOTES

1. As in Auden's *The Age of Anxiety*. For contemporary interest in anxiety, see Fred Berthold, Jr., *The Fear of God: The Role of Anxiety in Contemporary Thought* (New York, 1959).

2. We face here much the same problem as that confronted by Keith Thomas in his treatment of popular culture in *Religion and the Decline of Magic* (London, 1971); cf. his preface, p. x, on "the historian's traditional method of example and counter-example" as "the intellectual equivalent of the bow and arrow in the nuclear age." I am less confident than Thomas that models of scientific advance are applicable to historiography, and I suspect that "example and counter-example" will continue to be necessary to support many kinds of historical judgment, probably including those of greatest interest; but there is a serious methodological problem here.

3. W. H. Dodds, who took the title of his *Pagan and Christian in an Age of Anxiety* (Cambridge, 1965) directly from Auden. Also cf. the second volume of Theodore Zeldin, *France, 1848–1945*, which bears the title *Intellect, Taste and Anxiety* (New York, 1977).

4. Iris Origo, *The Merchant of Prato: Francesco di Marco Datini, 1335–1410* (New York, 1957), esp. her introduction, p. xi; Christian Bec, *Les marchands écrivains: Affaires et humanisme à Florence, 1365–1434* (Paris, 1967), pp. 127–28; P. S. Lewis, *Later Medieval France: The Polity* (London, 1968), pp. 242–45, 273; Philippe Dollinger, *La Hanse* (Paris, 1964), chap. 8; David Herlihy, "Some Psychological and Social Roots of Violence in the Tuscan Cities," in *Violence and Civil Disorder in Italian Cities*, ed. L. Martines (Berkeley and Los Angeles, 1971), p. 149.

5. E. Jane Dempsey Douglass, *Justification in Late Medieval Theology: A Study of John Geiler of Keisersberg* (Leiden, 1966); David C. Steinmetz, *Misericordia Dei: The Theology of Johannes von Staupitz in Its Late Medieval Setting* (Leiden, 1968); Michael Seidlmayer, *Currents of Medieval Thought*, trans. D. Barker (Oxford, 1960); Millard Meiss, *Painting in Florence and Siena after the Black Death: The Arts, Religion and Society in the Mid-Fourteenth Century* (Princeton, 1951); M. B. Becker, "Individualism in the Early Italian Renaissance: Burden and Blessing," *Studies in the Renaissance* 19 (1972): 273–97; E. Delaruelle et al., *L'église au temps du Grand Schisme et de la crise conciliaire*, Histoire de l'Église, vol. XIV (Paris, 1962), vol. 2; Charles Trinkaus, *In Our Image and Likeness: Humanity and Divinity in Italian Humanist Thought* (Chicago, 1970); Heiko Oberman, *Forerunners of the Reformation* (New York, 1966); Jean Delumeau, *Naissance et affirmation de la Réforme* (Paris, 1965); Steven E. Ozment, *The Reformation in the Cities: An Essay on the Appeal of Protestant Ideas to Sixteenth Century Society* (New Haven, 1975); A. G. Dickens, *The English Reformation* (London, 1964); Michael Walzer, *The Revolution of the Saints: A Study in the Origins of Radical Politics* (Cambridge, Mass., 1965).

6. Eugenio Garin, *Science and Civic Life in the Italian Renaissance*, trans. Peter Munz (New York, 1969), pp. 2–3.

7. Lynn White, Jr., "Death and the Devil," in *The Darker Vision of the Renaissance: Beyond the Fields of Reason*, ed. Robert S. Kinsman (Berkeley and Los Angeles, 1974), pp. 25–46. The germ of this interpretation may perhaps be discerned in Huizinga's *Waning of the Middle Ages*, which H. Stuart Hughes has read, though Huizinga did not himself use such language, as a study in the management of "unbearable anxiety" (*History as Art and as Science: Twin Vistas on the Past* [New York, 1964], p. 54). But the notion seems also imbedded in Burckhardtian individualism; cf. the extreme case of Filippo Maria Visconti, whose personality is described in *The Civilization of the Renaissance in Italy*, trans. S. G. C. Middlemore (London, 1944), pp. 24–25.

8. Robert S. Kinsman, in *The Darker Vision of the Renaissance*, Introduction, p. 14. This medieval condition *may*, of course, be related to modern "anxiety."

9. This emerges from a comparison of passages in the recent translation of the *Institutes* by Ford Lewis Battles (London, 1961), where the word "anxiety" appears, with Calvin's own Latin and French. See especially II, viii, 3; III, ii, 17 and 23; III, xxiv, 6.

10. *Petrarch's Secret or The Soul's Conflict with Passion: Three Dialogues between Himself and S. Augustine*, trans. William H. Draper (London, 1911), p. 56; *The Imitation of Christ*, trans. Leo Sherley-Price (London, 1952), p. 28.

11. *The Memoirs of Philippe de Commynes*, trans. Isabelle Cazeaux, 2 vols. (Columbia, S.C., 1969–73), 1:230.

12. *The Family in Renaissance Florence*, trans. Renée Neu Watkins (Columbia, S.C., 1969), examples on pp. 49, 78, 58, 47, 88, 41, 191, 46, 54–55.

13. *The Complete Works of Saint Teresa of Jesus*, trans. E. Allison Peers, 3 vols. (London, 1950), 1:5, 75, 78, 257; *The Collected Works of St. John of the Cross*, trans. Kieran Kavanaugh and Otilio Rodriguez (Washington, D.C., 1973), pp. 88, 594, 619, 620.

14. The following generalizations are based on, among other works, M. D. Chenu, *La théologie au douzième siècle* (Paris, 1957); R. W. Southern, *The Making*

of the Middle Ages (New Haven, 1953), and *Medieval Humanism and Other Studies* (New York, 1970); John Mundy, *Europe in the High Middle Ages, 1150–1309* (London, 1973); Jacques Le Goff, *Les intellectuels au Moyen Age* (Paris, 1957). The theological dimension of this optimism is particularly well described by Gerhart B. Ladner, "The Life of the Mind in the Christian West around the Year 1200," in *The Year 1200: A Symposium* (New York, 1975), pp. 4–6. That the *mentalité* even of peasants may have been relatively relaxed is suggested by Emmanuel Le Roy Ladurie, *Montaillou, village occitan de 1294–1324* (Paris, 1976).

15. In the words of Rolandino Passaggeri, quoted by Mundy, *Europe in the High Middle Ages,* p. 486.

16. "It is ful faire a man to bere him evene / For al-day meteth men at unset stevene" (lines 1523–24). I quote the modern English version of Nevill Coghill (London, 1960).

17. As most recently by Paul Lawrence Rose, *The Italian Renaissance of Mathematics: Studies on Humanists and Mathematicians from Petrarch to Galileo* (Geneva, 1975), p. 7. See more generally Carlo Cipolla, *Clocks and Culture 1300–1700* (New York, 1967).

18. Quoted by John Larner, *Culture and Society in Italy, 1290–1420* (London, 1971), p. 28.

19. Calvin, *Commentaries on the Book of Genesis,* trans. John King (Edinburgh, 1847), 1:84; Pascal, *Pensées,* no. 5 (in the arrangement in the translation of E. F. Trotter [New York, 1941]).

20. *Epistolae familiares,* X, 1, trans. David Thompson, in *Petrarch: An Anthology* (New York, 1971), p. 101.

21. *De ingenuis moribus,* trans. William Harrison Woodward, in *Vittorino da Feltre and Other Humanist Educators* (Cambridge, 1897), p. 112.

22. *Gargantua and Pantagruel,* trans. Jacques Le Clercq (New York, 1944), p. 71.

23. Quoted by Origo, *Merchant of Prato,* p. 187.

24. Leon Battista Alberti, *Opere volgari,* ed. Cecil Grayson, 3 vols. (Bari, 1960–73), 1:77. I use the translation of Watkins, cited above, n. 12.

25. Nicholas Mann, "Petrarch's Role as Moralist in Fifteenth-Century France," in *Humanism in France at the End of the Middle Ages and in the Early Renaissance,* ed. A. H. T. Levi (Manchester, 1970), pp. 6–28.

26. *Discorsi,* II, xxix. I follow the translation of Leslie J. Walker (New Haven, 1950).

27. Cf. Peter L. Berger and Thomas Luckmann, *The Social Construction of Reality: A Treatise in the Sociology of Knowledge* (Garden City, N.Y., 1966), pp. 27, 101. For a penetrating discussion of this point in theological terms, cf. Peter Knauer, *Gott, Wort, Glaube: Ein theologischer Grundkurs* (Frankfurt/Main, 1973), p. 157: "If one's own transitoriness is the final certainty, this means that all earthly certainty is finally dependent on complete uncertainty." Knauer's extended remarks on this point, a commentary on Hebrews 2:14ff., were called to my attention by the Reverend Frederick McGinness, S. J.

28. *Imitation,* pp. 58–59; cf. p. 66: "Always remember your end, and that lost time never returns."

29. See, for example, Huizinga's *Waning of the Middle Ages*; the works

by Seidlmayer, Meiss, and White cited above, n. 5; Alberto Tenenti, *Il senso della morte e l'amore della vita nel Rinascimento: Francia e Italia* (Turin, 1957); T. S. R. Boase, *Death in the Middle Ages: Mortality, Judgment and Remembrance* (London, 1972).

30. *De otio religioso,* in Thompson, *Petrarch: An Anthology,* pp. 153–54; *Epistolae familiares,* XIX, 6, quoted by Renée Neu Watkins, "Petrarch and the Black Death: From Fear to Monuments," *Studies in the Renaissance* 19 (1972): 215.

31. *Memoirs,* 2:433.

32. Commentary on Hebrews 2:15, in Calvin's *New Testament Commentaries,* trans. W. B. Johnston, 12 vols. (Grand Rapids, 1963), 12:31.

33. Douglass, *Justification in Late Medieval Theology,* p. 176; Susan Snyder, "The Left Hand of God: Despair in Medieval and Renaissance Tradition," *Studies in the Renaissance* 12 (1965): 41.

34. Cf. Dickens, *The English Reformation,* pp. 5–6.

35. Seidlmayer, *Currents of Medieval Thought,* p. 141; Dickens, *The English Reformation,* p. 12.

36. For this function of the Medici Chapel, see L. D. Ettlinger, "The Liturgical Function of Michelangelo's Medici Chapel," *Mitteilungen des Kunsthistorischen Instituts in Florenz* 22 (1978): 287–304.

37. Quoted by Ozment, *The Reformation in the Cities,* p. 28.

38. Quoted by Watkins, "Petrarch and the Black Death," p. 209.

39. See Douglass, *Justification in Late Medieval Theology,* p. 153, for the case of Geiler.

40. Quoted by Charles Trinkaus, "Italian Humanism and the Problem of 'Structures of Conscience,' " *Journal of Medieval and Renaissance Studies* 2 (1972): 28.

41. Letter to his father, 21 Nov. 1521, in *Luther: Letters of Spiritual Counsel,* ed. Theodore G. Tappert, Library of Christian Classics, vol. XVIII (London, 1955), p. 259.

42. *Lectures on Genesis,* ed. Jaroslav Pelikan, 8 vols. (St. Louis, 1958–66), 1:287.

43. Letter to Hess, Nov. 1527, in *Letters of Spiritual Counsel,* pp. 237–38.

44. *Institutes,* II, viii, 3; I, xvii, 11; I, xvii, 7; I, vi, 1; III, ii, 17; III, ii, 21. I use the translation of Ford Lewis Battles, cited above, n. 9.

45. *Life,* in *Works,* 1:236.

46. J. G. A. Pocock, *The Machiavellian Moment: Florentine Political Thought and the Atlantic Republican Tradition* (Princeton, 1975), p. 28, offers interesting remarks on the anxiety of rulers. For merchants, see n. 4 above. The vast literature of the period on friendship, a common concern of Petrarch, Commynes, Erasmus, Montaigne, and Bacon, among others, suggests that this aspect of life had become a problem; cf. Lionel Trilling, *Sincerity and Authenticity* (Cambridge, Mass., 1971). On sexual anxiety, see Herlihy, "Psychological and Social Roots of Violence," p. 134, and J. R. Hale, "Violence in the Late Middle Ages: A Background," in Martines, *Violence and Civil Disorder,* pp. 28–29. The ancient commonplace that denied the delights of love to the busy man was revived, as in Donne's "Break of Day": "The poor, the foul, the false, love can / Admit, but not the busied man."

47. Cf. Petrarch: "Shall I pride myself on much reading of books, which

with a little wisdom has brought me a thousand anxieties?" (*Secretum* in *Opere,* ed. Giovanni Ponte [Milan, 1968], p. 482); I follow the Draper translation, cited above, n. 10. See also Thomas à Kempis, *Imitation,* p. 28, and Alberti, *Opere volgari,* 1:247. In these illustrations, as in others presented here, one can detect echoes from such classical sources as Seneca; but the point, it seems to me, is that their Renaissance readers found them eminently relevant to their own predicament.

48. Alberti, *Opere volgari,* 1:161, 182.

49. These reflections were stimulated by an unpublished paper of my colleague Gene A. Brucker, "The Problem of Death in Fourteenth-Century Europe."

50. Quoted by Huizinga, *Waning of the Middle Ages,* p. 36. The italics here and in what follows are mine.

51. *Epistolae familiares,* XI, 7, and XIII, 6, in Thompson, *Petrarch: An Anthology,* pp. 107, 119.

52. Nicolas de Clamanges, quoted by Lewis, *Later Medieval France,* pp. 294–95.

53. *History of Florence,* trans. M. Walter Dunne (New York, 1960), p. 47.

54. In "Cyclops, or the Gospel Bearer," *The Colloquies of Erasmus,* trans. Craig R. Thompson (Chicago, 1965), p. 422.

55. In "Du jeune Caton," *Essais,* ed. Maurice Rat, 3 vols. (Paris, n.d.), 1:259–63.

56. See C. T. Davis, "Il Buon Tempo Antico," in *Florentine Studies,* ed. N. Rubinstein (London, 1968), pp. 45–69; and, for the general point, Harry Levin, *The Myth of the Golden Age in the Renaissance* (Bloomington, 1969). Huizinga has much on this point, passim.

57. *Memoirs,* 1:169.

58. Francesco Datini, quoted in Origo, *Merchant of Prato,* p. 68.

59. *Lectures on Genesis,* 2:65.

60. Letter to Boccaccio, 13 Mar. 1363, in *Lettere senili,* ed. Giuseppe Fracassetti (Florence, 1892), 1:69–70.

61. Quoted in Bec, *Les marchands écrivains,* p. 60.

62. In *Manifestations of Discontent in Germany on the Eve of the Reformation,* ed. Gerald Strauss (Bloomington, 1971), p. 21.

63. Johann Agricola, in ibid., p. 119.

64. *Lectures on Genesis,* 1:62.

65. See Jaroslav Pelikan's remarks in connection with Luther's attack on this movement, ibid., 1:211.

66. *De regno Christi,* trans. Lowell J. Satre, in *Melanchthon and Bucer,* ed. Wilhelm Pauck, Library of Christian Classics, vol. XIX (London, 1969), pp. 339–40. Similar sentiments were expressed by Luther in *To the Christian Nobility of the German Nation,* Art. 27, items 2–3.

67. In *Manifestations of Discontent,* p. 119.

68. Cf. *Secretum,* p. 488.

69. *Colloquies,* p. 48.

70. Cf. Garin, *Science and Civic Life,* p. 83.

71. Letter to Pirckheimer, in *Manifestations of Discontent,* p. 194.

72. There is much on this point in Trilling, *Sincerity and Authenticity.*

73. Datini in Origo, *Merchant of Prato,* p. 115.

74. Quoted by Gene A. Brucker, *The Civic World of Early Renaissance Florence* (Princeton, 1977), pp. 22–23.

75. *Della famiglia*, p. 297.

76. *Memoirs*, 1:265.

77. Quoted by Nancy S. Struever, *The Language of History in the Renaissance: Rhetoric and Historical Consciousness in Florentine Humanism* (Princeton, 1970), pp. 165–66.

78. Cf. Jack Goody, "Death and the Interpretation of Culture: A Bibliographic Overview," in *Death in America,* ed. David E. Stannard (Philadelphia, 1975), p. 7.

79. Students of an analogous transition in the modern world provide some support for this conclusion. The novel anxiety appearing among the populations of the new cities in developing countries seems to be a result not so much of the new urban experience directly as of the loss of a traditional culture. So Ari Kiev, *Transcultural Psychiatry* (New York, 1972), pp. 9–10, summarizes his conclusions: "Particularly stressful . . . is the loss of culture that is experienced by the educated yet still semi-primitive marginal African, who has become a member of a partially urbanized and Westernized society. Having renounced his old culture, yet so far having failed to assimilate the new, he is particularly prone to malignant anxiety. . . . The migration to the city removes the group protection, the psychological 'prop' of the African; he therefore finds himself psychologically isolated and vulnerable."

80. See especially Claude Lévi-Strauss, *The Savage Mind* (Chicago, 1966), passim; and Mary Douglas, *Implicit Meanings: Essays in Anthropology* (London, 1975), esp. p. 57.

81. For my understanding of culture as a mechanism for the management of anxiety, I am indebted to Berger and Luckmann, *Social Construction of Reality*; Clifford Geertz, *The Interpretation of Cultures* (New York, 1973); and above all to Mary Douglas, *Purity and Danger: An Analysis of Concepts of Pollution and Taboo* (London, 1966), and *Natural Symbols* (London, 1972).

82. I am here applying the conception of religions as maps through and beyond life developed in John Bowker, *The Sense of God: Sociological, Anthropological and Psychological Approaches to the Origin of the Sense of God* (Oxford, 1973). Bowker's idea of "compounds of limitation" is also relevant to the argument here.

83. Cf. Traiano Boccalini, *Ragguagli di Parnasso e scritti minori,* ed. Luigi Firpo, 3 vols. (Bari, 1948), 1:177–80.

84. *Secretum*, p. 516.

85. Especially in *Purity and Danger*.

86. *Secretum*, p. 458.

87. Quoted by Jerrold E. Seigel, *Rhetoric and Philosophy in Renaissance Humanism* (Princeton, 1968), p. 74.

88. Quoted by Le Goff, *Les intellectuels au Moyen Age,* p. 154.

89. In Quirinus Breen, *Christinnity and Humanism: Studies in the History of Ideas* (Grand Rapids, 1968), p. 57.

90. *Institutes*, III, iv, 1.

91. Quoted by Alexandre Koyré, *From the Closed World to the Infinite Universe* (New York, 1958), p. 44.

92. For the later Renaissance, see my "Changing Assumptions of Later Re-

naissance Culture," *Viator* 7 (1976): 421–40. On the penitential system, cf. Ozment, *Reformation in the Cities*; and Thomas N. Tentler, *Sin and Confession on the Eve of the Reformation* (Princeton, 1977).

93. In Jean Gerson, *Selections*, ed. Steven E. Ozment, *Textus minores*, vol. 38 (Leiden, 1969), p. 41.

94. *Pensées*, nos. 206, 72, 143, 146, 131, 692.

95. *Lettres philosophiques*, no. 25.

96. On the conception of a *Protestant* Counter-Reformation, cf. Delumeau, *Naissance et affirmation de la Réforme*, pp. 360–61, though it is here interpreted rather narrowly as a reaction against Calvinism. Nietzsche understood the phenomenon more deeply as a repudiation of the original Protestant opposition of faith to reason: i.e., to the structures of human culture; cf. Walter Kaufmann, *Nietzsche*, 3d ed. (New York, 1968), pp. 352–53.

97. The general point is succinctly stated by Struever, *Language of History*, esp. pp. 44–45.

98. Quoted by Michael Baxandall, *Painting and Experience in Fifteenth-Century Italy* (Oxford, 1972), p. 94. Baxandall is especially useful for the general importance of mathematics in Italian urban culture. See also Rose, *Italian Renaissance of Mathematics*, chap. 1, on mathematics in humanist education, and Larner, *Culture and Society in Italy*, p. 28, for general remarks on the growing importance of quantification in Italy. But the point was already touched on by Burckhardt, *Civilization of the Renaissance in Italy*, p. 46.

99. Cf. Damasus Trapp, "Augustinian Theology of the 14th Century," *Augustinianum* 6 (1956): 148.

100. Cited by Rose, *Italian Renaissance of Mathematics*, pp. 12, 16.

101. In "Apologie de Raimond Sebond," *Essais*, II.

102. *Pensées*, nos. 187, 233. Pascal also denounced (though recognizing its influence) the "probabilism" of Jesuit casuistry in no. 917: "Take away *probability*, and you can no longer please the world; give *probability*, and you can no longer displease it." The relationship of Jesuit probabilism to the new mathematics is far from clear; cf. Benjamin Nelson, " 'Probabilists,' 'Anti-Probabilists' and the Quest for Certainty in the 16th and 17th Centuries," *Actes du Xe congrès international d'histoire des sciences* (Paris, 1965), 1:269–73. But even here habits of numerical calculation seem to be at work. On the history of probability theory and its peculiar importance for "modern" culture, see Ian Hacking, *The Emergence of Probability* (Cambridge, 1975).

103. *Ricordi*, C20.

104. For my understanding of the significance of Cusanus, in addition to Ernst Cassirer's classic *Individuum und Kosmos in der Philosophie der Renaissance* (1927), I owe much to the doctoral dissertation of Ronald Levao, "The Idea of Fiction and the Concept of Mind in the Renaissance" (Berkeley, 1978), chap. 1.

105. Cf. Bec, *Les marchands écrivains*, p. 318.

106. *Della famiglia*, p. 170.

107. Ibid., pp. 293–94, for an example of this general concern.

108. Ibid., p. 54.

109. Ibid., p. 151.

110. On the systematic mentality and the concern for accuracy reflected in

mercantile records, see Armando Sapori, *The Italian Merchant in the Middle Ages,* trans. Patricia Ann Kennen (New York, 1970), pp. 29–31, 105; and for a hint of the more general significance of these qualities cf. the advice of a Venetian merchant to his son that he should frequently review his records because "he who does not frequently review his expenditures believes what is not true" (quoted in James C. Davis, *A Venetian Family and Its Fortune, 1500–1900* [Philadelphia, 1975], p. 26).

111. *Della famiglia,* pp. 119–20, 239.

112. Ibid., pp. 9 (prologue), 237.

113. See Hans Baron, *The Crisis of the Early Italian Renaissance,* rev. ed. (Princeton, 1966), esp. pp. 191–211.

114. As in part 6 of *Lettres philosophiques,* no. 25.

115. Noted by Struever, *Language of History,* p. 152.

116. In their epistles to the second books, respectively, of *Il Cortegiano* and *Discorsi.*

117. Cf. Huizinga, *Waning of the Middle Ages,* p. 80.

118. Cf. Steven E. Ozment, "The University and the Church: Patterns of Reform in Jean Gerson," *Medievalia et Humanistica,* n.s. 1 (1970): 121, which uses this point to bring out the essential difference between medieval and Protestant conceptions of reform.

119. As, for example, *Institutes,* epistle, and III, v, 10.

120. Cf. Levin, *Myth of the Golden Age,* pp. 30–31.

121. *Life,* in *Works,* 1:69–70.

7   The Politics of Commynes

This essay originated in a seminar at Harvard in the spring of 1947 conducted by Myron P. Gilmore, who eventually directed my dissertation. It reflected, only a year after my discharge from the army, what would be my constant concern to place the results of a particular investigation in the largest possible context of significance. The essay was published in the Journal of Modern History *23 (1951), 315–328, and is reprinted here with the permission of the publisher.*

•   •   •

A major problem for the historian of political thought in the period of the Renaissance is to trace the transition from the religious, idealistic, or constitutional ideas of the Middle Ages to the secular, realistic, or absolutist views of the early modern era.[1] A decade ago Felix Gilbert discussed this problem in connection with humanist political thought and its background in Italian political conditions.[2] But this evolution in political ideas was not confined to Italy, and this article proposes to examine the process in a writer from across the Alps, Philippe de Commynes.

Commynes has certain advantages as a case study in intellectual transition. A period on its way to great changes is generally characterized by the persistence of traditional forms whose content has altered; and the professional intellectual is perhaps too sensitive to the requirements of consistency. Hence the search for the origins of general changes in attitude may sometimes most profitably be carried on among unsystematic and informal thinkers. Commynes was no scholar; he was ignorant of Latin,[3] and his *Mémoires* are almost entirely free of classical allusion. His reading was confined to vernacular histories and to translations of

190

a few classics, such as Livy and the *City of God*.[4] And his own work is in no sense a formal treatise. It was ostensibly written to serve merely as material for a history of Louis XI, to be written in Latin by Angelo Cato, archbishop of Vienne.[5] In fact, however, Commynes certainly conceived also of an independent use for his *Mémoires*; and this is the only reason for considering him as a political thinker at all. "I judge," he wrote, "that simple and vulgar fellows will not bother to read these memoirs; but princes or courtiers will, I think, find in them some good lessons."[6] His aim is thus the instruction of princes, and his work belongs to the general class of mirrors and guidebooks for rulers.

The *Mémoires* of Commynes are mainly a historical narrative and describe, chronologically, events in which the author was concerned. The first six books deal with the period of Louis XI and Charles the Bold; the last two take up again, more than a decade later, to describe the Italian venture of Charles VIII. Into the narrative framework are woven comments on men and events whose value for the historian depends as much on their suggestiveness as on their intrinsic meaning. Thus the methodological problem in getting at the political ideas of Commynes is considerable, for they must somehow be sorted out from the unsystematic statements and allusions buried in the narrative. This informality has the advantage of permitting a more intimate acquaintance with the writer, so that his feelings and desires, his political emotions, so to speak, as well as his explicit convictions, are in evidence. It presents also, however, the usual disadvantages of lack of system. Important questions for the formal theorist, such as the problem of the origins of government, are left unsettled. Lack of system also exposes the student to the temptation to achieve understanding by the imposition of schemes and categories which have little basis except in his own mind.

This has, indeed, been one of the major barriers to any clear understanding of Commynes in the past. Thus nineteenth-century liberals like V.-L. Bourrilly[7] and Paul Janet[8] discovered modernity in Commynes by reading history backward from their own political ideals. And the most famous of all modern essays on Commynes, that of Sainte-Beuve, though it acutely recognizes his pragmatic attitude, is also perhaps the worst offender in its complete isolation of Commynes from his own historical context.[9] There are elements of modernity in Commynes, but there is much besides.

Commynes's opinions were closely connected with the circumstances of his life. His family was of recent middle-class origin: his grandfather, Colard Vanden Clyte, was a prominent citizen of Ypres, who supported the ducal against the communal party and was rewarded by a position as counselor to Louis the Bad. He was also given by his sovereign a wife who brought with her the lands of the ancient family of Commynes. But Philippe de Commynes, born about 1447, was the son of a younger son and inherited nothing but debts.[10] His position at the Burgundian court was thus based on his father's professional services and on his own abilities, not on family or wealth.

In the service of Charles the Bold, Commynes first met Louis XI at Péronne in 1468, and four years later he deserted Burgundy for the service of France. Commynes never offers an explanation for this act, but adequate reasons are not hard to see. He was ambitious but could rise only by making himself useful. Charles, however, was proud and self-reliant, neglecting all opinions but his own;[11] hence the usefulness to him of an intelligent man was limited. Louis, on the other hand, promised Commynes both responsibility and the status which he could scarcely have hoped for from Charles. Besides gifts of money and a pension, he received from Louis the huge feudal principality of Talmont, which had authority over seventeen hundred subfiefs; and within a few years he was also given a noble wife, whose dowry included the barony of D'Argenton.[12] Commynes's new responsibilities included important diplomatic functions and service as the most intimate sort of royal adviser. It has been suggested that some of the political ideas in the *Mémoires* and even some of the phraseology are Louis's;[13] perhaps the king was paying as much for a ready ear as for able counsel.

Up to this point Commynes's career seems to have been that of a self-made man and, indeed, of the new and modern professional servant of government. One might thus expect him to side with the monarchy in its tendencies to absolute and bureaucratic control and against the principles of traditional feudal institutions. Yet the very rewards which Commynes received for his professional services to the king were such as to identify his interests with the traditional forces against which the monarchy was contending. And his achievement of status in the traditional social order explains what would appear to be a contradiction in the life of Commynes; for the Commynes who had been the loyal follower of Louis XI was to spend several months in one of his late master's famous iron cages because of his activities as a supporter of rebellious feudal activity.[14] After the minority of Charles VIII he returned to public life, but he was never again entirely trusted.[15] The *Mémoires* also suggest at times the exaggerated consciousness of status of the parvenu, as when Commynes expresses his contempt for the political capacities of the Flemish townsmen—of whom his grandfather had been one.[16]

"Commynes wants to be useful," Bourrilly pointed out,[17] and in a sense his *Mémoires* serve to extend in time and space the value of his professional services as a counselor to princes. Written in his retirement, the *Mémoires* also perhaps served to compensate the author for the loss of past importance.[18] He has constantly in mind the practical value of his own intelligence as an aid to princely government, and the parallel between this aspect of the work and his own career should not be overlooked. Many of the didactic passages in the book are consciously the sort of comment that an able adviser might make to a young prince at the scene of action. Often they are simply practical suggestions with little general implication, as when, in connection with the siege of Liège, Commynes points out the folly of making sallies from besieged towns.[19] Or, again, he gives detailed advice on diplomacy in terms which reflect his own experience and seem almost a wistful application for employment:

> When [a prince] wants to conclude peace, he ought to employ the most faithful servants he has, men of middle years, in order that their feebleness may not lead them to some dishonorable bargain. . . . He ought also to employ men who have received some favor or benefit from him and, above all, men of wisdom; for a fool never profits a man. And his treaties ought to be negotiated afar off rather than near; and when the ambassadors return, he ought to see them in private, or in the presence of only a few, so that, if their news be alarming, he can instruct them how to answer any questions. For everybody wants to hear the news from those who return from such business.[20]

A useful point of departure for a survey of Commynes's political ideas is his estimate of the government of the Papal States. Except for the disorders produced by the rivalry of the Colonna and the Orsini, says Commynes, the territories of the pope are "the best governed in the whole world, for they do not pay *tailles* nor any other taxes" and the rulers "are always wise and well advised."[21] Regardless of its historical accuracy, this description suggests both the elements and the conflicts contained in Commynes's ideal. He desires a state in which a wise prince, assisted by able counselors, preserves peace and order, without having to levy taxes. Commynes's politics may be summarized in terms of these four elements, and major aspects of its significance in terms of the questions which they raise. For how are peace and order possible without taxation, and what is the necessity for counselors when the ruler is wise?

The first requirement of good government, then, is the wise prince;

but in what does princely wisdom consist? Commynes begins his definition by generalizing from the characters of the princes he knew; and
we must answer this question first by considering his two great masters:
Louis XI, the type of wisdom; and Charles the Bold, the type of folly.
Commynes compares them consciously and in almost these balanced
terms. Charles for him seems to have been a simple man, whose basic
flaw was pride. He pictures him exulting on the field of Montlhéry:

> All that day Charolais stayed on the field, rejoicing greatly,
> regarding the glory of the victory as entirely his own, a thought
> which has since cost him very dear; for henceforth he regarded
> no man's advice, but relied on himself alone. Whereas before he
> had hated war and everything connected with it, his ideas now
> changed; for he continued in it until his death. And by it his life
> was ended and his house destroyed, or at least badly desolated.
>   Three great and wise princes, his predecessors, had raised him
> high; and few kings besides the king of France were more pow-
> erful than he. For large and beautiful cities no ruler surpassed
> him. But no man should take too much on himself, especially a
> great prince: he should acknowledge that favors and good for-
> tune come from God.[22]

This judgment is, of course, generally consistent with the moral emphasis
of Christianity; on the other hand, it happens to coincide nicely with
Commynes's personal grudge against Charles.

The character of Louis XI obviously fascinated Commynes, and again
his generalized judgment happens to agree with his choice of masters.
The contrast is clear: unlike Charles, Louis was wise enough to be humble, and he would go to great lengths to persuade men (presumably like
Commynes) into his service; he was, furthermore, "naturally a friend to
men of middle estate,"[23] as well as a great respecter of learning.[24] Unlike
Charles, he avoided battles, yet not from fear (though he had wisdom
enough to know when to be afraid) but from his understanding of the
folly of risking his fortunes by battle when his ends could be accomplished by other means.[25] Time after time Commynes praises Louis for
his wisdom or his skill: he was "the most skilful prince in the world in
the art of dividing men";[26] he was "wiser in making treaties than any
other prince of his time."[27]

On one occasion Commynes makes the same comparison in abstract
terms, though here some bitter memory has evidently led him to drop
the eulogistic note:

> I have seen princes of two sorts: one so subtle and so very suspicious that it is impossible to live with them without being suspected; the other sort trust their servants well enough but are themselves so stupid and ignorant of their own affairs that they can't tell who serve them well and who badly. This latter sort are changed in a moment from love to hate or hate to love. And, although there are few of either sort who are good or constant, I should always prefer to live under the wise than under the foolish, because there are more ways of avoiding their displeasure and acquiring their favor. For with the ignorant there is no way, since one deals not with them but with their servants.[28]

But, when he is not its object, Commynes expresses another view of the wisdom of suspicion for princes.[29]

Commynes frequently emphasizes the importance of education for the prince, and he attributes part of Louis's success to the quality of his youthful education.[30] For learning is a shortcut to experience; the wise and learned prince cannot be abused by a learned rogue but will be able to recognize and so employ the best and wisest men about him.[31] Thus, while Commynes seems to identify *learning* with *wisdom* (perhaps not unusual for a man not himself learned), he clearly distinguishes between learning and virtue. And he suggests that a learned but wicked man is particularly dangerous as a royal adviser, since he is likely to "have a law or a history on the tip of his tongue for any occasion, and even the best will be twisted into an evil sense."[32] On the content of the princely education, Commynes has only one suggestion: the prince should read history: "One of the best ways of making a man wise is to have him read ancient history, which will teach him how to behave himself, defend himself, and carry out any enterprise wisely by the example of our ancestors. For our life is so short that experience is not enough to teach so much."[33] If the ideal prince of Commynes is not necessarily an Erasmian philosopher, he is at least a practical humanist.

The religious sanctions of political authority, which medieval theorists could almost never forget, interest Commynes little. On one occasion he states that his denunciation of evil rulers is justified by "the great responsibility and high office God has given them in this world."[34] Another passage insists on the moral obligations of the prince, informs his reader that only a beast is unaware of the difference between good and evil, and concludes that if a prince occasionally mistakes evil for good and rewards it, he should be careful not to condemn the principle on which he acted, along with the mistake.[35] But these are isolated passages. On the whole, the interest of Commynes is in the practical wisdom of the prince—his caution and calculation, his cunning in diplomacy, his knowledge of men, and his grasp of the practical problems of government. The modernity of this emphasis scarcely needs comment.

The nature of wisdom is presumably about the same for counselors as for princes; and what is significant in Commynes's emphasis is perhaps the hint contained in it that no prince is quite adequate to rule by himself. Yet the traditional element suggested here should be interpreted only in the light of Commynes's career. As a former counselor, he was bound to defend the importance of his own function. What is perhaps more important is his emphasis on the professional qualifications of royal counselors. Nowhere does he suggest that the basis on which the counselor should be selected ought to be anything but wisdom and ability. He condemns both Edward of England and Charles VIII, as well as Charles the Bold, for their neglect of "wise and experienced" advisers.[36] His emphasis on the importance of wise counsel for the prince is one of the most frequently recurring themes in the *Mémoires*.

Commynes nowhere attempts an abstract statement of the ends of government, but he scarcely needs to be explicit about his longing for peace and order. Numerous passages illustrate this desire, which was general in a France exhausted by the Hundred Years' War and worn out by feudal disorders. In a list of the wrongs committed by tyrants, Commynes lists the quartering of soldiery on the people and complains of the suffering caused by these irregular and unpaid troops;[37] but the chief offenders in this respect, as he must have known, were the feudal levies which Louis, like Charles VII before him, was taking steps to replace with the regularly paid soldiery, which Commynes recommended. Again, he laments civil strife: when disorders begin, all men hope to see them soon ended; but it is rather to be feared that they will spread, since "though at the beginning only two or three princes or lesser men be involved, before the banquet has lasted two years, everybody will be sitting down to it."[38] His experiences in an army composed of allies led Commynes to this reflection: "It is almost impossible for many great lords of equal rank to continue for long in friendship without there being a lord above all, who should be wise and well esteemed in order to have the obedience of all. I have seen a great many examples of this with my own eyes."[39] He has not yet reached here the notion of power sufficient to keep the peace, but he has only a short distance still to go. And some of his remarks about Louis XI suggest that the idea of domestic order imposed by royal authority is indeed very near expression. So he criticizes Louis for his failure to annex the Burgundian lands directly after the death of Charles the Bold, because annexation, instead of splitting the territory up into small feudal grants, would have spared the people much strife.[40] Again, Commynes reports approvingly the reforms that Louis projected before his death, among them standardization of all laws, weights, and measures.[41] Most significant is a part of his final judgment of Louis, a passage which amounts to a kind of rationale of royal absolutism: "I have never seen a better prince. It is true that he oppressed his subjects, *but he allowed no one else to do so, friend or foe.*"[42]

This reference to Louis as an oppressor brings us to the last aspect of Commynes's ideal state—the absence of taxation; for the one great failing of his master was that he burdened the people with overwhelming taxes.[43] Commynes expressed his views on the subject of taxation emphatically and often. In this respect, furthermore, the traditional element in his thought is most pronounced; and the question of taxation also brings us to the "constitutionalism" of Commynes.

He started with the medieval view that the king should live on the ordinary domain revenues, and these he regarded as fully sufficient for all the normal purposes of government; "for this domain is very large; and if it is well managed, its income, including *gabelles* and certain *aides,* is more than a million francs."[44] Only the requirements of defense could justify a royal request for more money, which could legally be obtained only by taxation consented to by the estates of the realm. And perhaps the major example of tyranny on Commynes's list is the waging of war without first asking the advice of the estates whose money and lives are spent therein. He asks, "Is there a king or lord on earth who has the power, outside his own domain, to levy a penny from his subjects without the grant and consent of those who must pay it—except by tyranny and violence?"[45] The procedure at Tours in 1484 seems to him the proper approach to royal taxation; and to those who (significantly) were doubtful of the wisdom of summoning the estates even before the sixteenth century, Commynes replies: "Some might have thought then that this assembly was dangerous, and there were those, of mean condition and small virtue, who said then, and have said since, that it is treason only to speak of assembling the estates and that it diminishes the authority of the king. But they are committing a crime against God, the king, and the public welfare."[46] He also points approvingly to England, where he reports that the monarch could not make war without first assembling parliament, which is "the equivalent of the three estates." The English system he regarded as both proper in principle and satisfactory in practice.[47] The difference between France and England in respect to taxation, however, he declares with emphasis, is a matter of practice only, not of principle: "Our king has the least basis of any for saying, 'I have the right to levy taxes from my subjects as I please.' "[48] In fact, no Christian prince whosoever has any "authority based on reason to impose taxes without the consent of his people."[49] Any method of raising extraordinary revenue in France except by application to the estates is tyranny and makes the king liable to excommunication.[50]

Several aspects of Commynes's position on taxation should be noted. One is that it is not necessarily an accidental survival in him of feudal principle. It happens to coincide with his own financial interests as a feudal proprietor, for the imposition of royal taxes was bound up with the abolition of important sources of noble revenue. Furthermore, it had been a general aim of Louis XI to bring the privileged groups within the scope of royal taxation, as Gandilhon has recently shown;[51] so that Commynes may very well be thinking of his own experiences.

But, in the second place, Commynes's expression of constitutional principle is perhaps the only suggestion of what he believed about the relationship of the monarch to law. He is clearly assuming the existence of some sort of fundamental law, and this law is not peculiar to France. He is generalizing about feudal society, and he has in mind, as a basis for the principle, some kind of universal religious concept.

Finally, Commynes's views on taxation are in glaring conflict with the practical realities underlying his longing for domestic peace and stability. That he failed to realize the necessity for a regular, dependable, and thus independent royal income for the attainment of real order and tranquillity in France is an amazing example of the incompleteness of his political understanding. Even his practical sense was not sufficient to suggest to him, for example, the enormous difference between the papal domains and the kingdom of France, their problems and sources of income.

This conflict between the general conditions which Commynes desires in France and the restrictions he wishes to place on their attainment is underlined by his analysis of the reasons for the enormous increase in extraordinary taxation since the time of Charles VII. He sees clearly that this increase is bound up very closely with the maintenance of a professional army and discusses together the increases in taxation and the number of paid soldiers. He gives statistics: during the reign of Louis XI, while the *taille* rose from 1,800,000 francs to 4,700,000 annually, the army increased from 1,700 men-at-arms to somewhere between 4,000 and 5,000, plus about 25,000 other troops.[52]

To the use of mercenaries, foreign or native, Commynes is bitterly opposed. But if part of his reason is financial, he also fears the power given the king by a regular army. He violently assails Charles VII for beginning the practice of trying to control the kingdom with regular troops after the manner of the Italians.[53] His description of an incident in the history of Burgundy is revealing. Commynes begins by reporting how Charles the Bold assembled the Burgundian estates for the purpose of establishing the nucleus of a regular army of his own such as had already been established in France. His subjects were, however, afraid to put themselves under the sort of "subjection they saw in France because ꞏf these troops." So they granted to Charles only a part of what he asked, and the sequel showed how right their fears had been; for Charles exploited the limited permission which he had received, increased the number of his paid troops, and taxed the people heavily for their support. And Commynes concludes with a generalization about the advantages and disadvantages of a standing army: under a wise ruler, it may be useful; but if the ruler is a minor—the attack on the Beaujeus, who had imprisoned him, is obvious here—this army may well be used by those who govern for ends "not always profitable either for the king or for his subjects."[54]

Commynes's explanation of the origins of high royal taxes and an independent royal army suggests again that he ought to have realized that the maintenance of the peace required financial and military power. He says that Charles VII was the first king to levy taxes "at his pleasure and without consent of the estates of his kingdom"; but he agrees that at the time there was sufficient cause, because of both the expenses of reconquest and the necessity for dealing with ravaging free companies.[55] Furthermore, he noticed the necessity of money for carrying on the Italian war, and he describes cases in which troops refused to serve without pay.[56] But, instead of advancing any real solutions to the problems of public finance, Commynes contents himself with the counsel that princes ought to keep on good terms with such merchant-financiers as the Medici, "for they know not when they will have need of them, since sometimes a little money accomplishes much."[57]

With his discussion of taxation Commynes touches on what has been called "the greatest political revolution of the fifteenth century, that which made the *taille* permanent, and thus gave to the crown the most powerful weapon it could wield for the overthrow of the practices of the Middle Ages."[58] This "revolution" was also one of the major issues at Tours in 1484, when an attempt was made to reassert the responsibility of the crown to the estates in matters of extraordinary taxation and where the principles expressed by Commynes were asserted with great vigor.[59] The issue for the historian is this: Did these principles express the realities of the time, or were they merely a last protest of the old order which was passing? The conclusion of this paper is probably already obvious; but so distinguished a historian as A. J. Carlyle has been eager to defend the vitality of the principles expressed by the deputies at Tours and by Commynes.[60] This is his position: "It is impossible to maintain that the King of France had any recognized and constitutional right to impose taxation at his discretion. That he frequently did so is clear, and the right to do so was from time to time asserted by some persons, but it is also clear that the right was emphatically and constantly denied, and that the King from time to time and in quite unequivocal terms recognized that taxation should not be imposed without the consent of the Provincial or General Estates."[61]

The facts are these: the origins of independent royal income went back, as Commynes pointed out, to the reign of Charles VII. Until 1435 the estates seem to have been fully in control of taxation; but with the military successes of the crown came an inevitable increase in royal prestige, and, at the same time, war weariness and impatience with feudal excesses reached a climax. The only way to finish the expulsion of the English and to end the depredations of the independent feudal bands was to establish some sort of regular army. But a regular army required a regular source of income; and to provide this was the task of the estates-general which met at Orléans in 1439.[62] This assembly was a striking contrast to that of 1484. Where the later group fought to decrease the regular army,[63] the earlier actually pleaded that it be established;[64] and where the later fought to establish the financial responsibility of the crown, the earlier made the crown financially independent. Charles VII was given the right to levy an annual *taille* for the support of an army.

The problem of royal taxation was thus closely bound up with the problem of feudal independence; and perhaps as important for the political future of France as the permission for the king to tax without consulting the estates were certain provisions in the royal edict which resulted from the assembly of 1439.[65] This edict was the negative corollary of the extension of royal military and financial power: what had been given to the king had to be forbidden to the nobles. Of its forty-six articles, the first three deal with the establishment of the new royal army and forbid all private persons to raise troops without consent of the king, under the penalty of forfeiting "all honors and public offices, and the rights and privileges of nobility, and the loss of life and goods." Then follows a series of regulations which impose certain standards of discipline on the royal military force. Implicit in these regulations is an attempt to end precisely those disorders which were being committed by the feudal levies; and their aim seems to be not the improved efficiency of the royal fighting force but the protection of the populace. This fact is important because it is reflected in the even more significant articles with which the edict ends, those dealing with fiscal abuses of the feudal system. These articles seem to have as their general purpose the regularization of feudal income, its fixture at a predetermined level, and hence the protection of the subject from all arbitrary feudal taxation. Article 37 states this principle generally but emphatically:

> Item. And the king forbids all lords, barons and others, all captains and guardians of towns and fortresses, of bridges and roads, and all others, all officers, provosts, toll collectors and others, that henceforth none of them shall force . . . their subjects or others to pay them anything, or demand anything of them, wheat, wine, money or anything else, beyond the dues and rents which their subjects and others owe to them, and on pain of seizure of body and goods by the captains, officers, and lords, under pain of confiscation of all their goods; and from henceforth the king declares the lands, seigneuries and fortresses where such exactions are made, whether by the lords or by their servants or officers . . . seized and confiscated forever and without restitution.[66]

Succeeding articles make this principle more specific: tolls are forbidden, beyond what ancient custom had established; and the lords are expressly forbidden to impose *tailles* or to interfere in any way with the collection of the royal *taille*. Here two motives are apparent. One, stated explicitly, is the protection of the people.[67] The other is suggested by the fact that the feudal *taille* and interference with the royal *taille* are forbidden together; apparently it was anticipated that king and nobles would be competing for the same money.

Study of this edict makes fairly clear some of the factors behind the action of the estates of 1439. Feudalism had proved itself wanting, not only through its military anarchy, but also because its own solution to the problem of taxation was unsatisfactory. Thus the revolutionary measure of 1439 was accomplished by constitutional means, not by a royal coup. While the permanence of the new royal *taille* was not explicitly stated in 1439, the fiscal abuses which it aimed to correct were not of a temporary sort.

In any case, once the right of the king to the *taille* was given, it was successfully maintained; and it is unlikely that the right would have been questioned but for its relentless exploitation by Louis XI. Even Commynes and the deputies at Tours, while they may complain about taxes, are often not clear about whether they are objecting to the illegality or merely to the weight of taxation. Indeed, the analogy of the fiscal system to the circulation of the blood made by the deputies suggests centralization quite as much as it suggests the need for economy.[68]

It is thus evident that the independence of royal taxation had been, in practice, established in France even before the accession of Louis XI, and even as powerful a gathering as the Estates-General of 1484 was able to do little but protest. The real turning point in the situation had come long before the time of Commynes; and the needs of the nation for order and tranquillity were such that it is difficult to conceive of any return to the medieval system of taxation. While both Commynes and the deputies at Tours protested against the methods used to insure a degree of order in France, both gave evidence of a deep sense of the need for it.

The political ideas which we have so far examined in Commynes show the difficulty of classifying him clearly as either "medieval" or "modern" and thereby also reveal how well he deserves to be called a transitional figure. The deeper religious and ethical implications of these political ideas and of his general attitudes show the same sort of complexities on a more profound psychological level. In the remainder of this paper I should like to attempt some analysis of what is going on in these fundamental areas of Commynes's mind.

The obvious point of departure here is the basic assumption of his work that his political advice has value for the prince and that it ought to be given. The implications are of two sorts. One may be described as traditional: the assumption that the individual, even though he is a prince, is by himself inadequate. We have already seen the specific application of this implication to the problem of government in Commynes's insistence on the need for a council; but it has also a more general significance. The other implication of Commynes's self-appointed role as adviser to princes is connected with Jacob Burckhardt's description of the Renaissance state in Italy as a "work of art": the idea that, by rational planning and a careful adaptation of means to ends, the political forms of human life may be consciously controlled and directed. As one might expect, both tendencies appear in Commynes.

Besides its political application in the idea of a council, Commynes's sense of the inadequacy of the individual expresses itself in religious terms. Often, however, his piety is unconvincingly formal. Thus he concludes a discussion of the unreliability of princes: "But, all things considered, our only hope ought to be in God; for in him only is complete constancy and goodness, which are not to be found in this world. But this we learn too late and after we have needed the lesson. Yet better late than never."[69] And his generalization that all the evils of this life proceed from lack of faith[70] rings somewhat hollow in view of his own readiness to prescribe practical measures of correction. More functional is his emphasis on providence, at least as a symbol for the unknown cause in events otherwise beyond his capacity for explanation. His account of the Wars of the Roses is an example: "So everything went awry in England. Civil wars broke out among them which have lasted almost until today, because the house of York usurped the throne, or held it by good title—I do not know which; for the governance of such matters is done by God."[71] His use of supernatural explanation, however, also leads Commynes into a reflection which strikingly suggests the essential shallowness of his religious convictions and the way in which his mind is on the verge of thinking in other terms; he is meditating about the fate of the rebellious Constable of Saint-Pol: "We must admit that changeable Fortune looked at him with a frown. Or [Commynes hastily corrects himself] to give a better answer, we should say that such great mysteries do not come from Fortune at all and that Fortune is nothing but a poetic fiction: God must have abandoned him."[72] For once, Commynes shows himself aware of a problem of intellectual integration.

This general theme of individual inadequacy is twice strikingly applied to the practices of government and governors. In speaking of Montlhéry, Commynes seems to deny all meaning to the phrase "the art of war": "I cannot be persuaded that the wisdom of one man is sufficient to govern such a number of men or that things turn out in the field as they are planned in the council chamber,"[73] though here his desire to deny credit for victory to Charles the Bold is pertinent. Again, his reflections on the wise calculations of the Venetians, who disbelieved in the possibility of a French invasion of Italy, lead him to conclude that the plans of men are worth nothing when God chooses to intervene.[74] Commynes also stresses at times the fallibility of the individual, and he shows no inclination to except princes: "No prince is so wise but that he sometimes makes mistakes, and a great many if he lives long."[75] Even counselors are of use only because many heads are better than one:

> Thus it is very necessary that a prince have many advisers, for even the wisest frequently err, whether through partiality in the matters on which they speak, through love or hate, through the spirit of opposition, or sometimes through bodily indisposition: for no one should be made to give advice after dinner. Some might object that men subject to these faults ought not be in the council of a prince, but it must be answered that we are all hu-

man; and he who would be advised only by such as never fail to speak wisely . . . must look for them in heaven, for they are not to be found among men. But to make up for this, a man in the council will occasionally speak very wisely and well who does not generally do so; and thus one makes up for the defects of another.[76]

Here is a picture of men approaching the problems of government not with the creative exuberance of the conventional Renaissance but piteously vulnerable even to the indignities of dyspepsia!

Yet there are elements in this insistence on the need for advice which may lead to an entirely modern emphasis on planning and the reliance of men on their human powers alone and, as the emphasis is shifted to the adequacy of means for given ends, even to the ethical detachment of Machiavelli. And side by side with the traditional elements in Commynes we may find passages which illustrate these "modern" tendencies also. The contrast of Charles the Bold and Louis XI is again to the point: Charles is criticized for his disorderly ways and his failure to plan;[77] Louis is commended for his caution and the thoroughness which he applied to every activity.[78] And Commynes's advice to the ruler who is preparing for battle reflects a spirit not of chivalric heroism but of middle-class business enterprise: "Therefore, one should consider well before risking an unnecessary battle; and if it should come, consider beforehand every danger. For generally those who do a thing in fear make the best provision for it and more often win than those who go at it arrogantly."[79] The implication is, certainly, that the prince may, by taking thought, add, if not a cubit to his stature, at least a few acres to his kingdom.

Commynes's insistence on thoughtful planning finally merges into an almost unconditional admiration for "cunning,"[80] and in this may perhaps be detected some of the influence of Louis XI. It is what Sainte-Beuve had in mind when he described Commynes as "our Machiavelli."[81] For his master's cunning made a deep impression on Commynes, whose frank admiration even extends to the praise of Louis's attainments in the art of dissimulation. In this respect he is recommended as a model for young princes, since they, too, "if they are wise, will always try to represent their acts in the best light."[82] On one occasion Commynes seems suddenly to become aware of some moral problem connected with the use of trickery, for he begins a paragraph thus: "Because it is necessary to know the cunning and evil practices of this world as well as the good, though not in order to make use of them, but rather to guard against them, I shall describe an example of cunning, or of clever dealing as it might be termed."[83] This he proceeds to do with great relish. But he is not usually so scrupulous; indeed, he seems generally to identify cunning with wisdom: "Some men are not so cunning as others or so clever or so experienced in these affairs, and some do not even feel the need of wisdom; but in these matters it is the wise who come off best. I shall give you a very clear example of this. Never has a treaty been made between the French and the English in which the judgment and sharpness of the French have not proved superior. And it is proverbial among the English that they have always beaten the French in battle but always lost at the peace table."[84]

The final element in Commynes's calculating attitude is a kind of cynical realism. It expresses itself in aphorisms such as "Most men serve rather for the rewards hoped for than for the favors received."[85] And in a passage which has implications for the interpretation of his own life, he even applauds in a prince the ability to exploit the moral weakness of other men: "Naturally most men look how to advance themselves or how to save themselves, so that they can easily be won over to the strongest side. There are other men so good and true that they are not affected by such considerations, but they are few. The problem of desertion is especially dangerous when princes try to win men over; but when a prince will attempt this, it is a great sign of God's grace. For it indicates that he is not infected with the foolish vice of pride, which calls down the hatred of everyone."[86] The secular quality in his estimate of pride and the perversity of Commynes's invocation of Christian concepts in this passage are obvious. Thus it is not surprising to find, side by side with statements of formal piety, passages in which Commynes can recommend the use of ambassadors as spies[87] or can describe without comment the butchery of the citizens of Liège, who had trustfully regarded themselves as safe from attack on the Sabbath.[88] With an attitude like this, we are scarcely any longer in the Middle Ages.

Thus the double quality of Commynes's more specifically political views is repeated at a deeper level, and his value as a representative of the transition to modern times is underlined. If he emphasized the practical competence rather than the ideal virtues of the ruler, he could not dispense entirely with the language of religion. He stressed the professional qualifications rather than the status of royal advisers, but he also defended traditional privilege. He saw clearly, and even felt deeply, the needs of his time for peace and order; but he could not detach himself sufficiently from the ideas of the past to support those extensions of central authority which alone could satisfy them. His pragmatism, his interest in planning, and his tendency to detach politics from morality point to a new era; but a recurring pessimism suggests the waning of the Middle Ages. No single classification of Commynes will suffice to reconcile these paradoxes, and in this fact lies his major historical significance.

NOTES

1. For an excellent bibliographical discussion of this problem see Felix Gilbert, "Political Thought of the Renaissance and Reformation," *Huntington Library Quarterly,* IV (1941), 443–68.
2. "The Humanist Concept of the Prince and *The Prince* of Machiavelli," *Journal of Modern History,* XI (1939), 449–83.
3. J. M. B. C. Kervyn de Lettenhove, *Lettres et négociations de Philippe de Commines,* 2 vols. (Brussels, 1867), I, 49.
4. R. Chanteleuze, "Philippe de Commynes," *Le correspondant,* CXXII (1881), 250–52.
5. Philippe de Commynes, *Mémoires,* ed. J. Calmette and G. Durville, 3 vols. (Paris, 1924–25), I, xii and 1.
6. *Ibid.,* p. 222. The translations throughout are my own, although I have also consulted the Elizabethan version of Thomas Danett.
7. V.-L. Bourrilly, "Les idées politiques de Commynes," *Revue d'histoire moderne et contemporaine,* I (1899), 93–124.
8. Paul Janet, *Histoire de la science politique,* 2 vols. (Paris, 1872), I, 474.
9. C. A. Sainte-Beuve, "Memoirs of Philippe de Commynes," *Causeries du lundi. (Oct., 1849–March, 1850),* ed. E. J. Trechmann (London, n.d.), p. 204: "In a word, Commynes is so modern in his ideas and views, that in reading him we might allot him (which is very rare for an author of a different epoch) the place he would be sure to have held in our present social order."
10. Kervyn de Lettenhove, I, 40–41 and 45–48.
11. Commynes, I, 37–38.
12. Kervyn de Lettenhove, I, 90–108; Charles Fierville, "Documents inédits sur Philippe de Commynes," *Revue des sociétés savantes,* 7th ser., I (1879–80), 397–98.
13. Kervyn de Lettenhove, I, 113–14.
14. John S. C. Bridge, *A History of France from the Death of Louis XI,* 5 vols. (Oxford, 1921–36), I, 138.
15. *Ibid.,* II, 7. Bridge quotes a letter from Francesco della Casa to Piero de' Medici, June 28, 1493, which notes that Commynes was distrusted and enjoyed "no great authority."
16. Commynes, II, 203–4.
17. Bourrilly, p. 95.
18. The first part was written between 1489 and 1491; the second, after his second period of prominence, in 1495–98 (Commynes, I, xiii–xv).
19. *Ibid.,* pp. 149–50.
20. *Ibid.,* pp. 66–67.
21. *Ibid.,* III, 71.

22. *Ibid.*, I, 37–38.
23. *Ibid.*, pp. 67–68.
24. *Ibid.*, p. 130.
25. *Ibid.*, p. 250.
26. *Ibid.*, p. 96.
27. *Ibid.*, p. 170.
28. *Ibid.*, p. 93.
29. *Ibid.*, II, 289.
30. *Ibid.*, I, 69–70.
31. *Ibid.*, pp. 130–31.
32. *Ibid.*, pp. 129–30.
33. *Ibid.*, pp. 128–29.
34. *Ibid.*, II, 262.
35. *Ibid.*, I, 115–16.
36. *Ibid.*, pp. 204–5, and III, 1–2.
37. *Ibid.*, II, 216.
38. *Ibid.*, I, 223.
39. *Ibid.*, p. 91.
40. *Ibid.*, II, 167–68.
41. *Ibid.*, p. 278.
42. *Ibid.*, p. 324; italics mine.
43. *Ibid.*, p. 290.
44. *Ibid.*, III, 305.
45. *Ibid.*, II, 217.
46. *Ibid.*, pp. 219–20.
47. *Ibid.*, pp. 8–9.
48. *Ibid.*, pp. 218–19.
49. *Ibid.*, p. 340.
50. *Ibid.*, p. 222.
51. René Gandilhon, *Politique économique de Louis XI* (Paris, 1941), p. 274.
52. Commynes, II, 290.
53. *Ibid.*
54. *Ibid.*, I, 188–90.
55. *Ibid.*, II, 289.
56. *Ibid.*, III, 266–68 and 272–73.
57. *Ibid.*, p. 41. B. de Mandrot suggests that Commynes acted as an agent of the Medici at the French court (*Mémoires de Philippe de Commynes,* ed. B. de Mandrot [Paris, 1903], II, xlvii).
58. Georges Picot, *Histoire des états généraux* (Paris, 1872), I, 323.
59. Thus the deputies insisted that "the *tailles,* first established because of the war, should have ceased with the war" (Jehan Masselin, *Journal des états généraux de France,* ed. A. Bernier [Paris, 1835], pp. 414–15).
60. Of Commynes's principles he remarks, I think incorrectly, that they have special significance "not only because he was a man of great experience in political and diplomatic affairs, but because he was a great servant of the French Crown, and cannot be suspected of any desire to depreciate its authority" (R. W. and A. J. Carlyle, *A History of Mediaeval Political Thought in the West,* 6 vols. [Edin-

burgh and London, 1909–36], VI, 214). Commynes was not a great servant of the crown when he wrote, and he certainly had considerable reason to resent the authority of the central government.

61. *Ibid.*, VI, 202–3.

62. Picot, I, 319–24.

63. See Masselin, pp. 332–33, and *passim.*

64. Picot, I, 327.

65. Printed in *Recueil général des anciennes lois françaises,* ed. A. J. L. Jourdan, Decrusy, and F. A. Isambert, 29 vols. (Paris, 1821–33), IX, 57–71.

66. *Ibid.*, p. 68.

67. *Ibid.*, p. 70.

68. See Masselin, p. 669.

69. Commynes, I, 93.

70. *Ibid.*, II, 224.

71. *Ibid.*, I, 24.

72. *Ibid.*, II, 86–87.

73. *Ibid.*, I, 26.

74. *Ibid.*, III, 28–29.

75. *Ibid.*, II, 173.

76. *Ibid.*, I, 103.

77. *Ibid.*, pp. 105–6.

78. *Ibid.*, pp. 146–47.

79. *Ibid.*, p. 121.

80. He is fond of the words *habilité* or *habile.*

81. Sainte-Beuve, *loc. cit.*, p. 200.

82. Commynes, I, 172.

83. *Ibid.*, pp. 195–96.

84. *Ibid.*, pp. 220–21. Later Commynes, feeling the need for some explanation of the inferiority of English wits, ascribes it to climate, reminding us of Bodin (II, 37–38).

85. *Ibid.*, p. 246.

86. *Ibid.*, pp. 65–66.

87. *Ibid.*, pp. 218–19.

88. *Ibid.*, pp. 161–64.

8 Postel and the Significance of Renaissance Cabalism

This essay was my first publication after I received my doctorate and was teaching at the University of Illinois. It was an effort to place the subject of my dissertation in a larger context; I tried to explain why Christian thinkers of the Renaissance were attracted to a singularly esoteric expression of Judaism. The essay was published in the Journal of the History of Ideas 15 (1954), *218–232, and is reprinted here by permission of the publisher.*

* * *

One of the most extraordinary and yet obscure currents in the intellectual history of the Renaissance was the interest of Christian thinkers in the Jewish cabala. This concern extended from Pico's attempt to absorb cabala into a Christian synthesis of universal knowledge at the end of the fifteenth century well into the seventeenth, and included writers and scholars from every major European country. Yet, in spite of the wide distribution of cabalistic interest in both time and space, the problem of explaining the movement, in the sense of relating it to the general concerns of its historical setting, has not been very satisfactorily dealt with.

There have been two contrasting reasons for this failure. One has been the difficulty of determining the nature of cabala itself. The task is by no means yet complete, but much has now been accomplished, notably through the work of Gershom Scholem.[1] It is now possible to affirm enough about cabala to attempt some explanation of its attraction for the mind of the later Renaissance.

The word *cabala,* which literally means *tradition,* designates an esoteric school of religious thought within Judaism, characterized by both a certain doctrinal emphasis and a particular system of exegesis. Its origins are still obscure, but it evidently emerged out of the eclectic intellectual atmosphere of the diaspora, and it thus represents a synthesis of influences variously drawn from Pythagorean, Neoplatonic, Gnostic, and even Zoroastrian sources, the whole fused with an essential structure of orthodox Judaism.[2] This fact provides a part of the explanation for Christian interest in cabala. It introduced many of the conceptions of hellenistic thought, attractive but previously suspect, under the respectable auspices of sacred tradition.

The heterogeneous elements of cabala began to assume more or less systematic and written form in the Middle Ages, especially among the Jews of Spain and southern France. The fullest development of cabalistic doctrine, although it can hardly be described as a systematic statement, is contained in the *Zohar,* or *Book of Splendor,* which was probably written by Moses of Leon, a Castilian Jew who wrote in the second half of the thirteenth century. In the history of Jewish thought, the *Zohar,* and the tradition of Jewish mystical speculation which it represents, seem to express the effort of religious minds to correct the overintellectualism of the philosophers such as Moses Maimonides.[3] This fact also has considerable relevance for the explanation of Christian Renaissance cabalism. Within Judaism cabala represented very much the same sort of reaction against the alleged irrelevancies of formal philosophy that humanism, mysticism, and some aspects of Protestantism represented in the history of Christian thought.

Cabalistic teaching is of several sorts, among which it is convenient to distinguish the following. First, cabala includes doctrines concerned with the relation between God and the creation which are chiefly based on Neoplatonic and Gnostic schemes of emanation. The *Zohar* posits between God and the universe ten intermediaries, the sephiroth, which solve the perennial problem of explaining the immanent activity of a transcendent God. Second, it includes messianic and apocalyptic doctrines of a more specifically Jewish character. Finally, it includes techniques of scriptural exegesis which have the general aim of discovering profound spiritual significance in even the most apparently local and trivial passages of the Scriptures.[4] The excesses associated with these techniques, which rely heavily on computing and manipulating arithmetically the numerical equivalents of Hebrew letters and words, have received undue attention.[5] All aspects of cabalistic teaching attracted and were utilized by Renaissance cabalists.

But there has been, in addition to the obscurity of cabala, a second reason for the inadequate historical treatment of Renaissance cabalism. It has been approached too exclusively in terms of its permanent impression on European thought, and, measured by this standard, it has been dismissed as an inconsequential "fad" in contrast with the truly "significant" activities of the scientists.[6] But historical significance involves more than contribution to the future, and it may be suggested that even a passing fad can be sometimes made to yield valuable evidence of the character of an age. In fact, the fads of the Renaissance raise important questions. Why was the intellectual of the Renaissance liable to fads (granted that he was)? What, again, is the significance of the sorts of fads which attracted him? And, to return to our immediate concern, what were the needs which cabalism satisfied for him? The purpose of the present paper is to consider the last question from the standpoint of a French cabalist of the sixteenth century, Guillaume Postel.

Postel is of unusual interest for helping to answer the question.[7] Part of the reason lies in the fact (which has been insufficiently recognized) that his knowledge of cabala was probably more extensive and systematic than that of any other cabalist of his time. To mention only the best known among Renaissance cabalists, Pico, some two generations earlier, had relied mainly on a mediocre commentary on the *Zohar* for his knowledge, and Reuchlin's sources were chiefly pre-Zoharic.[8] But Postel was thoroughly acquainted with all the major documents of cabala, in addition to possessing a wide reputation as a student of Hebrew and of the Near East in general.

Postel first learned Hebrew as a student in Paris after about 1525, but the first traces of cabalistic influence on his thought appeared only after a sojourn in Rome between 1544 and 1547. During this time he became acquainted with two German Hebraists, Andreas Masius (Andreas van Maes) and Johann von Widmanstadt, and it is probable that he also frequented the Jewish colony in Rome. His first cabalistic writings are works written during or immediately after this period,[9] which thus marks the beginning of his career as a Christian cabalist of the Renaissance. Among his major achievements in this role were two translations of important cabalistic sources. He first produced a Latin version of a considerable portion of the *Zohar*,[10] and not long after he published a Latin translation of the important *Sepher Yezirah*, or *Book of Formation*.[11] He was also familiar with a third important cabalistic writing, the *Sepher Bahir*.[12] A large proportion of his writing after 1548 contains cabalistic elements,[13] and includes works which demonstrate a knowledge of all three of the major aspects of cabalistic teaching.

A second reason for Postel's special usefulness as a representative of Renaissance cabalism lies in his active participation in numerous important movements of his time, both academic and practical.[14] He was a distinguished scholar with an international reputation in philology, and at various times he held chairs among the Royal Readers in what was to become the Collège de France and in the University of Vienna. A philosopher of sorts, he concerned himself with the stock problems of his day. He travelled extensively in the Near East and wrote vernacular best-sellers on the Ottoman Empire. He concerned himself with ecclesiastical reform and religious unity during the struggles of the Reformation, acting as a kind of lobbyist for conciliation at the Council of Trent. He was also a crusade propagandist, a missionary enthusiast, and an erstwhile member of the Society of Jesus. Finally, he was a very personal sort of mystic with a considerable circle of friends and correspondents both inside and outside the Catholic fold; eventually his private speculations brought about his imprisonment for several years in a papal prison at Rome. The wide range of Postel's interests and activities makes it possible to see through him a number of highly interesting relationships between cabalism and other concerns of the sixteenth century.

Finally, Postel is useful for our purposes because his life, and with it his bibliography, were long. He lived to the age of seventy-one; before his death in 1581 he had managed to publish some sixty works, several of considerable length.[15] In addition he produced numerous personal letters and a huge quantity of manuscript works. These writings cover almost every subject of interest to the learned mind of his day, and in addition a considerable range of subjects intended to interest a nonacademic audience. In fact, as a publicist (and no other word comes close to summarizing the activities of his life) he deliberately wrote for several audiences. The number of his works, their variety, and the diversity of the readers at whom he aimed all help, again, in establishing the connections between cabalism and other interests of the time.

In what follows, therefore, I should like to survey the uses to which Postel put cabala, with the broad purpose of attempting to determine why one leading Christian intellectual of the Renaissance was attracted to such unlikely material. I have suggested above two general explanations. One is that cabala, as of Jewish origin, provided a sanction for hellenistic conceptions previously regarded with distrust. The other is that, as the reaction of religious against philosophizing Judaism, cabala reinforced an important aspect of Renaissance thought. Through Postel we can make our explanations more specific.

Cabala was valuable to Postel, in the first place, because it helped him to make sense of the universe. His problem was the typical one of desiring to reintegrate various aspects of thought and experience which had been dissociated and compartmentalized not only by the prevailing philosophical schools, but also by the metaphysical skepticism of the humanists. On the one hand, he felt the universe to be a vast system of correspondences in which the general is everywhere mirrored in the particular, every object has cosmic implications, and all created things exist in dynamic relationship to each other and to an ultimate reality. It was God's "first intention," he wrote, "to unify all things."[16] Accordingly, as his writings indicate, he considered the comprehension and description of this integrated universe a primary aim of human thought. His assumptions about the organization of the universe made him receptive to "that divine Plato, god of philosophers,"[17] as one might expect, and to astrology.[18]

On the other hand, Postel could not simply dismiss that growing sense of the gulf between God and the world which was the most profound expression of Renaissance pessimism. He followed Nicholas of Cusa in beginning his thought with the absolute antithesis between God and the world. God, he says, is eternal, infinite, unmoving, and immutable; the created world is in every respect the direct opposite. Hence Postel insisted on the necessity for mediation, without which it would be, he felt, impossible for man and the universe to enter into relationship with God, "for there is no passing from one extreme to the other without mediation."[19] Without mediation the universe, for Postel, must lack both unity and meaning.

He found his principle of mediation, and hence the unity and meaning of the universe, in cabala. Out of cabalistic materials he was able to construct a total and unified description of the universe which corresponded to his assumptions about its nature, and at the same time which did not deny the absolute transcendence of God. Two aspects of cabalistic doctrine provided him with the integrated world-picture which he craved.

The first of these was the cabalistic view of language. This was, of course, primarily applicable to Hebrew, which Postel esteemed as the true *clavis scientiae* and the *via veritatis perdita*.[20] Its active recovery by all mankind, he believed, is the only path both to a proper understanding of the universe as the systematic whole which God created, and to the restoration of direct communication with God. Here, it may be observed, is a hint concerning one impulse behind the development of Hebrew studies in the Renaissance.

But the cabalistic attitude toward language is also applicable in a secondary sense to all other languages, since, as Postel stresses, they are in every case merely historical corruptions of "the holy language."[21] The point is that, for the cabalist, language is far more than an arbitrary instrument of communication between men. It is a general unifying principle, capable of comprehending all particular things. It originated in the words taught by God to Adam and hence possesses an absolute relation to what it designates; it represents the self-expression of God and reflects his creativity.[22] This view of language provides Postel both with a rationale for his plodding philological labors and, more obscurely, with a basis for a philosophical realism with which to oppose the schools.[23]

Postel goes considerably farther with the hierarchy of the sephiroth as mediators between God and the universe. He employs them in the first place to unite the creation to God as the transmitters of motion and life. God, he wrote, the unmoved mover, moves the world not directly, since this would require motion, but by means of emanated powers "proceeding from himself and inseparable from his person." And he identified these promptly as the mediators of cabala: they are "named by the Hebrew prophets the powers of the first ten divine names or angels."[24] Postel also uses the sephiroth, as we shall see in a moment, to unite all things to each other. This was a task for which they were well adapted. The hierarchy of the ten sephiroth is identifiable with, and mystically related to, the intellectual, sensible, and material worlds (to use the conventional distinction employed by Postel himself), the intellectual, moral, and physical attributes of man, sexual differences, colors, the decade, and the letters of the alphabet.[25]

The standard practice among Christian cabalists was to identify the Trinity with the first three of the sephiroth;[26] but Postel, who intended more than the reconciliation of religious systems, preferred to work out a system of his own. He arbitrarily selected and combined elements from a number of the original sephiroth to compose a trinity which has only the vaguest relation to that of Christianity.[27] While Postel was not one to overlook anything in the sephirotic system that would serve his own purposes, he found its sexual dualisms most useful for tying the universe together. In an effort to combine the terminology, and above all the implications, of as many intellectual systems as possible, he described his own mediators as the *animus mundi*, or masculine principle of the universe, the *anima mundi*, or feminine and maternal principle, and the first-born child of their marriage. These three mediators serve, for Postel, a wide variety of functions. They are somehow involved in every aspect of the activity of the universe, whose health depends on their proper relationship.

They have, in the first place, metaphysical significance: the *animus mundi* is the first means by which the unmoved mover imparts existence and motion to the world: thus, as with the mediator of Nicholas of Cusa, he unites the opposites of finite and infinite.[28] The maternal principle is specifically the mediator between God and the material world, and makes possible local action.[29] They also have epistemological significance and thus serve an educative function in which the parents are joined by their son as forms of intellect:

> Three separate persons are necessary, under the heading of active or formal INTELLECT, passive or material INTELLECT, and made or created INTELLECT: a general father, who is the root of authority; a mother who is the general basis of reason; and a third, the son, to teach both authority and reason. The task of these three persons joined in one is the illumination of the world by means of the light of the knowledge of God; so that just as these same general categories are joined to God, all individual and particular members of the human race may be united to God, so that men may know as they are known.[30]

Then, in a strange combination of philosophy and myth, Postel goes on to identify them with the terms of the syllogism, in which he conceives the conclusion as the offspring resulting from the union of the paternal wisdom of authority (the major premise) and the maternal wisdom of reason (the minor premise).[31] And he declares: "The final intention of God is that through these three universal mediators the law of reason inscribed on the minds of all by intellect or the light of first principles may be manifested and preserved so that man may be truly a rational animal, the image and likeness of God."[32] Postel means that there is, actually, no essential conflict between revelation (the expression of authoritative wisdom) and the natural reason of man, and that, through the activity of his three mediators, this fact must become clear to the human race.

Postel had for some time been attracted by the conception of religious truth as a set of demonstrable propositions on which all men, as rational beings, can agree. This interest had led to the charge by his Protestant enemies that he was the founder of "a sect of those who through mockery of God call themselves Deists."[33] He was in fact close to the Florentine Neoplatonic tradition, although bringing to it a fresh zeal which apparently frightened certain of his evangelical contemporaries; but the Protestant charge had its point. His long *De orbis terrae concordia,* which he always regarded as the most important of his writings, had been intended above all to teach Christian doctrine by "philosophical reasons," as the title page (verso) states. He more than once had attempted to list points of agreement among world religions on the basis of their acceptability to natural reason.[34] In the passages we have just examined he is discovering in cabala a means of justifying this general enterprise.

Another application of Postel's cabalism served to bring out the religious value of natural reason. For he identifies the feminine principle, the *anima mundi,* not only with reason but also with spiritual insights in this world, in order to explain or to justify a kind of religious feminism.[35] His doctrine here is an adaptation of cabalistic teaching concerning the Shekinah, last of the mediating sephiroth and the most immediately active in the sphere of human experience.[36] Postel identifies the feminine spirit of the universe with the Holy Spirit, whose presence alone insures the sanctity of the Church[37] (and we may recall that he wrote at a time when this matter was by no means academic). But he also believed that the feminine principle, with its special concern for both reason and holiness, is best represented in this life (as one might suppose it should be) by real women: he particularly mentions St. Catherine of Siena on the one hand, and the bluestocking daughters of the late Thomas More and of his own old friend Guillaume Budé on the other.[38] Femininity was not, for Postel, merely a metaphysical convenience, but a vital fact of positive spiritual value in this world.

Postel's mediators thus do not merely govern the great abstractions which stand above experience; they also intervene in even the most concrete facts of daily life. They give meaning to such different relationships as those of higher and lower, form and matter, heaven and earth, sun and moon, grace and nature, church and state, and even the Old World and the New.[39] They are the fundamental psychological realities; every individual is composed of both animus and anima, of masculine and feminine elements.[40] And in something that approaches a theory of myth, Postel discerns in the masculine and feminine principles of the universe the prototypes of all sexually differentiated pagan gods: they are Father Time and Mother Nature and all their numerous offspring.[41] So they give unity and coherence to the universe.

In fact, the most puzzling aspect of Postel's thought was his effort to bring his cosmic mediating principles down to earth in material incarnations. His identification of the first mediator, the *animus mundi,* with the incarnate Word[42] is perhaps inevitable enough. But (perhaps partly in the interests of balance and symmetry) Postel insisted also on the actual incarnation of the feminine principle and her first-born son. He believed he had found the former in a pious woman of Venice whom he called his *Mother Joan* and the *New Eve*; she impressed him in part because, in spite of her lack of education and her ignorance of Hebrew, she had been able to expound to him the deepest mysteries of the *Zohar*.[43] In her, he wrote, he had seen "things so miraculous and great that they exceed all past miracles, save those of the new Adam, Jesus, my father and her spouse." Her destiny it was now to accomplish the regeneration of the world:

> It is completely certain that, from the substance of her spirit, it has been decreed and determined in heaven that all men who through the corruption of the old Eve have ever been corrupted, killed and turned against God, being rather damned than born, will be completely restored, like me . . . for it is necessary that the new Adam and the new Eve, two in one spiritual flesh, should be, Jesus the mental father, and Joan the spiritual mother of all.[44]

The first-born son of the mystical union between the New Adam/and the New Eve was none other than Postel himself, whose duty in the world was thus to spread abroad the New Gospel, as the heir to both authority and reason.[45] He had, as he wrote, a divine commission to restore mankind to a proper recognition of "the divine right of reason."[46] This puzzling personal twist in his thought has been interpreted both as the evidence of a sick mind and as a rather unorthodox device to win an audience.[47] However this may be, it reveals Postel as a religious revolutionary who has found in cabala, among other things, the inspiration, or at least the justification, for a new sect.

It is not difficult to find fault with Postel's system on intellectual grounds and to dismiss it as fantasy. It is neither rigorously nor systematically worked out. Nevertheless, it satisfied Postel. It satisfied him because it corresponded to his preconceptions about the universe, and particularly because it not only described the basic structure of the world but also bound together in a living relationship the vital forces of the universe. Its peculiar character is partly explained by the fact that Postel's requirements were imaginative and vital as well as intellectual.

But this system, which depended so largely on cabala, also satisfied Postel because it was bound up with other concerns in which his cabalism played a role. Cabala was useful to him not only because it made a special kind of sense out of the universe, but also because it suggested to him a course of action at a crucial point in the history of European civilization. Postel was extraordinarily aware of the general circumstances of the sixteenth-century world, in which there were emerging new and challenging international, intercultural and interreligious relationships.

He was profoundly concerned with the problem of Christian action in a world in which Protestantism had destroyed the old internal unity of belief and Islam was continuing to expand steadily in the Old World, while, on the other hand, Christianity seemed to be making rapid progress in the New. The peoples of Europe were more than ever before brought into touch with alien peoples and alien beliefs. Postel provides a striking example of awareness of the fact that the European mind was compelled to adapt itself to "new horizons."

The fundamental problem, as Postel viewed it, was world ideological conflict; and in the critical pass to which his world seemed to have come, cabala appeared to him the only solution. It alone could harmonize the wide diversities in fundamental belief among all human groups; it alone could resolve the opposition between the Greek heritage and the Hebraic, between reason and authority, nature and grace. We have already observed how Postel's version of cabala solved the problem in theory, but it did more. By making truth communicable, cabala made it applicable to the solution of human problems.

Above all Postel hoped to use his rationalization of Christianity in behalf of a great missionary program. The conversion of the unbeliever, particularly in the Near East, was the fundamental motive of his scholarly pursuits. It had led him into the Society of Jesus during its early years. It had been chiefly responsible for his interest in the rational demonstration of Christian doctrine. Like Pico before him, he believed that cabala would be of the greatest value as a missionary tool; its primary documents, he thought, demonstrated irresistibly the truth of the basic Christian dogmas. The *Book of Formation,* he asserted, because it supremely reconciles reason and authority, will be of the greatest service in the conversion of the world.[48] He insisted also that the whole of the Christian Gospel is implicit in and therefore deducible from the *Zóhar*. By the light of its doctrines, he wrote, compared with which all other teachings in the world are as darkness, even the obstinacy of the Jews will finally be overcome.[49] The real point here was, of course, that since the Jews would be the last and most difficult converts, the use of cabala by Christian missionaries insured the winning of the whole world.[50]

The missionary task struck Postel as of particular urgency, and in his sense of crisis we may discern another major reason for his attraction to cabala. He was certain that the world stood on the brink of momentous developments. This certainty in him was in part the product of despair: he felt the world to be "in greater darkness than it has ever been since Christ came to send workmen into the vineyard,"[51] and at times everything about him seemed to attest to the general disintegration of Christian society and Christian values. He was particularly alarmed over the decay of the church and of civil society, and he spent a considerable amount of his energy in denouncing it to contemporaries.[52] He was further disturbed over the steady shrinking of Christendom before a militant Islam on the east, while at the same time Protestantism revealed the presence of the enemy within the gates.[53] But through apocalypticism, Postel's pessimism was transmuted into optimism, and in decay itself he found the anticipations of rebirth; this appeared to him the lesson and law of history.[54] Meanwhile the contemporary scene provided him with positive evidence which at once made him hopeful and strengthened his sense of crisis. He was, for example, as profoundly aware of the significance of the discoveries of America and the Orient for the expansion of Christian European influence over the world as any modern historian. Recent progress in learning—Postel had in mind the revival of letters, and especially the development of Hebrew studies—was further evidence to him of great changes immediately impending. And he found even in artillery and the printing press, new weapons of material and intellectual power in Christian hands, additional proof that the world was about to make a fresh start.[55]

Cabala stimulated his apocalypticism, provided him with prophetic techniques, and furnished him with a description of the characteristics of the last age. His first calculations placed the dawn of the new age in 1556; so in 1553 he wrote to Schwenckfeld, exhorting him to be of good courage, since the day of the Lord was at hand.[56] When nothing momentous occurred in that year (Postel was then a prisoner in Rome), he postponed the date.[57] His conception of the millennium itself was largely taken from cabalistic messianism. He envisaged it as a return to the earthly paradise of Genesis, in which man is to be finally delivered from bondage to Satan and restored to his original innocence; hence it is the *restitutio omnium,* in which mankind will be united in a common speech (Hebrew), a common government, and a common religion based on cabala in which what had hitherto been the possession of a few initiates will become the common property of all mankind.[58] It is not, Postel stresses, to be confused with eternal salvation. It is, in fact, the Judaic messianic age superimposed onto Christianity. Postel's apocalypticism, of course, is nothing new, and the Renaissance awareness of innovation has by this time been sufficiently established. What is significant here is their combination, and in this combination cabala played a fundamental role.

It is obviously impossible to generalize about Christian cabalism in any but the most tentative fashion on the basis of a single individual, and in certain respects Postel was probably eccentric rather than typical. Nevertheless his case may be used as the basis for a few provisional conclusions about the historical significance of Renaissance cabalism. What is most important, perhaps, is the evidence here that cabalism is to be understood in the context of contemporary needs and preoccupations. The cabalists were interested in studying cabala, not out of idle curiosity or an interest in "pure scholarship," but in order to use it in their more general experience with the intellectual and practical world. It is clear enough that Postel's uses of cabala were primarily dictated not by the nature of cabala itself but by the requirements of the sixteenth-century scene as he understood it.

Some of the uses to which cabala was put were relatively conscious and explicit; others were perhaps less so. The cabalists were hopeful about the possibilities of cabala as a missionary tool; and here we may discern a preoccupation about European relations with the non-European world. They proposed to use cabala to solve intellectual problems which available intellectual traditions evidently seemed to them inadequate to settle. In this respect cabala is a chapter in the effort of the European mind to adapt itself to new data and new ideas; an error, perhaps, in the process of trial and error, but one which illuminates the problems of adaptation and the nature of the process itself. On the whole (in spite of Postel's erratic qualities), cabalism would seem, perhaps even more than humanism, to have been a conservative adaptation. It aimed at absorbing new materials into a scheme dominated by the assumptions and purposes of the past: the systematic unity of all things, the expansion of Christianity, the apocalyptic end of history. But more than this, Christian interest in cabala served to express the general restlessness of an age of striking innovation. Through it we can find some clue to the causes and character of that restlessness. And in at least one case cabala contributed to the idea of the Renaissance itself.

NOTES

1. Above all in *Major Trends in Jewish Mysticism* (New York, 1946).

2. See Joseph Leon Blau, *The Christian Interpretation of the Cabala in the Renaissance* (New York, 1944), 6–7, for a summary of views on the question of the origins of cabala.

3. On the contrast between cabalism and philosophy, see Scholem, *op. cit.*, 35–7; and the succinct but suggestive remarks of Georges Vajda, *Introduction à la pensée juive du moyen âge* (Paris, 1947), 203ff.

4. I follow here the summary of Blau, *op. cit.*, 2–6.

5. This fact is reflected in the present general and inaccurate use of the adjective *cabalistic*.

6. Blau, *op. cit.*, vii.

7. Postel has received considerable scholarly attention. Among general treatments three should be mentioned: Jacques Georges de Chaufepié, "Postel," *Nouveau dictionnaire historique et critique pour servir de supplément ou de continuation au dictionnaire . . . de Bayle*, III (Amsterdam, 1753), 215–36, which combines most earlier accounts; Georges Weill, *De Guilielmi Postelli vita et indole* (Paris, 1892), the first serious attempt to reconstruct Postel's career from the sources; and J. Kvačala, "Wilhelm Postell. Seine Geistesart und seine Reformgedanken," *Archiv für Reformationsgeschichte*, IX (1911–12), 285–330, XI (1914), 200–227, XV (1918), 157–203.

8. Blau, *op. cit.*, 28, 59–60.

9. *De nativitate mediatoris ultima;* Πανθενωσια. *Compositio omnium dissidiorum; Absconditorum a constitutione mundi clavis*, all printed by Oporinus (Basel, 1547); *Candelabri typici in Mosis tabernaculo . . . interpretatio* (Venice, 1548).

10. This was not published but circulated in manuscript. Two copies are extant. One was discovered by Joseph Perles (*Beiträge zur Geschichte der hebräischen und aramäischen Studien* [Munich, 1884], 78–80, note); the other is in the British Museum (Sloane MS. 1410).

11. Under the title *Abrahami Patriarchae liber Jezirah, sive Formationis mundi* (Paris, 1552).

12. Cf. the boast concerning his sources on the title page of his *Candelabri . . . interpretatio:* "a work highly useful . . . based on the Zohar and Bahir and many other very ancient monuments of cabala."

13. His cabalism largely accounts for the reputation for obscurity which he bore even in his own time. The official examiner of his writings during his trial for heresy before the Venetian Holy Office in 1555 reported wearily that he had been able to extract meaning from them only after the greatest effort, and that, although Postel's doctrines were "unheard of, not to say impious," no one, fortunately, could possibly understand them except the author. (In the documents connected with the trial printed by Weill, *op. cit.*, 119–20.)

14. For various aspects of Postel's career, see Abel Lefranc, *Histoire du Collège de France* (Paris, 1893), 184ff.; Henri Busson, *Les sources et le développement du rationalisme dans la littérature française de la Renaissance (1553–1601)* (Paris, 1922), 282–302; Geoffroy Atkinson, *Les nouveaux horizons de la Renaissance française* (Paris, 1935), 245–9; Lucien Febvre, *Le problème de l'incroyance au XVIe siècle. La religion de Rabelais* (Paris, 1947), 111–28; Henri Fouqueray, *Histoire de la Compagnie de Jésus des origines à la suppression* (Paris, 1910–22), I, 131ff.; Johann Fück, "Die arabischen Studien in Europa vom 12. bis in den Anfang des 19. Jahrhunderts," *Beiträge zur Arabistik, Semitistik und Islamwissenschaft* (Leipzig, 1944), 120–28.

15. An eighteenth-century Jesuit, François J. T. Desbillons, listed Postel's published writings in *Nouveaux éclaircissements sur la vie et les ouvrages de Guillaume Postel* (Liège, 1773), 111ff. Geoffrey Butler's bibliography, *Studies in Statecraft* (Cambridge, 1920), 117–31, is based on that of Desbillons but unhappily omits the latter's discussion of his sources and his frank reservations concerning some works listed.

16. Πανθενωσια, 6.

17. Postel's own phrase in *De orbis terrae concordia libri quatuor* (Basel, 1544), 15.

18. For his interest in astrology, see, among other examples, *De originibus* (Basel, ?1553), 70, where Postel traces astrological lore back to Abraham; and, for a political application, *Les raisons de la monarchie* (Paris, 1551), xx.

19. *Absconditorum clavis* (new ed., Amsterdam, 1646), 13–14: "siquidem ab extremo in extremum sine Medio non itur. . . ."

20. *De nativitate ultima*, 16.

21. As a philologist Postel had numerous opportunities to develop this traditional view in detail. See particularly the *De originibus* of 1538, *passim*.

22. Cf. Scholem, *op. cit.*, 17–18.

23. For his view of language and the problem of universals, see *De nativitate ultima*, 13–16.

24. *Le prime nove del altro mondo* (Venice?, 1555), f. 3v.

25. Blau, *op. cit.*, 3–4.

26. *Ibid.*, 15.

27. His system is most fully described in his *Apologia pro Serveto*, a work directed against Calvin but in fact little concerned with Servetus. It was first published by Johann Lorenz von Mosheim, *Versuch einer unpartheiischen und gründlichen Ketzergeschichte* (Helmstaedt, 1748), II, 466–99. Postel's meaning here, however, must be understood in the light of his other works.

28. The nature and functions of the *animus mundi* are particularly developed in the three works of 1547 (see above, note 9).

29. See the extended description of the *anima mundi* in the *Apologia pro Serveto*, 466.

30. *Ibid.*, 479: "Sub INTELLECTU *agente vel formali, Patiente vel materiali, et sub Facto, sive Compositorio*, requirendae tres individuariae Personae, una Patris generalis in quo Autoritatis radix, altera matris, in qua Rationis generalis Basis, et tertia Filii, tam Autoritate, quam ratione docentis, quarum trium Personarum una coniunctarum opera, Summa ad cognoscendum Deum Lux Mundo proponatur, ut sicut ipsi gradus generales sunt coniuncti Deo, sic etiam singula individua, et membra particularia tanquam universalis humanitatis partes . . . ut singuli homines cognoscant, sicut et cogniti sunt."

31. *Ibid.*, 480.

32. *Ibid.*, 478: "Nam finalis Intentio Dei in hoc tendit per has tres mediatoris universalis naturas, ut rationis Lex omnium mentibus per Intellectum sive per Lumen primorum principiorum inscripta manifestetur et servetur, ut homo Animal rationale hoc est IMAGO ET SIMILITUDO DEI revera sit."

33. *Histoire ecclésiastique des églises réformées au royaume de France*, G. Baum and Ed. Cunitz, eds. (Paris, 1883), I, 108. This work was first published at Antwerp, 1580.

34. For example, *De orbis concordia*, 290–92; Πανθενωσια, 11–13.

35. On Postel as feminist, see Émile Telle, *L'Oeuvre de Marguerite d'Angoulême reine de Navarre et la querelle des femmes* (Toulouse, 1937), 63ff.

36. On the Shekinah see Scholem, *op. cit.*, 226–7. Postel explicitly identified the *anima mundi* with the Shekinah, stating that by the maternal principle "I mean the Shekinah (ssechinach, hoc est), or localized and moving providence,

by means of which God disposes of all things and rules and sustains in place."
(*Apologia pro Serveto,* 466).

37. *Les très merveilleuses victoires des femmes du nouveau-monde* (Turin, 1869),
62–3 (1st ed., Paris, 1553).

38. *Ibid.,* 21–22.

39. For a general statement of Postel's dualistic principle, see *De Etruriae
regionis originibus, institutis, religione, ac morbus commentatio* (J. G. Graevius,
ed., *Thesaurus antiquitatum et historiarum Italiae, Etruriae, Umbriae, Sabino-
rum et Latii,* VIII, Part I [Lyons, 1723]), 36. For particular applications see
Apologia pro Serveto, 476; letter to Masius, Nov. 25, 1563 (in Chaufepié, *loc.
cit.,* 226); *Victoires des femmes,* 28, 50–51.

40. This idea is developed through a number of Postel's works, in which the
process by which traditional psychological terminology is gradually altered under
the impact of cabalistic doctrine can be traced. See for this development the
comparatively early *De orbis concordia,* 19–20; Πανθενωσια, 26–9; and *De Etruriae regionis,* 35, 51.

41. See above all *De Etruriae regionis,* 20ff.

42. This is a major concern of his *De nativitate ultima.*

43. See the letters to Masius, May 19, 1549, and Nov. 25, 1563 (Chaufepié,
loc. cit., 220, 225–6); *Victoires des femmes,* 19–20; *Le prime nove del altro mondo,
passim.*

44. *Victoires des femmes,* 19–20.

45. *Ibid.,* 20: "she said that I was to be her eldest son."

46. *L'Histoire mémorable des expéditions . . . faictes par les Gauloys ou Françoys
depuis la France iusques en Asie,* etc. (Paris, 1552), f. 2.

47. Eberhard Gothein, *Ignatius Loyola und die Gegenreformation* (Halle,
1895), 377; Desbillons, *Éclaircissements sur Postel,* 56–7.

48. *De universitate liber,* 2nd ed. (Paris, 1563), 4.

49. *De originibus* (1553), 84–6.

50. In this insistence on the value of cabala as a missionary tool, Postel shared
a conviction common among Renaissance cabalists. Their optimism was, in fact,
considerably encouraged by a number of conversions among Jewish intellectuals
of the time which were, at any rate, attributed to cabala (Blau, *op. cit.,* 65).

51. *De orbis concordia,* 133.

52. His most outspoken attacks on ecclesiastical abuses are in his
Πανθενωσία, which was dedicated to the delegates at Trent. For attacks on
abuses in civil society, see *De magistratibus Atheniensium liber* (Paris, 1541) and
De la république des Turcs (Poitiers, 1560).

53. He found much in common between these threats to Catholicism in
Alcorani seu legis Mahometi et Evangelistarum concordiae liber (Paris, 1543).

54. His view of history, which involves regular cycles of decay and regeneration, was first outlined in *Absconditorum clavis* and developed in subsequent
works.

55. All this is conveniently summarized in the second section of his major
work on the Turks, bearing the separate title *Histoire et considération de l'origine,
loy, et coutume des . . . Ismaelites ou Muhamédiques* (Poiters, 1560), 53–4.

56. This letter fell into the hands of Flacius Illyricus and was printed by him
under the title *Epistola Guilielmi Postelli ad C. Schwenckfeldium* (Jena, 1556).

57. For the original prediction, see especially his letters to Schwenckfeld and Melanchthon (in *Postelliana. Urkundliche Beiträge zur Geschichte der Mystik im Reformationszeitalter,* J. Kvačala, ed., *Acta et Commentationes Imp. Universitatis Jurievenis (olim Dorpatensis)* XXIII [1915], No. 9, pp. 8–10, 33–43). For suggestions concerning Postel's revision of this date, see his letters to Theodor Zwinger, described in *ibid.,* 80, 85.

58. *Absconditorum clavis,* 6ff.; *De originibus* (1553), 44, 56–7; *Description et charte de la Terre saincte* (Paris?, 1553?), 20. On Postel's notion of French political leadership in the last age, see Pierre Mesnard, *L'Essor de la philosophie politique au XVIe siècle* (Paris, 1936), 445ff.

9 Renaissance and Reformation

An Essay on Their Affinities and Connections

This essay was commissioned by the organizers of the Fourth International Luther Congress, held in St. Louis in 1971. I tried to demonstrate in it not only the affinities of the Reformation with the Renaissance but also the European-wide character of the impulses underlying the Reformation. I naively assumed that none of this would be controversial, and I was quite unprepared for the hostility it provoked among some delegates to the congress, chiefly from Northern Europe, who represented what I came to perceive as the Lutheran Establishment. This group was concerned to insist on the total originality of Luther and the uniquely German origins of the Reformation. The paper would, I think, be more generally accepted today.

It was first published in Luther and the Dawn of the Modern Era: Papers for the Fourth International Congress for Luther Research, *ed. H. A. Oberman, Studies in the History of Christian Thought, vol. 8 (Leiden: E. J. Brill, 1974), pp. 127–149. It is reprinted here by permission of the publisher.*

•   •   •

Since the peculiar mixture of responsibility and presumption in the title of my paper will scarcely have escaped the notice of this distinguished audience, I feel some need to explain at the outset that it represents an assignment on the part of those who planned our meeting. The significance of the problems to which it points is suggested by the great historians who have grappled with it in the past, albeit (a fact that should constitute something of a warning) with somewhat contrary results, among them Michelet, Dilthey, and Troeltsch.[1] Its practical importance lies in the need of most of us to place our more limited conclusions in some broader historical framework; we must therefore reconsider, from

225

time to time, the relationship between Renaissance and Reformation. In spite of this, the subject has recently received little systematic attention, and many of us are still likely to rely, when we approach it, on unexamined and obsolete stereotypes. Obviously I cannot hope to remedy this state of affairs in a brief paper. Yet the progress of Renaissance studies in recent decades invites a reassessment of this classic problem, and I offer these remarks as an essay intended to stimulate further discussion.

What has chiefly inhibited larger generalization has been the extension and refinement of our knowledge, and with it a growth both in specialization and in humility. Thus we are increasingly reluctant to make broad pronouncements about either the Renaissance or the Reformation, much less about both at once. For as scholars we are divided not only between Renaissance and Reformation, or between Italy and Northern Europe; even within these categories most of us are specialists who would claim competence only in a particular aspect of Renaissance Florence or Venice, in one phase or another of Renaissance humanism, in Machiavelli or Erasmus, in later scholasticism or the history of piety, in Luther or Calvin or the sects. Under these conditions few students of the Renaissance have cared to look as far as the Reformation; and although Reformation scholars have been somewhat bolder, they have rarely pursued the question of Renaissance antecedents farther than northern humanism. Humanism is, indeed, the one subject that has recently encouraged forays into the problem of this paper; but although Breen, Dufour, Spitz, Liebing, and especially Charles Trinkaus, among others, have made valuable contributions to discussion,[2] the problem is still with us, primarily, I think, because we have not fully made up our minds about the meaning of Renaissance humanism. A result of this difficulty has been a tendency to focus special attention on Erasmus as a touchstone for the Renaissance, a role for which—for reasons that will emerge later in this paper—I think he is not altogether suited.

It is, however, one measure of the complexity of our subject that we cannot approach the question of the relationship between Renaissance and Reformation without somehow first coming to terms with the implications of humanism. I should like to do so, however, obliquely rather than directly. It seems to me that although humanism, which assumed a variety of forms as it passed through successive stages and was influenced by differing local conditions, was not identical with the more profound tendencies of Renaissance culture, it was nevertheless often likely to give them notable expression, and for reasons that were not accidental but directly related to the rhetorical tradition; whatever their differences in other respects, most recent interpretations of Renaissance humanism have at least identified it with a revival of rhetoric.[3]

What has been less generally recognized is the deeper significance of this revival. The major reason is, I think, that in our time the term *rhetoric* has become largely pejorative; we are inclined to couple it with the adjective *mere*. But for the Renaissance there was nothing shallow about rhetoric. Based on a set of profound assumptions about the nature, competence, and destiny of man, rhetoric gave expression to the deepest tendencies of Renaissance culture, tendencies by no means confined to men clearly identifiable as humanists, nor always fully expressed by men who have generally been considered humanists. I shall try in this paper to describe these tendencies, which seem to me to have exerted intolerable pressures on central elements in the medieval understanding of Christianity. And I will suggest that similar tendencies underlay the thought of the great Protestant Reformers. Thus the significance of Protestantism in the development of European culture lies in the fact that it accepted the religious consequences of these Renaissance tendencies and was prepared to apply them to the understanding of the Gospel. From this standpoint the Reformation was the theological fulfillment of the Renaissance.

I

Fundamental to the cultural movements of the Renaissance was a gradual accumulation of social and political changes: an economy increasingly dependent on commerce rather than agriculture; a political structure composed of assertive particular powers; and a society dominated by educated laymen who were increasingly restive under clerical direction and increasingly aggressive in pressing their own claims to dignity and self-determination. A commercial economy and the more and more openly uncoordinated conduct of politics supplied the social base for a new vision of man's place in the world, and of the world itself. Social experience rooted in the land had perhaps encouraged a sense of broad, natural regularities ultimately responsive to cosmic forces and inhibiting to a sense of the significance of change; but the life of a merchant community and the ambitious operations of independent rulers made all experience contingent on the interaction between unpredictable forces and the practical ingenuity and energies of men. Under these conditions the possibility of cosmic order seemed remote, but in any case of little relevance to human affairs; and the obvious rule of change in the empirical world encouraged efforts at its comprehension and eventually stimulated the awareness of history, that peculiarly Hebraic and Christian—as opposed to hellenic or hellenistic—contribution to the Western consciousness. Meanwhile new political realities and the claims of laymen undermined the hierarchical conceptions that had defined the internal structure of the old unified order of the cosmos, within which the affairs of this world had been assigned their proper place.[4] It will also be useful to observe at this point that these developments were by no means confined to Italy; I will touch briefly at a later point on the implications of this fact for the Renaissance problem.

It is not altogether wrong to emphasize the positive consequences of these developments which, by freeing human activity from any connection with ultimate patterns of order, liberated an exuberance that found expression in the various dimensions of Renaissance creativity. Burckhardt's insight that the autonomy of politics converted the prince into an artist of sorts may require modification; yet the new situation made all human arrangements potentially creative in a sense hardly possible so long as the basic principles of every activity were deduced from universal principles. The notion of the state as a work of art points to the general process of secularization and reminds us that the culture of the Renaissance extended far beyond its brilliant art and literature, and was perhaps even more significant in its implications than in its accomplishments.

It had, however, another and darker side. It rested on the destruction of the sense of a definable relationship between man and ultimate realities. It severed his connection with absolute principles of order, not so much by denying their existence as by rejecting their accessibility to the human understanding. It deprived him of a traditional conception of himself as a being with distinct and organized faculties attuned to the similarly organized structure of an unchanging, and in this sense dependable, universe. Above all, therefore, it left him both alone in a mysterious world of unpredictable and often hostile forces, and at the same time personally responsible in the most radical sense for his own ultimate destiny. For he was now left without reliable principles and—because the directive claims of the church also depended heavily on the old conceptions—reliable agencies of guidance. These darker aspects of Renaissance culture eventually required, therefore, a reformulation of Christian belief, and we shall now examine them a bit more closely.

Renaissance thought has sometimes been represented as a reassertion of ancient rationalism against the supernaturalism of the Middle Ages. The formulation is, of course, both inaccurate and misleading. In the thirteenth century some intellectual leaders had been notably hospitable to Greek philosophy, and had tried to coordinate it with revelation. But it was precisely the possibility of such coordination that Renaissance culture—insofar as it differed from what had preceded it—characteristically denied; in this sense Renaissance thought was less rationalistic (if not necessarily less rational) than that of the Middle Ages.

In fact it was inclined to distinguish between realms, between ultimate truths altogether inaccessible to man's intellect, and the knowledge man needed to get along in this world, which turned out to be sufficient for his purposes. Thus the Renaissance attack on scholasticism had a larger implication as well as a specific target; it implied, and occasionally led to, the rejection of all systematic philosophy. From Petrarch, through Salutati and Valla, to Machiavelli, Pomponazzi, and the Venetians of the later Renaissance, the leaders of Renaissance thought rejected any effort to ground human reflection or action on metaphysics: and at the same time they insisted on the autonomy of the various dimensions of human concern and the relativity of truth to the practical requirements of the human condition. In this sense, although truth was robbed of some grandeur, it was also made more human; and if Aristotle was less and less respected as a vehicle of eternal wisdom, he could be all the more admired as a man.[5] Under such conditions philosophy could evidently contribute nothing to theology; indeed, its spiritual effects were likely to be adverse since it encouraged malice and pride.

Related to the attack on metaphysical speculation was an attack on hierarchy, which rested ultimately on metaphysically based conceptions of the internal structure of all reality. The repudiation of hierarchy was most profoundly expressed in Nicholas of Cusa's conception of the infinite, which made every entity equally distant from—and thus equally near to—God;[6] a similar impulse perhaps lurks behind Valla's rejection of Pseudo-Dionysius.[7] But partly because the formulations of Cusanus smacked too much of metaphysics, partly because the problem of hierarchy was peculiarly related to social change, the attack on hierarchy was likely to receive more overtly social expression. It took a general form in the effort to substitute a dynamic conception of nobility through virtue for the static nobility of birth,[8] a specific form in the impulse (often expressed in legislation and the practical policies of states)[9] to consider the clergy in no way superior to other men but, on the contrary, as equal in the obligations of citizenship (if generally less competent in practical affairs), at least as vulnerable to sin, and in as desperate a need for salvation as other men, whom it was their obligation to serve rather than to command. This suggested at least that social order was unrelated to cosmic order, but it also raised the possibility that order per se was of a kind quite different from what had been supposed.

For the age of the Renaissance was by no means oblivious to the need for order, which indeed historical disasters had converted into the most urgent of problems. But its very urgency intensified the necessity of regarding order as a practical rather than a metaphysical issue. Bitter experience seemed to demonstrate that order had to be brought down to earth, where it could be defined in limited and manageable ways. And, as the occasional intrusions of the clergy into politics appeared periodically to demonstrate, the attempt to apply ultimate principles to concrete problems was likely only to interfere with their practical solution. This was a central point not only for Machiavelli and his *politique* successors; it also molded the numerous constitutional experiments of the Renaissance, with their repudiation of hierarchically defined lines of authority in favor of order through a balance of interests and their appeal to immediate local needs and the right of local self-determination. The best arrangements, in these terms, were not those that most accurately reflected some absolute pattern but those that best served the specific and limited human purposes for which they were instituted.

But although a sense of the limitation of the human intellect was basic to the thought of the Renaissance, this negation had a positive corollary in a new conception of the human personality which also seemed to correspond better to the experience supplied by a new social environment. Men whose lives consisted in the broad range of experiences, contingencies, and human relationships that characterized existence in the bustling and complicated modern world could no longer find plausible an abstract conception of man as a hierarchy of faculties properly subject to reason; instead the personality presented itself as a complex and ambiguous unity in which the will, primarily responsive to the passions, occupied a position at the center. One result of this conception was to undermine the contemplative ideal; if man's reason was weak but his will strong, he could only realize himself in this world through action, indeed he was meant for a life of action. Another was to reduce suspicion of the body; in the absence of the old psychological hierarchy, the body could no longer be held merely base and contemptible. Action required its use, and the new integrity of the personality reduced the possibility of attributing the human propensity to evil primarily to the physical or sensual aspect of man's nature. Human passions now also acquired a positive value, as the source of action.[10] This new anthropology, articulated by Petrarch, Salutati, and Valla, required a reconsideration of the problem of immortality and led eventually to the ardent discussions of the soul in which Pomponazzi figured. It also pointed to the political and historical conceptions of Machiavelli and Guicciardini, who emphasized the primacy of will and passion, as well as to the psychological interests of a host of Renaissance writers.[11]

In addition man was defined as a social being; if he lost one kind of participation in a larger reality, namely his abstract position as a member of the human species in the cosmic hierarchy of being, he obtained another with, perhaps, more tangible satisfactions: his membership as a concrete individual in the particular human community in which he lived, now an essential rather than an accidental condition of his existence. Thus the values of human community now achieved full recognition. Human virtue was defined not as an abstraction but as a function of relationship with other men; man's active nature was understood to achieve full expression only in a life of social responsibility, and indeed his happiness was seen as dependent on human community. Furthermore, since effective participation in society required some wealth, the conception struck another blow at medieval asceticism.

On the other hand the demands of life in society also stimulated a vision of human existence very different from that implicit in the contemplative ideal. For life in society was patently marked by a conflict of opposing interests that could rarely (if men were honest) be identified with absolute good or evil; and to incessant struggle with other men was added, in social existence, the temptations that inevitably beset anyone who chooses to engage with rather than to withdraw from the world. The life appropriate to men in this world was thus not repose (however desperately one might long for it)[12] but a constant and morally ambiguous warfare, with the outcome ever in doubt. By the same token earthly life had also to be seen as dynamic, as subject to change in all its aspects. Human communities could be seen to rise, flourish, and decay; and the philological investigations of Renaissance humanists supplemented common experience by revealing the general outlines of ancient civilization and thus demonstrating how much had changed during the intervening centuries.[13] They also wrote histories that communicated not only this perspective on the past, with its implication that human culture is not an absolute but relative to its times, but in addition other aspects of the Renaissance vision of life: the active and social nature of man, the values of community, the inescapability of conflict and change.

This vision found its fullest expression in the rhetorical culture of the Renaissance. Humanist oratory was based on the conception of man as a social being motivated by a will whose energies stemmed from the passions. This conception led in turn to a distinctive concern with communication as the essential bond of life in society, as well as to a new human ideal of the well-rounded, eloquent, and thus socially effective man of affairs. The purpose of communication, in this view, could not be the transmission of an absolute wisdom, which the human mind was incompetent to reach, but the attainment of concrete and practical ends.

Such communication had above all to be persuasive; it had to affect the will by swaying the passions, rather than merely to convince the mind; in short it needed to penetrate to the center of the personality in order to achieve results in visible acts. And the significance of the need for persuasion should also be remarked. It implied a life in society that could not be controlled by authority and coercion through a hierarchical chain of command but depended instead on the inward assent of individuals. It was therefore no accident that the rhetorical culture of Italian humanism achieved its fullest development in republics. In addition the needs of broad communication pointed eventually to the development and use of vernacular languages, a more important concern of Renaissance humanism than has sometimes been recognized.[14]

II

It should be immediately apparent that this set of attitudes imposed great strains on traditional Catholicism.[15] It undermined the effort to base earthly existence on abstract principles identified with divine wisdom, and to relate the visible and changing world of ordinary experience to the invisible and immutable realm of the spirit. Both the comforts in this relationship and its implications for the guidance and control of lower things by higher were seriously threatened. From a Renaissance perspective the arguments by which it was supported seemed at best frivolous, at worst a specious rationalization of claims to power in this world on behalf of a group of men whose attention should be directed exclusively to the next. And behind such suspicions we may also discern the perception of man as primarily a creature of will and passion. In this light intellectual claims were likely to be construed as masks for motives that could not bear inspection; dogma itself might be no more than an instrument of tyranny. In addition, since a contemplative repose now seemed inappropriate to the actual nature of man, as well as a breach of responsibility for the welfare of others, the ideal form of the Christian life required redefinition. Finally, the problem of salvation was transformed. Alone in an ultimately unintelligible universe, and with the more fundamental conception of sin and the problems of its control opened up by the new anthropology, man could no longer count on the mediation either of reason or of other men in closer contact with the divine than himself. His salvation depended on an immediate and personal relation with God.

Here it is necessary to pause for a more searching look at one of the key terms of our title: *Renaissance*. The conceptions I have so far reviewed have been based largely on developments in Italy, and this would suggest a vision of the Renaissance, or of Renaissance culture, as initially and perhaps primarily an Italian affair. But this audience is well aware that the tendencies I have described were also present in a variety of movements outside Italy, if in somewhat different forms. It is obvious, for example, that later medieval piety exhibited similar impulses; and that, in spite of the antipathy of humanists to scholastic speculation (though here we need to be more precise about what was actually under attack), the later schoolmen played a major if largely independent part in bringing underlying assumptions to the surface and in attempting to accommodate theology to them.[16] Perhaps, therefore, the time has come to expand, as well as to make more specific, our conception of what was central to the age of the Renaissance, and also to abandon the traditional contrast between Italy and the North, which seems to me to have been in some measure the result of a failure to get beneath surface differences. If I have concentrated on Italian thought in this sketch, I have done so partly to bring out the fundamental unity of European spiritual development, partly because the affinities between Protestantism and later Scholasticism have been more regularly a concern of Reformation scholarship than the parallels with the Renaissance in Italy. What is nevertheless increasingly clear is that the process of redefining Christianity to bring it into correspondence with the new assumptions about man and the world was gradual, and that it was taking place simultaneously throughout Europe.

Largely because of the recent profound book of Charles Trinkaus, it is unnecessary to review in detail the process by which the pressures for religious change implicit in the assumptions of Renaissance culture operated among the humanists of Italy. They are already discernible in Petrarch, and they seem to have reached a climax in Lorenzo Valla. In a general sense they may be attributed to the special loneliness and despair of men who could no longer regard religious truth as a body of knowledge of the same order as other knowledge that was communicable through similar kinds of intelligible discourse. Nor could the institutional fideism encouraged by ecclesiastical authority as an alternative to rational theology provide a satisfactory solution to the problem. Not only did the idea of implicit faith clash with the growing sense of individual spiritual dignity among pious laymen; in addition, discredited by its impotence, its worldliness, the presumed irrelevance of its abstract theology, and a sacramental and disciplinary externalism increasingly inadequate to assuage the peculiarly intense guilt of the age, the church could no longer be regarded as a dependable guarantor of truth.

Thus, driven by a profound yearning for immediate contact with the eternal,[17] the humanists of the early Italian Renaissance moved perceptibly toward a simple religion of grace based on the Scriptures and apprehended by the individual through faith. Petrarch typically began with insights into his own inner conflicts and the discovery that these could only be resolved by throwing himself on God's mercy in a faith that was at once the highest form of knowledge and at the same time different in kind from all other knowledge; confusion on this point seemed to him the most dangerous error. Salutati, concerned as a sterner moralist to protect human freedom and responsibility within a religion of grace, wrestled with the problem of predestination. And with Valla justification by faith received an even fuller exploration, the role of priest and sacrament in the economy of salvation was correspondingly reduced, and that of Scripture, the Word whose authenticity could be established by philology and which spoke directly to the individual, was enlarged.[18]

Corresponding to the distinction between philosophy and faith was the demand for a sharper distinction between the church and the world; the separation of realms in one area seemed to lead naturally to separation in others. In its demands for a spiritual church, the new historicism of the Renaissance collaborated with the insistence of the Italian states on freedom from clerical interference and with their grievances against Rome as a political force.[19] The study of the historical church revealed the spiritual costs of the confusion of realms.[20] At the very least, as men of the Renaissance with some political experience were in a position to know, the effective use of power in the world was always morally ambiguous;[21] and meanwhile the growing participation of popes and prelates in secular politics had been accompanied by an increasing neglect of the spiritual mission of the church. Thus, if reform required a return to the past, the reason was above all that the early church had been true to its spiritual character.[22] Only a spiritual church, devoted to that which does not change, could stand above history and thus resist decay. Valla's attack on the Donation of Constantine was not an isolated document;[23] it reflects a concern with the church, its earthly role and its spiritual mission, that runs through much of Renaissance historiography, from Mussato at the beginning of the fourteenth century to Machiavelli, Guicciardini, and Fra Paolo Sarpi.[24]

The rediscovery of grace was closely related to the new vision of man; philosophy, as Petrarch recognized, was incapable of converting man at the crucial center of his being. "It is one thing to know," he declared, "another to love; one thing to understand, another to will." What was required was a transformation not merely of the intellect but of the whole personality, so that Christian conversion would find appropriate expression in a life of love and active responsibility for the welfare of others. And, as in the world, the essential means for such a transformation was not rational appeal to the intellect but rhetorical appeal to those deeper levels in man that alone could move the will. Thus Petrarch argued for the superiority over rational philosophers of moral teachers who could sow the love of virtue in the very hearts of men.[25] For Valla rhetoric was thus the only branch of secular learning (except for philology) applicable to theology.[26] The implications of this position for the importance and character of preaching seem clear.

A new conception of man was also reflected in a changed conception of God, in accordance, perhaps, not only with Renaissance emphasis on man's creation in God's likeness and image but also with Calvin's recognition of the reciprocal relationship between man's understanding of himself and his knowledge of God.[27] Like man, God could no longer be perceived as a contemplative being, as Aristotle's unmoved mover, operating in the universe not directly but through a hierarchy of intermediate powers.[28] Laymen active in the world required a God who was also active, who exercised a direct and vigilant control over all things, like that to which they aspired for themselves. God too had therefore to be perceived as primarily will, intellectually beyond man's grasp yet revealing something of himself—all, at any rate, that man needed to know—in his actions, above all as recorded in Holy Scripture. And from Petrarch's sense of the free, mysterious, and incalculable nature of God,[29] Salutati went on to defend the anthropomorphic representations of God in the Bible as a form of communication appropriate to men's capacities.[30] Valla was, as one might expect, even clearer that the God of philosophy could not be the God of faith.[31]

In spite of all this, it is nevertheless undeniable that the culture of the Italian Renaissance did not culminate in Protestantism, although even on this point our old sense of the immunity of Italy to the impulses of the Reformation is no longer altogether tenable.[32] Yet it remains true that the religious thought of Renaissance Italy remained no more than an incoherent bundle of fundamental insights, and it was unable to rid itself of fundamental contradictions; again, however, the contrast with Northern Europe seems hardly absolute. Above all it failed to complete its conviction of man's intellectual limitations, which pushed him only part of the way into the realm of grace, with full conviction of his moral impotence. Even here its vision of man suggests a deepening in the understanding of sin and the human obstacles to salvation; and there is abundant evidence of a pessimistic estimate of the human condition in

Petrarch, Salutati, Poggio, Valla, and later, in a different form, in Machiavelli and Guicciardini. Yet Renaissance emphasis on the central importance of the will frequently served chiefly to nourish the moralism that so deeply permeated later medieval piety,[33] contributing both to the notion of Christianity as the pursuit of moral perfection and of the church as essentially a system of government;[34] Renaissance humanism remained, in Luther's sense, Pelagian. The consequence was, however, that Renaissance culture in Italy, like Scholastic theology in the north, helped to intensify, from both directions at once, the unbearable tension between the moral obligations and the moral capacities of the Christian that could at last find relief only in either a repudiation of Renaissance attitudes or the theology of the Reformation. But it could not resolve the problem itself, and we must ask why this was so.

Part of the explanation is connected with the fact that some among the figures we have cited were lacking in theological interests, while the rest were amateurs whose major activity lay elsewhere. The result was an inability to develop the full implications of their assumptions, which was supplemented by prejudice against intellectual labor too closely resembling the Scholasticism they despised. In addition, closely attached to particular societies in which, traditionally, no distinction was made between Christianity and citizenship, they were unable to achieve a full sense of the radical disjunction between salvation and civilization that might have placed the Christian man fully in the sphere of grace. Thus they celebrated instead the positive implications of the spark of divinity in man.[35]

Of greater importance were the changing social and political conditions of the later fifteenth century which, at least in Italy, tended to undermine the assumptions underlying Renaissance culture, and thus to remove the sociological pressures for religious change. Foreign invasion and prolonged war produced general insecurity and a growing sense of helplessness, so that freedom presented itself rather as a threat than an opportunity; and the extension of despotism even to Florence reduced the dignity of civic life and encouraged an increasingly aristocratic and stratified social order. Meanwhile the recovery of the papacy from the long eclipse of the conciliar period brought a vigorous reassertion of the old cosmic intellectuality, of hierarchical principles, and of claims to clerical superiority in the world.[36] The result was a movement of general, if not total, retreat from the ideals of the earlier Renaissance.

The Neoplatonism of later Quattrocento Florence may be taken as an illustration. Although this movement retained and even developed further some of the tendencies I have identified as central to Renaissance culture, what seems to me most significant in Florentine Platonism is not what it had in common with the humanism of the earlier Renaissance but the ways in which it differed.[37] Thus it was spiritually akin to the thirteenth century in its concern to reunite philosophy and theology; for Ficino philosophy was not merely the handmaid of theology but her sister.[38] It also reasserted, if in a modified form, the conception of hierarchy; Ficino provided contemporaries with a Latin translation of Pseudo-Dionysius.[39] And with these conceptions inevitably went also a return to an understanding of man as a duality in which sovereign intellect should rule the contemptible flesh and salvation was held to consist in the separation of the spiritual man from the visible world so that he might enjoy the harmony and peace of intellectual contemplation; Ficino described the task of Christian conversion as "fishing for intellects."[40] The intellectuality here was also reflected in a spiritual elitism based on contempt for the ordinary man who lacked the capacity for such lofty detachment; it also pointed once again to the authority of a body of absolute truths guaranteed by the experts who were alone competent to grasp them.[41] With such an ideal the historical world, the changing realm of conflicting interests, of political and social responsibility, and of the intrinsic dignity of the individual layman, was unworthy of attention.[42] Rhetoric was no longer praised for its utility but denounced as an enemy of truth.[43] For truth had come to present itself in the old way again.

The problem of interpreting Erasmus, as indeed of other northern humanists of his generation, arises from the fact that he appeared on the European scene when conceptions of this kind, by no means confined to Florence, were generally attractive. They provided a resolution of a kind for the religious tensions of the age, at least for intellectuals; and the mind of Erasmus was partly formed by them.[44] The place of Erasmus in any discussion of the relationship between Renaissance and Reformation thus requires some distinctions.

This is hardly the place to attempt a general interpretation of the complex and ambiguous Erasmus, but he enters so regularly into discussions of the relations between Renaissance and Reformation that we cannot avoid him altogether. As Margolin has reminded us, one needs first of all to understand Erasmus himself; for this purpose it is inappropriate to measure his thought by standards external to it.[45] Yet this is a different problem from the problem of his historical significance; and from the standpoint of those tendencies in Renaissance culture I have been concerned to emphasize here, Erasmus seems to me at least equivocal. Sometimes he attacked the schoolmen in ways typical of the

Renaissance, not only shallowly, for the barbarities of their style, but also because the kind of truth they sought to explicate was beyond the legitimate capacities of men and because of the irrelevance of their speculations to the urgent needs of spiritual life;[46] yet in the moment of personal crisis forced on him by Luther, he turned to Scholastic theology and rebuked Luther for his sweeping criticism of Aristotle.[47] Nor is it altogether clear that his own *philosophia Christi* (the phrase itself suggests a concern to reunite what earlier humanists had tried to keep apart) was intended simply to reflect the practical reason of the Renaissance; at times he seems to have conceived it as an expression of ultimate wisdom, of the Logos itself.[48] Again, although he often gave eloquent articulation to the lay impulses of Renaissance piety, we must also take into account the elitist tendencies in his insistence on the allegorical meanings of Scripture and his frequent expressions of contempt for the crowd; he attacked Luther for "making public even to cobblers what is usually treated among the learned as mysterious and secret."[49] He liked to represent true Christianity as a religion of the heart[50] and defended marriage,[51] but his anthropology tended to the familiar dualism that opposed the body to the rational soul and made actions depend on beliefs;[52] such conceptions contributed substantially to his belief in the value of education.[53] He described the Christian as a soldier of Christ; but his own ideal, at both the social and personal level, consisted in harmony and peace.[54] But if I call attention here to the contradictions in Erasmus, my purpose is not to indict him for what some have considered one of his more lovable traits, but only to suggest that we should be cautious in identifying Erasmianism with the Renaissance. Thus the echoes of Erasmus in Zwingli, Bucer, Melanchthon, and Calvin are not necessarily proof that we are in the presence of impulses from the Renaissance; the reverse may well be true.

Nevertheless the ambivalence of Erasmus reminds us again that the Renaissance posed religious problems that it could not solve. It left man alone and in desperate need, but without the means or the assurance of salvation. It pointed to a religion of free grace, perhaps even (as in Valla) to *sola fide*; but in the end it turned away. Indeed its refusal to give up the dubious consolations of an intellectual definition of man, its failure to distinguish between the temporal works of civilization and the requirements of eternal life, and the strain which this added to its continuing insistence on human responsibility merely left the masses of men unusually vulnerable to a spiritual anxiety widely reflected in a heightened sense of sin and a fear of damnation that found no relief. Meanwhile the persistent moralism in Renaissance culture was supplemented by the demands of the church for conformity to external moral and ritual observance as the price of salvation. And as the burdens on the individual conscience grew heavier, so also did the weight of man's anxiety.[55]

Yet I would argue that among the major causes of anxiety on the eve of the Reformation was also the persistence, even in movements that in some respects disowned them, of the deep and by this time ineradicable assumptions of Renaissance culture. As long as Europeans could not come to terms in an explicit theology with the conceptions that remained implicit in their vision of man and the world, as long as the beliefs of the heart remained at war with those of the head, the Renaissance would not be complete. That it required completion was, in a sense, recognized by Erasmus himself in his conviction of the peculiar degree to which the world of his time thirsted for salvation, "by a longing ordained, as it were, by fate."[56]

III

It would be too evidently a work of supererogation to demonstrate at any length the fundamental importance for classical Protestantism of the tendencies I have identified as central to Renaissance culture. I shall therefore offer only a rapid review of the connections between them, and then attempt to deepen the argument of this paper by focusing briefly on two questions that seem to me to reveal in a special way the intimate connections between Renaissance and Reformation: the conception of God and the Protestant solution to the Renaissance problem of anxiety.

Renaissance skepticism, with its sense of the limits of the human understanding, its utilitarian conception of the knowledge appropriate to the human condition, and its clear separation between philosophy and religious belief, found expression in the Protestant insistence that the Scriptures alone communicate what is necessary for salvation. They place, therefore, a limit on speculation; they reveal God only as he chooses to reveal himself, and only insofar as such revelation is relevant to man's practical needs. Furthermore this revelation is to be grasped not after the manner of earthly wisdom, which often requires peculiar intellectual gifts, but by a unique act of faith from which no man is excluded by the absence of natural capacities or of education. Thus in a practical manner the Renaissance rejection of metaphysics, as it was taken up in Protestantism, finally liberated the individual believer from subjection to theological experts. In this way the Renaissance had prepared the way for the lay religion of the Reformation, with its attention to the spiritual dignity of the individual, a dignity that depended only on the humanity all men possess in common.

The same skepticism also encouraged flexibility in dealing with all practical problems. Metaphysical argument could no longer be exploited to support claims for the absolute superiority of one vocation, one form of government, or one kind of social organization over another. What mattered was the satisfaction of concrete human needs, such as the necessity of political order; Calvin seems to have recognized the political implications of Renaissance laicism in a preference for republican government that allied him not only with Zwingli and Bucer but also with the champions of Renaissance Florence and Venice, but the great Reformers were notably undogmatic about the forms of government.[57] Released from the bondage of metaphysics, the arrangement of this world's affairs could now be fully secular and thus be judged simply on the basis of practical results. The same pragmatism can also be observed in Protestant conceptions of ecclesiastical polity, at least where positive Scriptural prescription was lacking. By the same token wealth appeared neither good nor bad in itself, but only in the manner of its use.

At the same time Protestants generally accepted the new anthropology of the Renaissance. It was fundamental to their definition of sin, whose location chiefly in the lower levels of the personality they decisively rejected. Since the personality was for them a unity, they were clear that every part of it had been vitiated. Luther saw the pursuit of "spiritual values" as a serious temptation,[58] and Calvin attributed the localization of sin in the senses to pagan influence.[59] Man, for the Reformers, was the complex unity of Renaissance thought, but now even more sharply defined; the core of his being was certainly not his reason, and indeed even his will responded to deeper impulses. The Reformers tried to convey their meaning here, like some Italian humanists, by frequent references to *the heart,* the mysterious center of the personality, which determines man's beliefs and actions alike. And they shared the conviction of the rhetoricians of the Renaissance that the essential problem of communication lay in penetrating this vital core. Like Renaissance oratory, the Gospel had to be conveyed into the hearts of the many rather than into the intellects of the few, for it had to transform lives rather than—merely—to change minds. The living word of Christ was not dialectic but rhetoric.[60]

As in the Renaissance this conception of man was combined with an emphasis on life in society; the existence appropriate for the human condition was not solitary contemplation but rather responsible action among other men; thus the Christian commandment of love complemented the Renaissance sense of social obligation.[61] Similarly Protestantism shared the Renaissance vision of life as conflict and change. The Christian life was dynamic; it was marked by progress towards godliness through temptation, which had therefore to be regarded not as an evil from which men should flee but as God's method of disciplining and purifying the soul. Milton's rejection of a cloistered virtue reflected Reformation and Renaissance simultaneously.

The same dynamism was more broadly reflected in a sense of the importance of historical change. The Reformers shared the Renaissance vision of the past as a decline into Gothic darkness from a better age, and also its hope for renewal; like the humanists, indeed, Calvin associated the decadence of his own time with the decline of literary culture.[62] But there was a larger point here. The God of Protestantism was once again the God of history rather than the author of a static system of metaphysical absolutes; and the destiny of man was no longer perceived as conformity to an ultimate and unchanging general order of things, but as the indefinite realization of his spiritual capacities in time, in accordance with the particular circumstances of concrete existence.[63]

But in none of its dimensions does Reformation theology more clearly reflect the rhetorical culture of the Renaissance than in its conception of God himself. The God of Luther, and even more of Calvin, may be seen as a transcendent expression of the Renaissance ideal of the orator, who, as active and personal governor of all things, supremely unites wisdom and virtue with eloquence, and power with a direct love and concern for his human subjects that is manifested in a desire to communicate to them what their welfare requires and to win their inward assent.[64] In fact, as Luther early remarked, God's works are identical with his words;[65] just as he communicates himself in his Word, so his words, whether through the law by which man is enslaved, or by the Gospel which sets man free, actively accomplish his purposes for mankind.[66] Furthermore, as Calvin emphasized, God's discourse is not couched in the timeless abstractions of logic. He appeals rather to the imagination than to the intellect; and in addition, like a skilled orator, he speaks to men in a language adapted to their capacities and their needs, taking historical and cultural differences into account and adapting his communication to the times.[67]

As representatives of the underlying tendencies of Renaissance culture, the great Reformers were also forced to confront the problems raised by the profound anxieties implicit in Renaissance culture, anxieties of which they were deeply aware. Calvin, indeed, was prepared to exploit positively "that religious fear by which we ought to be affected" for its value in driving man to rely on God alone, and he employed his own considerable eloquence in a deliberate effort to intensify it.[68] Not the least of his contributions to the needs of the age was, in addition, a system of both external constraints and internalized discipline that supplied a practical substitute for the discredited metaphysical structures that had previously been a source of guidance and comfort.

Yet it was Luther, with his doctrine of *sola fide*, who took the essential step toward dissipating the religious anxiety of the Renaissance. The skepticism of the Renaissance had closed off access to God through the understanding, and its conception of man had radically altered the problem of salvation, which could no longer be conceived as the reduction of the soul to a proper order as the source of meritorious works. Luther accepted these contributions of the Renaissance, but he perceived too their radical implications for the spiritual impotence of man. He was able to do so, as he was later to recall, because he "learned to distinguish between the righteousness of the law and the Gospel."[69] Thus he was able to distinguish also, as the religious thought of the Renaissance had failed to do, between the civilization of men, in which the will may be adequate, and salvation, in which it is powerless. The result was to eliminate the major impediment to a full acceptance of man's dependence on God's love. Completing the insights of the Renaissance, Luther recognized that the full realization of human freedom depended paradoxically on the complete acceptance of the sovereignty of God, for the work of salvation as well as the words of revelation, which in the end proved identical. He saw that any other conception of freedom resulted only in enslaving men to their own anxieties and, by way of relief, to human ordinations. In this way Luther met the religious needs implicit in the new culture of the Renaissance, and in ways largely consistent with its fundamental assumptions.

NOTES

1. The complexity of the issues involved is nicely suggested by Troeltsch's own retreat from the famous "medieval" interpretation of Reformation theology in his classic *Die Soziallehren der christlichen Kirchen und Gruppen* of 1911. Hans Baron has called my attention to Troeltsch's little-known revision of his *Protestantisches Christentum und Kirche in der Neuzeit* (Leipzig and Berlin, 1922), in the second edition of part one of *Die Kultur der Gegenwart*, Abteilung IV. 1, II Hälfte, pp. 431–792.

2. Quirinus Breen, *Christianity and Humanism: Studies in the History of Ideas* (Grand Rapids, 1968), and *John Calvin, A Study in French Humanism* (Chicago, 1931); Alain Dufour, "Humanisme et Reformation," *Histoire politique*

et psychologie historique (Geneva, 1966), p. 37–62; Lewis W. Spitz, *The Religious Renaissance of the German Humanists* (Cambridge, Mass., 1963), and, most recently, "Humanism in the Reformation," in *Renaissance Studies in Honor of Hans Baron,* Anthony Molho and John Tedeschi, eds. (Florence, 1970), pp. 643–62; Heinz Liebing, "Die Ausgänge des europäischen Humanismus," *Geist und Geschichte der Reformation* (Berlin, 1966), pp. 357–76; Charles Trinkaus, *In Our Image and Likeness: Humanity and Divinity in Italian Humanist Thought* (2 vols.; Chicago, 1970), and "Renaissance Problems in Calvin's Theology," *Studies in the Renaissance,* I, (1954) 59–80.

    3. Among more important recent works, see Paul Oskar Kristeller, *Renaissance Thought: The Classic, Scholastic, and Humanist Strains* (New York, 1961); Hans Baron, *The Crisis of the Early Italian Renaissance* (rev. ed.; Princeton, 1966); Eugenio Garin, *L'umanesimo italiano* (Bari, 1958); Jerrold E. Seigel, *Rhetoric and Philosophy in Renaissance Humanism* (Princeton, 1968); Hanna H. Gray, "Renaissance Humanism: The Pursuit of Eloquence," *Journal of the History of Ideas,* XXIV (1963), 497–514.

    4. I have discussed these matters at greater length in *Venice and the Defense of Republican Liberty: Renaissance Values in the Age of the Counter-Reformation* (Berkeley and Los Angeles, 1968), esp. chs. 1 and 8.

    5. Cf. Petrarch, *De sui ipsius et multorum ignorantia,* Hans Nachod, trans., in *The Renaissance Philosophy of Man,* Ernst Cassirer et al., eds. (Chicago, 1948), p. 74: "I certainly believe that Aristotle was a great man who knew much, but he was human and could well be ignorant of some things, even of a great many things."

    6. Cf. Ernst Cassirer, *Individuum und Kosmos in der Philosophie der Renaissance* (Leipzig and Berlin, 1927), ch. 1.

    7. See Mario Fois, *Il pensiero cristiano di Lorenzo Valla nel quadro storico culturale del suo ambiente* (Rome, 1969), p. 492.

    8. For Poggio's celebrated dialogue on this subject—one of the better known pieces on the theme—see George Holmes, *The Florentine Enlightenment, 1400–1450* (London, 1969), pp. 148–50

    9. For Florence, for example, see Marvin B. Becker "Church and State in Florence on the Eve of the Renaissance (1343–1382)," *Speculum,* XXVII (1962), 509–27. More generally, see Nicolai Rubinstein, "Marsilius of Padua and Italian Political Thought of His Time," *Europe in the Late Middle Ages,* J. R. Hale et al., eds. (London and Evanston, 1965), pp. 44–75; and Daniel Waley, *The Italian City-Republics* (London, 1969), pp. 87ff.

    10. Cf. Hans Baron, "Secularization of Wisdom and Political Humanism in the Renaissance," *Journal of the History of Ideas,* XXI (1960), 140–41.

    11. See in general Trinkaus, *In Our Image and Likeness.* On Pomponazzi see also J. H. Randall's introduction to Pomponazzi's *De immortalitate animae,* in *The Renaissance Philosophy of Man,* esp. p. 273; and on Valla, Giorgio Radetti, "La religione di Lorenzo Valla," *Medioevo e Rinascimento: studi in onore di Bruno Nardi* (Florence, 1955), II, 616–17.

    12. Cf. Petrarch, *De ignorantia,* p. 49: "Shall we never have any respite? Must this pen always need fight? Shall we never have a holiday? . . . Shall I never find quiet repose by fleeing almost everything for which mankind strives and fervently exerts itself? . . . Most avidly craving for peace, I am thrust into war."

13. For an introduction to this aspect of the Renaissance, see the fine piece of Theodor E. Mommsen, "Petrarch's Conception of the 'Dark Ages,' " *Speculum,* XVII (1942), 226–42, and Donald R. Kelley, *Foundations of Modern Historical Scholarship* (New York, 1969), esp. ch. 2.

14. Baron, *Crisis,* esp. pp. 332 ff., and Dufour, p. 58. Dufour emphasizes the concern for vernacular communication as a bond between humanists and Reformers.

15. On the general point Trinkaus is particularly valuable.

16. The affinities between Italian humanism and some tendencies in later scholasticism have been recognized by Garin, *L'umanesimo italiano,* pp. 10–11, and *Medioevo e Rinascimento: studi e ricerche* (Bari, 1961).

17. Cf. Heiko A. Oberman, "Some Notes on the Theology of Nominalism, with Attention to Its Relation to the Renaissance," *Harvard Theological Review,* LIII (1960), 47–76.

18. Trinkaus, I, 40–41, 55, 76, 127, 147; II, 575. On Valla, see also Radetti, pp. 609–10.

19. On the uses of history, see Walter Ullmann, *Principles of Government and Politics in the Middle Ages* (London, 1961), pp. 228–29.

20. This is a central conception, for example, in the first part of Machiavelli's *Istorie fiorentine.*

21. Cf. Guicciardini: "Political power cannot be wielded according to the dictates of a good conscience. If you consider its origin, you will always find it in violence—except in the case of republics within their territories, but not beyond. Not even the emperor is exempt from this rule; nor are the priests, whose violence is double, since they assault us with both temporal and spiritual arms." *Maxims and Reflections of a Renaissance Statesman,* Mario Domandi, trans. (New York, 1965), p. 54.

22. Cf. Machiavelli, *Discorsi,* Bk. III, ch. 1, on the need for regular revivals in religion.

23. See Radetti, pp. 610–12.

24. For Mussato, Manlio Dazzi, "Il Mussato storico," *Archivio Veneto,* Ser. 5, VI (1929), 361; for Machiavelli, see, for example, *Istorie fiorentine,* bk. I, ch. 1; for Guicciardini, *Storia d'Italia,* Bk. IV, ch. 12; for Sarpi, see my *Venice,* pp. 358 ff.

25. *De ignorantia,* pp. 103–4.

26. Hanna H. Gray, "Valla's *Encomium of St. Thomas Aquinas* and the Humanist Conception of Christian Antiquity," *Essays in History and Literature Presented to Stanley Pargellis* (Chicago, 1965), p. 45.

27. *Institutes,* I, i.

28. For the point in Valla, see Radetti, p. 616.

29. Trinkaus, II, 768–69.

30. Baron, *Crisis,* pp. 295–96.

31. Radetti, p. 616.

32. For example, George H. Williams, *The Radical Reformation* (Nashville, 1962), pp. 16 ff., and various works of Delio Cantimori.

33. Cf. Heiko A. Oberman, *Forerunners of the Reformation* (New York, 1966), pp. 10–12, and Jean Delumeau, *Naissance et affirmation de la Réforme* (Paris, 1968), p. 356, quoting J. Toussaert: "un Christianisme à 80% de morale, 15% de dogme et 5% de sacrements."

34. Ullmann, p. 51 and *passim*. Cf. E. Delaruelle et al., *L'église au temps du Grand Schisme et de la crise conciliaire* (Paris, 1962), II, 899, 902.

35. Cf. Trinkaus, I, 74–76 (on Salutati's amalgamation of Christianity with civic life), 88–89; and Nicola Abbagnano, "Italian Renaissance Humanism," *Journal of World History,* XI (1963), 278.

36. See L. D. Ettlinger, *The Sistine Chapel before Michelangelo: Religious Imagery and Papal Primacy* (Oxford, 1965). The development is nicely reflected also in the changing ecclesiology of Eneas Silvius Piccolomini.

37. In this emphasis I differ somewhat from Kristeller and Trinkaus, though I am deeply indebted to both.

38. Paul Oskar Kristeller, *The Philosophy of Marsilio Ficino* (New York, 1943), p. 322. On the general point cf. Holmes, p. 243.

39. See Josephine L. Burroughs, in *Renaissance Philosophy of Man,* p. 185. For the modification in the idea of hierarchy, P. O. Kristeller, "Ficino and Pomponazzi on the Place of Man in the Universe," in his *Studies in Renaissance Thought and Letters* (Rome, 1956), p. 286.

40. Letter to Pico, quoted by Leland Miles, *John Colet and the Platonic Tradition* (London, 1961), p. 7. On the general point, Burroughs, p. 191.

41. Edgar Wind, *Pagan Mysteries of the Renaissance* (New Haven, 1958), pp. 14 ff.

42. Eugene Rice, *The Renaissance Idea of Wisdom* (Cambridge, Mass., 1958), pp. 49 ff.

43. See the letter of Pico Della Mirandola to Ermolao Barbaro, in Breen, *Christianity and Humanism,* pp. 16 ff. On the general point, Seigel, p. 258.

44. Roland Bainton, *Erasmus of Christendom* (New York, 1969), pp. 59–60.

45. J. C. Margolin, *Recherches érasmiennes* (Geneva, 1969), p. 31.

46. See the general discussion by Eugene Rice, "Erasmus and the Religious Tradition," in *Renaissance Essays,* P. O. Kristeller and P. P. Wiener, eds. (New York, 1968), pp. 175–79.

47. See Philip S. Watson's introduction to *Luther and Erasmus: Free Will and Salvation* (London, 1969), p. 14. For Erasmus's criticism of Luther's attack on Aristotle, see his letter to Jodocus Jonas, 10 May 1521, *Opus Epistolarum Erasmi,* P. S. and H. M. Allen, eds. (Oxford, 1906–1958), IV, 488.

48. Cf. Matthew Spinka's introduction to the *Enchiridion,* in *Advocates of Reform from Wyclif to Erasmus* (London, 1953), pp. 285–86; and Heinrich Bornkamm, "Faith and Reason in the Thought of Erasmus and Luther," *Religion and Culture: Essays in Honor of Paul Tillich,* Walter Leibrecht, ed. (New York, 1959), p. 138.

49. Letter to Jonas, Allen, IV, 487–88.

50. See, for one example among many, his *Paraclesis,* in *Ausgewählte Werke,* Annemarie and Hajo Holborn, eds. (Munich, 1933), p. 144; here Erasmus expresses the hope that there should "everywhere emerge a people who would restore the philosophy of Christ not in ceremonies alone and in syllogistic propositions but in the heart itself and in the whole life." John C. Olin, trans., in *Christian Humanism and the Reformation* (New York, 1965), p. 99; cf. his letter to Paul Volz, 14 Aug. 1518, Allen, III, 374.

51. Cf. his approval of Colet's position on this matter, letter to Jonas, 13 June 1521, in Allen, IV, 521.

52. As with other aspects of Erasmus's thought, it is possible to find the

most contradictory passages on this point among his various pronouncements, but it seems to me difficult to ignore the dualism underlying his influential *Enchiridion*; and it is notable that although he has much to say about the immortality of the soul, he says remarkably little about the resurrection of the body. For the dependence of actions on beliefs, see the adage *Aut fatuum aut regem*, Margaret Mann Phillips, trans., *The Adages of Erasmus* (Cambridge, 1964), p. 217: "The first requisite is to judge rightly about each matter, because opinions are like sources from which all the actions of life flow, and when they are infected everything must needs be mismanaged."

53. Noted by Bornkamm, pp. 135–36.

54. Cf. Johan Huizinga, *Erasmus and the Age of the Reformation*, F. Hopman, trans. (New York, 1957), pp. 119–20; and Bernd Moeller, *Reichsstadt und Reformation* (Gütersloh, 1962), p. 49.

55. Cf. Delumeau, pp. 33, 48 ff.; Trinkaus, II, 767–69; Joseph Lortz, *Die Reformation in Deutschland* (3rd ed.; Freiburg, 1948), I, 11–12; Delaruelle, II, 872–74.

56. *Axiomata*, in *Erasmi opuscula*, W. K. Ferguson, ed. (The Hague, 1933), p. 337, trans. Olin, p. 149.

57. Cf. *Institutes*, IV, xx, 8.

58. *Römerbrief*, *WA*, LVI, 258–59.

59. *Institutes*, II, ii, 4.

60. Melanchthon's esteem for rhetoric is well known, and for Calvin see Breen, "John Calvin and the Rhetorical Tradition," *Church History*, XXVI (1957), 14 ff. But Luther's attitude to rhetoric has received less attention, although he discussed it from time to time in the *Tischreden*, for example 193 (called to my attention by Professor Steven Ozment) and 3528. *WA Tr*, I, 85–86; III, 378.

61. For Luther see the massive documentation in George W. Forell, *Faith Active in Love: An Investigation of the Principles Underlying Luther's Social Ethics* (New York, 1954). There is a good deal to the point for Calvinism in Michael Walzer, *The Revolution of the Saints* (Cambridge, Mass., 1965), esp. ch. 1.

62. *Institutes*, III, iv, 7, for example.

63. For the general point in Luther, see John Headley, *Luther's View of Church History* (New Haven, 1963), and the stimulating suggestions of Gerhard Ebeling, *Luther: An Introduction to His Thought*, R. A. Wilson, trans. (Philadelphia, 1970), pp. 87–88, 161–62.

64. Headley, p. 2; Trinkaus, "Renaissance Problems in Calvin," pp. 68, 72.

65. *Dictata super Psalterium*, *WA*, III, 152,

66. Ebeling, esp. pp. 66–67, 119–21.

67. *Institutes*, II, viii, 10; II, xi, 13; III, xviii, 9, xxiv, 9; IV, viii, 5–7.

68. *Institutes*, III, ii, 23. On the general point, Walzer, *passim*.

69. *WA Tr*, V, 210, 5518.

10 Venice, Spain, and the Papacy

Paolo Sarpi and the Renaissance Tradition

This essay, another by-product of my book Venice and the Defense of Renaissance Liberty, *sought to place Sarpi in the broader context of civic humanism and Renaissance historiography. It thus argued for the persistence of Renaissance values in Venice long after, as it has been assumed, they had disappeared from Italy. The essay was first published in an admirable Italian translation by my Berkeley colleague, the late Arnolfo Ferruolo, in the* Rivista Storica Italiana *74 (1962), 697–716. Translated into English by Catherine Enggass, it appeared again in* The Late Italian Renaissance, 1525–1630, *ed. Eric Cochrane (New York: Harper and Row, 1970), pp. 353–376. It is reprinted here with the permission of the publishers.*

• • •

Although Paolo Sarpi is one of the great figures of the seventeenth century, not only of Italy, but of all Europe, and although many historians, Italian and non-Italian, have studied his career and thought, he remains an enigma and a subject of controversy. It is true that we have good editions of his most important writings and an increasing body of information concerning his life and surroundings. Yet there is still no satisfactory general work on Sarpi, nor is there any generally accepted interpretation of his personality, his thought, and his purposes.

In the past, attempts to interpret his career have taken two main directions. On one hand, they have tried to ascertain whether Sarpi's hostility to the papacy and his loyalty to his native Venice were chiefly religious or political in motivation. On the other, these interpretations have sought to establish whether he was, as he protested, a loyal Catholic, or whether he was rather a secret sympathizer with Protestantism and

247

a heretic at heart.[1] These questions, however, have too often led to mere polemics, and Sarpi has chiefly been exploited by both sides in the great controversies that continue to divide Italy. Largely for this reason the endeavor to answer these questions has been inconclusive. Some scholars have even come to believe that Sarpi himself was singularly evasive and enigmatic regarding his true position and purposes.[2] I should like to suggest, rather, that not Sarpi but the questions have been at fault. They are based, in my opinion, on certain modern distinctions that are hardly applicable to Sarpi and his times.

The first problem, whether Sarpi's motives were essentially religious or political, depends on a tendency to distinguish between religion and politics, and hence between church and state. That distinction is characteristic only of more modern times. For Sarpi, as for the supporters of the pope, the struggle between Venice and the papacy was only one more chapter in the age-old debate about the location of supreme authority in Christendom.[3] It is important to recognize (as we too often fail to do) that this debate was not, after all, between the rival powers of church and state. As Pope Nicholas the Great wrote in the ninth century, "The Church is the world"; and this famous definition meant that the struggles between popes and emperors were always seen as taking place within the church. The issue was not between church and state or between politics and religion (although each side accused the other of mere worldliness), but between two rival conceptions of church order and between two religious agencies.[4] For Sarpi the state was a religious institution with divinely appointed responsibilities and a major role in the church. In promoting the cause of Venice against the papacy, he was defending an ancient religious position; and as historians we have no reasonable grounds to doubt his sincerity. The distinction between a political Sarpi and a religious Sarpi thus seems to me false: the political Sarpi does not exclude, but rather helps to explain, the religious Sarpi.[5] The second problem, whether Sarpi was truly a Catholic, seems to me equally anachronistic. For several generations before the appearance of Martin Luther a rich doctrinal ferment, both various and free, had permeated Western Christendom; and this variety persisted among men who continued to think of themselves as Catholics long after the last session of the Council of Trent. What true Catholicism was, what the authority of the council was, and what its decrees meant, were still open questions for many thoughtful Catholics in Sarpi's time.[6] If doubts about these matters were displayed less openly in Italy than in France, the reason was as much lack of opportunity as religious conviction.[7] From this point of view it was therefore quite legitimate to attack Tridentine Catholicism as a merely factional position which did not adequately reflect Catholic tradition, and even, without any disloyalty toward Catholicism, to share certain Protestant formulas. We are not justified in assigning the consolidated, monolithic Catholicism of the nineteenth and early twentieth centuries to the early seventeenth century. Nor are we justified in imputing subversive Protestant intentions to Sarpi.[8] Sarpi must be taken literally. He was struggling against what he considered a false Catholicism in favor of a true one.

Since the study of Sarpi by way of these questions has not proved fruitful, I should like to put the problem on a different basis. It seems to me that one must start by identifying in Sarpi a certain *forma mentis* and certain fundamental attitudes that correspond to a particular political situation and to a related moment in the history of culture. This observation, however commonplace it may appear, will be far more helpful in our endeavor to understand Sarpi than any effort to seek the origin of his thought in particular literary sources. Books and ideas are important historically not because of their intrinsic value and abstract force, but because of the fertile ground they find in certain readers; and the historian's major problem is that of determining not the lineage of a position, but the reasons for its attraction for a specific individual or group. It is in this sense, for example, that we must interpret Sarpi's preference for the philosophy of William of Ockham over that of any other Scholastic.[9] Sarpi was not identifying himself with a school. He was simply reporting his discovery of a kindred spirit.

For this reason we must approach Sarpi by way of a certain context of sympathies and values. These alone, I believe, will bring us to the heart of the question. First of all, it seems to me that Sarpi is best understood as a representative of certain attitudes prevalent in the late Middle Ages and the Renaissance. These attitudes have been variously described. Georges Delagarde has defined them as "l'esprit laïque" and has given particular attention to their expression in the thought of Marsilio of Padua and William of Ockham.[10] Eugenio Garin and Hans Baron have defined them somewhat differently and have preferred to associate them with the Italian humanistic tradition, especially in Florence.[11] Notwithstanding the differences between them, both positions insist upon the relationship of these tendencies in philosophy to the attempts of townsmen to free themselves from certain medieval forms of thought and social organization. It is against this general background that I wish to consider Sarpi, though without placing him too precisely within any particular tradition. If in the course of this discussion I make frequent allusions to the Renaissance, my intention is only to suggest a general framework of values. I do not claim, for example, that Sarpi was a humanist in any exact sense. He had no interest in rhetoric; and although he received a classical education, he did not attach much importance to ancient models of thought and expression. Nevertheless, profound influences from the Renaissance can be discerned in him.

Whatever else may be said about them, the republican communes of Renaissance Italy clearly provided an atmosphere favorable to the development of wide interests and broader spiritual horizons; and the responsibilities of civic life stimulated both patriotism and a new historical consciousness. Local tyranny and the Spanish domination eventually destroyed this political framework in most of the Italian states, and the Counter-Reformation generally suppressed what was left of the culture that the older political order had supported. But Venice, as has been too little recognized, was a unique exception to the rule. Venice retained the liberty that was lost by the rest of Italy.[12] At the same time, she jealously guarded her religious autonomy in the face of all attempts at centralization by Rome: and neither the Inquisition nor the Index managed to acquire much power within her dominions.[13] Thus, however much the world around her had changed, Venice remained the unwavering champion of Renaissance values as late as the first decade of the seventeenth century.[14] And the serious threat to these values posed by the papal offensive of 1606, which was encouraged by Spain, had almost the same effect on the Venetians, and on Sarpi in particular, as the Milanese aggression against Florence had had on Bruni's generation two centuries earlier.

Much of Sarpi's position is rooted in these circumstances and events. His youthful openness to all human thought and experience is typical of the varied and stimulating life of the Italian city. Endowed with an inexhaustible curiosity, he cultivated every branch of natural sciences. He actively participated in the philosophical inquiries of the University of Padua. He studied law and history. He talked with everyone, Italian or foreign, who could feed his curiosity about le cose humane ("the affairs of men"). And he longed to travel in order to see with his own eyes what his foreign acquaintances reported.

The variety of Sarpi's interests is one of the most significant aspects of his personality.[15] But the way in which he dealt with these interests is even more suggestive. What is impressive in Sarpi is his directness, his concreteness, and his flexibility in the face of any kind of experience. Perhaps the central conclusion of his early philosophical speculation was that the mind can return again to the real world of immediate experience.[16] This conclusion seems to be reflected in aspects of his later thought as well. For Sarpi, man must always start from the concrete and the particular, since general principles are deceptive. And it is his constant attachment to this conclusion that explains the rigidity of the positions he subsequently took.

After Romano Amerio's investigations, Sarpi's scientific empiricism and his positive conception of law can no longer be open to question.[17] It will therefore be more useful to illustrate this attitude in other aspects of his thought. The attitude underlies his work as a historian. The historian, he says, must avoid general principles and base his work on concrete situations and the accumulation of particular detail. At one point in his *History of the Council of Trent* Sarpi suddenly seems to realize that his meticulous attention to particulars might bore his readers. He therefore stops to explain: "To someone reading this report, its attention to trivial things and causes may seem excessive. But the writer of the history, taking a different view, has thought it necessary to show what tiny rivulets caused the great lake that occupies Europe."[18] Thus the flow of time seems to be composed of innumerable tiny droplets, each of which requires individual attention. This same attitude is manifested in Sarpi's view of education, as his friend and collaborator Fra Fulgenzio Micanzio tells us. Sarpi resolutely refused to deal systematically in his teaching with any author, because he held that this method was in general followed "not [to gain] knowledge or to improve the mind, but to speak with subtlety, to show one's cleverness, and to make oneself more pertinacious than sincere as an investigator of the truth." He preferred instead to teach "in the Socratic and obstetric manner," that is, to employ that method which emphasized particular human insights and the immediate and concrete response of the student.[19]

I have insisted on Sarpi's concrete and direct method because I think it crucial to our understanding both of the man and of his place in the development of Western culture. Efforts have been made to identify this tendency in Sarpi with particular systems of thought—with nominalism, for example.[20] I will not deny certain affinities between Sarpi's thought and that of Ockham. But I think that the attempt to classify Sarpi in this way obscures the essential quality of his mind. He did not have a system of his own, and he deeply opposed all systems as falsifications of reality. We must look first of all at Sarpi himself, at his concern with all things human and at his refusal to be constrained by any intellectual construction that he believed might cut him off from the richness and paradoxes of human experience.

This interpretation of Sarpi as a Renaissance man gains substance when two other aspects of his career are considered: his view of history and his connections with the Venetian Republic. Sarpi's view of history reveals the same sense of discontinuity between his own age and antiquity that had been characteristic of the Florentine historians; and his writings likewise reveal how well he had learned, like them, that institutions develop and change in time by natural processes. But in one way Sarpi went further than they: he applied this insight systematically to the church. He did so with regret, since he believed that the church ought to be identical and continuous with its primitive forms. In this sense he was a foe of history: he saw time as the great corrupter.[21] Nevertheless he recorded the changes that he observed; and though dealing with that institution to which some superiority over history was generally attributed, he noted the relativity of particular arrangements and pronouncements in terms of the concrete historical circumstances in which they occurred.[22] His extension of this Renaissance theme to the church is perhaps Sarpi's greatest technical contribution to Western historiography.

But Sarpi's major link with the Renaissance tradition appears in his attitude toward society and in his political thought and activity. His career falls naturally into two parts. Until 1605 he devoted himself to study, although his *vita contemplativa* was interrupted from time to time by the demands of his order. But with the crisis provoked by the interdict, he was suddenly called to take part in the affairs of the world; and from then until his death he was strenuously committed to the *vita activa*. Thus Sarpi in his own life was forced to grapple with a problem that had been crucial to the development of Florentine humanism. He was not the only one of his circle to be so involved. The problem had been faced by his close associate Nicolò Contarini;[23] and the comment of Fra Fulgenzio on this abrupt change in Sarpi's life shows us the traditional way in which Venetians regarded this central problem of the Renaissance circle. "At this period," Fulgenzio wrote, "it might be said that he terminated his tranquil studies and his private life; and from then until the end of his life he entered into another world, or rather into the world. And it pleased God to call him to labors to which he would never have thought to apply himself. But man is not born for himself. [He is born] principally for his country and for the common good."[24] It is interesting to observe the ardor with which Sarpi threw himself into the fray and what little regret he felt for the serene life of study he had forsaken. He seems, indeed, to have been waiting all his life for this moment.[25] Indeed, as though this activity corresponded to some profound personal need, his health, which had always been poor, suddenly improved.[26]

Yet even in action Sarpi did not base himself on general principles. What attracted him was not the abstract moral obligation of social duty but service to a particular community. Sarpi loved Venice as Salutati and Bruni had loved Florence; and his pride in the political achievements of the Republic and in the long duration of her freedom frequently recurs in his writings, both public and private. For him the cause of Venice against the papacy was that of "our liberty, which Divine Providence has preserved inviolate for one thousand and two hundred years . . . amongst innumerable dangers."[27]

But under the pressure of papal attack Sarpi also developed a theoretical justification for the authority of the Venetian government. It was one which, in its glorification of the powers inherent in the community, suggests a radical extension of certain elements of Renaissance patriotism. The obvious feature of Sarpi's political thought is the large authority it attributes to the "prince," a term by which he seems to have meant administrative office in general as well as the person holding it. Like other theorists of his time, Sarpi derived the sovereign authority of the prince directly from God;[28] and he attributed to sovereignty a remarkable comprehensiveness. Sovereignty, he declared, is necessarily indivisible and inalienable. Above all, it is absolute in its own realm. "Sovereignty is a power absolute by nature from which nothing can be exempted or excepted," he declared. "And the moment that it yields to any condition or exception, it loses its supreme being and becomes dependent."[29]

This sentiment may suggest that Sarpi was only another of the many exponents of seventeenth-century absolutism. But such a suggestion should be corrected in the light of another important aspect of his political thought. Although Sarpi's term "prince" is applicable to every supreme political authority, from the French monarchy to the Venetian *dogato,* he was thinking primarily of his own Republic. Absolute sovereignty of divine derivation is for Sarpi evidently consonant with republican government; it would therefore be somewhat misleading to associate him too closely with conventional theories of divine right. In reality Sarpi was concerned with the duty of the prince to the community; and this duty had for him a meaning very close to the function of government for Locke. "The prince and the senate have not sinned," Sarpi maintained; "they have rather obeyed the commandments of God in seeing to the preservation of the lives, honor, and property of His subjects."[30] Sarpi's absolutism, then, is not an unregulated and arbitrary power but unlimited authority to be exercised for the common good.[31]

If Machiavelli is the only touchstone of Renaissance political thought, this association of Sarpi's politics with the Renaissance would be quite unconvincing. As Chabod has emphasized, Sarpi's political philosophy has little in common with Machiavelli's, and it reveals rather more affinity with that of the French jurists of the period.[32] Sarpi's divergences from Machiavelli are many. The most notable is his insistence that the moral and religious obligations of the prince are greater than those of the ordinary citizen.[33] But Sarpi's intention was to defend what he considered the ancient rights of a free republic and not, as was Machiavelli's, to propose extraordinary remedies to halt a process of degeneration. So conservative a purpose really somewhat resembles that of those French theorists who were trying to bolster the position of an established monarchy. On the other hand, Sarpi's aim had also some precedent in a more vital period of Florentine history; his real spiritual precursor seems to me to be Salutati, who loved and served Florence and who praised the laws of his community as instruments of God's will.[34]

To identify Sarpi with the Renaissance past may appear somewhat anachronistic, and it therefore calls for some further elaboration. The seventeenth century is certainly not the fifteenth; the world had altered greatly since the time of Bruni and Salutati. But to establish Sarpi's relationship with the Renaissance will provide a point of departure for the next stage in our investigation. We must now examine how the Renaissance motives in Sarpi were adapted to new conditions and how they were modified in the process. Indeed, this appears to me to be the unique value of Sarpi, and indeed of the whole Venetian episode, for the historian. The special political conditions basic to Renaissance culture no longer existed in other parts of Italy, and what remained of it was defensive or merely academic. In Venice alone at this late date can we find central attitudes of the Renaissance still alive and engaged in an encounter with a changing world. Sarpi was the major Venetian exponent of these values, and because of a mentality extraordinarily open and sensitive to change, he was also the outstanding witness to their transformation.

The changes that had taken place since the "golden age" of the Renaissance were of several kinds; and it will be useful to distinguish here two major sorts of alteration, both of which deeply affected Sarpi and gave a particular direction to those of his characteristics that I have associated with the Renaissance. The first of these changes was political; and it resulted from the altered relation of Venice, as of the rest of Italy, to the powers of Europe. The emergence of a system of well-organized and ambitious states able to determine the destiny of Italy had made her role in European affairs increasingly passive. Venice's own field of action was more and more restricted, and her very existence as an independent state often seemed to depend on developments and decisions elsewhere.[35] With his broad interests and clarity of vision, no one realized this better than Sarpi.[36]

Sarpi recognized that the impotence of Italy came in part from her political division.[37] But he also saw that her principal problem was of a moral nature. For that reason he included even his beloved Venice, during the years after the Interdict, in his indictment of Counter-Reformation Italy. Echoing Machiavelli, he wrote sorrowfully of his native city: "Now we have breathed out all our virtue; . . . we have drunk some opiate from the vessel that puts everyone to sleep."[38] On the other hand, all was not yet lost for Sarpi as long as Venice retained her freedom. But she needed powerful allies, such as France or the Netherlands,[39] and Sarpi would not have rejected an alliance even with the Turks. When a Turkish attack on Rome seemed in prospect, he commented: "It causes sorrow here, people fearing the Turk in Italy; but it would be a universal salvation."[40]

But however conscious Sarpi might be of Venice's weakness and vulnerability, he retained his sense of the dignity of the Republic and his pride in the political values she represented. For Sarpi, Venice was the courageous defender of a common cause: "She alone upholds the dignity and true interests of an independent prince."[41] As such she merited the respect and assistance of the great powers; but she should beware of being absorbed by them. Therefore, the first rule for a state that "wanted an understanding with the Republic" would be "to demonstrate the desire for associates, not dependents."[42] In spite of all her vicissitudes, Venice continued to represent for Sarpi a complex of values that had to be preserved at any cost.

Closely connected with his estimate of the political situation was Sarpi's doctrine of "opportunity" (*opportunità*), a doctrine which helped him to solve a very serious problem. In a world so menacing, so inimical to the development and even the survival of everything most dear to him, how was a man or a government to act? To struggle openly and continuously against superior force would only ensure destruction. Yet to do nothing was unthinkable. Sarpi resolved this dilemma by proposing a policy of alert vigilance, of patient waiting for the opportune moment which would be presented by Divine Providence, and then of striking with vigor.[43] The doctrine of "opportunity" reveals how much the mood of the Renaissance had changed since the time of Machiavelli. In so far as the doctrine counseled shrewdness and flexibility, it may have precedents in Machiavelli. But for Sarpi it became a measure of human impotence. *Virtù* could no longer even hope to triumph over *fortuna*. Man is not incapable of controlling events. At the most he can only cooperate with the opportune moment. The wise man, therefore, must patiently resign himself to long periods of inactivity. Indeed, there is no certainty that God will even present him with a genuine *opportunità*. Sarpi himself began to suspect that it would not come in his generation and that, at best, he could work only for posterity. "It is well to instruct posterity," he pointed out, "at least with writings, so that when the evil of the present changes, they can regain liberty if it should be lost to us."[44]

A pessimism bordering on desperation with regard to the limits of human action is obviously not a characteristic generally associated with the Renaissance; and we are entitled to attribute Sarpi's gloom in great measure to altered political circumstances. Yet even here I think that his position was a natural development of the Renaissance emphasis on particular, concrete experience and of its rejection of all-embracing intellectual systems created by men. For the Renaissance mentality had two rather different aspects. On one hand, it tended to liberation and bold adventures of the mind; and this positive tendency could seem most prominent in a time of relative hope. But on the other hand, it rejected adventure in the present and withheld confidence in the future; and it manifested a profound skepticism concerning the limits of the human understanding and a resignation to man's imprisonment in the chaotic immediacy of direct experience. It is hardly surprising that for Sarpi this second tendency reflected the real truth about man's position in the universe. Indeed, notwithstanding his persistent pessimism regarding the probable course of events, he steadfastly refused to predict the future,[45] thereby revealing a deeper pessimism than would have been suggested by the certainty of disasters ahead. For Sarpi the world would always present surprises. He was convinced not only that all human calculation was useless but also that events usually turned out completely opposite to man's expectations.[46] Man, for Sarpi, was helpless in a world he could never hope to comprehend.

With this aspect of Sarpi's thought we have come to the other large set of changes that had altered the world since the time of the Renaissance, those released by the Reformation. If the political scene justified one kind of pessimism, the Christian view of man suggested another, though the two were closely related. The religious tendencies of the period were also reflected in Sarpi's thought. His most important writings, including his great *History,* are works in which he tried to present the values and attitudes we have just examined within a religious context.

He did not sacrifice these values to a religious perspective. Indeed, it seems to me that the key to an understanding of his religious position is to be found precisely in his effort to preserve these values and to reconcile the demands of Christian belief to all that he held most dear. For Sarpi, as for each of us in some sense, the validity of a religious position was to be tested by its consistency with what he otherwise knew to be true.

It seems to me, therefore, that Sarpi's religious position was based on the same renunciation of the general in favor of the particular that we have observed in other aspects of his thought—on the pessimism implicit in this point of view, and especially on the feeling of the help-lessness of man as a moral being, which in some degree parallels and in some degree underlies his helplessness to understand and to control events. For Sarpi, the weakness of man was, among other things, cer-tainly moral. "Every human action," he wrote, "lacks perfection";[47] and this gloomy vision seems to pervade the *History of the Council of Trent,* a work singularly lacking in heroes and one which appears at times to be almost a deliberate demonstration of the depravity of man. But this vision does not exclude all consolation. Sarpi also saw that man's moral deficiencies implied his dependence on divine grace, and this explains the attraction he felt for extreme forms of the Pauline-Augustinian tra-dition.[48]

Sarpi's sense of human limitations is equally evident in his attitude toward Christian doctrine. Here his affinities with the thought of the Renaissance are even clearer. I have in mind something more general than the influence of that evangelism which was so deeply rooted in sixteenth-century Venice. Regarding human reason as incapable of pass-ing from particulars to general truth, and considering all intellectual conclusions as possessing a merely operational validity and as being incapable of final verification, Sarpi considered reason irrelevant to sal-vation. The truths of Christianity could only be approached by faith:[49] hence his bitter criticism of the systematic theological discussions which produced the doctrinal formulations of Trent. This aspect of the *History,* although it has been little noticed, is almost as important as his antago-nism to Rome for the comprehension of his work.[50] To apply the subtle definitions and distinctions of human reason to the content of the faith was for Sarpi a shocking contamination of heavenly with earthly things, the product of human vanity, contentiousness, and presumption. It was therefore doomed to futility.[51]

The same skepticism also underlies Sarpi's tolerance of religious dif-ference and his aversion to persecution. Since a precise, systematic, rational, and coherent definition of the faith is so far beyond human capabilities, diversity of opinion must be permitted, and condemnation should be slow. For Sarpi, the doctrinal cleavages of Europe were largely verbal;[52] and since words cannot penetrate to the heart of reality, they were also essentially frivolous. This position, rather than an expression of *politique* indifference or the consequence of a direct inspiration from Protestant doctrines, explains his willingness to collaborate, for both political and religious ends, with Lutherans, Calvinists, and Anglicans. These "heretics" could not be excluded from the Church of Christ on dogmatic grounds, for no human authority could be considered intellectually competent to determine their orthodoxy.

We have thus arrived at another fundamental element in Sarpi's religious position: his theory of the church.[53] Here his emphasis on the particular as the exclusive reality in human experience merges with the other major Renaissance element in his thought, to which it is closely related: affection for a particular social community. Sarpi's concept of the church is based on his insistence upon the fundamental importance of the individual believer. The church thus becomes merely an aggregation of individuals, *convocatio fidelium*.[54] Moreover, Sarpi insisted on the right and duty of individual judgment in religious matters, which he held to be superior to the collective judgment of the church as expressed by ecclesiastical authority. The Venetians might therefore in good conscience defy the papal ban.[55] Obviously, this theory also implied a revision in the relations between layman and priest. If the authority of the church resided in the individual believer, then the priest was only a delegate of the faithful, and the authority of the clergy was based on consent.[56] In this way Sarpi was evidently attempting to supply a historical and theoretical foundation for the secular and anticlerical lay spirit that was so deeply rooted in the civic consciousness of the late Middle Ages and Renaissance. But the essence of his position is that the clerical conception of the church is a violation of the true structure of reality, which resides in individuals rather than in comprehensive systems.

The basis of authority in the church thus resided in the individual believer. But the believer in turn belonged to a national and confessional community. Hence, Sarpi saw the universal Church Militant essentially as the sum of all individual churches—Roman, Gallican, Greek, Anglican, and even Lutheran and Reformed.[57] His ideal, in fact, was not an organizational unity but a loose confederation of autonomous units. For this reason he showed little enthusiasm for any formal reconciliation and institutional unification between Catholics and Protestants.[58] Unity savored too much of authoritarian uniformity, and it was therefore the absolute negation of that freedom to which he so much aspired. Sarpi's idealization of division in the church was perhaps the primary reason for his approval of the Protestant Reformation.[59] Papalism as a theory of ecclesiastical government was obviously contrary to his conception of the proper organization of the church. Moreover, the papal concept of monarchy as the imposition of a general principle of authority over all particular churches and persons was radically opposed to Sarpi's almost instinctive location of essential reality in the individual.

For Sarpi, just as truth is inaccessible to man, who can know nothing but the particular, so the Holy Spirit does not function through institutions or other visible and tangible entities. There is no meeting point between the ultimate and the immediate, the spiritual and the worldly. Sarpi therefore insisted on the exclusively spiritual character of the church: "It is called the kingdom of heaven, not only because it will attain perfection in heaven, but because while yet on earth it reigns and governs not by rules and worldly interests but by completely spiritual ordinances. By another name this is called the Church."[60] He conceived of the clergy as a spiritual body that by its nature is far removed from laws, government, property, or questions of an earthly character in general.[61]

When the clergy concerns itself with such matters, another serious inversion of values occurs. His position here offers Sarpi the opportunity for another attack on Rome. In his view the papacy was generally guilty of confusing the temporal with the spiritual, thus contaminating spiritual things;[62] and the Roman Church had degenerated into a political instrument employed by shrewd rulers to govern the masses for their own interest.[63] To this extent Sarpi was Machiavellian. He accepted the "Averroist myth,"[64] and hence a political interpretation of papal policies. The political efficacy of religion, he held, was demonstrable.

Feeling strongly that such a church did not serve the Christian faith, however, Sarpi wished for something better. Yet how could a purely spiritual church function in the world? With his reply to this question we have come to what, in the more religious atmosphere that followed the Reformation, I would describe as a religious expression of the civic spirit of the Renaissance. Sarpi attributes a wide responsibility to the civil authority, or "prince," as he calls it, both for what concerns the institutional and secular aspects of the church and for what relates to its spiritual life. The institutional direction of the church naturally belongs to the prince, since he is the legitimate ruler of all temporal things.[65] But its spiritual direction also belongs to him. If the authority of the church definitively resides in the lay community and is merely delegated to the clergy, the head of the church is unquestionably the representative of this community. Therefore it is the prince who in the last analysis determines both spiritual and material matters.[66] Thus Sarpi was able to declare that the Venetian Republic and other political governments have frequently and rightly intervened in ecclesiastical matters, "not as princes and political authorities, but as believers and representatives of the whole body of believers."[67] The prince has been delegated by God to govern both the spiritual and temporal orders on behalf of the community. If we keep in mind his predilection for Venice, Sarpi's position evidently serves to combine civic and religious impulses; his radical ecclesiology expresses patriotic devotion and faith in his own community. From this point of view citizenship is the only social condition of importance, and the clergy themselves are first of all simply citizens like other men.[68] In this sense the Republic of Venice was not a secular state at all. It was in the fullest sense the church itself, in so far as the church impinges on man's experience in this world. The exaltation of the Renaissance city-state could go no further.

It is not my intention either to claim systematic consistency for Sarpi's views or to maintain that they have much intrinsic ecclesiological interest. Nevertheless, I think that the historians can discover in him more than a curious renewal of the doctrines of Marsilio of Padua or a late expression of the "Byzantinism" so often attributed to Venice. No doubt Sarpi's doctrine owes something to both these sources. But his importance comes rather from the concrete historical circumstances that elicited his position. Sarpi was the champion of the values inherent in a particular community, values that were seriously menaced; and to defend them he attributed to the community a set of religious sanctions that went far beyond the patriotic affirmations of the Renaissance, even though they were moving in the same direction and serving the same ends. Sarpi reveals the persistence at a remarkably late date of a fundamental motif of the Renaissance; and he helps us to see its development and transformation under the pressure of new historical conditions. He succeeded in being both a patriot and a realist, and in his radical glorification of the state he suggests an important contribution of the Renaissance to the absolutism of early modern Europe.

But even deeper than his attachment to Venice was Sarpi's aversion to the general and the rigidly systematic and his preference for the particular and the immediate. Two rather different historical impulses may be seen converging in this aspect of his thought. One is the reflection of a previous era; the other is an anticipation of much that was most fruitful for the later development of Western thought. Living in a less happy age, he recognized the darker implications of these impulses, and he adapted them to the construction of a more religious world view. There is no question here of a calculated and cynical exploitation of religious values for political and secular ends, as in the case of Machiavelli. Sarpi was a product of the Reformation as well as of the Renaissance, and one of the most striking features of his thought is precisely the way in which it so honestly combines two movements frequently considered antithetical. If, indeed, Sarpi's religious position appears finally closer to Wittenberg and Geneva than to Rome, it is not because he was attracted by Protestantism as such, but rather because the position expressed in the Protestant creeds seemed to him more consonant with the values he held so deeply as a free citizen of a free republic. In this way Sarpi can perhaps provide some insight into major tendencies of both the Renaissance and the Reformation, and above all into their profound connection.

NOTES

1. One example, among many, appears in the *Consiglio in difesa di due ordinazioni della Serenissima Repubblica,* published in *Istoria dell'Interdetto e altri scritti* of Sarpi, ed. M. D. Busnelli and G. Gambarin (Bari: Laterza, 1940; hereafter referred to as *Scritti*), vol. II, p. 16: "Just as until the present I have put forward in my writings only clear and unquestioned doctrine, so in the future I will be able to state quite simply all that I know to be Christian and Catholic doctrine." Cf. Luigi Salvatorelli, "Paolo Sarpi," in *Contributi alla storia del Concilio di Trento e della Controriforma* (Florence, 1949), pp. 142–43.

2. On Sarpi as a problem in historiography, see Giovanni Getto, *Paolo Sarpi* (Rome, 1941; but now republished, substantially unaltered, by Olschki in Florence, 1967), pp. 7–43 (pp. 1–52 of the Florentine edition); Vincenzo M. Buffon, *Chiesa di Cristo e Chiesa Romana nelle opere e nelle lettere di Paolo Sarpi* (University of Louvain, 1941), pp. 31–32; Federico Chabod, *La politica di Paolo Sarpi* (Rome and Venice: Isituto per la Collaborazione Culturale, 1962), pp. 13–18; Gaetano Cozzi, "Paolo Sarpi: il suo problema storico, religioso e giuridico nella recente letteratura," *Il diritto ecclesiastico,* LXIII (1952), 52–88; and Giovanni Gambarin, "Il Sarpi alla luce di studi recenti," *Archivio veneto,* L–LI (1953), 78–105.

3. Cf. Chabod, *La politica di P. S.,* p. 48.

4. See the penetrating book by Henri X. Arquillière, *L'Augustinisme politique: Essai sur la formation des théories politiques du Moyen-Age* (Paris: Vrin, 1934).

5. Cf. Salvatorelli, "Paolo Sarpi," p. 139.

6. Cf. Hubert Jedin, *Das Konzil von Trient: ein Überblick über die Erforschung seiner Geschichte* (Rome: Edizioni di Storia e Letteratura, 1948), pp. 62 ff.

7. Arturo Carlo Jemolo, *Stato e Chiesa negli scrittori politici italiani del Seicento e del Settecento* (Turin: Bocce, 1914).

8. Cf. Buffon, *Chiesa di Cristo e Chiesa Romana*, p. 32. On this point I agree with Getto, *op. cit.*, pp. 116–17, and I agree still more with Salvatorelli in his penetrating study *Le idee religiose di fra Paolo Sarpi*, Classe di Scienze Morali . . . Memorie, vol. V (Rome: Accademia Nazionale dei Lincei, 1953), p. 338.

9. Letter to François Hotman, 22 July 1608, in Sarpi, *Lettere ai Gallicani*, ed. Boris Ulianich (Wiesbaden: F. Steiner, 1961), p. 173. Cf. Buffon, *Chiesa di Cristo e Chiesa Romana*, p. 185.

10. Georges Delagarde, *La naissance de l'esprit laïque au déclin du Moyen-Age*, 6 vols. (Paris, 1942–48; but see now the new edn. in 5 vols. published by Nauwelaerts at Louvain, 1956 *et seq.*).

11. Cf. in particular Eugenio Garin, *L'umanesimo italiano* (Bari: Laterza, 1952); and Hans Baron, *The Crisis of the Early Italian Renaissance* (Princeton: Princeton University Press, 1955).

12. Gaetano Cozzi, *Il doge Nicolò Contarini* (Venice and Rome: Istituto per la Collaborazione Culturale, 1958), p. 81.

13. Cf. Chabod, *La politica di P. S.*, p. 119, and Clemente Maria Francescon, *Chiesa e Stato nei consulti di fra P. S.* (Vicenza, 1942), p. 251. The Republic's protection of Cesare Cremonini from the Inquisition is of special interest in this regard. See Spini, *Ricerca dei libertini* (Rome, 1950), pp. 146–47.

14. Cf. Salvatorelli, "Venezia, Paolo V e fra P. S.," in *La civiltà veneziana nell'età barocca* (Venice and Rome: Istituto per la Collaborazione Culturale, 1959), p. 91.

15. This is the impression that emerges very forcefully from the first biography of Sarpi, the *Vita* by Fulgenzio Micanzio, first published at Leiden in 1646 and more readily available in the Milan, 1824, or the Florence (Barbèra), 1958, editions of the *Istoria del Concilio Tridentino*, here cited in the 1658 edition (no place); see p. 178 for Sarpi's interest in travel. See also Chabod, *La politica di P. S.*, p. 32.

16. Cf. Romano Amerio, *Il Sarpi dei Pensieri filosofici inediti* (Turin, 1950), pp. 13–15, and the citations in Sarpi, *Scritti filosofici e teologici*, ed. Amerio (Bari: Laterza, 1951).

17. In *Il Sarpi dei Pensieri filosofici inediti*. Notable examples of Sarpi's empiricism are to be found in his letters to Jérôme Groslot de l'Isle of 6 January and 12 May 1609, in *Lettere ai Protestanti*, ed. Manlio Duilio Busnelli (Bari: Laterza, 1931; hereafter cited as *Lettere*), vol. I, pp. 58 and 79. For his juridical thought, see "Consiglio in difesa di due ordinazioni" and "Consiglio sul giudicar le colpe di persone ecclesiastiche," both in *Scritti*; see especially pp. 6 and 52–53.

18. *Istoria del Concilio Tridentino*, ed. Giovanni Gambarin (Bari: Laterza, 1935), vol. I, p. 187. Cf. Getto, *P. S.*, pp. 175–76.

19. *Vita*, pp. 79–80.

20. Cf. Buffon, *Chiesa di Cristo e Chiesa Romana*, p. 10. Getto, on the other hand (*P. S.*, pp. 68–69 and 92), sees Sarpi as a "Stoic sage."

21. "Considerazioni sulle censure," in *Scritti*, vol. II, p. 209: "Many things which in their beginnings are good become pernicious as they then change."

22. See his discussion of the council as an institution in Christian history: *Istoria del Concilio Tridentino*, vol. I, pp. 5–6 and 214–18; of the cult of the Virgin, *ibid.*, vol. I, pp. 287–90; of ecclesiastical government, *ibid.*, vol. I, pp.

350–52; and of ecclesiastical benefices, *ibid.,* vol. I, pp. 400–403. Naturally I do not exclude the importance of Protestant historiography in Sarpi.

23. Cozzi, *Contarini,* pp. 56–57.

24. *Vita,* p. 76.

25. Note the conclusion of Sarpi's first formal *consulto,* the "Consiglio in difesa di due ordinazioni," in *Scritti,* vol. II, p. 16.

26. Micanzio, *Vita,* pp. 93 and 145.

27. "Risposta al Breve circa li prigioni" in *Scritti,* vol. II, p. 71. Sarpi's words reflect a general Venetian ethos; see Ernesto Sestan, "La politica veneziana del Seicento" in *La civiltà veneziana nell'età barocca,* p. 54.

28. As in "Scrittura sopra la forza e validità della scommunica," in *Scritti,* vol. II, pp. 38–39.

29. From the *consulto, Della giurisdittione temporale sopra Aquileia,* cited by Francescon in *Chiesa e Stato nei consulti di fra P. S.,* p. 114. Cf. also "Consiglio in difesa di due ordinazioni," in *Scritti,* vol. II, pp. 12, 14, and 15, and "Consiglio sul giudicar le colpe di persone ecclesiastiche," *ibid.,* p. 46.

30. "Considerazioni sopra le censure," in *Scritti,* vol. II, p. 251.

31. Note the skill with which Sarpi contrasts the authoritarianism of Pope Paul V and the free deliberations of the Venetian Senate in "Istoria dell'Interdetto," *Scritti,* vol. I, pp. 15 ff. *et passim.*

32. *La politica di P. S.,* p. 72.

33. "Considerazioni sopra le censure," in *Scritti,* vol. II, p. 249.

34. Cf. Garin, *L'umanesimo italiano,* pp. 31 ff.

35. Cf. Sestan, "La politica veneziana," pp. 45 ff.

36. Cf. Chabod, *La politica di P. S.,* p. 135.

37. Thus in the "Istoria dell'Interdetto," *Scritti,* vol. I, p. 57, Sarpi speaks of the Spanish view that "the distrust between the two greatest Italian [states] made their affairs more stable; and by having the pope conquer the Republic, they would also increase their temporal jurisdiction."

38. Letter to Groslot, 23 October 1607, in *Lettere,* vol. I, p. 4.

39. Cozzi, *Contarini,* pp. 133–34; letter to Groslot, 25 September 1612, in *Lettere,* vol. I, p. 244.

40. Letter to Groslot, 23 October 1612, *ibid.,* vol. I, p. 248.

41. "Istoria dell'Interdetto," in *Scritti,* vol. I, p. 4, *et passim.*

42. Letter to Groslot, 27 April 1610, in *Lettere,* vol. I, p. 119.

43. This doctrine appears in many of his works. Note, for example, the letter to Groslot of 25 November 1608, *ibid.,* vol. I, p. 50: "But in all things the occasion is the chief matter, without which all goes not only fruitlessly, but even with loss. When God shows us the opportunity, we must believe it to be His will that we take it. When [He does] not, we must await silently the time of His good pleasure." The doctrine is carefully examined by Salvatorelli in *Le idee religiose di fra P. S.,* pp. 312 ff. and 358 ff., and by Cozzi in "Fra P. S., l'Anglicanesimo e la 'Historia del Concilio Tridentino,' " *Rivista storica italiana,* LXVIII (1956), 569–71.

44. Letter to Groslot, 25 September 1612, in *Lettere,* vol. I, p. 243.

45. See, for example, the letter to Groslot of 26 October 1610, *ibid.,* vol. I, p. 149: "I, however, have observed many times that matters thought to be without hope turn out well and those that appear to have every chance of success

turn out badly. I thus prefer to wait to see what happens and make no predictions."

46. So the letter to Groslot of 14 September 1610, *ibid.*, vol. I, p. 135: "As to predicting the future, I dare not do it, because of the experience I have had with things that always turn out contrary to expectations."

47. Letter to Groslot, 4 August 1609, *ibid.*, vol. I, p. 88. Cf. Micanzio, *Vita*, p. 173.

48. Cf. Boris Ulianich, "Sarpiana: La lettera del Sarpi allo Heinsius," *Rivista storica italiana*, LXVIII (1956), 425–46, and Cozzi, "Fra P. S., l'Anglicanesimo e la 'Historia del Concilio Tridentino.' " Micanzio, *Vita*, p. 73, speaks of Sarpi's special interest in St. Augustine.

49. Cf. Amerio, *Il Sarpi dei Pensieri filosofici inediti*, pp. 13–15.

50. Note, for example, the debates on systematic theology in the *Istoria del Concilio Tridentino*, vol. I, pp. 298–99, 318, 343–44, 365, and 380–81. Cf. Cozzi, "Paolo Sarpi tra il cattolico Philippe Canaye de Fresnes e il calvinista Isaac Casaubon," *Bollettino dell'Istituto di Storia della Società e dello Stato Veneziano*, I (1958), 98–99, on Sarpi's attitude with regard to speculative theology among the Protestants. See also Chabod, *La politica di P. S.*, pp. 149–50.

51. This is the position taken subsequently by Galileo and the Galileans, and it may be traced to the close personal ties between Galileo and Sarpi.

52. Letter to Groslot, 7 July 1609, *Lettere*, vol. I, p. 86.

53. For a more complete documentation on what follows, see Buffon, *Chiesa di Cristo e Chiesa Romana*, and Boris Ulianich, "Considerazioni e documenti per una ecclesiologia di P. S." in *Festgabe Joseph Lortz* (Baden-Baden: B. Grimm, 1958), vol. II, pp. 363–444.

54. See for example the "Apologia per le opposizioni fatte dal cardinale Bellarmino," *Scritti*, vol. III, p. 69: "What is meant by 'Church'? If we follow the meaning of the word itself and the Holy Scriptures, [it is] the congregation of the faithful." For precedents of Sarpi's position among the medieval canonists, see Brian Tierney, *Foundations of the Conciliar Theory* (London: Cambridge University Press, 1955).

55. "Scrittura sopra la forza e validità della scommunica," *Scritti*, vol. II, p. 21: "And the theologians give as a certain and infallible rule that when a man is sure in his conscience of not having sinned mortally in the action for which he has been excommunicated, he can have a sure conscience about having no damage in his soul and of not being excommunicated [in they eyes of] God, nor deprived of the spiritual assistance of the Church." For Sarpi's opinion on the Jesuit doctrine of obedience, see "Istoria dell'Interdetto," in *Scritti*, vol. I, p. 107, and on the troubles of the Jesuits during the interdict crisis, see Pietro Pirri, S. J., *L'Interdetto di Venezia del 1606 e i Gesuiti* (Rome: Institutum Historicum S. I., 1959).

56. Thus Sarpi's approval of the electoral principle in ecclesiastical office. See the letter to Groslot of 17 February 1608, *Lettere*, vol. I, p. 65.

57. For Sarpi, the cause of Gallican autonomy was also the cause of the Universal Church. See letter to Groslot of 22 July 1608, *ibid.*, vol. I, p. 24.

58. Note the texts presented by Cozzi in "Sarpi, L'Anglicanesimo e la 'Historia . . . ,' " pp. 613–15, and "P. S. tra il cattolico Philippe Canaye . . . ," pp. 123–24, n. 284.

59. He represented Protestant doctrine as a radical remedy for "extinguishing tyranny" in the letter to Groslot of 22 July 1608, *Lettere,* vol. I, p. 23.

60. Cited in Buffon, *Chiesa di Cristo e Chiesa Romana,* p. 42, from the "Sommario di una considerazione sulla libertà ecclesiastica," Biblioteca Marciana, Venice, MS It., cl. XI, cod. 176, fol. 171.

61. Note Sarpi's caustic reply to the pope in "Nullità nelli brevi del pontefice," *Scritti,* vol. II, p. 90.

62. See the summary of this position in Amerio, *Il Sarpi dei Pensieri filosofici inediti,* pp. 35–36.

63. "Consulto sui rimedii . . . ," *Scritti,* vol. II, p. 159: "It becomes just and legitimate to reject and oppose those pontiffs who adopt any means (even though wicked and impious) in order to conserve and increase their temporal authority. . . . "

64. Note Spini, *Ricerca dei libertini,* pp. 15 ff.

65. Note the texts assembled with regard to this point by Francescon in *Chiesa e Stato nei consulti di Fra P. S.*

66. See Micanzio, *Vita,* pp. 161–62.

67. "Consiglio sul giudicar le colpe di persone ecclesiastiche," *Scritti,* vol. II, p. 49.

68. *Ibid.,* p. 50: "Ecclesiastics are citizens and members of the republic. But the republic is governed by the laws of the prince. Hence [ecclesiastics] are subjects; and in disobeying [the law] they sin before God no less than the laity."

11 Venice and the Political Education of Europe

This essay aimed to display the continuing influence of the Italian Renaissance over the political attitudes of Europe in later centuries, as mediated by the Venetian Republic. The essay originally appeared in Renaissance Venice, *ed. J. R. Hale (London: Faber and Faber, 1973), and it is reprinted here with the permission of the publisher.*

• • •

Renaissance Florence has long been considered the origin in European history of a concern with politics as an autonomous study. Faced with the problems of governing a turbulent but independent republic, anxious to insure her survival in a precarious world that seemed to be ruled only by power, and nourished by the rediscovered political culture of antiquity, thoughtful Florentines, in a process that reached a climax with Machiavelli and Guicciardini, began to articulate realistic principles of political effectiveness and to define its limits. In this sense Florence contributed to the education of modern Europe as a congeries of particular powers, like Florence the products of their separate histories, whose policies would be determined by some calculation of political interest.

The role of Venice in transmitting the attitudes and the lessons of Renaissance politics to the larger European world has been less clearly recognized, partly because of the preoccupation of recent historians with Florence, partly because the Venetian contribution to political discourse was relatively late.[1] The government of Venice impressed other Europeans primarily when Italy as a whole was no longer an inspiring spectacle; for this, as well as for other reasons, Venice presented herself as a unique example of political wisdom. Furthermore her own major spokes-

266

men, Gasparo Contarini, Paolo Paruta, Enrico Davila, and perhaps above all Paolo Sarpi, were men not of the fifteenth but of the sixteenth and early seventeenth centuries. This chronology, however, should not obscure the fact that Venice represented in the modern world the central political values of Renaissance republicanism, which she made available to the rest of Europe in a singularly attractive and provocative form.

The European perception of Venice was not entirely, or perhaps even primarily, the consequence of reading Venetian writers, although their works were widely studied and deeply admired. Furthermore, men saw in Venice what they wanted to see. Venice possessed, nevertheless, a definable political culture;[2] and what the Venetians had to say will therefore be helpful in understanding the general interest of Europeans elsewhere in the Venetian achievement.

The most general element in the political ideal to which Venetian writers exposed their audience was a ubiquitous secularism. They were not hostile to religion; indeed, like most of their compatriots, they were demonstrably men of faith, albeit of a kind uncongenial to the developing orthodoxy of the Counter-Reformation; and this fact doubtless contributed to the esteem for Venice among pious Gallicans and Protestants. Their secularism was expressed rather in an antipathy to speculative systems that impose an artificial coherence on all values and experience and thereby claim a right to supervise, among other matters, the political order. They were the enemies not of religion but of metaphysics, and of the notion that the conduct of human affairs should be determined by some comprehensive vision of the nature of things. Their secularism was thus the necessary condition of an autonomous politics, an autonomous culture, and the full appreciation of human freedom.

This characteristic of the Venetian mind found especially vigorous expression in the hostility to Scholasticism and to the dogmatic temperament in general that permeated Sarpi's treatment of the Council of Trent and makes him seem so clearly a predecessor of Gibbon. Sarpi displayed much the same zest as some leading figures of the seventeenth and eighteenth centuries in showing up the presumption in all intellectual system building, its tendency to close men off from the actualities of human experience, and its exploitation to disguise and advance a crude *libido dominandi*. The Venetian approach to human affairs—though Contarini was a partial exception—was earthbound and empirical. Its refusal to force the data of human experience into large systems was notably exhibited in the preference of Venetian writers for exposition through dialogues in which various points of view may find expression without explicit resolution. This familiar Renaissance form was employed by Paruta. It was also, slightly disguised, a favorite device in Sarpi's great work.

Their rejection of system was fundamental for the Venetians to the appreciation of a wide range of human concerns. If there was no universal pattern which bound all things into a single scheme, the subordination of one set of values to another, of one area of experience to another, and indeed of one class of men to another was no longer defensible, except perhaps on the most practical grounds. The implications for political life were here especially clear. Reason of state could no longer find its justification in eternal reason, and there was thus no alternative to a secular politics. The consequence was full recognition of the dignity of the lay estate and of political activity; and this tendency in Venetian discourse was, I suspect, a substantial element in its attractions for European readers. It provided another of Sarpi's major themes, but it emerged with particular clarity in Paruta's defence of civic life.[3] We may also take Paruta as an example of Venetian appreciation of the autonomy of other dimensions of human culture.

Paruta artfully set his dialogue on this subject at the final session of the Council of Trent. This setting enabled him to divide its participants into two groups: on one side, representing the systematic approach to politics, a number of learned bishops; on the other, several Venetian ambassadors. The issue was joined by one of the bishops who, having listened impatiently as the laymen discussed their embassies, their travels, and their experiences throughout Europe, belligerently denounced their worldly activities and contrasted the tedium of service to society with his own leisurely contemplation of higher things. He argued that active commitment to the service of an earthly community is inferior, both relatively in the degree of happiness it provides, and absolutely in the values it represents, to a life devoted to the eternal verities. The active life is a weariness to the flesh and filled with sinful temptations. Above all, it tempts men to prefer an earthly city to the City of God, and of course it is obvious to what city he refers. The wise man, he argued, perceives "that all men ought to be regarded as citizens of this great city of the universe, just as we have all been given one identical eternal law for our governance, one same heavenly father . . . one same head and ruler to govern us and give us everything that is good among us, God, best and greatest. No other homeland have we than nature, no other law, no other family, no other prince."[4] And Paruta's Venetians understood immediately that what was here proposed was a comprehensive ideal at every point antagonistic to their own: a life without particular foci of experience or particular attachments to persons or places; a life that finds no value in the daily emotional and sensory encounters of human existence; a life in which the entire moral experience provided by society has only a negative value. Their defense of civic life was mounted on many fronts, but precisely because only life in society can provide for the whole, complex range of human capabilities, which cannot legitimately be prejudged, subsumed under any single principle, and organized in hierarchies. They insisted on the claims to human affection not only of particular states, which supply the context for all other values, but of family and friends, of the arts, and even of wealth. Political life was *perfect* for Paruta, because of its range and its refusal to discriminate: that is, because of its secularity. The relation of these attitudes to some belief in the dignity and value of human freedom is also close. Hostility to the authoritarianism of the Counter-Reformation in matters of belief permeated the writings of Sarpi, who condoned coercion only where the social order was at stake; and the personal liberty afforded by Venice was a perennial element in the European image of the Republic. In various ways, therefore, the Venetians supplied an idealistic justification for modern patriotism.

As the reflections of Paruta have already suggested, the rejection of universal intellectual systems had a counterpart in the rejection of political universalism, and this bias in the political culture of Venice doubtless also contributed to its wider acceptability. The values attributed to Venice and the patriotism they called forth were equally applicable to other particular states, but not to a universal empire. Paruta himself devoted many pages to a criticism of ancient Roman universalism, which he judged both politically ineffectual and, in comparison with the small states of ancient Greece, artistically and intellectually sterile.[5] The same arguments were equally effective, as the Venetians were aware, against the universalism promoted by the Counter-Reformation papacy.

Venetian politics were based, therefore, on the need to defend the integrity of particular states. The Venetian interdict of 1606–1607, so widely publicized throughout Europe, was, among other things, the first of the great seventeenth-century conflicts over sovereignty; and Sarpi had argued the cause of Venice in terms well calculated to have a broad appeal. "I cannot refrain from saying," he advised his government, "that no injury penetrates more deeply into a principate than when its majesty, that is to say sovereignty, is limited and subjected to the laws of another. A prince who possesses a small part of the world is equal in this respect to one who possesses much, nor was Romulus less a prince than Trajan, nor is your Serenity now greater than your forebears when their empire had not extended beyond the lagoons. He who takes away a part of his state from a prince makes him a lesser prince but leaves him a prince; he who imposes laws and obligations on him deprives him of the essence of a prince, even if he possesses the whole of Asia."[6] And the case for the local settlement of local issues was still another important theme in his history of the council. As he made a Gallican prelate at the council remark, "It would be a great absurdity to watch Paris burn when the Seine and Marne are full of water, in the belief that it was necessary to wait to put out the fire for water from the Tiber."[7] Venetian political culture corresponded, then, to what was more and more clearly destined to be the shape of the European community of nations.

The rejection of systems and of the notion of hierarchy posed a serious danger to political existence, however, because it deprived society, both domestic and international, of its traditional principle of order. The Florentines had discovered the solution to this problem in the idea of balance, which was destined to supplant the hierarchical principle of order at almost the same time in both science and politics. Venice largely owed her survival, in a world dominated by great powers, to a calculated exploitation of the balance of power, and her writers tended to take this for granted. The case was quite different, however, for the internal structure of states; and Venetian publicists were long concerned to account for the order and effectiveness of the Republic by describing its balanced constitution. Contarini's classic work on this subject at times justified Venetian arrangements by appealing rather mechanically to the eternal order of nature, an argument which doubtless did not weaken his case with some of his later readers.[8]

But Contarini was too much of a Venetian to remain long with metaphysics; the order with which he was really concerned was that provided by effective government. "In our city," he boasted, "no popular tumult or sedition has ever occurred";[9] and his explanation of this remarkable fact was understandably of peculiar interest for Europeans whose own societies had been demonstrably less fortunate. The secret of Venetian success, Contarini revealed, was her constitution, which held the potentially antagonistic forces of the political arena in a complementary equilibrium. "Such moderation and proportion characterize this Republic," he declared, "and such a mixture of all suitable estates, that this city by itself incorporates at once a princely sovereignty, a governance of the nobility, and a rule of citizens, so that the whole appears as balanced as equal weights."[10] And since this happy arrangement of checks and balances was severely impersonal, it pointed also to a government of laws rather than of men. But its ultimate test was utilitarian. "The whole purpose of civil life consists in this," Contarini insisted:

"that, by the easiest way possible, the citizens may share in a happy life."[11] Venice supplied, therefore, both a secular ideal and the means for its fulfillment.

Venetian constitutionalism received even wider, if less explicit, dissemination through the great work of Sarpi, which submits the papacy, as a species of governance, to searching scrutiny and finds it wanting largely because of its failure to realize the admirable principles exhibited by the Venetian government. Sarpi argued that the church had originated as a free, spiritual, and democratic body; and he showed how it had degenerated, step by step, through the classic sequence of forms described by Machiavelli, until it had at last emerged as the naked tyranny of the contemporary papacy, a particularly odious example of government by men rather than by laws. Here too the popularity of Sarpi's masterpiece had far more than a religious meaning.

Sarpi's vision of the development of ecclesiastical government over the centuries brings us to a final major contribution of Venetian political culture to the rest of Europe: its increasingly sophisticated historicism, which brought into a single focus the secularism, the particularism, and the constitutionalism of the Venetian tradition. These impulses were combined with a grasp of history as a process largely transcending individual acts which, it seems to me, went substantially beyond the hints at this conception in Florentine historiography. Even Contarini's *De republica Venetorum,* which otherwise displayed little historical sense, had suggested the idea of temporal process in applying the familiar platitude that Venice, following the course of biological nature, might decay;[12] and Paruta, an admirer of both Thucydides and Guicciardini, coolly analyzed the evolution of curial institutions,[13] described the broad changes in Venetian policy over the centuries,[14] and dealt with Roman history as a long decline through such natural causes as her limited economic base, her defective constitution, her militarism, and her excessive greatness.[15] He also expounded the idea of the progress of civilization to account for the contemporary splendors of Venice.[16] Davila was deeply interested in the remote causes for the recent tribulations of France, finding them in her constitution.[17] And Sarpi blamed the papal tyranny not primarily on the wickedness of worldly and ambitious popes but on the general decay of political authority in the early Middle Ages. To those who attributed the Protestant revolt to the actions of a single, nefarious man, he replied that Luther "was only one of the means, and the causes were more potent and recondite."[18]

Notable among the Venetian writers was a strong sense of the autonomy of history, of the obligation to confront the data exposed by historical research directly, without dogmatic preconceptions, and so to get at truth. During the interdict an anonymous Venetian pamphleteer had been bold enough to express a doubt that Charlemagne had truly received the Empire as a gift from the pope, and Bellarmine had angrily accused him of "heresy in history." The Venetian had not hesitated to set the matter straight; he retorted, "There cannot be heresy in history which is profane and not contained in Holy Scripture."[19] Sarpi insisted more than once that historical truth was a matter not of authority but of fact; and authority, he noted, "cannot alter things already done."[20] The famous history of his Venetian contemporary Enrico Davila also owed much of its conviction to its cool objectivity and its apparent freedom from confessional prejudice, and Davila was explicitly sensitive to the problem of bias.[21] Sarpi's bias is, of course, strongly evident, but his professedly empirical method was well calculated to make it appear the product, rather than the motive and organizing principle, of his research. He once compared the council to a great lake fed by numerous tiny rivulets and gradually spreading out over Europe; the task of the historian, in this light, was to follow each of these brooklets to its source.[22] At the same time Sarpi was not naive; he recognized the problem of selection, comparing himself to a harvester who found some fields more productive than others.[23]

But there was nothing detached about the Venetian pursuit of historical truth; and if Sarpi devoted himself to ferreting it out, he did so because he thought it useful. When a Gallican correspondent requested his opinion on the delicate question of Pope Joan, Sarpi replied that he found no solid evidence for her existence and personally doubted it; but, he went on to say, "I should not care to trouble myself to prove something that, once proved, would be of no further use to me."[24] History, for Sarpi, was not a matter for idle contemplation but an instrument of the active life celebrated by Paruta; the truth was useful, he profoundly believed, because the truth would set men free. Historical study, as the pursuit of truth, was for him the natural solvent and enemy of dogma, which sought, in the interest of an illegitimate empire over mankind, to obscure the truth. History thus became, in Sarpi's hands, the great unmasker, and therefore the one sure means of approach to a better world. By revealing the lost perfection of the past and the causes of its decay, it could display both the goal towards which contemporary reformers must struggle and the problems with which they must contend. Sarpi thus transmitted the secularism, the empiricism, and the reformist impulse of the Renaissance to the militant reformers of a later age.[25]

The popularity of the major Venetian political writers and the esteem in which they were held is one symptom of the congeniality of these conceptions in early modern Europe. Their works were widely printed outside Italy, both in their original Latin or Italian texts and in translation; these were in addition to Venetian editions exported abroad. Contarini's *De magistratibus et republica Venetorum* was printed many times in Latin, and was translated into both French and English;[26] Naudé thought this "admirable work" essential for the understanding of a republic.[27] Paruta's eloquent *Della perfezione della vita politica* was turned into French, his more mature *Discorsi politici* into English and German, and his Venetian history into English;[28] Naudé described him as an "ornament of erudition,"[29] and he was widely admired as one of the great political thinkers of his time.[30] Davila's *Istoria delle guerre civili di Francia* was twice translated into English,[31] appeared many times in French and Spanish versions, and was also put into Latin.[32] Bolingbroke praised Davila as the equal of Livy;[33] and while he sat as vice president under Washington, John Adams composed a set of *Discourses on Davila*.[34] Even better known was, of course, Paolo Sarpi. His lesser writings were widely read outside of Italy, and editions of his *Istoria del Concilio Tridentino* multiplied rapidly. After its first appearance in an Italian version in London in 1619, it was quickly translated into Latin, French, German and English;[35] the English edition was among the few books carried to the New World by William Brewster, spiritual leader of the Plymouth colony.[36] It might have had a second English translation if Dr. Samuel Johnson had managed to carry out all the projects he devised for himself,[37] and it was twice more translated into French.[38] And Sarpi's distinction as a political sage was soon recognized. His enemies suggested this by associating him with Guicciardini;[39] among his admirers, Naudé ranked him with such ideal counselors of government as Epictetus, Socrates, Seneca, and Cato.[40] His French translator of the later seventeenth century, Amelot de la Houssaye (no blind admirer of Venice) praised him as a *bon Politique* and recommended his great history because of its excellent lessons for princes.[41] By the eighteenth century Sarpi's reputation for political cunning had so grown that spurious collections of political maxims circulated under his name, for example, in the Berlin of Frederick the Great, a book of worldly counsel under the title *Le Prince de F. Paolo*.[42] To these works, which directly transmitted the political culture of Venice to the rest of Europe, should be added various writings of Giovanni Botero, and especially of Traiano Boccalini, both widely read abroad and inclined to dwell on the virtues of Venice. Boccalini, in the first century of his *Ragguagli di Parnaso*, included an eloquent and diverting summary of all that had seemed most admirable in the Republic.[43]

But these books did not by themselves create an interest in Venice;

they are significant because they nourished, and can therefore help us to understand more clearly, a taste that had deeper sources. The Venetian achievement and the attitudes surrounding it corresponded to the emerging needs of the European nations. And Venice had particular advantages for bringing into focus the political conceptions of modern Europeans. For the Venetian state was not a utopia reflecting merely theoretical values but a living reality, a palpable part of their own world, superior in this respect even to the Florentine republic. She could be wondered at and admired, and the perennial admiration of travelers attracted other sorts of attention to her; her government and the kind of society that accompanied it could be studied empirically and in detail; and the degree to which it actually worked could apparently be evaluated. Venice therefore corresponded naturally to the growing taste for concreteness in political discussion that had emerged with the great Florentines.

She had also figured prominently in events of European resonance that demonstrated conclusively, before an international audience, her effectiveness in meeting crises of enormous danger and her capacity for survival. Her ability to resist the dreaded Turk was generally recognized, but she had also participated actively in the international conflicts of the West. In the war of the League of Cambrai she had withstood the onslaught of all Europe; and, though brought to the brink of destruction, she had nevertheless emerged as powerful as before. This miracle, indeed, had stimulated the work of Contarini, which so effectively conveyed an appreciation of the Venetian government to the rest of Europe.[44] It also transferred an impression previously confined largely to Italy, where it had already attracted the notice of Florence, to a larger world.[45]

Even more stimulating to the European imagination was the Venetian triumph over the pope in the great interdict of 1606–1607. This episode, which was followed with keen attention abroad, was the occasion for a flood of writings, for and against Venice, that circulated everywhere and in various ways called attention to the political values she claimed to incorporate; indirectly the interdict also produced Sarpi's great work on the Council of Trent. Various interdict writings were translated into French, German, and English; they were sold at the Frankfurt fair; Pierre de l'Estoile acquired them in duplicate so that he could circulate them among his friends;[46] the interdict was carefully reported and documents relating to it were extensively reproduced in the *Mercure François*.[47] Later writers on Venice would give special attention to the event. For Pierre d'Avity it showed Venice as "an immovable rock in the defence of the state."[48] To the duc de Rohan the Venetians in this affair "had transcended themselves" and given "an example of perfect conduct to posterity."[49] James Howell devoted a special section to this "high Contestation," of which "ev'ry Corner of Christendome did ring aloud, and sounds yet to this day."[50] Even Amelot de la Houssaye devoted the whole of his second volume to the "good cause" of Venice against the pope.[51]

The capacity for survival that Venice had revealed in the course of such trials demonstrated, in short, that she had access to a general political wisdom, universal, eternal, and utterly dependable, that might be made available to others in an age of peculiar turmoil and political discontent, and therefore an age with a special need for stable principles.[52] Thus Howell opened his *Survay*: "Were it within the reach of humane brain to prescribe Rules for fixing a Society and Succession of people under the same Species of Government as long as the World lasts, the Republic of *Venice* were the fittest pattern on Earth both for direction and imitation." And, he declared, "If ever any hath brought humane government and policy to a *science* which consists of certitudes, the Venetian Republic is She, who is as dextrous in *ruling* men as in *rowing* of a gallie or gondola."[53] The duc de Rohan was attracted to Venice because he perceived in her the triumph of rational calculation over passion: science, perhaps, in a more modern sense.[54] Other writers, including even Bodin, made the point more obliquely by noting the gravity of Venetian political deliberation,[55] or more simply (following Contarini) by attributing the form of the Venetian government to philosophers.[56]

Venice, then, was the embodiment of political reason, a virtue that had previously been manifested chiefly by the ancients. And because of certain peculiarities claimed for her history, she could be seen as the means by which ancient political wisdom had been transmitted to the modern world.[57] For she had, as her admirers insisted, come out of the ancient world but had avoided its general collapse. She was living proof, therefore, of what men longed to believe: that ancient political virtue could find effective expression in the modern world. Thus, in a poem attributed to Marvell, Brittania, after expressing disgust with conditions at home, declares:

> To the serene Venetian state I'le goe
> From her sage mouth fam'd Principles to know,
> With her the Prudence of the Antients read,
> To teach my People in their steps to tread.
> By those great Patterns such a state I'le frame
> Shall darken story, Ingross loudmouthd fame.[58]

The comparisons between Venice and the admirable polities of antiquity—occasionally those of Greece but primarily that of Rome—that fill seventeenth- and eighteenth-century discussions of Venice were therefore more than routine embellishment; they made a reassuring point. Venetian historians had themselves sometimes seen a parallel, and such writers as Fougasse and Gregorio Leti were inclined to press it.[59] Fougasse's English translator, W. Shute, pushed from similarity to continuity. "It seemes in the dissolution of the last Monarchie, the *Genius* of it made transmigration to *Venice*. In her the Wisdome, Fortitude, Iustice, and Magnanimitie of old *Rome* doe yet move and stirre . . . All but her Ruines, and the Cause of them, (her Vice) is removed to *Venice*."[60] But other writers did not hesitate to find Venice far superior to Rome, above all in meeting those ultimate criteria for governments, domestic stability and length of life. Boccalini, in describing Venice, recalled with scorn "those reformations of government, those restorations of state that, with infinite disturbance" beset the Roman Republic;[61] and Howell observed that all ancient commonwealths, including the Roman, "may be sayed to have bin but Mushrumps in point of *duration* if compared to the Signorie of Venice."[62] Such comparisons also reveal another dimension of the Venetian role in later political discussion. Venice helped to strengthen the cause of the Moderns against the Ancients, and thus she played a part in the gathering self-confidence of modern Europe. It is significant that Sarpi and Davila were among the modern historians whom Perrault found equal to the best historians of antiquity, Thucydides and Livy.[63] Even William Temple, if a trifle grudgingly, acknowledged Sarpi (with Boccaccio and Machiavelli) as one of "the great Wits among the moderns."[64]

The notion of Venice as the supreme European representative of a generalized political wisdom meant that she could function as the standard by which all particular arrangements might be judged. For an anonymous pamphleteer during the early stages of the Puritan Revolution, a Venetian observer seemed the appropriate mouthpiece for a sensible perspective on the disturbing English scene.[65] A French writer on Venice, finding her utterly different from every other European state, compared her in this respect to China, which had by now seen long service in showing up the defects of Europe.[66]

The general character of the political wisdom attributed to Venice also meant that Europeans from various traditions, concerned with quite different problems and with conflicting aspirations, could (with the partial exception of those Frenchmen, beginning with Seyssel and Bodin, who were committed to proving the superiority of monarchy over all other forms of government) all find inspiration in the Venetian model. They could discern in her whatever they happened to yearn for: both frugality and luxury, valor and love of peace, aristocratic responsibility and broad political participation, order and personal freedom. But whatever they chose to emphasize, they were in general agreement that Venice met certain fundamental criteria of effective government.

The first of these, as I have already suggested, was the capacity for long survival, and the durability of Venice inevitably implied other virtues. Avity declared that she had lasted "longer than any other [state] that has come to our knowledge";[67] Howell thought her closer to immortality than any other government;[68] Amelot de la Houssaye paid tribute to her long existence;[69] Harrington saw her "at this day with one thousand years upon her back . . . as young, as fresh, and free from decay, or any apperance of it, as shee was born."[70] And as Howell observed, "Length of Age argues strength of Constitution; and as in Naturall bodies, so this Rule holds good likewise in Politicall: Whence it may be inferred, that the Signorie of Venice from Her Infancy was of a strong Symmetry, well nursd, and swadled with wholsom Lawes."[71] The durability of Venice was a result of, and therefore implied, an effective government capable of maintaining domestic peace. Even Seyssel, though he felt compelled to minimize this troublesome fact, had described Venice as "the most perfect and best administered empire and state of community that one has seen or read of up to now";[72] and though Bodin emphasized (against those who admired her immutability) that Venice had altered over the years, he too was compelled to acknowledge the gradual and peaceful character of the changes she had endured.[73] Boccalini celebrated the good order of Venice; she had avoided the conflicts between rich and poor so disastrous for other societies, her nobles willingly forgave each others' injuries instead of seeking revenge, she had consistently managed to control her military leaders.[74] Howell observed that Venetians were not "of so volatil an humor, and so greedy of change as other Italians," and that Venice was therefore free "from all intestin commotions and tumults"; he also appreciated the cleanliness of her streets, an outward and visible sign of her inner devotion to order.[75] Harrington echoed these sentiments.[76] And this impression of Venice was destined for a particularly long life. The *Encyclopédie*, though aware of her decline in other respects, applauded in Venice "an internal tranquility that has never altered."[77]

It was usual to attribute the internal stability of Venice to the excellence of her laws, their strict enforcement, and their impartial application to all classes. In Venice alone among republics, Boccalini suggested, the ruling group had abstained from oppressive legislation in its own interest;[78] and her reputation in this respect was celebrated by Spenser in a sonnet which praised Venice above Rome because she "farre exceedes in policie of right."[79] Boccalini praised the vigorous administration of her laws, attributing to this her perpetual youth and beauty;[80] and Bodin admitted that "an injury done by a Venetian gentleman unto the least inhabitant of the city is right severely corrected and punished."[81] Behind each of these observations, we may assume, lurks some experience with situations in which so happy a condition did not prevail.

Corresponding to the internal peace Venice seemed to represent was a peacefulness abroad that was equally attractive to many other Europeans. The interest of French observers in this quality, to be sure, sometimes was ambivalent. Bodin remarked that the Venetians were "better citizens than warriors," though he also saw their pacifism as a cause of happiness;[82] and if Amelot de la Houssaye emphasized Venetian neutralism and aversion to war, he also noted their occasional disadvantages.[83] But the Englishman Howell had no doubts about the benefits of Venetian pacifism: "Another cause of the *longevity* of this Republic may be alleged to be, that She hath allwayes bin more inclined to *peace* than *war*, and chosen rather to be a Spectatrix or Umpresse, than a Gamestresse." She had been, indeed, the great peace-maker of Europe: "All Christendom is beholden unto this wise Republic, in regard She hath interceded from time to time, and labourd more for the generall peace and tranquility of Christendom, and by her moderation and prudent comportment hath don better Offices in this kind then any other whatsoever."[84]

In addition to all this, Venetians were regularly seen as exemplars of all the old-fashioned political virtues; these both proved the general excellence of the Venetian system and helped to explain its strength. As Howell declared, "Ther are few Citties which have brought forth men more celebrous for all the Cardinall Virtues than *Venice*"; he also noted, as though it were a further proof of the vitality of Venetian society, her numerous "scientificall contemplative men, and greater Artists."[85] Fougasse treated Venetian history as a rich body of patriotic examples, presumably for imitation;[86] and Gregorio Leti also discovered in Venice instructive models of "service to country and the effects produced by love accompanied by zeal."[87] Both Amelot de la Houssaye[88] and Louis Dumay[89] defended, in addition, the piety of Venice.

Two characteristics of the Venetian ruling group, however, especially impressed other Europeans. The first was the absence of personal ambition on the part of even its most talented members, as shown by their readiness to descend from positions of power to the anonymity of private life. As Amelot de la Houssaye remarked, the citizens of Venice "know how to obey."[90] A reflection of this virtue was the modesty of life that prevailed even among the wealthiest Venetians, a quality that made them so different from powerful men elsewhere.[91] The second remarkable trait of this group was its acceptance of the obligation to support the state by paying taxes. Boccalini had emphasized the point, in which he would be echoed by others: "The great marvel of Venetian Liberty, which filled the whole world with wonder, was that the same nobility who governed not only patiently paid existing taxes into the public treasury, but also, with incredible quickness and facility, often decreed new ones against themselves which were then rigorously exacted by the public collectors."[92] Of what other society in Europe, although most governments were perennially close to bankruptcy, could this have been said?

But the peculiar virtues of Venetians themselves required explanation, as Howell recognized: "Now, ther are few or none who are greater *Patriotts* than the Venetian Gentlemen, their prime *study* is the public good and glory of their Countrey, and *civil prudence* is their principall *trade* whereunto they arrive in a high mesure; Yet as it may be easily observd, though these Gentlemen are extraordinary wise when they are *conjunct,* take them *single* they are but as other Men."[93] Even here, therefore, we have been primarily concerned with the evidence that Venice was admirable, and that she was therefore a potential source of instruction for ailing polities elsewhere. With Howell's implicit question about the causes of virtue, we may now turn to the identification by other Europeans of those more specific elements in the Venetian system that seemed to explain its peculiar capacity for survival, the maintenance of order and the encouragement of the civic virtues. The question was of the highest importance. If these could be imitated elsewhere, they might be expected to produce similar results.

We may note first the general European approval of the secular character of the Venetian state. The point is largely left implicit, or it emerges superficially as applause for the exclusion from political responsibility in Venice of the clergy or members of clerically oriented families.[94] But Howell, who had been imprisoned as a royalist and wrote of Venice during the Puritan domination of England, expressed fuller appreciation for the Venetian effort to separate politics from religion: "She hath a speciall care of the Pulpit (and Presse) that no Churchman from the meanest *Priest* to the *Patriarch* dare tamper in their Sermons with temporall and State-affairs, or the transactions and designes of the Senat; It being too well known that Churchmen are the most perilous and pernicious Instruments in a *State*, if they misapply their talent, and employ it to poyson the hearts of the peeple, to intoxicate their brains, and suscitat them to sedition, and a mislike of the Government. . . . Yet they bear a very high respect unto the Church."[95] And Amelot de la Houssaye charged that much of the criticism of Sarpi came from a failure to distinguish politics and religion.[96] Venice was a lesson, therefore, for a Europe in which political order was still regularly disrupted by the imperious demands of religion: Venice revealed that the first condition of effective statecraft was that it must be secular and therefore autonomous.

Hand in hand with the separation of realms went the separateness of states; Venice was also admirable because she had insisted so strenuously on her particularity and her sovereignty. This, indeed, was the primary meaning of that Venetian freedom which was the most widely celebrated element in the myth of Venice; its attractiveness signified resistance to the idea of a universal empire and devotion to one's own fatherland. Bodin noted this aspect of Venice;[97] Fougasse thought nothing more certain than that, in this sense, Venice had been always free;[98] Voltaire was still to celebrate the perpetual independence of Venice as though it represented for him some great human value.[99]

In England the unconquerability of Venice was associated with virginity, a virtue recently given prominence by a beloved queen; and erotic language was used to embroider an interesting image. Coryat noted with satisfaction, in writing of Venice, the frustration of all those who, "being allured with her glorious beauty, have attempted to defloure her";[100] and Howell, who noted more soberly that "this *Maiden* city . . . had the Prerogative to be born a *Christian,* and *Independent,* whereof She Glorieth, and that not undeservedly, above all other States or Kingdomes," composed verses exploiting an obvious pun:

> Venice Great Neptunes Minion, still a Mayd,
> Though by the warrlikst Potentats assayd . . .
> Though, Syren-like on Shore and Sea, Her Face
> Enchants all those whom once She doth embrace . . .
> These following Leaves display, if well observd,
> How She so long Her Maydenhead preserved . . .
> Venus and Venice are Great Queens in their degree,
> Venus is Queen of Love, Venice of Policie.[101]

In what may also have some interest for the development of a poetic metaphor, these crudities were eventually refined by Wordsworth into a famous sonnet after the extinction of the Venetian Republic by Napoleon:

> ... Venice, the eldest Child of Liberty
> She was a maiden City, bright and free;
> No guile seduced, no force could violate ...

The independence of Venice was the basis for what was widely regarded as her admirably successful foreign policy. Because she was free, she could balance among the various powers of Europe, and so protect both her liberty and her peace. Howell, again, noted this with particular clarity: "Now, one of the wayes wherby the Republic of *Venice* hath endeavourd to preserve her Maydenhead and freedom so long, hath bin to keep the power of the potentat Princes in a counterpoise; wherby She hath often adapted her designes, and accommoded Her-self to the conditions of the times, and frequently changd thoughts, will, frends, and enemies. She hath bin allwayes usd to suspect any great power, to fear much, and confide little, to be perpetually vigilant of the operations of others, and accordingly to regulat her own consultations and proceedings; wherby She hath bin often accusd of exces in circumspection."[102] Amelot de la Houssaye also remarked on this tendency in Venetian policy, though with less approval; he would have preferred a Venice more consistently allied with France.[103]

As Howell will have suggested, the Venetian talent for balancing among changing political forces abroad pointed more profoundly to a general adaptability to shifting circumstance that was seen as the necessary condition both of her survival and of her apparent invulnerability to change. She could remain "forever young" because she had learned how to master the successive challenges of political life and in this sense to triumph over time. Nothing was more attractive to anxious European observers than this aspect of the Venetian achievement. This was the major impulse behind their admiration of her constitution and of those qualities of flexibility and finesse in her policy that less friendly and less secular minds perceived as unscrupulous, opportunistic, in short Machiavellian.

There was a good deal of discussion about the nature of the Venetian constitution, and the earlier view that it was a mixture of monarchic, aristocratic, and democratic elements maintained (somewhat like the equilibrium in Venetian relations abroad) in a perfect balance tended to give way by the later sixteenth century to the recognition that Venice was a pure aristocracy.[104] Although some observers were critical of the limitations on the doge as a reflection on the competence of kings and therefore a threat to good political order,[105] the elimination of a democratic taint from the image of the Republic doubtless increased the attractiveness of the Venetian model for the seventeenth and eighteenth centuries. As an aristocratic republic of the most responsible and effective type, Venice acquired a new kind of interest.[106] Much was therefore made of the general competence of her nobility, of the systematic way in which younger nobles were advanced through positions of steadily increasing responsibility, and of the contentment of the lower classes under this regime.[107]

But however it was regarded otherwise, the main point about the Venetian constitution as it was perceived abroad was that it was a regular structure ("a great and ingenious machine" in the suggestive words of Saint-Didier),[108] and that it worked. As early as Thomas Starkey, Englishmen had recognized its effectiveness in preventing tyranny;[109] Howell identified this as a factor in the survival of Venice and a safeguard against "trenching upon the Common Liberty, and doing injustice";[110] and Venice figured prominently in the constitutional discussions carried on in the England of Cromwell and the Holland of De Witt.[111] Even in the France of Louis XIV Saint-Didier was bold enough to describe at length the limits on the power of the doge, in a work that generally represented the Venetian government as perfect.[112] Other writers emphasized the virtues in the Venetian system of broad participation by citizens in the affairs of the government. Even Bodin may have hinted at this in recognizing that although Venice was "pure and simply Aristocratic," she was "yet somewhat governed by Proportion Harmonicall," language that suggests multiple participation.[113] The point was evidently important to Voltaire in his contrast between Rome and Venice: "Rome lost, by Caesar, at the end of five hundred years, its liberty acquired by Brutus. Venice has preserved hers for eleven centuries, and I hope she will always do so."[114] In the same interest some writers persisted in the old view that the Venetian constitution retained a democratic element, among them Howell,[115] Harrington,[116] Saint-Didier,[117] and perhaps even Rousseau, who declared: "It is a mistake to regard the government of Venice as a genuine aristocracy. For while the Venetian people has no part in the government, the Venetian nobility is itself a people."[118]

By permitting the representation of diverse and changing interests, the Venetian constitution kept the Republic in touch with changing conditions and needs; and in the flexibility and shrewdness of Venetian policy European writers found additional grounds for admiration and emulation. This was the general lesson to which numerous particular examples pointed; Venice could be seen to incorporate not only eternal reason but also (however inconsistently in particular cases) practical reason, reason of state. Venice, Howell declared, had "allwayes bin one of the most politic and pragmaticall'st Republics on Earth";[119] Louis Dumay expressed somewhat the same thought in saying that she had been preserved "rather by prudence than by valour."[120] The duc de Rohan put it more baldly in celebrating the degree to which the Venetians followed "all the maxims of their true interest,"[121] and Naudé most sharply of all in describing them as "steeped in a continual Machiavelism": in Naudé's eyes a point in their favor.[122]

Some manifestations of the political astuteness attributed to Venice seem innocent enough: for example, insistence on the equality of all nobles as a means of maintaining their unity, or the requirement of a *relazione* from ambassadors.[123] Others, though usually mentioned with admiration, are more ambiguous: the capacity of "the sagacious Senate" for double-talk,[124] the secrecy with which official deliberations could be carried on even in large assemblies,[125] the wisdom of keeping arms out of the hands of subjects,[126] the use of ambassadors as spies, the astuteness with which residents of the city were kept divided.[127] Still others are presented as useful, but with some sense of distaste and occasionally with an argument for their necessity: skill in the exploitation of political symbolism;[128] the oppression of subject peoples on the mainland;[129] the secret denunciations, internal spying, and terrorization of the people increasingly attached to the image of Venice.[130] Of particular interest from this standpoint was the political explanation some French writers advanced for the moral permissiveness regularly attributed, with peculiar fascination, to Venice. Bodin saw it as a device on the part of the rulers of Venice to manage the populace: "to make them more mild and pliable, they give them full scope and liberty to all sorts of pleasures."[131] A century later Amelot de la Houssaye gave a similar account of the notorious indiscipline of the Venetian clergy; it served both to discredit them with the people and to keep them content and loyal to the state, in spite of their exclusion from positions of influence.[132]

In another sense, too, Venetian flexibility appealed to other Europeans; as a political model she displayed a remarkable responsiveness to what were, for them, material realities that required just such recognition as they received in Venice. French writers observed in her, with some approval, a degree of social mobility. Bodin noted that, as in England, the nobles participated in trade, and that "a Venetian gentleman may marry a base woman, or a common citizen's daughter,"[133] and Amelot de la Houssaye thought the sale of titles of nobility in Venice a good custom since it renewed the ruling class, eased the tax burden, and increased attachment to the state.[134] The English were impressed with the commercial and financial foundations of her greatness. Howell praised her for opening up trade with the Levant, Africa, and the Indies, and for "her Bank of money," which, he asserted, "as it hath bin the Ground and Rule of all other banks, so is it the most usefull for Marchants or Gentlemen to any part of the world, nor do I see how Christendom can subsist conveniently without it."[135] John Dury lauded Venice for encouraging invention.[136] Nor did the Venetian system of poor relief, the government's sponsorship of public works, its responsibility for the provision of food to the populace, and its regulations for the control of epidemics go unnoticed.[137]

Although its importance was yet scarcely recognized, it may be worth pointing out also that the historical aspect of Venetian political culture had some relation to its pragmatism. Like the statesmen of Venice, her historians too were concerned not with eternal principles but with particular and changing circumstances, about which they sought the same kind of clear and certain knowledge of the actual world as that on which Venetian statesmen were supposed to base their decisions. History too was in this sense amoral, and Venetian historiography was admired because of its capacity to get at and effectively to reveal the truth.

Most of the admiration focused on Sarpi, whose *Concilio Tridentino* in many ways brought the Renaissance tradition of historical writing to a climax. He appeared to have solved supremely well both the scientific and the rhetorical problems of a modern historian. Amelot de la Houssaye, who thought him the equal of Thucydides, Xenophon, and Tacitus, praised his truthfulness, his responsibility to the realities of the human world, his exactness. "Everything," he declared, "is *ad rem,* everything is instructive, natural, without art, without disguise. He proceeds always bridle in hand, and always arrives where he is going."[138] Le Courayer praised his impartiality: "Has he not entirely filled the character of a perfect historian, who must not show either his religion or his country, but consider himself a citizen of the entire world, and make as a law for himself the simple exposition of facts, whether favourable or prejudicial to anyone whomsoever?"[139] The *Encyclopédie* admired the naturalness and energy of Sarpi's style and the "judicious reflections" with which he sowed his work;[140] and Samuel Johnson praised the moral qualities of his work, quoting Wotton with approval to the effect that in it "the Reader finds Liberty without Licentiousness, Piety without Hypocrisy, Freedom of Speech without Neglect of Decency, Severity without Rigour, and extensive Learning without Ostentation."[141] Both Hume[142] and Gibbon[143] acknowledged Sarpi and Davila among their own masters and models. Thus Venetian historiography, so closely related in the Renaissance republics to the needs of political life, continued to affect the ways in which later Europeans viewed the past; this, indeed, may have been the most persistent among the legacies of Venice.

Much of what in Venice interested European observers might also have been discerned in Florence, though perhaps less readily and, because the Florentine Republic had perished, less persuasively. But one final attribute of Venice that vividly impressed the European imagination was regarded as clearly unique: the remarkable personal liberty enjoyed by all Venetians. Because it was general and took many forms, and because of the peculiar capacity of personal freedom to induce anxiety, it produced a variety of reactions, often ambivalent. Thus Saint-Didier: "The liberty of Venice permits everything, for whatever life one leads, whatever religion one professes; if one does not talk, and undertakes nothing against the state or the nobility, one can live in full security, and no one will undertake to censure one's conduct nor oppose one's personal disorder."[144] In its religious dimension the freedom of Venice won the approval of Salmasius,[145] and Milton was grateful to Sarpi for his contribution as a historian to liberty of conscience.[146] But although Saint-Didier was impressed by the religious latitude allowed in Venice, he was dubious about it: "The tolerance there is so great that they close their eyes" to all sorts of deviations.[147] Leti doubted whether liberty in Venice was good for civil life.[148]

These ambiguous reactions to the personal freedoms of Venice were all based on a failure, perhaps even a refusal, to distinguish between liberty and license. It is apparent from them that no real separation between the two yet seemed possible; personal liberty was generally supposed to merge inevitably into license; and, however fascinating either of these conditions might be, liberty was therefore always dangerous. The almost obsessive preoccupation of foreigners with the licentiousness of Venice,[149] which was given increasing substance as she became a purveyor of pleasures to the upper classes of Europe, the gaudiest stop on the Grand Tour, should thus be seen as a kind of negative tribute to the more general freedom of Venetian society. The sexual temptation that Venice represented and its very confusion with more obviously political aspects of personal liberty pointed, indeed, to the possibility that orderly and effective government might after all be consistent with permissiveness in the more private dimensions of life, though the lesson was slow to emerge. Venice, in any case, could be seen increasingly to possess all kinds of freedom, and by the second half of the eighteenth century the appropriate distinction could at last be made. Thus the *Encyclopédie,* delicately distinguishing among the satisfactions of life, observed that in Venice one tasted both *la liberté et les plaisirs.*[150]

By this time, of course, the importance of Venice for the political education of Europe was nearing its end. Venice herself was in decline, and the discrepancy between the tawdry realities of the age of Casanova and the ideal Venice imagined by generations of admirers was increasingly difficult to ignore. Furthermore, a new source of political wisdom, a new political model, was now emerging; the *philosophes* were discovering in England an inspiration Venice could no longer supply. Yet the virtues Voltaire and Montesquieu discovered across the Channel were still suspiciously like those previously associated with Venice. England too was admired as a free nation, with a secular and constitutional government in which tyranny was prevented by dividing and balancing powers; and, like Venice, England seemed to be ruled by laws rather than men, gave merchants their due, based her policies on a realistic perception of the needs of her people, and afforded them a remarkable degree of personal liberty. Even the distortions in this vision of England had their origins in the Venetian model.

I do not mean to suggest that Europeans learned their politics from Venice, as a student learns, for example, his chemistry. Her pedagogy, to borrow a piquant phrase from Sarpi, was "obstetrical."[151] She kept alive, for whoever found them useful, the political attitudes and values of the Renaissance, through her own political writings and above all through her survival as living proof of their validity; and from time to time, when conditions were favorable, Europeans could recognize that these attitudes and values were also their own. In this way Venice helped to transmit the political tradition of the Renaissance to the Enlightenment, and thus she prepared the way for the fruitful recognition of the political achievement of England.

NOTES

1. But see J. R. Hale, *England and the Italian Renaissance: The Growth of Interest in Its History and Art* (London, 1954), which does recognize that before the eighteenth century Venice was the primary source of European impressions of the Italian Renaissance. See also Zera S. Fink, *The Classical Republicans: An Essay in the Recovery of a Pattern of Thought in Seventeenth-Century England,* 2nd ed. (Evanston, 1962).

2. For fuller treatment of the Venetian political tradition, see my *Venice*

and the Defense of Republican Liberty: Renaissance Values in the Age of the Counter-Reformation (Berkeley, 1968).

3. Della perfezione della vita politica, in his Opere politiche, ed. C. Monzani (Florence, 1852) I, 33–405.

4. Ibid., 41–57, 214–216.

5. In his Discorsi politici, in Opere politiche, II, 1–371.

6. Sopra la forza e validità della scommunica, in Istoria dell' Interdetto e altri scritti, ed. Giovanni Gambarin (Bari, 1940) II, 40.

7. Istoria del Concilio Tridentino, ed. Giovanni Gambarin (Bari, 1935) II, 250.

8. De magistratibus et republica venetorum (Venice, 1543).

9. I cite from the edition of J. G. Graevius, Thesaurus antiquitatum et historiarum Italiae (Leyden, 1722) V, col. 58.

10. Ibid., cols. 7–8.

11. Ibid., col. 4.

12. Ibid., cols. 56–57.

13. In his relazione of 1595 after his Roman embassy, Relazioni degli ambasciatori veneti al senato, ed. Eugenio Albèri (Florence, 1839–1863), II, iv, 355–448.

14. In his Historia vinetiana (Venice, 1605).

15. In his Discorsi, cited above.

16. Vita politica, 254–256.

17. Istoria delle guerre civili di Francia (Milan, 1807) I, 7–13.

18. Concilio Tridentino, I, 236.

19. Bellarmine's charge appeared in his Risposta a un libretto intitolato Risposta di un dottore di Theologia (Rome, 1606). It was directed against Giovanni Marsilio, who replied in his Difesa a favore della risposta dell' otto propositioni (Venice, 1606). Both works are included in Raccolta degli scritti usciti . . . nella causa del P. Paolo V. co' signori venetiani (Chur, 1607) I, 166–167 and 243 for these passages.

20. Concilio Tridentino, II, 437.

21. Guerre civili di Francia, I, 3–5.

22. Concilio Tridentino, I, 187.

23. Ibid., I, 4–5.

24. Letter to Jérôme Groslot de l'Isle, 28 Feb. 1612, in his Lettere ai Protestanti, ed. Manlio D. Busnelli (Bari, 1931) I, 219.

25. For a vision of Sarpi as reformer, see Pierre F. Le Courayer, Défense de la nouvelle traduction de l'histoire du Concile de Trente (Amsterdam, 1742) 38.

26. The French translation was by Jehan Charrier (Paris, 1544), the English by Sir Lewes Lewkenor (London, 1599).

27. Gabriel Naudé, Bibliographia politica (Frankfurt, 1673) III.

28. For these translations see Carlo Curcio, Dal Rinascimento alla Controriforma (Rome, 1934) 211, n. The translation of the history (London, 1658) was the work of Henry, Earl of Monmouth.

29. Bibliographia politica, 33.

30. Curcio, 211.

31. By Charles Cotterell and William Aylesbury (1647) and Ellis Farnesworth (1758).

32. The French translation (1644) was by I. Baudoin, the Spanish (1675) by P. Basilio Varen de Soto, and the Latin (1735) by François Cornazanus.

33. Henry St. John, Lord Viscount Bolingbroke, *Letters on the Study and Use of History* (London [1st ed., 1752], 1770) 136–137. For English interest in Davila, see also Christopher Hill, *Intellectual Origins of the English Revolution* (Oxford, 1965) 2, 278–279.

34. It was first published in Boston, 1805. It must be admitted that the work is very little concerned with Davila.

35. See Hubert Jedin, *Das Konzil von Trient, ein Überblick über die Erforschung seiner Geschichte* (Rome, 1948) 93.

36. Giorgio Spini, "Riforma italiana e mediazioni ginevrine nella Nuova Inghilterra," in *Ginevra e l'Italia* (Florence, 1959) 454–455.

37. For Johnson's interest in Sarpi, see, most recently, John Lawrence Abbott, "Dr. Johnson and the Making of *The Life of Father Paul Sarpi*," *Bulletin of the John Rylands Library,* XXXVIII (1966) 255–267. The first translation was by Nicholas Brent (1620).

38. The first was by the Calvinist Giovanni Diodati (Geneva, 1621); the later translations were by Abraham Nicolas Amelot de la Houssaye (Amsterdam, 1683) and Pierre F. Le Courayer (London, 1736).

39. For example, Cardinal Pallavicino, in his own *Historia del Concilio Tridentino*; on this point see V. Luciani, *Francesco Guicciardini and His European Reputation* (New York, 1936) 208.

40. *Science des princes, ou considérations politiques sur les coups d'état* (Paris, 1757) III, 238

41. Amelot, in the preface of his *Histoire du Concile de Trente* (2nd rev. ed., Amsterdam, 1686).

42. See Francesco Griselini, *Memorie anedote spettanti alla vita ed agli studi del sommo filosofo e giureconsulto F. Paolo Servita* (Lausanne, 1760) 260.

43. For the numerous translations of this work, see Luigi Firpo, *Traduzioni dei "Ragguagli" di Traiano Boccalini* (Florence, 1965).

44. Cf. Franco Gaeta, "Alcune considerazioni sul mito di Venezia," *Bibliothèque d'Humanisme et Renaissance,* XXIII (1961) 63. Among Europeans particularly impressed by this was Claude de Seyssel, *La monarchie de France* (1519), ed. Jacques Poujol (Paris, 1961) 107.

45. For earlier impressions of Venice, see Gina Fasoli, "Nascita di un mito," *Studi storici in onore di Gioacchino Volpe* (Florence, 1958) I, 445–479. For Florentine interest in Venice see also Rudolph von Albertini, *Das florentinische Staatsbewusstsein im Übergang von der Republik zum Principat* (Berne, 1955); Renzo Pecchioli, "Il 'mito' di Venezia e la crisi fiorentina intorno al 1500," *Studi Storici,* III (1962) 451–492; and Felix Gilbert, *Machiavelli and Guicciardini: Politics and History in Sixteenth-Century Florence* (Princeton, 1965).

46. *Mémoires-Journaux,* ed. G. Brunet (Paris, 1875–1896) VIII, 198–310.

47. I (1614) leaves 48–70, 89–104, 120–128.

48. Avity, *Les estats empires royaumes et principautés du monde* (Paris, 1635) 497.

49. Rohan, *De l'interest des princes, et des estats de la Chrestienté* (Paris, 1692) 122–123.

50. Howell, *S.P.Q.V. A survay of the signorie of Venice* (London, 1651) 142.

51. *Histoire du gouvernement de Venise et l'examen de sa liberté* (Paris, 1677).

52. On the general point see, for example, the recent works of E. Thuau, *Raison d'état et pensée politique à l'époque de Richelieu* (Paris, 1966), and Leonard Marsak, "The Idea of Reason in Seventeenth-Century France," *Cahiers d'Histoire Mondiale*, XI (1969) 407–416.

53. Pp. 1, 10.

54. See, for example, his *Interest des princes,* 102.

55. Jean Bodin, *The six bookes of a commonweale,* Richard Knolles, trans. (London, 1606), in the facsimile edition of Kenneth D. McRae (Cambridge, Mass., 1962) 563. The Knolles translation made use of both the slightly differing French and Latin editions.

56. Avity, 477, for example.

57. The point has been made by Fink, 34–35.

58. "Brittania and Rawleigh," in Andrew Marvell, *Poems and Letters,* ed. H. M. Margoliouth (Oxford, 1952) I, 188. Margoliouth thinks the poem is not Marvell's.

59. Thomas de Fougasse, *The generall historie of the magnificent state of Venice,* W. Shute, trans. (London, 1612) I, 25, 162, from the French edition of 1608; Gregorio Leti, *Ragguagli historici e politici delle virtu, e massime necessarie alla conservatione degli stati* (Amsterdam, 1699) I, 103–105. In this work Leti attempts to substitute Holland for Venice as a new model of political perfection, but he does so by magnifying in the Dutch the virtues elsewhere attributed to Venice.

60. In his epistle to the reader.

61. Traiano Boccalini, *Ragguagli di Parnaso,* ed. Luigi Firpo (Bari, 1948) I, 21–22.

62. P. 203. See also 204–207.

63. Charles Perrault, *Parallèle des Anciens et des Modernes* (Paris, 1688), in the facsimile edition of H. R. Jauss (Munich, 1964) II, 100.

64. *An Essay upon the ancient and modern learning,* ed. J. E. Spingarn (Oxford, 1909) 36.

65. *A Venice looking-glasse: or, a letter written very lately from London to Rome, by a Venetian clarissimo* (London, 1648). This has been attributed to Howell.

66. Alexandre Toussaint de Limojon, sieur de Saint-Didier, *La ville et la république de Venise* (Paris, 1680) 4.

67. P. 476.

68. P. 1.

69. P. 12.

70. James Harrington, *Oceana,* ed. S. B. Liljegren (Heidelberg, 1924) 185.

71. Opening words of the epistle to Parliament.

72. Pp. 107–108.

73. P. 433.

74. Pp. 22, 28–29.

75. Pp. 5, 8, 35.

76. Pp. 32, 137.

77. Article "Venise," *Encyclopédie, ou dictionnaire raisonné des sciences, des arts et des métiers* (Paris, 1751–1765) XVII, 12.

78. P. 24.

79. This prefaced Lewkenor's English translation of Contarini.

80. Pp. 21–22.
81. P. 785.
82. Pp. 428, 606.
83. Pp. 108, 114.
84. Pp. 4, 208. See also Boccalini, 26.
85. Pp. 200–204.
86. For example, I, 114.
87. II, 344.
88. P. 549.
89. Against Naudé, in his notes to Naudé's *Science des Princes* (Strasbourg, 1673). Dumay was a Counselor-Secretary to the Elector of Mainz.
90. P. 547. See also Boccalini, 25–26.
91. Boccalini, 24.
92. P. 23. See also Amelot de la Houssaye, 48–49; Howell, 5; and the Sieur de la Haye, *La politique civile et militaire des Venitiens* (Paris, 1668) 65–67.
93. P. 23.
94. Amelot de la Houssaye, 37; Howell, 183; Harrington, 173.
95. P. 7.
96. In the preface to his translation of Sarpi's *Concilio Tridentino*.
97. P. 128.
98. I, 23.
99. "Venise, et, par occasion, de la liberté," in Voltaire, *Oeuvres complètes,* ed. Louis Moland (Paris, 1877–1885) XX, 552–554, often included in the *Dictionnaire philosophique*.
100. Thomas Coryat, *Crudities* (Glasgow, 1905) I, 415–416.
101. P. 1 and prefatory verses.
102. P. 180.
103. P. 160.
104. Gaeta, 69–72.
105. And not only in France; see G. P. Gooch, *English Democratic Ideas in the Seventeenth Century* (Cambridge, 1954) 243.
106. Cf. Fougasse, I, 208; and Fink, 46.
107. Boccalini, 23, 26–27; Amelot de la Houssaye, 37 et seq., 49–50, 61.
108. P. 151.
109. *Dialogue between Pole and Lupset,* ed. K. M. Burton (London, 1948) 167.
110. P. 12; see also 6.
111. Gaeta, 71–72.
112. P. 178.
113. P. 112.
114. P. 554.
115. Pp. 10–11.
116. P. 19.
117. Pp. 152–153.
118. *Contrat social,* bk. iv, ch. 3.
119. P. 55. See also 4, with special reference to Venetian foreign policy.
120. II, 457–458 in Naudé, *Science des Princes.*
121. P. 128. See also 92, 122.

122. *Science des Princes,* I, 146; cf. 144.

123. Amelot de la Houssaye, 99–101, 54–55.

124. Howell, 92.

125. Boccalini, 30–31; Amelot de la Houssaye, 76–77; Saint-Didier, 227–228.

126. Amelot de la Houssaye, 102.

127. Dumay, in Naudé, *Science des Princes,* I, 163; III, 115.

128. Rosseau, *Émile,* in *Oeuvres complètes* (Paris, 1969) IV, 646 n.

129. Leti, I, 74–76, on the ground that it is the way of nature for the great to oppress the weak.

130. Saint-Didier, 274 et seq., where these practices are seen as both debasing and useful; cf. Amelot de la Houssaye, 309 et seq., where distaste and fascination seem equally mixed.

131. P. 711.

132. Pp. 99, 135–142, 383.

133. Pp. 235, 398.

134. Pp. 133–134.

135. P. 208.

136. *A seasonable discourse* (London, 1649), cited by Hill, 278.

137. Fougasse, I, 112–113; Howell, 18, 185; Dumay, in Naudé, *Science des Princes,* I, 204.

138. Preface to his translation of Sarpi, *Concilio Tridentino.*

139. *Défense de la traduction,* 72, 94.

140. Article "Venise," 8.

141. "Father Paul Sarpi," *Works* (London, 1820) XII, 6–7.

142. Letter to Walpole, 2 Aug. 1758, in *Letters,* ed. J. Y. T. Greig (Oxford, 1932) I, 152.

143. *Decline and Fall of the Roman Empire,* ed. H. H. Milman (Philadelphia, n. d.) V, 537 n. 89.

144. P. 353.

145. René Pintard, *Le libertinage érudit dans la première moitié du XVIIe siècle* (Paris, 1943) I, 104.

146. *Areopagitica and Other Prose Works* (London, Everyman's Library, 1927) 8.

147. P. 171.

148. I, 260.

149. As in Coryat, I, 401–409; Amelot de la Houssaye, 88, 142 et seq., 331–332; and even Howell, 8: "She melts in softness and sensualitie as much as any other [place] whatsoever; for, 'tis too well known, ther is no place where ther is lesse Religion from the girdle downwards."

150. Article "Venise," 12.

151. Fulgenzio Micanzio, *Vita del Padre Paolo* (n.p., 1658) 79.

III

HISTORY AND HISTORIANS

12 Three Types of
Historiography in
Post-Renaissance Italy

This essay, another by-product of my Venice book, was first presented at the
annual meeting of the American Historical Association at Philadelphia in
1963. It distinguished three major types of historiography in early modern
Italy, correlating them with the widely differing political conditions in the
peninsula. The essay was first published in History and Theory *4 (1965),*
303–314, and is reprinted here with the permission of Wesleyan University
Press.

· · ·

Italy between the fourteenth and the eighteenth centuries was not a
unity in any significant respect, but, perhaps even more than in the
preceding age, only a collection of localities differing widely in economic
and social structure, political organization, traditions, culture, and speed
and direction of development. Profitable discussion of Italian affairs in
this period must therefore make careful distinctions of place. This caveat
is, indeed, particularly true for the period following the Peace of Bologna, early in 1530, which brought to an end the Italian phase of the
Hapsburg-Valois wars; it marked the conclusion of a long ordeal which,
however tragic for the peoples of Italy, had at least supplied a common
thread for the history of the peninsula. It is thus hardly an accident that
after Guicciardini's *Storia d'Italia* (written between 1537 and 1540, but
published only in 1561) there was not another general history of Italy
until well into the next century.[1] Any account of historiography in Italy
after the publication of his masterpiece must therefore recognize a variety
of tendencies, related for the most part only dialectically, corresponding
to the variety among political centers. Each of these had interests and

295

preoccupations of its own which imposed special requirements on historical composition.

Under these circumstances the historiography of three Italian centers assumed particular importance during the later sixteenth century. Although, under the Medici principate, the memory of the republican past was now fading, the contribution of Florentine republicanism to the formation of the modern historical consciousness gives a special interest to historical writing in Florence during this period of radically altered circumstances. Rome invites our attention because of her eagerness to press all forms of cultural expression into the service of the Counter-Reformation, as well as by her revitalized commitment to an ecclesiastical and political universalism which had profound implications for the interpretation of history. In Venice, meanwhile, in reaction to a now increasingly obvious decline in political and economic influence, this period saw a remarkable resurgence of the kind of republican enthusiasm once characteristic of Florence, with similarly fruitful results for the writing of history.

I

In Florence during the later sixteenth century, tendencies already apparent in Guicciardini were carried to extremes, and a historiography which had been based on the presumed utility of history for politics gradually disintegrated.[2] The principle of utility had presupposed a certain confidence both in the ability of the historian to lay bare the workings of the political world, and in the ability of the ruler in some measure to control it on the basis of knowledge. But the helplessness of Florence to determine her own destiny in a world dominated by great powers had demonstrated the futility of the attempt to guide events; and the imposition of princely despotism gradually converted a responsible citizenry into passive subjects who lacked the motive to cultivate a larger political understanding through the study of history. Historiography, therefore, like classical studies in the same period, moved from the *piazza* into the *studio,* detached itself from active politics, and reflected a steady decline in human confidence.

The process took several generations, but it is already apparent in Guicciardini, whose concern with history was largely contemplative; for him, the only mastery man finally could hope to achieve over events was to understand them, and even in this effort man could not transcend particular phenomena and their very particular relationships.[3] In fact, the limitation was useful to establish the independence of history from politics, but it was also a confession of defeat. Guicciardini's successors were even less confident about the powers of the human understanding. In the historical vision of Varchi, man is a helpless victim in a swirling chaos of fragmented detail and compulsive egotism, in which even the best-laid plans are bound to fail.[4] Increasingly the historian was limited to the exposition of detail whose authenticity he could vouch for with growing assurance, but whose meaning he hardly dared to suggest.

For several decades there remained in Florence enough former republicans to compose history with that sense of psychological nuance and of historical relationships which comes from personal experience and involvement, but at last these had died out altogether; and by the end of the century the official historiographer of Florence was a professional pedant from Naples, Scipione Ammirato. Ammirato was a collector of facts. His only practical function at the Tuscan court was to give satisfaction to his patron, and his *Istorie fiorentine* (1600) is both the end of the great tradition and its repudiation.[5] In this work we can examine, therefore, the culmination of one important tendency in the historiography of post-Renaissance Italy.

Ammirato's engaging humility, as he compares himself with both the ancients and his modern predecessors—for he evidently saw himself as continuing a tradition[6]—appears more than justified. As he informed his readers, he aimed only at conformity to the unexceptionable principles of order, piety, and fidelity to truth,[7] and his history is defective in both analysis and synthesis. Indeed, Ammirato would hardly presume to attempt either. He is almost totally unable to distinguish themes and forces; he has no discrimination, no psychological insight, no dramatic sense; his organization is too primitive even for the division of narrative into paragraphs. His work is conventionally clerical, and it also finds occasion to praise the Medici, comparing the first Cosimo, for example, to the great Romans of antiquity.[8] But gratuitous bias of this kind is not excessive, and the real weakness of the work lies in the opposite direction: in the absence of formal control. The history seems finally little more than an irrelevant accumulation of erudite and antiquarian detail, without insight into the meaning of events.

Yet even an empiricism run wild can, under certain circumstances, offer compensations; and Ammirato's work exhibits one useful virtue: a remarkable zest for the accumulation of facts. He was not imaginative, but he was vastly diligent and meticulous. His accounts of the Florentine past mark a great advance over those of all previous historians simply in their command of the detailed material of political narrative.[9] His additions to the record, to be sure, do not much advance our under-

standing of Florentine history. They generally serve no function whatsoever, except perhaps in providing such satisfactions as crude data may
afford to those in search of certainties in a time of deep insecurity. Yet,
the fact that historiography should have been reduced to this is itself of
some interest for the understanding of post-Renaissance Italy. Besides,
scholarship of this kind also points toward the erudite accumulations of
historical materials for which modern historians are still so heavily indebted to the seventeenth and eighteenth centuries.

II

While Florence suggests the end of the Renaissance tradition through
sheer attrition, Rome in the period of the Counter-Reformation seems
engaged in a direct attack on the historical accomplishment of the Renaissance. She evidently found several elements in later Renaissance historiography distasteful: in particular, the freedom with which historians
treated ecclesiastical history, as though it were no different qualitatively
from profane history; in general, their tendency to regard the study of
the past as an autonomous science in which all phenomena are to be
understood as a part of the natural order, and only conclusions derived
from adequate evidence can be accepted as legitimate.

Much of the impact of Rome on Italian historiography in this period
was thus merely restrictive. Because free investigation so often led in
undesirable directions, ecclesiastical authority sought again and again to
censor or suppress historical writings. A celebrated instance is the great
work of Guicciardini. The first Italian text of the *Storia d'Italia* to include
such passages as the author's full discussion of Alexander VI or the
extended retrospective essay on the temporal power of the papacy did
not appear until 1621, and then only in Geneva.[10] Expurgation and
suppression were also accompanied by an effort to make history "safe"
through its diversion from research into rhetoric, and through the revival
of the Ciceronian cliché *historia magistra vitae*, which reduced history to
ethics teaching by example. These purposes were served by various clerical treatises on the art of historical composition, notably those of Agostino Mascardi and Sebastiano Macci.[11]

Rome's fear of free intellectual activity was of obvious importance
for cultural expression in most of Italy, and it no doubt helps to account
for Ammirato's reluctance to interpret events.[12] On the other hand, it
seems to me a mistake to blame the cultural contraction which characterized Italy in general during this period, and of which the distrust of
history was merely one symptom among others, simply on the Counter-

Reformation. In fact, the relationship may be essentially the reverse of what is conventionally supposed; the influence of Italy, for a variety of reasons exhausted and insecure, may well have been as decisive for the defensive mentality of the Counter-Reformation as was the challenge of Protestantism. The fathers at Trent were—most of them—Italians as well as ecclesiastics, and the predominance of Italians at the Curia increased in the course of the century.[13]

In any case, however, the negative attitude of the Counter-Reformation toward historical study was not merely tactical; it also had deeper sources. For the categories by which the major Catholic thinkers of this period sought to comprehend all dimensions of reality were primarily systematic and rational, not historical; and discussion of the origins and development of phenomena seemed not only dangerous, but also essentially irrelevant to a world of eternal verities. Bellarmine himself largely ignored the Renaissance historians; and insofar as he required a framework of historical conceptions, he depended on the traditional four monarchies and a universal chronology which divided the history of the world into three ages, each lasting for two thousand years.[14] The Jesuit *Ratio studiorum* allowed almost no place for historical study, which, as Polman has noted, failed to develop significantly wherever the Society of Jesus was influential.[15]

If some of that zeal for research which characterized Ammirato also operated in Rome, the resemblance was superficial. The "positive theology" which the Catholic Reformation inherited from the Erasmians was, to be sure, concerned with the recovery, authentication, and study of ancient documents, and required the techniques of historical research; but its purposes were not those of the historian.[16] And insofar as thinkers in Rome seriously concerned themselves with the past, they did so less to ascertain its actual character through free investigation than to construct an orthodox interpretation consistent with the interests of the church. In Rome, therefore, in contrast to Florence, a kind of vision still operated in connection with the past; but the vision was antecedent to investigation, not based upon or even responsive to it. A nice instance of the Roman attitude is provided by Bellarmine himself, offended by a Venetian pamphleteer who had ventured to express doubt that Charlemagne had, in fact, received his empire as the gift of the pope.[17] This daring position, Bellarmine wrote, amounted to "heresy in history" as well as "temerity in theology"; it was "repugnant to all the historians and to the sacred canons."[18] Thus the Counter-Reformation proposed to absorb history, even earlier than the physical sciences, into the larger structure of dogma.

The great historiographical monument to this attitude is, of course, the *Annales ecclesiastici* (1588–1607) of Baronius, a work whose significance in cultural history as well as in the history of historiography deserves more serious attention. We are now chiefly inclined to think of the *Annals* as a massive repository of the sources of ancient and medieval ecclesiastical history, even when we recall its original polemical intent. But actually the work is of great substantive interest, as an effort to impose a certain interpretation on the history of the church; and it has another kind of interest because of the degree of its success. Its thesis is the essential invulnerability of the visible church, despite its operating in the world, to historical change. It argues that all the claims and characteristics of the modern church to which the enemies of Rome were now taking exception had been present, at least in embryo, from the beginning.[19] Thus it attempts to show that the historical world is really a coordinate of the systematic order described, at about the same time, in the theological writings of Bellarmine. To these it seems to be related as if it were part of a larger strategy: as though Bellarmine's task had been to demonstrate rationally what ought to be true; that of Baronius, to demonstrate historically that it always had been true.

In the course of this undertaking the *Annals* give the first extended development of one of the hardiest myths in European historiography: the conception of medieval Christendom as a unified polity recognizing papal superiority in principle, and essentially responsive to papal direction.[20] Even *Unam sanctam* (a composition which enjoyed new popularity in Rome during this period)[21] had been only the enunciation of an ideal; it did not claim that the ideal had been realized. Now, however, in the second half of the sixteenth century, this claim was fully developed, as a kind of concession, perhaps, to the new historical consciousness of the age. There was an effort to show that all who rejected the leadership of the pope, including his authority over temporal affairs—whether direct or indirect makes little difference—were guilty of rebellion against an established order whose traditional character was fully supported by historical evidence. Thus a new historical orthodoxy was elaborated whose influence is still with us. As late as the middle of the nineteenth century, a new edition of the *Annals* claimed for Baronius an authority in history comparable to that of Thomas Aquinas in theology.[22]

III

The Roman conception of history as a branch of dogma is of interest in part because of its continuing importance; in part because of its intimate relationship to the general atmosphere of fear, rigidity, and the search for secure authority in every sphere that characterized post-Renaissance Italy; and in part also because it helps to throw into relief the quite different historical consciousness developing during this period in Venice. That Venice should have become the scene of a vigorous historiography in the later sixteenth century must come as something of a surprise. In this as in other respects Venice had been singularly backward during the fifteenth century. When at last she had an official historian, the appointment of Bembo (1530), a self-confessed contemplative and a professional literary man without experience in practical affairs,[23] seems singularly inappropriate; and for nearly three decades during the middle of the sixteenth century, Venice was comfortable without any historiographer at all.[24]

The remarkable flowering of Venetian history which came at last during the later decades of that century, and which continued into the seventeenth, seems to express the slow reaction of a peculiarly conservative society to the fact of its gradual but steady decline in world importance. It may be associated with the mixture of self-confidence, alarm, and apprehension induced by the victory of Lepanto. It is also related to a shift in the control of the government from a smaller group of powerful families whose capital was now mainly invested in large-scale agriculture on the mainland, to a larger group of less wealthy nobles still engaged in commerce and convinced that the maintenance of Venetian greatness depended on the continuance of a traditional economy.[25] For this group, therefore, a more broadly based republic and a constant appeal to tradition as the sanction for present policy went hand in hand.

Thus Venetian historiography was in close contact with vital issues of political and social existence, but at the same time it was enriched by the sophisticated discussions about method carried on at Padua, now clearly the most vigorous intellectual center in Italy and the official academy of the Venetian patriciate. Here all the issues raised by Renaissance historical practice were debated and evaluated in the light of classical theory; and, because of the special Venetian predilection for Greek studies, men debated not only the relative merits of Livy and Tacitus, but also those of Herodotus and Thucydides, generally to the advantage of the latter.[26] During the middle decades of the century, even Paduan discussion about history was largely directed to the formulation of a rigid Ciceronian orthodoxy which made of it only a body of examples illustrating the static principles of morality or politics. (It is perhaps significant that these were the years when Venice had no official historian.) But this tendency was gradually supplanted by a new spirit which was given a strong impetus by the *Dialoghi* on history composed by Francesco Patrizzi. Patrizzi's skeptical tendencies undermined the authority of history as a repository of examples for the guidance of men in all ages, and at the same time he emphasized the importance of the formal elements in historical thought so conspicuously lacking in the work of Scipione Ammirato: organization, the selection of detail, the subordination of all elements to a major theme.[27]

Training in such a school enabled the Venetians to appraise critically those tendencies in contemporary historical practice that we have observed elsewhere. So Nicolò Contarini, a prominent member of the reform group, one of the official historians it maintained, and eventually doge of Venice, attacked the adulation and the suppression of truth characteristic of so many histories of the age; his own work admitted quite candidly that all was not well, even with Venice.[28] Another member of this circle, Paolo Paruta, also official historian of Venice and a dedicated servant of the state, composed a series of dialogues in praise of civic life, in one of which a Venetian patrician finds Guicciardini almost the equal of Thucydides, notably because he refused to present fact "simple and naked," clothing it rather "in its causes and in all the circumstances that accompany it"[29]—one immediately thinks of contemporary historians of whom this could not have been said. Such discussion also equipped the Venetians to contest the assimilation of history into dogma. To Bellarmine's charge of heresy in history, our Venetian pamphleteer gave the reply direct: "There cannot be heresy in history which is profane and not contained in Holy Scripture . . . [on the coronation of Charlemagne] the historians are not in agreement. . . . "[30] Another Venetian, somewhat later, responded dryly to a papalist effort to assert as an article of faith that the popes have perpetually and exclusively thirsted for the salvation of souls: "I believe he bases this on the goodness and sanctity of the present Highest Pontiff, disregarding the many histories of the lives of the popes, some by contemporaries who would swear that popes can have some other kind of thirst. This is to make an article of faith out of a matter of fact, which cannot be certain."[31]

It is possible here only to hint at the bulk and richness of Venetian historical composition during this period; few societies can have cultivated a historical consciousness with such intensity. Official historians like Paruta, Contarini, and Andrea Morosini had, naturally, to view events from a Venetian point of view, but they gave substantially greater attention to internal development than conventional court historiography.[32] The *Relazioni* of the Venetian ambassadors frequently contain historical analyses of considerable acumen,[33] and they often collected historical materials in their places of assignment: in the same generation, for example, Francesco Priuli at the imperial court, Ottaviano Bon in Constantinople, and the secretary Giambattista Padavino in Switzerland.[34] Giovan Michele Bruto, one of the most colorful of the Venetians, traveled in Spain, became a Dominican in middle age, spent a year in Savonarola's San Marco in Florence where (one suspects) the *quaestiones* of Thomas were even yet not the sole subject of discussion, and emerged to write a republican history of Florence under the Medici which, tearing away the masks, interprets Cosimo as an ambitious and unscrupulous despot and glorifies tyrannicide in the name of liberty—and this as late as 1562. Bruto eventually became both a Protestant and historiographer at the Catholic court of Hungary.[35] Giovan Francesco Biondi, a Protestant refugee in England, wrote a history of the Wars of the Roses;[36] and Enrico Davila's famous account of the civil struggles in France,[37] in its psychological interest and its analysis of causes, invites comparison with Guicciardini's work. We can also, perhaps, place beside these literary histories, as evidence of Venetian interest in the historical dimension of human experience, her leadership in the representation of historical events in art. A great fire in 1577 destroyed much of the ducal palace, including earlier cycles of paintings in the Great Council Chamber and the Hall of the Scrutinio, and a new plan was executed which depicted the glorious exploits of Venice throughout her past. The importance of the scheme was emphasized by the publication of a book to explain its various iconographical devices.[38] Thus Venice was to be comprehended not merely as the ideal polity described in Gasparo Contarini's *De republica venetorum* but also as an historical entity.

The most distinguished product of the Venetian historical school, however, and certainly its most influential book, was Paolo Sarpi's *Istoria del Concilio tridentino,* smuggled out of Venice and first published in London in 1619.[39] This work is, in spite of its ostensibly ecclesiastical character, a remarkable vehicle of the Venetian historical consciousness, and at the same time a deliberate refutation of both the method and the thesis of Baronius. It is, in effect, an assertion of the priority of historical truth over dogma wherever questions of fact are at stake, even in the history of the church. Sarpi's significance, therefore, consists first of all in his having applied the positive method of modern secular history, still best exemplified by the Florentine school, to ecclesiastical institutions and events. So he conceived his task as the careful accumulation of detail by research. He once compared his subject (the vision itself is eloquent) to a great lake spreading out over Europe: a lake, however, fed by numerous tiny rivulets, each of which the historian must follow to its source and measure drop by drop.[40] At the same time, Sarpi's purpose is to describe the formation of the lake, not to enumerate the droplets, and he uses his method to demonstrate the falseness of the claim that the church is invulnerable to change. In a series of retrospective essays related to the major issues debated at Trent, he aims to show that the institutional church, the church, that is to say, in those dimensions accessible to historical examination, is as much a child of time as any agency of the secular world. Above all he interprets its constitutional development as a product of the same tensions and human passions that have molded governments everywhere. Sarpi views the evolution of ecclesiastical polity as the slow degeneration from an original republicanism, of which Venice in his own time could be taken as the only surviving model, into a tyranny such as (if one may read between the lines) had engulfed other republics, notably Florence in the last century.

Furthermore, in developing this republican vision of church history which so strikingly transfers the preoccupations of Renaissance historiography to a new dimension, Sarpi exhibits all of the psychological insight and dramatic sense that had disappeared from Italian historiography elsewhere. The history of the Council of Trent is presented, with a mixture of distaste and admiration, as a kind of drama in which the popes, hopelessly at a disadvantage in a world controlled by power, fearful of the loss through reform of all they had gained in over a thousand years of self-aggrandizement, succeed nevertheless in winning total victory. Sarpi depicts the growth of reformist pressures and the gathering of the challenge to papal leadership at the council; France is hostile, Spain and the Empire demand reform, the Italians are restive; the crisis grows steadily more threatening; and then, at the last moment, defeat is deftly averted; the fox manages at the end to outwit and to survive among the lions. Indeed, one hardly knows in the end whether the work is best described as an anti-Machiavellian or a Machiavellian tract.

The extraordinary popularity of Sarpi's work[41] did not derive solely from its presenting a thesis of such evident utility for religious controversy; it was due most of all to the fact that his history was a masterpiece on a subject of great general interest. It was a masterpiece, however, as the historical compositions of Ammirato and Baronius were not, precisely because it maintained the fruitful tension between the two essential elements of any vital historiography: empirical investigation and the creative vision, related to living needs, which it disciplines and by which it is informed. Apparently only Venice, in later sixteenth-century Italy, could still support their union. Histories written by Venetians were therefore able to interest readers well into the eighteenth century; thus they served as a link between the historical consciousness of Renaissance Italy and later European historical discourse.

NOTES

1. The first that has come to my notice is Girolamo Briani, *Istoria d'Italia* (Venice, 1632), which, in eighteen books, moves from Hannibal to 1527. This was followed by several other general accounts of Italian affairs, chiefly, however, dealing with the seventeenth century.

2. For what follows see, in general, Rudolph von Albertini, *Das florentinische Staatsbewusstsein im Übergang von der Republik zum Principat* (Bern, 1955).

3. For Guicciardini see, in addition to Albertini, Vittorio de Caprariis, *Francesco Guicciardini: dalla politica alla storia* (Bari, 1950), esp. 89ff.

4. For Varchi, see, in addition to Albertini (esp. 332–333), Michele Lupo Gentile, "Studi sulla storiografia fiorentina alla corte di Cosimo I de' Medici," *Annali della R. Scuola Normale Superiore di Pisa*, XIX (1906).

5. I use the edition, in three volumes, Florence, 1647. A biography of Ammirato is in preparation by Rodolfo de Mattei.

6. *Istorie fiorentine*, I, 4D and 2.

7. *Ibid.*, 2.

8. *Ibid.*, II, 1102C.

9. Cf. the remarks of Ferdinand Schevill, *Medieval and Renaissance Florence*, new ed. (New York and Evanston, 1963), I, xxiii.

10. V. Luciani, *Francesco Guicciardini and His European Reputation* (New York, 1936), 14ff.

11. Agostino Mascardi, *Dell'arte istorica* (Rome, 1636); Sebastiano Macci, *De historia* (Venice, 1613). On Mascardi, see A. Belloni, *Il Seicento* (Milan, 1929), 447–448; on Macci, see Giorgio Spini, "I trattatisti dell'arte storica nella Controriforma italiana," in *Contributi alla storia del Concilio di Trento e della Controriforma* (Florence, 1948), 130–131.

12. Nevertheless even the edition of the *Istorie fiorentine* of 1647 ran into trouble with the censors. See the preliminary note by the printer explaining the omission of a section (for the year 1511) on pp. 294–295 of the third volume.

13. On this point see Jean Delumeau, *Vie économique et sociale de Rome dans la seconde moitié du XVIe siècle* (= *Bibliothèque des Écoles Françaises d'Athènes et de Rome*, Fasc. 184) (Paris, 1957–1959), I, 219.

14. For Bellarmine's historical thought, see E. A. Ryan, *The Historical Scholarship of Saint Robert Bellarmine* (Louvain, 1936).

15. Pontien Polman, *L'élément historique dans la controverse religieuse au XVIe siècle* (Gembloux, 1932), 500.

16. Cf. Ryan, *Bellarmine*, 149–150.

17. The skeptic was probably Giovanni Marsili, in the anonymous *Risposta d'un dottore in theologia ad una lettera scrittagli da un reverendo suo amico sopra il breve di censure, dalla santità di Papa Paolo V. publicate contro li Signori Venetiani* (Venice, 1606). I use the edition included in the *Raccolta degli scritti usciti fuori*

in istampa e scritti a mano, nella causa del P. Paolo V co'signori venetiani (Coira, 1607), p. 143 for the passage cited.

18. Roberto Bellarmino, *Risposta del Card. Bellarmino a un libretto intitolato Risposta di un Dottore di Theologia* (Rome, 1606), also in the *Raccolta* cited above, 166–167.

19. Cf. Polman, *L'élément historique*, 527.

20. A recent instance is provided by Hubert Jedin's authoritative history of the Council of Trent. I quote from the translation of Ernest Graf, *A History of the Council of Trent,* I (London, 1957), 5–6: "Up to the fateful turn of the Middle Ages, about the year 1300, the supremacy of the Papacy in the Church and in the *Respublica christiana* had remained unchallenged. Caesarism had collapsed after a long struggle. . . . The fourth Council of the Lateran, the two Councils of Lyons and that of Vienne, showed the Pope as the unquestioned head of Christendom."

21. It is cited frequently by the partisans of the papacy in the numerous anti-Venetian writings occasioned by the interdict of 1606–1607. Bellarmine, for example, appealed to its authority in the *Risposta del Card. Bellarmino ad un libretto intitolato Trattato, e risolutione sopra la validità delle Scommuniche, di Gio Gersone* (Rome, 1606), also in the *Raccolta* cited above, 310 bis.

22. So the "Monitum" of Louis Guerin, in the *Annales ecclesiastici,* I (1864): "Qui Baronium nominaverit, is nobis in memoriam revocaverit virum in historia ea auctoritate praeditum, qua ejus municeps, sanctus Thomas Aquinas, in theologia valet. *Annales* enim *Ecclesiasticos* unum esse hoc in genere absolutum opus, nemo non profitetur."

23. In point of fact, he was the second official historian of Venice, Andrea Navagero having been appointed fifteen years earlier; and Navagero, as a layman and diplomat, would seem to have been a more appropriate kind of choice. Navagero died, however, without having written anything. For the decrees of these appointments, see Carlo Laggomaggiore, "*L'Istoria Veneziana* di M. Pietro Bembo," *Archivio Veneto,* Ser. 3, IX (1905), 331–334.

24. Bembo was followed by Daniele Barbaro who, however, abandoned his history in favor of an ecclesiastical appointment in 1550; what he had written was evidently so little valued that it disappeared until found and published by Tommaso Gar, *Archivio Storico Italiano,* VII, part 2 (1884), 949–1112. After 1550 Venice had no official historian until the appointment of Paolo Paruta in 1580.

25. See, in general, the excellent discussion of this period of Venetian history in Gaetano Cozzi, *Il doge Nicolò Contarini: Richerche sul patriziato veneziano agli inizi del seicento* (Venice and Rome, 1958), esp. 1–52.

26. For Paduan historiography see, in general, Spini, "Trattatisti dell'arte storica," n. 11 above.

27. Patrizzi's skepticism is emphasized by Julian H. Franklin, *Jean Bodin and the Sixteenth-Century Revolution in the Methodology of Law and History* (New York, 1963), 96–102. See also Franz Lamprecht, *Zur Theorie der humanistische Geschichtsschreibung, Mensch und Geschichte bei Francesco Patrizzi* (Zurich, 1950); and Beatrice Reynolds, "Shifting Currents in Historical Criticism," *Journal of the History of Ideas,* XIV (1953), 471–472.

28. For discussion and excerpts from Contarini's *Le Historie Venetiane,* see

Cozzi, *Contarini,* 197ff. and appendix. An edition of Contarini's history is now in preparation under the auspices of the Fondazione Giorgio Cini.

29. *Della perfezione della vita politica,* in *Opere politiche,* C. Monzani, ed. (Florence, 1852), I, 200–203.

30. Giovanni Marsili, *Difesa a favore della risposta dell'otto propositioni* (Venice, 1606), in *Raccolta,* 243.

31. Fulgenzio Micanzio, in an official *consulta* of April 6, 1623, on the *Sui reditus ex Anglia consilium* of Marc-Antonio de Dominis, given in Bartolomeo Cecchetti, *La Repubblica di Venezia e la Corte di Roma nei rapporti della religione* (Venice, 1874), II, 246.

32. Paolo Paruta, *Historia Vinetiana* (Venice, 1605); for Contarini, see above, note 28; Andrea Morosini, *Historia Veneta ab anno 1521 usque ad annum 1615* (Venice, 1623).

33. An example is the relation, on his return from Rome in 1558, of Bernardo Navagero, in *Le relazioni degli ambasciatori veneti al senato,* ed. Albéri, ser. 2, III (Florence, 1846), esp. 371ff.; this is a significant early attempt to understand historically the political role of the church.

34. Marco Foscarini, *Della letteratura veneziana ed altri scritti intorno ad essa* (Venice, 1854), 423–426, 437. This work, by a cultivated doge of the later eighteenth century, is generally useful for Venetian historical writing.

35. For Bruto see Andrea Veress, "Il veneziano Giovanni Michele Bruto e la sua storia d'Ungheria," *Archivio Veneto,* Ser. 5, VI (1929), 148–178.

36. *L'Istoria delle guerre civili d'Inghilterra tra le due Case di Lancastro, e Iorc* (Venice, 1637).

37. *Istoria delle guerre civili di Francia* (Venice, 1630).

38. By the Florentine Girolamo Bardi, *Dichiaratione di tutte le istorie, che si contengono ne i quadri posti novamente nelle Salle dello Scrutinio, e del Gran Consiglio, del Palagio Ducale della Serenissima Republica di Vinegia* (Venice, 1587).

39. On the circumstances of its publication, see Gaetano Cozzi, "Fra Paolo Sarpi, l'anglicanesimo e la *Historia del Concilio Tridentino,*" *Rivista Storica Italiana,* LXVIII (1956), 559–619.

40. *Istoria del Concilio Tridentino,* Giovanni Gambarin, ed. (Bari, 1935), I, 187.

41. On this point see Hubert Jedin, *Das Konzil von Trient, ein Überblick über die Erforschung seiner Geschichte* (Rome, 1948), 93.

13 Gallicanism and the Nature of Christendom

This piece aimed to demonstrate the historical significance of Gallicanism and its view of the French past. Gallicanism, the ideology of most Frenchmen during the early modern period, involved a belief in the historical and legal autonomy of the French church within the Roman Catholic fold. Now virtually ignored by historians, it was of major importance, as I argue here, in the transition from medieval to modern conceptions of politics. The piece first appeared in Renaissance Studies in Honor of Hans Baron, *ed. Anthony Molho and John Tedeschi (DeKalb, Ill.: Northern Illinois University Press, 1971), pp. 811–830, and is reprinted here with the permission of the publisher.*

. . .

Over forty years ago Lucien Febvre insisted on the crucial importance of distinguishing between *religious* and *ecclesiastical* history, between powerful spiritual movements related to the major currents of European social and political development and the particular events and institutional forms through which, almost incidentally, they may find expression. The Reformation, in Febvre's perspective, was thus a movement of European scope that brought into focus, in areas destined to stay Catholic as well as in those that broke away from the medieval church, tendencies that had been gathering force for centuries. The problem for the historian, he suggested, was to identify these forces and then to show how they operated in various situations and were modified by local conditions.[1]

Although his brilliant essay was directed finally to explaining the origins of the Reformation in France, Febvre confined his attention largely to the sources of French Protestantism, which, as it turned out, failed to win over more than a minority of Frenchmen. But the general impulses behind the Reformation were often as effective among Catholics as among Protestants, as Febvre was well aware; and a better illustration of his point may perhaps be found in Gallicanism, which bridged the centuries before and after the Reformation proper, and which was attractive to generations of Frenchmen, among them not only personages of evident gravity, learning, and intelligence, but also in many cases men close to the center of public life.

Gallicanism has not been very positively regarded by historians, nor has it been closely associated with the problems posed by either the Reformation or the Renaissance. Standard general histories of France have viewed it largely as a dimension of politics, and it has suffered from the same distaste attached to other aspects of the Old Regime.[2] On the other hand historians who have studied Gallicanism systematically have tended to see in it little more than an incoherent bundle of currents of opposition to the Holy See, based on an ignorance of history and defective theology and animated by a selfish indifference to the larger needs of the Christian community.[3] For both, Gallicanism emerges as, in a rather precise sense, a transparent species of ideology, an elaborate mask for the special interests of crown and class. Students of ecclesiastical rather than of religious history (in Febvre's sense), its major historians, have assigned it only a limited significance even in the history of the church. Thus, in a manner ironically reminiscent of recent insistence that the revolution at the end of the eighteenth century was a national achievement, Victor Martin maintained that Gallicanism, native in origin and utterly self-absorbed, was "a movement specifically French." "Exported outside the kingdom," he declared, "it quickly died or was radically transformed."[4]

Martin was obviously asking precisely the sort of question that Febvre had called on historians of the Reformation to reject, and this paper will not pursue Martin's question by arguing that Gallicanism had a large influence beyond the borders of France. I think that it had, in fact, some external effect, though the problem of what constitutes an "influence" and why a movement of thought exerts influence under some conditions but not others is in any case more complicated than is sometimes supposed. The primary interest of Gallicanism lies rather in what it reveals about the concern of pious Frenchmen, like other Europeans, to redefine Christianity and the idea of Christendom, and thus to bring religious life into a closer correspondence with the changing structures of European society. From this standpoint Gallicanism can hardly be viewed as a narrowly national movement; the more Gallican Frenchmen were, the more emphatically they affirmed their membership in a larger

European community. Thus it should hardly be surprising to discover that Gallican theorists were sometimes well aware of their affinities with men elsewhere; and, conversely, both as a practical and a speculative posture, Gallicanism was an object of general European interest, among Catholics as well as Protestants.

Although Gallicanism can be traced back at least to the fourteenth century and perhaps earlier,[5] achieved a political climax of sorts in the later seventeenth century, and may be discerned again lurking behind the Civil Constitution of the Clergy and even later, the most significant chapter in its venerable history for the purposes of this paper was the heroic age of Gallican speculation extending from the end of the Council of Trent to the ministry of Richelieu. During this period Gallicanism enjoyed its maximum freedom from royal control, and it was therefore most spontaneous and responsive to a variety of contemporary impulses, both positive and negative. Notable among the latter was the challenge of the Counter-Reformation, during these years in its most militant mood and resolved to impose on Catholic Europe the whole pattern of universalist, hierarchical, and theocratic values elaborated by the papal theorists of the thirteenth and fourteenth centuries. This theoretical system had now been given concrete application in the decrees of Trent, whose significance was as much symbolic as practical.[6] Gallicanism, during this period, saw itself clearly as the major obstacle, in France and perhaps in all Europe, to a reactionary offensive stemming from Rome.

During this period, in addition, although the case of Edmond Richer shows that Gallicanism still found vigorous spokesmen among the clergy, its major champions came from the relatively independent magistracy, a group peculiarly fitted by its cosmopolitan culture as well as its specialized training to respond creatively to the general needs of the age.[7] That the Gallican leadership in these years consisted so largely of lawyers deserves some emphasis.[8] Supported by the prestige of imperial Rome and dedicated to the practical requirements of the *vita activa,* the civil law had long ignored the constraints of theology, and lawyers had perhaps earlier than any other social group insisted on a practical independence from ecclesiastical supervision; as early as the thirteenth century it was said that a good jurist was necessarily a bad Christian.[9] Legal training was thus particularly calculated to nourish a sense of the dignity of the lay estate and the prerogatives of the secular power.

Much of what was most significant in the Gallicanism of the later sixteenth and early seventeenth centuries may be associated with attitudes traditional among lawyers. Fundamental among these was an assumption that the entire institutional order was pluralistic rather than unitary; in both Italy and France lawyers had early accustomed themselves to working within a framework composed of a congeries of particular states rather than an all-inclusive system, and thus they had long opposed the directive claims of the papacy. Their concern with clearly defined spheres of activity and established procedures gave them a certain bias towards constitutionalism, and the same tendencies nourished a spiritual conception of the church. Legal study had also relied heavily on a species of historical research potentially applicable to revealing the evolution of institutions through time. Guillaume Budé had already exhibited something of this interest in France during the earlier sixteenth century; and it was destined to develop during succeeding generations into an increasingly sophisticated historicism. This tendency among the Gallican magistrates combined with a professional interest in the relation between law and the immediate needs of time and place to produce a type of mind notable for its openness, its flexibility, and its resistance to dogmatic rigidities in all aspects of human experience. The Gallicanism of the lawyers during this period can therefore enlarge our understanding of the later Renaissance in France as well as of the Reformation.

Fundamental to Gallicanism in every period of its history was the assumption that Christendom properly consisted not of a unified, hierarchically organized system, but of discrete and parallel entities.[10] This was taken to mean not only the independence of rulers from ecclesiastical supervision but also the legitimate existence of separate and independent states. As early as John of Paris (to whose authority later Gallicans appealed), Frenchmen had argued for a pluralistic political order;[11] and by the later sixteenth century Gallicans simply assumed that, since traditions and problems differed widely throughout Europe, it was essential that institutions should vary locally, and that they should be locally and flexibly administered. Above all they were persuaded that what was appropriate for Italy was by no means necessarily suited to France.[12] They were immediately concerned with the organization of the church, but this concern had a more general relation to the structure of European politics.

In its application to the church, the substitution of numerous parallel authorities for an arrangement in hierarchy led to a marked bias for the separate and independent authority of bishops,[13] and even some tendency to insist on the independent, divinely bestowed authority of each individual priest.[14] Their larger concern with local needs was also basic to Gallican hostility (most eloquently expressed in the pamphlets of Saint-Cyran, in this matter a close ally of Gallicanism) towards the regular clergy, international rules governing administrative affairs being themselves generally suspect.[15] This feeling was, of course, most vigorously directed against the Jesuits. The same interest was basic to Gallican support for conciliarism, one of the constants in the history of Gallicanism, equally shared by magistrates and theologians.[16] The council was superior to the pope in their view, however, for practical as well as theoretical reasons, a fact of some interest for appraising the Gallican mind. Gallicans preferred councils because many heads are better than one and because the needs of the church are not single and general but plural and particular, the needs of individual churches and individual churchmen which can only achieve satisfactory expression in an assembly.[17] The principle may be partly a feudal residue, partly a reflection of Aristotle; but the realities it reflected were those of the fragmented modern world.

The limited role in the church that Gallicans attributed to the pope was a corollary of these views; they saw the church as a constitutional apparatus properly governed by duly established machinery according to general laws and set procedures. The pope was no longer, for them, the apex of a hierarchy, the church's ultimate point of contact with the divine authority claimed for the whole, but hardly more than *primus inter pares,* the president of a college in which no member was essentially higher or lower than another since each was appointed directly by God. Gallican theorists considered the pope neither infallible in matters of doctrine nor broadly competent in the administration of the church;[18] they were utterly opposed to the doctrine of a papal *plenitudo potestatis.* No element in the pope's authority could be regarded, in their view, as unlimited; to the extent that he ruled the church, he did so as a constitutional monarch, and resistance to him was legitimate on conventional constitutional grounds.[19] On this point the connections between secular and ecclesiastical thought seem unusually close.[20] For the Gallican writers, however, the church, itself a congeries of particular churches, had not one but many constitutions: a universal constitution based on natural and divine law as implemented by the general council, but also a series of local constitutions based on local traditions and needs. "In France," declared Pithou, referring specifically to the church but certainly invoking a larger set of political conceptions, "absolute and infinite power has no place but is contained and limited by the canons and regulations of the ancient councils of the church received in this kingdom."[21] The Gallican liberties may thus be understood as an elaborate parallel to the fundamental laws of France, and the Parlement of Paris was felt to be the proper guardian of both.[22]

The pluralistic vision of the institutional order and the constitutionalism of the Gallican magistrates were directly related to a conception of the church that distinguished sharply between its mystical and spiritual dimension and the external and administrative framework through which the church operates in specific situations. If they gave special attention to the latter, it must be remembered that they were lawyers, professionally engaged with the definition of legal rights in concrete situations which they had to take into account. But as Christians in a period of deepening piety, in which they participated, they were aware that faith had other and more profound dimensions.[23] And as Christian lawyers, they were faced with the problem of coordinating the particular institutional and local realities with which they were in regular professional contact and the inescapable fact that Christianity in some sense also transcended the local scene, that the church was in some sense (if not in what was a regular part of their own experience) a universal and single body.

Like many of their contemporaries in other parts of Europe, Catholic as well as Protestant, they did so by sharpening the distinction between the spiritual and temporal realms and limiting the church to the former.[24] It is, indeed, not entirely clear what functions they were disposed to allow to the spiritual power; they were not systematic theologians in most cases, and perhaps it is best to speak rather of tendencies than of a mature theory of the church. Among these tendencies was an inclination to regard as the true church only what was immutable and therefore vulnerable neither to the vagaries of time nor to their own professional attention. Whatever history or the law could touch, whatever could be affected by the things they knew best, appeared to them as profane and tainted, as therefore not the true body of Christ, which by definition was spiritual, holy, subject to no shadow of turning.

This conclusion is difficult to demonstrate. No Gallican, as far as I am aware, quite said as much, and it must be deduced as the assumption underlying numerous general pronouncements. Here, for example, is a proposition of Jacques Leschassier, one of the most scholarly of the Gallican magistrates: "Among the political laws of the church, the divine or apostolic is the eternal and perpetual, the others are temporal and provisional, made for human and temporal reasons; and the church tends, by its duty and according to the opinion of all good Christians, to the restitution of the apostolic law."[25] The attitudes to history and reform suggested by this statement will concern us in a moment; here what should be noticed is its appeal to an ideal model from which every historical accident must somehow be shucked away. Among such accidents Leschassier clearly included not only all political dominion and property but rights of disposal over every temporal thing, which he explicitly denied either to the pope or to any clerical body. Pithou took much the same position, and the order of his argument implied (though it did not make explicit) the view that much and perhaps all the external administration of the church belonged to the temporal power. Thus he first denied the pope any general authority over temporal matters in France, and then he insisted that it belonged to the king to call national ecclesiastical councils responsible for the discipline of the clergy.[26] There appears to have been a sense in which the Gallican liberties did not properly concern the spiritual "estate" at all, but only (to apply a distinction of Richer) the "government."[27]

This position too had important implications for the role of the pope; the spirituality of the church as well as its decentralization severely limited his authority. It meant that the pope had no right to interfere in any way with political affairs or to call temporal magistrates to account.[28] On this the Gallican magistrates, with their keen sense of the dignity of the lay condition as well as their concern as lawyers to maintain the rights of the crown, felt strongly; and whenever it arose they came into action. Many Gallican treatises were occasional, called into existence by efforts to assert papal authority over rulers. Pius IV's summons to Jeanne d'Albret to appear before the Holy Office produced the *Mémoire* of Du Mesnil; Gregory XIV's attack in 1591 on the rights of Henry of Navarre to the French throne resulted in works by Coquille, Fauchet, and Faye;[29] the assassination of Henry IV (so widely attributed to a Jesuit and therefore papalist plot) was shortly followed by the treatise of Richer and certainly helps to explain Richer's wide support;[30] Pierre Pithou composed a history of the interdict, the device by which popes had long sought to impose their authority on rulers, and now a potential danger to France.[31] Although these men did not deny the right of the pope to excommunicate kings as individuals, they consistently rejected the alleged political implications of such action; they denied the pope's authority to depose any ruler or to release his subjects from obedience.[32]

The large supervisory role Gallicanism assigned to the crown in the national church had several sources, among them the idea that his authority was derived directly from God (a belief much facilitated by the general denial of hierarchy) and the long tradition that saw the king as no mere layman but an ecclesiastical functionary bound by sacred oath to defend the church from all its enemies, notably including those in Rome.[33] At the same time there had been a strong tendency from an early point for Gallican theorists to emphasize that the church consisted of the whole congregation of believers, laity as well as clergy;[34] and this view too implied the special responsibility of the king as primary layman. Finally, the distinction between the church's spirituality and its institutionality suggested parallel leadership, and Gallican theorists were prompt to attribute the direction of the institution to the crown. The duty of the king, as Leschassier remarked, was "not to baptize and to preach, but to provide for baptizing and preaching and to guard the rights of the church."[35] Popes deceived themselves, declared Le Jay, if they supposed that they alone were concerned with the harmony of the church, a responsibility that devolved also on kings and princes;[36] and Leschassier explained that it was above all to be exercised through their "sovereign judges," the "natural and legitimate protectors of the ancient law."[37] Thus through a series of venerable conceptions the Gallican magistrates, at once pious and practical, managed to combine the most transcendent ideal for the church with practical accommodation to the world as they knew it.

The obvious contrast between this ideal and the contemporary church of their own experience cried out to them (as to other religious reformers) for explanation, and to this task they brought the techniques for the historical study of law at work in France and, under the influence of Jacques Cujas, already evident in the transition from the more systematic and general *mos italicus* to the more specific and historically oriented *mos gallicus*.[38] Gallicanism thus participated fully in the broader movements that made of this period the first great age in French historiography.[39] But while some secular historians in France were moving toward an idea of progress, the Gallican historians of the church proposed a return to ancient and even primitive models; they sought an antidote to history.[40]

The Gallican view of church history thus resembled the vision of the European past shared by both medieval religious reformers and Renaissance humanists. In this perspective an original perfection had been succeeded by a long degeneration that had coincided precisely with the medieval centuries, and this in turn would be followed by a restoration in which, at least among humanists and Gallicans, the contemporary flowering of philological scholarship (as the key to grasping the whole pattern) would play the essential role. But Gallicanism, through its contact with legal study, was as a program of reform more concrete than medieval reformism or humanism. It perceived that change in the church (as in the law) responded to specific historical circumstances, and it was therefore concerned not merely with a general educational and spiritual revival but also with the actual structure of institutions and their modes of operation. Its historical analysis was also sharper. It had not only a general theory but also an interest in the actual processes and stages of historical change; the technical defects in its scholarship, which were those of its time, and the distortions stemming from its preconceptions should not be allowed to obscure these substantial merits.

A favorite Gallican text, cited by Pithou as a kind of summary at the end of his own major treatise, came from the book of Proverbs: "Pass not beyond the ancient bounds which thy fathers have set."[41] The verse was more than a conservative slogan. It was an invitation to historical scholarship: the health of the church, it suggested, depended on a clear definition of the limitations on ecclesiastical action and organization established by the early church. For lawyers this implied the need for a systematic reconstruction of ancient canon law; and therefore, in contrast to earlier Gallicans, who had appealed to ancient practice merely in general, the Gallican magistrates of the seventeenth century made a serious attempt to describe it in specific detail. They published a series of canonical collections antedating Gratian, but they were chiefly interested in the practice of the first five centuries when, as they believed, popes were properly submissive to the temporal power and the church universal consisted of a federation of local churches, all respecting each other's autonomy and mutually related through general councils convened by emperors.[42]

The most erudite among the Gallican students of the early church was probably Leschassier, whose *De la liberté ancienne et canonique de l'Eglise Gallicane* argued that the church had possessed an "ancient and common law," an antique *codex canonum* originated by the apostles, formulated through councils, and clearly recognized at Ephesus and Chalcedon, that had generally guaranteed "ancient and canonical liberty."[43] For Leschassier this ancient instrument for the defense of the church against "servitude" (i.e., centralization) had supplied the model for the more specific liberties of the Gallican church; the ancient church, he believed, had recognized papal authority only *legaliter et regulariter,* legally (according to Roman law) and canonically.[44] But it was all too obvious that, even in France, the original liberty of the church had not survived. The loosely federal constitution of the first centuries had collapsed under pressure from Rome, and thus the Middle Ages assumed a distinct identity.

This vision of the past is significant in several ways. It invested the autonomy of the Gallican church with the sanction of antiquity, and at the same time it depicted the Gallican liberties as rooted in the universal liberty enjoyed by the entire church during the first centuries of its existence, not merely in peculiar and shifting local conditions. As an argument for reform it had, therefore, a very general bearing. It was both (in a precise sense) radical and dangerous. It is also of considerable historiographical interest. By recognizing that even in France the ancient liberty of the church had disappeared, it implies a break with the myth of national continuity so inhibiting to the emergence of the Renaissance consciousness in northern Europe. It also suggests a concern to identify the crucial elements, moments, and discrete stages in a long and general historical process of subversion and recovery in which (in contrast to the polemical historiography of contemporary Protestantism) the essential causes were natural and all too human rather than diabolical.

Their conception of the church as essentially spiritual helped the Gallican magistrates to take this cool view of its history, for a visible institution whose career is punctuated by distinct events and phases was for them not properly the church at all, and it could therefore be discussed like any other earthly phenomenon. The Gallican treatment of the historical church was in this respect much like that of their Venetian contemporary, Paolo Sarpi.[45] Thus Coquille attributed the success of papal claims to temporal authority to the inherited prestige of ancient Rome, only by historical accident the see of Peter.[46] For Charles Faye earlier popes had been generally submissive to secular authority, and the relationship between popes and emperors had been proper until the time of Hildebrand. But then, "finding that this violent remedy profited the church, that institution exchanged its ancient humility for pride, cruelty, and tyranny, fastened papal attention on temporal concerns, and brought scandal that caused schism and heresy."[47] Leschassier associated the rise of ecclesiastical tyranny directly with internal developments in canon law, which had been compelled to express the "worldly greatness" that had penetrated the church. Under papal auspices the ancient code of the church universal had been gradually replaced by a specifically Roman canon law from which articles protecting local liberty were systematically excluded. He considered the process well under way with the code of Dionysius Exiguus and essentially completed by Gratian and his followers. After Gratian Christendom (except for the magistrates of Paris) entirely forgot "that the church had ever had any other law than this."[48]

Not every Gallican admitted that even the church in France had shared in the general eclipse of liberty. Charles Faye, for example, claimed that she had remained twelve hundred years the same, without any alteration in her "laws and form of establishment and police." In this respect he believed that the French church had been unique; every other church had changed for the worse.[49] But Leschassier knew better; he was explicit that in spite of staunch resistance, the Gallican church had fallen into the same "miserable servitude" as the rest of Christendom. From this condition she had only been rescued by Saint Louis, but that ruler's assertion of the autonomy of the French church against Innocent IV had begun a steady recovery that was still continuing in Leschassier's own time. In his conception, therefore, there had already been three phases in the history of the church in France: an ancient era of freedom, an intervening period of tyranny, and a new age of freedom. The first and third were qualitatively identical: "the ancient and the modern . . . are one same liberty measured differently." The ancient was based on the code of the church universal, while "the modern is contained in the ordinances of our kings, in their concordats and in the judgments of their sovereign courts; and this second liberty has been introduced by necessity, as subsidiary to the first." Modern Gallicanism was the ancient church universal reborn in one nation, and thus the model as well for ecclesiastical reform everywhere.[50]

The Gallican magistrates contemplated the accomplishments of Trent and the various reforms sponsored by Rome in the light of these conceptions. In their view these developments pointed not to the true *reformation* of the church but rather to a universal extension and consummation of that *deformation* so successfully prosecuted by the medieval papacy. Genuine reform, they believed, could proceed only along the lines marked out by Gallicanism; a reformed Christendom meant, for them, a collection of autonomous units modeled on France. As Leschassier declared, "The modern councils, which contain the servitude of the church, must yield to the ancient, which contain its liberty, since this is a common canonical and ancient right."[51]

These rather summary remarks about the attitudes and content of Gallicanism should be enough to suggest why the works of Gallicans were of considerable interest to other Europeans, not only because Gallicanism presented itself as a potential ally against the pope but for more positive reasons. Gallicanism suggested that a certain undogmatic spiritual unity was consistent with the political pluralism required by the emerging identities of particular states. It associated dogmatic rigidity with the corrupt medieval past, and Gallican writers occasionally took a remarkably broad view about the definition of Christian belief;[52] for Catholics Gallicanism offered a real alternative to the restrictive and often uncongenial orthodoxies required by the papacy. Basic to this attitude was also an intellectual style (among the Gallican magistrates if not necessarily among their theological allies) that also made their position widely attractive. Precisely during a time when the Roman reform movement sought to reinvigorate rational and systematic modes of thought, denounced or tried to control free historical investigation, and took an increasingly dim view of the new science, the Gallicanism of the magistrates sought truth in the concrete and empirical world, worked towards increasingly sophisticated techniques of free historical investigation and analysis, and accepted the autonomy of science as well as of politics; a sympathetic interest in the new astronomy was only one reflection among others of the remarkably open attitude to all human experience that characterized the Gallican magistracy.[53] Gallicanism thus brought into focus tendencies central to a whole generation of Europeans.

It should be clear, then, why lines of communication were open between Gallican leaders and like-minded men, perhaps especially government officials, in other parts of Europe; and they operated in both directions. Gallican writings occupied a prominent place in the Calvinist Melchior Goldast's monumental *Monarchia S. Romani imperii* (Hanover and Frankfurt, 1611–1613).[54] They were also read in England, occasionally in English translation;[55] and conversely the oath of allegiance that the Gallican Third Estate proposed to impose on the realm at the Estates General of 1614 was modeled on the Anglican oath of James I.[56]

The connections between Gallicanism and Venice, as another Catholic power, are, however, particularly instructive. After several decades of withdrawal from European affairs, the Serenissima, still regarded as a major state, was during the later sixteenth century drawing closer to France, whose recovery after the Religious Wars she welcomed as a makeweight on the Italian peninsula to Spain. An interest in French thought accompanied thoughts of political alliance, and both were mediated by ambassadors like Philippe Canaye, who, although forbidden direct contact with the Venetian patriciate, communicated with its more important members through such influential personages as Paolo Sarpi.[57] The mentality of this group, among which Galileo spent his most happy and fruitful years, is suggested by its interest in such works as the essays of Montaigne and Francis Bacon. It was cosmopolitan, skeptical, generally suspicious of both the motives and the results of intellectual system building, and in politics resolved to defend the autonomy of the secular world and the absolute independence of the Republic.[58]

Venetian interest in Gallicanism was notably stimulated by the papal interdict of 1606–1607 and the tense years following that traumatic event. The Venetians helped Canaye himself to recognize the larger importance of Gallicanism. Possibly a bit misled by Venetian flattery, he wrote home from Venice: "The greater the effort to stifle our Gallican liberties, the more they are studied and embraced by all nations, so that here they are described as a law of nations necessary to the conservation of every kind of state."[59] Such prominent Gallicans as Leschassier and Louis Servin were induced by the Venetian ambassador in Paris to compose treatises in behalf of Venice, whose cause against Rome was discovered to be much the same as that of France;[60] and Sarpi, who had long been interested in the doctrines of Cujas, busied himself in securing copies of Gallican treatises to circulate among the Venetian leaders.[61] In these works the Venetians found, if not novel arguments, valuable support for their general insistence that the autonomy they required for themselves represented the legitimate and historic organization of the church universal.

But here too the exchange moved in both directions, in spite of the complacency of Canaye. Gallicans admired and found encouragement in Venetian resistance to Rome, and they read the Venetian treatises with as much avidity as the Venetians read theirs. The magistrates of Paris followed the Venetian interdict with deep interest, collecting and passing around each scrap of news, and reacting with varying degrees of enthusiasm to the Venetian pamphlets as they reached Paris. For Pierre de l'Estoile, Paolo Sarpi, the leading Venetian theorist, was a kind of saint.[62] Nor did the impression that the Venetian interdict left in France die quickly. The papal nuncio in Paris noted with alarm a year after the interdict came to an end how much encouragement "the contumacy of the Venetians" still gave to the French. In his view it continued to justify and to excuse "the faults and errors" of the French, among whom "papal jurisdiction is almost completely destroyed."[63] After the assassination of Henry IV, the author of the famous *Anticoton* praised Venice for expelling the Jesuits. If France had been equally wise, he meant to imply, the king would still have been alive.[64]

Viewed in this broader context, therefore, Gallicanism takes on a new and larger meaning. Religious thought has a unique capacity to bring into focus fundamental changes in the whole range of human values and attitudes which may find only partial expression in other aspects of human activity. And Gallicanism reveals, perhaps more generally than any other development in the religious history of France during the later medieval and early modern periods, how fully France participated in the spiritual and cultural crisis of the Renaissance and Reformation.

NOTES

1. "Une question mal posée: les origines de la réformee française et le problème des causes de la réforme," first published in the *Revue historique*, CLXI (1929), and included in *Au coeur religieux du XVIᵉ siècle* (Paris, 1957), pp. 3–70.

2. A good example is the treatment by Ernest Lavisse, *Histoire de France*, VII (Paris, 1905), Part I, 387–400, Part II, 14–37.

3. An extreme, though not altogether unrepresentative, example of this view is M. Dubruel, "Gallicanisme," *Dictionnaire de théologie catholique*, VI, Part 2 (Paris, 1924), cols. 1096–1137; see, for example, cols. 1108–1109: "Ces théories sont des constructions factices imaginées pour justifier des résistances aux développements théoriques et pratiques de la primauté de Pierre," etc. Among the most important recent works on the subject are Joseph Lecler, "Qu'est-ce que les libertés de l'Église gallicane," *Recherches de science religieuse*, XXIII (1933), 385–410, 542–568, and XXIV (1934), 47–85; Aimé George Martimort, *Le Gallicanisme de Bossuet* (Paris, 1953), with massive bibliographies; and the magisterial works of Victor Martin, *Le Gallicanisme et la réforme catholique* (Paris, 1919), *Le Gallicanisme politique et le clergé de France* (Paris, 1929), and *Les origines du Gallicanisme* (Paris, 1939).

4. *Origines du Gallicanisme*, I, 39.

5. *Ibid.*, I, esp. 29 ff.; Lecler, pp. 388–395.

6. For the Council of Trent as a stimulus to Gallicanism, see Lecler, pp. 542 ff.

7. A systematic study of this group, its social and political backgrounds and its culture, is badly needed. There are scattered suggestions in René Pintard, *Le libertinage érudit dans la première moitié du XVIIᵉ siècle* (Paris, 1943), and George Huppert, *The Idea of Perfect History: Historical Erudition and Historical Philosophy in Renaissance France* (Urbana and Chicago, 1970).

8. It may be observed that the general importance of lawyers in the political and cultural history of the Renaissance is now receiving increased attention, for example in Myron P. Gilmore, *Humanists and Jurists* (Cambridge, Mass., 1963), and Lauro Martines, *Lawyers and Statecraft in Renaissance Florence* (Princeton, 1968).

9. Martin, *Origines du Gallicanisme*, I, 137–138.

10. In this connection cf. Edmond Richer, *De la puissance ecclésiastique et politique* (Paris, 1612), p. 11: "non donc la seule puissance est de Dieu: il y en a de mediocres & d'inferieures: & comme ce que Dieu a conioint ne doit estre separé: aussi ne se doit on aproprier, ce qu'il a attribué à ceux qui nous sont adioincts."

11. For John of Paris, see Otto Gierke, *Political Theories of the Middle Age*, tr. Frederic William Maitland (Cambridge, 1900), p. 20 and n. 61. Richer appealed to his authority, p. 48.

12. There is a witty reflection of this attitude in Paolo Sarpi, *Istoria del Concilio Tridentino*, ed. Giovanni Gambarin (Bari, 1935), II, 250, which quotes the bishop of Valence as observing that "it would be a great absurdity to watch Paris burn when the Seine and Marne are full of water, in the belief that it was necessary to wait to put out the fire for water from the Tiber." See also, in this

work, the remarks attributed to the French chancellor at Poissy (II, 300). On the general point see Martimort, pp. 106 ff.

13. Cf. Martimort, pp. 19–20, 76 ff. The same kind of episcopalianism was prominent in Saint Cyran; cf. Jean Orcibal, *Jean Duvergier de Hauranne, abbé de Saint-Cyran, et son temps* (Paris, 1947), pp. 353–354.

14. As in Richer, p. 10. Cf. p. 18, where Richer insists also on the participation of priests in church councils.

15. Cf. Orcibal, pp. 35 ff., and Martimort, pp. 21–22.

16. On the general point see Martimort, pp. 41 ff. For some particular expressions of conciliar sentiment, cf. Pierre Pithou, *Les Libertez de l'Eglise Gallicane* (in his *Opera* [Paris, 1609], pp. 511–533), p. 522; Jacques Leschassier, *De la liberté ancienne et canonique de l'Eglise Gallicane* (Paris, 1606), pp. 29–30; Richer, pp. 18–23.

17. Cf. Richer, p. 18, on the superiority of a council: "& celà se iuge en partie par inspiration divine, partie par la lumière naturelle: veu que plusieurs yeux voyent plus loing & aperçoivent mieux qu'un seul: & il n'a esté concedé de Dieu ou de Nature à un seul d'estre sage, de peur qu'il ne s'en eslevast." There is an interesting parallel here with the defense of royal rule through councils in Philippe de Commynes, *Mémoires,* ed. J. Calmette and G. Durville (Paris, 1924–1925), I, 103.

18. Martimort, pp. 23 ff. on the general point.

19. Cf. Charles Faye, *Discours des moyens pour lesquels messieurs du clergé . . . ont declaré les Bulles Monitoriales . . . nulles & injustes* (Paris, 1591), in *Traitez des droits et libertez de l'Eglise Gallicane,* ed. Pierre Dupuy (Paris, 1731), I, 98–99, which denies that the pope is universal bishop and insists on the limits of his authority in France. For the same point, see Guy Coquille, *Autre discours,* in his *Oeuvres* (Bordeaux, 1703), pp. 192–196; Pithou, pp. 522–526; Richer, pp. 7–9, 14, 17, 22–23, 29.

20. This tendency may be viewed as an application to the church of the general resurgence of French constitutionalism in the later sixteenth century, as noted by William Farr Church, *Constitutional Thought in Sixteenth-Century France* (Cambridge, Mass., 1941), pp. 74 ff.

21. *Libertez de l'Eglise Gallicane,* pp. 513–514.

22. On the general point cf. Martimort, pp. 84 ff. See also Martin, *Gallicanisme et la réforme,* pp. 350, 353, for examples of parlementary condemnations (to the distress of Rome) of heresy. For a typical assertion of the responsibilities of the clergy in ecclesiastical matters, cf. Leschassier, pp. 31–32. Leschassier argues that the defense of the church "est le plus grand honneur qui puisse estre en la main de iuges souverains, que de rendre à l'Eglise la saincteté de ses anciens reglemens."

23. On this point see Martimort, pp. 97–98.

24. As in Richer, pp. 29–32, who here makes a general Gallican point with particular sharpness.

25. *Liberté de l'Eglise Gallicane,* p. 31.

26. *Libertez de l'Eglise Gallicane,* pp. 514 ff. Pithou's list of actions prohibited to the pope is remarkably comprehensive.

27. Richer attacks papalists because they "confondent l'estat de l'Eglise avec le gouvernement" (p. 39).

28. Martimort, pp. 62–63, on the general point. Cf. Pithou, p. 513, and Leschassier, p. 29.

29. Coquille, *Discours des droits ecclesiastiques et libertez de l'Eglise de France*; Claude Fauchet, *Traicté des libertez de l'Eglise Gallicane*; Faye, as cited above, note 19. The two first works are also in Dupuy, I, 70–86, 190–210.

30. Cf. Leopold Willaert, *Après le concile de Trente: la restauration catholique (1563–1648)* (Paris, 1960), I, 387.

31. *De l'origine et du progrès des Interdicts ecclésiastiques*, included in Dupuy, I (separately paged).

32. On the general point, Martimort, pp. 66–67. Cf. Pithou, p. 518; Faye, 99 ff.; and *Maintenue et Defense de Princes souverains et Eglises chrétiennes, contre les attentats, usurpations et excommunications des Papes de Rome*, printed in *Mémoires de la Ligue* (Paris, 1601–1604), IV, 374–616.

33. See on this point the classic work of Marc Bloch, *Les rois thaumaturges: étude sur le caractère surnaturel attribué à la puissance royale, particulièrement en France et en Angleterre* (Strasbourg, 1924); Martimort, p. 83.

34. Martin, *Origines du Gallicanisme*, I, 33; Lecler, p. 392.

35. *Liberté de l'Eglise Gallicane*, pp. 30–31, appealing to the authority of Charlemagne and Constantine.

36. *Le tocsin* (Paris, 1610), p. 31.

37. *Liberté de l'Eglise Gallicane*, p. 33.

38. Cf. Julian Franklin, *Jean Bodin and the Sixteenth-Century Revolution in the Methodology of Law and History* (New York, 1963) and, more generally, J. G. A. Pocock, *The Ancient Constitution and the Feudal Law* (Cambridge, 1957), pp. 1–29.

39. As a number of scholars are now showing us. In addition to the works of Huppert and Franklin, cited above, see Werner L. Gundersheimer, *The Life and Works of Louis Le Roy* (Geneva, 1966); Samuel Kinser, *The Works of Jacques-Auguste de Thou* (The Hague, 1966); Franco Simone, *Il Rinascimento francese: studi e ricerche* (Turin, 1961); George W. Sypher, "La Popelinière's *Histoire de France*: A Case of Historical Objectivity and Religious Censorship," *Journal of the History of Ideas*, XXIV (1963), 41–54, and "Similarities Between the Scientific and the Historical Revolutions at the End of the Renaissance," in the same journal, XXVI (1965), 353–368; Donald R. Kelley, "*Historia Integra*: François Baudouin and His Conception of History," *Journal of the History of Ideas*, XXV (1964), 35–57, and "Guillaume Budé and the First Historical School of Law," *American Historical Review*, LXXII (1967), 807–834.

40. On the general point, see Lecler, pp. 547 ff.

41. *Libertez de l'Eglise Gallicane*, p. 533. The text is Proverbs 22:28.

42. For a typical discussion of how much of antiquity could serve as a model for the contemporary church, see *Lettre de Monseigneur le cardinal Du Perron. Envoyé au Sieur Casaubon en Angleterre* (Paris, 1612), pp. 22–25. On the general interest of the Gallican magistrates in the study of ancient canon law, see Martimort, pp. 90–91.

43. A general account of Leschassier's views may be found in Lecler, pp. 554–557.

44. Pp. 9, 25.

45. On Sarpi's vision of church history, see my *Venice and the Defense of*

Republican Liberty: Renaissance Values in the Age of the Counter-Reformation (Berkeley, 1968), esp. pp. 571ff.

46. *Devis entre un Citoyen de Nevers, & un de Paris,* in *Oeuvres,* I, 200: "Quand la Ville de Rome commandoit à tout le monde, le Pape étant élû à Rome étoit reconnu Souverain."

47. *Discours,* p. 100.

48. *Liberté de l'Eglise Gallicane,* pp. 16 ff., 27.

49. *Discours,* pp. 103, 115.

50. *Liberté de l'Eglise Gallicane,* pp. 4–8.

51. *Ibid.,* p. 30.

52. For example, Faye, *Discours,* p. 105, which quotes Augustine in support of the proposition that a man sincerely concerned to know the truth cannot be considered a heretic. Cf. Coquille's favorable treatment of Luther, *Devis,* p. 204.

53. Cf. Ludwig von Pastor, *The History of the Popes,* tr. Dom Ernest Graf (London, 1898–1953), XXV, 300. See too Sarpi's *Lettere ai Gallicani,* ed. Boris Ulianich (Wiesbaden, 1961); these letters deal repeatedly with scientific interests.

54. In addition to numerous treatises by older Gallican writers such as Gerson and John of Paris, Goldast included works of Richer, Leschassier, Louis Servin, and other contemporary Gallicans.

55. For example, Richer, *A Treatise of Ecclesiasticall and Politike Power* (London, 1612).

56. See Martin, *Gallicanisme et la réforme catholique,* pp. 367 ff.

57. For Sarpi's contacts with Gallican leaders, see Ulianich's long introduction to his edition of the *Lettere ai Gallicani.*

58. See, in general, Gaetano Cozzi, *Il doge Nicolò Contarini: Ricerche sul patriziato veneziano agli inizi del Seicento* (Venice, 1958), esp. pp. 1–52.

59. Letter to Hotman de Villiers, Oct. 12, 1606, in his *Lettres et ambassade* (Paris, 1635–1636), III, 233.

60. Leschassier, *Consultatio Parisii cujusdam de controversia inter sanctitatem Pauli V et Sereniss. Rempublicam Venetam, ad virum clariss. Venetum,* and Servin, *Pro libertate status et reipublicae venetorum Gallo-franci ad Philenetum epistola,* both printed in Paris in 1606.

61. See his *Lettere ai Gallicani* and his *Lettere ai Protestanti,* ed. Manlio Duilio Busnelli (Bari, 1931), passim.

62. On the general point, see his *Mémoires-Journaux,* ed. G. Brunet (Paris, 1875–1896), VIII, 254 ff.; on Sarpi, p. 255.

63. Roberto Ubaldini to Cardinal Borghese, Aug. 5, 1608, in "Per l'epistolario di Paolo Sarpi," ed. Pietro Savio, *Aevum,* X (1936), 74, n. 1.

64. (Paris, 1610), pp. 46–47. This work is now generally attributed to César de Plaix.

14   *The Waning of the Middle Ages* Revisited

The author of The Waning of the Middle Ages, *Johan Huizinga, is the historian who has most influenced my work, both more generally in his conception of the scope of cultural history and more specifically in his preoccupation with the relation between culture and anxiety. The essay is reprinted by permission of* Daedalus, Journal of the American Academy of Arts and Sciences, *"Twentieth-Century Classics Revisited," 103, no. 1 (Winter 1974), 35–43.*

•   •   •

We have come a long way since Bury informed us so firmly that history is a science, no more and no less. Historiography has now become so various and eclectic that it is often difficult to see it as the expression of any specific discipline; historians today seem to be united only by some common concern with the past and by a common allegiance, at least in principle, to respect for evidence, the exercise of critical intelligence, and openness of mind. They differ, on the whole amicably, about the questions they ask; and in answering these questions they draw freely on all the resources of their own intellectual and artistic culture. Their work often reveals highly personal qualities, sometimes latent, sometimes explicit and without apology; and although historical criticism can still find nothing better to say about much undistinguished work than that it is "definitive," it is likely to praise significant historical writing for its "imaginative power," its "vision," or its "originality." Johan Huizinga was a herald of this great change, and his *Waning of the Middle Ages* was one of the earliest and most influential models of the new history of the twentieth century.[1]

He had, of course, distinguished predecessors. But Jacob Burckhardt,

325

to whom Huizinga was closer than has sometimes been recognized, had little general influence on the way history was written, however important he may have been for shaping the idea of the Renaissance; and Wilhelm Dilthey left no major work to illustrate his views, but only scattered essays and theoretical pronouncements not widely read by working historians. The historical profession continued on the whole, therefore, to follow what it thought of as scientific method, regarding its evidence as so much objective data to be accumulated bit by bit and then used like bricks for the construction of an edifice that was presumed to represent the past *wie es eigentlich gewesen ist*. Because politics had been more fully recorded than anything else, the core of most historical composition was political narrative; and although other aspects of human experience in the past were not altogether ignored, they tended in the typical history to be held aside for discussion at the end in chapters that seemed more like appendices than like an integral part of the historian's conception. Man, in this historiography, seemed little more than *Homo politicus*. By precept, but above all by example, Huizinga taught us how to write history differently.

He could do so partly because he was not a historians' historian but always, to his profession, something of an outsider. Largely self-trained, he observed his fellow historians—their methods, their questions, and their assumptions—with remarkable detachment and a refined irony that, it must be admitted, sometimes seemed calculated rather to annoy than to persuade. There was, perhaps, a good deal of *Homo ludens* in Huizinga himself; and one suspects that he enjoyed teasing his professional colleagues by deliberately ignoring, in his own work, some of their favorite concerns, or by pointing out how little their solemn categories had to do with any objective historical reality. His manner, indeed, made him appear in some respects more iconoclastic than he was. Nevertheless, his rebellion against the tendencies dominant in the historical establishment of his time was fundamental; he rejected its scientific pretensions, its belief—attached to conceptions of geological and biological evolution— in progress, and its naive confidence that the facts speak for themselves.

The narrowing of the historian's audience, for which he partly blamed these tendencies, also troubled him. In "The Task of Cultural History," a lecture delivered in 1926, seven years after the appearance of *The Waning of the Middle Ages,* Huizinga exposed the concerns underlying that work. He proclaimed that history should serve as "the implement with which culture accounts for its past," and he argued that it must therefore "find its sphere and its sounding board in life in general in its own day" and be read as widely as possible. Few among the great historians since the Renaissance, he pointed out with perhaps a hint of malice, had been university men; and the growing confinement of history within universities seemed to him symptomatic of an increasingly unhealthy relation between scholarship and the general culture of educated men.[2] From this standpoint *The Waning of the Middle Ages* presents itself as a conscious effort to restore the health of the profession to which Huizinga belonged by striking out in a new direction. He was seeking, in that book, to reclaim history for the culture of his own time, and to do so in part by redefining the relationship of the historian to his subject along what might crudely be described as humanistic rather than scientific lines, in part by incorporating into historical thought new kinds of evidence and new conceptions drawn from other human (rather than scientific) disciplines: literature and aesthetics but also social studies in which, like few other historians of his generation, he was widely read.

The importance of *The Waning of the Middle Ages* does not, in fact, lie in its general thesis, which—a point not always realized—was a bit old-fashioned, even reactionary. Huizinga relied heavily on Burckhardt's *Kultur der Renaissance in Italien* (I cite the German title because *Kultur* brings out, better than the English *Civilization,* the filiation between Burckhardt and Huizinga, the self-conscious historian of culture). Huizinga began with Burckhardt's view of cultural history as a study of the attitudes, values, and behavior patterns of men in groups in the past, a conception that largely ignored conventional political narrative. Such history turned out to have obvious affinities with sociology, anthropology, and psychology, and Huizinga, three-quarters of a century later, was in a better position to recognize this than Burckhardt.

Huizinga was also Burckhardtian in a more specific way. Far from attacking Burckhardt's conception of the Renaissance wholesale, *The Waning of the Middle Ages* accepted and reiterated its general validity. Burckhardt's work, after all, had been limited to Italy; and, by stressing the priority of Italy in the formation of modern culture, Burckhardt was also saying that the rest of Europe in the fourteenth and fifteenth centuries had remained essentially medieval. Huizinga's book revealed how well the courtly culture of France and the Netherlands supported this view, and the central thesis of the book was its least original quality. Indeed, from time to time Huizinga paid explicit tribute to the Burckhardtian orthodoxies. He made much of Michelangelo's remarks about Flemish painting to show the contrast between Italy and the North, and he thought Burckhardt equally right about literature. "Thinking of the Italian literature of the same period, the fresh and lovely period of the *quattrocento,*" Huizinga wrote, "we may perhaps wonder how the form and spirit of the Renaissance can still seem so remote from the regions on this side of the Alps."[3] Huizinga's true target was not Burckhardt but those scholars, such as Konrad Burdach or the art historian Louis Courajod, who were attempting to annex parts of medieval culture to the Renaissance in a quite un-Burckhardtian spirit, to deny the uniqueness of Italy, and to claim the Renaissance as a European phenomenon.

Not that Huizinga was a slavish disciple. Like any able scholar working in the tradition of a respected master, he reviewed Burckhardt's insights critically, tested them with fresh evidence, and limited some of Burckhardt's claims; Burckhardt, after all, had invited such treatment by modestly calling his own great work "an essay." Huizinga had the advantage of knowing more about Northern Europe in the Middle Ages than Burckhardt, and he perceived that, in some matters of detail, Burckhardt had been mistaken about the peculiarities of the Italian Renaissance; medieval culture, too, had known Stoic concern with the inconstancy of Fortune and the natural equality of man, thirst for glory, and a bold naturalism, to cite a few examples.[4] Again, the popularity of Petrarch and Boccaccio in France led Huizinga to take a brief but closer look at these supposed founding fathers of the Renaissance, and he discovered in them more ambiguity, more that seemed medieval, than had commonly been discerned.[5] The result was a more nuanced but still fundamentally Burckhardtian perception of the Italian Renaissance that strikingly foreshadowed some of the most fruitful achievements of recent scholarship—for example, Hans Baron's treatment of the ambiguities of the fourteenth century or Charles Trinkaus's study of the moral and religious thought of the Italian humanists.[6]

But Huizinga also felt compelled to deal in a more basic way with the problem of innovation and tradition so central to Renaissance scholarship. Medievalists since Burckhardt had shown conclusively that a broad and respectful knowledge of the classics had been common during the Middle Ages, so that classicism in itself could no longer be taken as an essential criterion of Renaissance culture. Yet Huizinga was fully persuaded, following Burckhardt, that there was some crucial difference between medieval and modern culture, however inaccurately this had been defined. And in his effort to solve this problem we can begin to sense both his originality and something of the larger resonance of his work. His solution took the shape of a distinction between the forms of a culture and its content or spirit. The true significance of the Renaissance, he argued, did not lie in its use of classical forms, since these had been known before, but in the convergence of these forms with a new spirit.[7] He was traditional enough to identify this new spirit with an authentic classicism, but the principle has led to a new precision in the understanding of what was peculiar to the Renaissance. By reuniting a genuinely classical spirit to classical forms, Renaissance culture could perceive the great Greeks and Romans as inhabitants of a world very different from its own, remote in time as well as in quality.

Huizinga's distinction between form and spirit, however vague it may have seemed at the outset, thus opened the way to the emphasis of twentieth-century scholars on the peculiar historicism of the Renaissance, that sense of temporal perspective which made it possible for the first time for men to contrast themselves with other men in the past and to consider themselves modern. From this standpoint, the men of the Renaissance were indeed the first modern men, not quite for Burckhardt's reasons but because they were the first Europeans to consider themselves so. Huizinga did not explore all this himself, but the insight, with its recognition of the historical significance of subjectivity, was typical of his kind of cultural history. It also had other implications important for later historians of the Renaissance. For Renaissance historicism pointed to the relativity of all human culture, including historical and perhaps even scientific thought, to historical conditions. Huizinga's conception of his own historical activity was thus closely related to his understanding of what had occurred in fourteenth- and fifteenth-century Europe.

Thus, even as he wrestled with the Renaissance problem, Huizinga was opening up, in *The Waning of the Middle Ages,* a new way of thinking about every part of the past; and here, of course, lies the larger importance of the book. It was reassuring to historians in its adherence to guild standards: it was based on objective data critically scrutinized. Nevertheless, it departed radically from prevailing assumptions about the relation between the historian and his materials. Huizinga was, in fact, proposing a far more dynamic, creative, and personally responsible conception of the historian's task than a "scientific" idea of history had permitted. He saw clearly that the ability of the historian to make sense of the past did not depend primarily on his adding to an already unmanageable body of data but on the questions he asked, and that these were products of the historian's personal insight and imagination. "Ten fools can answer more questions than one wise man can ask," he declared, inverting an old proverb.[8] Huizinga, by his own example, was exhorting the historian to make creative use of his unavoidable subjectivity and his dependence on the culture of his time. This, for him, was the only way to restore a healthy relation between history and culture.

More specifically, the general task of historical composition, as Huizinga saw it, was not to review and describe "all" the evidence (though this had to be meticulously evaluated) but to penetrate beneath it to its underlying principles; we can thus discern here a more general application of his distinction between the forms and the content of culture. But this task could not be accomplished mechanically, by following the rules of an objective methodology. It required the full engagement of the historian both as a percipient individual and as a sensitive representative of his own culture, able to ask the questions that mattered in his own time. This conviction was a fundamental addition to Burckhardt's idea of cultural history. "Only when the scholar turns to determining the patterns of life, art, and thought taken all together can there actually be a question of cultural history," he wrote. But "the nature of those patterns is not set. They obtain their form beneath our hands."[9] Following this principle the historian could present all that men had done in the period of his concern—the totality of human culture in a given place and time—in a way that was not only historically authentic but that also illuminated the broader possibilities of the human condition. For, in Huizinga's thought, man was always at the center of the historical stage; none of his activities could be hypostatized (the efforts of historians notwithstanding); all that man did was significant at least as a form of expressive behavior, telling us what, at some moment in the past, he was like at the center of his being.

The result was both a new concreteness and a new principle of synthesis, at once Burckhardtian and going beyond Burckhardt in its ability to give coherence to the historian's total enterprise. After Huizinga, for example, intellectual history, as the simple history of ideas, could no longer be fully satisfying; it had to be an integral part of life itself, pointing ultimately to deeper impulses flowing from social and political experience or from collective psychology.

His focus on the human being at the center of history allowed Huizinga to enlarge the scope of history in ways that remarkably anticipated many of the new directions history has taken in this century, for his conception of cultural history has tended to become the definition of what, for many of us, all history should now aspire to be, even when our particular studies seem far removed from his. Nor can we blame him for failing to pursue all the provocative suggestions offered, sometimes almost casually, in *The Waning of the Middle Ages*. Few of his successors have been able to follow more than one or two of them.

Much of the excitement of the book lay, therefore, in its demonstration of what could be done with kinds of evidence few previous historians had known how to exploit fruitfully. Huizinga was instructive not so much because he used artistic and literary materials as for what he made them reveal. The peculiar responses of the senses, not only of the eye and ear but also of touch, smell, and even taste became, under his guidance, historically significant. The passions as well, the manner in which they were regarded, the ways they found expression, became a part of culture. So did dreams, fantasies, delusions, fads, games, symbolic structures: these were no longer too frivolous to merit the attention of a serious historian, or errors happily transcended by a more enlightened age, but profoundly instructive reflections of the human condition. Apparently without the help of Freud, Huizinga was also aware of the erotic element in human culture, an insight that informed some of his most evocative chapters. And in spite of the elitism for which he has so often been condemned, Huizinga pointed too, in one of his pregnant asides, to the special importance for the historian of the humbler dimensions of life:

> The specific forms of the thought of an epoch should not only be studied as they reveal themselves in theological and philosophic speculations, or in the conceptions of creeds, but also as they appear in practical wisdom and everyday life. We may even say that the true character of the spirit of an age is better revealed in its mode of regarding and expressing trivial and commonplace things than in the high manifestations of philosophy and science.[10]

He was equally open to methodological innovation and in some cases he practiced it. He would, I think, have been deeply sympathetic to quantitative research; consider how useful he would have found the computer for solving the following problem, which he posed with a clarity not always characteristic of later quantifiers: "To determine the taste in colors characteristic of the epoch would require a comprehensive and statistical research, embracing the chromatic scale of painting as well as the colors of costume and decorative art."[11] Meanwhile the work of sociologists like Weber encouraged him into occasional ventures in cross-cultural comparison; thus he bolstered his remarks about the aristocratic ideal of manly perfection in Europe by noting similar conceptions in India and Japan.[12] And, more profoundly, his approach to the life of the past took the form of a kind of cultural functionalism. The structures of culture, in his view, were of interest to the historian because they met the most serious social needs. Much of the special quality of Huizinga's thought is conveyed in a characteristic effort to apply this principle:

The passionate and violent soul of the age, always vacillating between tearful piety and frigid cruelty, between respect and in-
solence, between despondency and wantonness, could not
dispense with the severest rules and the strictest formalism. All
emotions required a rigid system of conventional forms, for
without them passion and ferocity would have made havoc of
life. By this sublimating faculty each event became a spectacle
for others; mirth and sorrow were artificially and theatrically
made up. For want of the faculty to express emotions in a simple and natural way, recourse must needs be had to esthetic representations of sorrow and joy.[13]

All this can be said of the greatness of Huizinga and the distinction
of *The Waning of the Middle Ages,* and yet it is also a flawed book which
even a historian sensitive to its virtues cannot find altogether satisfactory.
For Huizinga was an outsider not only in respect to his own profession
but also in relation to the culture of his own time, and he was therefore
imperfectly fitted to mediate between the two. He was uncomfortable
in an increasingly democratic world, and the development of mass culture
left him with a sense of foreboding to which he gave formal expression
with *In the Shadow of Tomorrow* (1935). The mood of that book was
already present in *The Waning of the Middle Ages* and largely accounts
for its defects as well as its peculiar point of view. Huizinga saw his own
time as a period in which culture was also waning; and just as he was
blind to much that others have seen as positive in the modern world,
he ignored, though he was not altogether unaware of, the positive elements in the Northern European scene during the later Middle Ages.

Thus Huizinga's reaction against assumptions of progress made him
reluctant to grapple with change, and his portrait of Northern Europe
in the later Middle Ages is even more static than Burckhardt's of Italy.
His resistance to the significance of change was reflected in a skepticism
about historical periodization; and although this was wholesome in itself,
it weakened his presentation of the peculiarities of the fourteenth and
fifteenth centuries, which he never clearly distinguished from what had
gone before. This unsolved problem is reflected in the original Dutch
title of his book, whose ambiguity is concealed by its English translation:
Waning is too unequivocally negative for *Herfsttij,* which suggests not
only autumnal decline but also the ripe fruits of the harvest.[14] Huizinga
often seems unclear whether he is describing a "primitive" and "childlike"—these are among his favorite adjectives—or a decadent and sophisticated culture.

A related defect was his basic lack of concern with explanation. Again his impulse here was in part a healthy reaction against the facile treatment of causality by some of his contemporaries, especially Marxists, but he weakened a good point by stating it in a way that was not only playful but perhaps frivolous:

> Knowing in the historical sense rarely if ever means indicating a strictly closed causality. It is always an understanding of contexts. . . . This context is always an open one, which is to say that it may never be represented in the metaphor of links forming a chain, but only in that of a loosely bound bundle of sticks to which new twigs can be added as long as the band around them allows it. Perhaps more suitable than a bundle of sticks might be a bunch of wildflowers. In their variety and their difference in value new notions added to the conception of a historical context are like newly found flowers in the nosegay: each one changes the appearance of the whole bouquet.[15]

The conception may have fitted the historical "still-lifes" that came out of his own study, but it was hardly helpful in accounting for the "waning" of the Middle Ages; and he could not altogether avoid the problem of cause. Yet when he did deal with it, he took refuge in a kind of organic cultural determinism that seems more like evasion than explanation. The waning of medieval culture, he suggested, was a product of fatigue, the result of the long and strenuous elaboration of its potentialities: "What may be called a stagnation of thought prevails, as though the mind, exhausted after building up the spiritual fabric of the Middle Ages, had sunk into inertia."[16] But this was a betrayal of his own deepest insights. It implies that, in spite of his sociological interests, some part of his mind still clung to the notion of an autonomous culture developing, in the custody of a cultivated elite, according to its own internal dynamics.

Yet this also helps to explain why he refused to look seriously beyond aristocratic culture at the forces that were making the old nobility superfluous and at the energies already at work in the formation of a new culture—a serious limitation that also reflected his indifference to both change and cause. He did not choose to face the double significance of the notion of decadence at the heart of his book, the symbiosis of old and new, decay and growth. Every positive development he either minimized, like nominalism, or omitted, like the movements of religious renewal. He was not unaware of what was positive in the fourteenth and fifteenth centuries, and the end of his book suggested what a more balanced depiction of the later Middle Ages would have included: "A high and strong culture is declining, but at the same time and in the same sphere new things are being born."[17] He was even inconsistent enough to admire the novelties of Italy. But the contrast between "a high and strong culture" and "new things" sticks in the mind. Huizinga did not much care for new things, and so he left them out of what he nevertheless often seems to want us to accept as the essential truth about the later Middle Ages.

Yet, in spite of its defects, in spite of the fact that so much in *The Waning of the Middle Ages* has now become the common possession of historians so that its work has in this respect largely been done, the book is still well worth reading. It can be enjoyed as a work of high art, full of color and life, as in its marvelous opening chapter with its bells and processions, its public executions and public tears. Or it can be read as documentation of an important transition in the cultural history of our own century, as illuminating for its ambivalence and confusion as for its movement from one stage to the next. But the work will continue to be read above all, I think, for another reason. Just as man, in all his multifaceted complexity, is for Huizinga at the center of history, so Huizinga the man, in all his brilliance and complexity, remains at the center of the history he wrote. Since Huizinga revealed so much of himself in his work and since he had a singularly original and stimulating mind, provocative even when it seems most limited and perverse, *The Waning of the Middle Ages* has the kind of vitality that causes historical writing to be read long after its own time.

NOTES

1. *Herfsttij der Middeleeuwen: Studie over Levens- en Gedachtenformen der Veer-tiende en Vijftiende Eeuw in Frankrijk en de Nederlanden* (Haarlem, 1919). I cite the convenient Anchor edition, *The Waning of the Middle Ages: A Study of the Forms of Life, Thought and Art in France and the Netherlands in the XIVth and XVth Centuries,* tr. F. Hopman (New York, 1954). This essay owes much to Rosalie Colie, "Johan Huizinga and the Task of Cultural History," *American Historical Review,* 59 (1964), 607–630. For discussion of Huizinga in the context of the Renaissance problem, see also Wallace Ferguson, *The Renaissance in Historical Thought: Five Centuries of Interpretation* (Boston, 1948), esp. pp. 373–376.

2. "The Task of Cultural History," *Men and Ideas: Essays by Johan Huizinga,* tr. James S. Holmes and Hans van Marle (New York, 1959), pp. 40–42.

3. Huizinga, *Waning,* pp. 265, 322.

4. Ibid., pp. 18–19, 64–67, 70, 332–334.

5. Ibid., p. 325–326.

6. Hans Baron, *The Crisis of the Early Italian Renaissance: Civic Humanism and Republican Liberty in an Age of Classicism and Tyranny,* rev. ed. (Princeton,

1966); Charles Trinkaus, *In Our Image and Likeness: Humanity and Divinity in Italian Humanist Thought* (Chicago, 1970).

7. *Waning,* p. 335; also pp. 324–325 and *passim.*

8. Huizinga, "Task," p. 27.

9. Ibid., p. 28.

10. Huizinga, *Waning,* p. 225.

11. Ibid., p. 270.

12. Ibid., pp. 77.

13. Ibid., pp. 50–51.

14. This was pointed out to me by Heiko Oberman. The title of Oberman's own *The Harvest of Medieval Theology: Gabriel Biel and Late Medieval Nominalism* (Cambridge, Mass., 1963) is intended both to recall Huizinga and to correct the one-sidedness of Huizinga's vision.

15. Huizinga, "Task," p. 39.

16. Huizinga, *Waning,* p. 295.

17. Ibid., p. 335.

15   From History of Ideas to History of Meaning

In the summer of 1980, the editors of the Annales, *of* Past and Present, *and of the* Journal of Interdisciplinary History *jointly sponsored a conference at the Villa Serbelloni, the conference center of the Rockefeller Foundation, to discuss the directions historical research might and should take in the decade of the eighties. I was asked to prepare this essay for the conference as a position paper on the present condition and the probable future of intellectual history. I was chiefly concerned with what intellectual history could still be now that the idealism implicit in much history of ideas has been generally abandoned. Reprinted from* The Journal of Interdisciplinary History *12 (1981), 279– 291, with the permission of the editors of* The Journal of Interdisciplinary History *and the MIT Press, Cambridge, Massachusetts, © by the Massachusetts Institute of Technology and the editors of* The Journal of Interdisciplinary History.

• • •

Intellectual history, until recently, was regarded with particular respect. It was probably the most interdisciplinary area of historical study and therefore seemed both unusually demanding and unusually prestigious. It was considered important. But during the last two decades, the impression has grown among historians that the kinds of material likely to be studied by intellectual historians are not very useful for telling us what we most need to know about the past.[1]

As those of us who scrutinize the small number of job listings for our students have observed, intellectual history seems now to be considered less essential to the curriculum than other kinds of history. Fewer students care to be identified as intellectual historians, and the remaining practitioners of intellectual history are more and more uncertain about their methods and purposes. And it is increasingly difficult to say what, at least in the abstract, intellectual history is about. For these reasons, as well as for others that will emerge later in this article, the question of the immediate future of intellectual history requires more radical treatment than may be appropriate for other dimensions of historiography.

The decline of intellectual history appears obvious, and probably irreversible. But despite a long identification with the problems and methods of intellectual history, I do not deplore this development. For although intellectual history has indeed declined as an isolated specialty, in another form it has never been more important. The resources of intellectual history, or of something related to and growing out of it, can be useful to historians precisely in the degree to which intellectual history is not treated separately but is generally assimilated by other kinds of historians. This is what has recently been happening. That intellectual history is now disappearing as one of the conventional specialties into which historians segregate themselves is a sign of the growing maturity of intellectual history, and of historiography more generally. We no longer need intellectual history because we have all become intellectual historians: some of us, no doubt, unintentionally, reluctantly, and without fully realizing what has happened. Since the explanation for this situation will itself require some exploitation of the resources of conventional intellectual history, it will also provide an example of the tasks that even an old-fashioned and specialized intellectual historian can continue to perform in any decade, notably for other historians: in this case the liberation—not always welcome—that can result from identifying and laying bare for inspection our own deepest assumptions about ourselves and the world. This useful service may suggest that the specialized techniques of intellectual historians are worth keeping alive.

Conventional intellectual history itself has a history that is instructive about its present predicament. Since this history is still largely unwritten, my observations about the origins and lineage of intellectual history will necessarily be somewhat speculative; but the word "intellectual" here holds some promise as a point of entry. This word is an adjective, based on a noun that refers to a faculty alleged—in a certain venerable tradition of thought which historians have never found very congenial— to reside in the human personality. This tradition is that of philosophical idealism, which, since its beginnings in classical antiquity, has depended on—and constantly reinforced—a characteristic anthropology that has had a major influence on the understanding of the human animal in the West.

According to this view, the human personality consists of a hierarchy of discrete faculties, among which intellect—more or less closely identified with reason—is highest. In the earlier stages of this tradition, the intellect was believed to constitute the divine element in man and so to distinguish him from the other animals; and a sense of the peculiar virtue and importance of the intellect and its works, although variously expressed, has always been a major element in this tradition. The association of the intellect with the brain gave the head ethical significance and converted it into a potent metaphor; the highest became best. And for two thousand years, in what was the main stream of Western thought, the erect stature of man was the visible sign of his distinction from and his superiority to nature. It raised him above the material earth and enabled him to contemplate the heavenly bodies, from which he first learned the eternal principles of order. As Plato himself had testified, this was the origin of philosophy, the noblest of human activities.[2]

This remote background helps to explain both the special prestige once attached to intellectual history and the reasons for its recent decline. Intellectual history was perceived as the study of the working and the works of the human intellect through the centuries; and, since the intellect was the highest faculty in man, it followed that intellectual history was the highest type of history. As Hegel believed, it also could be seen as the source of such clues as we could have to the direction and meaning of all history. These ideas are still very much alive in the notion, which pervades much contemporary social and political speculation, that man, by taking thought, can add cubits to his stature: that is, that "intellectuals" can shape the world for the better. Furthermore, since society, in this tradition, was also conceived—following the general principle underlying all order—as a hierarchy, this line of thought also directed historical investigation toward the intellectual activity of elites. And such notions exerted a power over us, even just half a century ago, that was all the greater because we were unaware of them. A generation of academically precocious youths, too myopic or too light to be good in sports, found compensation in turning from physical activity to the higher concerns of the intellect. In this context intellectual history had obvious attractions.

But the marriage between an intellectuality that was focused on the progressively clearer grasp of the eternal, and history, which tended increasingly to view all things as mutable and even its own presuppositions as historical artifacts, was uncomfortable from the outset; and even in its purer forms intellectual history, although it was often hardly very historical, did not succeed in being philosophical.

Lovejoy's treatment of the history of ideas is an illuminating example. His detachment of his "unit ideas" from a larger context of changing human needs and conditions suggests the autonomy of intellect in the idealist tradition; but when he faced the question of the significance of such conceptions as the great chain of being, Lovejoy could only reduce them to mysterious psychological impulses, inexplicable cravings for simplicity or complexity which were themselves variations on what he called "metaphysical pathos."[3]

The satisfaction of dealing with the morphology of ideas at the highest level in courses entitled "intellectual history" was rarely sufficient for historians, and the teachers of such courses tended increasingly to analyze a conventional body of texts (the standard works of "great thinkers") with the tools of psychohistory or one or another approach to the sociology of knowledge. In the degree to which it was genuinely historical, intellectual history was thus undermining its own claims to special respect.

Meanwhile these developments internal to the profession were complemented by the more important changes taking place in the larger world that historians inhabited—changes that radically subverted the claims of intellect not only to receive privileged treatment but even to any discrete existence. It is hardly necessary to review the role of Charles Darwin, Karl Marx, and Sigmund Freud in disintegrating the intellectual conception of man, although of the three Freud may prove to have been the most radical in his impact on anthropology. For Freud associated man's upright posture explicitly with his fall from a condition of primordial bliss; he saw in the erect stature of the human animal the sign, perhaps even the prehistorical cause, of that schism in the personality which, perversely dividing *humanitas* into an honorable portion above the neck and a shameful region below the waist, produced not wisdom and order, but neurosis, conflict, and despair. At any rate we can hardly any longer define man as an intellectual animal. However we regard him, he is both less and more than this—and infinitely more interesting, which is the major explanation for the fact that an autonomous intellectual history is now likely to seem, like the discrete intellect of the old anthropology, at best an irrelevant abstraction from real life.

Nevertheless the materials with which intellectual historians have traditionally worked cannot be dismissed as without interest or value for students of the past. Rather they must now be understood in a new way, as expressive or adaptive behavior of a kind still identifiable as (probably) peculiar to the human animal, and also as a subset of a larger category of such human behavior, to which they now solicit our attention. This category consists of all efforts to discover or to impose meaning on our experience, although some sense of meaning is also both a condition and a product of experience. These efforts are not the work of the "intellect" or of any particular area of the personality. They are rather a function of the human organism as a whole; they are carried on both consciously and unconsciously; and they are presupposed by, and merge with, every more specific human activity, including the begetting of children and their upbringing within families. I cite these examples not in order to put such matters down, but to reinforce the general point that the concern with meaning, which I take to be the remnant chiefly worth saving from intellectual history, has been profitably appropriated for their own purposes even by historians of those dimensions of human experience farthest removed from the sublime concerns of intellectual history.

The amalgamation of concerns once primarily limited to so-called intellectual historians with other kinds of history by way of a (usually only implicit) concern with meaning is the most significant development of the recent past from the standpoint of my argument in this article. The works that have most interested those of us who have sometimes thought of ourselves as intellectual historians, and that also have made the greatest impact on historiography, are virtually impossible to classify in terms of our conventional categories, but they come into focus as studies in the construction of meaning. I would cite from my own field (not because it is unanimously admired or because all of its conclusions have been accepted, but because it stimulated a whole generation of Renaissance scholars in various directions and in this way transformed a major area of European historiography) Baron's *The Crisis of the Early Italian Renaissance*. The very title of this work lets us know that we cannot put it into one of our standard categories, and indeed that such classification would be useless for understanding it. It draws on the resources of both political and intellectual history, and it touches also on social and economic matters. But it is basically an extended account of a collective discovery of meaning in the destiny of the Florentine polis.[4]

A similar point could be made of May's *The Enlightenment in America*; although its title seems to classify it as intellectual history, it is also heavily concerned with political, social, and institutional analysis as it reveals how Americans, who must first be understood in their own complex setting, struggled to find meaning in a complex set of European ideas. Again we can only classify a work like Eisenstein's *The Printing Press as an Agent of Change* as an assessment of the impact of technology on the construction of meaning in various aspects of European experience. This work also provides us with an instance of the increasing tendency of historians to substitute the word "cultural" in places where they might earlier have employed the word "intellectual." No doubt this is partly because "cultural" seems less restrictive than "intellectual," but it also is an expression of an at least obscure association of "culture" with meaning in a larger sense.[5]

Thus, if I discern any trend in the work of historians who were once clearly (but have perhaps not recently been) identified with intellectual history, it is an increasing concern with the location, the description, and perhaps the explanation of what passes for meaning in a variety of historical situations. Once this is recognized, a good deal of what seems most vague (and perhaps therefore irritating) about intellectual history will come into focus.

It explains, for example, a tendency for intellectual historians to exploit artistic expression. From the standpoint of a strictly "intellectual" history, this presents a serious conceptual difficulty, for art and intellect are not obviously synonymous and, since Plato, have often been at odds. But the difficulty evaporates once we have recognized that the arts have always been a primary vehicle for the expression of meaning (or more recently, sometimes, meaninglessness).

Intellectual historians have long sensed (without perhaps fully understanding) their affinities with art historians like Erwin Panofsky. Baxandall's *Painting and Experience in Fifteenth-Century Italy* is an unusually valuable study of the artistic creation of fundamental meanings by an art historian. The possibilities of collaboration between art historians and a more general kind of cultural historian are suggested by *A Renaissance Likeness* by Partridge and Starn, which explores a whole milieu by the intensive study of a single painting. Schorske's *Fin-de-Siècle Vienna* combines an interest in artistic meaning with the use of psychoanalysis to penetrate to other levels of meaning, which again are hardly to be described as "intellectual."[6]

In reporting on the past and future of intellectual history, I am (somewhat to my own surprise) describing the metamorphosis of an old and familiar, although never very satisfactorily developed, field of historical activity into something new and strange that is likely to be far more useful. In its new state, however, it can also be seen to assimilate various kinds of history, some of them clearly growing in interest, which are otherwise hard to classify. A distinguished example is Thomas's *Religion and the Decline of Magic.* How are we to classify this work in terms of our conventional categories? It is not exactly intellectual history,

if only because intellectual activity as a high thing was almost by definition confined to the upper classes. That Thomas's book deals with
structures of popular belief is hardly sufficient to call it social history,
although the identity of social history sometimes raises difficulties for
me almost as serious as those created by intellectual history. But if we
recognize this work as an example of a new historical genre that might
be called, for want of a more elegant term, the history of meanings, we
have placed it within its own family of works, the members of which—
once we recognize that they belong together—can illuminate each
other.[7]

Immediately one thinks of further candidates for membership in this
group: some of the essays of Davis; Le Roy Ladurie's *Montaillou*; Levine's *Black Culture and Black Consciousness,* with its eloquent use of folk-
lore; or Jordan's *White over Black* which, whatever else it may be, is a
report on the tragic results of one kind of assertion of meaning.[8]

In the same way other major kinds of recent work, too often ignored
in historiographical discussions because they do not fit our conventional
categories, can be seen as subsets of the history of meanings, and therefore well worth serious attention. One of the most important of these
clearly is religious history, which is concerned in the most direct and
ultimate way with the exploration of meaning, and in its institutional
dimension with structures for the preservation, cultivation, and transmission or meaning. Thomas's work belongs partly in this category, and
a substantial proportion of the activity of historians of every period and
part of the world is now devoted to religious phenomena. Again this
remarkable circumstance is easy to overlook because of an inherited
system for the classification of historical scholarship in which it has no
place.

The titles of a few major works concerned with the period with which
I am most familiar convey some sense of the difficulty of classifying
them according to our usual labels: among them are books by Reeves,
Ozment, Tentler, O'Malley, and Rothkrug.[9]

Still other kinds of scholarship can be brought into focus in this way.
One thinks immediately of the history of education, which has normally
had as its primary purpose the transmission of meanings from one generation to the next; a recent example is Strauss's *Luther's House of Learning.* The history of historiography, and perhaps of other branches of
learning, also assumes more general significance when it is understood
to be centrally concerned with meaning; every work of historical composition is, after all, a bit of documentation of what passes for meaning
in the community and period out of which it arises. Such studies as

White's *Metahistory* may be highly "intellectual" (a term that now seems to mean something like "difficult to read"); but the awkward intrusion of the word "imagination" in the title suggests that it is not very usefully called "intellectual history." A similar point can be made about Pocock's *The Machiavellian Moment*. But meaning can also be expressed through institutions: constitutions, for example, judicial systems, or even bureaucracies. Thus Brentano's *Two Churches* is a distinguished investigation of the construction of meaning as well as utility out of materials not usually associated with such activity.[10]

The kind of history that I am describing is characterized not (like traditional intellectual history) by the sources that it utilizes but by the questions that it asks. By the same token, it does not exclude attention to the creation of meaning by elites; it leaves open the considerable possibility that this may be of the greatest interest. It may be objected, indeed, that this redefinition of intellectual history is far too broadly conceived: that, indeed, in an outburst of disciplinary imperialism from the most unexpected quarter, and by the most arbitrary redefinition of my assignment, I have claimed almost everything in historiography for my province. I hope that this is not the case; but I do see, in the conception of man as an animal who must create or discern meaning in everything that he does, the most promising resource that has yet presented itself for overcoming the consequences—so devastating for the historical understanding in the long run, no matter how convenient in the short—of our proliferating specialization. The only antidote for this tendency in historiography, now so widely deplored, is a shift in emphasis from raw historical experience (i.e., what happens to people) to what human beings have made out of that experience. Such a shift should remind us, too, that the creative interpretation of experience also shapes experience, which is only in the abstract independent of the meaning imposed upon it.

As to the future, it is my hope that tendencies already discernible— the decline of traditional intellectual history as an area of specialization, the exploitation of its resources instead by historians who do not care to identify their work as intellectual history, and an expanded concern with the meanings expressed by every kind of human activity in the past—will grow stronger, be more explicitly embraced, and develop the more deliberate strategies that are likely to emerge when scholarship becomes conscious of what it is doing. I have one or two suggestions about what this might mean, but first it seems to me that a caveat against reductionism is in order.

I have referred to the role of Darwin, Marx, and Freud in the destruction of a traditional model of man; we owe them a great deal for this and will continue to benefit in various ways from the insights that they have released. But we should not, by following them, correct one kind of mistake only to make another. It is unlikely to help us much simply to reverse the hierarchy, and to put matter in the place of mind, or biological in the place of intellectual experience. This would still be too traditional; the structural principle—the principle that organizes phenomena as *sub* (or *infra*) and *super*—would remain the same. A more novel anthropology (which is at the same time very old, since it too has a history), an anthropology that is more wholesome (in the sense of integrated and therefore irreducible), is fundamental to the notion of man as a creator of meanings, a conception that can only engender a sense of the unpredictability of the human condition and therefore of mystery and awe, sensations as appropriate to the historical as to the poetic understanding.

History, as has often been observed, is parasitical; but as it changes, so does the host on which it feeds. Traditional intellectual history was chiefly nourished by traditional philosophy; but as intellectual history has been transformed, it has been turning to the arts. I expect this tendency to grow stronger and to expand from literary, and visual art into music and dance, and from elite to popular expression in all the arts.

But art as expressive and integrative behavior points finally to anthropology, now as an academic discipline, and especially to cultural anthropology, which is likely to be the fundamental external resource for the kind of study that is being born out of a dying intellectual history. This is so for several reasons. The anthropological model which generally (with some exceptions) informs anthropology as a discipline underlies the conception that I have outlined of man as a creator of meanings. This model largely rejects the conception of man as a hierarchy of discrete faculties. It accordingly rejects also the assignment of privileged status *a priori* to one or another area of human activity. Since it conceives of the human personality as a mysterious whole, it is opposed to all reductionism. And, of course, it is centrally concerned with the construction and symbolic expression of meaning in every dimension of human activity. In short it is useful to the historian precisely because it is the least specialized among the social sciences; this is why, increasingly, it insists on a kind of "thick description" that many historians are finding so congenial. Most anthropologists have been content so far with a kind of systematic and static description that is fundamentally ahistorical (although even this has been useful for the—almost equally static—

study of *mentalités* by historians); and I have heard anthropologists confess that their discipline has not dealt very satisfactorily with problems of cultural change. But the recent work of some anthropologists, for example Sahlins, Bourdieu, and Bloch, has been increasingly historical. It may be that future work in anthropology will be even more useful for historians, and also that historians can be of some help to anthropologists.[11]

A second and closely related discipline that will probably be necessary for the development of intellectual history is linguistics. For if man (to quote once again a much-quoted remark) is "an animal suspended in webs of significance he himself has spun," he spins these webs primarily from—or with the help of—language. Through language man orders the chaos of data impinging on his sensorium from, in a singularly mysterious and problematic sense, "out there," organizing them into categories and so making them intelligible for himself, manageable, communicable, and therefore socially useful as well as essential to his private adaptation to the world. Indeed, as the humanists of the Renaissance maintained (the point was perhaps more profound than they could realize), language is the basis of society. The human and social world with which historians are all, in one way or another, concerned, might therefore be described as a vast rhetorical production; and rhetoric is also likely to become a major tool of the new intellectual history. For the operations that bring this human world into existence in consciousness and endow it with meaning are comparable to such basic rhetorical transactions as division and comparison, or metonymy and metaphor.[12]

A few historians have pointed in this direction; but the connections between a language and the perceptions of reality peculiar to those who speak it, as well as the significance of linguistic change, although often recognized in the abstract, have not yet seriously engaged historians.[13] Because of the basic role of language at once in perception, thought, and social existence, linguistics seems—in the most literal sense—of fundamental importance for historians, as indeed for other social scientists. Changes in language are likely to provide us with clues, of a kind previously lacking, to the human significance of various kinds of developments about which we have so far been able to form only the most unverifiable impressions. Here, indeed, might lie one of the possibilities, which may be rare in the kind of history with which I am concerned, for the application of quantitative methods.

I have noted that traditional intellectual history depended heavily on traditional philosophy, and, in conclusion, it is worth observing that traditional philosophy has been slowly dying, although with occasional remissions, during the same period, at about the same speed, and for probably the same reasons as traditional intellectual history. But it has gradually been replaced by a quite different kind of wisdom than traditional philosophers were supposed to enunciate. It is thus possible that intellectual history, transformed in the manner that I have envisaged here, may also be able to renew its connections with philosophy, similarly transformed. Under new conditions, history and philosophy might once again have much to offer each other. Historians could help explain what has been happening to philosophy, and philosophers might help historians to scrutinize their own metahistorical assumptions. In this way one of the least historical among academic disciplines might at last join hands with one of the least philosophical. This is another possibility for the next decade.

NOTES

1. See, for example, the opening paragraphs of Robert Darnton, "Intellectual and Cultural History," in Michael Kammen (ed.), *The Past Before Us: Contemporary Historical Writing in the United States* (Ithaca, 1980), 327–354.

2. Plato, *Timaeus,* 47a.

3. Arthur O. Lovejoy, *The Great Chain of Being: A Study of the History of an Idea* (Cambridge, Mass., 1948), 10–14.

4. Hans Baron, *The Crisis of the Early Italian Renaissance: Civic Humanism and Republican Liberty in an Age of Classicism and Tyranny* (Princeton, 1955). The works cited in this article were chosen for illustrative purposes. I have not surveyed recent literature, although I have tried to range widely enough with my examples to suggest that the tendencies described in my text are not confined to particular areas of study.

5. Henry May, *The Enlightenment in America* (New York, 1976); Elizabeth Eisenstein, *The Printing Press as an Agent of Change: Communications and Cultural Transformations in Early Modern Europe* (Cambridge, 1979).

6. Michael Baxandall, *Painting and Experience in Fifteenth-Century Italy* (Oxford, 1972); Loren Partridge and Randolph Starn, *A Renaissance Likeness: Art and Culture in Raphael's Julius II'* (Berkeley, 1980); Carl E. Schorske, *Fin-de-Siècle Vienna: Politics and Culture* (New York, 1980).

7. Keith Thomas, *Religion and the Decline of Magic: Studies in Popular Beliefs in Sixteenth- and Seventeenth-Century England* (London, 1971).

8. For example, Natalie Davis, "The Reasons of Misrule" and "The Rites of Violence," in *Society and Culture in Early Modern France* (Stanford, 1975), 97–123, 152–187. Emmanuel Le Roy Ladurie, *Montaillou, village occitan de 1294 à 1324* (Paris, 1975); Lawrence W. Levine, *Black Culture and Black Consciousness: Afro-American Folk Thought from Slavery to Freedom* (New York, 1977); Winthrop D. Jordan, *White over Black: American Attitudes toward the Negro, 1550–1812* (Chapel Hill, 1968).

9. Marjorie Reeves, *The Influence of Prophecy in the Later Middle Ages: A*

Study in Joachimism (Oxford, 1969); Steven Ozment, *The Reformation in the Cities: An Essay on the Appeal of Protestant Ideas to Sixteenth-Century Society* (New Haven, 1975); Thomas N. Tentler, *Sin and Confession on the Eve of the Reformation* (Princeton, 1977); John W. O'Malley, *Praise and Blame in Renaissance Rome: Rhetoric, Doctrine, and Reform in the Sacred Orators of the Papal Court, c. 1450–1521* (Durham, N. C., 1979); Lionel Rothkrug, "Religious Practice and Collective Perceptions: Hidden Homologies in the Renaissance and Reformation," *Historical Reflections/Réflexions Historiques,* VII (1980), published as a special issue.

10. Gerald Strauss, *Luther's House of Learning: Indoctrination of the Young in the German Reformation* (Baltimore, 1978). Hayden White, *Metahistory: The Historical Imagination in Nineteenth-Century Europe* (Baltimore, 1973); John G. A. Pocock, *The Machiavellian Moment: Florentine Political Thought and the Atlantic Republican Tradition* (Princeton, 1975); Robert Brentano, *Two Churches: England and Italy in the Thirteenth Century* (Princeton, 1968).

11. Marshall Sahlins, *Culture and Practical Reason* (Chicago, 1976); Pierre Bourdieu (trans. Richard Nice), *Outline of a Theory of Practice* (Cambridge, 1977); Maurice Bloch, "The Past and the Present in the Present," *Man,* XII (1977), 278–292.

12. The quoted remark is Clifford Geertz's paraphrase of Max Weber in *The Interpretation of Cultures* (New York, 1973), 5. Cf. Bouwsma, "The Renaissance and the Drama of Western History," *American Historical Review,* LXXXIV (1979), 10–11.

13. For example, Nancy S. Struever, *The Language of History in the Renaissance: Rhetoric and Historical Consciousness in Florentine Humanism* (Princeton, 1970); Pocock, *Politics, Language, and Time* (New York, 1971); Marjorie O'Rourke Boyle, *Erasmus on Language and Method in Theology* (Toronto, 1977).

16   The Renaissance
and the Drama of
Western History

*This essay was my presidential address before the American Historical Asso-
ciation at its annual meeting in 1978. I chose to discuss, for this occasion, what
could be salvaged for the conception of the Renaissance as the great turning
point in the history of the West, now that historians have largely lost confidence
in the old dramatic scenario on which its significance depended. The address
was published in the* American Historical Review *94 (1979), 1–15.*

•   •   •

I should like to discuss a remarkable historiographical event—an event
so recent that it may have escaped general notice, yet of considerable
importance both for historians and for the larger culture of which we
are a part. This event is the collapse of the traditional dramatic organization of Western history. We have long depended upon it, as inhabitants of the modern world, to put the present into some distant
temporal perspective and, as professional historians pursuing our particular investigations, to provide us with some sense of how the various
fields of history are related to each other as parts of a larger whole. Thus,
the subject seems appropriate for a general session of our annual meeting.
The subject is also appropriate for me, as a historian of the Renaissance,
because of the pivotal position of the Renaissance in the traditional
pattern. Indeed, the historian of the Renaissance has long been the
principal guardian of that pattern. But historians of the Renaissance
have lately been unable—or unwilling—to fulfill this old responsibility.
Hence, this essay is also a kind of oblique professional autobiography,
though I point this out only for the sake of candor, not as a further
inducement to your attention.

Nothing seemed less likely than this development when I entered the profession some thirty years ago or, indeed, before the last two decades. Earlier in this century, the Burckhardtian vision of the importance of the Renaissance for the formation of the modern world had been under attack in the "revolt of the medievalists"; and in 1940 Wallace K. Ferguson had described the Renaissance as "the most intractable problem child of historiography."[1] But Ferguson had himself never been without hope for straightening out his problem child; and less than a decade later, after studying the history of the case from many directions, he predicted for it a tranquil and prosperous maturity. The time was ripe, he declared, for "a new and more comprehensive synthesis."[2] The revolt of the medievalists had apparently been beaten back; indeed, by teaching us greater care in distinguishing the new from the old, they seemed only to have strengthened our sense of the originality and modernity of the Renaissance. In the years after the war a group of unusually distinguished scholars brought new excitement to Renaissance studies; the concreteness and depth of their learning seemed to confirm Ferguson's expectations.[3]

During the fifties, therefore, it was common for Renaissance specialists from various disciplines to celebrate, by reading papers to each other, their triumph over the medievalists and the world-historical significance of the Renaissance. Our agreement was remarkable. The editor of one volume of such papers noted with satisfaction "the virtual disappearance of the disposition to deny that there was a Renaissance." And he ventured to predict, obviously recalling controversies now happily over, "that future soldier scholars will beat their swords into ploughshares and that what has long been the Renaissance battleground will be transformed into a plain of peace and plenty." On the other hand, he also hinted that the occasion evoking these papers was a bit dull. "The atmosphere of charitable catholicity was so all pervading during the symposium," he remarked, "that even the moderators' valiant efforts to provoke controversy were largely futile."[4] That the Renaissance was the critical episode in a dramatic process that would culminate in ourselves had become an orthodoxy that few cared—or dared—to question.

The notion of an abiding consensus among historians of any complex subject may now seem rather surprising, and this agreeable situation was probably in part a reflection of the general consensus of the Eisenhower years, when we were all beating our swords into ploughshares. That same irenic mood, that same amiable but slightly complacent consensus, also left its mark on other fields of history. The gentle complaint of our editor, disappointed in his hopes for a little fun at a scholarly symposium, hinted at the charge of dullness brought by bored professors against their boring students of the silent generation—upon which we would soon enough be looking back with a degree of nostalgia. For since the 1960s the world around us has dramatically changed, and with it historiography.

These two sets of changes are not unrelated, and the result for the Renaissance has been rather different from what Ferguson foresaw. In his vision the Renaissance was to retain its pivotal position in the old scenario, but our knowledge of it would be better pulled together. But this has not occurred. Although the consensus of the golden 1950s has not been seriously challenged, we are now remarkably indifferent to the world-historical importance of the Renaissance.[5] We go about our particular investigations as though the Renaissance problem had evaporated; we neither affirm nor bother to deny that there was a Renaissance. And the venerable Renaissance label has become little more than an administrative convenience, a kind of blanket under which we huddle together less out of mutual attraction than because, for certain purposes, we have nowhere else to go.[6]

I do not mean to exaggerate the abruptness of this development. In retrospect we can see that the role of historians in the postwar rehabilitation of the Renaissance was always somewhat ambiguous. We accepted what was said in praise of the Renaissance by representatives of other humanistic disciplines; the importance of the Renaissance for them enhanced our own importance. But, like Garrett B. Mattingly on one such occasion, we were sometimes "puzzled" about what we might contribute to a Renaissance symposium.[7] The normal skepticism of a professional historian in the presence of large views has now given way, however, to agnosticism and even indifference about what was once the central claim of Renaissance scholarship.

This result may have been implicit in Ferguson's call for synthesis, with which most of us were sympathetic even in the 1950s without fully realizing its implications. It implied the integration of all of our data, an aspiration that seemed unexceptionable. But the ideal of "synthesis"— at least for a generation not yet dialectically sophisticated—was essentially static. Synthesis tended to shift the emphasis in Renaissance studies from process, on which the traditional estimate of the Renaissance depended, to structure or, minimally, from the long-range processes which gave European history a larger narrative shape to particular, ostensibly self-contained (and in this sense inconsequential), more limited processes. This tendency was supplemented by an influence from another direction: our supposedly innocent but in fact deeply insidious course catalogues. We should treat the course catalogue with more respect.

Partly because we are inclined to take it so lightly, it is one of the most potent forces in historiography: it tends to organize the past, for the sake of "coverage," as a sequence of chronologically bounded segments, the number of which reflects the size of our departments. The individual historian is then made responsible for one of these segments, with the expectation that he will deal with it in all of its aspects. And the assignment defined for him by the catalogue, when he is young and malleable, is likely to shape his general understanding of what it means to "do" history.[8] Thus, the influence of the catalogue has various consequences, among which the most positive is to deepen the historian's sense of complexity. But the catalogue also discourages him from intruding into adjacent segments that "belong" to his colleagues; and by the same token it encourages him, however conscious he may be of the arbitrariness of the dates bounding his assignment, to treat his segment as self-contained. At the very least, he feels compelled out of esthetic motives to portray it as some kind of intelligible unity.[9]

Historians of the Renaissance have responded to these pressures in two ways. First, we began to distinguish more and more clearly between "the Renaissance" itself, a cluster of cultural movements pregnant with the future, and the "age of the Renaissance," the more general context within which we encountered these movements. The "age of the Renaissance" was invoked to accommodate in some unstable tension with the novelty and modernity of Renaissance culture whatever seemed inconsistent or in tension with it. But we tended at first to regard these anomalies as so many medieval residues, destined to yield ineluctably, in the long run, to its modernizing forces. This approach was hardly the method of synthesis.

But at the same time we were increasingly uncomfortable with the rather mechanical work of sorting our data into two heaps, one marked "continuities," the other "innovations." This discomfort led to a second move that seems on the surface to have brought us closer to synthesis: we began to describe the age of the Renaissance as the age of transition *to* the modern world. And this formula, which now appears with some regularity in our textbooks, has provoked little dissent. Indeed, the formula appears to exclude the possibility of dissent, for it is nicely calculated to accommodate every anomaly and at the same time to protect the significance of the Renaissance. This, of course, is its purpose. To the objection that every past age might equally be represented as transitional, we can reply that this one was *unusually* transitional, that it was an age of *accelerated* transition.[10] This position now gives a semblance of agreement to Renaissance scholarship, enabling us to engage in a wide variety of tasks, comfortable in the belief that our larger claims are secure—and effectively indifferent to them.

Nevertheless, there are difficulties in this apparently unexceptionable strategy. For one thing, it neglects to state the criteria by which one age can be considered more transitional than another; by begging this question, which was at the heart of our controversy with the medievalists, it invites a new revolt from that direction as well as protests from other quarters. The strategy also seems to me conceptually confused, a reflection of the chronic temptation of the historian to identify "history" as the actuality of the past with "history" as the construction he makes of its records. For history as actuality, an "age" is simply a considerable span of time; for history as construction, an "age" is a segment of the past on which he can impose some intelligibility. The notion of an "age of transition" thus exploits what is essentially a structural conception to assert for the Renaissance a continuing significance that actually derives from its place in a process.

This confusion points to a further problem, since the notion of a transitional age depends on the intelligibility of the "ages" it supposedly connects. The Renaissance as "transition" suggests something like an unsteady bridge between two granitic headlands, clearly identifiable as the Middle Ages and the modern (or, at least, the early modern) world. As a Renaissance specialist, I am reluctant to commit myself about the present stability of these two adjacent historiographical promontories. But my impression is that neither medieval nor early modern historians would be altogether comfortable with the image.[11] And as an inhabitant of the modern world, I find it rather too amorphous, unintelligible, and contradictory, at least as a whole, to provide any stable mooring for such a bridge. I am, in short, doubtful whether we are yet in any position to represent our own time as an intelligible age.

But a reflection of this kind takes us beyond internal historiographical pressures to the impact of contemporary experience on historiography. And such experience may, in the end, be the major cause for the present disarray of Renaissance scholarship: since we are baffled by the modern world, we are hardly in a position to argue for the relevance to it, at least in the traditional way, of the Renaissance.[12] For the argument that attached the Renaissance to the modern world was based on two assumptions: that the modern world does, in fact, constitute some kind of intelligible entity, and that modernity has emerged by way of a single linear process. Neither of these assumptions is, at least for me, self-evident. To be a competent historian of the Renaissance is, of course, hard enough, even without engaging in extracurricular ventures of this kind; but my efforts to sample the work of those scholars who have struggled to define the modern condition leave me as uncertain as the modern world itself.[13] And I am further bewildered by the suggestion that we have now entered into a "postmodern" age. Meanwhile, the collapse of the idea of progress has profoundly subverted our sense of the direction of history. We can agree, perhaps, only that the present is the complex product of a remarkably tangled past.

Other pressures from the surrounding world have also weakened the ability of the historian of the Renaissance to defend the old dramatic organization of Western history and have at the same time promoted an alternative. Brought into focus by the social and cultural ferment of the 1960s, so stimulating to historiography in other areas, these pressures have left the Renaissance in a partial eclipse. They pose a radical challenge—one that we have largely ignored—to our own doubtful compromise between process and structure.[14]

This challenge is related to a generous concern with the historiographically neglected and suffering majority of mankind that has diverted attention from those elites whose achievements have been the mainstay of claims for the Renaissance. From this standpoint historical significance tends to be defined largely as a function of numbers, of mass, and, hence, of the masses; this interest in the masses may suggest an ideological and even sentimental content in the supposedly cold and scientific impulse toward quantification. But mass also suggests matter and, therefore, points to the material basis of human existence, with a concomitant tendency to rely on the architectural model—so disruptive of traditional historiography—of superstructure and infrastructure, against the idealism often implicit in the preoccupation of historians of the Renaissance with high culture. A further consequence of this interest has been an emphasis on the more inert aspects of the past, with reduced attention to what had traditionally been seen as the source of the most dynamic forces in modern history. Meanwhile, the peculiar insecurity of the last two decades seems to have intensified the occasional yearning of the historian to regard himself as a scientist; and the methods recently devised to promote this aspiration and to open up new social groups to investigation have not been suited to the ways of Renaissance study, which has depended chiefly on the cultivated judgment and creative imagination of the individual historian.

These impulses have conspicuously been at work in the new social history, which has produced results of great interest, if chiefly for a later period, and which seems to me itself a remarkable feat of the historical imagination. This much is, I think, indisputable, however skeptical one may be of its scientific pretensions[15] and of the claims of some of its practitioners to have overcome at last the distinction between history as actuality and history as construction. And it is particularly instructive from the standpoint of our present difficulties with the Renaissance, because it displays the results of a deliberate and wholehearted acceptance of that notion of an "age" with which the historian of the Renaissance has dealt so gingerly. It may also help to explain why he has preferred compromise.

I am referring to the concept of the *longue durée,* the intelligible age par excellence, whose implications for the Renaissance emerge with special clarity in a recent essay by Emmanuel Le Roy Ladurie.[16] This piece offers a general interpretation of the extended period between about the eleventh and the nineteenth centuries. Situated between two intervals of innovation and expansion, this true age is, for Le Roy Ladurie, an intelligible unity, given fundamental coherence by a kind of grim Malthusian balance. The productivity of agriculture was limited, population was limited by it, and the material conditions of life for the vast majority were virtually unchangeable. By the democratic criterion of numbers, this long period was, except in insignificant detail, changeless; Le Roy Ladurie has accordingly described it as "motionless."

From this standpoint the period of the Renaissance appears as little more than, in a double sense, the dead center of a much longer age in which the conventional distinction between medieval and early modern Europe has been obliterated. At most, the Renaissance is a *conjoncture* that is intelligible only in a far larger temporal context. But the full implications of the argument emerge only in Le Roy Ladurie's reply to the objections that might be raised against it by more traditional historians:

> One might object to this conception of motionless history . . . because it is a little too negligent of such fundamental innovations of the period as Pascal's divine revelation, Papin's steam engine and the growth of a very great city like Paris, or the progress of civility among the upper classes as symbolized by the introduction of the dinner fork. Far be it from me to question the radically new character of these episodes. But what interests me is the *becoming,* or rather the *non-becoming* of the faceless mass of people. The accomplishments of the elite are situated on a higher and more isolated plane and are not really significant except from the point of view of a noisy minority, carriers of progress without doubt, but as yet incapable of mobi-

lizing the enormous mass of rural humanity enmeshed in its Ricardian feedback.[17]

One has only to substitute—for Pascal, Papin, Paris, and the dinner fork—any random set of Renaissance accomplishments—Petrarch's historical consciousness, the Copernican Revolution, the Florentine city-state with its civic rhetoric, and double-entry bookkeeping, for example—to appreciate the mordant implications here for the Renaissance.

Although the plausibility of this argument, which appears to illustrate the consequences of a thoroughgoing "synthesis," has perhaps been one element in the present disarray of Renaissance historiography, its approach also has limitations (as I am hardly the first to point out)[18] that make it less decisive for the Renaissance than it may first appear. Largely an adaptation of French structuralism, Le Roy Ladurie's thesis carries with it the antihistorical bias of that movement: structuralist analysis of the past has never been well adapted to deal with change. The consequences are apparent when Le Roy Ladurie, too good a historian to ignore this problem, must account for the end of his *longue durée,* when motion was finally restored to human affairs, the constraints on agriculture loosened, the old Malthusian cycle was broken, the migration from field to factory could begin, and the masses were at last expelled from the traditional world into, presumably, a new age.

At this point Le Roy Ladurie's rich ironies seem to serve chiefly as a rhetorical justification for the limitation of his vision to what, as he so disarmingly puts it, "interests" him. Here we become aware of a difference in both strategy and tone. Since the masses were helpless to bring about this ambiguous denouement, that ridiculous noisy minority becomes unexpectedly important. Now it represents "forces of elitist renovation which had been building up slowly over the course of centuries" and which finally succeeded, after about 1720, in "setting off an avalanche."[19] This "build-up of forces" might suggest that Paris and the steam engine—and even, more obscurely, Pascal and the fork—are after all, if one is interested in that "avalanche," worth some attention. And back of them lies the Renaissance—not, perhaps, as an "age" but (in the terms of its traditional interpretation) as a critical moment in a process that would in the long run significantly transform the world. The impulses not altogether arbitrarily associated with the Renaissance—its individualism and its practical and empirical rationality—were, though immediately limited to a statistically insignificant minority, destined for some importance even from the standpoint of the majority.[20] I do not mean to deny the value of structural description;

indeed, it provides essential safeguards against anachronism for the historian primarily interested in process.[21] But structures can hardly exhaust the concern of the historian; the past is not simply a world we have lost.

The inability of a history of structures to deal with change has, however, a further consequence. Its neglect of the continuities that link the past with the present and one "age" to the next opens the way to an interpretation of change as cataclysm, with the implication that the modern world is genetically related to the past only remotely. Our own time thus appears as something like a biological mutation, whose survival value remains an open question. For the structural approach to the past may ignore but cannot, after all, repudiate process altogether. One set of structures obviously does, somehow, give way to another. The effect of this approach is to promote, however inadvertently, a discontinuous concept of process. Thus, for the myth of continuity with the Renaissance it substitutes what I will call the myth of apocalyptic modernization. In calling this a myth, I mean nothing pejorative.[22] A myth is, for the historian, the dynamic equivalent of a model in the social sciences, and we can hardly do without it. The crucial transition from chronicle to history depended on the application of some principle of mythical organization to previously discrete data: the myth of the hero, the myth of collective advance, the myth of decline. That the weakening of one mythical pattern should have left a kind of vacuum for another myth to fill is hardly surprising.

So the apocalyptic myth—a product partly of our own self-importance and partly of the mingled hopes and anxieties generated by recent experience—has emerged, though it is not itself peculiarly modern. A modification of the basic Western myth of linear time of a type periodically recurrent under conditions of stress, the apocalyptic myth provides an alternative to the idea of continuous development, with which it can be variously combined. Indeed, it is not altogether different from the Renaissance notion of radical discontinuity with the Middle Ages. In discussing it critically, I am aware of a certain analogy with the medievalists' protests against the idea of the Renaissance.

Largely, as a result of those protests, historians of the Renaissance generally gave up the apocalyptic dimension of the original Renaissance myth, at least as it related to the past. Without renouncing the novelties of the Renaissance, they recognized its continuities with the Middle Ages, themselves increasingly seen as complex. In other words, they made distinctions, within both periods, among contrary tendencies. But these careful distinctions took care of only half of the Renaissance problem. Thus, if we are still in disarray, the explanation may ultimately be that we have failed to modify in the same way that element in the Renaissance myth that pointed to the future: its perception of the modern world—the goal of the historical process—as a coherent entity. Since we can no longer support our claims for the Renaissance origins of the modern world so conceived, we have fallen silent. If this is true, the full solution to the Renaissance problem would thus depend on our giving as much attention to the complexities and contradictions of our own time as we have given to those of the Middle Ages and the Renaissance and on being equally selective about the relation of the Renaissance to the modern world. Among its other advantages, this solution might enable us to put the apocalyptic myth itself in some perspective; we might then notice that some reaction against it is already under way in the social sciences.[23]

Such selectivity might enable us to claim for the Renaissance a substantial role in the formation of those tendencies in our own world that perhaps have a better claim to modernity than does the present apocalyptic mood: the skeptical, relativistic, and pragmatic strains in contemporary culture.[24] These strains would suggest, in place of the apocalyptic myth, something like the myth of Prometheus, itself of some interest to Renaissance thought[25]—Prometheus who, by tricking Zeus and stealing the fire that made possible the arts, endowed man with the power to create a world in which he could survive alone. Such a myth might be interpreted to mean that the world man inhabits is formed, not through some transcendent and ineluctable process—whether cataclysmic or uniform—but only out of his own shifting needs and unpredictable inventiveness. From this standpoint, the basic peculiarity of the modern world might be seen as the present consciousness of human beings of their power to shape the world they inhabit, including the social world and, by extension, themselves. A (for us) poignant reflection of this situation might be the unique predicament of the modern historian, who is in a position to choose, among various possibilities, the myth most useful to impose dramatic organization on his data—a problem of which previous historians were largely unaware. In modern culture, then, the determinism and helplessness implicit in the apocalyptic myth are opposed by a still lively belief in human freedom.

The modern sense of the creative freedom of mankind now finds stimulating expression in a concept of culture that underlies the work of a group of distinguished contemporary anthropologists.[26] According to this view of the human condition, the universe man inhabits is essentially a complex of meanings of his own devising; man, as Max Weber perceived him, is "an animal suspended in webs of significance he himself has spun."[27] These webs make up his culture or, more exactly, since they are utterly various, his cultures. Furthermore, as philosophers and linguists have made increasingly clear, he spins these webs from language. Through language man orders the chaos or data impinging on his sensorium from, in a singularly mysterious and problematic sense, "out there," organizing them into categories and so making them intelligible, manageable, and useful. The human world might, therefore, be described as a vast rhetorical production, for the operations that bring it into existence are comparable to such basic rhetorical transactions as division and comparison, or metonymy and metaphor.[28] This concept denies not that an objective universe exists but only that man has direct access to it or can know what it is apart from what he makes of it, out of his own limited perceptual and intellectual resources and for his own purposes, whatever these might be.[29]

The epistemological decisions embedded in language are thus the precondition of human apprehension of an external world; culture in this sense is prior to both materialism and idealism, which represent contrary efforts to assign ontological status to—in the language of sociology, to legitimize—a world whose actual source in the creativity of man violates the all-too-human need for transcendence.[30] From this standpoint history presents itself not as a single process but as a complex of processes, which interests us insofar as we are interested in the almost infinite possibilities of human existence. Beyond this, history as construction often tends to be a misleading and sometimes pernicious reification.

Here, I am only advancing on an old position in the historiography of the Renaissance from a somewhat new direction. For the kind of history this approach suggests was very much that of the most distinguished historians of the Renaissance of the last hundred years, Jacob Burckhardt and Johan Huizinga, notable pioneers in what both called cultural history. Misled by their concentration on evidence drawn from the culture of elites, we have tended to see in their work no more than the study of "superstructure," losing sight of the generous conception of culture underlying their work. For Burckhardt, the proper subject of *Kulturgeschichte* was not simply the arts, which were relatively neglected in his account of the Renaissance, but "what moves the world and what is of penetrating influence, . . . the indispensable."[31] For Huizinga, cultural history required the identification of "deeper, general themes" and "the patterns of life, thought, and art taken all together," which he was prepared to pursue in every dimension of human experience.[32] And both had such reservations about the modern world that neither would have found much satisfaction in representing it as the goal of history.

This conception of culture is perhaps the contemporary world's most general legacy from the Renaissance: the recognition that culture is a product of the creative adjustment of the human race to its varying historical circumstances rather than a function of universal and changeless nature, and the perception that culture accordingly differs from time to time and group to group. This insight of the Renaissance suggested that mankind, by its own initiatives, could, for better or worse, shape its own earthly condition. Hints of this idea can be found earlier, of course, both in antiquity and in the Middle Ages; and even in the Renaissance the idea was limited to certain groups in which it only occasionally became explicit—as it did for Petrarch and Nicholas of Cusa (though only at certain moments), for Sir Philip Sidney, and for Montaigne. But this shocking view of the human condition made its first durable impression on the Western consciousness then and has continued to shape our world.

The high culture of the Renaissance immediately revealed some of the implications of the new conception of culture. Scholars became aware of the distinct, historically contingent cultures of antiquity, while the voyages of exploration discovered the varieties of contemporary culture in America and the Orient. Although the first European responses to these revelations tended to be ethnocentric, the relativism of Montaigne suggested that another kind of reaction was already possible. Meanwhile, cultural expression was being conceived, more modestly, not as a total and authoritative reflection of external reality but as a particular human insight, conveyed by isolated proverbs, pensées, familiar essays, small areas of practical or esthetic order, of which the autonomous painting of Renaissance art provides a nice symbol.

Perhaps the most profound indication that a radical shift in the understanding of culture was taking place—and, hence, a shift in the sense of man's relation to the world and to himself—can be seen in the Renaissance crisis of language, that basic instrument in the formation of culture.[33] The first sign of that crisis was a growing uneasiness, at first among the most abstract thinkers but then more broadly, that the human vocabulary was failing to mirror the objective world. *Words,* it was widely lamented, no longer corresponded to *things.* This lament was often taken to mean that the vocabulary should be reformed so that this traditional identity could be restored: a demand, in effect, for a return to the dependence of culture upon external nature. But then an alternative solution to the problem began to unfold. Skepticism about the capacity of the human mind to grasp the structures of nature directly led to growing doubt about the possibility of such an identity, to a recognition of the conventionality of language and its susceptibility to change, to the perception of language as a human creation, and eventually to the conclusion that, as the creator of language, man also shapes through language the only world he can know directly, including even himself.

This insight was a major impulse behind the brilliant imaginative literature of the Renaissance, which was one channel for the diffusion of this new concept of language. So was the steady displacement of Latin, the language of absolute truths both sacred and profane, by the European vernaculars, not only in literature but in law and administration. The variety of the vernaculars suggested that language was based on the consensus of particular peoples, arrived at by the processes of history; and the growing expressiveness of the various languages of Europe appeared to demonstrate that linguistic change signified not that the primordial identity of language with the real world was being corrupted—the traditional view propounded by Socrates in the *Cratylus*—but that language is a flexible tool. The rich elaboration of vernacular languages was not only the deliberate project of elites but a spontaneous and increasingly popular eruption to meet the shifting requirements of existence.

There was thus nothing ethereal about this portentous cultural shift. If a common culture is the foundation of community and limits the possible modes of social organization and social action, it is also responsive to changing social needs, themselves culturally defined. And, like other historical phenomena, the subtle and reciprocal dialogue between culture and society is open to investigation.[34] The expanding linguistic resources of Renaissance culture simultaneously facilitated and reflected the development of a more complex urban and monarchical society. The sense that language does not simply mirror, passively, the structures of external nature but functions as a tool to serve the practical needs of social existence eventually stimulated reflection about the uses and creative possibilities of language. And we can see in those reflections the germ of a new vision of human culture.

Whether given practical expression in the creative modification of language or, at another level, in the Renaissance idea of self-fashioning,[35] the notion of man as creator of himself and the world was heady stuff. It found expression in the modern expectation that government, the economy, and education should constantly reconstruct society, the environment, and man himself in accordance with the constantly changing expectations of mankind. There are doubtless limits to such an enterprise, both in the malleability of physical and biological reality and in man's own moral capacities,[36] that this aspiration tends to overlook. These limits and the attempts to exceed them help to explain a perennial impulse since the Renaissance to react against the creativity and freedom of Renaissance culture toward various types of philosophical and scientific determinism and, thus, also to explain the contradictions of the modern world. Perhaps the Renaissance vision of man with its vast practical consequences has needed, from time to time, to be chastened in this way. But it has so far survived as the major resource with which to oppose the temptation to escape from the anxieties of the human condition into new versions of authoritarianism.

I began these remarks by announcing the collapse of the dramatic scheme that has long organized our vision of the general career of Western history. Since I think that drama is vital to historiography, because it enables us to impose form on the processes of history and so to make them intelligible, this seems to me an ominous development, especially since it has invited the substitution of another dramatic scheme that would deprive us of our roots in the past. But, although I have argued for the continuing significance of the Renaissance, I have not tried simply to defend the traditional pattern, which seems to me seriously defective, in ways that the legacy of Renaissance culture also helps us understand. The old dramatic pattern, with its concept of linear history moving the human race ineluctably to its goal in the modern world, depended on concealed principles of transcendence inappropriate to the human understanding of human affairs. The trinity of acts composing the great drama of human history and its concept of the modern epoch as not just the latest but the last act of the play bear witness to its eschatological origins,[37] and such notions seem to me peculiarly inappropriate to so human an enterprise as that of the historian. But I also find the traditional scheme unsatisfactory because it is not dramatic enough. It fails to accommodate the sense of contingency and, therefore, suspense—the sense that the drama might have turned out otherwise—that belongs to all human temporal experience. Though it has survived for over five centuries, for example, I see no reason to assume that the anthropological vision we owe to the Renaissance is destined to triumph forever over the forces arrayed against it, and much in the modern world suggests the contrary.

But the more human concept of the drama of history that had its effective origins in the Renaissance understanding of culture overcomes these various disadvantages. Its pluralism implies the possibility of a multiplicity of historical dramas, both simultaneous and successive; and so it relieves us of the embarrassment, inherent in a linear and eschatological vision of time, of repeatedly having to reclassify in other terms what for a previous generation seemed modern. Since it perceives history as a part of culture and also, therefore, a human creation, it permits us constantly to reconstruct the dramas of history and so to see the past in fresh relationships to ourselves. Above all, since it insists on no particular outcome for the dramas of history, it leaves the future open.

NOTES

I should like to acknowledge at the outset the helpful criticism this paper received from Thomas A. Brady, Jr., of the University of Oregon and from my Berkeley colleagues Gene Brucker and Randolph Starn.

1. Ferguson, *The Renaissance* (New York, 1940), 2.

2. Ferguson, *The Renaissance in Historical Thought* (Boston, 1948), 389.

3. For some of the works that particularly influenced me at this time, in addition to those of Ferguson, see Paul Oskar Kristeller, *The Classics and Renaissance Thought* (Cambridge, Mass., 1955); Hans Baron, *The Crisis of the Early Italian Renaissance: Civic Humanism and Republican Liberty in an Age of Classicism and Tyranny*, 2 vols. (Princeton, 1955); Eugenio Garin, *L'umanesimo italiano* (Bari, 1958); and the various essays of Erwin Panofsky, especially "Renaissance and Renascences," *Kenyon Review*, 6 (1944): 201–36.

4. Tinsley Helton, ed., *The Renaissance: A Reconsideration of the Theories and Interpretations of the Age* (Madison, Wisc., 1961), xi–xii. The papers in this volume were presented at a symposium at the University of Wisconsin, Milwaukee, in 1959. For other symposia, see *The Renaissance: A Symposium* (New York, 1953); and Bernard O'Kelly, ed., *The Renaissance Image of Man and the World* (Columbus, Ohio, 1966).

5. Randolph Starn has called attention to this; see his review of Nicolai Rubinstein, ed., *Florentine Studies: Politics and Society in Renaissance Italy* (London, 1968), in *Bibliothèque d'Humanisme et Renaissance*, 32 (1970): 682–83. Also see his "Historians and 'Crisis,'" *Past & Present*, no. 52 (1971): 19.

6. For explicit recognition that the term functions chiefly as an administrative convenience, see Brian Pullan, *A History of Early Renaissance Italy from the Mid-Thirteenth to the Mid-Fifteenth Century* (London, 1973), 11.

7. Mattingly, "Some Revisions of the Political History of the Renaissance," in Helton, *The Renaissance: A Reconsideration*, 3.

8. The effect of this periodization by course sequences has doubtless been intensified by the decline of introductory surveys of European history.

9. There may be analogies here with the consequences of specialization in other occupations, notably medicine.

10. In his *Renaissance in Historical Thought*, Ferguson tied the notion of transition to synthesis; he combined the two strategies in *Europe in Transition, 1300–1520* (Boston, 1962), the first large-scale presentation of the period in these terms, though this project was already foreshadowed in his "The Interpretation of the Renaissance: Suggestions for a Synthesis," *Journal of the History*

of Ideas, 12 (1951): 483–95. For other works that rely on the idea of transition, see Eugene F. Rice, Jr., *The Foundations of Early Modern Europe, 1460–1559* (New York, 1970), ix; Lewis W. Spitz, *The Renaissance and Reformation Movements* (Chicago, 1971), vii, 3; and Pullan, *Early Renaissance Italy,* 11. The widespread assumption that textbooks such as these are no part of our "serious" work seems to me both troubling and mistaken.

11. It may be noted that medievalists who write about the Renaissance tend to see it not as a "transition" but as having a distinct identity of its own. See, for example, Denys Hay, *The Italian Renaissance in Its Historical Background* (Cambridge, 1961), 14–25; and Robert S. Lopez, *The Three Ages of the Italian Renaissance* (Charlottesville, Va., 1970), 73.

12. For a work that is especially sensitive to this problem, see Rice, *Foundations of Early Modern Europe,* x.

13. I have been helped to see the complexity of this problem by Richard D. Brown's work; see his *Modernization: The Transformation of American Life, 1600–1865* (New York, 1976), 3–22.

14. For a stimulating exception, see John Hale, *Renaissance Europe: The Individual and Society, 1480–1520* (London, 1971). But its short time-span excuses it from the need to deal with larger processes, and in spite of Hale's attempt to write "majority" history, much of his detail is drawn—inevitably—from "minority" sources.

15. This issue is muddied by the ambiguity of the term "science." For a useful discussion of its somewhat different meanings in French and English usage, see J. H. Hexter, "Fernand Braudel and the *Monde Braudellien . . . ,*" *Journal of Modern History,* 44 (1972): 500.

16. Le Roy Ladurie, "L'histoire immobile," *Annales: Economies, sociétés, civilisations,* 29 (1974): 673–82, translated by John Day as "Motionless History," *Social Science History,* 1 (1977): 115–36. Clyde Griffen kindly called this article to my attention.

17. Le Roy Ladurie, "Motionless History," 133–34.

18. For a notable critique, see Hexter, "Fernand Braudel and the *Monde Braudellien,*" 480–539. Also see, for a criticism of the neglect of process in much of the new social history, Eugene and Elizabeth Fox Genovese, "The Political Crisis of Social History: A Marxian Perspective," *Journal of Social History,* 10 (1976): 215. As Robert M. Berdahl points out, many non-Marxists can agree with this; see his "Anthropologie und Geschichte: einige theoretische Perspektiven und ein Beispiel aus der preussisch-deutschen Geschichte," [now published in *Klassen und Kultur,* ed. Robert M. Berdahl et al. (Frankfurt, 1982), 263–287].

19. Le Roy Ladurie, "Motionless History," 134.

20. The long-range significance of these tendencies of the Renaissance is still recognized, however, in some recent work. See Jean Delumeau, "Le développement de l'esprit d'organisation et de la pensée méthodique dans la mentalité occidentale à l'époque de la Renaissance," in Thirteenth International Congress of Historical Sciences, Moscow 1970, *Doklady Kongressa,* 1, pt. 5 (Moscow, 1973): 139–50; and Peter Burke, *Culture and Society in Renaissance Italy, 1420–1540* (London, 1972), 225.

21. The very real danger of anachronism seems to have led Charles Trinkaus to renounce the "traditional genetic-modernist bias," i.e., the scrutiny of the past

in the interest of understanding the present; Trinkaus, "Humanism, Religion, Society: Concepts and Motivations of Some Recent Studies," *Renaissance Quarterly,* 29 (1976): 677, 685–86. Though I agree that it is subject to abuse, I see nothing illegitimate in principle in genetic explanation, and I am quite sure that its abandonment by historians would only leave it to others less sensitive to its difficulties.

22. For this complex word, see Raymond Williams, *Keywords: A Vocabulary of Culture and Society* (New York, 1976), 176–78. For a generally instructive work on the role of myth in historiography, see Hayden White, *Metahistory: The Historical Imagination in Nineteenth-Century Europe* (Baltimore, 1973).

23. See Shmuel N. Eisenstadt, "Sociological Theory and an Analysis of the Dynamics of Civilizations and Revolutions," *Daedalus,* 106 (1977): esp. 61–63.

24. Isaiah Berlin has helped me bring these strains into focus; see his *Vico and Herder: Two Studies in the History of Ideas* (New York, 1976).

25. See Charles Trinkaus, *In Our Image and Likeness: Humanity and Divinity in Italian Humanist Thought,* 1 (Chicago, 1970): 244–45. Also see, for a significant and more recent application of this myth, Donald R. Kelley, "The Metaphysics of Law: An Essay on the Very Young Marx," *AHR,* 83 (1978): 350.

26. For studies that reflect this concept of culture, see Pierre Bourdieu, *Outline of a Theory of Practice,* trans. Richard Nice (Cambridge, 1977); Mary Douglas, *Purity and Danger: An Analysis of Concepts of Pollution and Taboo* (London, 1966), *Natural Symbols* (London, 1970), and *Implicit Meanings: Essays in Anthropology* (London, 1975); Louis Dumont, *From Mandeville to Marx: The Genesis and Triumph of Economic Ideology* (Chicago, 1977); Clifford Geertz, *The Interpretation of Cultures* (New York, 1973); Marshall Sahlins, *Culture and Practical Reason* (Chicago, 1976); Victor Turner, *The Ritual Process: Structure and Anti-Structure* (Ithaca, N.Y., 1969); and, seminal for the role of language in culture, Edward Sapir, *Culture, Language, and Personality: Selected Essays,* ed. David G. Mandelbaum (Berkeley and Los Angeles, 1949).

27. Geertz, *Interpretation of Cultures,* 5.

28. The historian's creation of the world of the past out of language provides a close analogy.

29. For much of this I am indebted to the theoretical essays of Harry Berger, Jr. See, in particular, his "Outline of a General Theory of Cultural Change," *Clio,* 2 (1972): 49–63, and "Naive Consciousness," *Papers on Language and Literature,* 8 (1973): 1–44.

30. See Sahlins, *Culture and Practical Reason,* esp. ix–x.

31. As quoted in Karl J. Weintraub, *Visions of Culture: Voltaire, Guizot, Burckhardt, Lamprecht, Huizinga, Ortega y Gasset* (Chicago, 1966), 138.

32. Huizinga, *Men and Ideas: History, the Middle Ages, and the Renaissance,* trans. James S. Holmes and Hans van Marle (New York, 1959), 28. Also see Weintraub, *Visions of Culture,* 230–31.

33. For a general discussion of Renaissance views of language, see Karl-Otto Apel, *Die Idee der Sprache in der Tradition des Humanismus von Dante bis Vico,* Archiv für Begriffsgeschichte, no. 8 (Bonn, 1963). For some of the studies that have influenced my own understanding of these matters, see Michael Baxandall, *Giotto and the Orators: Humanist Observers of Painting in Italy and the Discovery*

of Pictorial Composition, 1350–1450 (Oxford, 1971); Salvatore I. Camporeale, *Lorenzo Valla: Umanesimo e teologia* (Florence, 1972); Thomas M. Greene, "Petrarch and the Humanist Hermaneutic," in K. Atchity and G. Rimanelli, eds., *Italian Literature: Roots and Branches* (New Haven, 1976), 201–24; Gordon Leff, *William of Ockham: The Metamorphosis of Scholastic Discourse* (Manchester, 1975), esp. 124–237; J. G. A. Pocock, *Politics, Language, and Time: Essays on Political Thought and History* (New York, 1971); and Nancy S. Struever, *The Language of History in the Renaissance: Rhetoric and Historical Consciousness in Florentine Humanism* (Princeton, 1970). It is increasingly apparent that those self-conscious antagonists, Renaissance humanists and later Scholastics, in fact collaborated in this development.

34. For an especially useful discussion of this relationship, see Bourdieu, *Outline of a Theory of Practice*, esp. 72–95.

35. On this radical application of the Renaissance concept of human creativity, see A. Bartlett Giamatti, "Proteus Unbound: Some Versions of the Sea God in the Renaissance," in Peter Demetz, ed., *The Disciplines of Criticism* (New Haven, 1968), 431–75; and Stephen J. Greenblatt, "Marlowe and Renaissance Self-Fashioning," in Alvin Kernan, ed., *Two Renaissance Mythmakers: Christopher Marlowe and Ben Jonson* (Baltimore, 1977), 41–69.

36. Hence, the condemnation of the Renaissance in Protestant neo-orthodoxy; see Herbert Weisinger, "The Attack on the Renaissance in Theology Today," *Studies in the Renaissance*, 2 (1955): 176–89. This hostility continues to inhibit recognition of the filiation between the Reformation and the Renaissance.

37. The structural principle of the conventional ancient-medieval-modern division seems to persist in more recent trinitarian schemes—i.e., primitive-traditional-modern and aristocrat-bourgeois-proletarian.

IV

ESSAYS IN APPLIED HISTORY

17 Models of the Educated Man

In the summer of 1974, I participated in an Aspen Institute conference that brought together a wide range of scholars and educational administrators from Europe and the United States to discuss the kind of education appropriate for the latter part of the twentieth century. I was asked to prepare for the conference this paper surveying various past models of education, drawing such conclusions from the exercise as seemed appropriate. The piece was published in The American Scholar *44 (1975), 195–212.*

• • •

Those of us who are troubled by the confusion in contemporary education, perhaps especially if we continue to believe in a liberal or general education, are sometimes tempted to look to the past for guidance. But the lessons of history are rarely unambiguous. For one thing, its messages are various. Like Scripture, it can generally be made to support what we want it to support; and in the case of education, the Western cultural tradition incorporates not just one but a whole series of educational ideals, which rest on quite different assumptions and point in different directions. Beyond this, however, it is not always clear just how the present learns from the past. If history can help us, it will not be because those apparently ideal moments in the past which appeal to our nostalgia can simply be recalled under our own very different circumstances. It is these difficulties surrounding the relevance of history to education that this essay seeks to examine.

At the outset, it may be observed that the conventional contrast between general and specialized education appears, in historical perspective, less than absolute; the earliest hints of a general education ideal were the products of professionalism. Particular occupational groups, notably warriors and scribes, developed high standards of competence; and, in doing so, they exhibited a tendency to idealization that seems regularly to accompany the formation of a professional ethos. Indeed, only at the stage of idealization have these groups first come to our attention: warriors through the competitive heroism of the Homeric epics, scribes through the Old Testament book of Proverbs. This idealization may be partly understood as a response to social need. Warriors were more effective if their brutality was restrained and if they were not only good fighters but also loyal and congenial comrades; scribes, if they were honest, fair, and consistent in their administrative duties. But a more personal impulse was also at work, a profound aspiration to personal excellence and social respect, a desire for recognition as the most admirable warrior or scribe. In this way, professional roles were elevated into ideal human types, with implications extending far beyond the professional group.

We may first see this aristocratic ideal in the evolution of the ancient warrior from predator into hero and, when the fighter again became prominent in the Middle Ages, of freebooter into knight and eventually courtier and gentleman. Each may be seen as a variant of the same general model of the educated man, which may conveniently be described as aristocratic. Warrior, knight, courtier, and gentleman have in common a concern with conspicuous achievement, prestige, or leadership. Each, as an ideal type, implies that education should be directed to the formation of effective men who, through their independence, ambition, initiative, and personal strength can take a prominent role in the world. For such men, both self-respect and the ability to maintain the respect of others are essential; an important aim of their education must therefore be a sense of personal honor. But the ultimate test of their education is the ability to perform great deeds, a concern that led to an emphasis on the educational value of examples of glorious achievement in the past. This was why Greek aristocrats studied Homer, medieval knights listened to the *chansons de geste,* Rabelais included chronicles of chivalry in Gargantua's curriculum. But preparation for achievement also required practice, whether in the use of arms or, at a later stage in the development of this ideal, in more refined kinds of virtuosity. It is also obvious that the ideal was highly elitist; its essence lay in the ability to rise and to remain above other men.

But although such education was professional, the leadership for which it prepared was peculiar in that it demanded not specialized formation alone but the development of all dimensions of the personality. It called on a man to excel simultaneously in bodily strength, skill, and stamina, in vigor of personality, social gifts, reliability, and good sense. It was concerned at once with physical, moral, and social development. Chaucer's knight had learned not only the use of arms but music, which he could compose as well as play, dancing, drawing, the arts of speech, even carving at the table. In addition, the aristocratic ideal has always been unique in its careful attention to shaping and refining the erotic impulse.

Yet in its earlier stages, this ideal did not quite provide for the development of the whole man because of its neglect of, even contempt for, learning and intellect. It required a wide variety of personal skills, but it was largely indifferent both to substantive knowledge and to the value of a disciplined mind. But by the sixteenth century, the aristocratic ideal proved flexible enough to make room for literary education, increasingly important for political leadership in a more complex world. Books were needed now, especially histories, because the variety in the modern world was exceeding what a man could learn from his own experience. Thus the aristocratic ideal of the educated man as one who has *become* something was at least partly transformed into one who has *learned* something. But learning, like personal skill, was still subordinated to great achievement and retained its elitism: even this enlarged general education was exclusively for rulers. As time went on, the aristocratic prejudice against learning did not disappear; rather, it survived in the aristocrats' attitude toward universities. From the beginning they had disdained the university because it was the domain of "clerks" and not primarily concerned with forming gentlemen. And although aristocrats sometimes felt the need to attend universities, they retained a deep conviction of the difference between formal schooling and education for life in the world, an education that only the world itself could provide. Indeed, since the universities in the seventeenth and eighteenth centuries remained clerical institutions in an increasingly secular world, they were not attractive to men of talent. They could not fit any man for a life that put a premium on civilized manners, sociability, urbanity— in short, the worldly arts.

So in the eighteenth century the aristocratic ideal was transmuted once again into the conception of a person at ease in the world, whose mind was polished rather than trained, who might know very little beyond the arts of getting along, and who learned them not in the universities (which could not teach them) but in public assemblies, private clubs, and drawing rooms. Thus the aristocratic ideal grew socially more comprehensive. It seems least admirable in the degree to which it remained narrowly tied to the old aristocracy, as witness that most curious of educational documents, Lord Chesterfield's *Letters*. It is most impressive in the extent to which it permeated the ambitious bourgeoisie; its breadth and flexibility are illustrated in the English novel of manners. In the end, the ideal of the gentleman as formed by the world did not stress the dissimulation and self-seeking urged on poor Philip Stanhope, but something more like the generous civility of Tom Jones—a quality not unrelated to civilization and capable of extension to new social groups.

A rather different emphasis came out of the educational ideal of ancient scribe culture—the scribe ideal. The distinction of the scribe was his literacy, which not only differentiated him from the warrior but also elevated him above peasants and manual workers. Literacy, therefore, meant social superiority, a circumstance not irrelevant to the perennial notion that things of the mind are higher than those of the body. The literacy of the scribe associated education with books and led eventually to the notion of education as familiarity with a standard literary corpus, the classics. Hence scribe education, in contrast to aristocratic education, pointed to the need for schools, and eventually universities, which could supply bookish learning. Books also made possible the accumulation of substantive knowledge; thus scribe culture suggested that education might consist in the acquisition of a body of knowledge and that the educated man is a learned man.

Scribe education aimed to produce a human type significantly different from the aristocratic ideal. It sought to form not heroes but practical men whose ability to manage their own affairs and those of a complex society would ensure for themselves good health and long life, material prosperity, and the respect of others. Its moral ideal included such useful but equivocal virtues as prudence, calculation, and foresight, economic enterprise and thrift, vigilance and reticence. While the aristocrat displayed himself to the world, the scribe gave it wary service. But the literacy of the scribe also imposed on him the higher responsibilities of the teacher, and the wisdom books of scribe culture often transcend mere worldly wisdom to teach a lofty ideal of honesty, justice, loyalty, temperance, charity, cheerfulness, and personal stability. The educational ideal of scribe culture had, therefore, a strong ethical component, not altogether different from, but more complex and less heroic than, that of the aristocrat.

It differed, however, on one crucial point. Scribe culture is important for introducing into educational thought a primary concern with intellectual formation. The education of the scribe advanced from proficiency in the use of language to the higher arts of verbal and rational discourse, and its concentration here was in sharp contrast to aristocratic concern with the shaping of the total personality. There is, in the scribe ideal, no interest in the body or in the dramatic and aesthetic presentation of the self. For the scribe, the intellectual faculties are preeminent; all other dimensions of the personality must be subordinate to them. Only when the intellect is sovereign can man be freed from the limitations of a merely material existence or from enslavement to the bodily passions. Thus, in scribe education, concerned with the liberation of man by cultivating his "higher" mental faculties, lies the origin of the idea of the liberal arts that shape and free the mind, and hence of a liberal education. The scribe ideal is preoccupied with what can be planted in the mind, and even the scribe ethic is secondary to scribe intellectuality, in the sense that it is acquired by precept rather than by practice, from books rather than from direct experience. Thus the ideal scribe, whose duties required that he be a model of social responsibility, became an authority first on the virtues, then on virtue itself, and finally on the uses of the mind—which, as the highest faculty in man, might provide him access to the highest powers in the universe and the highest way of life. From the scribe ideal comes the attenuated idea of the educated man as philosopher and sage. The philosopher-king is thus a kind of hybridization of the aristocratic and scribe ideals.

The aristocratic and scribe ideals obviously touched each other, and the transformations of the aristocratic ideal can be understood partly as a result of their interaction. A courtier had to acquire some of the verbal skill of the scribe, and the worldly culture of the eighteenth-century gentleman exhibits some of the worldly wisdom of the more mundane kind of scribe culture. But the assimilation of the two types was never complete: central elements in the aristocratic ideal survived among the ruling groups of the West, notably its concern for great achievement and the persistent suspicion of bookishness reflected in the worry of eighteenth-century parents over sons who pursued their studies with excessive diligence and, within the memory of some of us, the idea of the gentleman C.

Both these early ideals entered into the formation of a third major conception of the educated man which has, nevertheless, some claim to discussion as a separate type—the civic ideal. The idea of the educated man as citizen appeared first in the Greek polis, reappeared in Rome and again during the Renaissance, and has remained a prominent strain in modern educational discourse. In this conception, education *civilizes* men, in the root meaning of the word. It is based on a notion of man as a political animal whose potentialities are realized in the degree to which he is effectively socialized and a participant in the life of his community. This ideal immediately appears to subordinate individual talents to collective needs and sees the educated man as one who understands and performs his social duty; the state thus becomes the essential force in education.

Aristocratic elements may be discerned in the civic ideal. It was concerned to develop the whole man, not only intellectually but physically, emotionally, and morally, for honorable achievement on behalf of the community; hence its devotion to poetry, on the ground that poetry alone could reach the deeper levels of the personality. The exploitation of aristocratic competitiveness to identify excellence also kept this educational tradition solidly elitist. At the same time the civic ideal relied heavily on literacy—first because written laws replaced imitation as the primary vehicle of instruction in civic virtue, and then because civic education depended on literature to transmit collective ideals. Hence it relied on a standard body of written classics to provide a common culture that was eventually seen as the bond uniting all civilized men, a perennial justification for a classical education. So, in this conception, education is no longer the possession of a particular professional group; it becomes, for the first time, fully identified with general culture. Yet along with its balance, the civic tradition obviously stressed the moral ends of education, an emphasis expressed in the French ideal of the *honnête homme* and the Victorian concern with character. Its educated man is first of all a good man.

But this moral emphasis generally rested on the assumption, frequently unexamined, that virtue is a function of enlightenment; it assumed that virtue can be taught because it can be planted in the mind. Hence in practice the civic ideal, like that of the scribe, gave primary attention to the development of the intellect. It regularly emphasized the importance of disciplining the mental faculties, a conception already present in the sophistic idea of the arts as purely theoretical studies that exercise the intellect and give it ineradicable powers. Thus the idea of the educated man as the man of virtue pointed to the notion of the educated man as the intellectually disciplined man. But this tradition also found a place for emphasis on the values of substantive learning. Renaissance thinkers saw learning as vicarious experience that enabled the individual to transcend the limits of his own existence and thus prepare himself for all the contingencies of life. Bacon saw learning as a source of perspective. Newman appreciated the well-stocked mind

almost as much as the well-formed mind. Such a mind, he wrote, tes-
tifying to the comprehensiveness of this ideal, "is almost prophetic from
its knowledge of history; it is almost heart-searching from its knowledge
of human nature; it has almost supernatural charity from its freedom
from littleness and prejudice; it has almost the repose of faith, because
nothing can startle it; it has almost the beauty and harmony of heavenly
contemplation, so intimate is it with the eternal order of things and the
music of the spheres." But knowledge, Newman made clear, could assume such significance only to a disciplined mind.

The social emphasis in this view of education did not, however, always
signify conformity to conventional ways of thought and behavior. This
is apparent in Bacon's emphasis on the critical powers of the trained
mind, one of whose responsibilities is to expose the fraudulent idols of
the tribe. Bacon's educated man was not only the civilized and socialized,
but also the independent man, whose mind is always "capable of growth
and reformation." Thus this conception also contains the germ of the
notion of the educated man as one who, though still working for the
benefit of society, stands apart from it in order to expose and remedy
its errors: the autonomous rational man of the Enlightenment, whose
education has freed him from the superstitions of the past, who has
indeed a duty—again we sense the moralism of the civic ideal—to oppose the collectivity when it is wrong.

The notion of such detachment of the educated man from society
suggests the possibility of his alienation from society and thus another
ideal, that of personal self-cultivation. This ideal, though it draws on
some elements in the civic ideal, severs man's bond with the social world
and makes the pursuit of individual perfection an end in itself. This ideal
has tended to emerge when an effective role in the world's affairs is
foreclosed to educated men by historical conditions, as in the hellenistic
world with the decline of the polis, during the earlier Middle Ages, and
in the later Renaissance with the loss of civic freedom. Under such
conditions, general education lost its social value, and the ideal of the
educated man was narrowed to include those human qualities, chiefly
intellectual, most appropriate to the cultivation of private excellence.
This could mean, in its more trivial modes, the formation of taste and
refinement, aesthetic and intellectual snobbery.

It could also find loftier expression. Plato suggested this in his disillusioned advice to the wise man to renounce politics and turn instead
"to the city he bears within himself" and there "to cultivate his own
garden"—the conclusion also of *Candide,* the most readable educational

novel of the eighteenth century. Education in this sense sought to produce an isolated sage who devotes himself to higher things, perhaps, because he knows the world so well, even a misanthrope. Learning here is no longer seen as a resource with which to manage the world but as a private consolation for the sufferings inflicted by the world and a means to escape from it. Thus Seneca recommended the avoidance of public affairs in favor of "sacred and sublime studies which will teach you the substance, will, environment, and shape of god, what destiny awaits your soul, where Nature lays us to rest when we are released from our bodies." He prescribed such an education as an antidote to the urgency, complexity, and confusion of life: "Everyone accelerates life's pace, and is sick with anticipation of the future and loathing of the present."

Seneca still paid tribute to the disciplined mind and to the virtue stemming from it, but now as resources for transcending the ordinary human condition. His kind of education is no longer the development of powers for use in the world, but rather of the defensive strategies of the personality to avoid contamination by it. His ethic is all control; his educated man is the man who refuses full engagement with life through a perfect *apatheia*. Such self-discipline is still intended to serve human freedom, but freedom now in an entirely private definition. Its proper use is the contemplation of the eternal verities. Liberated from all earthly bonds, the soul of the educated man "makes its way to the heights," where its freedom is at last complete.

This conception of the educated man is, of course, quintessentially elitist; Stoics of every age have taken pride in their distance from "the crowd." Here, however, the elitism is that of the scribe rather than of the aristocrat. It is likely to recur with some regularity among scholars who, although they are generally regarded, and above all regard themselves, as the custodians of education, live sequestered from men in more active careers, by whom they vaguely feel despised. There is, at any rate, a slightly familiar note in a letter of an eminent Cambridge don written in 1871: "For me it is one of the great happinesses of the happy life here that one can live with such men, not with men who are starving their minds or making their moral natures hopelessly ugly in order to be millionaires or, as the crown of their career, expectant baronets. Here, at all events, there is a true and refined republicanism; for there is no rank except what culture gives; and the society is composed of people who have foregone the pursuit of wealth or rank because they preferred prizes of another kind . . . they are bound to each other by the ties of interests which can never become slack, and which no self interest can dissolve." The author of this sentimental—and to one experienced in the ways of universities today somewhat implausible—tribute to Cambridge life was the distinguished classicist Sir Richard Jebb. If Jebb's vision of the educated man had been nourished by his knowledge of antiquity, he had evidently exploited it rather selectively.

The Christian-secular ideal, the traditional Christian conception of education, borrows from several of the ideals so far described but differs from them all in one crucial respect. This is, paradoxically, its secularity. Christian education is necessarily secular because, for the Christian, the most important capacity of man is his ability to respond to the love of God; and since this response depends on grace, it is beyond the power of education. This circumstance makes possible a way of approaching education radically different from those so far described. At the same time, the Christian view of education illuminates a dimension of the other conceptions to which we have not yet given sufficient attention. The pagan culture originally underlying these other ideals was not secular, in the sense that it sought to understand every dimension of human experience—physical nature, politics, and anthropology—within the context of a single holy and cosmic order governed throughout by a uniform set of rational principles. Thus the same patterns of order, the same subordination of low things to high things, supplied the model of perfection for the larger cosmos in which they were obviously realized, for society, and for man; and this meant that politics and human nature were seen as perfectible in the degree to which they were brought into conformity with the divine order of the cosmos. From this standpoint, education was the process of bringing man into harmony with nature by strengthening the sovereignty of his higher faculties and, ipso facto, making him harmonious within himself. In this sense, the educational ideals of antiquity were generally religious.

Christianity took issue with this notion of the sacred character of education. For the Christian, education could neither make man truly virtuous nor unite him to God, and any claims to the contrary were perilous to the soul. The heart of the Christian position was thus a distinction between the aims of education and the end of man. This explains the "almost" in Newman's celebration of knowledge and sets him somewhat apart from other champions of a liberal education. "Knowledge is one thing," Newman declared, "virtue is another; good sense is not conscience, refinement is not humility, nor is largeness and justice of view faith. Philosophy, however enlightened, however profound, gives no command over the passions, no influential motives, no vivifying principles." Here the intellectuality central to classical anthropology has given way to a different estimate of man.

Accordingly, Christian thinkers valued education, drew heavily on the resources of other patterns of education, but assigned it more limited goals. Though they denied that it could endow men with the holiness demanded by God, they recognized its capacity to civilize. They valued this lesser species of excellence, for it was both humanly convenient and pleasing to God that men who nevertheless remain sinful in the sense that they are full of potential sins should be restrained, through the internalized disciplines of a sound education, from the commission of overt sins. Christians also valued the knowledge conveyed by education, only stipulating that it must not be confused with sacred wisdom and that, in Augustine's pregnant phrase, it was used rather than enjoyed. Thus Christianity did not so much repudiate earlier ideals of education as reinterpret them along more utilitarian lines. This humility was also reflected in a more democratic understanding of education. Besides the standard subjects of a literary education, Augustine recognized the place of "teachings which concern the bodily senses, including the experience and theory of the useful mechanical arts."

In addition, the secularity of the Christian ideal was liberating. For it implied that man is not compelled to adopt an authoritative (and authoritarian) model of education imposed on him by the abstract order of things, that he is not a slave to forces outside himself but can freely choose the kind of education best suited to his needs, as he defines them for himself in the particular and concrete circumstances of his existence. Yet this existential dimension of the secular ideal has often so burdened man's resources for deciding how to use his freedom that he may be tempted to escape from it into new kinds of naturalistic determinism.

This dilemma may help to explain the emergence, since the end of the eighteenth century, of still another educational ideal: the romantic-naturalist ideal. Like the secular ideal, it differs radically from most of what has gone before, but now through the idea that the task of education is to protect and aid human nature to unfold according to its own innate principles of development. The models so far treated, however various in other respects, at least agree that the human personality is basically malleable and that the task of education is to shape it in accordance with predetermined ends. But the telos of man in the naturalistic model is no longer derived from social, ethical, or religious sources and imposed on human nature, so to speak, from the outside; it is immanent in man. Thus, while other conceptions find their justification and explanation in history and anthropology, in ethical and social philosophy, or in cosmology and theology, this model looks to biology, developmental psychology, and learning theory. Its ruling principle is not some ideal of the mature person but the nature of the child.

A mark of this conception is that it seeks to restrain the teacher from interfering with the development of his pupils: he is not to beat them, an injunction with more than humanitarian significance, in order to shape them to his own preconceptions, but to encourage them by gentleness and understanding. They are to enjoy education because education, properly constructed, should be consistent with the obvious needs of their own natures. Nor, in this conception, does the teacher decide which human faculties to develop or in what order. Every capacity for personal development is seen as equally worthy of encouragement, since each is by definition natural. And each unfolds in a natural order in which—another significant feature of the conception—the rational powers are last to emerge; that is why Rousseau's Émile did not learn to read until early adolescence. In this ideal, intellectual development is secondary—not only in its order in the curriculum of nature but also in the values it represents—to the perfection of the body, the life of the senses, the feelings, the imagination, and adjustment to all the circumstances of daily life. At the same time, there is more room for individuality, since reason is a common possession of men while their other potentialities tend to differentiate men from one another. In important respects, therefore, this model suggests a less social idea of man, although, by its indiscriminateness and its lack of objective norms, it is also singularly democratic.

Meanwhile, the idea of an educated man has also been deeply affected by the "knowledge revolution," out of which has emerged the conception of education as preparation for research. As long as knowledge was limited, relatively simple, and not very technical, education could be fairly eclectic. Although it regularly emphasized the formation of character, it could attempt at the same time to discipline the mental faculties, provide a common culture, and supply a minimum of substantive knowledge. Yet obviously the sheer bulk of the knowledge now deemed necessary for an educated man has squeezed out of education—and for the most part even out of our understanding of it—everything but the acquisition of knowledge in some manageable form. One result has been a broad decline in the idea of a general education, which for all practical purposes has become little more than a nostalgic memory. Indeed the body of requisite knowledge has become so vast that no one can hope to master more than a small segment of it. So, in the popular mind, an educated man is now some kind of specialist; and in a sense we no longer have a single conception of the educated man, but as many conceptions as there are learned specialties.

Yet even in this situation, which seems to preclude a common educational ideal for man, we may discern a development somewhat analogous to the evolution of the aristocratic and scribe models. The need for knowledge, and above all for new knowledge, seems to be pointing to the formation of still another ideal. For the proliferating new specialties have at least this in common: that all are supposed to expand indefinitely through research; and a new conception of the educated man seems to be emerging precisely from this circumstance. It is closely related to the changing conception of the university, whose primary task is certainly no longer the formation of virtuous men nor the study of inherited learning, but the discovery of new knowledge. In this context, an educated man is above all a man who is open to new knowledge and able to advance it.

Once again what immediately presents itself as only the narrowing of education into specialized training for the scholar, and more specifically the scientist (the scientific conception of scholarship having invaded, with mixed results, even the humanities), points to a modification in the idea of the man best suited to the broader service of a changing society. Training in research is thus perceived as a moral force, as forming men who are bold, critical, imaginative, industrious, innovative, independent, and active. Whether these qualities are all the world now requires is, of course, a question worth serious consideration; nor is it certain that the virtues of the laboratory are readily transferable to other aspects of life. And in any case, although the research ideal clearly fits some of our needs, it leaves unanswered the question what we are to do with all our new knowledge. In this respect the research ideal, like the Christian, is fully secular.

The foregoing analysis may be of some interest to the historian of Western culture; but it remains to ask what, practically, we are to do with it. In earlier periods, history was conceived as a body of examples to be imitated or abhorred in the critical decisions of life, and therefore essential to any educated man. But it is obvious that we cannot exploit history in this way. We cannot choose for ourselves the most attractive among past educational ideals, if only because each was firmly embedded in its own time. Yet the relativity of each ideal to its historical context may suggest at least one "lesson of history": that any fruitful reflection about the purposes of education must now begin with a definition of our own social and cultural condition. We shall need to ask not only what our world is like and what it needs but such fundamental questions as whether it is sufficiently consolidated to permit the formulation of any single educational ideal, whether it is likely to be, or (perhaps the hardest of all) whether we really want it to be.

But the relativity of education to its time has a further implication. It suggests the impossibility of establishing any educational ideal on the cosmic principles that infused some of the most attractive among the ideals of the past. Whether we like it or not, we are, at least for the time being, restricted to a secular conception of education, with all the burdens of choice this implies. Even the naturalistic ideal cannot, I believe, relieve us of the burdens of freedom—partly because the supposed orthodoxies of science, especially when applied to man, have generally proved no more stable than other dimensions of thought and just as dependent on cultural change; partly because the very importance of education for the needs of society means that we cannot allow it simply to happen but must continue to define its aims in accordance with changing collective needs.

The rich accumulation of ideals I have here described may also help to illuminate our educational predicament in another way. I suspect that few of us can review these alternatives without the sense that each of them expresses some part of his own deepest assumptions on the matter. For, however little practical influence some of them now exert, all of them linger on in some part of our minds, obscurely clashing with one another and variously challenging, accusing, and confusing us. This suggests that we face a problem not altogether new but now aggravated beyond anything known before: that we have inherited too much and from too many directions to be able to manage our cultural resources. Thus we now have no classics because we have too many classics. To pose our problem in its starkest and most dismal terms, how can an educational ideal bring into focus a culture that Joyce compared to the scattered debris on the field of Waterloo and that only achieved coherence in his peculiar artistic vision? Unlike antiquity, which had the practical advantage of knowing culture but not cultures, in our age we have effectively lost the ability to recognize a barbarian when we meet him. Or if some apprehension of this kind crosses our minds, we may try, with a vague sense of guilt, to repress it. On the other hand, the cultural relativism that is now probably an ineradicable element in our world may itself, in ways I cannot altogether foresee, provide some positive foundation for an educational ideal. It has, at any rate, some ethical content, as our guilt at being repelled by those unlike ourselves may imply. It suggests respect for variety and humility about ourselves, and it may lead us in the direction of an open and pluralistic ideal of education. Whether such an education is likely to meet other contemporary needs, such as the need for a minimal sense of community in a large and complex modern society, is of course another, and very large, question.

But perhaps the educational ideals of the past can also be instructive in less portentous ways. They can, in any event, tell us something about how conceptions of education come into existence, how they are related to social and political realities, what requirements a viable educational ideal must meet, and the kinds of assumptions on which it is based. It is evident that the needs of societies for particular kinds of trained persons have been decisive in the development of education and even of ideas about general education. Such needs obviously differ according to whether a society is primitive or advanced, warlike or peaceful, agrarian, commercial, or industrial. Moreover, the specialized training required by specific needs displays a regular tendency to assume a more general significance, and the idealization of a professional type has commonly evolved into an ideal for man in general. Past experience suggests, therefore, that the familiar antithesis between specialized and general education is somewhat misleading. The larger significance of social need for education is also evident if we look at the problem from the standpoint of the individual. The emphasis then shifts from the kind of man needed by society to the kind of education needed by man for survival in society, and this too is likely to suggest something more than a narrowly vocational training.

Along with social need, we may identify another set of variables that has proved crucial to defining the purposes of education. In that process, much has regularly depended on how the human personality is perceived, though this generally remains an unexamined assumption underlying educational discourse; the anthropological presuppositions of a culture are perhaps the least likely elements in it to receive critical scrutiny. Obviously, however, men's notions of what education can or should accomplish depend on the degree to which they consider human nature malleable and in which of its dimensions; on their analysis of the human organism and the value attributed to its various potentialities; and, again, on whether they perceive man as autonomous, unique, and free to determine his own ends or as part of a larger system of reality—metaphysical, cosmological, or biological—that determines objectively the proper shape and direction of human development. Some of the superficiality in educational discussion stems from failure to recognize issues of this kind. And since we can generally identify the assumptions of another age more readily than those of our own, reflection on earlier conceptions of education may provide some training in the critical scrutiny of our own anthropological preconceptions.

But here a word of caution about the literature of education: it has been notoriously optimistic. Doubtless because most of it is composed by pedagogues, it has usually stressed the malleability of human nature. One suspects that much of its enthusiasm (especially when it comes from experienced teachers) is chiefly hortatory, or exaggerated for strategic reasons. Still, recent expressions of outrage over the views of Jensen, Herrnstein, et al. suggest (among other issues in this controversy) the degree to which confidence in the power of nurture over nature has become a piece of orthodoxy that cannot be challenged without considerable personal risk. But although writers on education often sound as if they consider each individual a tabula rasa on which the educator may imprint whatever messages he wishes, it is also worth observing that such enthusiasm has not, historically, been a necessary condition for taking education seriously.

Past experience appears to suggest, then, that any satisfactory educational ideal for our own time must be appropriate to our kind of society and government. If we are to reach agreement about education, we must first agree about the nature of our social and political arrangements, taking into account both their structure and their capacity for change. In addition, an appropriate educational ideal must have some correspondence to our understanding of human nature, its limitations and its possibilities: what it is, what it can be, what it ought to be. These are hard, perhaps impossible, questions. But until they are answered I cannot foresee any solution to our difficulties.

One further troubling question needs to be raised here: the value and practical significance of deliberate efforts to formulate an educational ideal. This is, finally, the knotty question of the relation between social theory and social reality, of the place of ideas in history and of the function of the intellectual. I am far more comfortable in raising this question than in trying to answer it. Accordingly, I should like to state it more specifically as well as historically: what has been the relationship between those who have thought most constructively about education in the past and the time and place in which they existed? Are we to understand their reflections about education as descriptive, or prescriptive, or in some way both at once? It may be that no single answer will cover every case and that, like political theory, educational theory is sometimes largely descriptive in a normative sense, sometimes largely prescriptive and idealistic. But it seems to me in general that the educational proposals in the past which have proved most influential have chiefly put into words the values and convictions already implicit, if not in educational practice, at least in the more vigorous cultural movements of their times. Thus the role of the educational theorist may be somewhat like that of a statesman: not so much to create a new ideal for education as to sense what is already present in a latent form. His greatest talent, aside from his articulateness, is his ability to perceive with skill and sensitivity the changing needs of his time; thus he expresses, clarifies, and consolidates perceptions that have remained, for others, still below the level of consciousness. But the ability to do this well, like the ability to manage the tangled affairs of states, requires talent of the highest order.

18   Socrates and the
        Confusion of
        the Humanities

This essay owes its existence to my membership, during the academic year 1976–1977, in the National Humanities Institute, funded by the National Endowment for the Humanities, in New Haven. Under the leadership of Robert E. Hiedemann, a number of us who had been fellows at the institute contributed essays on appropriate topics to a volume dedicated to Maynard Mack, its distinguished director. My essay, included here, was a slightly tongue-in-cheek reaction to a certain preciousness about the humanities that I sensed in some of my colleagues. The volume in which it appeared was entitled The American Future and the Humane Tradition: The Role of the Humanities in Higher Education, *ed. Robert E. Hiedemann (New York: Associated Faculties Press, 1982), pp. 11–22. It is reprinted here with the permission of the publisher.*

· · ·

The impression that the humanities are now in special trouble—perhaps even, as we sometimes say, in a "crisis"—is widespread among teachers in the traditional humanistic disciplines, and it is doubtless true that we have immediate grounds for concern. After a period of remarkable expansion and exuberance in higher education, when there were students enough for us all, enrollments are declining; and students, worried about the future, seem to be drifting into programs better designed to prepare them for jobs than anything we have to offer. This essay is directed, however, not to this immediately distressing situation, but to more fundamental problems in the humanities that, indeed, our present difficulties may have inclined us to forget. For these difficulties have encouraged us to look without and to deplore the times, when our basic problems—as we knew better in the period of our prosperity—were in ourselves. The present situation may therefore be unfortunate for the

385

humanities above all because it has tended to diminish our perspective. It encourages us to imagine in the past some kind of Golden Age, or series of Golden Ages—fifth-century Athens, the Augustan age, the twelfth century, the age of the Renaissance, the nineteenth century, now perhaps even the happy decades after the war—when the humanities were properly appreciated.

Such nostalgia is hardly supported by what we know of the humanities in the past; as nearly as I have been able to determine, teachers and scholars in the humanities have always felt defensive and insufficiently valued. In the nineteenth century, when everybody who was anybody received a classical education—the touchstone of the humanities in the past—Matthew Arnold was apprehensive about the spread of Philistinism. Renaissance humanists felt much the same. So Petrarch exclaimed of his own time, "Oh inglorious age, that scorns antiquity its mother, to whom it owes every noble art—that dares to declare itself not only equal but superior to the glorious past!"; and his followers continued in this vein for the next two centuries, not realizing that they were living in the Renaissance. We hear the same sad complaint in the greatest humanist of the twelfth century, John of Salisbury, who imagined himself besieged by a new horde of barbarians. "What is the old fool after?" he imagined them asking of himself; "Why does he quote the sayings and doings of the ancients to us? We draw knowledge from ourselves; we, the young, do not recognize the ancients." It may even be possible to read a hint of the perennial unpopularity of the humanities into the tragic fate of Socrates, though his case, as I will try to show, is more problematic.

What this appears to suggest is that, in thinking about the plight of the humanities, we are confronted with some chronic disease that is far more important to diagnose than any acute illness that may have developed during the last decade. It is this deep-seated and perennially debilitating malaise that I will try to identify here. To do so, I will begin by setting side by side two important features of the long history of the humanities. One has to do with the origin of humanistic education among the Greeks, as historians now understand it. The other involves the veneration for Socrates, and for what he supposedly stood for, in a series of writers, most of them prominent in the long tradition of humanistic discourse. The juxtaposition of these matters is intended to throw into relief a deep and persistent ambiguity in the humanities that seems to me to have confused us about both our role and our public. We would like to believe that we have something of supreme value, perhaps even a kind of saving grace, to offer to a world in desperate need of redemption. But the world has seemed oddly indifferent to this gracious offering, with the result that we who represent the humanities have for centuries felt unappreciated, frustrated, sometimes even aggrieved.

Underlying this unhappiness is a deep-seated ambivalence about the significance of the humanities. Here the early history of education in the humanities is instructive. It appears to have emerged out of the ancient rivalry between philosophy, with its rational pursuit of ultimate truth, and rhetoric, which assumed that this quest was hopeless and was prepared to make the best of the sensible, contingent, and shifting world of appearances. This opposition was the analogue, in antiquity, of the familiar tension between the two cultures of our own time, with philosophy then corresponding to natural science now. And the crucial point here is that education in the humanities stems not from the position represented by Socrates (unless Plato has quite misled us about this great figure), but from his antagonists, the Sophists, among whom Protagoras was probably the most influential, as he is for us the most vivid, individual personality.

An immediate implication of this glimpse at our origins might be that the inclusion of philosophy among the humanities today, insofar as philosophy is still conceived as the rational pursuit of final truth, itself reflects some confusion about the humanities. It also suggests that, if we are to understand the humanities as the expression of some coherent tradition, we ought to think very seriously about what Protagoras stood for. Basic to his position seems to have been a thorough skepticism about the possibility, for human beings, of what for Plato (and presumably for Socrates) constituted genuine knowledge. For Protagoras, the human mind is confined to the subjective and transitory realm of appearances; it cannot penetrate through or beyond them to a realm of objective and immutable (i.e., scientific) truth, notably to such truth about the human condition; the mind is confined to the human world of probability and convention. This is the significance of Protagoras's famous dictum, so unacceptable to Socrates and to all who have yearned for transcendence, that man is the measure of all things. Protagoras was agnostic. Diogenes Laertius attributed to him this saying: "About the gods I have no knowledge whether they exist or do not exist. There are many obstacles to such knowledge, for instance, the obscurity of the subject and the shortness of human life." This meant that, for Protagoras, education could not consist in the encouragement or transmission of what, for philosophers, was true wisdom, but only in the formation of useful or probable opinion; he had nothing to offer in the way of salvation. And although his educational objectives were to be met by the effective use of language, he conceived of language not as an access to objective reality (as Socrates suggests that it ought to be in the *Cratylus*) but simply as a conventional instrument for human communication, derived not from *physis* but from *nomos*. The Sophists were, in this tradition, rhetoricians, with close ties to those arts that rely on language to create a variety of human worlds: to legal and political discourse, but also to historical and dramatic composition, and notably to poetry, the art especially distrusted by Socrates.

And in the culture of antiquity it was not philosophy that triumphed, but rhetoric. For a thousand years rhetoric dominated education, subordinating systematic rationality to the arts of language, and relying for this purpose on a corpus of received texts esteemed for what they could convey through language. Rhetoric, not philosophy, gave us the humanities. The position represented by Protagoras was further developed by Gorgias and other rhetoricians, converted into a more systematic pedagogy by Isocrates, transmitted to Rome by Greek teachers of rhetoric, and assimilated by the Latin orators. Only in the later hellenistic period, with the triumph of an increasingly authoritarian empire, did philosophy begin to develop any general prestige among educated men, for whom it represented solace in a situation in which public communication, and accordingly the rhetorical art, had reduced value; and the notion that philosophy was concerned with higher and better things than this world can afford also proved attractive to some Christians, who saw in it an opportunity to emerge from their long cultural isolation. But although a considerable revival of philosophy, and of dialectic as its primary instrument, took place in medieval Christendom, and rhetoric endured a corresponding decline, the ancient tradition of education in the humanities was periodically rediscovered. With the Renaissance it again became a dominant force in education, until it began to falter once more in the later nineteenth century. Or, more precisely, it dominated the education of the upper classes, a qualification that may have some bearing on the curious place of Socrates in the post-classical career of the humanities.

For meanwhile something quite odd had occurred. Protagoras, the figure with the best claim to be considered as the founding father of education in the humanities, has either been forgotten in this connection or transformed into some kind of enemy of true learning, even for those who owe him most: and "sophist" has become a term of opprobrium. On the other hand Socrates, the foe of Protagoras, has been metamorphosed into the model and patron saint—*Sancte Socrate, ora pro nobis*—of the whole humanistic enterprise. Given the circumstances I have described, however, it is hardly surprising that he has been a singularly ambiguous model and that what he has chiefly sanctified has been a vast confusion about the significance of the humanities.

This has not been, on the whole, the fault of professional philosophers. Thus there is nothing ambiguous in the account of Socrates given by Aristotle, who perceived him strictly as a philosopher. "Socrates," Aristotle said, "concentrated on ethics and not on external nature, though in ethics he sought the universal and was the first to set his mind to definitions." This seems to mean that Socrates adopted—but also refined—the rational methods that philosophers had previously employed in speculating about external nature, and that he redirected them to the investigation of human nature. Thus his importance consists in the fact that he pursued the old philosophical quest, with its assumption of an ultimate truth awaiting discovery by human reason, in a new area of inquiry. It also seems clear that, by this interpretation, Socrates would be difficult to transform into a model for the humanities. He remains, in Aristotle's presentation, a philosopher and, in the context of ancient thought, a scientist, albeit an ethical scientist.

The improbable transformation of Socrates into a model for the humanities seems to have been a result of the observation, which was correct, that Socrates was concerned with ethics, while at the same time it was forgotten that he did so *as a philosopher,* in the ancient meaning of that term. The result was to assimilate into humanistic learning, inadvertently, the philosophical pursuit of final truth; and because ethics was thought vital to salvation, the humanities were transformed from a body of discourse concerned with the best possible adaptation to a merely human world, into a set of disciplines claiming access to some kind of ultimate wisdom, with a bearing on the final destiny of man.

The transformation began early; Socrates was celebrated in antiquity itself for having shifted the attention of philosophy from cosmology to ethics and, in this sense, from heaven to earth. In this way, it was supposed, he had made it relevant to the human situation. Thus for Diogenes Laertius, Socrates was "the first person who conversed about human life, [for], perceiving that natural philosophy had no immediate bearing on our interests, he began to enter upon moral speculations, both in his workshop and in the marketplace." Augustine transmitted this estimate, giving a Neoplatonic interpretation to Socrates' motives: he had recognized that ethical study purifies the mind and thus prepares it for the contemplation of eternal truth. Medieval thinkers, John of Salisbury included, venerated Socrates on this basis, and this estimate of Socrates became the orthodoxy of the Renaissance. Savonarola and

Erasmus shared it; and Vives notably pressed Socrates into the battle of the two cultures: "Since he was the wisest of all mortals, he did not hesitate to proclaim his ignorance of the things of nature; he preferred to encourage men to give up the study of those mysteries and apply the same energies to the reformation of their moral life." But the point here was always, not simply that Socrates had shifted philosophy from heaven to earth, a notion possibly consistent with the Sophistic origin of the humanities, but that the heavenly insights of philosophy had, through Socrates, been given a terrestrial application. Socrates brought philosophy down from heaven, but this meant that he had obtained it in heaven.

Furthermore it was generally believed that, from the profundity of Socrates' ethical thought, it necessarily followed that he had been the best of men; his life demonstrated that to know the good is to do the good, and more broadly the competence of philosophy—again in the ancient sense—to rule over human affairs. Epictetus made the connection between Socrates' thought and his life explicit: "Thus Socrates became perfect, improving himself by everything, following reason alone." Montaigne described the soul of Socrates as "the most perfect that has come to my knowledge." Rousseau praised him for his practical virtues; for Hegel he was the model as well as the founder of morality; Mill thought him "the man who probably of all then born had deserved best of all mankind." Even Nietzsche, whose understanding of the moral life was somewhat different, hoped that "if all goes well, the time will come when, to develop oneself morally-rationally, one will take up the memorabilia of Socrates rather than the Bible." What Nietzsche most admired in Socrates was his capacity for "joy in life and in one's own self." His Socrates was distinguished by "the gay kind of seriousness and that *wisdom full of pranks* which constitutes the best state of the soul of man." All of this seems to imply, however goodness is defined, the ability of an education in the humanities to make men good.

But although Nietzsche contrasted Socrates with Jesus ("Moreover, he had the greater intelligence"), it has been more common to identify the two, especially by those who have wanted to claim for Christianity the status of a higher philosophical wisdom and to equate such wisdom with sanctity. Justin Martyr proclaimed that Christ had been "known in part even by Socrates." Aeneas Sylvius—later pope—believed that "the doctrine of the life of the world to come" had been taught by Socrates; Ficino thought that the self-renunciation of Socrates had foreshadowed Christ; Zwingli included Socrates among the virtuous pagans in Paradise; Rousseau maintained that Socrates had worked for the glory of God and the Christian church. On the other hand still another view associated Socrates with the civic tradition. Diogenes Laertius thought him "very much attached to democracy," and Vives represented him as "the first who applied philosophy to the service of people and cities." But the notion of a civic Socrates was vigorously rejected by Kierkegaard, for whom Socrates was wholly indifferent either to being, or to making anyone else, a good citizen; for Kierkegaard the Socratic ethic was strictly individual.

Interpretations of the Socratic method, and above all of the motives behind it, have been equally diverse. Socrates' protestations of his own ignorance were taken at face value by some of his earliest admirers, for whom he was simply a humble seeker after a truth he did not himself possess, but which he nevertheless hoped to attain. So, for Diogenes Laertius, "in an argumentative spirit [Socrates] used to dispute with all who would converse with him, not with the purpose of taking away their opinions from them, so much as of learning the truth, as far as he could do so, himself." It was in this spirit—the positive spirit of classical philosophy—that the Socratic dialogue, if it was noticed at all, tended to be understood. Aeneas Sylvius claimed to discern its influence in, of all places, the debates among the theologians at the Council of Basel, who "held a long discussion, some maintaining the negative, some the positive view, knowing that this was the old Socratic method of arguing against another's opinion. For Socrates thought that in this way what was closest to the truth could most easily be discovered." John Ponet represented his own *Short Catechisme* as an application of Socratic method, through which, "by certain questions, as it were by pointing, the ignorant might be instructed, and the skilful put in remembrance, that they forget not what they have learned." According to this common view, the Socratic method is a positive strategy for discovering an objective and impersonal truth.

Others, perhaps truer to the posture if not to the declamatory style of Protagoras, have been less sure of the innocence of Socrates. In early Christian thought he could also be seen as an aggressive agnostic, preparing for the Gospel by displaying the pretentious folly of paganism and, by implication, of classical philosophy. Augustine believed that he had "hunted out and pursued the foolishness of ignorant men who thought they knew this or that—sometimes confessing his own ignorance, and sometimes dissimulating his knowledge." For Augustine, Socrates had discovered and taught nothing positive, even in ethics; this explained, for him, the radical disagreements among those who claimed to be his disciples, and confirmed Augustine's mature view of philosophy as "the city of confusion." This vision of Socrates as a deliberately destructive critic of all facile belief was revived in the Enlightenment, in a rather different interest, by Diderot, who posed as a potential martyr in the cause of atheism and free expression and identified himself closely with Socrates, who "at the moment of his death was looked upon at Athens as we are now looked upon at Paris; . . . he was at the very least a turbulent and dangerous spirit who dared to speak freely of the gods." And Kierkegaard, contrasting Socrates sharply with Plato on the basis of a distinction between "questioning in order to discover content and questioning in order to disappoint and humiliate," compared him to Samson: he "seizes the columns bearing the edifice of knowledge and plunges everything down into the nothingness of ignorance." Nietzsche may have had something similar in mind in describing Socrates as "not only the wisest talker who ever lived" but also "just as great in his silence." There is strange company here; but whatever the historical accuracy of this vision of Socrates, it suggests something closer than anything else we have examined to the original inspiration of education in the humanities.

This rapid survey leads to various reflections, all somewhat disheartening. One is that the invocation of Socrates inevitably results either in the distortion of Socrates to bring him into conformity with our notion of the humanities, or in the distortion of the humanities to make them conform to our image of Socrates. The first would imply indifference to history, the second a betrayal of what gave the humanities, at the outset, their specific identity. The second would seem to be more serious, from the standpoint of the humanities, and raises a question of motive, or at least function, for it seems to me not enough to say that the ambiguous portrait of Socrates in Plato has misled us; consciously or unconsciously, we have made choices. I would suggest that, except for the last group noticed above, whose reading of history may not be altogether plausible, Socrates has been invoked by teachers in the humanities because of their discontent with the humble status assigned them by Protagoras, in a world in which "philosophy," because of the sublimity of its concerns and the certainties to which it laid claim, had become—as for some it remains—a word to conjure with. The patronage of Socrates has allowed them—and us—to cherish the humanities and at the same time to lay claim to a wisdom infinitely more prestigious than anything in the more mundane tradition of Protagoras.

For, underlying the remarkable diversity among our conceptions of Socrates, one common impulse can be discerned: the belief that, as the Delphic Oracle was reported to have said of Socrates, he was "of all mortals the wisest." Each vision of Socrates represents one interpretation or another of what it means to be wise. The model of Socrates allows us, therefore, to avoid that radical choice between the authoritative wisdom claimed for classical philosophy and the humbler, more tentative, and practical insights, appropriate to the merely human condition, that gave birth to the humanities. Socrates enables us to have it both ways. And this seems to me unusually dangerous in the world we presently inhabit, a world that has either ceased to believe in wisdom—as a good deal in contemporary philosophy suggests—or has good reason to distrust any human claims to wisdom. The humanities, in the tradition of Protagoras, seem to me to have abiding value; but claims to the wisdom of Socrates, who "sought the universal," only reduce our credibility and justify the indifference of contemporaries. I do not mean to suggest that all teachers in the humanities are haunted in this way by the ghost of Socrates; and even for those who are, any claim to wisdom is likely to be subliminal and in any event now too embarrassing to be pressed. But there is abundant evidence of the importance of this claim among our predecessors; and, perhaps because I can still sense its numinous charm in myself, I am persuaded of its continuing and seductive power.

The basic problem here is that the admirable but ambiguous Socrates encourages us to cling obscurely to a conception of man, embedded in ancient philosophy, that few of us, on a conscious level, can now accept. In this view the various agencies of the human personality are distinguished as real entities and regarded as higher or better and lower or worse, with the clear implication that the higher should rule the lower. This higher faculty is variously identified with reason or the soul, and contrasted with the body and the passions. It is also seen as the spark of divinity within, and therefore man's point of contact with a realm of higher and eternal truths and values. This conception was often associated with man's upright stature, which made him unique among animals. Cicero's Stoic gave this notion classic expression; providence, he explained, raised men "to stand tall and upright, so that they might be able to behold the sky and so gain a knowledge of the gods. For men are sprung from the earth not as its inhabitants and denizens, but to be as it were the spectators of things supernal and heavenly, in the contemplation whereof no other species of animals participates." With the intrusion of philosophy into the humanities, this conception became the essence of *humanitas;* the task of the humanities was henceforth to assist man in developing his potentialities for the contemplation of higher things, and the coordination of lower things, notably his own faculties, in accordance with his heavenly vision. And it seems to me that this notion of man, however detached from its pagan theological context, persists among us, with its implication that, in their concern with higher things, the humanities can somehow finally save mankind from whatever dismal fate might otherwise await it.

Yet here we are also divided against ourselves. For in our world the human personality is understood as a mysterious psychosomatic unity in which the classical distinction between its higher and lower faculties— a distinction that Socrates presumably endorsed—has lost all meaning. That remarkable modern humanist Sigmund Freud, indeed, fixed on the erect posture of man as precisely the mark of his fall from primordial bliss; it signified the schism of the personality, the perverse separation of *humanitas* into an honorable portion above the waist and a shameful region below, which brought not salvation but neurosis and despair. Yet the claims of the humanities to a privileged position in education seem to me still to rest, for many of us, on this traditional understanding of man. The notion of man as divided into higher and lower elements is the basis of a persistent belief that the humanities are concerned with higher things, with perhaps a hint of contempt for the ordinary concerns of daily life; and in our world this is only too likely to reinforce the prejudice against the humanities as precious and impractical, at best concerned with the improvement of leisure and the provision of social distinction.

This anthropology is also, therefore, the vehicle of an implicit elitism that lingers on in the humanities and continues to make them seem of doubtful relevance to the tasks of mass education with which most of us are confronted. For just as the humanities, in their admixture with the attitudes of classical philosophy, have distinguished between the higher matters of their own concern and the lower preoccupations of ordinary life, so they have traditionally distinguished between the higher men for whom they are appropriate and those lower beings to whom they must remain inaccessible, however much we may aspire to "raise" the barbarians in our midst, through instruction in the humanities, to a higher and more human level of existence. This aspiration is itself, of course, unexceptionable; I only mean to suggest the possibility, by describing it in such language, that the social attitudes embedded in the philosophical tradition that Socrates represents among us (however democratic he may sometimes appear) may interfere with our task in a very different setting.

But there is a further problem for us in the latent influence of philosophy represented among us by Socrates: its authoritarianism. If human culture is a body of sublime insights derived by man's higher faculties from the heavens above, then its values must apply equally to all men in all times. This conception of what we have to offer puts us in the position of a kind of (not altogether secular) priesthood, but in addition it implies that other men have an obligation to attend to our teaching. This is perhaps why we sometimes feel aggrieved that they remain so indifferent and refractory. And this is all the harder to bear since, because we too are inhabitants of the modern world, we can neither express nor defend this discontent. In another part of ourselves, we know that it is no longer possible, indeed that it would hardly be desirable, to promote the notion of a single high Culture; consciously we now recognize only cultures in the plural. We know only that the human world is fascinatingly diverse and that we can discern in it, or impose on it, many meanings, but no longer—at least as responsible teachers—a single Meaning. But Socrates, except perhaps in the ahistorical vision of an Augustine or a Kierkegaard, justifies our yearning for something more.

I do not mean to suggest that this yearning much affects what presently goes on in our programs in the humanities, though I suspect that it inhibits our respect for a good deal of what we feel compelled to do; and indeed Socrates may be so protean a figure that we could exploit him—though this is not commonly done—to sanction even our current activities. This is suggested by the hodgepodge of ancient reports about the philosopher thrown together by Diogenes Laertius. This writer, who happily did not himself claim to be very wise, noted among other matters the fame of Socrates as a usurer and bigamist, his mysterious immunity from the plague, his devotion to physical fitness, and his reputation for valor, most of which would appear to have only marginal significance for the humanities. But Diogenes also tells us that Socrates was devoted to the performing arts. He was a distinguished sculptor, and in addition he played the lyre and "used frequently to dance." A talented poet, he helped Euripides write plays. He was also a sharp literary critic; he "used to pull to pieces" the work of other poets, with such devastating effect that he drove Meletus, an aggrieved poet, to join the prosecution at his trial. And finally he was himself a clever rhetorician, "a man of great ability, both in exhorting men to, and dissuading them from, any course . . . very ingenious at deriving arguments from existing circumstances": in short, much like Protagoras. I realize that the suggestion that we might appeal to Socrates in support even of what we are now doing is likely to seem absurd, but this sense of its absurdity might also obliquely confirm the fact of our discontent with the humbler tasks that have now fallen to our lot.

For, as I have tried to suggest in this essay, the real significance of our persistent devotion to the model of Socrates is that he helps us to evade the radical choice between the lofty responsibilities that classical philosophy aspired to fulfill and those more human tasks that the humanities can effectively perform. It is in this sense that I think it *is* appropriate to speak of a "crisis" in the humanities, for this word literally signifies a crossroads, where a decision must be made. This crisis is not a product of the recent past; we have been standing, immobile, at this crossroads for nearly two thousand years. But such a decision, as I have also tried to show, would not require the repudiation of the treasures of antiquity, though it might compel us to view some of them in a rather different light; for the culture of antiquity—and this is also at the heart of the problem—was far more diverse than many of us now commonly recognize. The decision would compel us, instead, to treat the resources of antiquity with greater discrimination. Indeed, it would require us to follow antiquity in a choice that, unlike us, it was prepared to make. Such a choice would enable us, I believe, to speak with greater inner confidence, and therefore greater effect, to our contemporaries.

19 Christian Adulthood

An issue of Daedalus *is often preceded by intensive discussion in preliminary conferences, out of which specific assignments emerge for dealing with a proposed topic. In 1974 such a conference was held, presided over by Erik Erikson, to discuss comparative models of human adulthood. Because I took exception to remarks at this conference about the significance of Christianity in this context, I was assigned to prepare an essay on the subject. Reactions to my essay have sometimes been surprising. One commentator described it as "a classic of gerontology." Reprinted by permission of* Daedalus, *Journal of the American Academy of Arts and Sciences, "Adulthood," 105, no. 2 (Spring 1976), 77–92.*

• • • •

The elasticity of Christianity, as it has accommodated itself to two thousand years of cultural change, is well known; and it poses special problems for the identification of a peculiarly "Christian" conception of what it means to be an adult. It is also likely to make any attempt at such definition seem arbitrary. I shall nevertheless try to show in this essay that Christianity does contain a characteristic conception of healthy human maturity, but to do so it will be necessary to distinguish between what I shall call *historical* and *normative* Christianity. Historical Christianity reflects the composite of those cultural impulses that make up what is commonly thought of as Christian civilization; much of it is not specifically Christian, although it constitutes a large part of what has been believed by Christians. Its conception of "adulthood" is often an eclectic mixture of somewhat contrary impulses, and it is likely to be unstable. But normative Christianity is an ideal type. It is normative in the sense that it builds on and is consistent with those biblical norms

397

about human nature and human destiny that give to Christianity whatever precise identity it may possess. It is also, therefore, heavily indebted to Judaism. It is not ahistorical, but it can rarely be found in a pure form. Its conception of adulthood can be stated with some coherence.

The conception of maturity in historical Christianity can be further described as a mixture of two quite different notions, which I shall call the idea of *manhood* and the idea of *adulthood*. The significance of this second distinction may be suggested by the differing etymologies of the two terms. The Germanic *man* is considered by most linguists to be derived from an Indo-European verb meaning "to think" (cf. the Latin *mens*); it thus refers to a supposedly qualitative difference between human beings and other animals, and "manhood" would thus imply entrance into a fully rational existence. But *adult* comes from the Latin *adolescere*, "to grow up." It is (or can be) neutral about the nature of growth; it implies a process rather than the possession of a particular status or specific faculty. The two terms, which are often confused in our culture, can also be taken to represent the two major but contrasting impulses in the Western tradition. *Adulthood*, as I will use it here, is related to the anthropology of the Bible; and its suggestion of process hints at the distinctively dynamic qualities of the Hebrew language.[1] But *manhood* is a creation of classical antiquity, and it reflects the need of classical culture to organize all experience in terms of absolute, static, and qualitative categories.

The idea of manhood is elaborated in the classical formulations of *paideia* or *humanitas,* which pointed, for the Greek and Latin educational traditions, to the peculiar excellence of the human species. Unlike adulthood, manhood tends, with rare exceptions, to be sexually specific, and thus it is one source of the tendency to deny full maturity to women.[2] It also differs from adulthood in its rejection of individuality, and it is oriented to the goal rather than the processes of human development. We can see this in the relative indifference of classical humanism to the psychology of the child and its significance for the formation of the man.[3] Childhood, in this conception, was conceived not as the positive foundation of maturity but as formlessness or chaos, and manhood was the result of the imposition on this refractory matter, by education, of an ideal form. With the achievement of manhood, childhood was decisively and happily left behind.

Embedded in this conception were both the metaphysical distinction between form and substance, with its hints of anthropological dualism, and a characteristic distinction, within man, among the several elements of the human personality: soul and body, or reason, will, and passion.

These were seen not merely as analytical devices but as real, qualitative distinctions corresponding to distinctions in the structure of all reality. Similarly, childhood and manhood had to be qualitatively distinct; they could not coincide, for insofar as a human being was still a child he could not be a man. Here we may discern the characteristic resistance of ancient rationalism to ambiguity and paradox.

In this view, some of man's faculties were also ontologically superior and sovereign, others inferior, dangerous except in subordination, and thus demanding suppression. Manhood was specifically associated with the rule of reason, which was at once the spark of divinity in man, his access to the higher rationality of the divinely animated cosmos, and the controlling principle of human behavior; the function of reason was to order the personality into conformity with the larger order of the universe as it was apprehended by the mind. The principles of reason thus come from "above," and the ideal man is therefore a fully rational being who pits his reason against the chaotic forces both within himself and in the world.

The assimilation of this conception into historical Christianity has been responsible for its tendencies to an idealism in which the religious quest is understood as a commitment to higher things, with a corresponding contempt for lower. Anthropologically, this has often pitted the soul (more or less associated with reason) against the passions and the body; it has also been responsible for the doubtful association of Christianity with the notion of the immortality of a disembodied soul. And certain conclusions have followed for the ideal of human maturity often encountered in historical Christianity. This conception is the source of a Christian ethics of repression, directed (like the pagan ethics of the hellenistic world) chiefly against sexuality as the most imperious of the bodily passions; of Christian distrust of spontaneity, a quality especially associated with childhood; and of the notion of the mature Christian—this might be called the Christian ideal of manhood—as a person who has so successfully cultivated his own bad conscience, his guilt for his persistent attraction to lower things, that he can only come to terms with his existence by a deliberate and rigorous program of self-discipline and self-denial in the interest of saving his soul. The Christian man, in this conception, has consciously separated himself as far as possible from his childhood, in obedience to a higher wisdom that is readily distinguishable from folly.[4]

We can encounter this conception of Christianity in many places, notably among its modern critics. Nietzsche's morbid caricature of Christianity owed a good deal to the conception,[5] though Nietzsche also understood the significance of biblical Christianity better than many of his Christian contemporaries.[6] And of course this kind of Christianity is now peculiarly vulnerable to attack. A case in point is a recent work by a British psychologist, whose position will both help to bring out the human implications of the classical strand in historical Christianity and throw into relief what I will present as normative Christianity. This writer addressed herself especially to the historical impact of Christianity on human development. Noting Jesus' association of childhood with the kingdom of heaven, she remarked:

> Socrates encouraged his young followers to develop towards maturity; Jesus tried to reduce his to the level of children. The Gospels contain numerous statements in which the attitudes of children are compared favorably with those of adults. . . . These statements are so often quoted with approval that probably few pause to consider whether it is really a good thing for adults to think and behave like children. What attracted Jesus towards "little children," obviously, was their unquestioning trust in adults, and his ideal was to be surrounded by adults who had a similar trust in him.

This writer's somewhat uncritical commitment to the classical ideal of a manhood that leaves childhood behind seems reasonably clear, though her sense of the implications of that ideal and of the historical roots of the kind of Christianity she indicts is somewhat confused. But her attitude is not uncommon, and her depiction of one prominent strand in historical Christianity is not unfounded. She discerns in Christianity an authoritarian impulse that, rejecting true adulthood, aims to reduce adults to a childish malleability, and so proves also destructive of the positive qualities of childhood. Christianity, in her view, is a "harsh, joyless, guilt-obsessed religion that makes happiness suspect and virtue unattractive." It is, in essence, an "ascetic, other-worldly religion which for centuries has served to stifle the free intelligence and to limit disastrously the range of human sympathies." It is dominated by "a self-centred preoccupation with one's own virtue and one's own salvation," and accordingly the Christian has a "negative, passive, masochistic character and [an] obsession with suffering and sacrifice."[7]

But this indictment neglects to notice that similar charges against historical Christianity have been periodically made from within the Christian community, a fact which suggests that we may find in Christianity itself a very different understanding of the Christian position. Thus it has not escaped the attention of Christians that the authority claimed for Christian belief has at times tended to degenerate into an authoritarianism that contradicts the central meaning of Christianity. It is undeniable, for example, and certainly by Christians, that the Christian clergy have in some periods claimed, as Christ's successors, to be "fathers" with a more than legitimate paternal authority over the laity, their "children." In 1301, for example, Boniface VIII brought a long tradition of such paternalism to a climax in a stern letter to the king of France. "Hearken, dearest son," he wrote, "to the precepts of thy father and bend the ear of thy heart to the teaching of the master who, here on earth, stands in place of Him who alone is master and lord."[8] But the practical authoritarianism in Christian history is easily exaggerated; the claims of ecclesiastical authority have rarely gone unchallenged. Those of Pope Boniface, indeed, resulted in a major disaster for the papacy at the hands of men who also considered themselves Christians. Some Christians have also rejected in principle the attitudes he represented. Calvin, for example, placed a highly unfavorable construction on clerical paternalism. "Hence it appears," he declared, "what kind of Christianity there is under the Papacy, when the pastors labor to the utmost of their power to keep the people in absolute infancy."[9] Indeed, the papacy itself has shown recent indications of sympathy for Calvin's position. The *aggiornamento* of John XXIII has been widely interpreted as an admission of the coming-of-age of the laity, and Pope John himself suggested a new understanding of adulthood in his transparent inability to take seriously his own status and dignity as an adult. Paradoxically, this was somehow interpreted by many of those who observed him as the most persuasive evidence of his maturity.

The paradox of Pope John takes us to the heart of the conception of adulthood in normative Christianity, which I shall now approach directly through a text in the Pauline letter to the Ephesians:[10]

> So shall we all at last attain to the unity inherent in our faith
> and our knowledge of the Son of God—to mature manhood,
> measured by nothing less than the full stature of Christ. We are
> no longer to be children, tossed by the waves and whirled about
> by every fresh gust of teaching. . . . No, let us speak the truth in
> love; so shall we fully grow up in Christ. He is the head, and on
> him the whole body depends. Bonded and knit together by ev-
> ery constituent joint, the whole frame grows through the due
> activity of each part, and builds itself up in love.

Here we are immediately introduced to several important themes. One is the strictly metaphorical meaning of "childhood," whose characteristics may be encountered in men of all ages; another is the association of maturity with personal stability. Still another is the identification of full adulthood with the loving solidarity of mankind, and this will concern us later. But it is of particular importance for our immediate purposes that the measure of true adulthood is finally "the full stature of Christ," for this is an absolute standard, in relation to which no man, whatever his age, can claim to be fully an adult. This peculiarity of Christian adulthood especially struck Calvin, who emphasized it in commenting on the text:[11]

> As [the apostle] had spoken of that full-grown age toward which we proceed throughout the whole course of our life, so now he tells us that, during such a progress, we ought not to be like children. He thus sets an intervening period between childhood and maturity. Those are children who have not yet taken a step in the way of the Lord, but still hesitate, who have not yet determined what road they ought to choose, but move sometimes in one direction, and sometimes in another, always doubtful, always wavering. But those are thoroughly founded in the doctrine of Christ, who, although not yet perfect, have so much wisdom and vigor as to choose what is best, and proceed steadily in the right course. Thus the life of believers, longing constantly for their appointed status, is like adolescence. So when I said that in this life we are never men, this ought not to be pressed to the other extreme, as they say, as if there were no progress beyond childhood. After being born in Christ, we ought to grow, so as not to be children in understanding . . . although we have not arrived at man's estate, we are at any rate older boys.

Here the paradox is fully stated: that the Christian, however ripe in years, cannot think of himself as a completed man. Christianity has, then, a conception of full adulthood; the goal of human development is total conformity to the manhood of Christ. But since this is a transcendent goal, the practical emphasis in Christian adulthood is on the process rather than its end. Since it is impossible to achieve perfect maturity in this life, the duty of the Christian is simply to develop constantly toward it. The essential element in the Christian idea of adulthood is, accordingly, the capacity for growth, which is assumed to be a potentiality of any age of life. It is in this sense that the Christian life is like adolescence, that stage in which the adult seems, however ambiguously, trembling to be born.

But adolescence also suggests the coexistence, within the personality, of the child and whatever it is that he promises to become, and this points to another peculiarity of the Christian view: its insistence on the continuity, rather than the absolute qualitative difference, between the child and the man. The developing adult is assumed to incorporate positively the individual and (in fact) irrepressible character of the child. Adulthood assumes that the child cannot be left behind, but is the basis of the more mature personality. Thus the child lives on in the man, so that child and man are somehow identical, a conclusion, from the standpoint of classical manhood, that is paradoxical and absurd. It is evident also that the idea of adulthood is related to various other Christian paradoxes: that the last shall be first, that foolishness is wisdom, and that God, who is himself "highest," should lower himself to become a corporeal man—and indeed, as though this metaphysical confusion were not sufficiently degrading, that he should come not as a hero or a king but as a humble figure who is put to death for others. The paradox of adulthood points to the folly of the cross.

Similarly adulthood does not recognize real qualitative and hierarchical distinctions *within* the personality; it sees man, whether child or adult, as a living whole. It may sometimes use such terms as "spirit," "soul," "mind," or "flesh"; but this vocabulary (which also reflects the difficulties of translating the thought of one culture into the language of another) is intended to describe various modes of activity of what is, in itself, an undifferentiated unity. The anthropology of normative Christianity can only be pictured, not as a hierarchy of discrete faculties, but as a circle organized around a vital center, the core of human being (cf. Latin *cor*, "heart"), whose qualities, for good or evil, permeate the whole.[12] Thus, where classical anthropology sought to understand man by identifying the several faculties of the personality and ranking them according to their objective value, normative Christianity has been inclined to accept and even to celebrate the mysteries of the total personality.[13]

This conception of Christian adulthood is, of course, not only normative; it has also found concrete historical expression, though I think it has rarely been dominant in the history of Christianity.[14] Nevertheless, the availability to Christians in all subsequent ages of the canonical Scriptures and the constant effort to penetrate to their meaning have meant that, however obscured by misunderstandings arising out of the cultural limitations of their readers, a biblical conception of adulthood has always played at least a counterpoint to the classical conception of manhood. It has never altogether disappeared from later Western culture, however muted it may have become; it has regularly helped to block radical intrusions of the classical idea of manhood into Christianity (I suspect that both Arianism and Pelagianism are linked to that conception); and occasionally, though usually only briefly, it has swelled out unmistakably as a major theme. It is prominent in the mature Augustine, in the more Pauline manifestations of the Catholic and Protestant Reformations, and in twentieth-century neo-orthodoxy and biblical theology, with their heightened cultural relativism and their enhanced sensitivity to history.

This conception of adulthood is in fact so inextricably linked to normative Christianity as a whole that we can trace it through a series of basic and specifically Jewish and Christian doctrines and, in this way, explore its implications more deeply. Its foundations can be discerned in the biblical account of the Creation, which incorporates a number of insights basic to Christian thought. This is not, as in the creation myths of surrounding peoples, the culmination of a primordial struggle between a creator and the forces of chaos, coeternal with, perhaps even anterior to, him; it is a true beginning. This has various implications. God created the universe; and, as this was eventually understood, He created it out of nothing,[15] a doctrine that establishes both the absolute transcendence of God and His full sovereignty over every aspect of creation.[16] And since the Creation specifically included the heavens as well as the earth, the story subverts the classical distinctions between high things and low.[17] If hierarchies of any kind are admissible in the biblical universe, they cannot, at any rate, have any sacred basis. They possess only relative value; all created things are, in the only relationship of absolute significance, on the same level, as creatures.[18] For man this means not only that he must recognize his creatureliness but that he must see it in every aspect of his being. No part of him is divine, and therefore none can claim to rule by divine right over the others.[19] Among its other implications, this precludes the possibility of repression as a way of ordering the personality. Because man was created as a whole, indeed in God's own image, every aspect of man is good and worthy of development, for "God saw all that he had made, and it was very good" (Gen. 1:31).[20]

In addition, this good creation is depicted as a work of time, and, as the sequel reveals, God has built into it the dimension of process and change. Time and change, so dimly regarded in the classical world of thought, are therefore also necessarily good; the biblical God underlined their positive significance by presenting Himself, after the Fall, as the Lord of history who encounters and reveals Himself to man in temporal experience.[21] The Old Testament is fundamentally historical, and the

New is based on a further series of historical events in which God uniquely enters and sanctifies time.[22] In this conception the past acquires peculiar significance. It is that aspect of time which man can know through memory, which indeed he must ponder deeply because it gives meaning to the present and promise to the future.[23] The past demonstrates God's care and will for man and therefore it cannot be ignored or repudiated. This explains why the Scriptures so frequently summon man to *remember* the past, for in an important sense it is contemporaneous with all subsequent time.

The significance of the past also points to the indelible importance of all human experience. It gives meaning to the particular temporal experiences that have shaped each individual during the whole course of his life, so that the biblical idea of time is the foundation for the conception of the worth of the individual personality.[24] But it also gives meaning to the collective experiences of mankind into which all individual experience is ultimately submerged, a conception basic to the discovery of the great historical forces that transcend individual experience.[25] Fundamental to the Christian view of man is, therefore, an insistence on a process of growth in which the past is not left behind but survives, shapes, and is absorbed into the present.[26] The unalterable past provides a stable base for the identity alike of each individual and of every society. St. Augustine's *Confessions,* with its vivid delineation of a personality changing yet continuous with its past, is a product of this conception.[27] The absence of genuine biography in the classical world has often been remarked.[28] By the same token, the great classical histories sought to reveal the changeless principles governing all change, while the biblical histories were concerned with change itself as God's work and with its shaping impact on men.

The Christian life, then, is conceived as indefinite growth, itself the product of a full engagement with temporal experience involving the whole personality. The Christian is not to evade the challenges, the struggles, the difficulties and dangers of life, but to accept, make his way through, and grow in them. He must be willing to disregard his vulnerability and to venture out, even at the risk of making mistakes, for the sake of growth.[29] This understanding of life finds expression in the figure of the Christian as wayfarer (*viator*) or pilgrim; Christian conversion is thus not, as in the mystery religions, an immediate entrance into a safe harbor but rather, though its direction has been established, the beginning of a voyage into the unknown.[30] As movement in a direction, it also implies progress, but a progress that remains incomplete in this life.[31] The "other-worldliness" of Christianity is significant, in this context, as the basis of the open-endedness of both personal and social development.

From this standpoint, just as the essential condition of Christian adulthood is the capacity for growth, the worst state of man is not so much his sinfulness (for sins can be forgiven) as the cessation of growth, arrested development, remaining fixed at any point in life. In these terms, just as adulthood requires growth, its opposite—what might be called the Christian conception of immaturity—is the refusal to grow, the inability to cope with an open and indeterminate future (that is, the future itself), in effect the rejection of life as a process.

There is, however, a close connection between the rejection of growth and the problem of sin; the refusal to grow is, in an important sense, the source of all particular sins. The story of the Fall reveals the connection, and may also be taken as the biblical analysis of the causes and the consequence of human immaturity. It contrasts essential man, as God created him, with actual man, man as he appears in history, who is fearful of the future and afraid of growth. The story explains this as a result of man's faithlessness. For the fall is caused not by a breach of the moral law but by man's violation of the relationship fundamental to his existence; it belongs to religious rather than to ethical experience. Primordial man, whose goodness stems from his dependence on God, is depicted as rejecting the creatureliness basic to his perfection and claiming independent value and even divinity for himself. He seeks to become "like gods," and implicit in this pretension is the rejection of his own further development. By complacently making himself *as he is* the divine center of his universe, he rejects the possibility of change and learns to fear all experience. Thus he loses his openness to the future and his capacity for growth; in short he repudiates his capacity for adulthood.[32] The claim to divinity, therefore, paradoxically results in a pervasive anxiety. And out of this anxiety man commits a whole range of particular ethical sins, the end products of his faithlessness. Thus, too, he begins to suffer particular sensations of guilt.[33]

A further symptom of his immaturity may be seen in man's perennial tendency, implicit in his claim to divinity, to absolutize his understanding of the universe in a frantic effort to hold his anxiety in check. This, I take it, would be the Christian explanation for the relatively small influence of a biblical understanding of the human situation in Christendom itself. Man solemnly invests his culture, which is in fact always contingent on his own limited and self-centered vision and need, with ultimate meaning, thereby imprisoning himself within a man-made, rigidly bounded, and internally defined universe that further destroys the possibility for growth. He philosophizes, claims access to the real truth of things, to being-in-itself. This is the significance normative Christianity would assign to the absolute qualitative distinctions of classical culture, a man-made substitute for biblical faith. Harvey Cox has described such constructions as a "play-pen," a nice image in its implications for human development.[34] Their power to inhibit human sympathy, with its special value for personal growth, is suggested by the need of the Greek (in an impulse with which we are all quite familiar) to see the man who differed from himself as a barbarian. Without faith— what Tillich has called the courage to be, which is also the courage to become—the only escape from man's intolerable fear of chaos is the idolatry of cultural absolutism. So, without faith, man tends to bigotry, for any grasp of the universe other than his own is too dangerous for him to contemplate. It is in this light that we can understand the full implications of the pagan charge that the early Christians were enemies of culture. In a sense this was true then, and it remains true; for normative Christianity all culture is a human artifact, and no absolute validity can be attached to its insights. Such a position is always likely to be disturbing, as every social scientist has discovered.

Yet normative Christianity does not deny the practical values of culture. It simply insists that, just as man is a creature of God, so culture is a creature of man, not his master. Secularized in this way, culture can serve many useful human purposes, and it can even become a vehicle of Christian purposes when men fully recognize their dependence on God.[35] But culture can never be ultimately serious. Indeed, there are tensions in the Scriptures that suggest that some dimensions of biblical religion itself may be understood as products of culture, or at any rate set in a larger context within which, like culture, they can be seen to possess only relative authority. Job discovered this in his confrontation with an inscrutable but infinitely holy God, and we can also sense something of this in the tension in the Old Testament between prophetic religion and the law. The law is like culture in the sense that it defines and particularizes sins, and the prophets do not deny the validity of such definition. But prophetic religion also insists, not simply that there is more to be said about man's situation before God than this, but, in addition, that definition is significant only in relation to the indefinite and open.[36]

If the Christian analysis of the evils in historical existence can be understood as a diagnosis of immaturity, the Christian conception of salvation can be similarly construed as a description of the only way to recover that capacity for growth in which true adulthood consists. The basic problem here is to replace anxiety with faith, so that man can enter an open future with confidence and grow through his experience. But here he encounters a problem he cannot solve. Faith is a function of man's dependence on God, but it is precisely this relationship that man in historical existence has repudiated. In effect he has destroyed the "true self" God made, and he must therefore be remade. And as Augustine asked, "If you could not make yourself, how could you remake yourself?"[37] Described psychologically, the predicament in which man finds himself is one of entrapment and bondage—in short, of total helplessness.[38] Furthermore, because man was created a living whole and repudiated his creatureliness as a whole, there is no area of his personality left untouched by his alienation from God and thus from his true self. This is the precise meaning of the often misunderstood doctrine of total depravity: it signifies that man has no resources by which he can save himself.

Yet exactly here, in the recognition that this is the case, lies the first step toward the resumption of growth. Once man sees himself as he is, acknowledges his limits, perceives the contingency of all his own constructions, and admits that they have their sources only in himself, he is well on the way to accepting his creaturehood and open to the possibility of faith. Faith begins, then, not in illusion but in an absolute and terrifying realism; its first impulse is paradoxically the perception that faith itself is beyond man's own control, that there is no help in him, that his only resource is the grace of a loving God. The Christian, as Barth remarked, is "moved by a grim horror of illusion." "What is pleasing to God comes into being when all human righteousness is gone, irretrievably gone, when men are uncertain and lost, when they have abandoned all ethical and religious illusions, and when they have renounced every hope in this world and in this heaven. . . . Religion is the possibility of the removal of every ground of confidence except confidence in God alone. Piety is the possibility of the removal of the last traces of a firm foundation upon which we can erect a system of thought."[39] Salvation thus begins with confession, the admission of sin and ultimately of faithlessness, which is therapeutic in the sense that it demands total honesty and is directed to the removal of every false basis for human development. Augustine's *Confessions* might be described as the Christian form of psychoanalysis, the retracing, in God's presence and with His help, of the whole course of a life, which aims to recover the health of faith.[40]

By confession and repentance, themselves a response to faith, man recognizes his helplessness and thus becomes open to help. This help is revealed and made available by God himself through the saving work of Christ, in which God again demonstrates his infinite concern with history. The response to Christ in faith expresses man's full acceptance of that creatureliness which is the essential condition of his authentic existence and growth; the answer to sin is not virtue but faith. By faith man is dramatically relieved of his false maturity, his claims to a self-defined "manhood," and enabled to begin again to grow. This is why conversion can be described as a "rebirth," which resembles birth also in that it is not subject to the control of him who is reborn; baptism, the ritual of rebirth, is an initiation into true existence. Freed from the anxieties of self-sufficiency by faith, man can grow, both individually and collectively. Indeed, only now has he the strength to face directly the contingency, the inadequacy, the slavery and sinfulness of all merely human culture. He can risk seeing it clearly because, with faith, he has also received the gift of hope. From this standpoint the Gospel is the good news because it frees man for adulthood.

But this is an adulthood that involves, always, the whole man; thus its goal is symbolized not by the immortality of the soul but by the resurrection of the body as representing the total self that must be made whole. As Augustine exclaimed in old age, "I want to be healed completely, for I am a complete whole."[41] Christian maturity is manifested, therefore, not only in the understanding but more profoundly in the affective life and in the loving actions that are rooted in the feelings. Christ is above all the model of absolute love. Conformity to this loving Christ is the goal of human development; in Augustine's words, "he is our native country." But he is also the key to Christian adulthood, for "he made himself also the way to that country."[42] The Christian grows both in Christ and to Christ.

Again we encounter a set of paradoxes, the first of which is that man's full acceptance of his creatureliness, the admission of his absolute dependence on God in Christ, proves to be the essential condition of human freedom. For the only alternative to the life of faith is bondage to the self, to the anxieties and the false absolutisms embedded in human culture, by which man is otherwise imprisoned. Faith, in these terms, is the necessary condition of true autonomy, of freedom not from the constraints of experience—the Stoic ideal—but freedom to grow in and through them that is essential to adulthood. The Pauline injunction to work out one's own salvation in fear and trembling suggests this freedom, and suggests also the strains attendant on growth, but it would be impossible to fulfill without the faith that "it is God which worketh in you both to will and to do of his pleasure" (Phil. 2:13). This kind of freedom supplies the strength to challenge authority maturely, without the rebelliousness, arrogance, and destructiveness symptomatic of insecurity, or to criticize the definition of one's own life and to examine the dubious sources of one's own actions.[43]

At the same time, obedience to God paradoxically proves a far lighter burden than obedience to human ordinances or the requirements of culture, even though—another paradox—it is, in any final sense, impossible. For Christian righteousness consists not in a moral quality that must be maintained at all costs but in a relationship of favor and peace with God that is the source (rather than the consequence) of moral effort. If the Christian is in some sense virtuous, his virtue arises from love rather than duty, and if he fails, he can count on forgiveness. Thus, though he must recognize and confess his guilt as part of his more general realism, he is not to nourish or cling to it, for this would amount to the rejection of God's love. Repentance means allowing our guilt to be God's concern, and all guilt, otherwise so paralyzing for the moral life, must be swallowed up in love and gratitude. Christian adulthood is a growth away from, not toward, guilt.

By the same token it cannot be repressive, not only because no power in the human personality is entitled to excise or even to control any other (this is the happy implication of total depravity), but above all because such an effort, since it cannot touch the quality of the heart, would be superficial and in the end futile. Christian thinkers have sometimes displayed great insight into the nature of self-imposed control. Calvin's description of the process implies some acquaintance with its physiological consequences, as well as realism about the social necessity for restraint in a world in which those, too, who are growing in Christ must recognize that they are not fully and dependably adult: "the more [men] restrain themselves, the more violently they are inflamed within; they ferment, they boil, ready to break out into external acts, if they were not prevented by this dread of the law. . . . But yet this constrained and extorted righteousness is necessary to the community."[44] But the ideal of Christian adulthood is not control but spontaneity; it is, in Augustine's words, to "love and do what you will."[45]

The spontaneity in the Christian ideal of adulthood points to still another paradox: its deliberate cultivation of, and delight in, the qualities of the child, now understood less metaphorically.[46] Childhood, after all, assumes growth, and it is in this respect fundamentally different from childishness, which rejects it; in this sense childhood is a model for adulthood. Indeed, childhood welcomes the years, unaware that they bring decay and death, and the deep and fearless interest of the child in his experience permits him to ask simple but profound questions that, later, may seem wearisome or too dangerous to be entertained. The child is not afraid to express wonder and astonishment.[47] Thus the confident trust in life of a healthy child, so different from the wariness that develops with age, has often been taken in Christian thought as a natural prototype of faith; in this sense, the adult Christian life is something like a return to childhood. As Kierkegaard remarked, it seems to reverse the natural order: "Therefore one does not begin by being a child and then becoming progressively more intimate [with God] as he grows older; no, one becomes more and more a child."[48] But there is, in this reversal, realism about the actual results of maturation, which ordinarily destroys the openness and wonder of childhood and replaces it with disguises and suspicion, with sophistication and a "knowingness" that chiefly serve to exclude a profounder knowledge. For the man, a return to the values of childhood is only possible when the inadequacies of his pretended manhood have been recognized in repentance and confession and he can take the way of faith. Then the growth of the man can again be like that of the child.[49]

This suggests a further peculiarity in the Christian view of adulthood: its lack of interest in chronological disparity. All Christians, insofar as they are growing in Christ, are equally becoming adults—or equally children.[50] Baptism is no respecter of age. An important consequence of this is to limit the authority and influence of parents, for where parent and child are both growing up in Christ,[51] the parent cannot be the only, or even the primary, pattern of maturity.[52] The Christian parent has failed unless his child achieves sufficient autonomy to establish his own direct relation to Christ. Nor is there sexual differentiation in the Christian conception: girls and boys, women and men are equally growing up in Christ.

But there is still another respect in which Christian adulthood merges with childhood: in its appreciation for play. This may be related to Paul's contrast between the wisdom of this world and the divine foolishness by which its hollowness is revealed.[53] The recurrent figure of the Christian fool, both child and saint, has sought to embody this conception. But it also has lighter, if equally serious, implications. The security of dependence on a loving God makes it unnecessary to confront life with a Stoic solemnity; the Christian can relax, even (again paradoxically) when he is most profoundly and actively confronting the sinfulness of the world. He can enjoy playfully (which also means to delight in, for itself, not to exploit instrumentally, for himself) the goodness of the Creation. His culture can be an unbounded playground for free and joyous activity. He can risk the little adventures on which play depends. The loving human relationships of the Christian life can find expression in mutual play, through which we give pleasure to one another. Play is a natural expression of the joy of faith, which makes it possible to engage in life, even the hard work of life, as a game that has its own seriousness (for without their special kind of seriousness games could scarcely interest us), and that yet can be enjoyed precisely because the ultimate seriousness of existence lies elsewhere, with God.[54] But play is also related to that seriousness. Bushnell saw play as "the symbol and interpreter" of Christian liberty and pointed to its place in the eschatological vision of Zechariah 8:5: "And the streets of the city shall be full of boys and girls, playing in the streets."[55]

I have treated these various elements in the Christian conception of adulthood as aspects of an ideal for individual development, but to leave the matter at this would be to neglect an essential dimension of the Christian position. Like Judaism, Christianity has usually seen the individual in close and organic community with others. The Pauline description of growing up in Christ, though it has obvious implications for the individual, is primarily concerned with the growth of the Christian community; it is finally the church as one body, and perhaps ultimately all mankind, that must reach "mature manhood." The primary experiences through which the Christian grows are social experiences. One encounters Christ and the opportunity to serve him in others; the maturity of the individual is realized only in loving unity with others.[56] The power of growth is thus finally a function of community, and, at the same time, maturity finds expression in identification with other men; Christ, the model of human adulthood, was supremely "the man for others."[57] Through this identification of the individual with the body of Christ, the Christian conception of adulthood merges finally into history and eschatology.

NOTES

1. Cf. Thorlief Boman, *Hebrew Thought Compared with Greek,* tr. Jules L. Moreau (New York, 1970), esp. pp. 28–33, 45–69.

2. An exception can be found in Seneca's letter to his mother, known as the *Consolation to Helvia,* in which he recommends a standard program of literary and philosophical studies to console her for his exile.

3. Cf. H. I. Marrou, *A History of Education in Antiquity,* tr. George Lamb (New York, 1964), pp. 297–98.

4. A good example of this ideal is John Chrysostom's address to Christian parents on the upbringing of children, translated by M. L. W. Laistner in his

Christianity and Pagan Culture in the Later Roman Empire (Ithaca, 1951), pp. 85–122. "Thou art raising up a philosopher and athlete and citizen of heaven," Chrysostom declared; for this he recognized "wisdom" as "the master principle which keeps everything under control," the height of which is "refusal to be excited at childish things." The purpose of education for him is to make the Christian boy "sagacious and to banish all folly": that is, to make him a precocious little Stoic sage. He is to "know the meaning of human desires, wealth, reputation, power" that he "may disdain these and strive after the highest." And the fruit of his maturity consists in the ability to control his passions: if he can only learn "to refrain from anger, he has displayed already all the marks of a philosophic mind."

5. Cf. *The Antichrist,* no. 51, tr. Walter Kaufmann: "We others who have the *courage* to be healthy and also to despise—how we may despise a religion which taught men to misunderstand the body! which does not want to get rid of superstitious belief in souls! which turns insufficient nourishment into something 'meritorious'! which fights health as a kind of enemy, devil, temptation! which fancies that one can carry around a 'perfect soul' in a cadaver of a body, and which therefore found it necessary to concoct a new conception of 'perfection'—a pale, sickly, idiotic-enthusiastic character, so-called 'holiness.' Holiness—merely a series of symptoms of an impoverished, unnerved, incurably corrupted body." From the standpoint of normative Christianity, this seems fair enough as a characterization of much that has professed to represent Christianity. Wagner's *Parsifal* is a familiar and particularly morbid expression of this conception.

6. For a perceptive essay on Nietzsche's relation to Christianity, see Karl Barth, *Church Dogmatics,* III:2 (Edinburgh, 1960), pp. 231–42.

7. Margaret Knight, *Honest to Man* (London, 1974), pp. 41–42, 193, viii, 21, 196. The popular character of this work by no means reduces its value for our purposes.

8. Quoted by John Mundy, *Europe in the High Middle Ages* (London, 1973), p. 323.

9. *Calvin's New Testament Commentaries,* XI, tr. T. H. L. Parker (Grand Rapids, 1972), p. 183 (on Ephesians 4:14).

10. Ephesians 4:13–16. I use the translation in *The New English Bible.* The precise authorship of this epistle is a matter of dispute, but there seems to be little doubt about its Pauline inspiration.

11. *New Testament Commentaries,* XI, pp. 182–84. On Paul's metaphorical use of childhood, see Paul Ricoeur, *The Symbolism of Evil,* tr. Emerson Buchanan (Boston, 1969), p. 149.

12. For biblical anthropology in general, see Hans Walter Wolff, *Anthropology of the Old Testament,* tr. Margaret Kohl (Philadelphia, 1974), esp. pp. 7–9. On Paul's anthropological terminology, so often misunderstood in historical Christianity, cf. Günther Bornkamm, *Paul,* tr. D. M. G. Stalker (London, 1971), p. 131.

13. Cf. Augustine, *Confessions,* tr. R. S. Pine-Coffin (London, 1961), p. 224: "What, then, am I, my God? What is my nature? A life that is ever varying, full of change, and of immense power. . . . This is the great force of life in living man, mortal though he is." There is much of this attitude also in Pascal's *Pensées,*

for example, no. 434: "What a chimera then is man! What a novelty! What a monster, what a chaos, what a contradiction, what a prodigy! Judge of all things, imbecile worm of the earth; depositary of truth, a sink of uncertainty and error; the pride and refuse of the universe!" Barth, *Church Dogmatics*, III:2, pp. 110–11, has this: "[Man's] existence is he himself, who in his very subjectivity, in his very indefinability, is seeking after the mystery of himself."

14. The common notion of the "infinite elasticity of Christianity" (in Hegel's phrase) is somewhat misleading; this quality might, with approximately equal justice, be called the infinite elasticity of Hellenism.

15. There is a useful survey of this idea in the early church in Barth, *Church Dogmatics*, III:2, pp. 152–53. I do not mean to suggest that Creation *ex nihilo* is clear in the Genesis account; cf. E. A. Speiser, *Genesis* [The Anchor Bible] (Garden City, 1964), pp. 13–14. But Job 26:7 suggests it, and it is clearly spelled out in 2 Macc. 7:28.

16. Cf. Reinhold Niebuhr, *The Nature and Destiny of Man* (New York, 1941), I, pp. 133–34.

17. Cf. Barth, *Church Dogmatics*, III:2, pp. 350–51.

18. Wolff, *Anthropology*, p. 162.

19. Augustine appears to be struggling toward this conception in *De natura et gratia*, ch. 38: "I am of the opinion that the creature will never become equal with God, even when so perfect a holiness is accomplished within us as that it shall be quite incapable of receiving an addition. No, all who maintain that our progress is to be so complete that we shall be changed into the substance of God, and that we shall thus become what He is should look well to it how they build up their opinion; upon myself I must confess that it produces no conviction." But there is a tentativeness here that suggests the difficulty of the idea of man's creatureliness for the hellenistic Christian.

20. Niebuhr, I, p. 167, suggests that "sometimes the authority of this simple dictum . . . was all that prevented Christian faith from succumbing to dualistic and acosmic doctrines which pressed in upon the Christian church."

21. Augustine's *Confessions* is, of course, a kind of extended essay on this theme; cf. his *On Christian Doctrine*, tr. D. W. Robertson, Jr. (Indianapolis, 1958), p. 64: "the order of time, whose creator and administrator is God."

22. Cf. Emil Brunner, "The Problem of Time," in *Creation: The Impact of an Idea*, ed. Daniel O'Connor and Francis Oakley (New York, 1969), p. 124.

23. Cf. Augustine, *Confessions*, 222–23: "Who is to carry the research beyond this point? Who can understand the truth of the matter? O Lord, I am working hard in this field, and the field of my labors is my own self. I have become a problem to myself, like land which a farmer works only with difficulty and at the cost of much sweat. For I am not now investigating the tracts of the heavens, or measuring the distance of the stars, or trying to discover how the earth hangs in space. I am investigating myself, my memory, my mind." See also Rudolf Bultmann, *Primitive Christianity in Its Contemporary Setting*, tr. R. H. Fuller (Cleveland, 1956), pp. 144–45.

24. On this point, cf. Charles Norris Cochrane, *Christianity and Classical Culture* (New York, 1957), p. 456; Niebuhr, I, p. 69; Bultmann, p. 180; and Kierkegaard, *The Concept of Dread*, tr. Walter Lowrie (Princeton, 1957), p. 26: "the essential characteristic of human existence, that man is an individual and

as such is at once himself and the whole race, in such wise that the whole race has part in the individual, and the individual has part in the whole race."

25. Eric Auerbach, *Mimesis,* tr. Willard Trask (Garden City, 1957), chs. 1– 3, is especially perceptive on this characteristic of biblical, as opposed to classical, literature.

26. Kierkegaard's conception of the stages on life's way may perhaps be taken as a reflection of this tendency in Christian thought; Kierkegaard's three stages do not simply replace each other, but the later stages absorb the earlier.

27. Cochrane, pp. 386ff.; Peter Brown, *Augustine of Hippo: A Biography* (Berkeley, 1967), p. 173.

28. As in Bultmann, p. 130.

29. This seems to be implied in the *Divine Comedy,* in which the way to Paradise begins with the full moral experience of the Inferno.

30. Cf. Brown, p. 177, on Augustine's understanding of conversion as a beginning. As Augustine remarks in *Christian Doctrine,* p. 13, the Christian life is "a journey or voyage home." The notion of life as movement was also important for Luther: "For it is not sufficient to have done something, and now to rest . . . this present life is a kind of movement and passage, or transition . . . a pilgrimage from this world into the world to come, which is eternal rest" (quoted by Gerhard Ebeling, *Luther: An Introduction to His Thought,* tr. R. A. Wilson [Philadelphia, 1970], pp. 161–62). Calvin devoted particular attention to this theme (*Institutes,* III, vi, p. 5): "But no one . . . has sufficient strength to press on with due eagerness, and weakness so weighs down the greater number that, with wavering and limping and even creeping along the ground, they move at a feeble rate. Let each one of us, then, proceed according to the measure of his puny capacity and set out upon the journey we have begun. No one shall set out so inauspiciously as not daily to make some headway, though it be slight. Therefore, let us not cease so to act that we may make some unceasing progress in the way of the Lord. And let us not despair at the slightness of our success; for even though attainment may not correspond to desire, when today outstrips yesterday the effort is not lost. Only let us look toward our mark with sincere simplicity and aspire to our goal; not fondly flattering ourselves, nor excusing our own evil deeds, but with continuous effort striving toward this end: that we may surpass ourselves in goodness until we attain to goodness itself. It is this, indeed, which through the whole course of life we seek and follow. But we shall attain it only when we have cast off the weakness of the body, and are received into full fellowship with him" (Battles tr.). Bunyan's *Pilgrim's Progress* vividly dramatizes the conception.

31. Ricoeur, pp. 272–74, is instructive on the conception of progress implicit in Paul's understanding of the transition from the law to the grace of Christ: "the fall is turned into growth and progress; the curse of paradise lost becomes a test and a medicine." Augustine interpreted his own life as a progression in understanding: "I am the sort of man who writes because he has made progress, and who makes progress—by writing" (quoted by Brown, 353). For Thomas à Kempis, the Christian life is marked by a concern "to conquer self, and by daily growing stronger than self, to advance in holiness" (*Imitation of Christ,* tr. Leo Sherley-Price [London, 1952], p. 31). For Luther, progress was a condition of all existence, for "progress is nothing other than constantly

beginning. And to begin without progress is extinction. This is clearly the case with every movement and every act of every creature." Thus one must "constantly progress, and anyone who supposes he has already apprehended does not realize that he is only beginning. For we are always travelling, and must leave behind us what we know and possess, and seek for that which we do not yet know and possess" (quoted by Ebeling, pp. 161–62).

32. Bultmann, esp. p. 184.

33. This interpretation of the Fall owes a good deal to Ricoeur. For the transition from anxiety to sin, see Niebuhr, I, pp. 168, 182–86.

34. *The Secular City* (New York, 1965), p. 119.

35. For a survey of Christian attitudes to culture, see H. Richard Niebuhr, *Christ and Culture* (New York, 1951).

36. Ricoeur, pp. 58–59, 144–45, 321.

37. Quoted by Gerhart B. Ladner, *The Idea of Reform: Its Impact on Christian Thought and Action in the Age of the Fathers* (Cambridge, Mass., 1959), p. 406.

38. Ricoeur, p. 93.

39. *The Epistle to the Romans*, tr. Edwyn C. Hoskyns (London, 1933), pp. 68, 87–88.

40. Cf. Brown, p. 175.

41. Quoted by Brown, p. 366.

42. *Christian Doctrine*, p. 13.

43. Cf. Paul Tillich, *The Eternal Now* (New York, 1956), p. 158.

44. *Institutes,* II, vii, p. 10. Melanchthon was particularly subtle about human behavior that does not correspond to the impulses of the "heart"; the result is not, in fact, rationality, but, to follow Lionel Trilling's distinction, *both* insincerity *and* inauthenticity: "Therefore it can well happen that something is chosen which is entirely contrary to all affections. When this happens, insincerity takes over, as when, for example, someone treats graciously, amicably, and politely a person whom he hates and wishes ill to from the bottom of his heart, and he does this perhaps with no definite reason" (*Loci communes theologici,* tr. Lowell J. Satre, in *Melanchthon and Bucer,* ed. Wilhelm Pauck [London, 1969], p. 28).

45. Quoted by Anders Nygren, *Agape and Eros,* tr. Philip S. Watson (New York, 1969), p. 454.

46. On the virtues of a childlike spontaneity, cf. Horace Bushnell, *Christian Nurture* (New Haven, 1916; first ed., 1888), p. 5: "A child acts out his present feelings, the feelings of the moment, without qualification or disguise."

47. Cf. Niebuhr, *Beyond Tragedy* (New York, 1937), pp. 143–48.

48. *Journals and Papers,* tr. Howard V. and Edna H. Hong (Bloomington, 1967), I, p. 122, no. 272.

49. Niebuhr, *Beyond Tragedy,* pp. 148–52. At the same time Augustine's portrayal of infancy in the *Confessions* should warn us, in its realism, that Christianity is not merely sentimental about childhood, in which it can also detect the flaws of maturity. But this is again to suggest their identity.

50. Bushnell noted, p. 136, that the apostolic church included children and observed, pp. 139–40, that "just so children are all men and women; and, if there is any law of futurition in them to justify it, may be fitly classed as believing men and women."

51. Cf. Bushnell, 10: "since it is the distinction of Christian parents that

they are themselves in the nurture of the Lord, since Christ and the Divine Love, communicated through him, are become the food of their life, what will they so naturally seek as to have their children partakers with them, heirs together with them, in the grace of life?"

52. Barth emphasizes this, *Church Dogmatics,* III:4, p. 248. It is a significant feature of the Christian conception, indeed in a patriarchal society a revolutionary feature, that the Son, rather than the Father, is the model of adulthood. Lest this peculiarity seem to invite too simple an interpretation, however, the paradoxical unity of Father and Son in the Trinity must also be kept in mind.

53. Cf. Tillich, *Eternal Now,* pp. 155–57.

54. For Christianity and play, I have been stimulated by Lewis B. Smedes, "Theology and the Playful Life," in *God and the Good: Essays in Honor of Henry Stob,* ed. Clifton Orlebeke and Lewis B. Smedes (Grand Rapids, 1975), pp. 46–62. In view of common misunderstandings about the normative Christian attitude to sexuality, it is worth quoting Smedes—who certainly represents the normative position—on the playfulness of sex, p. 59: "The sexual component of our nature testifies that man was meant to find the most meaningful human communion in a playful relationship. In mutual trust and loving commitment, sexual activity is to be a playful festivity. It attests that human being is closest to fulfilling itself in a game. To be in God's image, then, includes being sexual, and sexuality is a profound call to play." Smedes also has useful comments on recent theologies of play.

55. Bushnell, pp. 290–92.

56. Cf. Augustine, *City of God,* XIX, v: "For how could the city of God . . . either take a beginning or be developed, or attain its proper destiny, if the life of the saints were not a social life?" Luther was emphatic: "We ought not to isolate ourselves but enter into companionship with our neighbor. Likewise it . . . is contrary to the life of Christ, who didn't choose solitude. Christ's life was very turbulent, for people were always moving about him. He was never alone, except when he prayed. Away with those who say, 'Be glad to be alone and your heart will be pure' " ("Table Talk," no. 1329).

57. Cf. Barth, *Church Dogmatics,* III:2, pp. 222ff.

V

CODA

20 The History Teacher as Mediator

The American Historical Association has made efforts over the years to contribute to the improvement of history teaching and in particular to take an interest in the problems facing history teachers in secondary schools and community colleges. One way of doing this has been the participation of its elected presidents in regional conferences on the teaching of history. It was in this capacity that I attended such a conference at North Texas State University in Denton, Texas, in the fall of 1978. The general theme of the conference was posed as a question: "Is the art of history safe in the hands of the profession?" In spite of my lack of acquaintance with the problems of teaching history at the grass roots, so to speak, or of any other special qualifications, I was expected to give an address appropriate to this theme. My response to the challenge, which appears here, has not been published before.

● ● ●

It is a curious reflection on the historical profession that I have only once been invited to express my views about the teaching of history. There is something distinctly odd about this. Our society, after all, supports us not simply because we are historians, but primarily because we are *teachers* of history. It does so on the assumption that we are the guardians, not simply of a professional discipline, but of something that, in a deep sense, belongs to society itself, something precious and even essential to its life, with which we have been entrusted not only to preserve and cultivate it for ourselves, but above all so that we may transmit it from generation to generation. And yet—I keep returning to the point as to a wonderful paradox—this is the only piece I have written during a career of nearly forty years in which I have tried to say something about the teaching of history.

There are other paradoxes about the present occasion. One is that our conferences about the teaching of history, rare as they may be, tend to be held only at certain kinds of institutions, as though only these are seriously concerned with teaching history; and I find this troubling. Another paradox—particularly poignant for me—is the strategic location, within the program of this conference, of my own presentation. Although I have never before been known to express myself on the subject of teaching, I am here, by virtue of my office of President of the American Historical Association, giving your keynote address. This is a considerable, and hardly justifiable, mark of trust on the part of those who planned this conference. I feel a strong need to assure you at the outset, therefore, that I actually am a teacher, that I conceive of everything I have written as somehow pedagogical, and that my primary satisfactions as a historian are associated with the classroom.

Some of these paradoxes are, I suppose, not so difficult to resolve. Historians have recently begun to worry about teaching because of widespread reports about a decline of enrollment in history courses. I am in no position to evaluate these reports, which I am inclined to regard a bit skeptically. They are rather impressionistic, they are not based on much hard data, and in the end—when we have such data—it will be very important to look carefully not only at aggregate figures but at what kinds of courses are suffering, and where. I think it will be important to recognize also that, if enrollments in history are declining, so are enrollments in other subjects, and not only in the humanities; in physics, for example, and in most areas not perceived as directly vocational. So if historians are in trouble, our problems probably reflect rather general changes in higher education. Nor can they be altogether solved by any adjustments we may make by ourselves, even by better teaching. And these larger changes seem to reflect, in turn, both that demographic shift we have heard so much about and a change in the economic climate. Students are worried about what will become of them after graduation, and this worry affects what they choose to study. There is no point to our reproaching them; we ought to sympathize with them as they confront, after all, a genuine problem. All these matters, nevertheless, suggest that we may have sound reasons for concern about the teaching of history, and I do not mean to minimize them.

I should like to direct these remarks, however, to what seems to me an even deeper reason for concern: to a dimension of our situation that, at the same time, I think we can do something about, provided that we recognize and attend to it. For I have been brooding about the central theme of our conference: *Is the art of history safe in the hands of the profession?* I have chosen not to regard this as strictly a rhetorical question, to be answered with: *Of course it is.* I suppose my own answer will turn out to be, *Not altogether, but it might be*—again provided that we admit to some real problems. And I want also to focus a little attention on two other terms in the question: to the notion of history as an *art,* and finally to our understanding of what it means to do *history* itself.

Let me approach these matters by noticing the role of the history teacher as a mediator between two communities, on both of which he depends and both of which he must serve. On the one hand, he is a member of the more particular professional or disciplinary community of historians. But he is also a member of a more general community, or perhaps more precisely of a series of more general communities that might be conceived as a set of concentric circles: local, regional, national, and finally international. In some way history belongs simultaneously both to the professional community and to all these larger communities. This seems to me a truth that we, as professional historians, sometimes tend to forget: that history is not our exclusive property. And I want to propose that it is the particular responsibility of the *teacher* of history to bear it constantly in mind and to mediate between the two sorts of community in the interest of both. For if we are anxious about the future of history as a body of discourse, the deepest reason for it may be a vague suspicion that this work of mediation has somehow broken down. And I think that this suspicion is well founded.

I am not much concerned about the possibility that the larger community might somehow—without assistance from us—simply lose interest in history. We ought, I should think, to find it reassuring, at least in the long run, that some kind of interest in the past, however it may vary from culture to culture, seems almost universal; the only exceptions seem to be the primitive groups studied by anthropologists in which all experience is interpreted within the context of a timeless present. But it is my impression that every historical society, as it reflects about itself, takes time and change into account and raises historical questions, questions about its origins, questions about the way in which its identity has taken shape over time. An interest in history seems to be almost as natural as the child's question, "Where did I come from?" and indeed to flow out of it, biology passing into history, with its social analogue, "Where did *we* come from?" At any rate I know of no chapter in the Western past, beginning with the Jews and the Greeks, without a lively interest in history; an interest, furthermore, sometimes greater among groups lower on the social scale than among elites, whose dominance may be threatened by the sense of contingency implicit in a historical perspective.

Nor does our own time seem exceptional in this respect; whatever the problems of history teachers may be, I do not think they arise out of any indifference to the past that is peculiar to our own time. I share the ambiguous reaction of many historians to some recent expressions of popular interest in history; but the existence of this interest seems too difficult to deny when *Roots* becomes a best-seller, when the television networks consider it reasonable to invest great sums in historical dramatizations watched by millions on prime time, or when large crowds stand in line for hours to see Egyptian or early Irish artifacts. Or when, to come closer to ourselves, there have never been, per capita, more teachers of history at, however inadequate they may be, better salaries. Or—and this may be more surprising—more financial support, sometimes including federal money, both for novel ways of teaching history and for even the most esoteric kinds of historical research. I do not mean to suggest that this support is enough; I am only trying to put our situation into some social and historical perspective. There has always been, and I see no reason to doubt that there always will be, a great reservoir of public interest in history, on which we can depend.

It is important to notice, however, the kinds of historical questions that appear to interest the public, since these are by no means necessarily those that interest professional historians. They are sometimes relatively practical questions, questions about the direct relevance of the past to the present, in a collective sense self-centered questions, directed to self-understanding. On the other hand, even such questions seem to be consistent with an interest in many kinds of history, including the study of the remote past and of quite alien situations. The reason for this is, I suspect, that human beings learn about themselves not only by retracing those processes by which they have been directly shaped but also by contrasting their own familiar world with what may be utterly remote from it. It can be at once a source of instruction in the possibilities of human existence, and a liberation, to enter vicariously and imaginatively, through history, into situations quite different from our own.

All of this may suggest something of what the general community seeks from historians, who from this standpoint may be seen as the providers of a social utility. The interest of the general community in history is a product neither of idle curiosity nor of scientific detachment but goes to the heart of its own existence; in this sense it is, in a collective as well as an individual sense, an existential interest. Furthermore, it wants this interest to be satisfied in language it can understand and to which it can respond not only intellectually but imaginatively, for its concern with the past requires attention not only to narrow matters of fact but to the wholeness of past life, to its felt quality. This means that the history teacher—and I think this is as true of what he conveys in the classroom as it is of his books—cannot, to communicate effectively, simply be well-informed. He must cultivate his own powers of imagination and expression in order to convey, attractively and with contagious excitement, the full quality of the past. I need hardly remind historians that history itself originated as a rhetorical art, and that effective historical communication was traditionally thought to depend on the inseparability of utility and delight. We all know that those great historians who continue to be read—Herodotus, Gibbon, the Huizinga of *The Waning of the Middle Ages* (to cite some of my own favorites)— have remained alive because they met this standard. And it seems to me quite wrong to argue that we read them still only as "literature"; we cherish them because, through their style, they are able to convey a vision of the past that still nourishes us.

On the other hand, I am of course not arguing that it is the duty of the history teacher simply to give the public—our students in both the narrower and the larger sense—uncritically what it wants. And this brings me to that other community with which the history teacher is involved, the disciplinary community of historians. Historians exist, to be sure, because there is a social need for knowledge of the past. But they also exist, as a distinct group, because of their special competence in obtaining and mobilizing this knowledge. The participation of the history teacher, as a historian, in a professional community with its own autonomous standards of judgment protects and sharpens this competence. This is the justification of the professional community: that professionalism is itself socially useful. It assists the historian to resist the all-too-human demand for simple answers to difficult questions, to resist the tendency of mankind to prefer confirmation in its collective self-esteem to the unflattering truth, to resist the pitiful yearning to forget what is unlovely in the past even when this is essential to self-understanding, to resist the pressure to exploit the past selectively and even cynically. The existence of the professional community gives to the history teacher a space of relative freedom in which it is possible to distinguish between what the general community might like to believe and what it can responsibly be taught.

Yet, as historians well know, particular professional communities, although they come into existence to meet social needs, exhibit a remarkable tendency, as they develop, toward autonomy and isolation. They tend to behave as though they exist chiefly to promote the interests of their own members, even when these interests conflict with those of the larger society. Professionals are thus inclined to present themselves—and even to regard themselves—less as the servants of the public than, in their own sphere, its masters, as the priestly guardians of a body of knowledge and activity beyond the capacity of the laity to evaluate, as authorities with an exclusive competence to determine what is best for others, sometimes even as a privileged caste relieved of the need to concern itself with the public interest. This is why "professionalism," once an unambiguously honorable term, is now viewed with growing distrust by the lay public: that is to say by those who contemplate the professions from the outside. Historians have been among the first to observe how other professions with major social impact, law and medicine in particular, have been increasingly estranged from the public by their own internal development. It is time, I would suggest, to scrutinize ourselves with the same cold eye, if only because it may help to explain some of our present difficulties.

Since history belongs, in a deep sense, to everybody, the consequences of an overweening professionalism for historical study seem both particularly inappropriate and particularly unfortunate. The central difficulty arises, I would suggest, from the fact that, when he sees himself only as a professional, the historian addresses himself chiefly to his fellow professionals, the group to which he chiefly owes his prestige and advancement. The first result is that he loses his ability to communicate effectively with a larger audience; and while the utility of his work can be recognized only by a smaller and smaller public, it is less and less likely to evoke delight. I dare say that historians are not altogether immune to delight; but there is a kind of austerity about our professionalism that assigns to delight only marginal value, and we protest only mildly if at all when we encounter an awkward, lifeless, or unnecessarily difficult style of discourse. In this connection our increasing reliance on quantitative method may be symptomatic. Quantification is obviously a valuable new resource for historiography, but it is a measure of the inroads of our professionalism that we have been so little troubled by the problems of communication it creates. Except in pure mathematics, numbers function linguistically, I should think, as adjectives; they modify nouns, and it is these nouns that give them life. Thus numbers do not constitute after all, as their enthusiasts sometimes claim, a separate language. They must somehow be assimilated, as elegantly and imaginatively as possible, into the traditional task of the historian, which is the creation and communication of the past through a common language. This is our special art.

But a further consequence of the tendency of professionals to direct their discourse primarily to each other is the fragmentation of the historical discipline into an indefinite series of increasingly remote and tiny specialties. There are good reasons for specialization; historical knowledge is difficult, and specialization may be the price of competence. Yet this seems to me only the respectable tip of the iceberg; specialization also serves less presentable motives. Psychologically, it is a source of personal security in a harshly competitive world, for the atmosphere within professional groups is not exactly gentler and more friendly than that within the larger society of which they are a part. This is why (if I may speak for myself) publication is so fraught with fear and trembling. In this situation specialization functions somewhat like territoriality among animals. We stake out our turf by leaving little tokens of our presence about; so we mark out a familiar place that looks and smells like home, within which we know our way and feel reasonably safe, where the perennial risks of professional existence are at least kept to a minimum, and which we are prepared to defend against venturesome intruders—though it must be admitted that specialization as a defensive strategy sometimes fails, since the most deadly struggles for dominance may be waged over the smallest territories. But meanwhile we become like those physicians who seem, to an increasingly suspicious laity, indifferent to the general health of the patient, though they may know everything about a particular set of endocrine glands. But we, perhaps, have less excuse; the specialties in medicine exist because patients have specific as well as general needs. Our specialties are too often generated only to serve ourselves.

But the major problem here is that our specialization tends to estrange us from that larger community to which history "belongs" in a livelier sense, perhaps, than to us. Instead of recognizing and building on the fact that history is public property, we have often seemed to want to take it away from the public, among other devices by claiming that history is a science and therefore the preserve of scientists. This claim may, in some respects, be justified, as similar claims may be justified in the case of physicians or librarians; and of course much depends on what one means by "science," a word whose significance seems to be determined somewhat by the kind of language game one chooses to play. Here I want only to call attention to its social function. It converts history from a common heritage that, by our teaching, we invite the public to appropriate and cherish, into a thing, our thing, which we as teachers are seeking to impose on students, an operation that understandably invites resistance. The claim to be scientists also justifies us in pursuing our own questions, not those of the public, to follow our own rather than its interest in the past.

Now, even from the standpoint of what I take to be our proper social role, this independence is not wholly misguided. In the long run we can often contribute more to the understanding of those matters on which we are obligated to inform the public by devising our own strategies. My question is whether we are in fact motivated by this ultimately pedagogical concern, and whether we are serving it. Let me give a couple of examples to illustrate why I am doubtful.

The first, which may be less compelling, is the present vogue, among professional historians, of a kind of ahistorical structuralism. This sort of historiography describes, often in highly sophisticated ways, isolated and relatively static moments in the past in all their social and cultural complexity. It can be marvelously ingenious and persuasive, and it is also remarkably suited to a profession consisting of specialists, since it takes little responsibility for relating one such moment to another. This approach to the past can, of course, be profoundly useful even for a historiography that is concerned, as historians have traditionally been and as our public largely remains, with the processes of history. It illuminates the complexity of the relations between past and present, and it provides a kind of insurance against anachronism. But it also results in a virtual denial of the continuities of history. It reduces our knowledge of the past to a series of unrelated flashbacks, so that all that can then be said about the relation of the past to ourselves—at least all that is now being said even about so recent a time as the seventeenth and eighteenth centuries—is, to cite the title of a distinguished book, that the past is "a world we have lost." The past, in this construction, ceases to be *our* past, and some of the advocates of this kind of history have been aggressive in denying the very legitimacy of seeking self-understanding through the study of history. No position, it seems to me, could be better calculated to isolate the historical profession; and insofar as isolation signifies distinction, this may indeed be its unconscious purpose. To me it seems professionally suicidal. It is also opposed to the commonsensical view that, however obscurely, the past lives on in the present, a view for which, if we care to look, there seems to me always abundant evidence.

My second illustration is the low esteem of professional historians for textbooks. Though sometimes written by distinguished historians, textbooks—if my own observations are correct—are rarely prepared because the author believes he has something to present that will significantly improve the teaching of his subject. What has in fact happened is that he has succumbed to the blandishments of a publisher; after all, who would write a textbook on his own initiative, as he would write something else, before signing a contract and receiving an advance? The author writes his textbook as quietly as possible, and with apologies and elaborate explanations of his financial need to any colleague who discovers what he is up to. The fact is that our textbook writers would honestly prefer, with an occasional honorable exception, to be writing something else: something "serious," with the implication that pedagogy is not, for a professional historian, altogether serious. Under these circumstances it is hardly surprising that textbooks are not reviewed in our professional journals, or that they are rarely well regarded by the teachers who must rely on them. Generally speaking one chooses a textbook *faute de mieux*.

I have presented here a one-sided and somewhat unflattering description of the professional community of historians. But I have done so in order to focus on what seems to me an extremely serious problem, one that concerns us all, arising out of the widening gulf between the two communities that the history teacher simultaneously inhabits. Obviously the validity and integrity of what we teach depends on the disciplines that our professional community enforces. Good history—useful history—depends on high professional standards. But these standards do not exist only to serve the internal development of an autonomous professionalism. And given our present difficulties it is a matter of some urgency to insist on the need for a historical discourse that is finally directed to the larger social community, *ad urbem et orbem,* and that speaks to its concerns. What is at stake, after all, is *its* history, which is not a commodity that it can afford to do without, and which it will not do without unless we manage to persuade the public, by our own professionalism, that history is irrelevant and dispensable.

This suggests the strategic importance of the historian as teacher, with a double role, facing both the profession and the public; and it is a singular advantage of our profession that the overwhelming majority of historians are also teachers, a fact that remains potentially significant even when our professionalism tempts us to forget it. It is as a teacher, open in both directions, that the historian can mediate between his professional community and the larger community—from which, it may be added, his professional status has not separated him: he remains a part of the world he also addresses, a part of his own audience. This probably means that he must ponder the concerns of the larger community, and his own as that member of it with whom he is best acquainted, as thoughtfully as he studies the past. In short, as a condition of dealing effectively, as a teacher, with the past in the present, he must try to understand the present as well as the past. I suspect that, however essential, this may prove for most of us the more difficult assignment. In this way, as mediator, the history teacher might contribute both to keeping the historical profession alive and to keeping the life of his own time rooted in a sense of history.

Index

Compositor: J. Jarrett Engineering, Inc.
Text: 10/13 Galliard
Display: Galliard
Printer: Bookcrafters
Binder: Bookcrafters